Lecture Notes in Artificial Intelligence 12948

Subseries of Lecture Notes in Computer Science

More information about this subseries at http://www.springer.com/series/1244

Sergei M. Kovalev · Sergei O. Kuznetsov ·
Aleksandr I. Panov (Eds.)

Artificial Intelligence

19th Russian Conference, RCAI 2021
Taganrog, Russia, October 11–16, 2021
Proceedings

Editors
Sergei M. Kovalev
Rostov State Transport University
Rostov-on-Don, Russia

Aleksandr I. Panov
Russian Academy of Sciences
Moscow, Russia

Sergei O. Kuznetsov
National Research University Higher School
of Economics
Moscow, Russia

ISSN 0302-9743 ISSN 1611-3349 (electronic)
Lecture Notes in Artificial Intelligence
ISBN 978-3-030-86854-3 ISBN 978-3-030-86855-0 (eBook)
https://doi.org/10.1007/978-3-030-86855-0

LNCS Sublibrary: SL7 – Artificial Intelligence

This Springer imprint is published by the registered company Springer Nature Switzerland AG
The registered company address is: Gewerbestrasse 11, 6330 Cham, Switzerland

Preface

Welcome to the proceedings of the 19th Russian Conference on Artificial Intelligence (RCAI 2021). RCAI 2021 was held in Taganrog (Rostov region) and organized by the Russian Association for Artificial Intelligence and Southern Federal University. As a long-standing member of the European Association for Artificial Intelligence (EurAI, formerly ECCAI), the Russian Association for Artificial Intelligence has a great deal of experience in running important international AI events.

The first Soviet (Russian, from 1992 onwards) Conference on AI was held in Pereslavl-Zalessky in 1988. It was then held every other year till 2018, when the conference became annual. The conference gathers the leading specialists from Russia and other countries in the field of Artificial Intelligence. The participants of RCAI 2021 were mainly the members of research institutes of the Russian Academy of Sciences and universities all over the Russian Federation. The topics of the conference included data mining and knowledge discovery, text mining, reasoning, decision-making, natural language processing, vision, intelligent robotics, multi-agent systems, machine learning, AI in applied systems, ontology engineering, etc. Each submitted paper was reviewed by three reviewers, experts in the field of Artificial Intelligence, to whom we would like to express our gratitude. The conference received a total of 80 submissions, of which 26 were selected by the International Program Committee to be published in this volume. We hope that this publication will stimulate further research in various domains of Artificial Intelligence.

We dedicate this volume to the memory of our dear colleagues who passed away this year.

Valerii B. Tarasov (1955–2021) graduated from Moscow Bauman State Technical University and lectured there for several decades. Prof. Tarasov had a very broad scope of scientific interests in AI and related fields, he made important contributions in the fields of soft computation, semiotic modeling, and multi-agent systems. Prof. Tarasov was a cofounder and devoted member of the Russian Association for Artificial Intelligence and the Russian Association for Soft Computations, as well as the organizer of numerous conferences on soft computation.

Anna E. Yankovskaya (1939–2021) graduated from Tomsk State University and taught and undertook research at Tomsk Engineering University for several decades. Prof. Yankovskaya was a member of scientific councils of the Russian Association for Pattern Recognition and the Russian Association for Artificial Intelligence, along with European Academy of Science and International Association for Pattern Recognition. Her major contributions in discrete mathematics and AI are related to a matrix representation of knowledge, logical control, pattern recognition, test synthesis, and decision making.

August 2021

Sergei M. Kovalev
Sergei O. Kuznetsov
Aleksandr I. Panov

Preface

Contents

Cognitive Research

Data Mining, Machine Learning, Classification

Knowledge Engineering

Cognitive Research

Heterogeneous Formal Neurons and Modeling of Multi-transmitter Neural Ensembles

Nikolay Bazenkov(✉)

V. A. Trapeznikov Institute of Control Sciences of the Russian Academy of Sciences, Moscow, Russia

Abstract. A multitransmitter neural ensemble is a group of neurons interacting not via isolated synaptic connections, but via the emission of neurotransmitters directly into the shared extracellular space (ECS). There are multiple experimental evidence that non-synaptic interactions play the important role in biological neural circuits. We propose a model of multitransmitter neural ensembles where each neuron is represented as a finite state machine. An algorithm of neural interactions via the shared ECS is proposed. This framework allows one to capture the variety of spiking behavior observed in biological neurons. The model is intended primarily for simulation of simple neural ensembles where each neuron has a unique internal properties and plays the specific role in the ensemble activity. We show how the model can imitate such neural activity classes as tonic spiking, bursting, post-inhibitory rebound etc. To illustrate the key features of the proposed framework, we have modeled two examples of pattern-generating neural ensembles: a half-center oscillator and a feeding network of a pond snail.

Keywords: Central pattern generator · Neural network · Finite state machine · Neurotransmitter · Discrete modeling

1 Introduction

1.1 Motivation

Numerous experimental evidences suggest that the diversity of neurotransmitters and their receptors underlies the richness and flexibility of behavioral repertoire in all animals with a nervous system including humans. Nevertheless, the chemical heterogeneity inherent to natural neural populations remains beyond the formalization that still sees the synaptic wiring diagram as the key explanation of behavioral phenomena.

The research was partially supported by the Russian Foundation for Basic Research (projects Nos. 19-04-00628, 20-07-00190).

S. M. Kovalev et al. (Eds.): RCAI 2021, LNAI 12948, pp. 3–16, 2021.
https://doi.org/10.1007/978-3-030-86855-0_1

The objective of the study is to provide a model illustrating how the chemical composition of the extracellular space (ECS), transmitter specificity, and neuronal membrane properties can sufficiently shape coordinated rhythmic activity of neural ensembles. The model does not involve axonal connections and the neurons communicate purely by "broadcast" non-synaptic mechanisms. Extracellular space shared between all neurons approximates connectivity schemes present, for example, in neural ganglions of invertebrates as well as in numerous experimental neuronal populations grown in cultures from pluripotent cells. We propose this simplified view intentionally to emphasize the fact that the diversity of neurotransmitters and electrical properties is in some cases sufficient to organize the observed activity patterns.

Another goal is to provide a discrete model taking into account individual membrane properties essential for biological neural networks. Current computational modeling of biological ensembles mainly uses models of spiking neurons based on differential equations describing the dynamics of ionic currents during spike initiation. We propose a much rougher model which operates in larger timescales while preserves, as we believe, the properties essential for functioning of rhythm-generating neural ensembles.

1.2 Contribution

Combining both objectives, we propose a heterogeneous active neural network. It consists of a set of active formal neurons interacting by neurotransmitters emitted to the shared extracellular space. The network dynamics and output is shaped by transmitter-receptor pairing and individual membrane properties. Early an asynchronous discrete neural network was proposed where neurons function in continuous time [4,14]. Here we develop a parallel branch of research where neurons are represented by finite state machines operating in discrete steps. The early version of the model was proposed in [3].

Each neuron in the model is represented by a finite-state machine (FSM). Discrete states correspond to different functional modes of the membrane, ionic currents and intracellular metabolic processes. The FSM input is a value representing external excitation or inhibition. Neural output and transition to the next state depends both on the current state and the input. The model is formally described in Sect. 3.

The network itself may be analyzed as an aggregated finite state machine where the network state consists of the individual neurons' states. The network activity may be explored and analyzed by the transition graph of this network FSM. Our model may be extended to the probabilistic framework if the deterministic FSMs are replaced by hidden Markov models.

We focus on neural properties essential for central pattern generators (CPG), relatively simple neural ensembles able to produce rhythmic output in the absence of external stimuli. Experimental evidence from studies of CPGs is a powerful illustration of the way network activity is altered by neurotransmitters [2,16]. Our model combines neural properties that we believe are important for coordinated rhythmic activity of CPG. We illustrate our model with two examples relevant for CPG studies: the half-center oscillator and the feeding network of a pond snail *Lymnaea stagnalis*. The examples are provided in Sect. 4.

2 Related Work

There exist numerous mathematical models of individual neurons and large neural networks. Biophysically accurate conductance-based models rely on Hodgkin-Huxley equations [8] which describe in detail ionic currents driving the membrane potential dynamics. This approach is suitable for small networks, especially when biophysical details are the primary research interest. For large networks these models are mainly intractable, though a number of simplified modifications were proposed [7,18,19].

Conductance-based models are widely used for CPG modeling. In [24] a feeding network of a pond snail is formalized and simulated by a two-compartmental model. In [21] the crustacean stomatogastric CPG and its primary activity patterns are simulated by a conductance-based model. In [9] the spinal CPG based on Hodgkin-Huxley neurons controls locomotion of simulated cat hindlimbs. Kinetic equations of transmitter interactions are sometimes introduced into conductance-based models [6].

Phenomenological models such as integrate-and-fire [1] are often used for simulations of large-scale neural networks [11]. They omit the complex structure of ionic currents and focus on observable dynamics of membrane potential and spiking behavior. It is shown that multiple firing patterns such as tonic spiking, post-inhibitory rebound, and bursting may be produced by a relatively simple model including two differential equations [10].

Our paper is in line with the research of Boolean networks. After the famous work of McCulloch and Pitts [17] networks of Boolean threshold elements and their extensions [13,26] were widely used to model biological systems such as gene regulatory networks [12]. There are few discrete models of small neural circuits. In [22], rhythmic patterns generated by CPG are classified as binary sequences. A model of bio-inspired neurons incorporating cellular homeostasis and synaptic plasticity is suggested for simulating adaptive and robust behavior in multi-goal tasks [20]. A logical model of Aplysia buccal CPG was proposed in [23], the authors used Symbolic Analysis Laboratory language as a formal description of CPG neurons and interconnections. In [25], a Boolean network is proposed to control feeding activity of *Aplysia*. We believe that logical modeling may be an important tool in computational neuroscience since it allows one to highlight the interactions and internal structure essential for a given case while omitting unrelated details.

3 Model Formulation

3.1 Neurons and Their Interactions

The network consists of the set of neurons $N = \{N_1, \dots, N_n\}$ and the set of neurotransmitters $C = \{c_1, \dots, c_m\}$. The time is divided into discrete timesteps

$t = 1, 2, \ldots$. At each timestep the neurons emit some amounts of the neurotransmitters into the shared extracellular space (ECS). The neurotransmitters cause either excitation or inhibition to the neurons. Under the neurotransmitters' influence the neurons change its internal states and output.

Neural Outputs. Each neuron's output during timestep t may be one of the discrete levels $y_i(t) \in Y_i = \{0, y_i^1, \ldots, y_i^{K_i}\}$, $y_i^k > 0$ corresponding to different rates of firing. The release of neurotransmitters is specified by the matrix $D = ||d_{ij}||_{n \times m}$ where $d_{ij} \geq 0$ is the amount of neurotransmitter c_j neuron N_i emits while firing spikes with the rate $y_i = 1$. So, neuron N_i emits $y_i(t)d_{ij}$ of neurotransmitter j during timestep t.

Extracellular Space (ECS). Each neuron emits neurotransmitters to the ECS, shared by all neurons in the ensemble. The amount of neurotransmitter j in the ECS during timestep t is defined as

$$x_j(t) = \sum_{i=1}^{n} y_i(t)d_{ij} + u_j(t), \quad (1)$$

where $u_j(t)$ is an external injection of j-th neurotransmitter to the ECS.

Neural Inputs. Neural response to a specific neurotransmitter is defined by their receptors. The model does not involve the diffusion of neurotransmitter across ECS. So, we consider that once the neurotransmitter was released, all neurons with appropriate receptors will respond to it. The receptors are defined by matrix $W = ||w_{ij}||_{n \times m}$. The weight $w_{ij} \in R$ defines how neurotransmitter j influences neuron i. The possible effects are the following: inhibition ($w_{ij} < 0$), excitation ($w_{ij} > 0$), no effect ($w_{ij} = 0$).

The effects of neurotransmitters are aggregated to the total input

$$\Delta_i(t) = \sum_{j=1}^{m} w_{ij}x_j(t). \quad (2)$$

The value Δ_i is further transformed to the discrete activation level $z_i \in \{z_i^1, \ldots, z_i^{L_i}\}$ which represents qualitatively different levels of excitation or inhibition. The discrete transformation is defined by the thresholds $\theta_i^0 = -\infty$, $\theta_i^1 > \theta_i^0$, $\theta_i^2 > \theta_i^1, \ldots, \theta_i^{L_i} = \infty$ as follows:

$$z_i = z_i^l, \text{if } \theta_i^{l-1} < \Delta_i \leq \theta_i^l. \quad (3)$$

Since discrete input $z_i(t)$ depends on neurotransmitter concentrations, which, in turn, depends on neural activity, the discrete input may be viewed as a function of the activity: $z_i(t) = z_i(y_i(t))$. Figure 1 illustrates the activation levels for the case where $z_i \in \{-1, 0, 1\}$.

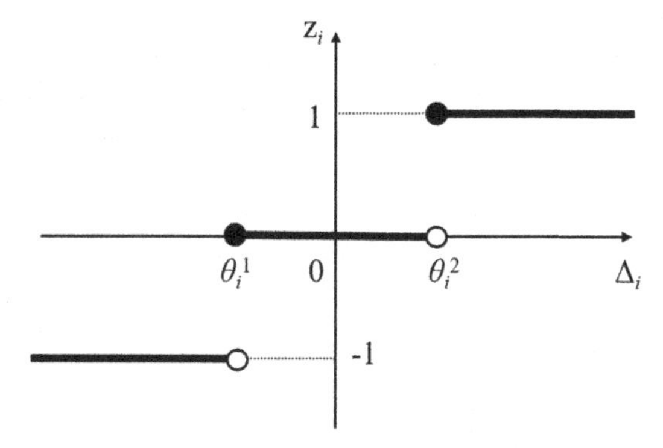

Fig. 1. Discrete neural input with three activation levels

Internal Structure: Finite State Machines. The membrane properties and internal processes in a neuron are represented by a finite state machine (FSM). In our model, the input of the FSM is the discrete activation level z_i. The output is the firing rate y_i. The internal states $S_i = \{s_i^0, \ldots, s_i^{P_i}\}$ represent different functional states of the membrane. For example, a separate state may correspond to the hyperpolarization, which triggers post-inhibitory rebound. The state transitions are defined by the function $Q_i : S_i \times Z_i \to S_i$. The output is defined by the function $F_i : S_i \times Z_i \to Y_i$. FSM may be fully specified by a table, where rows correspond to the state and columns correspond to the inputs. A cell at the intersection of p-th row and l-th column contains the new state $Q_i(s_i^p, z_i^l)$ and the output $F_i(s_i^p, z_i^l)$.

Table 1. FSM table

State	Input, z_i		
	...	z_i^l	...
...	...		...
s_i^k		$Q_i(s_i^k, z_i), F_i(s_i^k, z_i)$	
...	...		...

The equivalent representation of an FSM is a directed graph, where the nodes correspond to states and the edges correspond to transitions.

3.2 Classes of Neural Activity

Here we present how the basic classes of neural activity may be reproduced by the proposed model. These classes are one of the most common in biological neural ensembles, though the variety of neural behavior is much broader [10]. Note that the FSM framework is a flexible tool to model diverse behavior and the model is not limited to the presented classes.

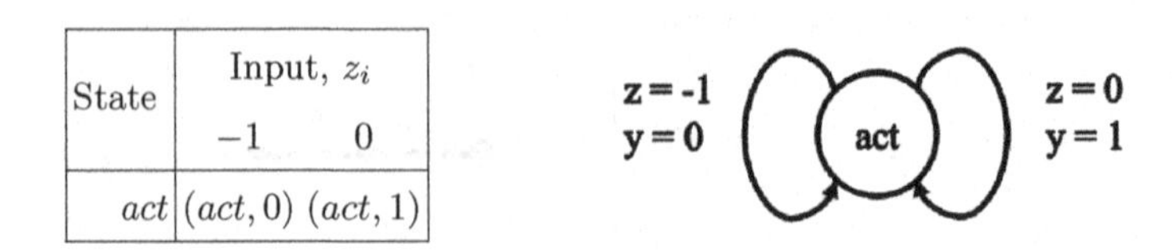

State	Input, z_i	
	-1	0
act	$(act, 0)$	$(act, 1)$

Fig. 2. Tonic neuron

Tonic Firing. A neuron firing regular spikes in the absence of external input may be represented as an automaton with a single state, defined as *act* (active). The input is one of the two possible values: 0 (no input) and -1 (inhibition). The neuron's output is $y_i = 1$ when it receives input $z_i = 0$, and $y_i = 0$ when the input is $z_i = -1$. The transition graph is shown in Fig. 2.

Tonic Neuron with Post-Inhibitory Rebound. Post-inhibitory rebound (PIR) is the ability of a neuron to produce a powerful burst of spikes emitted after a strong inhibition. This property plays an important role in pattern-generating neural ensembles. In the discrete model PIR is represented by the additional state added to the tonic neuron. If a neuron receives a strong inhibition represented by $z_i = -2$, it transits to the state *inh* (inhibited) and remains in this state until the inhibition is removed, e.g. the input becomes $z_i = -1$ or $z_i = 0$.

After the release of inhibition, the neuron produces a stronger than normal ($y_i = 1$) output $y_i = 2$ (Fig. 3).

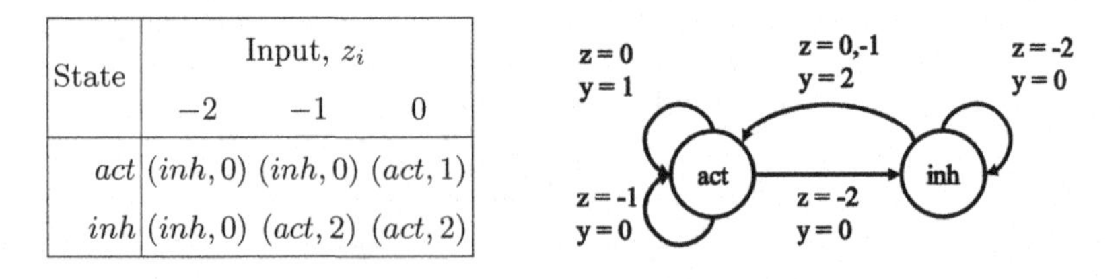

State	Input, z_i		
	-2	-1	0
act	$(inh, 0)$	$(inh, 0)$	$(act, 1)$
inh	$(inh, 0)$	$(act, 2)$	$(act, 2)$

Fig. 3. Tonic neuron with post-inhibitory rebound

Follower Neuron. A follower neuron is active only after external excitation. The FSM structure is shown in Fig. 4. The neuron remains in the default *rest* state until an excitatory stimulus $z_i = 1$ is received. Then it transits to the *burst* state and fires a burst at the next step. The neuron remains active until the excitation is removed.

Oscillatory Neuron. Neurons able to fire bursts of spikes periodically play an important role in the generation of biological rhythms. They may act as pacemakers driving the whole rhythm. A simple FSM, which mimics the behavior

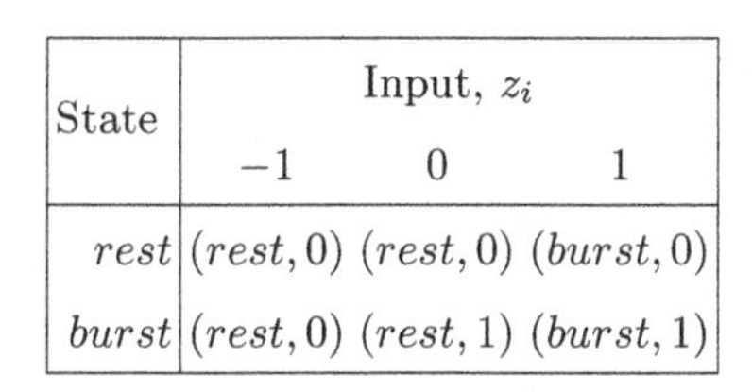

State	Input, z_i		
	−1	0	1
rest	(*rest*, 0)	(*rest*, 0)	(*burst*, 0)
burst	(*rest*, 0)	(*rest*, 1)	(*burst*, 1)

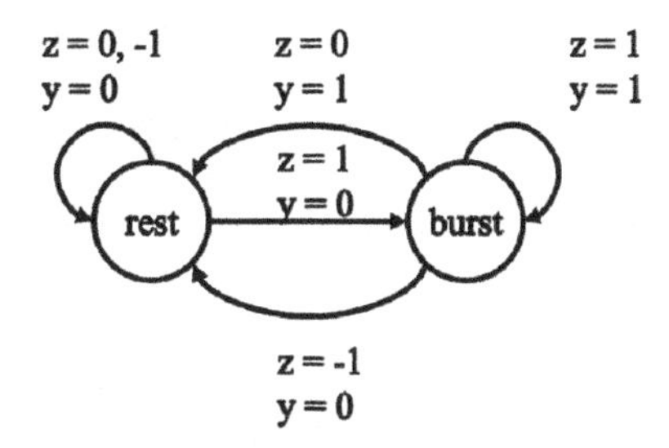

Fig. 4. Follower neuron with one-step delay.

of oscillatory neurons, is shown in Fig. 5. After the *recharge* state, the neuron transits to *burst* state. Then it fires a burst of spikes $y_i = 1$. After each burst, the neuron is inactive during the recharge period. In the example, the recharge duration is one step. To extend the period, we would need to add more states corresponding to the recharge period.

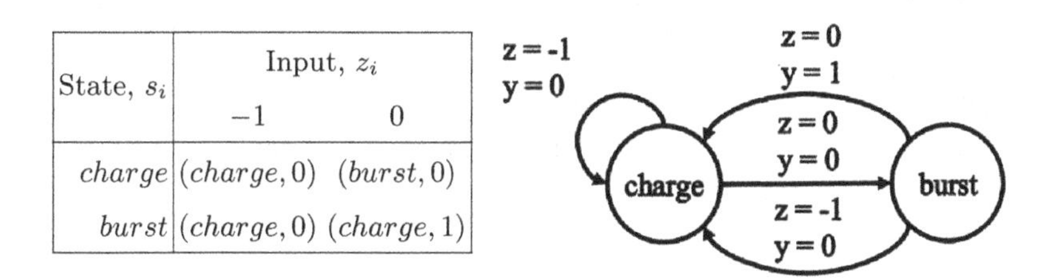

State, s_i	Input, z_i	
	−1	0
charge	(*charge*, 0)	(*burst*, 0)
burst	(*charge*, 0)	(*charge*, 1)

Fig. 5. Oscillatory neuron

3.3 Network Dynamics

The time is simulated as discrete timesteps. The model state at timestep t consists of the neural states $s(t) = (s_1(t), \dots, s_n(t))$. Each timestep corresponds to a certain time interval, long enough for the neurons' activity $y(t) = (y_1(t), \dots, y_n(t))$ and transmitters' concentration $x(t) = (x_1(t), \dots, x_m(t))$ to be considered constant during this interval. The transitions between the timesteps occur both due to neural interactions and internal neural processes.

State Transitions. The transition from the previous timestep $t-1$ to the next t is organized as follows. The internal neural states $s(t-1)$ and activity $y(t-1)$ are given and $s(t)$ and $y(t)$ should be computed. The states and activity are computed in the following two stages.

1. Compute the next neural states according to the transition functions:

$$s_i(t) = Q_i(s_i(t-1), z_i(t-1)),\ i = 1, \ldots, n \tag{4}$$

2. The neural activity $y(t)$ is computed as a solution to the equations

$$y_i(t) = F_i(s_i(t), z_i(y(t))),\ i = 1, \ldots, n. \tag{5}$$

Here $z_i(y_i(t))$ is given by Eqs. (3), (2)

The first point is straightforward. The internal states are computed according to the transition table of the corresponding FSM (see Table 1). The second point is less obvious. In the transition table, only a single transition cell may be active during a timestep. The transition depends on the input $z_i(t)$, which, in turn, depends on the transmitters' concentrations $x_j(t)$. The concentrations depend on neural activity $y_i(t)$, which depends on the neural inputs $z_i(t)$. We are looking for a vector $y(t)$, which provides a solution to each of these equations. This mechanism reflects the fact that each neuron is not isolated but functions as a part of the ensemble.

The system (5) may admit multiple solutions, which for small networks, may be enumerated by the following naive algorithm.

1. Initialize the set of possible activity vectors as $Y^* = \emptyset$
2. For each neuron i enumerate all outputs which are possible given its current state $s_i(t-1)$: $\overline{Y}_i = \{y_i : \exists z_i, F_i(s_i(t-1), z_i) = y_i\}$
3. For each vector $\overline{y} \in \overline{Y}_1 \times \ldots \times \overline{Y}_n$ check the Eqs. (5). If $\overline{y}$ is a solution, add it to the set Y^*.

Note that the transitions depend on the external injections of neurotransmitters through the neural activations z_i depending on $x(t)$, see Eqs. (1–3). So, it is possible to inject a neurotransmitter to intentionally block or activate certain transitions.

Activity Graph. As explained in the previous subsection, for a model state $s(t) = (s_1(t), \ldots, s_n(t))$ there may exist multiple activity vectors $y(t)$ being a feasible solution to the (5). Each activity triggers a transition $s(t) \Rightarrow s(t+1)$. We may plot all model states and their transitions as a directed graph $G = (S, T)$, $T \subseteq S \times S$ where each node corresponds to a model state $s \in S = S_1 \times \ldots \times S_n$ and each edge represents a transition $s \Rightarrow s'$, $s, s' \in S$.

Each edge corresponds to the neural activity $y(t) = (y_1(t), \ldots, y_n(t))$ produced during the transition $s \Rightarrow s'$ and the ECS state $x(t) = (x_1(t), \ldots, x_m(t))$. We call graph G an activity graph. It is a useful tool for visual analysis of network behavior. Cycles in the graph show which activity patterns are repeating. Each cycle is a stationary mode of the network functioning. A network having a non-trivial cycle in the activity graph is able to produce rhythmic activity and, therefore, is as a central pattern generator.

Activity graph of a given network under the specified external neurotransmitter injections may be created by enumerating all transitions for every possible state $s \in S$ as proposed in the previous subsection. For an arbitrary network, the graph is not necessarily connected. That said, biologically plausible neural ensembles should have a strongly connected component which corresponds to the normal operation mode of the ensemble. An external injection of some neurotransmitters may alter the activity graph. Actually, for a single network, there may exist multiple activity graphs selected by the injection of specific neurotransmitters.

4 Biological Rhythms

4.1 Oscillation by Mutual Inhibition

One of the basic mechanisms of rhythm generation is called a half-center oscillator (HCO) [15]. It is present, for example, in the spinal CPG of vertebrates [9]. It is shown in Fig. 6A. HCO consists of a pair of neurons, which do not produce an organized rhythm in isolation but do produce an alternating phasic activity being coupled by inhibitory connections. In this case, the rhythm emerges from mutual inhibition and does not require the pacemaker neuron.

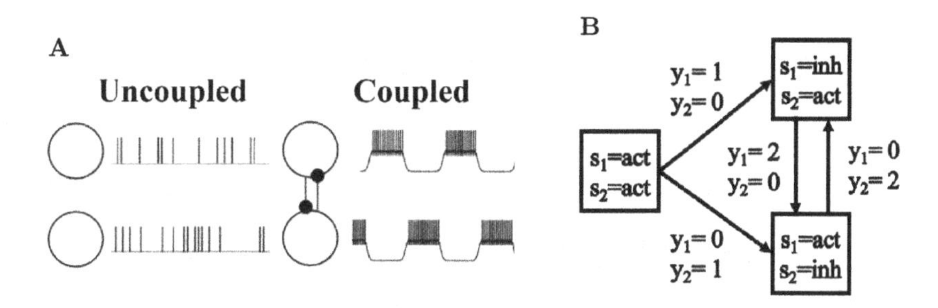

Fig. 6. Half-center oscillator. Isolated neurons show irregular tonic activity. Coupled neurons show strong alternating bursts.

The neural circuitry of HCO may be modeled as follows by the proposed framework. As shown in the Table 2, the network consists of two tonic neurons, N_1 and N_2, with post-inhibitory rebound described in Subsect. 3.2. The inhibitory links are implemented via two different neurotransmitters. Define them as transmitters *ach* and *glu*. N_1 produces *ach* and is inhibited by *glu*, and N_2 does the opposite.

The activity graph of the network is shown in Fig. 6B. There exists a single cycle among two network states: (act, inh) and (inh, act). This cycle produces activity $(2, 0), (0, 2), \ldots$ which corresponds to the alternating bursts shown in Fig. 6A. The simulation begins from the state (act, act) and never returns to it.

Table 2. Connectivity in the model of HCO.

Neurons	Receptors		Output	
	ach	*glu*	*ach*	*glu*
N_1	0	−1	1	0
N_2	−1	0	0	1

This example shows how the FSM model may be used to represent network properties essential for the given activity pattern. In the next section, we present a more complex example and show how the network activity is controlled by the external neurotransmitter.

4.2 Three-Phase Feeding Rhythm of a Pond Snail

The feeding generator of a pond snail *Lymnaea stagnalis* is a well-studied example of a CPG. As shown in Fig. 7, the network consists of three interneurons responsible for separate phases of the feeding rhythm: protraction, rasp and swallow. In [24], a model based on Hodgkin & Huxley equations was proposed; it is a 38-dimensional system of ordinary differential equations which were solved numerically. Here we propose a simplified discrete model that emphasizes the logic of the interactions and neuronal roles in the CPG.

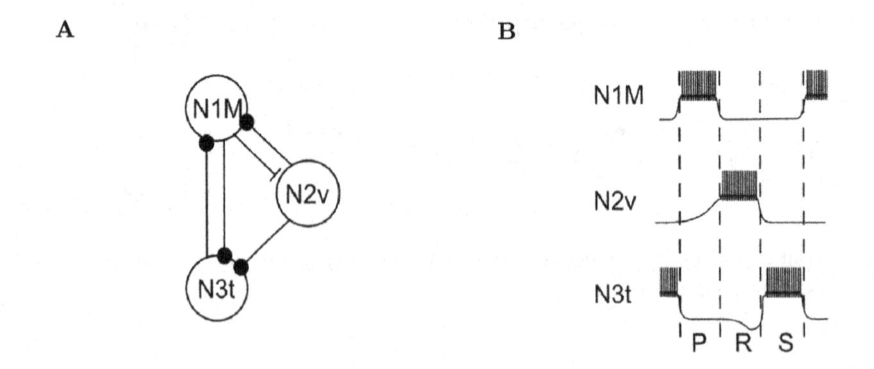

Fig. 7. Feeding CPG of the pond snail Lymnaea stagnalis [5,24]. The core network structure consists of three interneurons driving separate phases of the feeding rhythm: radula protraction (P), rasp (R) and swallowing (S). **A:** Interactions between CPG neurons. Dots indicate inhibitory influence, the bar indicates excitatory influence from N_1 to N_2; **B:** Phases of the feeding rhythm: protraction, rasp, and swallow.

The network shown in Fig. 7 consists of three neurons N_1, N_2, N_3 producing two neurotransmitters: *ach* and *glu*. Let us consider what properties the neurons should possess to produce the forward feeding rhythm by the proposed model. N_1

neuron is an endogenous oscillator that drives the whole rhythm. N_2 is a follower that must be excited by N_1 to activate. N_3 is a tonic neuron with weak default output and strong post-inhibitory rebound. The types are assigned according to the paper [24].

Table 3. Neural types and interactions in the model feeding CPG

Neurons	Type	Receptors		Output	
		ach	*glu*	*ach*	*glu*
N_1	Oscillatory	0	−1	1	0
N_2	Follower	0	−1	0	4
N_3	Tonic	−1	−0.3	0	0.5

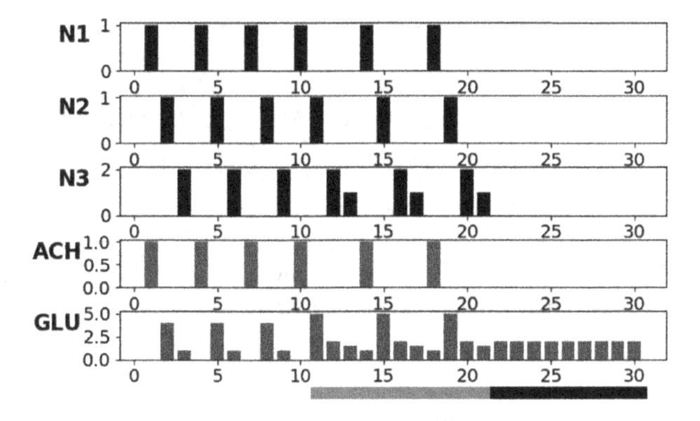

Fig. 8. Simulated feeding rhythm. The three top plots show the activity of neurons, bottom plots show the concentrations of each neurotransmitter. Injection of *glu* alters the rhythm: $u_{glu} = 1$ (grey bar), $u_{glu} = 2$ (black bar).

The network parameters are shown in Table 3, and the produced rhythm is shown in Fig. 8. The rhythm is altered under the external injection of *glu* neurotransmitter. First, the medium level of additional transmitter ($u_{glu} = 1$) is injected, which prolongs the activity of N_3. Then the high level of the transmitter ($u_{glu} = 2$) completely stops the rhythm.

The activity graph is shown in Fig. 9. The basic rhythm is expressed by solid lines. It contains the starting state when N_3 is active while N_1 is in the *charge* state. This activity is weak and cannot inhibit N_1 when it starts bursting. The output of N_1 is strong enough to inhibit N_3 while it is in *act* state and activate N_2. But the N_1 activity is insufficient to push N_3 into *inh* state. Then N_2 produces a single burst, which strongly inhibits N_3 transiting into *inh* state. At the next step, N_3 emits a powerful post-inhibitory activity which prevents N_1

from bursting. After this, N_3 transits to *act* state, and the rhythm continues from N_1 activity.

The additional node ($s_1 = charge$, $s_2 = rest$, $s_3 = act$) emerged in the graph under the medium injection of *glu*. It corresponds to the prolonged activity of N_3, due to additional inhibition of N_1 by the external neurotransmitter. Under the high *glu* concentration, the rhythm collapses to a single loop when no neurons are active. The most obvious biological interpretation of this state is when the animal is satiated and does not need to consume food.

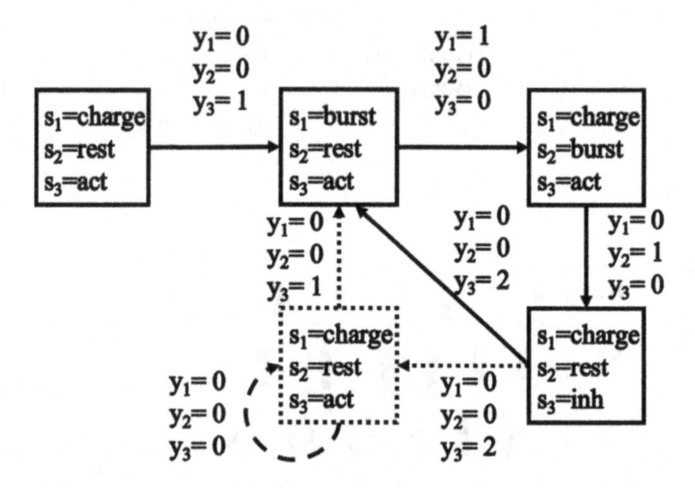

Fig. 9. Activity graph combined from different levels of *glu* injection. **Solid lines:** no injection, $u_{glu} = 0$; **Dotted lines:** $u_{glu} = 1$; **Dashed lines:** $u_{glu} = 2$

5 Conclusion

Multi-transmitter neural ensembles differ from the conventional view of synaptic connections as the main mechanism of neural interaction. Here we have proposed a formalized model where neurons with complex internal structure communicate not by isolated synapses but via the shared extracellular space.

The neurons represented as finite state machines may be used to capture the essential features of various activity patterns. Oscillatory bursting, tonic firing, reactive bursting, and post-inhibitory rebound were used in the paper to illustrate the model.

These types of neural activity were sufficient to reproduce two basic examples of biological pattern-generating ensembles: half-center oscillator and a snail feeding network. We show what role each activity type plays in the rhythm organization. The number of neurotransmitters may be less than the number of neurons. In this case the selective influence is achieved through different sensitivity to the neurotransmitter concentration and individual internal structure of the neurons.

The proposed framework provides a useful representation of neural rhythms: the activity graph. It may be used to explore the state transitions related to changes in neural activity. It is a convenient tool to explore how the rhythm is altered by an external neurotransmitter.

The simulated examples show that rhythmic activity patterns may be produced by a multitransmitter ensemble. There are many ways to enrich the model. For example, isolated synaptic connections may be introduced in the framework while the FSM representation and the activity graph will not change.

Acknowledgment. The author thanks Oleg Kuznetsov, Liudmila Zhilyakova, Varvara Dyakonova, and Dmitry Sakharov for helpful discussion on the mathematical framework and biological motivation.

References

1. Abbott, L.F.: Lapicque's introduction of the integrate-and-fire model neuron (1907). Tech. Rep. 6 (1999)
2. Bargmann, C.I.: Beyond the connectome: how neuromodulators shape neural circuits. BioEssays **34**(6), 458–465 (2012). https://doi.org/10.1002/bies.201100185
3. Bazenkov, N., Dyakonova, V., Kuznetsov, O., Sakharov, D., Vorontsov, D., Zhilyakova, L.: Discrete modeling of multi-transmitter neural networks with neuronal competition. In: Samsonovich, A.V., Klimov, V.V. (eds.) BICA 2017. AISC, vol. 636, pp. 10–16. Springer, Cham (2018). https://doi.org/10.1007/978-3-319-63940-6_2
4. Bazenkov, N.I., Boldyshev, B.A., Dyakonova, V., Kuznetsov, O.P.: Simulating small neural circuits with a discrete computational model. Biol. Cybern. **114**(3), 349–362 (2020). https://doi.org/10.1007/s00422-020-00826-w
5. Crossley, M., Staras, K., Kemenes, G.: A two-neuron system for adaptive goal-directed decision-making in Lymnaea. Nature Commun. **7**(1), 1–13 (2016). https://doi.org/10.1038/ncomms11793
6. Destexhe, A., Mainen, Z.F., Sejnowski, T.J.: Kinetic models of synaptic transmission. Methods Neuronal Model. **2**, 1–25 (1998)
7. Fitzhugh, R.: Mathematical models of excitation and propagation in nerve. In: Biological Engineering, pp. 1–85 (1969)
8. Hodgkin, A.L., Huxley, A.F.: A quantitative description of membrane current and its application to conduction and excitation in nerve. J. Physiol. **117**(4), 500–544 (1952). https://doi.org/10.1113/jphysiol.1952.sp004764
9. Ivashko, D.G., Prilutsky, B.I., Markin, S.N., Chapin, J.K., Rybak, I.A.: Modeling the spinal cord neural circuitry controlling cat hindlimb movement during locomotion. Neurocomputing **52–54**, 621–629 (2003). https://doi.org/10.1016/S0925-2312(02)00832-9
10. Izhikevich, E.M.: Simple model of spiking neurons (2003). https://doi.org/10.1109/TNN.2003.820440
11. Izhikevich, E.M., Edelman, G.M.: Large-scale model of mammalian thalamocortical systems. Proc. Nat. Acad. Sci. U.S.A **105**(9), 3593–3598 (2008). https://doi.org/10.1073/pnas.0712231105
12. Karlebach, G., Shamir, R.: Modelling and analysis of gene regulatory networks (2008). https://doi.org/10.1038/nrm2503

13. Kuznetsov, O.P.: Complex networks and activity spreading. Autom. Remote Control **76**(12), 2091–2109 (2015). https://doi.org/10.1134/S0005117915120012
14. Kuznetsov, O.P., Bazenkov, N.I., Boldyshev, B.A., Zhilyakova, L.Y., Kulivets, S.G., Chistopolsky, I.A.: An asynchronous discrete model of chemical interactions in simple neuronal systems. Sci. Tech. Inf. Process. **45**(6), 375–389 (2018). https://doi.org/10.3103/S0147688218060072
15. Marder, E., Bucher, D.: Central pattern generators and the control of rhythmic movements. Curr. Biol. **11**(23), R986–R996 (2001). https://doi.org/10.1016/S0960-9822(01)00581-4
16. Marder, E., Goeritz, M.L., Otopalik, A.G.: Robust circuit rhythms in small circuits arise from variable circuit components and mechanisms (2015). https://doi.org/10.1016/j.conb.2014.10.012
17. McCulloch, W.S., Pitts, W.: A logical calculus of the ideas immanent in nervous activity. Bull. Math. Biophys. **5**(4), 115–133 (1943). https://doi.org/10.1007/BF02478259
18. Morris, C., Lecar, H.: Voltage oscillations in the barnacle giant muscle fiber. Biophys. J. **35**(1), 193–213 (1981).https://doi.org/10.1016/S0006-3495(81)84782-0
19. Nagumo, J., Arimoto, S., Yoshizawa, S.: An active pulse transmission line simulating nerve axon. Proc. IRE **50**(10), 2061–2070 (1962). https://doi.org/10.1109/JRPROC.1962.288235
20. Nikitin, O., Lukyanova, O.: Control of an agent in the multi-goal environment with homeostasis-based neural network. In: Procedia Computer Science, vol. 123, pp. 321–327. Elsevier B.V. (2018). https://doi.org/10.1016/j.procs.2018.01.050
21. Prinz, A.A., Bucher, D., Marder, E.: Similar network activity from disparate circuit parameters. Nature Neurosci. **7**(12), 1345–1352 (2004). https://doi.org/10.1038/nn1352
22. Roberts, P.D.: Classification of temporal patterns in dynamic biological networks. Neural Comput. **10**(7), 1831–1846 (1998).https://doi.org/10.1162/089976698300017160
23. Tiwari, A., Talcott, C.: Analyzing a discrete model of *Aplysia* central pattern generator. In: Heiner, M., Uhrmacher, A.M. (eds.) CMSB 2008. LNCS (LNAI), vol. 5307, pp. E1–E1. Springer, Heidelberg (2008). https://doi.org/10.1007/978-3-540-88562-7_27
24. Vavoulis, D.V., Straub, V.A., Kemenes, I., Kemenes, G., Feng, J., Benjamin, P.R.: Dynamic control of a central pattern generator circuit: a computational model of the snail feeding network. Eur. J. Neurosci. **25**(9), 2805–2818 (2007). https://doi.org/10.1111/j.1460-9568.2007.05517.x
25. Webster-Wood, V.A., Gill, J.P., Thomas, P.J., Chiel, H.J.: Control for multifunctionality: bioinspired control based on feeding in *Aplysia californica*. Biol. Cybern. **114**(6), 557–588 (2020). https://doi.org/10.1007/s00422-020-00851-9
26. Zhilyakova, L.Y.: Small networks of MIMO agents with two activity types. In: Kuznetsov, S.O., Panov, A.I., Yakovlev, K.S. (eds.) RCAI 2020. LNCS (LNAI), vol. 12412, pp. 100–114. Springer, Cham (2020). https://doi.org/10.1007/978-3-030-59535-7_8

Methods for Recognition of Frustration-Derived Reactions on Social Media

Dmitry Devyatkin[1(✉)], Natalia Chudova[1], Anfisa Chuganskaya[1], and Daria Sharypina[2]

[1] Federal Research Center "Computer Science and Control", Russian Academy of Sciences, Moscow, Russia
devyatkin@isa.ru
[2] Moscow Institute of Physics and Technology, Moscow, Russia

Abstract. In this paper, we attempted to find speech features of different reactions to frustration to detect and classify them in social media texts. Frustration is a highly motivated situation in which it is impossible to achieve a goal when unexpected external or internal obstacles are encountered to meet the need. We use a well-recognized typology of the reactions and focus on context-aware but straightforward models and classification features, which can be easily interpreted. The experiments show that pure lexis cannot be used as the only feature for the classification. Only the models, which combine different-level linguistic features, implicitly like in BERT or in the models with the linguistic patterns, provide fair results. From a psychological point of view, some misclassifications of the obtained reaction data can be related to their assignment to one class of extrapunitive reactions. Discussions in social networks suggest a high level of human activity, a desire to seek a solution to the problem in a broader social interaction. Thus, the focus on extrapunitive reactions and an increased emotional component in the form of aggression is a feature of that interaction type. On the one hand, we provide a method to classify the social network messages; on the other hand, the training results can be interpreted and analyzed by experts in psychodiagnostics.

Keywords: Social media mining · Rosenzweig's frustration test · Linguistic patterns · Heterogeneous semantic networks · BERT

1 Introduction

The study of mental states through the analysis of speech production is one of the leading research topics in network communication. We can note that the research interest and relevance of mental state analysis based on the study of messages on social media is pretty high. But from the psychology and psychodiagnostics side, most of those works' lack of theoretical elaboration of mental state typologies or their signs makes the obtained data hard to interpret. In the automatic network content analysis, the current state is that research, educational, healthcare, and government organizations can hardly use the outcomes. Namely, the results of those works are exciting and sometimes plausible [1]. Still, they lack clear justification and demonstrate only the potential of the methods

S. M. Kovalev et al. (Eds.): RCAI 2021, LNAI 12948, pp. 17–30, 2021.
https://doi.org/10.1007/978-3-030-86855-0_2

with which they are obtained to become full-fledged population psychodiagnostics and epidemiological psychiatry methods.

In this paper, we study different types of reactions to frustration to detect and classify them in social media texts. Frustration is a highly motivated situation in which it is impossible to achieve a goal when unexpected external or internal obstacles are encountered to meet the need. The Rosenzweig typology of the frustration reactions is well-recognized in psychology but has not been applied to analyze social media yet. However, the types of frustration reaction are the predictors that explain the subsequent affective speech and behavioral responses of social media users from apathy and depression to rage and aggression, from self-blame to anger at others. The use of more in-depth tools for psychological analysis of network content makes it possible to increase the predictive ability of methods for automatic analysis of network interaction situations.

Our recent study [2] proposes a method that can classify the responses of subjects in the Rosenzweig Frustration Test. In these works, a linguist created between three and 12 linguistic descriptions for each response type. These descriptions were formalized and used to construct linguistic patterns of the reactions [3]. The linguistic patterns obtained in this way form high-level features of text fragments, making it possible to identify statements related to various types of reactions accurately. It seems the method is indifferent to the frustrating situations themselves. Typologically, one can observe similar speech reactions in any case of frustration, including in those situations that occur in social media communication. Based on that result, we attempt to create a method to reveal reactions to frustration in social media texts, which results would be psychologically and linguistically interpreted. In the current study, we are trying to answer the following research questions, which would help build that method.

1. Which are the linguistic features to reveal a type of frustration reaction on social media? Can the features we utilized to classify the Rosenzweig Frustration Test responses be applied to analyze social media?
2. Are those linguistic features not related to the content of the frustrating situation? If so, regardless of the subject of discussion, communicants who describe their frustrating reactions use universal mechanisms of expression (speech patterns), making it possible to identify the type of reaction to frustration in a wide range of contexts.
3. Which classification approaches and models are applicable to build such a method?

In contrast to Rosenzweig's test responses, social media messages are often short and grammatically incorrect; they also have many spelling mistakes. To tackle that problem, we combine and test several types of linguistics features including lexis, and morphology, with psychologically aware linguistic patterns, semantic and deep embeddings from BERT transformer models, and then use those features to train quite simple well-interpreted models.

The rest of the paper is organized as follows. Section 2 contains a thorough description of the Rosenzweig's frustration reaction typology and frustration test. Section 3 briefly provides the results of the recent studies in the mental state detection. Section 4 describes the annotated corpus of frustrated texts, collected from the Pikabu social network. Eventually, Sects. 5 and 6 contain the description of the features and models we applied to classify the reactions. They also provide the results of the experimental evaluation on the corpus.

2 Rosenzweig's Frustration Test

S. Rosenzweig proposed the most complete and systematic description of the types of frustration response [4]. This typology contains people's mental defense levels: the cellular (immunological) level, the autonomous level (providing protection from physical aggression and based on feelings of fear and anger), and the highest level (protection of the "Self," protection from psychological aggression and based on anxiety).

Rosenzweig identified three types of frustrators, which are obstacles that cause a frustrating state: deprivation as the lack of external (for example, food in a situation of starvation) or internal (for example, the lack of the ability to read or walk to get to the object of need) means to achieve the goal, loss of somebody or something external (a beloved one, property) or internal (of some skill), external or internal conflict. This classification is a cornerstone of his Picture-association test. The material of that test contains 24 pictures, which schematically depict two or more people in a situation of incomplete dialogue. The respondent's task is to add the first answer that comes to mind for the actor who has an empty cloud for the statement. The experimenter records the execution time and features of the respondent's behavior (comments, nonverbal manifestations) [5]. S. Rosenzweig proposes interpreting the test results in two scales.

First, according to the direction of frustration reactions:

1. Extrapunitive — the reaction is directed at the external environment; the external cause of frustration is condemned. The situation needs to be resolved by another person. This reaction is denoted as *E*.
2. Intropunitive — the reaction is self-directed and reflects the experience of guilt and responsibility for correcting the situation. In the results of the study, it is denoted as *I*.
3. Impunitive — a frustrating situation is seen as insignificant, unavoidable, surmountable over time. It is encoded with the letter *M*.

Second, the respondent's response to frustrating situations is divided by types:

1. Fixed on the obstacle (OD) — obstacles that cause frustration are strongly emphasized, whether they are favorable, unfavorable, or insignificant. This type of reaction is designated as *E', I', M'*.
2. With a focus on self-defense (ED)-focus on your "I": blaming someone, denying or admitting your guilt. It is denoted as *E, I, M*.
3. With a focus on meeting the need (NP) — the need to find a constructive solution to a conflict situation in the form of demanding help from others, taking on such a responsibility, and confidence that time will lead to a resolution of the situation.

They are marked as *e, i, m*.

The combination of these two directions of interpretation gives nine types of frustration reactions (for example, a picture with a driver and a pedestrian who is splashed with water from a puddle):

1. *E'* extrapunitive reaction with the fixation on the obstacle — "How terrible!".
2. *I'* intrapunitive reaction with the fixation on the obstacle — "I remained almost clean".
3. *M'* impunitive reaction with the fixation on the obstacle — "Nothing happened; it's a little splashed with water".
4. *E* extrapunitive reaction with a fixation on self-defense — "You are quite careless driver".
5. *I* intropunitive reaction with a fixation on self - defense — "It's my own fault, I should have stay away".
6. *M* impositiva reaction with a fixation on self-defense — "Nothing special, all right".
7. *e* extrapunitive reaction with the fixation on the satisfaction of needs — "You must return my clothes a clean look".
8. *I* intropunitive reaction with the fixation on the satisfaction of needs — "I will wipe that with a napkin".
9. *m* impunitive reaction with a fixation on satisfying the need - "Nothing, it will dry itself".

The proposed scheme of frustration analysis reactions by S. Rosenzweig allows studying individual speech reactions of respondents. It has become a reliable scheme for analyzing human behavior. The answers of the respondents in such projective test are based on scenarios of actual behavior in a conflict situation. Various modifications are created to evaluate, for example, coping strategies or ethnic prejudices [6].

3 Related Work

Most recent research efforts are devoted to investigating specific emotional states, where the task is to identify the linguistic styles of certain groups of users. For example, Brubaker, Kivran-Swaine, Taber, and Hayes studied how users experienced the loss and grief of losing a friend or a beloved person by analyzing posts on MySpace [7]. They analyzed more than 2,000 post-comments of MySpace users and compared the messages with emotional distress and without it. The study also suggests a typology of such comments. It includes ambivalent comments that ignore emotional content, memories of the deceased, prosaic messages with a general funeral style, messages with a positive understanding of loss, comments with pronounced emotional distress without a positive reframe. The linguistic style of texts with emotional distress is defined by the extensive use of first-person singular pronouns, past verbs, adverbs, prepositions and conjunctions, negatives, and vocabulary expressing anger. Comments without emotional stress have a higher level of use of second-person pronouns, speech reflecting positive emotions, and sadness. That study shows that while most people write, often using funerary-style language, people expressing emotional distress focus on themselves and isolation.

In the paper [8], Coppersmith, Harman, and Dredze analyzed post-traumatic stress disorder (PTSD) by scrutinizing Twitter messages. The researchers selected 244 users with a diagnosis of PTSD (based on self-reports of respondents in their posts and a keyword search of these posts followed by manual verification) and 6,000 randomly selected users for a control sample without PTSD [Coppersmith & al., 2014]. Using the Linguistic Inquiry Word Count (LIWC) [9], the researchers analyzed nine features: first -, second -, and third-person pronouns, profanity, anger, positive emotions, negative emotions, death, and other words. Second-person pronouns were employed significantly less frequently by users with PTSD, while third-person pronouns and words from the anxiety vocabulary were used considerably more often. The researchers also analyzed tweets from areas where military bases were located, with soldiers returning from war zones in other countries and surroundings. They revealed statistically significant trends in posts with PTSD at military bases in opposition to civilian areas. In the paper [10], researchers use the part-of-speech (POS) tags of the first three words and the last three words in the texts. They also include the position of the first sentiment-loaded word and the first affect-loaded word as a feature. To capture differences in syntactic structures, they consider POS tags present in the message. Namely, they build a probability distribution over the POS tags present in the current text and POS tags in past messages and use the Jensen-Shannon divergence value between the two distributions as a feature. They also use lexical density, which is the fraction of information-carrying words present in the text (nouns, verbs, adjectives, and adverbs).

[11] also studies complex linguistic features to identify hate speech. Researchers collected more than 2 million texts, comparing discussion actors around neutral topics to those more likely to be hate-related. They combined word embeddings, sentiment, and emotional features, lexis, and POS tags, applied bidirectional Long-Short-Term Memory (LSTM) [12], and obtained promising results. However, such an approach can be used only if the training corpus is big enough; in another scenario, those complex models cannot be trained reliably.

The recent approach to deal with that problem is the use of pre-trained context-aware language models. On the one hand, they consider complex features; on the other hand, they do not require such big datasets to be fine-tuned. [13] focuses on the emotional cause identification problem, which is detecting the causes behind a specific emotion expressed in the text. Most of the previous studies are restricted to the clause-level binary classification, which has ignored the crucial factor that not all words in the clause express emotions. In this study, the researchers suggest a new problem: emotion-cause span extraction, capable of obtaining more accurate and effective emotion causes. They propose a joint learning framework for emotion-cause span extraction and span-based emotion classification to address the emotion-cause span extraction task better. They used BERT [14] to encode multiple words and serve contextualized token representations. Furthermore, they propose a multi-attention mechanism with emotional context awareness and a relative position learning mechanism on word-level, which can further capture the mutual interactions between the emotion clauses and candidate spans. The experimental results show the reliability of the emotion-cause span extraction task and the effectiveness of the proposed framework.

[15] presents a BERT-based approach to detect hate speech. Such variance can be introduced by various factors, such as the BERT encoder layers, the fine-tuning architecture, or the hyperparameter settings. Each architectural design choice leads to different

results for a specific task. Hence, researchers are interested in reducing this variance given some settings. This study shows the use of a genetic algorithm to search, select and create a suboptimal fine-tuned BERT architecture for a hate speech detection task. The automatic search provided by the genetic algorithm helps to reduce the time and cost involved in manual trial and error design methods. The experiments show that the resulting architectural design and hyperparameter settings are good choices for the hate speech detection task. Although validated only on hate speech detection tasks, that method can easily be extended and generalized to other text classification tasks.

There are also several studies related to cognitive distortion detection. As for the previous case, the primary problem here is the lack of training corpora. For example, [16] presents an approach to classify text into one of several distortion types. They tested various classifiers based on Logistic regression, SVM, recurrent neural networks (Gated Recurrent Units) [17], and gradient boosting on decision trees (XGBoost) [18]. The best-performing model is logistic regression again because the corpus is quite small.

To summarize, frustration-derived reaction type detection requires representative datasets to train the complex classification models with rich contextual linguistic features. The creation of such a dataset involves a lot of manual data collection and annotation. Besides, the most complex classification models lack interpretability, which is a crucial option for psychodiagnostics. Therefore, in this study, we mainly focus on context-aware but straightforward models and classification features, which can be easily interpreted and verified.

4 Pikabu Frustration Dataset

The experimental dataset contains 528,097 clauses manually annotated with 11 classes. We use the DOCATO (DOCument lAbeling TOol) visual tool to collect and label the texts [19].

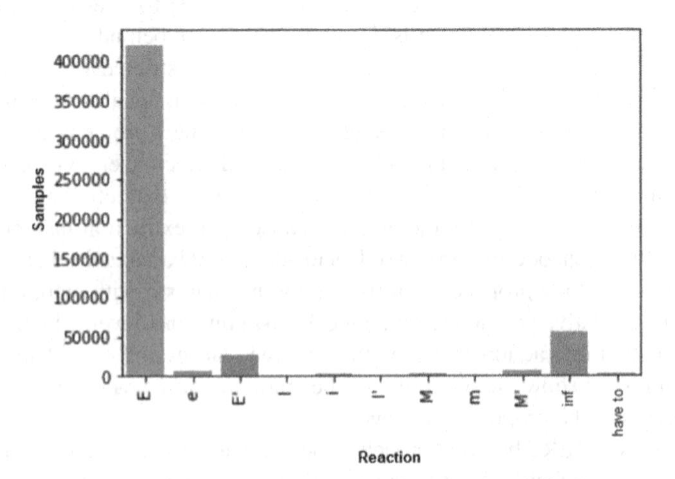

Fig. 1. Type distribution in the labeled frustration reaction corpus

In total, the texts of 1,943 unique posters and commenters were analyzed. After marking up the building, three psychologists identified 3,490 cases of responding to frustration, including: E: 1579, e: 200, E': 390, I: 64, i: 129, I': 79, M: 147, m: 41, M': 201, informing: 528, instructing: 132 (Fig. 1).

These clauses have been extracted from the Pikabu social network messages related to various controversial topics. Therefore, one can use the corpus to reveal topic-independent features, which are not strongly correlated with the content of the frustrating situation. We collected those messages in such a way to make each class (reaction) multi-topical to avoid the use of topic-related lexis by the frustration-derived reactions classifier. Because of the texts' nature, the dataset is severely imbalanced. Namely, the *E* class is more than a dozen times bigger than the second-largest class. In addition to pure texts, the dataset contains information about relationships between the messages (post-comment), which makes it possible to catch the context for each message.

In addition to types of frustration reactions from the method described above, we have included two categories in the markup:

- "*Inf*" — informational messages that provide general information about the situation or explain the circumstances;
- "*have to*" — messages of a normative or deontic modality, which is characterized by the words "*надо* (*nado*, Russian for *need to*), *нужно* (*nuzhno*, Russian for *necessary*)" and is in the nature of a normative recommendation without specifying a subject for performing actions in a particular frustrating situation.

These categories were introduced for the corpus of online discussions due to their significant representation. The dataset is free to use and available at [20] in JSON format.

5 Features for the Frustration Detection

First of all, the original texts have been preprocessed. We converted them to lowercase and then separated them into tokens-words. After tokenization, we applied JamSpell for typo correction, and then lemmatize with Pymorphy2 [21]. Besides, we extracted the textual context of each message with a fixed size window. The context was preprocessed similarly to the original texts.

In experiments, we used four types of features: lexical, psycholinguistic, semantic patterns, and deep BERT embeddings.

Lexical features include vector representations of texts. We obtained Bag-of-Words (BoW) vectors, *tf-idf* vectors, and vectors from the Doc2Vec model [22]. Token Bigrams and trigrams were also used to build BoW vectors and *tf-idf* vectors in addition to unigrams. Lemmatized tokens and context are inputs for that vector representation building.

We also tried to filter non-informative lexical features with the approach from [23]. Namely, we evaluate *idf* score of each token *t* in the corpus considering messages as documents, and also we evaluated the *idf* score for each separate part of the corpus related to particular reaction type c. Finally, we calculate the difference between those scores and filter the tokens with negative Δidf score (expression 1):

$$\Delta idf(t, c) = idf(t) - idf(t, c) \tag{1}$$

Psycholinguistic features were obtained via the Linguistic Inquiry and Word Count (LIWC) tool for automatic extraction of frequency features from texts: the frequency of punctuation marks, tokens with particular lexico-semantic group (positive and negative emotions), words of a specific part of speech (prepositions, adverbs, pronouns). These features were extracted from texts with corrected typos without lemmatization. Those tools return 302 psycholinguistic features in total. Those features are widely used to detect tension or aggression in texts [24]; therefore, we decided to test them.

Pattern-based features are high-level features built with the context-free linguistic pattern developed by the authors to analyze the results of the Picture-association test [2]. The cornerstone of the patterns is the relational-situational model of a clause.

The relational-situational model is a heterogeneous semantic network (HSN) with the following structure [25]:

$$H =< D, N, S, R, F >, \tag{2}$$

where

$D = \{D_1, D_2, \ldots, D_m\}$ is a set of feature sets;

S is a set of tuples like $< n_j, \Delta_j >$ and n_j– a value of a syntaxeme from a name set N, $\Delta_j \subseteq D^k = D_l \times D_t \times \ldots . \times D_q$—features of the syntaxeme for each $j = 1, 2, \ldots, |S|$ and $k \leq m$.

R is a set of relationships on N^2;

and F is a set of functions $D^k \rightarrow D_j$, $j = 1,..,m$.

That HSN represents a text clause, whose vertices are syntaxemes, and edges define syntax or semantic relationships between the vertices. The syntaxemes are minimal indivisible semantic–syntactic structures of a language. In our case, set D includes various morphological features of the syntaxemes (POS tags, grammatical cases, and moods, etc.) and word embeddings of the syntaxemes' lexis. We use pre-trained FastText [26, 27] to build the character-level embeddings and tackle lexical richness and potential misspellings.

Let every clause of the analyzed text can be represented with this model; therefore, all the text is the following sequence of HSNs: $\boldsymbol{H} =< H_1, H_2, .., H_t >$.

Define the context-free patterns as a tuple $\boldsymbol{T} =< H_1, H_2, .., H_n >$ of HSNs. Since the HSNs from $\boldsymbol{T}$ are patterns, they hold only the feature descriptions essential for the identification. Here we presume that all the HSNs from $\boldsymbol{T}$ and $\boldsymbol{H}$ have the same feature sets D.

Eventually, we define a reflection: $\varphi : \boldsymbol{H}^t \times \boldsymbol{T}^n \rightarrow \{0, 1\}^{tn}$ in the following way. For every text clause model $< D, N_i, S_i, R_i, F_i > \in \boldsymbol{H}$ and every pattern $< D, N_j, S_j, R_j, F_j > \in \boldsymbol{T}$, we set $\varphi_{ij} = 1$ if $N_i \cap N_j = N_j$, and $R_i \cap R_j = R_j$, otherwise we set $\varphi_{ij} = 0$. Figure 2 shows an example of such matching, where the whole network represents a clause, and the red fragment is the part that matches a pattern. We have built 60 of such patterns based on the cognitive-communicative action markers revealed for the specific reactions by psychologists and linguists. After removing the pattern-based features containing only zero values for the entire corpus, there are 56 features left.

The pattern-based feature-set generation is a process, which analyzes the message clauses the dependency and SRL parsers [28], builds their HSNs and matches them with the context-free patterns.

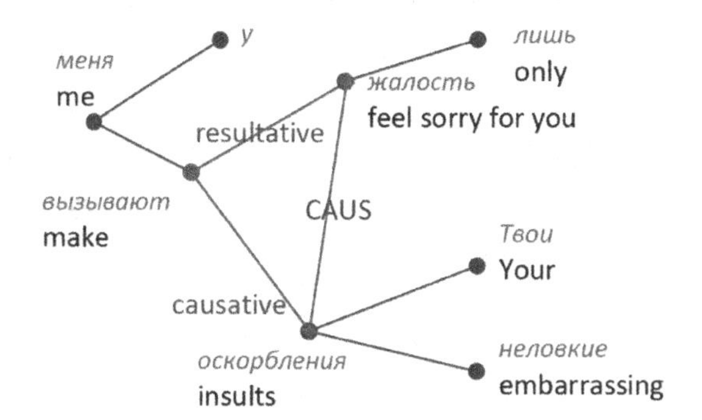

Fig. 2. A pattern example (red) and the HSN of the text that matches it (Color figure online)

Finally, we use the following ideas to intersect syntaxeme values in the pattern and text HSNs. The analyzer matches two syntaxemes from different HSNs if they have the same morphology features and syntax dependencies, and the cosine similarity between their lexis embeddings is greater than the determined threshold.

It is worth noting that this pattern-matching process is context-free. That means one can use the algorithms, which have good performance and applicable for analyzing big texts. As a result, each text clause is represented with a binary vector, which encodes if the clause matches the patterns.

Since these vectors are sparse, it is reasonable not to use them for further training directly but to build some dense embeddings before. All features were used in the experiments both in the raw form and in the compressed form obtained using truncated SVD. In the experiments, we trained the models on different groups of features separately and on their combinations.

6 Methods and Results of the Frustration Detection

In the experiments, we used models based on support vector machines (SVM) with linear and RBF kernels, logistic regression, random forest, and gradient boosting (XGB) [29]. RBF SVM, XGB, and random forest [30] yield the best scores, so these models were used in the final experiments. We have also revealed that all the models show a significant increase in classification scores if we use a sliding window to consider the context of the messages. Therefore, the frustration reaction classification should be tackled as a sequence labeling problem.

All models were trained using weights to balance the classes. We used F_1-micro metric and stratified five-fold cross-validation to select the values of the hyperparameters, including the size of the window for context extraction and the number of components in truncated SVD. Models were evaluated on the holdout sub-corpus with the same class distribution as the original dataset.

F_1-micro values for the best feature and model combinations are shown in Table 1.

Table 1. Frustraction reaction classification scores for different feature combinations and models (all classes)

Features	Raw			With compression		
	SVM	Random forest	XGB	SVM	Random forest	XGB
BoW-vectors	0.46	0.41	**0.48**	0.44	**0.48**	0.47
Filtered BoW vectors	0.45	0.37	**0.47**	0.42	**0.47**	0.48
Psycholinguistic markers	0.38	0.46	**0.47**	–	–	–
Patterns	0.50	**0.61**	0.59	–	–	–
BoW-vectors + psycholinguistic markers	0.46	0.47	**0.48**	0.45	**0.48**	0.47
BoW-vectors + patterns	0.47	0.60	**0.62**	0.46	0.54	0.55
Filtered BoW vectors + patterns	0.45	0.60	**0.61**	0.45	0.54	0.56
Psycholinguistic makers + patterns	0.49	**0.59**	**0.59**	–	–	–
BoW-vectors + psycholinguistic markers + patterns	0.47	0.59	**0.61**	0.54	0.52	0.54
Filtered BoW-vectors + psycholinguistic markers + patterns	0.45	0.59	**0.60**	0.52	0.52	0.54
RuBERT	0.51					

We also tested a BERT-based model. We used the Conversational RuBERT model pre-trained on Russian texts from social networks by DeepPavlov [31]. The model weights were fine-tuned for the frustration reaction classification task. Fine-tuning was done using the texts with corrected typos and contexts. We used a validation sample for the hyperparameters values selection and holdout sample for model evaluation.

The experiments show the combination of the patterns, and lexical BoW vectors shows the best accuracy of the reaction type classification. Because the experimental corpus is multi-topic and all reaction types are well represented for each topic, we conclude those features are topic-independent. At the same time, the "markers" feature set does not seem to be very helpful for the problem. The shallow analysis of the results shows that a significant share of misclassifications is related to the "have to" and "inf" classes. We believe that because they belong to a different classification typology, they should be treated as a multi-output classification problem. Therefore at the current step, we decided to perform the detailed experiments without those classes. Regarding the classification models, XGB with a sliding window shows the best scores, although it might be because of a quite small size of the experimental corpus. Table 2 shows the detailed results on the holdout part of the corpus. The overall F_1-micro score, in that case, is 0.73.

Table 2. Detailed frustration classification scores (Rosenzweig's types only)

Type	Precision	Recall	F_1-score
E	**0.77**	**0.89**	**0.89**
E'	**0.67**	0.45	0.54
M	**0.74**	**0.69**	**0.71**
M'	**0.62**	**0.72**	**0.67**
e	0.48	0.28	0.35
i	**0.64**	0.36	0.46

Figure 3 shows the confusion matrix for the best combination of model and features. It is worth noting that the method extracts *E, M, M'* types pretty accurately. The precision scores are fair for all the types except *i*.

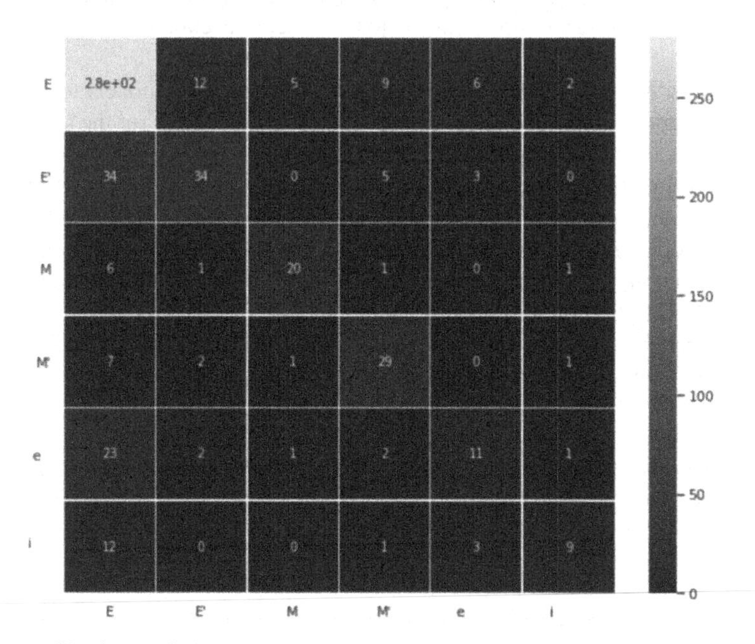

Fig. 3. Confusion matrix for the best model and feature combination

The largest share of misclassification is related to the E/E' and E/e pairs. We believe that is partly because of imbalance of the data; therefore the accuracy for those types can be improved when we extend the corpus.

7 Conclusion

The clarity and reliability of the research scheme based on the S. Rosenzweig typology of frustration reactions allowed us to obtain fair results to detect those reactions in social media texts. Namely, more than 73% of the analyzed messages have been classified correctly with the XGB classifier with a sliding window. The experiments show that pure lexis cannot be used as the only feature for the classification. Only the context-dependent models, which combine different-level linguistic features, implicitly like BERT or explicitly like the models with the linguistic patterns, provide fair results. On the other hand, those features seem to be independent from the content of the frustrating situation because the experimental corpus is multi-topic.

From a psychological point of view, the problem of classifying the obtained data of reactions by types E, E', e may be related to the assignment of them to one class of extrapunitive reactions. The difficulty is caused not by the emphasis on the direction of frustration (extrapunitive) but by the type of reaction of a person (to an obstacle, with a focus on oneself or a decision over time). In general, this may be related to the nature of the data on which the study was conducted. Discussions in social networks suggest a high level of human activity, a desire to seek a solution to the problem in a broader social interaction. Thus, the focus on extrapunitive reactions and an increased emotional component in the form of aggression is characteristic of this type of interaction. We are going to implement several improvements to reach better accuracy.

1. The corpus should be extended and balanced, allowing the models to catch more complex dependencies and increasing the classification scores for the small classes.
2. The significant share of misclassifications is related to the fact that the social media texts have lots of grammar mistakes, misspellings. Obscene language and idioms are also widely used. Non-conventional language use leads to incorrect morphology and syntax dependency parsing. It seems that end-to-end approaches can tackle the problem, but they are hardly interpreted. We shall apply Manning's attention probe method [32] to find relationships between the BERT attentions and our frustration reaction patterns. Eventually, those relationships can be used to regularize the BERT better when fine-tuning and still leave the results helpful for the psychodiagnostics.

Acknowledgements. This study is supported by Russian Foundation for Basic Research, grant No. 18–29-22047 mk.

References

1. Ophir, Y., Tikochinski, R., Asterhan, C.S., Sisso, I., Reichart, R.: Deep neural networks detect suicide risk from textual Facebook posts. Sci. Rep. **10**(1), 1–10 (2020)
2. Devyatkin, D., Chudova, N., Salimovskyi, V.: Method for automated recognition of frustration-derived aggression in texts. In: Velichkovsky, B.M., Balaban, P.M., Ushakov, V.L. (eds.) Advances in Cognitive Research, Artificial Intelligence and Neuroinformatics. AISC, vol. 1358, pp. 663–670. Springer, Cham (2021). https://doi.org/10.1007/978-3-030-71637-0_76
3. Devyatkin, D., Kadzhaya, L., Chudova, N., Mishlanov, V., Salimovsky, V.: Automatic identification of cognitive actions constituting speech genres of scientific theoretical text. In: Proceedings of the Linguistic Forum 2020: Language and Artificial Intelligence, Moscow, Russia, 12–14 November, vol. 2852. CEUR Workshop Proceedings (2020)
4. Rosenzweig, S.: An Outline of Frustration Theory. In: Hunt, V.N.Y. (ed) Personality and Behavior Disorders (1949)
5. Rosenzweig, S.: The picture-association method and its application in a study of reactions to frustration of personality. J. Pers. **14**, 3–23 (1945). https://doi.org/10.1111/j.1467-6494.1945.tb01036.x
6. L'vova, E., Shlyagina, E., Gusev, A.: Using the Rosenzweig frustration picture test in the study of coping behaviour in the situation of uncertainty. Natl. Psychol. J. **4**, 19–27 (2016)
7. Brubaker, J., Kivran-Swaine, F., Taber, L., Gillian, H.: Grief-stricken in a crowd: the language of bereavement and distress in social media. In: Proceedings of the Sixth International AAAI Conference on Weblogs and Social Media, pp. 42–49. The AAAI Press, Palo Alto (2012)
8. Coppersmith, G., Harman, C., Dredze, M.: Measuring post traumatic stress disorder in Twitter. In: Proceedings of the 8th International Conference on Weblogs and Social Media, ICWSM, pp. 579–582 (2014)
9. Tausczik, Y.R., Pennebaker, J.W.: The psychological meaning of words: LIWC and computerized text analysis methods. J. Lang. Soc. Psychol. **29**(1), 24–54 (2010)
10. Suri, S., Sharma, K., Papneja, S.: Frustration detection on reviews using machine learning. In: Proceedings of the 2020 International Conference for Emerging Technology (INCET), pp. 1–5. IEEE (2020)
11. Rajadesingan, A., Zafarani, R., Liu, H.: Sarcasm detection on Twitter: a behavioral modeling approach. In: Proceedings of the Eighth ACM International Conference on Web Search and Data Mining, pp. 97–106 (2015)
12. Hochreiter, S., Schmidhuber, J.: Long short-term memory. Neural Comput. **9**(8), 1735–1780 (1997)
13. Li, M., Zhao, H., Su, H., Qian, Y., Li, P.: Emotion-cause span extraction: a new task to emotion cause identification in texts. Appl. Intell. 1–13 (2021).https://doi.org/10.1007/s10489-021-02188-7
14. Devlin J., Chang, M. W., Lee, K., Toutanova, K.: Bert: pre-training of deep bidirectional transformers for language understanding. arXiv preprint https://arxiv.org/abs/1810.04805 (2018)
15. Madukwe, K.J., Gao, X., Xue, B.A.: GA-based approach to fine-tuning BERT for hate speech detection. In: Proceeding of the 2020 IEEE Symposium Series on Computational Intelligence (SSCI), pp. 2821–2828. IEEE (2020)
16. Shickel, B., Siegel, S., Heesacker, M., Benton, S., Rashidi, P.: Automatic detection and classification of cognitive distortions in mental health text. arXiv preprint arXiv: https://arxiv.org/abs/1909.07502 (2019)
17. Chung, J., Gulcehre, C., Cho, K., Bengio, Y.: Empirical evaluation of gated recurrent neural networks on sequence modeling. arXiv preprint arXiv: https://arxiv.org/abs/1412.3555 (2014)

18. Friedman, J.H.: Greedy function approximation: a gradient boosting machine. J. Ann. Stat. 1189–1232 (2001)
19. Suvorov, R., Shelmanov, A., Smirnov, I.: Active learning with adaptive density weighted sampling for information extraction from scientific papers. In: Filchenkov, A., Pivovarova, L., Žižka, J. (eds.) Artificial Intelligence and Natural Language, vol. 789, pp. 77–90. Springer, Cham (2017). https://doi.org/10.1007/978-3-319-71746-3_7
20. Labeled Frustration Corpus. http://nlp.isa.ru/frustration. Accessed 24 July 2021
21. Korobov, M.: Morphological analyzer and generator for Russian and Ukrainian languages. In: Khachay, M., Konstantinova, N., Panchenko, A., Ignatov, D., Labunets, V. (eds.) Analysis of Images, Social Networks and Texts, vol. 542, pp. 320–332. Springer, Cham (2015). https://doi.org/10.1007/978-3-319-26123-2_31
22. Le, Q., Mikolov, T.: Distributed representations of sentences and documents. In: Proceedings of the International Conference on Machine Learning, PMLR, pp.1188–1196 (2014)
23. Suvorov, R., Sochenkov, I., Tikhomirov, I.: Method for pornography filtering in the web based on automatic classification and natural language processing. In: Železný, M., Habernal, I., Ronzhin, A. (eds.) Speech and Computer, vol. 8113, pp. 233–240. Springer, Cham (2013). https://doi.org/10.1007/978-3-319-01931-4_31
24. Donchenko, D., Ovchar, N., Sadovnikova, N., Parygin, D., Shabalina, O., Ather, D.: Analysis of comments of users of social networks to assess the level of social tension. Procedia Comput. Sci. **119**, 359–367 (2017)
25. Osipov, G.S., Smirnov, I.V., Tikhomirov, I.A.: Relational-situational method for text search and analysis and its applications. Sci. Tech. Inf. Process. **37**(6), 432–437 (2010). https://doi.org/10.3103/S0147688210060080
26. Bojanowski, P., Grave, E., Joulin, A., Mikolov, T.: Enriching word vectors with subword information. Trans. Assoc. Comput. Linguist. **5**, 135–146 (2017)
27. Benko, V., Zakharov, V.P.: Very large Russian corpora: new opportunities and new challenges. In: Computational Linguistics and Intellectual Technologies, pp. 79–93 (2016)
28. Larionov, D., Shelmanov, A., Chistova, E., Smirnov, I.: Semantic role labeling with pretrained language models for known and unknown predicates. In: Proceedings of the International Conference on Recent Advances in Natural Language Processing (RANLP 2019), pp. 619–628 (2019)
29. Chen, T., He, T., Benesty, M., Khotilovich, V., Tang, Y., Cho, H.: XGBoost: extreme gradient boosting. R package version 0.42 **1**(4), 1–14 (2015)
30. Breiman, L.: Random forests. Mach. Learn. **45**(1), 5–32 (2001). https://doi.org/10.1023/A:1010933404324
31. Burtsev, M., et al.: DeepPavlov: open-source library for dialogue systems. In: Proceedings of ACL 2018, System Demonstrations, pp. 122–127 (2018)
32. Manning, C.D., Clark, K., Hewitt, J., Khandelwal, U., Levy, O.: Emergent linguistic structure in artificial neural networks trained by self-supervision. Proc. Natl. Acad. Sci. **117**(48), 30046–30054 (2020)

Identification of the Network State Based on the ART-2 Neural Network with a Hierarchical Memory Structure in Parallel Mode

Vladimir Polyakov, Dmitriy Bukhanov, and Maxim Panchenko(✉)

Belgorod State Technological University named after V.G. Shukhov, Belgorod, Russia

Abstract. A new memory structure for artificial neural networks of adaptive-resonance theory is proposed, which has a hierarchical form. For each new memory level, the previous classification value is refined by increasing the similarity parameter. This architecture was used to determine the network state in intrusion detection systems. The paper describes an algorithm for learning the proposed structure of the ART-2m network in parallel mode. A comparative analysis of the time characteristics of the network with the proposed structure when operating in series and parallel modes is carried out. Experiments were carried out using the NSL KDD-2009 sample, the results of which show the possibility of using ART-2m in intrusion detection systems. Most states were determined with sufficient accuracy that is greater than 80%.

Keywords: Adaptive resonance theory · Intrusion detection systems · Data mining

1 Introduction

According to Positive Technologies reports on vulnerabilities in corporate information systems, the percentage of systems in which critical vulnerabilities have been discovered doubles annually [1]. The report also states that penetration into a computer network occurs with less effort for intruders. Timely identification of the computer network state (CNS) will improve the security of computer systems. To solve the problem of CNS identification, intrusion detection systems (IDS) are most often used [2]. An IDS is a software or hardware-software complex located inside the network or on its external perimeter.

The basis of any IDS is the implementation of the method for identifying the CNS. According to the method of detecting the state of a computer network, IDS can be divided into two types. IDS of the first type detecting the state of a computer network by known features (signatures). The disadvantage of such systems is the impossibility of detecting a new type of network attacks. IDS of the second type detect deviations of the values of network parameters from the norm (network traffic anomalies). The disadvantage of such systems is a large number of false positives, but unlike systems of the first type,

S. M. Kovalev et al. (Eds.): RCAI 2021, LNAI 12948, pp. 31–40, 2021.
https://doi.org/10.1007/978-3-030-86855-0_3

they can detect new types of attacks. Methods of data mining (DM) have proven useful as methods for analyzing the parameters of network activity in such IDS.

In [3], cluster analysis was used as one of the methods of data mining. To identify the CNS, the use of the *k-means* algorithm was proposed. It is important to note that the best classification results (81.61%) were obtained with the number of output clusters equal to the number of identified states of the computer network. The disadvantage of such approaches is that it is necessary to know in advance the number of identified states. This hinders timely detection of new network attacks and also leads to the need to retrain the entire system when a new state appears.

In [4], the authors propose to use a Neuro-fuzzy system for data classification, which, in comparison with other neuro-fuzzy classification systems, such as Radial Basis Function Neural Network and Adaptive Neuro-Fuzzy Inject System, shows significantly better results. The disadvantage of such systems is the insufficient speed of work for use in real-time systems, as well as the need to retrain and add new rules and then check the consistency and completeness of the knowledge base.

Due to the complexity and heterogeneity of objects of computer security, there are IDS [5], which are aimed at solving specific problems. For example, such systems can, in addition to data received from incoming traffic, receive data from a dedicated cloud storage router. The use of this approach allows one to obtain high results in the classification of CNS, but such solutions are difficult to adapt for other problems.

Among the most promising methods for classifying the state of a network are methods based on artificial neural networks (ANN). In [6], the authors present experimental data using multilayer perceptron and Kohonen networks to identify abnormal behavior within the network. Their studies show good results, for some types of attacks, apart from DoS attacks like *Smurf* and *Neptune*, which are detected by 2–3 parameters, they exceed 80% accuracy. This is higher than the results of similar experiments conducted by other authors. In [7], to increase the efficiency of classifying the state of a computer network, the use of preprocessing of input monitoring data was proposed. After preprocessing, the data goes into the classifier based on the Kohonen network. The studies conducted by the authors show quite good results. When new types of network attacks appear, it is necessary to retrain the entire classifier, which can lead to the inability of the used neural network architecture to classify the new image. This is a disadvantage of the considered systems and may lead to a revision of the ANN architecture.

In view of the above-described shortcomings, the use of the adaptive resonance theory, namely ART-2, was proposed, which is capable of working with continuous input signals, as a method of data mining. General provisions on ART-2 architecture were presented in [8, 9]. In [10], a modification of the memory structure in the F2 field of the ART-2 network is proposed, which makes it possible to organize a tree-like memory structure.

2 Description of the Structure of the ART-2m Network

The basic principle of the ANN adaptive-resonance theory, formulated by Grossberg, involves finding a resonance between the upward signal from the sensory layers to the downward signals from the memory layers. Based on the theorem formulated in [8] on the finiteness and stability of the learning process, it is possible to organize a tree-like structure of memory in the recognition field. Figure 1 shows the structure of the ART-2 network with multilevel memory, which was named ART-2m.

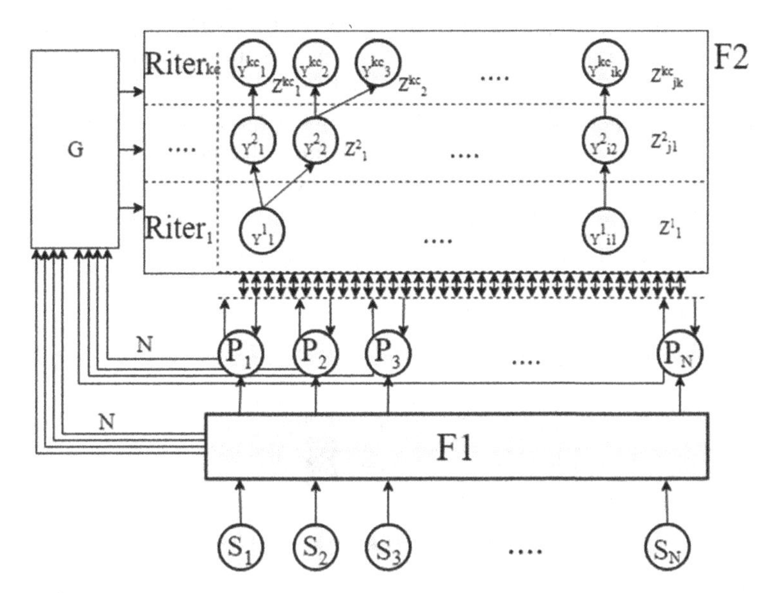

Fig. 1. The structure of the ART-2m network

The algorithm of such a network is described in detail in [10]. ANN ART-2m consists of three types of fields: *F1*, *F2* and *G*. *F1* is an input processing field that receives an input image, which is a tuple of *N* parameters describing the state of the network ($S = \{s1, s2, \ldots, sN\}$). *F2* is a memory field representing a set of *Y* neurons, which are characterized by level (maximum level is a *kc*), similarity parameter $Riter_j$ and weights z_{ij}, where $i = 1..N, j = 1..kc$. Field *G* evaluates resonance between the upstream signals from the *F1* field and the downstream signals from the *F2* field.

The proposed structure of the ART-2m network has the following features:

1. The search for an active neuron, in the weights of which the image is stored, occurs not only based on the frequency of the submitted images of the corresponding classes, but also based on semantic connections that are formed at the time of training the network. This allows one to significantly reduce the number of checks since all memory is now represented in a tree structure.
2. The possibility of parallelizing computations in the *F2* field, which is due to the impossibility of firing a memory neuron of the *Y*-layer, which is not semantically connected with the current neuron.

Due to the change in the memory architecture, the development of an effective learning and recognition algorithm for the ART-2m network was required.

3 Algorithm of ART-2m Network Functioning in Parallel Mode

The upgraded architecture of ART-2m allows parallelizing the process of pattern recognition due to the fact that the memory structure is tree-like. There are three most advanced technologies for parallelizing computations: *OpenMP* (the parallelization of computation at the level of control threads), MPI (process-level computation parallelization), and parallelization using graphics cores (*OpenCL* and *Cuda*).

The most suitable parallelization technology in the IDS software for the classification of CNS based on ART-2m is parallelization into computational threads. Figure 2 shows a block diagram of the functioning process of the ART-2m network in parallel mode.

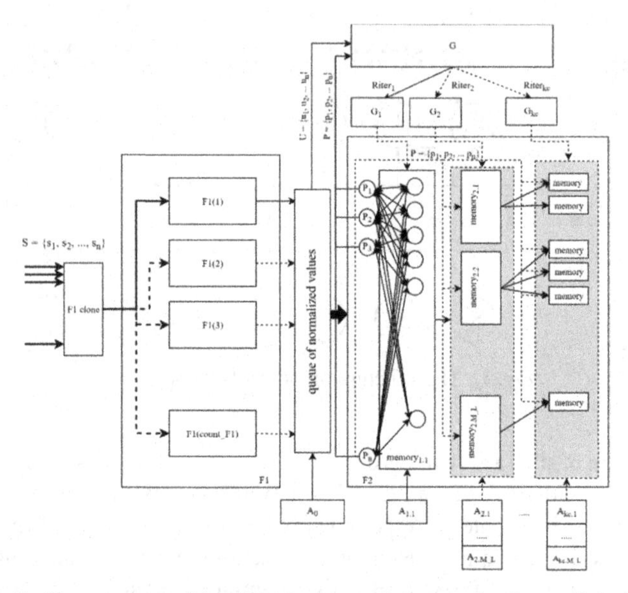

Fig. 2. The structure of the ART-2m network functioning in parallel mode

Data for CNS classification are presented as a vector *S* = *{s1, s2, ..., sN}* and enter the *F1* field into the *F1_clone* block. *F1_clone* decides to create a computation flow for normalizing input signals and generates *F1(c)* blocks, where *c* = *1..count_F1* (*count_F1* is a tuning parameter that defines the maximum number of threads in the *F1* field). The result of the *F1(c)* block enters the queue of normalized values. To synchronize this process, arbiter *A0* is used, which controls the sequence of writing data from blocks *F1* and reading field *F2*. When implementing the arbiter *A0*, mutexes were used, which are objects of the operating system kernel.

After entering the first record of normalized values into the queue, processing starts in the *F2* field. Reading data from the queue of normalized values and their further processing is performed in a new control flow and represents the following sequence of steps:

Step 1.1. Search resonating neuron in the current memory level $memory_{jk}$, where $k = 1..M\_L$ (*M_L* is a number of $memory_j$ at the *j*-th memory level). If a resonating neuron is found and the current memory level $memory_{jk}$ is not the last (the similarity parameter $Riter_j$ is less than the specified precision), then move to **step 1.2.** If a resonating neuron is not found and the current memory level $memory_{jk}$ is not the last one, then create a new neuron in the current $memory_{jk}$, initialize its weights and move to **step 2**, otherwise create a new neuron in the current $memory_{jk}$, initialize it weights, unlocking access to $memory_{jk}$ and closing the processing flow.
Step 1.2. Train the weights of the current resonating neuron, unblocking access to $memory_{jk}$, go to next $memory_{j+1,k}$ and move to **step 1.1.**
Step 2. Creating a new memory level $memory_{j+1}$, blocking it, calculating the similarity parameter using recurrent relation $Riter_{i+1} = Riter_i + 0.75(1 - Riter_i)$ creating a memory neuron of the current layer $j + 1$, initializing its weights, and move to **step 3**.
Step 3. Unlocking access to $memory_{j+1}$. Go to a new memory level, considering it current and move to **step 1.**

Synchronization of operations on neuron weights is performed by arbiters *Ajk*, which are implemented based on mutexes. In the algorithm of the ART-2m network, the following memory structure was used:

```
class Neuron {
public:
        ...
protected:
double      grade_;
double      type_;
double      nw_;
MemoryLevel* tree_;
std::vector<double>
weights_;
              ...};
```

```
class MemoryLevel {
public:
                    ...
protected:
std::mutex
mem_mutex;
std::vector<Neuron>
neurons_;
double
r_;
...
}.
```

where the *Neuron* class is a neuron containing the following fields: neuron weights (*weights_*); grade (*grade_*), which is calculated when training the network and determines whether the neuron is active; class of computer network state, in real representation (*type_*); pointer to next memory level (*tree_*) and the parameter of normalization of the neuron weights (*nw_*). If tree_ is *NULL*, then the neuron is the resultant.

The *MemoryLevel* class is one of the memory levels. It contains the following fields: OS kernel object, thread synchronization tool mutex required for parallel processing of network input (*mem_mutex*), vector of neurons (*neurons_*) and the similarity parameter of the current memory layer (*r_*).

4 Description of the Sample for Training

The NSL KDD-2009 [11] sample of signatures was used as test data for the formation of training and test samples of attacks, which is based on the KDD'99 database. Unlike the 1999 sample, there are no redundant images in the NSL KDD-2009. Each image is a connection consisting of a sequence of packets recorded at a certain time interval from one source IP address to another destination IP address using the corresponding protocol. Each such image has a label, which is a type of computer network state. The sample contains 22 types of network attacks and type of a stable network state. These types of attacks are combined into classes such as *DoS*, *R2L*, *U2R*, and *Probe*.

The data on the state of a computer network based on the KDD sample is a reference for testing problems of classifying the state of a computer network. In [12], the analysis of the KDD sample itself is carried out and all parameters of network connections are divided into four classes. The first class includes the parameters of TCP connections, the second is the IP-layer parameters, the third is the parameters calculated using a two-second time window, and the fourth is the parameters used to detect those attacks that last more than two seconds. Also, in the work, an analysis of the accuracy and speed of classification was carried out with a combination of various classes of parameters. The classification quality was assessed using the ROC (Receiver Operating Characteristic) curve.

5 Experimental Results

During the research, two types of experiments were carried out. The first experiments were carried out to evaluate the performance gain in parallel mode. The work speed, the number of transit neurons, and the number of execution threads were assessed. The second type of experiments was aimed at obtaining the results of the accuracy of the network states classification. Figure 3 shows the graphs of the system functioning in serial and parallel modes.

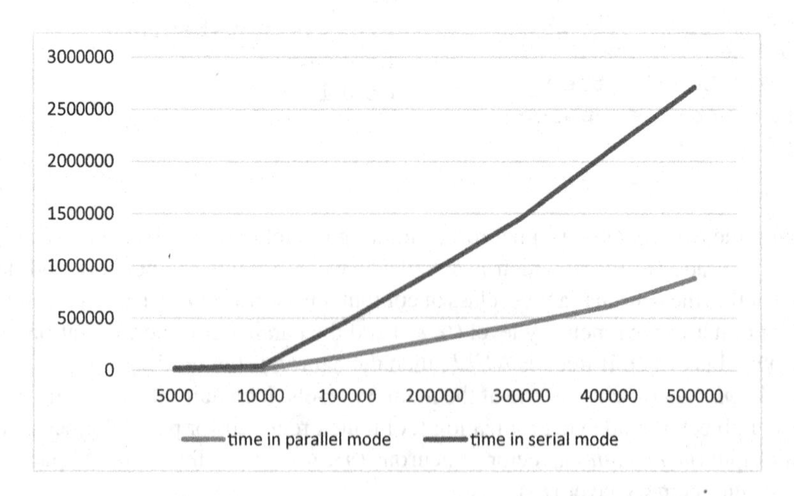

Fig. 3. Time characteristics for serial and parallel modes

From the results of the experiment, it can be seen that the increase in speed occurs after 10,000 images. This is due to the fact that additional structures and additional checks related to thread synchronization are used to parallelize computations.

Figure 4 shows the excess number of neurons. When training the network, five transient neurons are added to one resulting neuron. When training on a KDD sample of 400,000 images, the number of transit nodes is approximately 4,000 with 8,000 resulting ones, which means that with an increase in the number of different images, the number of new redundant nodes becomes less than the resulting ones.

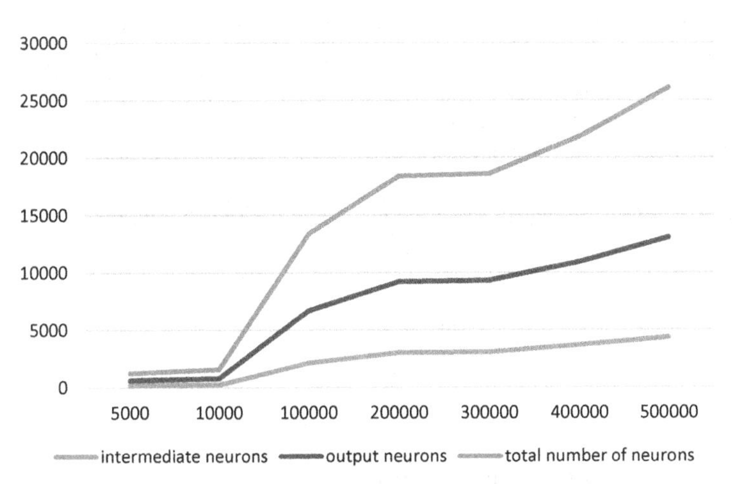

Fig. 4. The analysis of the redundancy of the memory structure with a different number of recognition patterns

The analysis of the number of transit and resultant nodes suggests that the proposed classifier based on ART-2m works more efficiently in classification problems with a large amount of different classified data.

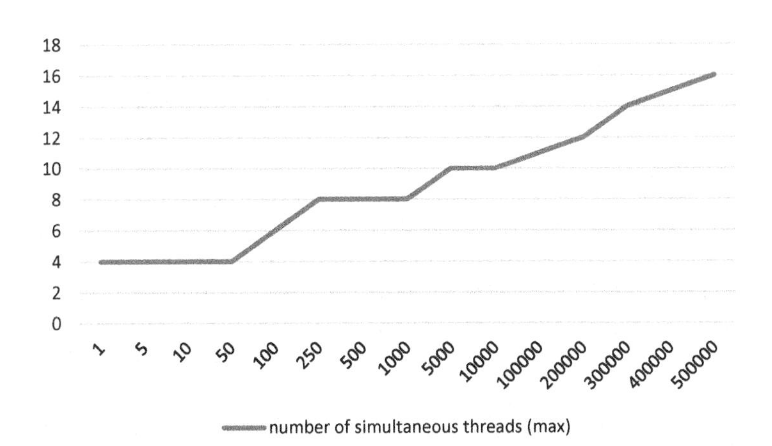

Fig. 5. The number of control flows for working in the F2 field depending on the number of analyzed images

Figure 5 shows the dependence of the number of generated flows in the *F2* field when classifying a different number of images. These experiments were carried out on a personal computer with an INTEL Core i5 6400 processor.

Since each control flow is created and executed in the *F2* field for each image from the queue of normalized values, the obtaining and further processing of the image from the queue formed by the *F1* field occurs in a random sequence. The number of created control threads that will train memory in the *F2* field will depend on the current free operating system resources. In the experiments, with an increase in the amount of processed data, an increase in the number of control flows occurs.

Tables 1 and 2 show the results of the experiment in comparison with the results of the experiments of the authors of other works [6, 7, 13]. Precision and recall were chosen as a measure of classification. The data for calculating these metrics is taken from an $n \times n$ confusion matrix (where n is the number of different determined states), the diagonal elements of which contain correctly defined states.

$$\text{precision}_c = \frac{A_{c,c}}{\sum_{i=1}^{n} A_{c,i}},$$

$$\text{recall}_c = \frac{A_{c,c}}{\sum_{i=1}^{n} A_{i,c}},$$

where A is a value of the confusion matrix cell.

Table 1. Results of experiments for determining the quality of classification of CNS types

State type	ART-2m		Direct distribution network		Kohonen network	
	Precision	Recall	Precision	Recall	Precision	Recall
normal	1	0.98	1	0.99	0.99	0.99
neptune	0.98	0.98	1	0.99	1	0.99
back	0.93	0.99	0.87	0.99	0.72	0.66
land	0.75	0.71	0.89	1	0.6	1
pod	1	1	0.55	1	0.24	0.78
smurf	1	1	1	1	1	0.99
teardrop	1	0.99	0.99	1	1	0.99
buffer_overflow	0.35	0.35	0.04	1	0.03	0.75
loadmodule	0.44	0.67	0.02	1	1	0.5
perl	1	1	0.28	1	1	0.5
rootkit	0.5	0.06	0	1	0.16	0.14
guess_passwd	0.98	1	0.7	1	0.16	0.96

(*continued*)

Table 1. (*continued*)

State type	ART-2m		Direct distribution network		Kohonen network	
	Precision	Recall	Precision	Recall	Precision	Recall
ftp_write	0.63	0.16	0.04	1	1	0.25
imap	0.82	0.82	0.14	1	0.3	0.83
multihop	0.43	0.5	0.25	1	1	0.57
phf	0	0	0.02	1	0.02	1
spy	1	1	0.02	1	1	0.5
warezclient	0.74	0.91	0.23	0.94	0.82	0.69
warezmaster	0.1	1	0.09	0.95	1	0.95
ipsweep	0.8	0.86	0.93	0.99	0.99	0.97
nmap	0.55	0.51	0.77	1	0.68	0.92
portsweep	0.56	0.67	0.93	1	0.99	0.98
satan	0.78	0.82	0.94	0.99	0.97	0.98

Table 2. Results of experiments for determining the quality of classification of CNS classes.

State class	ART-2m		Double layer perceptron		k-nearest neighbors		Decision tree	
	Precision	Recall	Precision	Recall	Precision	Recall	Precision	Recall
normal	1	0.98	1	0.99	0.66	0.98	0.67	0.95
dos	0.98	0.98	1	0.99	0.96	0.79	0.96	0.8
u2r	0.44	0.18	0.03	0.96	0.79	0.16	0.75	0.22
r2l	0.72	0.88	0.25	0.97	0.93	0.03	0.96	0.11
probe	0.7	0.91	0.97	0.99	0.81	0.66	0.86	0.63

The average classification accuracy of the CNS in the studied sample was 95.88. The experiments show comparable results. But unlike the other methods of data mining, the use of an ART-2m classifier guaranteed additional training. It should be noted that in most works, the phf attack is not detected. The implementation proposed based on ART-2m also failed to identify this CNS. This is primarily due to the fact that the phf attack is the script that may be held for a long time, and the data presented in KDD are discrete packets characterizing one connection. To identify these types of attacks, the use of other tools, for example, analyzing not only one packet, but also the entire traffic of the corresponding protocol was required.

6 Conclusion

The paper proposes a hierarchical memory structure for an artificial neural network of the ART-2 type. Such an organization of memory allow us to eliminate the shortcomings of the classical neural network of the adaptive-resonance theory, namely, to accelerate the search for a resonating neuron and provide the ability to organize computations in parallel mode. It also makes it possible to improve the recognition accuracy by adding new memory levels with a stricter similarity parameter. An algorithm for the parallel functioning of the ART-2m network was proposed. The results of the experiments show the possibility of using ART-2m in intrusion detection systems.

Acknowledgment. This work was supported by Russian Foundation for Basic Research, project 19-29-09056 mk and Ministry of Education of Russia (grant IS) project No. 13.

References

1. Positive Technologies. Vulnerabilities of corporate information systems, p. 21 (2018)
2. Petrenko, S.A.: Methods for detecting intrusions and anomalies in the functioning of cyber systems. Proc. Inst. Syst. Anal. Russian Acad. Sci. **41**, 194–202 (2009)
3. Duque, S., bin Omar, M.N.I.: Using data mining algorithms for developing a model for intrusion detection system (IDS). Procedia Comput. Sci. 61, 46–51 (2015)
4. Ghosh, S., et al.: A novel neuro-fuzzy classification technique for data mining. Egypt. Inform. J. **15**(3), 129–147 (2014)
5. Idhammad, M., Afdel, K., Belouch, M.: Distributed intrusion detection system for cloud environments based on data mining techniques. Procedia Comput. Sci. **127**, 35–41 (2018)
6. Emelyanova, U.G., et al.: Neural network technology for detecting network attacks on information resources. Softw. Syst.: Theor. Appl. 2(3) (2011)
7. Markov, R.A., et al.: Research of neural network technologies to identify information security incidents. Young Sci. **23**, 55–60 (2015)
8. Carpenter, G.A., Grossberg, S.: ART 2: self-organization of stable category recognition codes for analog input patterns. Appl. Opt. **26**(23), 4919–4930 (1987)
9. Carpenter, G.A., Grossberg, S., Rosen, D.B.: ART 2: an adaptive resonance algorithm for rapid category learning and recognition. Neural Netw. **4**(4), 493–504 (1991)
10. Bukhanov, D.G., Polyakov, V.M.: Adaptive resonance theory network with multilevel memory. Sci. Bull. Belgorod State Univ. **45**(4), 665–673 (2018)
11. The NSL-KDD Data Set. [Electronic resource]. http://www.unb.ca/cic/datasets/nsl.html. Accessed 20 Jan 2021
12. Aggarwal, P., Sharma, S.K.: Analysis of KDD dataset attributes-class wise for intrusion detection. Procedia Comput. Sci. **57**, 842–851 (2015)
13. Kajemskiy, M.A., Shelukhin, O.I.: Multi-class classification of network attacks on information resources using machine learning methods. Proc. Educ. Inst. Commun. **5**(1), 107–115 (2019)

Data Mining, Machine Learning, Classification

Ranking Weibull Survival Model: Boosting the Concordance Index of the Weibull Time-to-Event Prediction Model with Ranking Losses

Kseniia Cheloshkina(✉)

Laboratory of Bioinformatics, Faculty of Computer Science, National Research University Higher School of Economics, Moscow, Russia
kcheloshkina@hse.ru

Abstract. The concordance index is a widely used metric for the evaluation of time-to-event prediction models. It describes the proportion of correctly ranked pairs of observations by time to event and hence is closely related to ROC AUC. In this paper, we propose enriching such baseline model as Weibull time-to-event feed-forward network, which optimizes classic in survival analysis log-likelihood with additional concordance-aware loss components. Here we demonstrate that a combination of parametric survival analysis methods with a learning-to-rank approach forces the model to achieve higher concordance. The experiments over real-world datasets demonstrate the highly competitive performance of the proposed method called RWSM (Ranking Weibull Survival Model) in terms of the concordance index.

Keywords: Survival analysis · Learning-to-rank · Contrastive learning

1 Introduction

Time-to-event prediction is a popular task in healthcare and medical diagnosis. It also has found industrial use, for example, in a task of customer churn modeling, credit scoring, prediction of time-to-failure of mechanical systems, etc. In industry, this problem is often solved with binary classifiers, which are able to output the probability distribution of event for one fixed time horizon. By contrast, classical survival analysis models provide full time-to-event probability distribution. Additionally, these models suggest interpretability of the results. But since interpretability imposes restrictions on the form of relationship between the dependent variable and the predictors, it often comes at a cost of accuracy loss in comparison with binary classifiers. Another difference is the ability to take into consideration the censoring of data that underlies survival analysis methods but is not taken into account in the case of binary classifiers. Given these distinctions, boosting the survival analysis model's performance will provide different applications with the opportunity to use full time-to-event probability distribution.

S. M. Kovalev et al. (Eds.): RCAI 2021, LNAI 12948, pp. 43–56, 2021.
https://doi.org/10.1007/978-3-030-86855-0_4

All survival analysis methods could be grouped into two general approaches: statistical and machine learning. The former group of methods is presented by parametric, non-parametric, and semi-parametric methods. The most popular models in the group are Cox proportional hazards (CPH) model and Accelerated Failure Time (AFT) model. The latter group consists of modifications of classical machine learning approaches to account for censored data: survival SVM, random survival forest, Cox boosting, etc. One of the recent research directions is a combination of classical survival models with deep learning.

Inspired by deep learning advances, researchers propose methods to combine survival analysis with neural network architectures and make them applicable to their custom industry problems. [9] applies survival analysis to model click probability distribution. Usually, this task is solved as a learning-to-rank problem by using point-wise or pairwise approach. The authors proposed the deep recurrent survival ranking (DRSR) model, which combines the survival model and recurrent neural network (RNN) to model click probability distribution at the document given the history of clicks and non-clicks (contextual info). In [19], survival analysis solves the problem of early fraud detection. The RNN model outputs a hazard rate with no assumptions of underlying time-to-event distribution and motivates the model to capture the events as early as possible by transformation of classic loss function (likelihood).

In the paper, we propose an approach to incorporate survival times order information into survival analysis model to boost concordance index. It is realized by the extension of the Weibull time-to-event prediction model with additional ranking loss functions: in the form of cross-entropy loss and contrastive loss. The proposed model possesses two important characteristics: 1) provides full time-to-event probability distribution and 2) takes into account censoring and survival times order, while not implying the interpretability of results in general case. The framework is implemented in TensorFlow and available at Github (https://github.com/KseniiaCheloshkina/ranking-survival).

The rest of the paper is organized as follows. In Sect. 2, we describe the concordance index and discuss different deep learning approaches to survival analysis. In Sect. 3, we introduce the proposed approach, while Sect. 4 demonstrates experimental results on several real-world datasets.

2 Related Work

2.1 Concordance Index

Since the survival analysis main goal is to get full time-to-event probability distribution, for evaluation of survival analysis models special metrics should be used which differ from those reported for classification models. The commonly used metrics are the concordance index [7], brier score, binomial log-likelihood, and their integrated versions.

Due to its close relationship with ROC AUC [8], the concordance index is the most widely used evaluation metric. In general, the concordance index describes the probability that, for a pair of observations, the predicted ordering of survival times will coincide with the true ordering. This way, concordance index measures how well observations are ranked by their survival times.

Let t_i be a time to event and y_i an event label for i-th observation (y_i is equal to 0 if observation is right censored and 1 if event occurred). Then observations i and j are *comparable* if both are events ($y_i = 1, y_j = 1$) or only the observation with greater time-to-event is censored ($(t_i, y_i = 1), (t_j, y_j = 0), t_i < t_j$). In comparable cases (set of pairs E), true ordering of survival times coincides with the ordering of corresponding time-to-event. In other cases (observations are both censored or only the observation with smaller time-to-event is censored), we could not reliably determine whose survival time is greater so that observations are *incomparable*.

Since, in general, for one pair of comparable observations, the ordering of predicted survival probabilities $\hat{S}_i(t)$ could change over time, the concordance index (or C-index) is calculated for a fixed time horizon t_0:

$$c(t_0) = \frac{1}{|E|} \sum_{(i,j) \in E, t_i < t_j} 1_{\hat{S}_i(t_0) < \hat{S}_j(t_0)} \tag{1}$$

Similarly to ROC AUC, the concordance index is equal to 0.5 in the case of a random choice model and 1 for a perfect model.

Integrated versions of concordance index [1] do not use a fixed prediction time but rather set it equal to minimal time-to-event in pair $t_0 = min(t_i, t_j)$:

$$c^{td} = P\left(\hat{S}_i(t_i) < \hat{S}_j(t_i) \middle| t_i < t_j, (i,j) \in E\right) \tag{2}$$

Later, in the discussion of the experiments' results, we will report this time-dependent version of the concordance index.

The concordance index is a well-interpreted metric, and for many industrial applications, it is closely related to business metrics, that is why it is of most interest to use the methods aimed at direct optimization of the concordance index. Earlier, the methods aimed at forcing linear models or neural networks to optimize the concordance index instead of Cox's partial likelihood were discussed in [16,17]. In [4], the authors proposed GBMCI, which is a gradient boosting method optimizing a smoothed approximation of the concordance index based on covariates.

2.2 Deep Learning in Survival Analysis

With the growth of deep learning, its advances were applied to the field of survival analysis. One of the main research directions extends the classical Cox model with deep learning components to further boost the performance. Basically, the linear predictor ($\beta^T x$) in the Cox model may be replaced with a more complex function such as a multilayer perceptron [5]. In [18], the authors propose a framework for deep survival models (deep neural net ending up with a Cox survival model) with Bayesian optimization of hyperparameters. As a further development of the idea, Kvamme [12] removed the proportionality constraint of the Cox model by the introduction of alternative loss function for optimization of a neural network model. In the DeepSurv framework [10], the authors proposed getting personalized treatment recommendations by the inclusion of an additional categorical variable of the treatment group in the deep survival model. The DeepHit approach [13] models competing risks for discrete time. The neural network outputs time-to-event probability mass distribution and optimizes combined loss function

$$loss = \alpha loss_{rank} + loss_L \tag{3}$$

composed of log-likelihood component:

$$loss_L = \sum_{i=1}^{N} \Big(y_i log(y_{e_i}(x_i)) + (1 - y_i) log(\hat{S_{t_i}}(x_i)) \Big) \tag{4}$$

and ranking component

$$loss_{rank} = \sum_{i,j} \left(y_i 1_{t_i < t_j} \exp\left(\frac{\hat{S}_i(t_i) - \hat{S}_j(t_i)}{\sigma} \right) \right) \tag{5}$$

In [14], the authors proposed MTLSA (Multi-Task Learning Model for Survival Analysis), which translates the survival analysis problem into a set of related binary classification problems with one classifier for each time interval. Each binary classifier only focuses on modeling the local problem (event at day t), while the network has a shared representation for all related tasks and additionally applies a penalty to force feature selection.

In [2], the authors propose an idea of applying data augmentation and convert a survival task into a standard Poisson regression task. Per the paper, time-to-event distribution is divided into discrete intervals assuming piece-wise constant hazard rates, and then data are transformed to piece-wise exponential data (PED). The authors demonstrate that Poisson log-likelihood is proportional to piece-wise exponential log-likelihood and hence any machine learning algorithm that can optimize a Poisson likelihood (GBM, deep NN, etc.) can be used in the context of time-to-event analysis.

In the Deep Adversarial Time-to-Event (DATE) model [3], a conditional generative adversarial network (GAN) is used to model non-parametric time-to-event distribution. Additionally, the authors provide an approach to measure time-to-event uncertainty.

3 The Proposed Model

In this section, we first discuss a parametric approach to modeling time-to-event and introduce Weibull distribution as one of the most popular choices for this group of methods. Then we describe the proposed framework and base model. Next, we transform the task of boosting concordance into a learning-to-rank problem, and for this purpose, we enrich the base model with additional loss functions.

3.1 Modeling Time-to-Event with Weibull Distribution

As has been mentioned earlier, one group of statistical methods for survival analysis is presented by parametric methods. The parametric methods assume that time-to-event has specific distribution with the most popular choices of it such as exponential, log-logistic, log-normal, gamma, and Weibull distribution for continuous time. In the simplest case, a univariate model could be fitted to an entire dataset that outputs distribution parameters corresponding to the maximal likelihood. These kinds of models could be impractical if empirical distribution significantly differs from the assumed distribution. But if the assumption holds, optimal parameters could be used to generate the entire time-to-event distribution and get survival probabilities for any time t.

One of the most useful distributions in survival analysis is Weibull distribution for continuous data. It has interpretable shape and scale parameters (α and β) and is an example of unimodal distribution. For $T \sim Weibull(\alpha, \beta)$ probability density function $F(x)$, survival distribution function $S(t)$, hazard function $\lambda(t)$ and cumulative hazard function $\Lambda(t)$ are expressed as follows:

$$F(t) = 1 - \exp\left[-\left(\frac{t}{\alpha}\right)^{\beta}\right] \tag{6}$$

$$S(t) = \exp\left[-\left(\frac{t}{\alpha}\right)^{\beta}\right] \tag{7}$$

$$\lambda(t) = \left(\frac{t}{\alpha}\right)^{\beta-1}\frac{\beta}{\alpha} \tag{8}$$

$$\Lambda(t) = \left(\frac{t}{\alpha}\right)^{\beta} \tag{9}$$

In survival analysis likelihood l for an observation with time-to-event t and an event label, y is specified as either a probability of the event at time t if the observation is not censored or the probability of the event being later than t, otherwise:

$$l = P(T = t)^{y} P(T > t)^{1-y} \tag{10}$$

which could be expressed in terms of cumulative hazard function:

$$\log l = y \log \lambda(t) - \Lambda(t) \tag{11}$$

To find optimal α and β parameters of the distribution for a sample, it is necessary to sum up log-likelihoods for all observations and maximize the sum. By contrast, it could be supposed that time-to-event t_i for an observation is distributed as $Weibull(\alpha_i, \beta_i)$ with its own optimal α_i and β_i parameters. If covariates information x_i is provided, it could be used to predict these parameters by maximizing log-likelihood. This idea was exploited in [15] where the author proposed WTTE-RNN method (Weibull Time-To-Event Recurrent Neural Network). Here it was proposed to pass time-dependent feature vectors into a recurrent neural network stacked with an output layer consisting of two units representing α and β parameters and maximizing log-likelihood.

3.2 General Framework

Here we formulate a general framework for concordance-aware modeling of time-to-event with Weibull distribution.

The purpose of the model is to predict the parameters α and β of Weibull distribution based on input features. Given a feed-forward neural network $g(x)$ input features x_i are passed through the network to get representation $g_i = g(x_i)$. This representation is further processed by the output layer $o(x)$, which is a linear layer with specific activation functions. The output $o_i = o(g_i)$ is a pair (α, β), which could be further used to generate whole time-to-event distribution. Assuming continuous time T and given cumulative hazard function (9), substituting it into (11) gives log likelihood for Weibull distributed time T. To get final loss function it is needed to sum up for all n observations and turn the task into minimization problem. Additionally, to make the model numerically stable (to prevent it from exploding α values), it is important to add a penalty on mean α value. Then the next loss function should be optimized:

$$loss_{ll} = \sum_{i=1}^{n} \left(-y_i \left(\beta_i \log \left(\frac{t_i}{\alpha_i} \right) + \log \beta_i \right) + \left(\frac{t_i}{\alpha_i} \right)^{\beta_i} \right) + w_\alpha \frac{1}{n} \sum_{i=1}^{n} \alpha_i \quad (12)$$

Note that neural network $g(x)$ is a feed-forward network. In the case when it is necessary to take into account time-varying features or recurrent events, a feed-forward neural network could be replaced with a recurrent neural network (RNN) to process sequences. For this purpose, loss function should be slightly changed by the introduction of the sum over time-steps $j = 0, .., T$ as proposed in [15] as well:

$$loss_{ll} = \sum_{i=1}^{n} \sum_{j=0}^{T} \left(-y_{i,j} \left(\beta_{i,j} \log \left(\frac{t_{i,j}}{\alpha_{i,j}} \right) + \log \beta_{i,j} \right) + \left(\frac{t_{i,j}}{\alpha_{i,j}} \right)^{\beta_{i,j}} \right) \quad (13)$$

Besides, this framework could be adjusted to another time-to-event distribution (continuous or discrete).

As the primary goal of the framework is to improve concordance of time-to-event predictions, it is necessary to introduce the information on the true survival times ordering into the model. We approach this issue by specifying additional loss components and a batch generator. Here we define a base batch generator, which will allow us to form pairs of observations for the incorporation of the information on their survival times ordering into the model.

Batch Generation: At each iteration, we would like to feed into the model samples from all time-to-event distribution. For this purpose, the distribution is divided into m time bins with equal number of observations in each and q_i being the index of the time bin for observation i with time-to-event t_i. Each batch consists of k examples from each of m time bins where examples from specific time bins are taken uniformly from the corresponding event time distribution. The batches are generated as long as there are at least k examples in each time bin. The base model in the proposed framework optimizes loss function (12) and is trained on batches generated by the specified procedure. To achieve the concordance index uplift, additional loss components will be added that penalize the model if the ordering of predicted survival times differs from the true ordering (only for comparable observations).

3.3 Improving Concordance by Adding Cross-Entropy Loss

One of the most natural methods to account for the correctness of the ranking of a pair of observations is the introduction of additional loss function in the form of cross-entropy.

The procedure takes pairs of comparable examples from different time bins, for which predicted survival probabilities are ordered incorrectly, and calculates an error based on the difference in the probabilities and difference in time bins. The pairs are sampled on-the-fly (online) from all available combinations of examples provided by the batch generator described above. Besides, the pairs are "hard mined", which suggests that for each example we consider only the hardest pairs with the greatest error.

Pairs Hard Mining for Cross-Entropy Loss. First, the batch is generated as proposed earlier resulting in a set of k examples from each of m time bins. Then for each example, the hardest positive and the hardest negative examples are selected (if available). For this purpose the next variables are defined for each pair of examples:

- Comparability label in terms of c-index

$$w_{i,j}^{comp} = \begin{cases} 1 & \text{if observations } i \text{ and } j \text{ are comparable} \\ 0 & \text{otherwise} \end{cases} \tag{14}$$

- Time bins distance weight

$$w_{i,j}^{dist} = 1 + \frac{|\Delta q_{i,j}|}{m} \tag{15}$$

  where $\Delta q_{i,j} = q_i - q_j$
- Survival predictions difference

$$\Delta S_{i,j} = \begin{cases} S_i(t_i) - S_j(t_i) & \text{if } t_i < t_j \\ S_i(t_j) - S_j(t_j) & \text{otherwise} \end{cases} \tag{16}$$

A pair of examples is considered positive if they are comparable ($w_{i,j}^{comp} = 1$) and $\Delta q_{i,j} > 0$. In other words, a positive pair is a pair of comparable examples with time-to-event of observation i greater than time-to-event of observation j. If the model is correct, then predicted survival probabilities for the moment t_j should be ordered in the same direction (the greater the time-to-event, the greater survival probability). Hence, "hard positive pairs" are presented by positive pairs with reverse order ($\Delta S_{i,j} < 0$). If there are examples, which form, together with example i, hard positive pairs, then the hardest positive pair is selected for example i that have the greatest error:

$$\arg\min_j err_{i,j}^{ce+} \tag{17}$$

where

$$err_{i,j}^{ce+} = w_{i,j}^{comp} w_{i,j}^{dist} \Delta S_{i,j} 1_{\Delta q_{i,j}>0} 1_{\Delta S_{i,j}<0} \tag{18}$$

Then the error err_i^{ce+} is added to a set of all "hardest positive pairs" U_+ :

$$err_i^{ce+} = \min_j err_{i,j}^{ce+} \tag{19}$$

Similarly, a pair of examples is considered negative if they are comparable ($w_{i,j}^{comp} = 1$) and $\Delta q_{i,j} > 0$. The hardest negative pair for example i is formed with example j such that:

$$\arg\max_j err_{i,j}^{ce-} = \quad \arg\max_j \left(w_{i,j}^{comp} w_{i,j}^{dist} \Delta S_{i,j} 1_{\Delta q_{i,j}<0} 1_{\Delta S_{i,j}>0} \right) \tag{20}$$

Following this batch generation technique, the corresponding loss function could be expressed in cross-entropy form to force the model to fix the ordering errors:

$$loss_{ce} = -\left(\sum_{i \in U_+} \log \sigma(err_i^{ce+}) + \sum_{i \in U_-} \log(1 - \sigma(err_i^{ce-})) \right) \tag{21}$$

This loss component could be added to log-likelihood main loss as specified in (12) with a coefficient:

$$loss = loss_{ll} + w_{ce} loss_{ce} \tag{22}$$

3.4 Improving Concordance by Adding Contrastive Loss

Another option of expressing the ranking objective is using a contrastive loss function, standard for metric learning (or pairwise ranking loss function, [6]). Here we apply this idea to our domain in the following form. First, we get representations (linear projections) of Weibull parameters and then calculate the Euclidean distance between these representations for all examples. The goal is to minimize the distance between representations of examples in the same time bin and maximize the distance between representations of examples from different time bins with a penalty proportional to the difference in time bins. For each example in the batch, we select the hardest negative and the hardest positive example if available.

Pairs Hard Mining for Contrastive Loss. First, the output layer with Weibull parameters α and β for each example in the batch is linearly transformed to get representations. These representations $o_i = h([\alpha_i; \beta_i])(h(x) = Hx, H \in R^{2x2})$ are inputs for contrastive loss component.

Then the next variables are defined for each pair of examples in the batch:

- Indicators of t_i and t_j being in the same time bin or not

$$w_{i,j}^{q+} = \begin{cases} 1 & \text{if } \Delta q_{i,j} = 0 \text{ and } i \neq j \\ 0 & \text{otherwise} \end{cases} \tag{23}$$

$$w_{i,j}^{q-} = \begin{cases} 1 & \text{if } \Delta q_{i,j} \neq 0 \\ 0 & \text{otherwise} \end{cases} \tag{24}$$

- Euclidean distance $D_{i,j}$ between representations

$$D_{i,j} = ||o_i - o_j||_2 \tag{25}$$

- Time bins distance weight

$$w_{i,j}^{dist} = 1 + \frac{|\Delta q_{i,j}|}{m} \tag{26}$$

where $\Delta q_{i,j} = q_i - q_j$

The positive pairs P_+ are presented by comparable examples within the same time bin ($w_{i,j}^{q+} = 1$). For each example i in the batch, the "hardest positive example" is selected - an example $j((i,j) \in P_+)$ with maximum positive distance $D_{i,j}$. Then the error is

$$err_i^{cntr+} = w_{i,j}^{comp} w_{i,j}^{q+} D_{i,j} 1_{D_{i,j}>0} \qquad j = \arg\max\{D_{i,j} | (i,j) \in P_+\} \tag{27}$$

Set U_+ is defined as a set of all examples in the batch for which the hardest positive example is found.

A set of negative pairs P_- is composed of pairs of comparable examples with $w_{i,j}^{q-} = 1$. The "hardest negative example" is found for each example i in the batch: it is an example $j((i,j) \in P_-)$ with minimum distance $D_{i,j}$.

The error is estimated as

$$err_i^{cntr-} = w_{i,j}^{comp} w_{i,j}^{q-} \max(0, w_{i,j}^{dist} - D_{i,j}) \text{ where } j = \arg\min\{D_{i,j} | (i,j) \in P_-\} \tag{28}$$

Then a set U_- is created, which consists of all examples in the batch for which negative loss is defined: add an example i if the hardest negative example with $err_i^{cntr-} > 0$ exists.

Then the contrastive loss component will be estimated as

$$loss_{cntr} = \sum_{i \in U_+} err_i^{cntr+} + \sum_{i \in U_-} err_i^{cntr-} \tag{29}$$

and included in the final loss with a coefficient:

$$loss = loss_{ll} + w_{cntr} loss_{cntr} \tag{30}$$

Training. As in this setting the network has two heads, the model could be trained in two modes: by joint optimization of log-likelihood and contrastive loss as stated in (30) or by sequential optimization. Since the survival analysis task is the primary task the model should solve, while contrastive loss should be used only to further boost the performance, we propose the following procedure:

- First r_{main} epochs optimize $loss_{ll}$. This helps find appropriate α and β parameters' ranges
- The next r_{contr} epochs fine-tune "contrastive head". For this purpose, optimize only $loss_{cntr}$ loss function with all neural network weights freezed except $h(x)$
- The last r_{both} epochs optimize the final loss function (30) with all weights unfrozen.

4 Experiments

To evaluate the proposed method and compare it with the existing methods, we used two real-world datasets. The first is the one commonly used in the literature, the Molecular Taxonomy of Breast Cancer International Consortium (METABRIC) dataset, which has a relatively small sample size. One large data set is used for comparison - from the WSDM KKBox's churn prediction challenge.

4.1 Data

For the experiments, we used versions of the datasets provided by pycox Github repository [11]. The summary of datasets' statistics is presented in Table 1.

The METABRIC dataset is a dataset for time-to-event prediction of breast cancer patients. It consists of nine covariates: four gene indicators, and the rest are the patient's clinical features. They were transformed as follows: five numerical columns were standardized, while the rest were taken as is. Additionally, we removed observations with zero duration because they introduce instability into the model. To evaluate model performance on such a small dataset, five-fold CV resampling procedure was used. For splitting the dataset into folds, time-to-event distribution was divided into five equal-sized bins (with an equal number of observations in each), and strata were formed from the time bin number and event label.

Table 1. Datasets summary

Dataset	Size	Features	Censored
METABRIC	1 901	9	42%
KKBOX	2 646 746	15	28.5%

The KKBOX dataset used for evaluation ("kkbox_v1" in pycox package [11]) is the modification of the original survival dataset created from the WSDM - KKBox's Churn Prediction Challenge 2017. The dataset was published at Kaggle to solve a problem of customer churn prediction: in this case, the unsubscription from the music streaming service KKBOX. In pycox package [11]), the dataset has been already divided into the train, test, and validation sets in proportion 67.5/25/7.5 with stratification by event label. During preprocessing for categorical features like "gender", "city", and "registered_via", one-hot encoding was applied, while seven continuous columns were standardized and five binary columns were taken without changes, resulting in a total of 40 features.

Table 2. Concordance index for METABRIC (mean validation score in 5-fold CV) and KKBOX (test score).

Method	METABRIC	KKBOX
Base	0.658	0.856
+ Cross-entropy loss	0.659	0.857
+ Contrastive loss	**0.669**	0.855
CoxPH (DeepSurv)	0.634	0.843
CoxCC	0.638	0.843
DeepHit	0.656	**0.859**

4.2 Results

METABRIC. As the main goal is to check the ability of the proposed method to boost the concordance index, we did not perform an exhaustive search of the most appropriate neural network architecture. For the METABRIC dataset, four units dense layer without activation was used as a feed-forward network.

Except for the neural network optimizers' settings, the most influential hyper-parameters are the alpha regularization hyper-parameter w_α, cross-entropy weight w_{ce} and contrastive weight w_{cntr}.

For each model, we performed grid search over these hyper-parameters and optimizers' parameters (learning rate, decay, step-rate); Adam or SGD optimizers were used in the study.

The next parameters ranges were checked: 1e-6–1e-9 for w_α, 0.1–5 for w_{ce} and 0.1–5 for w_{cntr}. All models were trained for 80 epochs. A model with contrastive loss was trained with sequential optimization spending 40 epochs on log-likelihood loss optimization, 25 epochs on contrastive loss optimization, and 15 epochs on joint optimization of both losses. The results for the best model of each type are presented in Fig. 1 and Table 2.

It could be seen that the model with cross-entropy loss has only slight uplift in terms of the concordance index, while the model with contrastive loss significantly outperforms the baseline. We compared proposed models to recent

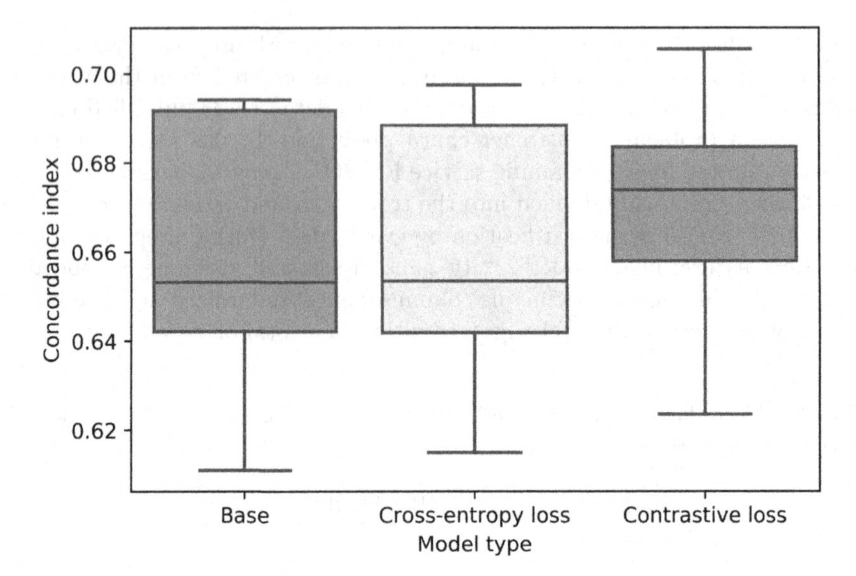

Fig. 1. Distribution of the concordance index on the validation fold in five-fold CV for the METABRIC dataset.

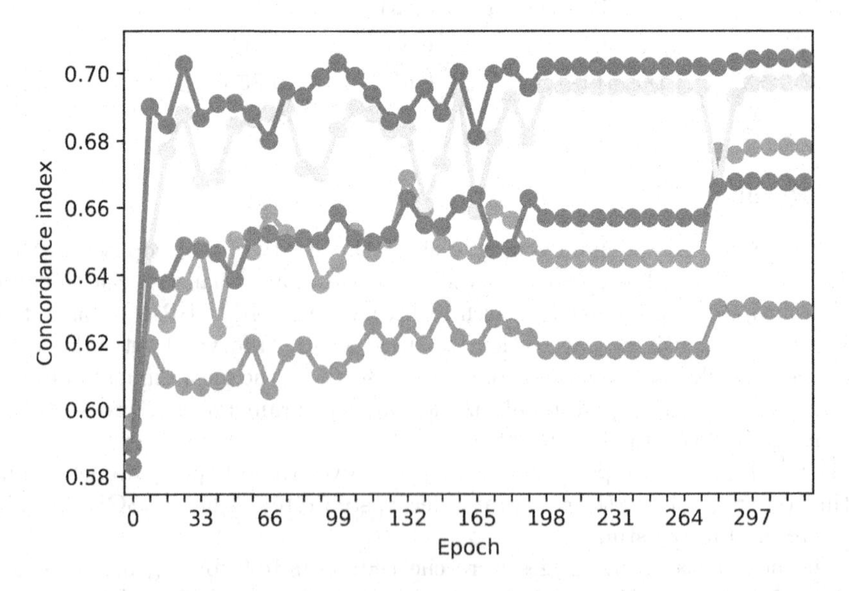

Fig. 2. Model with contrastive loss: the concordance index on validation set for each fold in the METABRIC dataset.

state-of-the-art methods keeping the same runtime (~30 s). Results presented in Table 2 demonstrate the competitiveness of the approach. Moreover, if we increase the number of epochs to train the model with contrastive loss up to 330 (200/80/50 epochs by stages, resulting in total 130 s runtime), even higher uplift could be achieved resulting in the mean c-index 0.675. For this model in Fig. 2, the concordance index is plotted for each validation fold by epoch number, and it is clearly seen that for most of the folds, an increase in the c-index is observed at the last optimization stage.

KKBOX. For the KKBOX dataset, a feed-forward net is composed of three layers (64, 32, and 16 units) with ReLU activation, where for categorical features embeddings are used. For each of the three model types, hyperparameters search was performed with the same hyperparameter ranges as for the METABRIC dataset. Training each model for 30 epochs ($\sim$1 h for base model and model with cross-entropy loss, 4.5 h for model with contrastive loss and 15/10/5 epochs per stage) we got the concordance index as shown in Table 2. Given the performance for benchmark models, which were fitted for comparable time, it could be seen that proposed methods outperform Cox-based models (DeepSurv and CoxCC), while having slightly lower quality than DeepHit.

5 Conclusion

In the paper, we introduced an approach to include survival times ordering information into the time-to-event prediction model. Taking as a baseline the Weibull survival model, which passes covariates through a feed-forward network to predict distribution parameters, we proposed extending it with pair-wise ranking losses. Cross-entropy loss forces the model to keep the order of survival probabilities the same as their time-to-event, penalizing the incorrect rankings by a value proportional to the difference in survival probabilities and the difference in time. Contrastive loss makes the model keep distance between parameters embeddings small for examples from the same time bin and large for examples from different time bins. It is worth noting that the proposed loss functions can be computed in batches, enabling the models to scale well to large data sets. Using two real-world datasets (small METABRIC and large KKBOX datasets), we demonstrated the competitiveness of the approach for the purpose of the concordance index improvement.

References

1. Antolini, L., Boracchi, P., Biganzoli, E.: A time-dependent discrimination index for survival data. Stat. Med. **24**(24), 3927–3944 (2005)
2. Bender, A., Rügamer, D., Scheipl, F., Bischl, B.: A general machine learning framework for survival analysis. arXiv preprint arXiv:2006.15442 (2020)
3. Chapfuwa, P., et al.: Adversarial time-to-event modeling. In: International Conference on Machine Learning (2018)
4. Chen, Y., Jia, Z., Mercola, D., Xie, X.: A gradient boosting algorithm for survival analysis via direct optimization of concordance index. Comput. Math. Methods Med. **2013** (2013)

5. Faraggi, D., Simon, R.: A neural network model for survival data. Stat. Med. **14**(1), 73–82 (1995)
6. Hadsell, R., Chopra, S., LeCun, Y.: Dimensionality reduction by learning an invariant mapping. In: 2006 IEEE Computer Society Conference on Computer Vision and Pattern Recognition (CVPR 2006), vol. 2, pp. 1735–1742. IEEE (2006)
7. Harrell, F.E., Califf, R.M., Pryor, D.B., Lee, K.L., Rosati, R.A.: Evaluating the yield of medical tests. Jama **247**(18), 2543–2546 (1982)
8. Heagerty, P.J., Zheng, Y.: Survival model predictive accuracy and roc curves. Biometrics **61**(1), 92–105 (2005)
9. Jin, J., et al.: A deep recurrent survival model for unbiased ranking. In: Proceedings of the 43rd International ACM SIGIR Conference on Research and Development in Information Retrieval (2020)
10. Katzman, J.L., Shaham, U., Cloninger, A., Bates, J., Jiang, T., Kluger, Y.: Deepsurv: personalized treatment recommender system using a cox proportional hazards deep neural network. BMC Med. Res. Methodol. **18**(1), 24 (2018)
11. Kvamme, H.: pycox: Survival analysis with pytorch (2020). https://github.com/havakv/pycox/releases/tag/v0.2.1
12. Kvamme, H., Borgan, Ø., Scheel, I.: Time-to-event prediction with neural networks and cox regression. J. Mach. Learn. Res. **20**(129), 1–30 (2019)
13. Lee, C., Zame, W., Yoon, J., van der Schaar, M.: Deephit: a deep learning approach to survival analysis with competing risks. In: Proceedings of the AAAI Conference on Artificial Intelligence, vol. 32 (2018)
14. Li, Y., Wang, J., Ye, J., Reddy, C.K.: A multi-task learning formulation for survival analysis. In: Proceedings of the 22nd ACM SIGKDD International Conference on Knowledge Discovery and Data Mining, pp. 1715–1724 (2016)
15. Martinsson, E.: Wtte-rnn: Weibull time to event recurrent neural network. Ph.D. thesis, Chalmers University of Technology & University of Gothenburg (2016)
16. Steck, H., Krishnapuram, B., Dehing-Oberije, C., Lambin, P., Raykar, V.C.: On ranking in survival analysis: Bounds on the concordance index. In: Advances in Neural Information Processing Systems, pp. 1209–1216 (2008)
17. Yan, L., Verbel, D., Saidi, O.: Predicting prostate cancer recurrence via maximizing the concordance index. In: Proceedings of the tenth ACM SIGKDD International Conference on Knowledge Discovery and Data Mining, pp. 479–485 (2004)
18. Yousefi, S., et al.: Predicting clinical outcomes from large scale cancer genomic profiles with deep survival models. Sci. Rep. **7**(1), 1–11 (2017)
19. Zheng, P., Yuan, S., Wu, X.: Safe: A neural survival analysis model for fraud early detection. In: Proceedings of the AAAI Conference on Artificial Intelligence, vol. 33, pp. 1278–1285 (2019)

Predicting Different Health and Lifestyle Behaviors of Social Media Users

Karim Khalil[1](✉), Maksim Stankevich[2], Ivan Smirnov[1,2], and Maria Danina[3]

[1] Peoples' Friendship University of Russia (RUDN University), Moscow, Russia
[2] Federal Research Center "Computer Science and Control", Russian Academy of Sciences, Moscow, Russia
{stankevich,ivs}@isa.ru
[3] Psychological Institute of the Russian Academy of Education, Moscow, Russia

Abstract. The rise of social media platforms and a growing interest in applying machine learning methods to ever increasing amounts of data creates an opportunity to use data from social media to predict lifestyle choices and behaviors. In this study, we examine the possibility of using machine learning methods to classify users of the Russian-speaking social networking service VK based on different health related activities and habits. Participants of this study took a survey that had questions about different health-related behaviors and activities and the intensity with which users follow them. We describe the process of gathering, processing, and using this data to train a set of machine learning classifiers, and we evaluate the performance of these models in our experimental results. The features that were best able to classify most of the behaviors were collected from user subscription data. The best results were achieved on the questions about limiting the alcohol use and limiting the laptop and smartphone use (0.73 and 0.74 ROC AUC) with features generated from user profile and subscription data.

Keywords: Health · Lifestyle · Social networks · Classification

1 Introduction

Disease prevention is a critical issue addressed by behavioral medicine, and one of the main areas of research of behavioral medicine is the maintenance and promotion of healthy behavior. This type of behavior depends on many factors, both external (social, organizational) [12] and internal (motivational, emotional) [14]. Psychology offers many ways to assess and measure various health-related behaviors using questionnaires and self-reports [5,10], which, however, do not provide a feasible way to observe markers of such behavior in real life. At the same time, user behavior on social media and networking services is a promising source of data on both external and internal determinants of such behavior. An automated way of classifying users based on their lifestyle and health-related

The reported study was funded by RFBR under the research project No. 18-29-22041.

S. M. Kovalev et al. (Eds.): RCAI 2021, LNAI 12948, pp. 57–66, 2021.
https://doi.org/10.1007/978-3-030-86855-0_5

behaviors is an area of great interest in the field of public health. In the study [7], the researchers examined the possibility of using data gathered from social media as a predictor for whether users lead healthy or unhealthy lifestyles. Based on user answers to a health behavior survey, a healthy lifestyle score was used to split users into groups of users that lead healthy and unhealthy lifestyles. These classifiers were able to produce results reaching 0.75 ROC AUC on some feature sets. In this study, we use a similar approach, but instead, we utilize individual questions in a health-related survey as qualities to predict about users.

2 Related Work

The topic of monitoring public health using social media is gaining traction in the scientific community. In the study [3], the researchers sought to use natural language processing techniques to determine social media users' attitudes toward hookah tobacco smoking (HTS). The authors attempted to detect users with ambivalent or mixed views toward HTS. Detecting users that have not made up their mind on HTS allows public health programs to target these users and send them information that could change their opinion about HTS. Targeting users that have mixed feelings about HTS is more efficient and protects anti-smoking campaigns from countercampaigns from smoking advocates.

Another study [6] adopted a different approach to using data gathered from social media as a public health tool. The researchers garnered 4.5 million tweets that related to diabetes, diet, exercise, and obesity (DDEO) and analyzed them to find correlations between those topics. The study shows that the strongest correlation between the topics in the collected tweets was between obesity and exercise. There were also correlations between DDEO topics and other topics. For example, diabetes often appeared along with the topics of "blood pressure" and "heart attack." This type of information can help medical professionals better understand public opinions in regards to DDEO.

Automatic detection of eating disorders is an area that researchers of one [15] study focused on. Data was gathered from eating disorder forums and examined by clinically licensed psychologists, which then determined whether the poster needed medical intervention. Natural language processing techniques in combination with machine learning algorithms were trained using this data. The results of the study found that the machine learning algorithms were able to classify the top 50 intervention-worthy posts in their respective top-50 lists.

Researchers in another study [1] attempted to check whether it was feasible to determine if the content of tweets could be used to identify whether the posts were about alcohol use. Using data gathered from social media as another device to measure where and when people are using alcohol can be an important tool for public health officials in measuring risk factors and overall health of a society. Researchers in another study [4] attempted to perform a similar experiment with data collected from Instagram. User-generated tags and annotations obtained using automatic image tagging algorithms were used as a way of mapping the prevalence of the so-called "lifestyle" diseases like smoking, obesity, and drinking

Table 1. List of questions on the health and lifestyle survey

(1) limiting consumption of fast food
(2) limiting intake of foods high in sugar
(3) eating fruits and vegetables
(4) limiting consumption of red meat
(5) limiting consumption of alcohol
(6) limiting use of cigarettes
(7) taking vitamins and dietary supplements
(8) maintaining a regular diet
(9) maintaining regular hobbies
(10) getting proper rest from work and study
(11) getting regular room/workplace ventilation
(12) taking a walk regularly
(13) partaking in physical activity and active sports
(14) doing morning exercises
(15) limiting laptop and smartphone use
(16) using dark and night screen modes
(17) consuming health literature
(18) having regular medical examinations

to different locations that were extracted from the geotags in the Instagram posts.

These types of experiments were performed not only on English-speaking social media and networking services. Researchers from Spain and Portugal [11] used natural language processing and machine learning methods to classify Twitter posts from the Iberian Peninsula. The researchers attempted to extract data about the incidence of a set of health conditions: depression, pregnancy, flu, and eating disorders. The study showed that these methods can be used to detect the presence of certain diseases and conditions in society.

3 Dataset

The data that was used in this study was gathered from the Russian social media and networking service VK. This is a social media platform that allows users to share photos, texts, and music on their public "walls." VK also allows users to add friends, comment on other people's posts, share posts that other people upload, and curate sources of information that they want to see regular posts from. With the users' consent, this information can be downloaded through the use of the VK API. Participants of this study consented to the gathering and processing of their profile information.

Table 2. Results of the survey. The table indicates how users answered to the following questions and whether or not that response was considered to be a response that a healthy person would give (healthy = green, unhealthy = red)

Question	Never	Rarely	Sometimes	Often	Always	Healthy*	Unhealthy*
1	179	1419	862	394	83	1598 (1114/384)	477 (353/124)
2	97	695	929	881	335	792 (545/247)	1226 (861/365)
3	15	217	664	1094	947	2041 (1410/631)	896 (646/250)
4	400	944	793	576	224	1344 (933/411)	800 (553/247)
5	1306	1059	391	140	41	1306 (914/392)	181 (132/49)
6	2229	249	107	108	244	2229 (1559/670)	352 (249/103)
7	1036	946	485	255	215	470 (318/152)	1036 (732/304)
8	67	321	756	846	947	1793 (1254/539)	388 (277/111)
9	49	301	691	1008	888	1896 (1316/580)	350 (249/101)
10	165	615	838	773	546	1319 (933/386)	780 (555/225)
11	50	226	463	833	1365	2198 (1537/661)	276 (194/82)
12	46	390	767	893	841	1734 (1183/551)	436 (316/120)
13	211	803	795	605	523	1128 (788/340)	1014 (724/290)
14	1036	887	458	278	278	556 (379/177)	1923 (1359/564)
15	1139	932	576	209	81	290 (211/79)	1139 (799/340)
16	668	487	431	558	793	1351 (951/400)	1155 (802/353)
17	686	672	647	528	404	932 (648/284)	686 (482/204)
18	322	978	893	449	295	744 (519/225)	322 (217/105)

* Total number of samples and train/test split

The metric that we used to determine whether users conformed to certain health-related behaviors was gathered from the answers to an online health-related survey that we asked participants of this study to take. This survey is part of an expanded questionnaire of motivational determinants of health-preserving behavior, developed on the basis of the self-determination model of health-preserving behavior [8,13]. Users were asked various lifestyle and health-related questions ranging from their dietary habits to the frequency of their medical examinations. The survey asked about the frequency with which a user conforms to a health-related behavior on a scale of 1 to 5 with 1 being "never" and 5 being "always"; the full list of questions can be found in Table 1.

The results were analyzed by a group of experts which determined whether the answer to each question corresponded to healthy or unhealthy behavior. This allowed us to create individual groups of users who have healthy or unhealthy lifestyles based on their answers to the questions in the survey. The results of the survey are presented in Table 2. We considered users that answered "never" or "rarely" to questions about healthy habits as unhealthy, and users that answered "often" or "always" to these questions as healthy. The inverse is true for questions about unhealthy habits. In order to balance users leading healthy and unhealthy lifestyles, we made some exceptions in whether we used data from users that answered "rarely" or "often" to some questions.

A total of 2,937 users took the survey and agreed to have their data used in this study. There was a total of 30,311 original posts gathered from these users and 33,539 reposts. The gathered data consisted of 13,435 unique groups. We pruned all of the groups that had fewer than five subscribers.

We split our data into a train and test set. This was done in a way that would preserve some level of balance between classes for each of the individual questions that we attempted to classify.

4 Features

Using our data, we generated feature sets analogous to feature sets used in another study [7]. Two types of n-grams and psycholinguistic markers were generated from the posts that were authored by the subjects of this study. We similarly generated n-grams from posts that the subjects of this study reposted on their walls and did not author themselves. User profile information was also used as a feature set (friend count, number of subscriptions, ratio of posts made at night). Subscription and repost matrices were used as feature sets in this study. These feature sets encompass the relationship between the users and the sources of information that they subscribe to or repost content from. A new feature set that we created for the purposes of this study consisted of the group themes that are attributed to different groups that users are subscribed to on VK. Public groups on VK have attributes that are accessible to us via the VK API. These attributes include information on the theme of the group and the size of the group. We used these themes to create a feature set containing all of the themes that we encountered in the pool of groups that the users participating in this survey were subscribed to. This group theme feature set consists of columns of the top 139 themes that we encountered and rows of all of the users. Some examples of the group themes that are in our dataset are "Pets and Wild Animals," "Discussion Club," and "Science." The cells in this feature set contain the ratio of groups with a given theme that the user is subscribed to over the total number of groups that the user is subscribed to. This feature set also contained several columns with information on the number of groups that the given user is subscribed to and the sizes of the groups that the user is subscribed to. Listed below are the feature sets that were used in this study and the annotations by which we will be referring to them from this point on.

- Psycholinguistic markers (PM)
- Unigrams from original posts (UG)
- Bigrams from original Posts (BG)
- Unigrams from reposts (UGR)
- Bigrams from reposts (BGR)
- Subscription matrix (SM)
- Repost matrix (RM)
- Profile information (PI)
- Group themes (GT)

5 Method and Evaluation Setup

We used scikit-learn [9] and xgboost [2] packages in order to perform our classifications. The following machine learning methods were evaluated:

- Adaptive Boosting (ABC)
- Gradient Boosting Classifier (GBC)
- Logistic Regression (LR)
- Multi Layer Perceptron Classifier (MLP)
- Naive Bayes (NB)
- Random Forest (RF)
- Support Vector Machine (SVM)
- XGBoost (XGB)

Each of the 18 questions was considered to be a binary classification problem. Users were considered to be users who leaned toward either healthy or unhealthy behaviors. The datasets for some of the questions remained unbalanced even with our efforts of balancing the results. We used various resampling strategies to attempt to improve the quality of the trained models. An individual grid search was performed for each of the following resampling strategies.

- Adaptive Synthetic Sampling (ADASYN)
- Condensed Nearest Neighbour (CNN)
- Near Miss (NM)
- Random Over Sampler (ROS)
- Random Under Sampler (RUS)
- Synthetic Minority Oversampling Technique (SMOTE)

We were optimizing models based on the ROC AUC score during the training process. The results of the models training on the resampled data were compared to the results of the models that were trained without the resampling step. The models that were trained without the resampling step were also optimized based on the ROC AUC score.

There was another set of models that we trained on the unbalanced questions. We did not use a resampling strategy for them, but the models were configured to favor the minor class.

We used the best performing model parameters for each question in each training strategy. The resulting models were scored on our testing set, and the ROC AUC scores of each of these models was used to determine which training strategy and classifier and feature set provided the best results.

6 Results

We used the ROC AUC score as our evaluation metric. In Table 3, we aggregated the best performing classifiers for each of the questions in our survey. Questions that received ROC AUC scores of lower than or equal to 0.6 (3, 4, 7, 9, 10,

Table 3. Classification results on different feature sets and feature set groups

	Original posts			Reposts		Profile data			
Question	PM	UG	BG	UGR	BGR	SM	RM	PI	GT
(1) limiting fast food	0.6	0.59	0.57	0.57	0.57	**0.63**	**0.63**	0.57	**0.63**
(2) limiting foods high in sugar	0.57	0.53	0.53	0.58	0.58	**0.62**	0.59	0.57	0.59
(3) eating fruits and vegetables	0.54	**0.57**	0.53	0.55	0.54	0.54	0.55	0.55	0.55
(4) limiting red meat	0.56	0.52	0.55	0.55	0.55	0.59	0.56	0.53	**0.6**
(5) limiting alcohol	0.58	0.54	0.55	0.6	0.54	0.68	0.6	**0.73**	0.72
(6) limiting cigarettes	0.67	0.64	0.57	0.57	0.55	**0.69**	0.54	0.62	0.65
(7) vitamins and supplements	0.54	**0.6**	0.54	0.58	0.52	0.56	0.55	0.58	0.55
(8) regular diet	0.56	0.6	0.58	0.55	0.56	0.63	0.58	0.65	**0.63**
(9) regular hobbies	0.57	0.57	0.57	0.55	**0.58**	0.54	0.52	0.52	0.51
(10) proper rest	**0.56**	0.55	0.55	0.55	0.5	0.53	0.53	0.52	0.55
(11) room/workplace ventilation	0.56	0.56	0.56	**0.57**	0.53	0.54	0.5	0.55	0.56
(12) walking regularly	0.55	0.63	0.54	0.57	0.6	0.6	0.59	**0.64**	0.6
(13) physical activity	0.58	0.59	0.55	0.63	0.57	0.6	0.54	0.59	**0.64**
(14) morning exercises	0.57	0.58	0.56	0.58	0.61	**0.62**	0.53	0.55	0.55
(15) limiting laptop/phone	0.64	0.6	0.54	0.66	0.67	**0.74**	0.65	0.68	0.69
(16) dark/night screen modes	0.51	0.54	0.51	0.57	0.51	0.54	0.51	0.54	**0.57**
(17) health literature	0.6	0.61	0.58	0.63	0.62	0.67	0.6	0.6	**0.68**
(18) regular medical examinations	0.6	**0.65**	0.6	0.55	0.57	0.63	0.57	0.63	0.58

11, 16) are not going to be examined further because the performance of the classifiers on each of the feature sets that we attempted to train them on is too close to the performance of a random classifier (ROC AUC score of 0.5). The rest of the questions that received ROC AUC scores of greater than 0.6 (1, 2, 5, 6, 8, 12, 13, 14, 15, 17, 18) were considered to have performed adequately well and deserved to be examined further.

Feature sets generated from user profile data tended to perform better than feature sets that were generated from text on user walls, with the subscription matrix and group themes feature sets generally outperforming the other feature sets. Features generated from user text and features generated from the relationship between the users and the sources of repost information tended to perform poorly compared to features generated from user profile data. However, the unigram feature set was able to outperform the other feature sets on question 18 (0.65 ROC AUC), which was asking whether the user had regular medical examinations. Two other noteworthy results can be found in questions 5 and 15. The profile information (PI) feature set achieved good results on question 5 (limiting the consumption of alcohol) getting a score of 0.73 ROC AUC. Question number 15 was about whether the user limited their laptop and smartphone use, and the subscription matrix (SM) feature set performed very well (0.74 ROC AUC) on that question. The new group theme (GT) feature set that we had created for this study often outperformed other feature sets. The group theme feature set is interpretable, and it may be possible to extract some interesting relationships between different questions that it performed well on.

7 Discussion

It is encouraging to see the group themes and profile information feature sets showing overall good performance on the task of classifying users based on their health related behaviors. These feature sets are interpretable and can be further studied to extract relationships between different groups of users based on the answers that they gave on the survey.

Let us consider the attributes on which the most significant (Student's t-test) differences were found between the groups of people that answered questions in a way that corresponded to healthy lifestyles. The findings are presented in the context of each behavior separately.

For users committed to a healthy diet, there was significantly less participation in the groups on the topics "Pets and Wild Animals," "Discussion Club", "Television Shows," and "Humor" and less participation in groups with small numbers of users, fewer gifts and audio files on their personal pages. These attributes characterize the use of social networking services for the purpose of entertainment, recreation, and communication. People who are not committed to healthy eating show themselves to be more active users of social networking services that use them for the purposes of entertainment. People who are more committed to healthy eating are significantly more likely to be members of the "Medicine," "Science," "Culture," "Languages," and "Music" groups, and have more followers and friends. The participation of health-conscious users in these groups can be indicative of the fact that these users are using social networking services for the purposes of education, self-improvement, and communication.

Users who actively consume alcohol were significantly more involved in the "City/Community" and "Pets and Wild Animals" groups; these users had more photos and albums. It can be assumed that users who drink alcohol more actively participate or plan to participate in city events and share events and impressions of their own life on social media. Similar results were obtained for users who were self-reported smokers. They are characterized by greater involvement in groups on "Cooking and Recipes," "Gender Relations," and "Society," and lesser involvement in groups on "Education"; these users tended to have more photos, videos, and posts uploaded at night, also indicating the use of social networks primarily for the purpose of entertainment and socializing.

Users who consciously limit their use of gadgets and the Internet also showed significant differences in social networking behavior. They are significantly less likely to be members of the "Youth" and "Television Show" communities and more likely to be members of the "Science" communities. As with other healthier lifestyles, these users have fewer gifts and audio files on their profiles. Another significant difference is that these users are more prolific posters.

Finally, users who marked active participation in medical examinations show significantly greater involvement in communities on the topics of "Self-care," "Urban Community," "Cooking and Recipes," and "Healthy Living," and these users also had a larger number of friends and music albums on their profiles.

Thus, the differences in these attributes indicate the different attitudes that groups of users have toward the use of social media platforms and their relationship to health-preserving behaviors. Active orientation toward a healthy lifestyle is manifested in a greater use of social networking services in an educational and developmental context with a focus on the topics of health, science, medicine, and self-care. Conversely, the tendency to lead an unhealthy lifestyle is manifested in users who turn to social networking services as a source of entertainment (expressed in the topics of communities, the number of gifts and media files present on their profiles). However, we do not have adequate experimental data to show that this is the cause of the relationship between social media use and real world behaviour. Further studies would have to be conducted in order to understand the motives behind people's social media use and the lifestyles that they lead.

8 Conclusion

In this study, we explored the task of classifying users of the Russian-speaking social media and networking service VK based on different health-related habits and preferences. Participants of this study took a survey that asked them different health-related questions such as their attitude toward smoking, alcohol, or fitness. These users agreed to have their public VK profile information to be processed and analyzed by us for the purposes of this study. We processed their public posts, the content that they are subscribed to and that they repost, and other profile information that was available for download via the VK API. Textual data was used to form sets of text-based feature sets that included psycholinguistic markers and n-grams. Profile information and information about user subscriptions and reposting history was used to form subscription matrices, repost matrices, and group themes feature sets.

The resulting machine learning models revealed that feature sets extracted from user subscription information were able to classify health-related behaviors better than feature sets extracted from the text that users author and share. The subscription matrix feature set and the group themes feature set were able to achieve scores of 0.74 and 0.72 ROC AUC for questions about limiting the laptop and smartphone use and limiting alcohol consumption. We consider these results to be indicative of the fact that human behavioral tendencies regarding health and lifestyle can be extracted from their social media profiles.

The analysis of social media profile data is a promising field of research that can provide innovative ways of supplementing public health systems and campaigns.

References

1. Aphinyanaphongs, Y., Ray, B., Statnikov, A., Krebs, P.: Text classification for automatic detection of alcohol use-related tweets: a feasibility study. In: Proceedings of the 2014 IEEE 15th International Conference on Information Reuse and Integration (IEEE IRI 2014), pp. 93–97. IEEE (2014)

2. Chen, T., Guestrin, C.: Xgboost: a scalable tree boosting system. In: Proceedings of the 22nd ACM Sigkdd International Conference on Knowledge Discovery and Data Mining, pp. 785–794 (2016)
3. Chu, K.H., Colditz, J., Malik, M., Yates, T., Primack, B.: Identifying key target audiences for public health campaigns: leveraging machine learning in the case of hookah tobacco smoking. J. Med. Internet Res. **21**(7), e12443 (2019)
4. Garimella, V.R.K., Alfayad, A., Weber, I.: Social media image analysis for public health. In: Proceedings of the 2016 CHI Conference on Human Factors in Computing Systems, pp. 5543–5547 (2016)
5. Hagger, M.S., Hardcastle, S., Chater, A., Mallett, C., Pal, S., Chatzisarantis, N.: Autonomous and controlled motivational regulations for multiple health-related behaviors: between-and within-participants analyses. Health Psychol. Behav. Med. Open Access J. **2**(1), 565–601 (2014)
6. Karami, A., Dahl, A.A., Turner-McGrievy, G., Kharrazi, H., Shaw, G., Jr.: Characterizing diabetes, diet, exercise, and obesity comments on twitter. Int. J. Inf. Manag. **38**(1), 1–6 (2018)
7. Khalil, K., Stankevich, M., Smirnov, I., Danina, M.: Detection of social media users who lead a healthy lifestyle. In: Kuznetsov, S.O., Panov, A.I., Yakovlev, K.S. (eds.) RCAI 2020. LNCS (LNAI), vol. 12412, pp. 240–250. Springer, Cham (2020). https://doi.org/10.1007/978-3-030-59535-7_17
8. McLachlan, S., Hagger, M.S.: Do people differentiate between intrinsic and extrinsic goals for physical activity? J. Sport Exerc. Psychol. **33**(2), 273–288 (2011)
9. Pedregosa, F., et al.: Scikit-learn: machine learning in python. J. Mach. Learn. Res. **12**, 2825–2830 (2011)
10. Ping, W., Cao, W., Tan, H., Guo, C., Dou, Z., Yang, J.: Health protective behavior scale: development and psychometric evaluation. PloS one **13**(1), e0190390 (2018)
11. Prieto, V.M., Matos, S., Alvarez, M., Cacheda, F., Oliveira, J.L.: Twitter: a good place to detect health conditions. PloS one **9**(1), e86191 (2014)
12. Short, S.E., Mollborn, S.: Social determinants and health behaviors: conceptual frames and empirical advances. Curr. Opin. Psychol. **5**, 78–84 (2015)
13. Teixeira, P.J., Silva, M.N., Mata, J., Palmeira, A.L., Markland, D.: Motivation, self-determination, and long-term weight control. Int. J. Behav. Nutr. Phys. Act. **9**(1), 1–13 (2012)
14. Williams, D.M., Rhodes, R.E., Conner, M.T.: Conceptualizing and intervening on affective determinants of health behaviour (2019)
15. Yan, H., Fitzsimmons-Craft, E.E., Goodman, M., Krauss, M., Das, S., Cavazos-Rehg, P.: Automatic detection of eating disorder-related social media posts that could benefit from a mental health intervention. Int. J. Eating Disord. **52**(10), 1150–1156 (2019)

Methods for Finding Consequences with Specified Properties

Boris Kulik[1(✉)] and Alexander Fridman[2]

[1] Institute for Problems in Mechanical Engineering of the Russian Academy of Sciences, Saint Petersburg, Russia
[2] Institute for Informatics and Mathematical Modelling, Kola Science Centre of the Russian Academy of Sciences, Apatity, Russia
fridman@iimm.ru

Abstract. In logical inference, two main tasks are relevant: verifying the correctness of an alleged consequence and inferring a consequence with predetermined properties. The entire theoretical potential of mathematical logic is mainly aimed at solving the former problem. As for the task of finding some desired consequences, it has obtained practically no useful developments. In this paper, we propose methods for solving the problem of finding consequences with certain properties on the basis on n-tuple algebra. These methods are shown to be applicable for solving constraint satisfaction problems as well.

Keywords: Inference · Interesting consequences · N-tuple algebra · Rule of generalization · Elimination of attributes · Constraint satisfaction problem

1 Introduction

In deductive systems, the following definition is considered generally accepted: the ***logical inference*** of a formula A from a set of premises P is a finite sequence of $A_1, \ldots, A_n$, where $A_n = A$, and each of A_i either is one of the premises, or is obtained from the preceding formulas of the sequence by one of inference rules [1]. In practice, methods such as the method of resolution, analytical or semantic tables are often used to check the correctness of the inference [2, 3], etc. However, such methods are not suitable for solving the problem of deriving consequences with given properties (sometimes they are called interesting consequences) since they assume the consequence is already known. To find a simple method for solving this problem, it is proposed to use the methods of n-tuple algebra [4, 5].

2 Briefs from N-tuple Algebra

N-tuple algebra (NTA) is a universal algebra of n-ary relations based on the properties of the ***Cartesian Product*** (CP) of sets. Relations in NTA can be represented by using four types of structures (***NTA-objects***). Each NTA object is immersed in a specific ***attribute*** space. The set of all values for an attribute is called its ***domain***.

S. M. Kovalev et al. (Eds.): RCAI 2021, LNAI 12948, pp. 67–80, 2021.
https://doi.org/10.1007/978-3-030-86855-0_6

The close connection between NTA and logic is that ***NTA objects are interpreted as the domains of truth for formulas of mathematical logic***. Instead of logical connectives $\wedge$, $\vee$, $\supset$ and $\neg$, NTA uses analogous operations of algebra of sets with n-ary relations, and instead of quantifiers, it applies operations with attributes (see below).

The names of NTA objects contain an identifier assigned with a sequence of attribute names, enclosed in square brackets, which define the ***relation diagram*** where this NTA object is specified. For example, the name $R[XYZ]$ means that the NTA object R is contained in the space $X \times Y \times Z$. NTA objects specified in the same attribute space are called of the ***homotypic*** ones.

Consider the types of NTA structures. They are C-n-tuples, C-systems, D-n-tuples and D-systems. These designations are associated with the words "conjunction" and "disjunction" since a C-n-tuple corresponds to a conjunction, and a D-n-tuple corresponds to a disjunction of logical formulas.

NTA structures are matrix ones, and their cells contain ***components*** (subsets of the corresponding attributes) rather than elements. When transforming NTA objects into formulas of mathematical logic, the components of the NTA objects correspond to unary predicates, and the NTA objects themselves correspond to formulas or n-ary predicates.

A ***C-n-tuple*** is a tuple of components bounded by square brackets, which can be represented as an ordinary relation if we calculate the CP of these components.

For example, the NTA object $T[XYZ] = [A * B]$ is a C-n-tuple, while $A \subseteq X$, $B \subseteq Z$, and the "*" component is a ***complete component***, its value is equal to the domain of the corresponding attribute (in this case, since it is in the second position, then $* = Y$). This C-n-tuple can be transformed into an ordinary relation by using a CP as follows: $T[XYZ] = A \times Y \times B$. It corresponds to the formula $T(x, z) = A(x)$ & $B(z)$, while components A and B are the truth domains for the predicates $A(x)$ and $B(z)$.

Consider the intersection of C-n-tuples. Let there be given two homotypic C-n-tuples $P = [A_1\ A_2\ \ldots\ A_n]$ and $Q = [B_1\ B_2\ \ldots\ B_n]$ (for homotypic NTA objects, there is no need to denote their relation diagrams). Then

$$P \cap Q = [A_1 \cap B_1\ \ A_2 \cap B_2 \ldots A_n \cap B_n].$$

Moreover, if at least one intersection $A_i \cap B_i$ is equal to $\emptyset$, then $P \cap Q = \emptyset$.

A ***C-system*** is a union of homotypic C-n-tuples that is written in the form of a matrix bounded by square brackets. So, $R[XYZ] = \begin{bmatrix} A_1 & * & A_3 \\ B_1 & B_2 & * \end{bmatrix}$ is a C-system where $A_1 \subseteq X$, $A_3 \subseteq Z$, etc. This C-system is transformed into an ordinary relation by using a CP as follows: $R[XYZ] = (A_1 \times Y \times A_3) \cup (B_1 \times B_2 \times Z)$.

The union of C-n-tuples, except for some specific special cases [4], cannot be represented as a single C-n-tuple. In general, the following is true:

$$\begin{bmatrix} A_1\ A_2\ \ldots\ A_n \end{bmatrix} \cup \begin{bmatrix} B_1\ B_2\ \ldots\ B_n \end{bmatrix} = \begin{bmatrix} A_1\ A_2\ \ldots\ A_n \\ B_1\ B_2\ \ldots\ B_n \end{bmatrix}.$$

If an NTA object is transformed into an ordinary relation, the elements of this relation are called ***elementary tuples***.

The intersection of C-systems is calculated as the union of all non-empty intersections of each C-n-tuple of one C-system with each C-n-tuple of another C-system. For instance, let two homotypic C-systems be given.

$$P = \begin{bmatrix} \{a, b, d\} & \{f\} & \{b\} \\ \{b, c\} & \{f, g\} & \{a, c\} \end{bmatrix}, \; Q = \begin{bmatrix} \{a, d\} & \{f, g\} & \{b, c\} \\ \{b, d\} & \{f\} & \{a, c\} \\ \{b, c\} & \{g\} & \{b\} \end{bmatrix}.$$

To calculate their intersection, we have to perform the following:

1) find the intersection of all pairs of C-n-tuples contained in different C-systems:

$$\big[\{a, b, d\} \;\; \{f\}\{b\}\big] \cap \big[\{a, d\} \;\; \{g\} \;\; \{b, c\}\big] = \big[\{a, d\} \;\; \{f\} \;\; \{b\}\big];$$

$$\big[\{a, b, d\} \;\; \{f\} \;\; \{b\}\big] \cap \big[\{b, d\} \;\; \{f\} \;\; \{a, c\}\big] = \emptyset;$$

$$\big[\{a, b, d\} \;\; \{f\} \;\; \{b\}\big] \cap \big[\{b, c\} \;\; \{g\} \;\; \{b\}\big] = \emptyset;$$

$$\big[\{b, c\} \;\; \{f, g\} \;\; \{a, c\}\big] \cap \big[\{a, d\} \;\; \{g\} \;\; \{b, c\}\big] = \emptyset;$$

$$\big[\{b, c\} \;\; \{f, g\} \;\; \{a, c\}\big] \cap \big[\{b, d\} \;\; \{f\} \;\; \{a, c\}\big] = \big[\{b\} \;\; \{f\} \;\; \{a, c\}\big];$$

$$\big[\{b, c\} \;\; \{f, g\} \;\; \{a, c\}\big] \cap \big[\{b, c\} \;\; \{g\} \;\; \{b\}\big] = \emptyset.$$

2) from the remaining non-empty C-n-tuples, we form a C-system:

$$P \cap Q = \begin{bmatrix} \{a, d\} & \{f\} & \{b\} \\ \{b\} & \{f\} & \{a, c\} \end{bmatrix}.$$

Any n-ary relation can be expressed by using C-systems, but new structures, namely D-n-tuples and D-systems, are required to express complements of relations and operations with them. To define these NTA objects, an intermediate structure is used, it is the diagonal C-system.

A ***diagonal C-system*** is a C-system of dimension $n \times n$, in which all off-diagonal components are complete (*).

For instance, $Q[XYZ] = \begin{bmatrix} A & * & * \\ * & B & * \\ * & * & C \end{bmatrix}$ is a diagonal C-system.

Any diagonal C-system is proved to be the result of computing the complement of a C-n-tuple. In particular, $Q[XYZ]$ is the complement of the C-n-tuple $[\overline{A} \; \overline{B} \; \overline{C}]$ where $\overline{A} = X \setminus A, \overline{B} = Y \setminus B, \overline{C} = Z \setminus C$.

A ***D-n-tuple*** is a diagonal C-system written as a tuple of its diagonal components bounded by reverse square brackets.

For example, the diagonal *C*-system shown above can be written as the *D*-n-tuple $Q[XYZ] =]A\ B\ C[$, whose complement is evidently equal to the *C*-n-tuple $[\overline{A}\ \overline{B}\ \overline{C}]$.

A ***D-system*** is a matrix of components bounded by reverse square brackets, in which the rows are *D*-n-tuples.

With the help of *D*-systems, it is easy to calculate complements of *C*-systems. To do this, it is enough to replace all the components of any *C*-system with their complements, and to use reverse square brackets instead of the square ones. The complement of a complete component * is the component ∅ called an ***empty component***.

For instance, the complement of the *C*-system $P[XYZ] = \begin{bmatrix} A & * & C \\ D & E & * \end{bmatrix}$ is calculated as the *D*-system $\overline{P}[XYZ] = \left]\begin{matrix} \overline{A} & \emptyset & \overline{C} \\ \overline{D} & \overline{E} & \emptyset \end{matrix}\right[$. Using de Morgan's law, we can prove that a *D*-system is the intersection of the *D*-n-tuples it contains.

In NTA, the components ∅ and * are called ***dummy components***.

The ***universe of an NTA-object*** (***U***) is defined as the CP of the domains of the attributes specified in the relation diagram of this object. For example, the universe of the NTA object *R*[*XYZ*] equals $\boldsymbol{U} = X \times Y \times Z$.

If in the calculation it is established that a *C*-system is equal to the universe, such system corresponds to a ***generally valid formula***, and if a check shows that a *D*-system is equal to an empty set, this system corresponds to an ***identically false formula*** or a ***contradiction***.

The rules for performing union and intersection operations for *C*- and *D*-structures are formulated and proved in [5]. NTA also proposes algorithms for checking the inclusion of any types of NTA objects into others and algorithms for transforming *C*-structures into *D*-structures and vice versa.

Quantifier operations are performed in NTA by using simple ***operations upon attributes***. These include, in particular, the ***addition of a dummy attribute*** (+*Attr*) and the ***elimination of an attribute*** (–*Attr*). Consider these operations.

The +*Attr* operation is performed by adding the name of a new attribute to the relation diagram of an NTA object and the corresponding new column with dummy components to the matrix representation. For instance, let $R_k[XZ] = \begin{bmatrix} A_1 & A_3 \\ B_1 & B_3 \end{bmatrix}$ be given. Then adding the dummy attribute *Y* to $R_k[XZ]$ yields the NTA-object $+Y(R_k[XZ]) = \begin{bmatrix} A_1 & * & A_3 \\ B_1 & * & B_3 \end{bmatrix}$. When performing the +*Attr* operation, the dummy components "*" are added to *C*-structures, and the dummy components "∅" are added to *D*-structures.

The +*Attr* operation corresponds to the ***rule of generalization*** (*Gen*) in predicate calculus [1]. The essence of this rule is that the formula ∀*x*(*A*) is deducible from an arbitrary formula *A*. With that, many monographs on mathematical logic do not indicate the status of the variable *x* in the formula *A* (free, bound, or absent). For predicate calculus, in which all axioms and derivable formulas are tautologies, the rule *Gen* in this formulation is quite correct. Conversely, in natural reasoning, where many sentences are not generally valid, it is impossible to derive ∀*x*(*A*(*x*)) from the formula *A*(*x*) with the free variable *x*. In this case, the rule *Gen* is correct only provided that the free variable *x* is not included in *A*. If a logical formula $R_k(x, z)$ corresponds to an NTA object $R_k[XZ]$, then adding a dummy attribute Y to $R_k[XZ]$ models deriving the formula $\forall y(R_k(x, z))$ from $R_k(x, z)$.

The $+Attr$ operation is also used to bring NTA objects with different relation diagrams to one diagram by adding missing dummy attributes. Considering this, ***generalized operations*** ($\cap_G$, $\cup_G$) are introduced, which differ from the usual operations of the same name SSin algebra of sets only in that, before their execution, NTA objects are reduced to the same relation diagram by using the operation $+Attr$.

Let us look at an example.

Example 1. Suppose $P[XY]$ is an NTA object representing the relation PARENTS[X, Y]. By renaming the attributes in $P[XY]$, we obtain the NTA object $P[YZ]$. To get the relation "persons-their children-their grandchildren," we calculate the generalized intersection:

$$P[XY] \cap_G P[YZ] = +Z(P[XY]) \cap +X(P[YZ]).$$

And in order to obtain the relation "persons-their grandchildren," it is necessary to calculate the composition ($\circ$) of these relations, which, in this case, can be done by the elimination of the attribute Y:

$$P[XY] \circ P[YZ] = -Y(P[XY] \cap_G P[YZ]).$$

Let the relation PARENTS[X, Y] be given as the C-system $P[XY]= \begin{bmatrix} \{a, b\} & \{c, f, g\} \\ \{f\} & \{h, k\} \end{bmatrix}$. Then

$$P[XY] \cap_G P[YZ] = \begin{bmatrix} \{a, b\} & \{c, f, g\} & * \\ \{f\} & \{h, k\} & * \end{bmatrix} \cap \begin{bmatrix} * & \{a, b\} & \{c, f, g\} \\ * & \{f\} & \{h, k\} \end{bmatrix}$$
$$= \begin{bmatrix} \{a, b\} & \{f\} & \{h, k\} \end{bmatrix}.$$

$$P[XY] \circ P[YZ] = [\{a, b\} \quad \{h, k\}].$$

Generalized operations are semantically equivalent to logical connectives of conjunction and disjunction. ***Generalized relations*** ($\subseteq_G$ and $=_G$) are introduced similarly. It is proved that the *NTA with generalized operations and relations is isomorphic to algebra of sets.*

Consider one more example.

Example 2. A bottle, a jug, a glass, and a pot contain milk, lemonade, kvass, and water. It is known that water and milk are not in the bottle; a vessel with lemonade is between the jug and a vessel with kvass; in the pot, there is neither lemonade nor water; the glass is located near the pot and the container with milk. How are these fluids placed in the vessels?

First, we introduce abbreviations: the bottle is B, the jug is denoted as J, the glass is marked G, the symbol for the pot is P, M stands for milk, L denotes lemonade, K is for kvass, and W means water.

We use liquids $\{M, L, K, W\}$ as attributes. The values of these attributes will be the vessels that can hold these fluids. Then we get the following premises.

1) "Milk and water are not in the bottle": $A_1[MW] = [\{J, G, P\}\ \{J, G, P\}]$;
2) "A vessel with lemonade is located between the jug and a vessel with kvass" means that lemonade and kvass are not in the jug:

$$A_2[LK] = [\{B, G, P\}\ \{B, G, P\}];$$

3) "There is neither lemonade nor water in the pot":

$$A_3[LW] = [\{B, J, G\}\ \{B, J, G\}];$$

4) "The glass is near the pot and the container with milk" means that milk is neither in the pot nor in the glass: $A_4[M] = [\{B, J\}]$.

To solve the problem, we sequentially calculate the generalized intersections of the premises:

$$A_1[MW] \cap_G A_2[LK] = [\{J, G, P\} * *\{J, G, P\}] \cap [*\{B, G, P\}\ \ \{B, G, P\}*] =$$

$$= [\{J, G, P\}\ \ \{B, G, P\}\ \ \{B, G, P\}\ \ \{J, G, P\}].$$

$$A_1[MW] \cap_G A_2[LK] \cap_G A_3[LW] =$$

$$= [\{J, G, P\}\{B, G, P\}\{B, G, P\}\{J, G, P\}] \cap [*\{B, J, G\} * \{B, J, G\}] =$$

$$= [\{J, G, P\}\{B, G\}\{B, G, P\}\{J, G\}].$$

$$A_1[MW] \cap_G A_2[LK] \cap_G A_3[LW] \cap_G A\,_4[M] =$$

$$= [\{J, G, P\}\ \ \{B, G\}\ \ \{B, G, P\}\ \ \{J, G\}] \cap [\{B, J\} * * *] =$$

$$= [\{J\}\{B, G\}\ \ \{B, G, P\}\ \ \{J, G\}].$$

Thus, we have calculated one of the possible consequences.

$$A[MLKW] = [\{\{J\}B, G\}\ \ \{B, G, P\}\ \ \{J, G\}].$$

In the resulting C-n-tuple, we need to select elementary tuples that do not have duplicate values in the attributes. There is no need to calculate the CP, which contains 12 elementary tuples. In this example, we can solve the problem by sequentially deleting unnecessary values from the components of the C-n-tuple.

First, you need to remove the element J from the attribute component W since this element is the only one in the attribute component M, and we may not delete it from there. We get $A[MLKW] = [\{J\}\ \{B, G\}\ \{B, G, P\}\ \{G\}]$. Next, we can delete the element G from the components of the attributes L and K. Then we obtain.

$$A[MLKW] = [\{J\}\ \ \{B\}\ \ \{B, P\}\ \ \{G\}].$$

It is now clear that the element B in the attribute component K is also redundant. As a result, we get the answer: $A[MLKW] = [\ \{J\}\ \ \{B\}\ \ \{P\}\ \ \{G\}\ ]$.

The operation of elimination of an attribute *–Attr* is performed by removing the name of this attribute from the relation diagram and removing the column with values of this attribute from the matrix representation. Unlike *+Attr*, the logical meaning of the operation *–Attr* depends on the type of the NTA object. Let an NTA object $R[XYZ]$ be given, and the logical formula $F(x, y, z)$ corresponds to it. If $R[XYZ]$ is a C-n-tuple or a C-system, then $-Y(R[XYZ])$ is equivalent to $\exists y(F(x, y, z))$, and if $R[XYZ]$ is a D-n-tuple or a D-system, operation $-Y(R[XYZ])$ yields $\forall y(F(x, y, z))$. All these relations are rigorously proved.

Applying the *–Attr* operation to a C-n-tuple or a C-system allows calculating a ***projection*** of this NTA object. If, for example, a C-system $R[XYZ]$ is given, its projections are denoted by $\mathrm{Pr}_{XY}(R)$, $\mathrm{Pr}_{Y}(R)$, $\mathrm{Pr}_{XZ}(R)$, etc. In particular, the projection $\mathrm{Pr}_{Y}(R)$ is calculated by eliminating two attributes: $-Z(-X(R[XYZ]))$. For any NTA-object $R[\ldots]$, the following correlation is proved:

$$R[\ldots] \subseteq_G Pr_{\boldsymbol{V}}(R), \tag{1}$$

where $\boldsymbol{V}$ is an arbitrary subset of attributes from the relation diagram of this object. If an NTA object is expressed as a D-n-tuple or a D-system, it must be transformed into a C-system prior to calculating any projection of it.

The concept of dummy attributes contained in a relation is closely related to projections of NTA objects. Let an NTA object $R[\boldsymbol{W}]$ be given, where $\boldsymbol{W}$ is a set of attributes, among which there is an attribute X, and $\mathrm{Pr}_{\boldsymbol{W}\setminus X}(R)$ is a projection of $R[\boldsymbol{W}]$, in which all attributes are present except X. Then X is a ***dummy attribute*** in $R[\boldsymbol{W}]$ if the following equality holds:

$$R[W] = +X\left(\mathrm{Pr}_{W\setminus X}(R)\right). \tag{2}$$

This means that each elementary tuple in the projection $\mathrm{Pr}_{\boldsymbol{W}\setminus X}(R)$ of $R[\boldsymbol{W}]$ corresponds to the set of all values (domain) of the attribute X.

In the NTA, a new method of checking the correctness of a consequence has been proposed and substantiated. Let the premises of a reasoning be written in the form of NTA objects $A_1, A_2, \ldots, A_n$. Then the logical formula represented by an NTA object B will be a consequence of these premises if and only if the following correlation is observed:

$$(A_1 \cap_G A_2 \cap_G \ldots \cap_G A_n) \subseteq_G B. \tag{3}$$

The NTA object obtained as a result of calculating the expression in the left side of (3) is called the ***minimal consequence*** in NTA. Below, we show how to obtain consequences with predetermined properties by using this expression.

3 Properties of "Interesting" Consequences

The publication [6] formulates the problem setting for the search of "interesting" consequences and contains an estimate of the number of possible consequences, according to which this number is infinite. However, in some cases, this estimate can be significantly reduced. Let us consider the case that is of frequent use in practice, when a system intended for logical analysis is immersed in a space containing a finite number of attributes, and each attribute is represented by a finite number of values.

Suppose that the system of premises A_i expressed as NTA objects is specified in an attribute space $X_1, X_2, \ldots, X_k$ with a finite number of values for each attribute. Using the metric properties of NTA [4] based on the metric properties of Cartesian products, we can calculate the number of elements (elementary tuples) in the universe $\boldsymbol{U} = X_1 \times X_2 \times \ldots \times X_k$ and in the NTA object A obtained as a result of the generalized intersection of the premises A_i. In [4, 5], the following theorem is formulated and proved.

Theorem 1. Let $\boldsymbol{U} = X_1 \times X_2 \times \ldots \times X_k$ be a universe in which all attributes have a finite set of values, and this universe contains the premises $A_1, \ldots, A_n$ expressed by NTA objects. Then the number of possible consequences from the premises A_i is equal to 2^N where $N = |\boldsymbol{U}| - |A|$ and $A = A_1 \cap_G \ldots \cap_G A_n$.

Let us first consider one obvious consequence of the correlation (3). Suppose that premises in (3) include a premise A_i. Then the following relation is true:

$$(A_1 \cap_G A_2 \cap_G \ldots \cap_G A_n) \subseteq_G A_i.$$

It implies that any premise in $\{A_1, A_2, \ldots, A_n\}$ is a consequence. It is clear that such consequences are easily deducible, but they are not of interest, evidently.

Let us consider other cases. Numerous examples of inference problems [2, 7] are characterized by the fact that verified consequences very often contain a relatively small composition of variables compared to the initial data.

Example 3. [2]. Prove that the premises $\neg P \vee \neg Q \vee R$; $P \vee R$; and $Q \vee R$ allow to infer the consequence R.

Here, the premises contain three propositional variables (P, Q and R), while the corollary contains only one variable (R).

In the famous Steamroller problem (No. 47 in [7]), which illustrates the complexity of inference, formalization results in only three logical variables, but it shortens the number of predicates used in this problem. These predicates include "wolves," "foxes," "plants," "less," etc. The corollary of this problem contains three predicates, while the premises formulate 10 different predicates.

Thus, *one of the properties of "interesting" consequences is the composition of variables and\or predicates reduced in comparison with the initial data.*

The second property of interesting consequences is closely related to the first one: in some cases, not only consequences with a reduced composition of variables, but also consequences in which certain variables are used. For instance, the initial premises in Example 3 allow to pose the following problem: check the existence of a corollary with two variables, among which the propositional variable Q is necessarily present. The same feature can be useful for predicates as well. Hence, *the second property of "interesting" consequences is a certain composition of variables and\or predicates in the reduced corollary.*

4 Methods for Calculating "Interesting" Consequences

If we use the traditional method of deductive analysis using inference rules, then in order to obtain consequences with certain properties, it is necessary to enumerate a large number of options since it is impossible to predict the result of applying the rules in advance. Therefore, it becomes necessary to develop more efficient methods for calculating consequences with predetermined properties.

When using NTA methods, the task is greatly simplified. When a set of NTA objects $\{A_1, \ldots, A_n\}$ is given, and these objects represent axioms (or premises), we can find the minimal consequence $A = A_1 \cap_G \ldots \cap_G A_n$. To obtain any consequence, it is sufficient to construct an NTA object B such that the relation $A \subseteq_G B$ holds.

The number of variables in a consequence can be reduced by calculating projections of A. Taking into account the correlation (1), it turns out that each projection is a consequence. Hence, the relation $A \subseteq_G \mathrm{Pr}(A)$ will hold for any projection $\mathrm{Pr}(A)$.

If A is a C-system (otherwise it can be transformed into a C-system by using certain algorithms [4, 5]), any of its projections can be easily calculated by elimination of attributes. However, not every projection presents an interesting consequence, since it may be equal to the universe; in this case, it does not contain any useful information.

Let us see how the search for "interesting" consequences in Example 3. In this and other problems, orthogonalization of diagonal C-systems is used to reduce the complexity of computational operations [4, 5]. For instance, the diagonal C-system $\begin{bmatrix} A & * & * \\ * & B & * \\ * & * & C \end{bmatrix}$ can be transformed into the equivalent diagonal C-system $\begin{bmatrix} A & * & * \\ \overline{A} & B & * \\ \overline{A} & \overline{B} & C \end{bmatrix}$. Orthogonalization can significantly reduce the number of C-n-tuples in intermediate computations and the resulting computation result due to increasing the number of empty intersections.

Using some correlations from [5], we express the premises in the form of C-systems:

$$\neg P \vee \neg Q \vee R \text{ will be written as } A_1[PQR] = \begin{bmatrix} \{0\} & * & * \\ \{1\} & \{0\} & * \\ \{1\} & \{1\} & \{1\} \end{bmatrix};$$

$$P \vee R \text{ equals to } A_2[PR] = \begin{bmatrix} \{1\} & * \\ \{0\} & \{1\} \end{bmatrix};$$

$$Q \vee R \text{ corresponds to } A_3[QR] = \begin{bmatrix} \{1\} & * \\ \{0\} & \{1\} \end{bmatrix}.$$

Next, we calculate the minimal consequence, that is, the generalized intersection of premises:

$$A[PQR] = A_1[PQR] \cap_G A_2[PR] \cap_G A_3[QR] = \begin{bmatrix} \{0\} & * & \{1\} \\ \{1\} & * & \{1\} \end{bmatrix}.$$

In the C-system $A[PQR] = \begin{bmatrix} \{0\} * \{1\} \\ \{1\} * \{1\} \end{bmatrix}$, the projection $\mathrm{Pr}_R(A)$ is incomplete and equal to $[\{1\}]$, which implies that the formula R is a consequence of the premises listed in Example 3. Thus, one of the methods for obtaining interesting corollaries is to find incomplete projections in a minimal consequence.

Consider another problem: calculate a corollary from Example 3, which contains two variables, and among them there must be a propositional variable Q. One of the possible solutions is easy to find since, among the premises of Example 3, there is the premise $Q \vee R$, which, as has been shown earlier, turns out to be one of the possible consequences. But is it possible to deduce another meaningful consequence in the relation diagram $[QR]$? For example, does the formula $\neg Q \vee R$ result from the premises of this problem? The answer is given by the following theorem.

Theorem 2. Let the minimal consequence $A(\boldsymbol{W})$ be computed for a set of premises $\{A_1, \ldots, A_n\}$, where $\boldsymbol{W}$ is the set of attributes, and $A(\boldsymbol{W})$ has an incomplete projection $\mathrm{Pr}_{\boldsymbol{V}}(A)$ where $\boldsymbol{V} \subset \boldsymbol{W}$. Then consequences can be obtained as any NTA object calculated by the formula $T \cup_G \mathrm{Pr}_{\boldsymbol{V}}(A)$, where T is an arbitrary NTA object.

Proof. According to (1), $A(\boldsymbol{W}) \subseteq_G \mathrm{Pr}_{\boldsymbol{V}}(A)$. Since $\mathrm{Pr}_{\boldsymbol{V}}(A) \subseteq_G T \cup_G \mathrm{Pr}_{\boldsymbol{V}}(A)$, it follows that $A(\boldsymbol{W}) \subseteq_G T \cup_G \mathrm{Pr}_{\boldsymbol{V}}(A)$, and according to (3), $T \cup_G \mathrm{Pr}_{\boldsymbol{V}}(A)$ is a consequence of the set of premises $\{A_1, \ldots, A_n\}$. *End of proof*.

Theorem 2 yields that any significant (that is, not equal to a tautology) corollary F_m allows to obtain a new formal consequence by the formula $G \vee F_m$ where G is an arbitrary formula.

With the help of Theorem 2, it is relatively easy to obtain a large number of new consequences, but many of them do not carry any useful information. Consider the case when A is a minimal consequence and the logical formula F_m corresponds to an incomplete projection $\mathrm{Pr}_{\boldsymbol{V}}(A)$. Let G be a formula such that the formula $G \vee F_m$ is not a tautology. Then, according to Theorem 2, the formula $G \vee F_m$ is a consequence, but it turns out that the formula $\neg G \vee F_m$ is also the correct consequence. Hence, it is clear that both the formula $\neg Q \vee R$ and the formula $Q \vee R$ are consequences in Example 3. Thus, the disjunctive joining of any formula to a correct corollary does not lead to a decrease in the uncertainty of the inference.

It remains to consider the case when the investigated projection is complete, i.e., equal to the universe. In Example 3, such a variant is given by the projection:

$$\mathrm{Pr}_{PQ}(A) = \begin{bmatrix} \{0\} * \\ \{1\} * \end{bmatrix} = [* *] = \boldsymbol{U}.$$

Suppose there is a complete projection in the minimal consequence A. The question is whether this case allows us to construct a corollary not equal to the universe in the relation diagram, which would coincide with the diagram of this complete projection.

The answer to this question is given by the following theorem.

Theorem 3. Let the minimal consequence $A(\boldsymbol{W})$ be computed for the set of premises $\{A_1, \ldots, A_n\}$, where $\boldsymbol{W}$ is the set of attributes, and $A(\boldsymbol{W})$ has a complete projection $\mathrm{Pr}_{\boldsymbol{V}}(A)$ with $\boldsymbol{V} \subset \boldsymbol{W}$. Then any NTA-object R, in which $\mathrm{Pr}_{\boldsymbol{V}}(R) \neq \boldsymbol{U}$, is not a consequence.

Proof. Suppose $Pr_Y(R)$ is a consequence. Then $A(\boldsymbol{W}) \subseteq R(\boldsymbol{W})$. Hence, any projection $Pr_X(A)$ satisfies the relation $Pr_X(A) \subseteq Pr_X(R)$. However, this relation is impossible for $Pr_X(A)$ by the conditions of the theorem, since $Pr_Y(A) = \boldsymbol{U}$, and the strict inclusion $Pr_Y(R) \subset \boldsymbol{U}$ holds. The resulting contradiction proves the theorem. *End of proof.*

The considered variants show that only the minimal consequence $A = A_1 \cap_G \ldots \cap_G A_n$ and its incomplete projections can be interesting possible consequences of the premises $\{A_1, \ldots, A_n\}$. It should be taken into account that dummy attributes (2) may exist in incomplete projections. For instance, in Example 3 the projection $Pr_{PR}(A) = \begin{bmatrix} \{0\} & \{1\} \\ \{1\} & \{1\} \end{bmatrix}$ is incomplete, but at the same time, its attribute P is dummy, since $Pr_{PR}(A)$ $= \begin{bmatrix} \{0\} & \{1\} \\ \{1\} & \{1\} \end{bmatrix} = [* \; \{1\}]$.

Hence, the problem of finding interesting consequences requires not only to find an incomplete projection of the minimal consequence, but also to minimize this projection, i.e., to find dummy attributes in it and eliminate them.

The foregoing allows to formulate the following algorithm for calculating interesting consequences.

Algorithm for inference of consequences with a reduced relation diagram

Let the premises $\{A_1, \ldots, A_n\}$ expressed in the form of NTA objects be given.

Step 1. Calculate the minimal consequence $A = A_1 \cap_G \ldots \cap_G A_n$.

Step 2. If A is a C-system, find its incomplete projections that do not contain dummy attributes; the obtained NTA objects are the desired consequences.

Step 3. If A is a D-system, transform it into a C-system and perform Step 2.

End of the algorithm.

The concept of the minimal consequence can be used not only to derive interesting consequences, but also to solve Constraint Satisfaction Problem (CSP) [8]. The publication [9] shows how to apply NTA methods for solving CSPs.

Let the given constraints be expressed in the form of NTA objects $\{C_1, \ldots, C_m\}$. To solve a CSP then, it is necessary to calculate the generalized intersection $C = C_1 \cap_G \ldots \cap_G C_m$. If $C = \emptyset$, this CSP has no solution, otherwise the NTA object C is a solution to the CSP. In contrast to the problem of finding consequences, for which the result of the solution is characterized by the property (3), no solution D of the CSP may satisfy the strict inclusion $C \subset D$, since the NTA object $D \backslash C$ would violate at least one of the constraints C_j. In logical inference, the relation (3) means that a consequence can go beyond any axiom in terms of volume, while in CSP, the fact that a result of computations C goes beyond at least one constraint means that the conditions of the problem are violated.

Let us now consider a mixed problem of satisfying constraints, where the constraints C_j are used in the initial data along with the premises A_i.

To solve this problem, it is necessary to separately calculate the minimal consequence $A = A_1 \cap_G \ldots \cap_G A_n$ and the result of solving the CSP problem $C = C_1 \cap_G \ldots \cap_G C_m$.

For non-empty A and C, the final solution depends on the correlations between them.

If $A \subseteq C$, then a general solution to the problem exists, and consequences can include only those NTA objects B that meet the following constraint: $A \subseteq B \subseteq C$.

If the relation $A \subseteq C$ is not true, there is no joint solution to the problem since no consequences in this case can satisfy the given constraints. Consider an example.

Example 4. Four friends Alan (*A*), Brian (*B*), Colin (*C*), and Dean (*D*) are fans of the hockey teams: the Detroit Red Wings (*W*), the Edmonton Oilers (*E*), the New York Rangers (*N*), and the Pittsburgh Penguins (*P*). Moreover, their preferences are determined by the following premises:

$\mathbf{A_1}$: if *A* is not a fan of *W*, then *B* is a fan of *W* or *P* and *C* is not a fan of *E*;
$\mathbf{A_2}$: if *B* is not a fan of *N*, then *C* is a fan of *P*;
$\mathbf{A_3}$: if *B* is not a fan of *W*, then *D* is a fan of *W*;
$\mathbf{A_4}$: if *B* is a fan of *W*, then *D* is a fan of *N*.

It is necessary to determine the preferences of each person. In the premises, conditional sentences can be expressed in the form of *C*-systems. To do this, we use the names of the friends $\{A, B, C, D\}$ as attributes, whose values will be the names of the teams. Then the expression "*A* is not a fan of *W*" can be written as $L_1[A] = [\{E, N, P\}]$, and the expression "*B* is a fan of *W* or *P* and *C* is not a fan of *E*" turns to the expression $L_2[BC] = [\{W, P\}\ \{W, N, P\}]$. The condition $\mathbf{A_1}$ "If $L_1[A]$, then $L_2[C]$" can be calculated using the generalized union:

$$A_1[ABC] = \overline{L}_1[A] \cup_G L_2[BC] = [\{W\} * *] \cup [* \{W, P\} \ \ \{W, N, P\}]$$
$$= \begin{bmatrix} \{W\} & * & * \\ * & \{W, P\} & \{W, N, P\} \end{bmatrix}.$$

The resulting *C*-system can be transformed to an orthogonal one. Then

$$A_1[ABC] = \begin{bmatrix} \{W\} & * & * \\ \{E, N, P\} & \{W, P\} & \{W, N, P\} \end{bmatrix}.$$

The following conditions are calculated similarly:

$$A_2[BC] = \begin{bmatrix} \{N\} & * \\ \{W, E, P\} & \{P\} \end{bmatrix};$$

$$A_3[BD] = \begin{bmatrix} \{W\} & * \\ \{E, N, P\} & \{W\} \end{bmatrix};$$

$$A_4[BD] = \begin{bmatrix} \{E, N, P\} & * \\ \{W\} & \{N\} \end{bmatrix}.$$

These conditions can be considered premises. Let us calculate the minimal consequence:

$$A[ABCD] = A_1[ABC] \cap_G A_2[BC] \cap_G A_3[BD] \cap_G A_4[BD].$$

As an illustration, consider one of the intermediate calculations:

$$K_1[ABC] = A_1[ABC] \cap_G A_2[BC] = \begin{bmatrix} \{W\} & * & * \\ \{E, N, P\} & \{W, P\} & \{W, N, P\} \end{bmatrix}$$

$$\cap \begin{bmatrix} * & \{N\} & * \\ * & \{W, E.P\} & \{P\} \end{bmatrix} = \begin{bmatrix} \{W\} & \{N\} & * \\ \{W\} & \{W, E, P\} & \{P\} \\ \{E, N, P\} & \{W, P\} & \{P\} \end{bmatrix}.$$

After performing all the calculations, the minimal consequence will be obtained as

$$A[ABCD] = \begin{bmatrix} \{W\} & \{N\} & * & \{W\} \\ \{W\} & \{W\} & \{P\} & \{N\} \\ \{W\} & \{E, P\} & \{P\} & \{W\} \\ \{E, N, P\} & \{W\} & \{P\} & \{N\} \\ \{E, N, P\} & \{P\} & \{P\} & \{W\} \end{bmatrix}.$$

If in addition to the premises $\boldsymbol{A}_1 - \boldsymbol{A}_4$, there are no other restrictions in this problem, its solution will include many uncertainties. Except for $\mathrm{Pr}_D(\boldsymbol{A})$, all projections with one attribute contain a complete list of teams. All paired projections also do not allow obtaining unambiguous results.

The situation will change significantly if we introduce the restriction "There are no equal preferences among friends." This limitation is called *Alldiff*; it is often used in CSP tasks.

In this case study, as in Example 2, it is possible to consistently delete unnecessary values from C-n-tuples and even entire C-n-tuples, in which singleton components are repeated in different attributes (for instance, the C-n-tuple $[\{W\}\ \{E, P\}\ \{P\}\ \{W\}]$).

As a result, we obtain the answer $\boldsymbol{C}$ that includes both premises and constraints:

$$C[ABCD] = [\{E\} \quad \{W\} \quad \{P\} \quad \{N\}].$$

But this answer is no longer a consequence since $\boldsymbol{C}$ is a strict subset of the minimal consequence. The problem can be considered solved, if formulas $\boldsymbol{A}_1 - \boldsymbol{A}_4$ can be used as constraints rather than premises.

5 Conclusion

Above, some procedures have been proposed for finding consequences from a given system of premises with the possibility to choose the desired properties of these consequences. In particular, it is possible to search for consequences with a reduced (in comparison with the initial system of premises) or a given set of variables.

In all cases, the concept of the minimal consequence is used, which is the generalized intersection of the NTA objects that model premises. Interesting corollaries are either equal to the minimal consequence or are its incomplete projections.

With usage of the minimal consequence, some methods for solving constraint satisfaction problems based on n-tuple algebra have been developed as well.

Acknowledgements. This research was supported in part by the Russian Foundation for Basic Research (grant No. 19-08-00079).

References

1. Mendelson, E.: Introduction to Mathematical Logic, 6th edn. Taylor & Francis Group, Milton Park, Oxfordshire (2015)
2. Chang, C.-L., Lee, R.C.-T.: Symbolic Logic and Mechanical Theorem Proving. Academic Press, New York (1973)
3. Vagin, V.N., et al.: Reliable and plausible inference in intelligent systems. In: Vagin, V.N., Pospelov, D.A. (eds.), 2nd edn, FIZMATLIT, Moscow (2008). (in Russian)
4. Kulik, B., Fridman, A.: N-ary Relations for Logical Analysis of Data and Knowledge. IGI Global (2017)
5. Kulik, B.A.: Logic and Mathematics: Complex Methods of Logical Analysis in Plain Words. Polytechnica, Saint Petersburg (2020). (in Russian)
6. Shalak, V.I.: Analysis vs deduction. Logical Stud. **24**(1), 26–45 (2018). (in Russian)
7. Pelletier, F.J.: Seventy-five problems for testing automatic theorem provers. J. Autom. Reasoning **2**, 191–216 (1986)
8. Rossi, F., Sperduti, A.: Learning solution preferences in constraint problems. J. Exp. Theor. Artif. Intell. **10**(1), 103–116 (1998)
9. Zuenko, A.A.: Inference on constraints with using matrix representation of finite predicates. J. Artif. Intell. Decis. Making **3**, 21–31 (2014). (in Russian)

Data Mining Methods for Analysis and Forecast of an Emerging Technology Trend: A Systematic Mapping Study from SCOPUS Papers

Nguyen Thanh Viet[1,2(✉)], Alla Kravets[1,3], and Tu Duong Quoc Hoang[1]

[1] Volgograd State Technical University, Volgograd, Russia
agk@gde.ru
[2] Pham Van Dong University, Quang Ngai, Vietnam
[3] Dubna State University, Dubna, Russia

Abstract. To stay competitive in an environment of rapidly changing science, it is important to monitor the development of existing technology and to discover new and promising technologies. Similarly, it is necessary for a firm to establish a technology development strategy through emerging technology forecast to gain a competitive edge while utilizing limited resources. Numerous methods of emerging technology trend analysis and forecast (TTAF) have been proposed; however, no study described data mining methods' review of this research area in a systematic and structured procedure. Hence, this paper intends to give a review of TTAF data mining methods and shortages by surveying and constructing challenging problems, research and resolving approaches. Moreover, the study highlights adopted data mining methods and types of data sources. Specifically, 50 documents from SCOPUS over a ten-year timespan between 2010 and 2019 were systematically reviewed, and each performing step was followed properly in accordance with systematic mapping study.

Keywords: Data mining · Emerging technology · Technology forecast · Technology analysis · Systematic mapping study · SCOPUS · Patent clustering

1 Introduction

Numerous emerging innovations with breakthrough improvements have quickly arisen over the past decades. Crucial technological progressions comprise nanotechnology, biotechnology, new material technology, and information technology. The appearance and evolution of the abovementioned emerging innovations not only have shifted existing productions but also have generated new ones that retain important influences on the social economic construction. Recognizing upcoming shifting tendencies of those technological emergences as soon as possible is essential for strategic planning in research and development (R&D) of enterprises and governments to obtain primacy in emulative commercial domains. Many decision-makers and employers are familiar with the seriousness of realizing the emerging patterns and detecting the upcoming development tendencies of relating technological emergences for sustained evolution and corporation's

S. M. Kovalev et al. (Eds.): RCAI 2021, LNAI 12948, pp. 81–101, 2021.
https://doi.org/10.1007/978-3-030-86855-0_7

competitiveness [1–3]. At the same time, each emerging technology could provide plenty of business opportunities and attract venture investments. For this reason, with numerous emerging technologies, evaluating properly and specifying the emerging technologies as early as possible is crucial for any management unit and industrial business.

Studying technically appropriate historic knowledge could help explore how variations in technology advancements are affected by past and existing shifts in associated technologies [4]. An essential facet for detecting technology tendencies is data. News, social media, blogs, and company reports reveal mostly the technologies that have recently reached the evolutionary peak thereof or have been accessible on the market so far. However, premature technology tendencies are usually disseminated originally in scientific publications. Thus, these data are crucial knowledge sources for prime trends and signs [5, 6].

Besides, patents supply the trustworthy and latest knowledge source for detecting technology evolutions [7]. In terms of the research of accessible technological data in patents, one can better discover and perceive the pathway of technological advancements and determine the technological evolutionary tendencies with the support of corresponding domain specialists. For this reason, up to now researchers have utilized patent data for studying technological trends [1, 8–12].

The evolutionary path and development trends of technology are the outcome of synergies between the actual technology and the technological environment in which it is expanded [13]. In addition, due to the inconstancy and uncertainty of emerging technologies, analyzing merely scientific publications or patents causes restrictions to the research of technological development tendencies [14]. Thus, in order to gain better comprehension of the development tendencies and evolutionary pathways of emerging innovations, one should focus more on environment aspects such as up-to-date and temporal data [15] that could alter or form the advancement and emergence progress of emerging technologies.

Numerous methods of emerging technology trend analysis and forecast (TTAF) have been proposed; however, to the best of our knowledge, no study described a data mining methods review of this research area in a systematic and structured procedure. Hence, this study intends to give a review of TTAF data mining methods and shortages by surveying and constructing challenging problems, research and resolving approaches. To do so, our work emphasizes adopted data mining methods and types of data sources. A careful systematic mapping study is carried out by employing guidance elaborated by Petersen et al. in 2008 [16] and 2015 [17]. In this survey, 50 publications from the SCOPUS database over a ten-year timespan between 2010 and 2019 are investigated systematically by complying with each step of systematic mapping study procedure precisely. Most frequent and important data mining methods and data source types were exposed and notable detections concerning the progression of TTAF research within the ten-year period were analyzed.

The rest of our paper is arranged as follows. Section 2 reports the existent viewpoints of the promising technology definition via the literature review. Section 3 describes the primary approach of this systematic mapping study and delineates operations of the research framework with study results. Section 4 summarizes basic ideas of the most impact method used in TTAF research, which will be discovered in the previous section. Finally, concluding remarks and a future research plan are presented in Section 5.

2 Existent Viewpoints for Determining Promising Technologies

Many studies have employed the term *promising technology* usually and commonly without yet clarifying it distinctly. Therefore, to assist decision-making, the prediction of a promising technology expects cautious investigations of its related facets. To comprehend these facets, we should primarily study the available literature associated with promising technologies. Consequently, we revise the recent studies on technological trend analysis and prediction, promising technologies and foresight, and then explain the viewpoints of what comprises a promising technology [18].

The first category (viewpoint) of a promising technology is a vacant technology. Researchers employing this viewpoint concentrated on innovatory dominance in the technology emulation, specifying prospective chances for entering potential markets that are receiving little recognition [19–23]. To explore vacant technologies, authors adopted visualizations such as patent maps, generated by patent network clustering, text mining, document-term matrix clustering, and analogous techniques.

The second category of a promising technology is a convergent technology, which has been examined recently as a dominant technology for the future [24–28]. Technological convergence is the trend of initially separate technologies to transform into more closely interrelated and even to be combined as they advance. Besides, current innovative tendencies which are overlapping and merging are assessed as convergent technologies. The technology convergences revise the borders of current industries and generate novel productions or whole domains. To predict convergence, interrelations between patents, such as the co-occurrence of the International Patent Classification (IPC), bibliometric analysis, or association rule analysis, have been utilized.

The third category of a promising technology is anticipating customer-based technologies; concurrently, market approval (or market pull) is the most essential problem to resolve. In case there is a technological innovation, we cannot consider it promising if its diffusion or utilization is restricted due to a commercial failure. Involving clients or end-users in predicting a promising technology has been studied [29–33].

The fourth category of a promising technology is a disruptive technology (or disruptive innovation), which changes the standard functioning of a manufacturing or a business; sometimes it even replaces a well-accepted technology or product in the market [34–38]. While sustainable technologies rely on the increasing upgrades in the current innovations, the practical implementation of disruptive technologies occasionally has not been verified yet.

The last category is the research of the latest occurrence and quick growth of emerging technologies [14, 39–41]. Rotolo et al. [14] characterized emerging technologies through the prism of five attributes: (1) radical novelty, (2) relatively fast growth, (3) coherence, (4) prominent impact, and (5) uncertainty and ambiguity. Furthermore, relevant documents and other techniques associated with emerging technologies' analysis and forecast will be revealed and discussed in the later sections of this paper.

In addition to those main categories, a promising technology can be specified by other perspectives. Some scholars proposed that the technology push and the market pull should be analyzed jointly, even though the features or criteria of these two factors are distinctive, based on the studies [42–44]. Additionally, some studies implemented technological forecasts based on the technology life cycle approach [45–49]. Moreover, promising technology could be both vacant and emerging [22], or have commercial potential and be emerging [50]. In these contexts, the phrase *promising technology* is supposed to contain multidimensional and compound features.

The viewpoints about promising technologies mentioned above are not comprehensive and distinctly not mutually exclusive; also, they are influenced by the motivation of the study and the properties of considered technologies. These viewpoints should be regarded before developing a framework for identifying promising technologies, which most of the available studies lack. Among the five viewpoints, this study adopted the emergence viewpoint of a promising technology to investigate data mining methods and data sources used for TTAF research.

3 Systematic Mapping Study

Dispersed published studies in TTAF pose challenges for successive researchers and practitioners to evaluate the latest evolution of the regarded field. Besides, until now, only a small portion of effort to provide systematic reviews of the adopted TTAF techniques or methods has been carried out in a well-organized procedure. To eliminate this shortage, our study offers a concise overview of TTAF method patterns and deficiencies. Different from systematic literature reviews, which involve detailed investigation of particular results and experiment configurations of research, the primary purpose of a systematic mapping (SM) study is to provide a survey of a particular research domain without requiring comprehensive examination of literature [16]. It concentrates on the structured categorization of selective documents, subjective examination, and defining the maturity of publications in the regarded timespan [51]. As far as we know, this study may be the first SM study on TTAF methods to emphasize a wider perspective of existent TTAF techniques and assist in a beneficial reference for upcoming studies with regard to TTAF issues.

This work follows the SM methodology procedure as originated by Petersen in 2008 [16] with upgraded instructions from 2015 [17]. The fundamental objective of SM is to create a classifying diagram for the selective documents. The whole process includes defining research questions, looking for related documents, refining documents, extracting keywords, extracting data, and mapping as depicted in Fig. 1. The subsequent subsections will present each procedure in a particular manner.

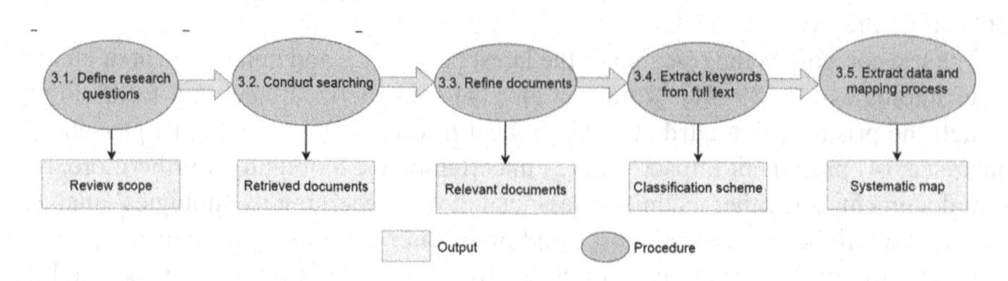

Fig. 1. The systematic mapping process

3.1 Defining Research Questions (RQs)

The central purpose of a SM study is to give a summary of a research domain and specify the quantity of obtainable results and achievements. This phase affects the extent of the entire examining process. Key research questions manifesting our aims are specified below:

Within the past 10 years (i.e. 2010–2019):

RQ1: What are the most common data source types for TTAF?
RQ2: What are the data mining methods (techniques) used in TTAF?
RQ3: What are the most cited (impact) documents in TTAF research?
RQ4: What are the most frequent indexes or scores that could be used for time series analysis?
RQ5: What are the technical gaps in TTAF research?

3.2 Conducting Search

The appropriate documents are explored by applying a search query to scientific databases as well as scanning manually across journal publications or conference proceedings. An efficient strategy to build a search query is to construct it in terms of an intervention, a population, an outcome, and a comparison [52]. Thus, search string keywords can be selected from each facet of the structure, which is formed by the RQs.

In this paper, a selective collection of publications was obtained by establishing keywords for creating a search query as below, adopting the SCOPUS database, setting the search period as 2010–2019, subject area as (Engineering, Computer Science), document type as (Article, Conference paper, Book chapter, Review), and written language as English. After eliminating the duplicates, the number of retrieved documents is 305.

Search query: (Monitor* OR Identif* OR Discover* OR Predict* OR Forecast* OR Analy* OR Detect* OR Explor*) AND (Technologi*) AND (Trend* OR Focus* OR Emerg* OR Disrupt* OR Development*).

3.3 Refining Documents

In the refining phase, most pertinent studies that resolve closely the predefined RQs remain after using the exclusion and inclusion criteria. At first, documents are assessed by examining the titles and abstracts. Introduction of full texts will be studied only when titles and abstracts fail to yield sufficient knowledge to determine the inclusion (or exclusion) of the considered document.

The following inclusion criteria are considered in the obtained search result, i.e. a publication (document) will be included if:

- (**IC01**): the publication addresses the elaborated research questions;
- (**IC02**): the publication full text is available;
- (**IC03**): the publication authors use data mining methods to analyze or forecast an emerging technology trend.

The following exclusion criteria are also regarded, i.e. a publication will be excluded if:

- **(EC01)**: the primary focus of the publication is not related to TTAF;
- **(EC02)**: the publication full text is not available;
- **(EC03)**: proposed methods in the publication are not based on data mining.
- **(EC04)**: publication focuses on identifying and forecasting technological reverse salient or identifying particular strategic reactions toward the technological change.

By checking publication titles and abstract, ones that did not comply with inclusion criteria and were duplicated were excluded. Finally, the initial bulk of 305 publications was reduced to 50 documents as the final list for further analysis. However, after studying these 50 documents' full texts, 12 documents were eliminated due to irrelevant research.

3.4 Extracting Keywords from the Full Text

Creating a classification scheme focuses on extracting dominant keywords and discovering categories from studying literature full texts. In [51], the authors emphasized that there were two typical methods for creating a classification scheme. The bottom-up method is a strategy of investigating selected publications and summing up a notable classification, whereas the top-down method is a strategy to build a scheme by applying entire expertise of a certain area. In this paper, we decided to build the scheme using the bottom-up method.

3.5 Extracting Data and Creating a Systematic Map

After building the classification scheme, the authors examined the eventual selective documents and extracted essential knowledge based on the RQs and the classification scheme. A systematic map that illustrates the defined issues with the kind of techniques is demonstrated below.

RQ1: What are the Most Common Data Source Types for TTAF?
Seven types of common data sources in TTAF research were identified. These types are: (a) miscellaneous: include diverse data sources such as patents, publications, news, social network data, etc.; (b) news; (c) patents; (d) patents & publications; (e) publications; (f) publications & news; and (g) unknown. Figure 2 shows percentages of the adopted data source types. By analyzing statistics, it was found that patent data sources were used most frequently and constituted half of the publications (50%). The following common data source types are patents & publications (16%), publications (10%), unknown (8%), miscellaneous (8%), publications & news (5%), and news (3%).

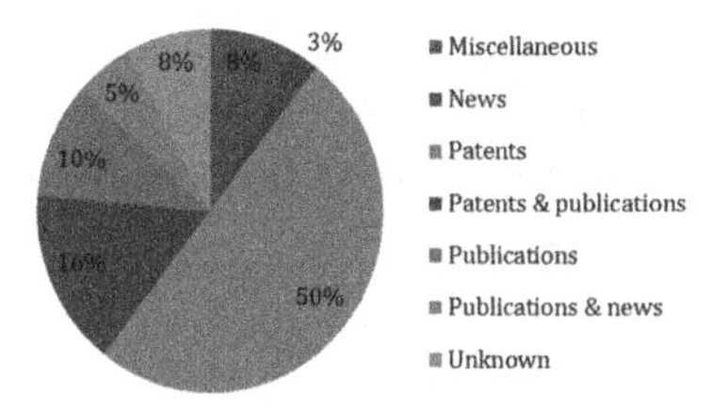

Fig. 2. Statistics of data source types

Table 1 specifies respective studies of different data source types on solving TTAF.

Table 1. Description of data source types

Data source type	Percentage	Specificity	References
Miscellaneous	8%	Patents, publications, news, social media data, etc	[53–55]
News	3%	Stack Overflow website	[56]
Patents	50%	USPTO, EU, Korea, Japan patent databases, PatBase, Wisdomain, Derwent Innovation	[8, 9, 18, 20, 57–71]
Patents & publications	16%	Patents (WIPO, Thompson Innovation, PATSTAT), publications (Web of Science, Scopus, DBLP, Springer, IEEE)	[72–77]
Publications	11%	Web of Science, Scopus	[78–81]
Publications & news	5%	Web of Science, Google News	[82, 83]
Unknown	8%		[84–86]

Figure 3 demonstrates the distribution of various patent databases adopted in TTAF research, which applied data mining methods on patent data only.

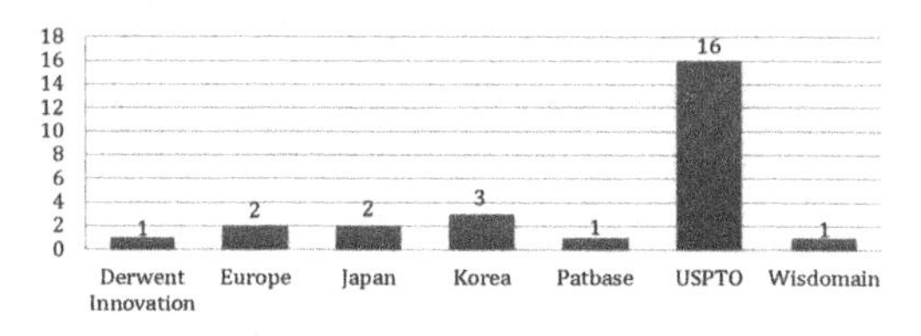

Fig. 3. A usage count of patent databases

RQ2: What are Data Mining Methods (Techniques) Used in TTAF?
Method labels were extracted after studying the full texts of abovementioned SCOPUS publications. Figure 4 illustrates the usage frequency of data mining methods with minimum appearance 2 (i.e. threshold = 2).

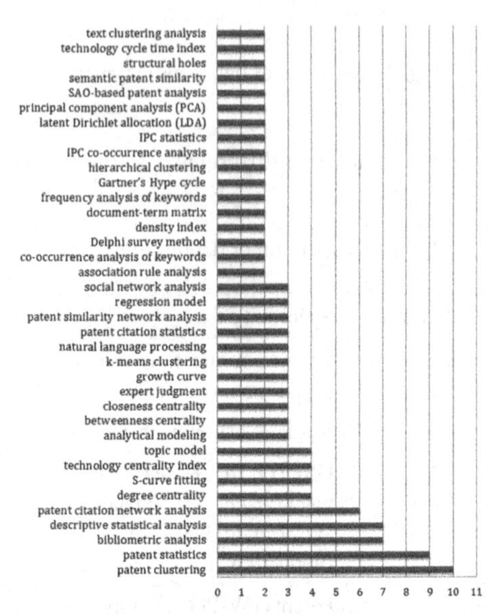

Fig. 4. Data mining method usage statistics (appearance threshold = 2)

Table 2 lists respective references of methods (appearance threshold = 3) used in TTAF research.

As presented in Table 2, one can see that most impact and frequent methods adopted in TTAF research are: patent clustering, patent statistics, bibliometric analysis, descriptive statistical analysis, patent citation network analysis, degree centrality, S-curve fitting,

Table 2. Identified methods (appearance threshold = 2) with respective references

Method	References	Method	References
Patent clustering	[8, 9, 18, 20, 58, 61, 62, 65, 66, 69]	Patent statistics	[63–65, 67, 69, 70, 74, 76, 80]
Bibliometric analysis	[18, 58, 72, 79, 80, 87, 88]	Descriptive statistical analysis	[55, 60, 63, 64, 67, 80, 89]
Patent citation network analysis	[18, 60, 62, 66, 67, 69]	Degree centrality	[60, 67, 70, 71]
S-curve fitting	[78, 80, 86, 87]	Technology centrality index	[58, 60, 61, 70]

(*continued*)

Table 2. (*continued*)

Method	References	Method	References
Topic model	[56, 77, 81, 83]	Analytical modeling	[78, 82, 86]
Betweenness centrality	[67, 70, 71]	Closeness centrality	[67, 70, 71]
Expert judgment	[89–91]	Growth curve	[78, 80, 86]
k-means clustering	[9, 72, 84]	Natural language processing	[8, 9, 68]
Patent citation statistics	[57, 63, 71]	Patent similarity network analysis	[8, 58, 61]
Regression model	[77, 80, 82]	Social network analysis	[67, 70, 71]
Association rule analysis	[20, 65]	Co-occurrence analysis of keywords	[72, 79]
Delphi survey method	[84, 89]	Density index	[58, 61]
Document-term matrix	[20, 65]	Frequency analysis of keywords	[72, 79]
Gartner's Hype cycle	[73, 78]	Hierarchical clustering	[58, 62]
IPC co-occurrence analysis	[59, 69]	IPC statistics	[69, 72]
Latent Dirichlet allocation (LDA)	[56, 77]	Principal component analysis (PCA)	[71, 84]
SAO-based patent analysis	[8, 9]	Semantic patent similarity	[8, 9]
Structural holes	[60, 70]	Technology cycle time index	[58, 61]
Text clustering analysis	[54, 65]		

technology centrality index, topic model, etc. In Section 4, we will describe the basic ideas of the most frequent method: patent clustering.

RQ3: What are the Most Cited (Impact) Documents in TTAF Research?
Lately Klavans and Boyack [92] suggested that direct citations are more dependable in detecting research fronts than bibliographic coupling and co-citation. Moreover, the

direct citation model was proved to be much selective than the co-citation model [66]. The influence of a publication is confirmed closely by being quoted by the others. In other words, the significance of a publication is explicitly proportional to the amount, quality, and authority of the ones that cite it.

Figure 5 demonstrates the top five most cited publications of TTAF research between 2010 and 2019 (citation data was collected from SCOPUS on March 25, 2021).

Authors	Ref.	Title	Year	Cited	Author Keywords	Source title
Albino V., Ardi	[63]	Understanding the development trends of low-carbon energy technologies: A patent analysis	2014	142	Eco-innovation; Environmental programs; Environmental sustainability; Low-carbon energy technologies; Patents	Applied Energy
Érdi P., Makov	[62]	Prediction of emerging technologies based on analysis of the US patent citation network	2013	122	Co-citation clustering; Network; Patent citation; Technological evolution	Scientometrics
Yoon J., Kim K.	[8]	Identifying rapidly evolving technological trends for R&D planning using SAO-based semantic patent networks	2011	113	Natural language processing (NLP); Patent mining; Patent network; Research and development (R&D) trend; Semantic patent similarity; Subject-action-object (SAO)	Scientometrics
Chang P.-L., W	[58]	Using patent analyses to monitor the technological trends in an emerging field of technology: A case of carbon nanotube field emission display	2010	107	Carbon nanotube field emission display (CNT-FED); Patent bibliometric analysis; Patent network analysis	Scientometrics
Yoon J., Park H	[9]	Identifying technological competition trends for R&D planning using dynamic patent maps: SAO-based content analysis	2013	100	Dynamic patent map; Natural language processing (NLP); Research and development (R&D) strategy; Semantic patent similarity; Subject-action-object (SAO) structure	Scientometrics

Fig. 5. Top five most cited publications among 50 retrieved documents

To verify the validation and impact of top-cited publications, we identify citation counts of the first four ranked publications by year to observe citation tendencies. Figure 6 illustrates the citation dynamics of these documents, and it means that the citation counts are still growing each year. This fact claims that these top-cited documents still influence later researches and TTAF topic is still urgent, practical, and significant.

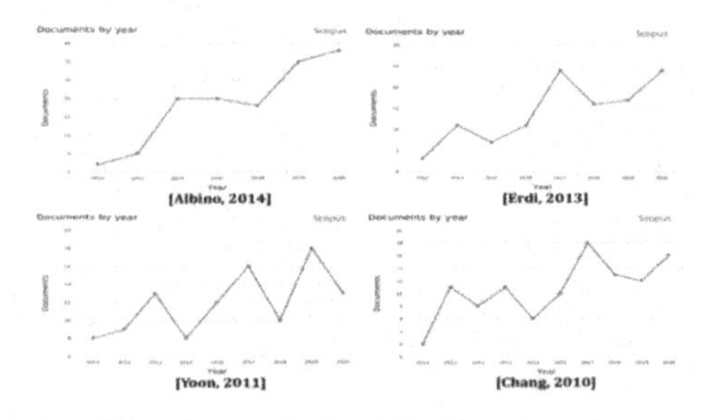

Fig. 6. Citation dynamics of first four ranked publications from the year of publication to 2020

RQ4: What are the Most Frequent Indexes or Scores that Could be Used for Time Series Analysis?

Time series are inspected to comprehend the past, forecast the future, and allow policy-makers or employers to make well-informed decisions precisely. Time series analysis quantifies the principal attributes of data and the random variability. Subsequently, a significant suggestion to implement TTAF research is analyzing and forecast quantified technological features in time series.

By observing the most adopted methods in TTAF research in Table 2, one can identify some significant indexes such as: the technology centrality index, degree centrality, betweenness centrality, closeness centrality (these ones are utilized popularly in the field of social network analysis — SNA). Accordingly, we focus on the definition of these indexes, which are highly promising for time series analysis in future researches.

Technology Centrality Index (TCI) [58, 60, 61, 70]. The index is suggested in patent network analysis, which is defined as:

$$TCI(p_k) = \frac{m}{n-1} \tag{1}$$

where m is the number of lines that are incident with patent (node) p_k, and n denotes the total number of patents (nodes). It computes the relative significance of a target patent by determining the density of its connection with other patents. The centrality index in the patent network indicates the proportion of connected links to all (n – 1) remaining patents. Therefore, the higher the centrality index, the greater the impact on other patents.

Degree Centrality [60, 67, 70, 71]. Degree centrality (C_D) is employed to compute the amount of undirected or directed connections a node holds with other nodes in a network, as presented in Eq. (2). In a network, this index can be adopted to compute a node's amount of straight linked neighbors. A node with a greater degree of centrality shows that it retains more significance and effect than the remaining nodes in the network.

$$C_D(p_k) = \sum\nolimits_{i=1}^{n} c(p_i, p_k) \tag{2}$$

where p_k is regarded as node p; n is the overall number of nodes; and$c(p_i, p_k) = [1,$ if node p_i and node p_k are linked;0, otherwise].

Betweenness Centrality [67, 70, 71]. Betweenness centrality (C_B) is employed to compute how regularly a node remains on the closest path between other nodes in a network, as presented in Eq. (3). It implies the node performs like a bridge linking any two other nodes in order to convey information within network. In a technological network, a node with greater betweenness centrality reveals that this technological node occupies a crucial place in the network composition because the dissemination and linkage between other technological nodes are influenced by the certain node.

$$C_B(p_k) = \sum_{i<j} \frac{s_{ij}(p_k)}{s_{ij}} \tag{3}$$

where s_{ij} is the number of closest paths from node i to node j; and $s_{ij}(p_k)$ is the number of closest paths from node i to node j which goes through the node p_k.

Closeness Centrality [67, 70, 71]. Closeness centrality (C_C) is employed to compute the distance from a node to the others in a network, as presented in Eq. (4). Closeness centrality is equivalent to the inverse of the sum of the closest distance between the target node and the others. A closer distance between the considered node and the others reveals that the node has a greater degree of proximity or closeness. Within a technological network, closeness centrality can quantify the general centrality of the regarded technology in terms of specifying its connection with other technologies.

$$C_c(p_k) = 1/\sum_{i=1}^{n} d(p_i, p_k) \quad (4)$$

where $d(p_i, p_k)$ is the number of linkages in the geodesic (closest distance) connecting node p_i and node p_k.

RQ5: What are the Technical Gaps in TTAF Research?

Most of the considered studies (92%, derived from Table 1) exploring the evolutionary path and development trends of emerging technologies are based on patents or scientific publications, or news alone from a technological perspective, whereas few scholars (8% of studies) have combined simultaneously information from publications, news, social media data, and patents to monitor the advent of emerging technologies and to identify future change trends from a technical-environmental perspective. A few experts recommended that several kinds of information sources supply various knowledge about the evolutionary pathway of technology advancement; also, the combined usage of different data sources will definitely provide a more general representation of technological trends [54, 55]. Thus, the analysis of only patents or publications is not sufficient to fully understand the evolutionary path and development trends of emerging technologies. Moreover, due to the comparative analysis of engineering knowledge included in patents and attention information of user feedback and reactivity to emerging technologies mentioned in social media, we could recognize and better discover the emergence of these technologies and attain the comprehension of evolutionary tendencies by analyzing the distinctions between social networks data and patents. Thus, the task of analyzing and predicting trends in technological development based on processing heterogeneous data from open sources — e.g., scientific publications, patents, social media, mass media, foresight projects, conferences, international projects, dissertations, presentations, etc. — becomes relevant and substantial.

Only 8% of studies [56, 65, 69, 76] employed time factors to observe and analyze the changes of technological properties. However, no document so far has utilized time series analysis to implement technological trend prediction.

4 Basic Ideas of Patent Clustering Methods in TTAF Research

As shown in Table 2, the most frequently used method in TTAF researches is patent clustering, which was utilized in 10 studies. The current section summarizes the basic ideas and general algorithm of this significant method.

In [58], the authors examine the relationship of Carbon nanotube field emission display (CNT-FED) patents using network analysis in overall network and cluster levels. At the general network level, this paper adopts an entire keyword-based similarity patent network to analyze the common relation and to reveal crucial patents. At the cluster level, the paper clusters patents together by close technologies to create a technological package. By analyzing the specific relation among patents in each cluster, the attributes of clusters and main technologies can be detected. In quantitative analysis, various indicators are used to study the structure of the patent network in cluster and general network levels, e.g. the technology centrality index, technology cycle time index, density index. This work employs a two-stage clustering strategy, which integrates nonhierarchical with hierarchical clustering algorithms to discover various clusters in the CNT-FED patent network. Thanks to the proposed approach, three distinct clusters with patents thereof were specified.

In [20], the authors propose a forecasting model for technological trend using Association rule mining (ARM) and a self-organizing map (SOM). The SOM is a competitive neural network for classification and clustering, which consists of two layers, input, and a feature. The researchers cluster all patent documents to a 2×2 feature map. First, the SOM normalizes input vector x and initializes weight matrix M. Second, the distance between the input and weight is computed using Euclidean distance. The closest m_j to x_i is updated as follows:

$$m_k = m_j + \alpha(x_i - m_j) \quad (5)$$

where m_j and m_k are current and new weights, and the constant α is the learning rate. Accordingly, the authors clustered all patent documents to feature maps. The vacant technology was found in the feature map of the SOM by identifying low-density areas.

[8] proposes a procedure for generating a patent network based on semantic patent similarity; this process consists of (1) collecting patent data sources, (2) extracting SAO (subject – noun phrase, action – verb phrase, and object – noun phrase) structures from patent text, (3) computing patent similarities by measuring semantic sentence similarities between SAO structures, and (4) visualizing a patent network. Then, the patent network can be clustered by the Bi-Component method. Employing the density analysis concept of patent clusters such as "Large size, high density," "Large size, low density," and "Small size, high density," inferences from a technological perspective can be developed.

[61] employs patent network analysis to study technology tendencies in flexible display fabrication domain via the technology cycle time (TCT) index and technology centrality index (TCI). The proposed approach adopts the keywords frequency in patents like the input basis to build a visual patent network. Furthermore, crucial technologies were detected by clustering analysis; besides, the density index estimation of each cluster specified the discovery of basic materials for electro-optic display as the most essential subject. These clusters could be considered as a reduced-scale patent network of the flexible display. The more concentrated links among patents are, the more similar these patents are due to technological contents. Alternatively, each patent in a cluster may attain a close technological level and create a technological package. By analyzing the complete relation among patents in each cluster, features of the clusters and dominant technologies were detected.

In [9], the semantic patent closeness was calculated by using the WordNet-based semantic similarities between their SAO (subject-action-object) forms of sentences [8, 93]. The authors employed the k-means clustering, where the optimal figure k of clusters is expected to produce the minimum average intra-cluster distance (distance between individual elements and the cluster center) and the maximum average inter-cluster distance (distance between cluster centers). Clusters with plenty of items, small average intra-cluster length, and large average inter-cluster length have a high possibility of becoming crucial, low-cost, or accepted technologies. Nevertheless, patent clusters with a small number of items, short average intra-cluster length, and long average inter-cluster length are likely not a crucial or certified technology but probably early signals for the evolution of a novel technology.

In [62], the search for emerging and evolving technology clusters was based on a citation network. With the clustering algorithm, the authors used advancing samples of citations from other patents toward a certain patent in numerous technological groups to compute patent closeness. To perceive the temporal advancement of technology fields, the "citation vector" was used to measure closeness between patents in the following way: (1) For each patent, compute the total citations gained by that patent from other ones in each of the 36 technology sub-categories. This provides 36 totals for each patent, which are regarded as items in a 36-element vector. (2) Compute the closeness between two patents by the Euclidean distance of their citation vectors and employ hierarchical clustering method on basis of this closeness value. (3) Repeat the previous phases for different time points $t_1 < t_2 < \ldots < t_n$. Compare the attained dendrograms by clustering procedure for various time points to explore structural shifts (e.g. disappearance and emergence of groups).

In [65], text parsing and filtering were used to decrease the number of terms and explore main phrases. In the text parsing procedure, only nouns and noun groups were analyzed to obtain apparent technology fields. Through these procedures, a weight term-by-document matrix with n rows (number of documents) and p columns (number of terms) were generated. Thereafter, singular value decomposition (SVD) was applied to decrease the size of weighted term-by-document matrix. In this process, the authors made the largest SVD dimension equivalent to 25, which was appropriate to perform clustering analysis. Subsequently, Expectation-Maximization (EM) method was selected for text clustering on the SVD matrix (the biggest amount of clusters was 20).

In [66], citation linkages between patents were adopted to generate clusters by employing the full collection of Solar Photovoltaic patents in a single clustering algorithm. Herein, the direct citation clustering was performed employing the algorithm devised by Waltman and Van Eck [94]. This algorithm utilized a variation of modularity-based clustering, which aims to maximize the rate of linkages inside clusters toward linkages between clusters.

In [18], patents with close contents were clustered to detect emerging technological fields. To do so, network analysis and bibliographic coupling were utilized. Among them, 21 clusters that contained a minimum of 10 patents were regarded to be main technologies. After specifying main technologies, the authors used text mining to each set of main technologies to seize technology features. Subsequently, typical keywords of each set were obtained from patent abstracts by adopting TF-IDF, applying the method in [7], and then each set was assigned a label on the basis of extracted keywords.

In [69], patent was regarded as a node, and a cited and citing relation was regarded as a non-directional link. Finally, the network was divided into clusters, using the topological clustering method. A fast clustering algorithm devised by Newman [95] was employed for clustering. The clustering approach was derived from modularity Q, which was established as follows:

$$Q = \sum_{s=1}^{N_m} \left[\frac{l_s}{l} - \left(\frac{d_s}{2l} \right)^2 \right] \tag{6}$$

where N_m is the number of clusters, l_s is the number of linkages between nodes in cluster s, and d_s is the total degrees of nodes in cluster s. Because large magnitude of Q revealed an appropriate splitting, clustering would be terminated when ΔQ was negative. Then, keywords were retrieved by computing TF-IDF.

5 Conclusion

Technological advancements considerably affect strategic decision-making. The premature recognition of feasible emerging or future technology tendencies can help reinforce the trade position and competitiveness of companies. This paper provides an overview of TTAF data mining methods (techniques) and shortages by surveying and constructing challenging problems, research and resolving approaches. An intensive systematic mapping study is conducted by reviewing 50 documents from SCOPUS over a ten-year timespan (2010–2019). Most frequent and important data mining methods and data source types were identified, and significant findings, which highlighted the evolution of TTAF research within the ten-year period, were investigated. Some interesting discoveries and facts include the following: (a) very few studies implemented TTAF research based on processing heterogeneous data from open sources; (b) the most impactful and frequent method adopted in TTAF research is patent clustering; and (c) no document utilized time series analysis to implement technological trend prediction.

To fill out the gaps of existing studies, we will develop strategies for working with different sources of information to analyze and predict technology trends and identify factors to consider when selecting them. To do this, it is necessary to compare, on a systematic basis, the results of technology monitoring obtained from various data sources (such as scientific publications, patents, mass media, social media, foresight projects, conferences, international projects, dissertations, and presentations). Furthermore, we will exploit time series analysis and forecast aspects to discover the dynamics of technological features such as the technology centrality index, degree centrality, betweenness centrality, closeness centrality, etc.

Acknowledgments. The reported study was funded by RFBR, projects Nos. 19–07-01200 and 20–37-90092.

References

1. Li, X., Zhou, Y., Xue, L., Huang, L.: Integrating bibliometrics and road mapping methods: a case of dye-sensitized solar cell technology-based industry in China. Technol. Forecast. Soc. Change **97**, 205–222 (2015). https://doi.org/10.1016/j.techfore.2014.05.007

2. Lee, C., Kwon, O., Kim, M., Kwon, D.: Early identification of emerging technologies: a machine learning approach using multiple patent indicators. Technol. Forecast. Soc. Change **127**, 291–303 (2018). https://doi.org/10.1016/j.techfore.2017.10.002
3. Zhou, Y., Dong, F., Liu, Y., Li, Z., Du, J., Zhang, L.: Forecasting emerging technologies using data augmentation and deep learning. Scientometrics **123**(1), 1–29 (2020). https://doi.org/10.1007/s11192-020-03351-6
4. Momeni, A., Rost, K.: Identification and monitoring of possible disruptive technologies by patent-development paths and topic modeling. Technol. Forecast. Soc. Change **104**, 16–29 (2016)
5. Nazemi, K., et al.: Visual trend analysis with digital libraries. In: ACM International Conference Proceeding Series (2015). https://doi.org/10.1145/2809563.2809569
6. Viet, N.T., Kravets, A.G.: Analyzing recent research trends of computer science from academic open-access digital library. In: Proceedings of the 2019 8th International Conference on System Modeling and Advancement in Research Trends, SMART 2019 (2020)
7. Noh, H., Jo, Y., Lee, S.: Keyword selection and processing strategy for applying text mining to patent analysis. Expert Syst. Appl. **42**, 4348–4360 (2015). https://doi.org/10.1016/j.eswa.2015.01.050
8. Yoon, J., Kim, K.: Identifying rapidly evolving technological trends for R&D planning using SAO-based semantic patent networks. Scientometrics **88**, 213–228 (2011)
9. Yoon, J., Park, H., Kim, K.: Identifying technological competition trends for R&D planning using dynamic patent maps: SAO-based content analysis. Scientometrics **94**, 313–331 (2013)
10. Chen, H., Zhang, G., Zhu, D., Lu, J.: Topic-based technological forecasting based on patent data: a case study of Australian patents from 2000 to 2014. Technol. Forecast. Soc. Change **119**, 39–52 (2017). https://doi.org/10.1016/j.techfore.2017.03.009
11. Kravets, A.G., Vasiliev, S.S., Shabanov, D.V.: Research of the LDA algorithm results for patents texts processing. In: 2018 9th International Conference on Information, Intelligence, Systems and Applications, IISA 2018 (2019). https://doi.org/10.1109/IISA.2018.8633649
12. Kravets, A., Gneushev, V., Biryukov, S., Skorikov, D., Marinkin, D.: Research of the LDA algorithm processing results on high-level classes of patents. In: CEUR Workshop Proceedings (2020)
13. Small, H., Boyack, K.W., Klavans, R.: Identifying emerging topics in science and technology. Res. Policy **43**, 1450–1467 (2014). https://doi.org/10.1016/j.respol.2014.02.005
14. Rotolo, D., Hicks, D., Martin, B.R.: What is an emerging technology? Res. Policy **44**, 1827–1843 (2015)
15. Injadat, M.N., Salo, F., Nassif, A.B.: Data mining techniques in social media: a survey. Neurocomputing **214**, 654–670 (2016). https://doi.org/10.1016/j.neucom.2016.06.045
16. Petersen, K., Feldt, R., Mujtaba, S., Mattsson, M.: Systematic mapping studies in software engineering. In: 12th International Conference on Evaluation and Assessment in Software Engineering, EASE 2008 (2008). https://doi.org/10.14236/ewic/ease2008.8
17. Petersen, K., Vakkalanka, S., Kuzniarz, L.: Guidelines for conducting systematic mapping studies in software engineering: an update. Inf. Softw. Technol. **64**, 1–18 (2015)
18. Noh, H., Song, Y.-K., Lee, S.: Identifying emerging core technologies for the future: case study of patents published by leading telecommunication organizations. Telecommun. Policy **40**, 956–970 (2016)
19. Choi, S., Jun, S.: Vacant technology forecasting using new Bayesian patent clustering. Technol. Anal. Strateg. Manag. **26**, 241–251 (2014). https://doi.org/10.1080/09537325.2013.850477
20. Jun, S.: A forecasting model for technological trend using unsupervised learning. In: Kim, T.-H., et al. (eds.) Database Theory and Application, Bio-Science and Bio-Technology. CCIS, vol. 258, pp. 51–60. Springer, Heidelberg (2011). https://doi.org/10.1007/978-3-642-27157-1_6

21. Yoon, B., Park, I., Yun, D., Park, G.: Exploring promising vacant technology areas in a technology-oriented company based on bibliometric analysis and visualization. Technol. Anal. Strateg. Manag. **31**, 388–405 (2019). https://doi.org/10.1080/09537325.2018.1516864
22. Yu, J., et al.: Identification of vacant and emerging technologies in smart mobility through the GTM-based patent map development. Sustainability **12**, 9310 (2020). https://doi.org/10.3390/su12229310
23. Jun, S., et al.: Identification of promising vacant technologies for the development of truck on freight train transportation systems. Appl. Sci. **11**, 499 (2021). https://doi.org/10.3390/app11020499
24. Lee, W.S., Han, E.J., Sohn, S.Y.: Predicting the pattern of technology convergence using big-data technology on large-scale triadic patents. Technol. Forecast. Soc. Change **100**, 317–329 (2015)
25. Lee, J., Sohn, S.Y.: Recommendation system for technology convergence opportunities based on self-supervised representation learning. Scientometrics **126**(1), 1–25 (2020). https://doi.org/10.1007/s11192-020-03731-y
26. Arzhanovskaya, A.V., Eltanskaya, E.A., Generalova, L.M.: Convergence of technologies in education: new determinant of the society development. In: Popkova, E.G., Sergi, B.S. (eds.) "Smart Technologies" for Society, State and Economy. LNNS, vol. 155, pp. 619–624. Springer, Cham (2021). https://doi.org/10.1007/978-3-030-59126-7_69
27. Farahani, B., Firouzi, F., Luecking, M.: The convergence of IoT and distributed ledger technologies (DLT): opportunities, challenges, and solutions. J. Netw. Comput. Appl. **177**, 102936 (2021)
28. Lee, C., Hong, S., Kim, J.: Anticipating multi-technology convergence: a machine learning approach using patent information. Scientometrics **126**(3), 1867–1896 (2021). https://doi.org/10.1007/s11192-020-03842-6
29. Ju, Y., Sohn, S.Y.: Patent-based QFD framework development for identification of emerging technologies and related business models: a case of robot technology in Korea. Technol. Forecast. Soc. Change **94**, 44–64 (2015). https://doi.org/10.1016/j.techfore.2014.04.015
30. Reyes-Mercado, P., Rajagopal.: Dynamics of disruptive innovations in outperforming global brands: a study in Mexico. Int. J. Bus. Excell. (2017). https://doi.org/10.1504/IJBEX.2017.080599
31. Munir, A.R., Ilyas, G.B.: Extending the technology acceptance model to predict the acceptance of customer toward mobile banking service in Sulawesi Selatan. Int. J. Econ. Res. **14**, 365–375 (2017)
32. Song, K., Kim, K., Lee, S.: Identifying promising technologies using patents: a retrospective feature analysis and a prospective needs analysis on outlier patents. Technol. Forecast. Soc. Change **128**, 118–132 (2018). https://doi.org/10.1016/j.techfore.2017.11.008
33. Benzidia, S., Luca, R.M., Boiko, S.: Disruptive innovation, business models, and encroachment strategies: buyer's perspective on electric and hybrid vehicle technology. Technol. Forecast. Soc. Change **165**, 120520 (2021). https://doi.org/10.1016/j.techfore.2020.120520
34. Laurell, C., Sandström, C.: Analysing Uber in social media - disruptive technology or institutional disruption? Int. J. Innov. Manag. **20**, 1640013 (2016)
35. Trubnikov, D.: Analysing the impact of regulation on disruptive innovations: the case of wireless technology. J. Ind. Compet. Trade **17**(4), 399–420 (2016). https://doi.org/10.1007/s10842-016-0243-y
36. Sun, J., Song, Z., Wang, K., Li, H., Tan, R.: How to find disruptive technologies systematically? In: Benmoussa, R., De Guio, R., Dubois, S., Koziołek, S. (eds.) New Opportunities for Innovation Breakthroughs for Developing Countries and Emerging Economies, vol. 572, pp. 159–173. Springer, Heidelberg (2019). https://doi.org/10.1007/978-3-030-32497-1_14
37. Krotov, V.: Predicting the future of disruptive technologies: the method of alternative histories. Bus. Horiz. **62**, 695–705 (2019). https://doi.org/10.1016/j.bushor.2019.07.003

38. Müller, J.M., Kunderer, R.: Ex-ante prediction of disruptive innovation: the case of battery technologies. Sustainability **11**, 5229 (2019). https://doi.org/10.3390/su11195229
39. Guderian, C.C.: Identifying emerging technologies with smart patent indicators: the example of smart houses. Int. J. Innov. Technol. Manag. **16**, 1950040 (2019). https://doi.org/10.1142/S0219877019500408
40. Altuntas, S., Erdogan, Z., Dereli, T.: A clustering-based approach for the evaluation of candidate emerging technologies. Scientometrics **124**(2), 1157–1177 (2020). https://doi.org/10.1007/s11192-020-03535-0
41. de Falani, S.Y.A., González, M.O.A., Barreto, F.M., de Toledo, J.C., Torkomian, A.L.V.: Trends in the technological development of wind energy generation. Int. J. Technol. Manag. Sustain. Dev. **19**, 43–68 (2020). https://doi.org/10.1386/tmsd_00015_1
42. Lee, D.J., Hwang, J.: Decision support for selecting exportable nuclear technology using the analytic hierarchy process: a Korean case. Energ. Policy **38**, 161–167 (2010)
43. Cagnin, C., Havas, A., Saritas, O.: Future-oriented technology analysis: its potential to address disruptive transformations. Technol. Forecast. Soc. Change **80**, 379–385 (2013)
44. Ma, T., et al.: A technology opportunities analysis model: applied to dye-sensitised solar cells for China. Technol. Anal. Strateg. Manag. **26**, 87–104 (2014). https://doi.org/10.1080/09537325.2013.850155
45. Gao, L., et al.: Technology life cycle analysis method based on patent documents. Technol. Forecast. Soc. Change **80**, 398–407 (2013). https://doi.org/10.1016/j.techfore.2012.10.003
46. Jamali, M.Y., Aslani, A., Moghadam, B.F., Naaranoja, M., Madvar, M.D.: Analysis of photovoltaic technology development based on technology life cycle approach. J. Renew. Sustain. Energ. **8**, 035905 (2016). https://doi.org/10.1063/1.4952763
47. Byun, J., Sung, T.E., Park, H.W.: Technological innovation strategy: how do technology life cycles change by technological area. Technol. Anal. Strateg. Manag. **30**, 98–112 (2018)
48. Madvar, M.D., Ahmadi, F., Shirmohammadi, R., Aslani, A.: Forecasting of wind energy technology domains based on the technology life cycle approach. Energy Rep. **5**, 1236–1248 (2019)
49. Lin, D., Liu, W., Guo, Y., Meyer, M.: Using technological entropy to identify technology life cycle. J. Informetr. **15**, 101137 (2021). https://doi.org/10.1016/j.joi.2021.101137
50. Zhang, L., Qi, Y., Huang, Y., Wang, X.: Research on commercial potential evaluation of newly & emerging technology: a case study of graphene. In: 10th International Conference on Software, Knowledge, Information Management and Applications (2017)
51. Maw, M., Balakrishnan, V., Rana, O., Ravana, S.D.: Trends and patterns of text classification techniques: a systematic mapping study. Malays. J. Comput. Sci. **33**, 102–117 (2020)
52. Kitchenham, B., Charters, S.: Guidelines for performing systematic literature reviews in software engineering. Technical report, Ver. 2.3 EBSE Technical Report. EBSE (2007)
53. Arskii, Y.M., Yashukova, S.P.: The methodical aspects of the information-analytical support of forecasts of scientific-technological development. Sci. Tech. Inf. Process. **37**, 201–206 (2010)
54. Ena, O., Mikova, N., Saritas, O., Sokolova, A.: A methodology for technology trend monitoring: the case of semantic technologies. Scientometrics **108**(3), 1013–1041 (2016). https://doi.org/10.1007/s11192-016-2024-0
55. Ernstsen, S.K., Thuesen, C., Larsen, L.R., Maier, A.: Identifying disruptive technologies: horizon scanning in the early stages of design. In: Proceedings of International Design Conference, DESIGN, vol. 4, pp. 1833–1844 (2018)
56. Johri, V., Bansal, S.: Identifying trends in technologies and programming languages using topic modeling. In: Proceedings - 12th IEEE International Conference on Semantic Computing, ICSC 2018, vol. 2018, pp. 391–396 (2018)
57. Schultz, L.I., Joutz, F.L.: Methods for identifying emerging general purpose technologies: a case study of nanotechnologies. Scientometrics **85**, 155–170 (2010)

58. Chang, P.-L., Wu, C.-C., Leu, H.-J.: Using patent analyses to monitor the technological trends in an emerging field of technology: a case of carbon nanotube field emission display. Scientometrics **82**, 5–19 (2010)
59. Gui, J., Zhang, Z., Sun, M., Lei, X.: IPC co-occurrence based technological trends discovery. In: Proceedings - 3rd International Conference on Information Management, Innovation Management and Industrial Engineering, ICIII 2010, vol. 4, pp. 459–462 (2010)
60. Cho, T.-S., Shih, H.-Y.: Patent citation network analysis of core and emerging technologies in Taiwan: 1997–2008. Scientometrics **89**, 795–811 (2011)
61. Chang, P.-L., Wu, C.-C., Leu, H.-J.: Investigation of technological trends in flexible display fabrication through patent analysis. Displays **33**, 68–73 (2012)
62. Érdi, P., et al.: Prediction of emerging technologies based on analysis of the US patent citation network. Scientometrics **95**, 225–242 (2013)
63. Albino, V., Ardito, L., Dangelico, R.M., Messeni Petruzzelli, A.: Understanding the development trends of low-carbon energy technologies: a patent analysis. Appl. Energ. **135**, 836–854 (2014)
64. Golembiewski, B., Vom Stein, N., Sick, N., Wiemhöfer, H.-D.: Identifying trends in battery technologies with regard to electric mobility: evidence from patenting activities along and across the battery value chain. J. Clean. Prod. **87**, 800–810 (2015)
65. Suh, J., Sohn, S.Y.: Analyzing technological convergence trends in a business ecosystem. Ind. Manag. Data Syst. **115**, 718–739 (2015)
66. Zhang, S., Han, F.: Identifying emerging topics in a technological domain. J. Intell. Fuzzy Syst. **31**, 2147–2157 (2016)
67. Perng, Y.-H., Huang, Y.-Y.: Investigation of technological trends in shading devices through patent analysis. J. Civ. Eng. Manag. **22**, 818–830 (2016)
68. Gim, J., Lee, J., Jang, Y., Jeong, D.-H., Jung, H.: A trend analysis method for IoT technologies using patent dataset with goal and approach concepts. Wirel. Pers. Commun. **91**(4), 1749–1764 (2016). https://doi.org/10.1007/s11277-016-3276-y
69. Kose, T., Yamano, H., Sakata, I.: Detecting emerging complex technological fields in robotics. In: Portland International Conference on Management of Engineering and Technology: Technology Management in the World of Intelligent Systems, Proceedings (2019)
70. Chang, S.-H.: Revealing development trends and key 5G photonic technologies using patent analysis. Appl. Sci. **9**, 2525 (2019)
71. Aaldering, L.J., Leker, J., Song, C.H.: Analysis of technological knowledge stock and prediction of its future development potential: the case of lithium-ion batteries. J. Clean. Prod. **223**, 301–311 (2019)
72. Wu, F., Tang, M., Huang, L.: Analysis on the technologies' trend of R&D industry based on WIPO patent and SCI documents. In: 2nd International Conference on Information Science and Engineering, ICISE2010 – Proceedings, pp. 117–120 (2010)
73. Lee, J., et al.: Towards discovering emerging technologies based on decision tree. In: Proceedings - 2011 IEEE International Conferences on Internet of Things and Cyber, Physical and Social Computing, iThings/CPSCom 2011, pp. 529–532 (2011)
74. Minke, C., Turek, T.: Technology cycle analysis for emerging technologies on the example of the vanadium redox flow battery. In: World Automation Congress Proceedings, pp. 382–387 (2014). https://doi.org/10.1109/WAC.2014.6935957
75. Joanny, G., et al.: Monitoring of technological development - detection of events in technology landscapes through scientometric network analysis. In: Proceedings of ISSI 2015 Istanbul: 15th International Society of Scientometrics and Informetrics Conference, pp. 1259–1260 (2015)
76. Dernis, H., Squicciarini, M., de Pinho, R.: Detecting the emergence of technologies and the evolution and co-development trajectories in science (DETECTS): a 'burst' analysis-based

approach. J. Technol. Transf. **41**(5), 930–960 (2015). https://doi.org/10.1007/s10961-015-9449-0
77. Nazemi, K., Burkhardt, D.: Visual analytics for analyzing technological trends from text. In: Proceedings of the International Conference on Information Visualisation, vol. 2019, pp. 191–200 (2019)
78. Gluhov, V., Leventsov, V., Radaev, A., Nikolaevskiy, N.: Analytical modeling of development and implementation of telecommunication technologies. In: Galinina, O., Andreev, S., Balandin, S., Koucheryavy, Y. (eds.) Internet of Things, Smart Spaces, and Next Generation Networks and Systems. LNCS, vol. 11118, pp. 428–440. Springer, Cham (2018). https://doi.org/10.1007/978-3-030-01168-0_39
79. Santa Soriano, A., Lorenzo Álvarez, C., Torres Valdés, R.M.: Bibliometric analysis to identify an emerging research area: public Relations Intelligence—a challenge to strengthen technological observatories in the network society. Scientometrics **115**(3), 1591–1614 (2018). https://doi.org/10.1007/s11192-018-2651-8
80. Sheikh, N.J., Sheikh, O.: Bibliometrics and patents: case of forecasting biosensor technologies for emerging point-of-care and medical IoT applications. In: Innovation Discovery: Network Analysis of Research and Invention Activity for Technology Management (2018)
81. Zhou, Y., Lin, H., Liu, Y., Ding, W.: A novel method to identify emerging technologies using a semi-supervised topic clustering model: a case of 3D printing industry. Scientometrics **120**(1), 167–185 (2019). https://doi.org/10.1007/s11192-019-03126-8
82. Abercrombie, R.K., Udoeyop, A.W.: A study of scientometric methods to identify emerging technologies. In: Proceedings of ISSI 2011 - 13th Conference of the International Society for Scientometrics and Informetrics, vol. 1, pp. 2–12 (2011)
83. Xie, Q.-Q., Li, X., Huang, L.-C.: Identifying the development trends of emerging technologies: a social awareness analysis method using web news data mining. In: Portland International Conference on Management of Engineering and Technology: Managing Technological Entrepreneurship: The Engine for Economic Growth, Proceedings (2018)
84. Huang, L., Yuan, Y.: Evaluation on the industrialization potential of emerging technologies based on principal component and cluster analysis. In: UKSim2010 - UKSim 12th International Conference on Computer Modelling and Simulation, pp. 317–322 (2010)
85. Kaiser, I.: Collaborative trend analysis using web 2.0 technologies: a case study. Int. J. Distrib. Syst. Technol. **3**, 14–23 (2012)
86. Kucharavy, D., Schenk, E., De Guio, R.: Long-run forecasting of emerging technologies with logistic models and growth of knowledge. In: Competitive Design - Proceedings of the 19th CIRP Design Conference, pp. 277–284 (2014)
87. Daim, T.U., Rueda, G., Martin, H., Gerdsri, P.: Forecasting emerging technologies: use of bibliometrics and patent analysis. Technol. Roadmapping **2**, 305–353 (2018)
88. Wang, H., Liu, K., Long, S.: Identifying the core knowledge domains of emerging technologies: the case of new energy vehicles. In: PICMET 2018 - Portland International Conference on Management of Engineering and Technology: Managing Technological Entrepreneurship: The Engine for Economic Growth, Proceedings (2018)
89. Gerdsri, N.: An analytical approach to building a Technology Development Envelope (TDE) for roadmapping of emerging technologies. Technol. Roadmapping **2**, 585–607 (2018)
90. Gorbachev, S.: Intellectual multi-level system for neuro-fuzzy and cognitive analysis and forecast of scientific-technological and innovative development. In: MATEC Web of Conferences, vol. 155 (2018)
91. Lee, K., Song, Y., Lee, S.: Identifying emerging technologies in the e-business industry: A needs-driven approach. In: DCNET 2012, ICE-B 2012, OPTICS 2012 - Proceedings of the International Conference on Data Communication Networking, e-Business and Optical Communication Systems, ICETE 327–334 (2012)

92. Klavans, R., Boyack, K.W.: Which type of citation analysis generates the most accurate taxonomy of scientific and technical knowledge? J. Assoc. Inf. Sci. Technol. **68**, 984–998 (2017)
93. Yoon, J., Kim, K.: Detecting signals of new technological opportunities using semantic patent analysis and outlier detection. Scientometrics **90**, 445–461 (2012). https://doi.org/10.1007/s11192-011-0543-2
94. Waltman, L., Van Eck, N.J.: A new methodology for constructing a publication-level classification system of science. J. Am. Soc. Inf. Sci. Technol. **63**, 2378–2392 (2012). https://doi.org/10.1002/asi.22748
95. Newman, M.E.J.: Fast algorithm for detecting community structure in networks. Phys. Rev. E **69**, 066133 (2004)

Machine Learning for Assessment of Cardiometabolic Risk Factors Predictive Potential and Prediction of Obstructive Coronary Arteries Lesions

Karina Shakhgeldyan[1], Boris Geltser[2], Vladislav Rublev[2](✉), Andrey Vishnevskiy[1], Elena Emtseva[1], and Mikhail Tsivanyuk[2]

[1] Vladivostok State University of Economics, Vladivostok, Russia
[2] Far Eastern Federal University, School of Medicine, Vladivostok, Russia

Abstract. The aim of this study was searching and validation of new obstructive coronary arteries lesions predictors and prognostic models development for its verification in patients with ischemic heart disease prior to invasive coronary angiography. Research included a step-by-step algorithm for predictors selection and validation as well as thresholds measurements with filtering and wrapping techniques. Cross-validation of predictive models based on multivariate logistic regression, support vector machine and random forest were made by averaging of 4 quality metrics. Based on selected predictors in continuous and categorical forms the best developed predictive model was logistic regression models ensemble with the following quality metrics: area under the ROC curve 0.85, accuracy - 0.80, sensitivity - 0.82, and specificity - 0. 73, which is higher than the existing CAD Consortium scale.

Keywords: Machine learning · Categorization of variables · Ensembles of models · Coronary arteries · Predictive models

1 Introduction

Coronary artery disease (CAD) takes one of the leading places in the morbidity and mortality structure among majority countries of the world [1]. Thus, annual CAD death rate is around 9,5 million people or more than 17% of all world death. Strategy of early CAD diagnostics is used for mortality reduction and according to the clinical recommendations of cardiological community is aimed to improve the technologies of risk stratification and prophylactics.

Coronary insufficiency is main known mechanism of CAD development due to an imbalance between myocardial oxygen demand and its actual delivery. The narrowing of coronary arteries (CA) lumen by more than 50% is the most common reason for this

This work was carried out with partial support of grants from the Russian Foundation for Basic Research within the framework of research projects No. 20-37-90081, No. 19-29-01077.

S. M. Kovalev et al. (Eds.): RCAI 2021, LNAI 12948, pp. 102–116, 2021.
https://doi.org/10.1007/978-3-030-86855-0_8

condition development. The exact degree of narrowing is specified during and invasive diagnostic procedure – coronary angiography (ICA). The latter is the gold standard of coronary blood flow functional anatomical status diagnostics and surgical treatment indications identification. Recently there are more and more studies indicating an increase number of persons with non-obstructive (less than 50% of the lumen) lesions of coronary artery (NOCAD) among patients with suspected CAD [2, 3]. Thus, hemodynamically significant CA stenoses in patients with clinical signs of CAD according to the results of ICA were detected only in 40% of cases [2]. According to the US national registry data, among of patients with suspected CAD NOCAD occurred in 58%. Registry data from Brazil, Finland and Switzerland describes NOCAD in 76%, 57% and 32% of patients, respectively [4].

Despite ICA's high diagnostic value, usage is associated with a certain risk of surgical complications. So, ICA is described as cause of death in 0.1–0.14% of patients. ICA-associated myocardial infarction is diagnosed in 0.06–0.07% cases. Allergic reactions to the contrast introduction and local post-puncture vascular complications were recorded in 0.23% and 2%, respectively, cerebrovascular complications - in 0.07–0.14% of patients.

Methods for assessing the pretest probability (PTP) of obstructive coronary arteries damage (OCAD) (before ICA) for patients with suspected CAD were firstly introduced in routine clinical practice around 40 years ago by American cardiologists George Diamond and James Forrester. Their article "Analysis of Probability as an Aid in the Clinical Diagnosis of Coronary Artery Disease", published in The New England Journal of Medicine in 1979 were presenting the Bayesian classifier model allowing to calculate OCAD probability for patients with suspected CAD before functional and laboratory tests [5]. Gender, age (from 30 up to 69 years) and clinical symptoms of CAD (typical and atypical angina pectoris, cardialgia) were described as predictors in this model based on ICA results of 4952 patients. For several decades, the Diamond-Forrester (DF) scale has been one of the most popular PTP OCAD methods [6]. Years after its usage showed a significant overestimation of CAD likelihood among surveyed, especially in the female population. In 2011 Genders TS, et al. modified the DF scale, adapting it for modern cohort of patients with age limit extension up to 80 years [7]. For a new CAD Consortium scale development, EuroAIM registry data of 2,260 patients from 14 Europe and United States medical centers were used. All included subjects were complaining chest pain, had no CAD history and were underwent ICA for its verification. Update and expansion of PTP models showed a significant increase of predictive power. In 2012, same authors improved calculator and proposed the CAD Consortium clinical model (base model + risk factors for cardiovascular diseases (CVD), including diabetes mellitus (DM), hypertension (HTN), smoking, hyperlipidemia, and body mass index (BMI)) and an extended model (clinical model + coronary calcium index according to multislice computed tomography). The latest model showed accuracy increase based on C-statistics indicators from 0.77 to 0.79, and the reclassification - by 35%. Advantages of this method was proven by results of Bittencourt MS, et al. (2016) study, where straight comparison of DF scale with two CAD Consortium models were made based on 2,274 patients clinical data [8]. Also, this study reaffirms the overestimation of CAD prevalence among the surveyed by DF scale. Withal, both clinical and extended CAD Consortium models provided higher prediction accuracy for OCAD detection: area under the ROC

- curve (AUC) for DF was 0.713, and for CAD Consortium 1 and 2 - 0.752 and 0.791, respectively. Besides, with these models, significantly more patients were attributed to the low OCAD probability group (24.6% and 30.0% vs 8.3% - by DF), and the persons proportion with a high OCAD risk was only 1.1% vs 18% by DF. Authors suggested that widespread of these methods in routine clinical decisions can tremendously reduce the need for invasive CAD diagnosis [9]. Juarez-Orozco LE, et al. (2019), developed new method for PTP OCAD determination based on the Bayesian classifier and data analysis of three large-scale studies results, describing patients with suspected coronary artery disease (n = 15815, mean age 59 ± 11 years) [10]. This method was included to the European Society of Cardiology recommendations for the diagnosis and treatment of chronic coronary syndrome [11, 12].

Recently, modern machine learning (ML) methods are more commonly used for predictive research in clinical cardiology, allowing to increase the forecast accuracy by identifying non-obvious patterns. At the same time, there is only a small number of articles where these methods were used for OCAD prediction.

The aim of this study was searching and validation of new OCAD predictors with determination of their threshold values and prognostic models development for its pre-test diagnostics in patients with CAD prior to ICA, based on ML methods.

2 Materials and Methods

2.1 Patient Characteristics

A prospective cohort study included 496 patients (314 men and 182 women) aged 30 to 80 years with a median of 62 years and a 95% confidence interval (CI) [60; 64], who were proceed to the emergency cardiology department of the Vladivostok Clinical Hospital No. 1 in 2017–2020. All patients underwent invasive ICA. Among the surveyed cohort, 2 groups were identified. The first included 345 (69.6%) patients with hemodynamically significant coronary artery narrowing (≥50%) according to ICA results, the second included 151 (30.4%) with NOCAD (<50%).

Before ICA patients clinical and functional status was evaluated by 29 indicators containing anamnestic, anthropometric, clinical and laboratory data associated with cardio-metabolic risk (CMR). Measurements of height (Ht), weight, waist circumference (W), hips (H), calculation of body mass index (BMI), WH ratios (WHR) (indexed to gender), WHt ratio (WHtR) were carried out. The levels of glucose, total cholesterol (TC), high density lipoprotein cholesterol (HDL cholesterol) and low (LDL cholesterol) density, triglycerides (TG), creatinine, uric acid (UA) were determined.

The indices of visceral adiposity (VAI), lipid accumulation product (LAP), atherogenicity (AIP) were calculated using the well-known formulas [13]. The insulin resistance index (IRI) was determined by the ratio of TG/HDL cholesterol [14], and the glomerular filtration rate (GFR) was determined using the CKD EPI formula.

2.2 Data Processing

The end point of the study was presented by the OCAD in the binary form feature ("absence" or "presence"). Input signs - a subgroup of potential predictors was expressed in the form of continuous and categorical variables. Filtration and wrapping methods were used for data processing and analysis [15]. Filtration was performed by mathematical statistics, and ML methods were used as a "wrapper". The first were represented by the Fisher, Mann-Whitney, Chi-square tests and one-way logistic regression (LR) with the calculation of weights for a normalized sample. The second - by ML methods: multifactorial LR (MLR), random forest (RF) and support vector machine (SVM).

Significance of features and testing of hypotheses was confirmed by a p-value <0.05. The quality of the models developed on training samples was assessed using a cross-validation test procedure, by averaging 4 metrics: area under the ROC curve (AUC), accuracy (ACC), sensitivity (Sen), and specificity (Spec). Cross-validation was performed using a k-fold approach on 10 stratified samples.

2.3 Study Design

The study design included 5 stages.

1. On the first, the probability of the presence of OCAD was calculated using the CAD Consortium method [7] and its predictive value was assessed.
2. On the second stage, in order to identify potential predictors linearly related to OCAD, 29 CMR factors were analyzed in the comparison groups. We did not use the most significant predictor of the CAD Consortium scale (pain syndrome), which is the most significant for diagnostics, in order to identify other, previously unused predictors. For continuous variables, the Mann-Whitney test was used, and for categorical variables - the chi-square test. The odds ratio (OR) and their 95% CI were assessed by the Fisher test.
3. At the third stage, using one-factor LR-models, the weighting coefficients of individual indicators were determined.
4. At the fourth stage, based on LR results, threshold values of factors with the highest predictive potential were identified.
5. At the fifth stage, the predictive models of OCAD were developed using the MLR, RF and SVM. Data analysis and model development were performed in R-studio and Python by R languages.

3 Results

During the first stage of the study, the probability of OCAD was assessed in accordance with the CAD Consortium scale recommended by the European and American Society of Cardiology. The quality metrics of the obtained assessment were: ACC - 0.7, AUC - 0.75, Sen - 0.68, Spec - 0.71, which confirmed the need of more advanced models development based on new predictors.

At the second stage of the study, an intergroup analysis of the factors characterizing the clinical and functional status of patients was carried out, which showed the presence of statistically significant differences in 15 parameters (Table 1). At the same time, the maximum level of reliability was recorded for indicators of gender (male sex), HDLC, AIP, and Creatinine (p-value <0.0001). The highest OR values were associated with males (OR = 2.5) and active smoking (OR = 2.3). A less noticeable, but statically significant likelihood of OCAD was associated with a family history of CVD (OR = 1.6). It should be noted that DM and hypertension (HTN) were recorded with the same frequency in patients with OCAD and NOCAD. According to the preliminary analysis, age, height, WHtR, weight and BMI of the surveyed, the concentration of glucose and CRP, systolic (SBP), diastolic (DBP) and pulse (PAP) blood pressure also did not affect the likelihood of OCAD.

Table 1. Patients clinical and functional characteristics (ME, 95% CI).

Parameter	1 group (OCAD), n = 345	2 group (NOCAD), n = 150	OR, 95% CI	p-value
Age, years	62 [61;64]	62 [59;64]		0,57
Male, (%)	241 (69,9%)	72 (48,3%)	2,5 [1,6; 3,7]	<0,0001
Smokers, (%)	135 (40%)	34 (23%)	2,3 [1,5; 3,7]	0,0001
Family history of CVD, (%)	102 (30%)	32 (21%)	1,6 [1,0; 2,6]	0,048
WHR, c.u	1,08 [1,05; 1,1]	1,05 [1,0; 1,1]		0,005
TC, mmol/l	5,6 [5,5; 5,9]	5,3 [5,1; 5,55]		0,012
TG, mmol/l	1,4 [1,35; 1,6]	1,3 [1,15; 1,4]		0,005
HDLC, mmol/l	1,2 [1,2; 1,25]	1,35 [1,3; 1,4]		<0,0001
LDLC, mmol/l	3,6 [3,4; 3,8]	3,3 [3,0; 3,4]		0,0003
IRI, c.u	1,2 [1,1; 1,35]	0,9 [0,8; 1,1]		0,0005
VAI, c.u	1,7 [1,4; 2,1]	1,2 [0,9; 1,6]		0,011
LAP, cm × μmol/l	49,6 [42,0; 60,3]	36,3 [30,7; 48,5]		0,04
AIP, c.u	3,55 [3,4; 3,9]	2,8 [2,4; 3,2]		<0,0001
Creatinine, μmol/ml	90 [88; 93]	79 [76; 83]		<0,0001
GFR, ml/min/1,73 m^2	73,2 [71,35; 74,8]	76.9 [73,2; 82,5]		0,012
UAA, μmol/l	379 [366; 393]	338 [320; 361]		0,007

At the third stage of the study, using standardized data, univariate LR models were constructed with the calculation of weight coefficients. This approach expands the possibilities for data processing and analysis due to a more detailed assessment of the degree and vector influence of potential predictors on the resulting variable.

Table 2. Patients Weights for univariate LR models for OCAD probability estimation (ME, 95% CI).

Parameter	Weights	P-value
Age	0,4 [−0,7; 1,5]	0,5
Male gender	0,9 [0,5; 1,3]	<0,0001
Smokers	0,8 [0,4; 1,3]	0,0002
Family history of CVD	0,5 [0,03; 0,9]	0,04
W	2,5 [0,3; 4,9]	0,03
WHR	3,4 [1,3; 5,8]	0,0029
TC	1,9 [0,4; 3,4]	0,013
TG	3,8 [0,1; 7,8]	0,05
HDLC	−3,9 [−6,3; −1,7]	0,0007
LDLC	2,1 [1,0; 3,3]	0,0003
IRI	1,6 [0,4; 2,9]	0,01
AIP	3,5 [1,9; 5,2]	<0,0001
Creatinine	4,7 [2,8; 6,8]	<0,0001
GFR	−3,35 [-5,7; −1,1]	0,004
CRP	6,1 [1,1; 13,8]	0,06
UA	1,7 [0,3; 3,1]	0,016

According to the results of the analysis statistically significant level of weighting coefficients took place in 13 variables (Table 2). The highest values of the weighting factors were associated with the Creatinine level (4.7; $p < 0.0001$), HDLC (−3.9; $p = 0.0007$) and AIP (3.5; $p < 0.0001$). The less valued indicators were WHR (3.4), GFR (−3.35), LDLC (2.1), TC (1.9), IRI (1.6), male sex (0.9), smoking status (0.8) and family history of CVD (0.5). At the same time, the weight coefficients of factors such as age, height, WHtR, weight, SBP, DBP, PAP, the presence of hypertension, diabetes, CRP and glucose levels, VAI and LAP were statistically insignificant. In the developed univariate models, most of the weighting coefficients had a positive value, which indicated an increase in the likelihood of OCAD in the presence of these signs or their levels increasing. On the contrary, negative values of the weights of HDLC and GFR indicate an increase in the risk of OCAD with a decrease in the level of these indicators.

At the fourth stage of the study, among the indicators selected at the previous stages, using one-factor LR, their threshold values with the highest predictive potential were identified (Table 3). To accomplish this task, indicators in a continuous form were transformed into categorical ones. It is known that categorization in continuous space leads to the loss of some information and the appearance of "quantization noise". However, in medical research, it is customary to operate with the concepts of norms and thresholds that are associated with risk factors that contribute to the development of diseases and their complications. Within a certain "normative" range, the values of the indicator are not interrelated with the development of the disease, but, starting from a certain threshold, this indicator can act as a risk factor for an adverse event. To confirm this hypothesis, the threshold values of the indicators were verified, which were used for further analysis.

Table 3. The range of threshold values for potential OCAD predictors based on univariate LR-models.

Thresholds	1 group (OCAD), n = 345	2 group (NOCAD), n = 150	OR, 95% CI	p-value
Age, years male ≥55 female ≥65	235 (68%)	84 (56%)	1,7 [1,1; 2,5]	0,01
W, см male ≥105 female ≥115	76 (22%)	13 (9%)	3,05 [1,15; 8,1]	0,025
WHR, c.u Female and male ≥0,9	255 (74%)	75 (50%)	2,9 [1,5; 5,7]	0,0017
WHtR, c.u. ≥ 0,69	48 (14%)	4 (3%)	5,7 [1,25; 26,35]	0,025
TC ≥ 5,9 mmol/l	148 (43%)	43 (29%)	2,0 [1,3; 3,0]	0,001
TG ≥ 1,6 mmol/l	157 (45,5%)	48 (32%)	1,75 [1,2; 2,6]	0,006
HDLC ≤ 1,1 mmol/l	129 (37,5%)	30 (20%)	2,4 [1,5; 3,9]	0,0002
LDLC > 3,5 mmol/l	181 (52,5%)	52 (35%)	2,1 [1,4; 3,1]	0,0004
IRI ≥ 1,5 c.u	134 (39%)	40 (27%)	1,75 [1,15; 2,7]	0,009
LAP ≥ 38,5 см*mmol/l	238 (69%)	67 (45%)	2,7 [1,3; 5,45]	0,003
AIP ≥ 3,4 c.u	190 (55%)	56 (38%)	2,0 [1,3; 3,1]	0,0006
Creatinine, µmol/ml female ≥94 male ≥87	190 (55%)	47 (31,5%)	2,6 [1,7; 4,05]	<0,0001
GFR < 75 ml/min/1,73 m^2	193 (56%)	69 (46%)	1,5 [0,1; 2,2]	0,049
UA ≥ 356 µmol/l	210 (61%)	61 (41%)	2,2 [1,35; 3,6]	0,0008

The analysis results allowed us to identify age ranges for male (≥55 years old) and female (≥65 years old), which increased the likelihood of OCAD (OR = 1.7, p = 0.01). In men with WC ≥ 105 cm and women with WC ≥ 115 cm, the probability of detecting hemodynamically significant CA lesions increased 3 times (p = 0.025). Increase in

WHtR ≥ 0.69 c.u. (OR = 5.7, p = 0.025) and WHR ≥ 0.9 c.u. (OR = 2.9, p = 0.0017) also increased the likelihood of OCAD regardless subjects gender. Comparable chances of having OCAD were associated with lipid metabolism disorders, manifested by an increase in TC concentration ≥5.9 mmol/l (OR = 2.0, p = 0.001), LDLC > 3.5 mmol/l (OR = 2.1, p = 0.0004) and TG ≥ 1.6 mmol/l (OR = 1.75, p = 0.006), as well as a decrease in HDLC level ≤1.1 mmol/l (OR = 2.4, p = 0.0002). Similar values of OR were correlated with indicators IRI ≥ 1.5 c.u. (OR = 1.75, p = 0.009), LAP ≥ 38.5 cm * mmol/l (OR = 2.7, p = 0.003) and AIP ≥ 3.4 c.u. (OR = 2.0, p = 0.0006). The risk of OCAD increased with a serum concentration of UA ≥ 356 μmol/L (OR = 2.2, p = 0.0008) and Creatinine ≥ 87 μmol/mL in men and ≥94 μmol/L in women (OR = 2, 6, p < 0.0001). At the same time, the GFR index <75 ml/min/1.73 m^2 increased the probability of OCAD by 1.5 times (p = 0.049). It should be noted that testing the predictive potential of individual factors in different numerical ranges allowed us to identify predictively significant threshold values even among indicators (WHtR and LAP), the intergroup differences in median values of which at the previous stages of the study were insignificant.

At the fifth stage of the study, based on the methods of MLR, RF and SVM, prognostic models were developed to assess the likelihood of OCAD prior to performing invasive ICA (Table 4). Developing the models, we tested both continuous and categorical forms of predictors. Those shapes that provided the best accuracy were included in the final version of the models.

Table 4. Evaluation of the predictive models accuracy for pretest OCAD verification.

№		AUC	ACC	Sen	Spec
MLR					
1	TC* + WHR*	0,65	0,56	0,60	0,57
	TC + WHR + HDLC	0,72	0,63	0,64	0,62
2	TC* + WHR* + HDLC*	0,75	0,67	0,54	0,82
3	TC* + WHR + HDLC*	0,75	0,66	0,56	0,68
4	TC* + WHR* + HDLC	0,75	0,7	0,67	0,68
5	TC* + WHR* + HDLC + TG*	0,75	0,7	0,7	0,69
6	**TC* + WHR* + HDLC + IRI**	0,8	0,73	0,74	0,71
7	**Ensemble of models (TC* + LDLC* + WHR* + WHtR* + AIP* + LAP* + UA* + HDLC + IRI)**	0,85	0,80	0,82	0,77
SVM					
8	TC* + WHR*	0,64	0,63	0,82	0,41
	TC + WHR + HDLC	0,68			
9	TC* + WHR* + HDLC*	0,73	0,65	0,65	0,65
10	TC* + WHR + HDLC*	0,75	0,71	0,7	0,72
11	TC* + WHR* + HDLC	0,7	0,65	0,65	0,64

(continued)

Table 4. (*continued*)

№		AUC	ACC	Sen	Spec
12	TC* + WHR* + HDLC + TG*	0,69	0,63	0,64	0,62
13	**TC* + WHR* + HDLC + IRI**	0,73	0,67	0,67	0,67
14	**Ensemble of models (TC* + LDLC* + WHR* + WHtR* + AIP* + LAP* + UA* + HDLC + IRI)**	0,74	0,65	0,64	0,68
RF					
15	TC* + WHR*	0,67	0,6	0,62	0,57
	TC + WHR + HDLC	0,69			
16	TC* + WHR* + HDLC*	0,71	0,63	0,53	0,77
17	TC* + WHR + HDLC*	0,7	0,66	0,66	0,65
18	TC* + WHR* + HDLC	0,72	0,67	0,65	0,69
19	TC* + WHR* + HDLC + TG*	0,64	0,56	0,56	0,56
20	**TC* + WHR* + HDLC + IRI**	0,69	0,65	0,67	0,61
21	**Ensemble of models (TC* + LDLC* + WHR* + WHtR* + AIP* + LAP* + UA* + HDLC + IRI)**	0,77	0,7	0,7	0,69

During models construction TC $\geq$ 5.9 mmol/l was determined as the basic predictor by the direct selection method (Forward Selection procedure). The step-by-step inclusion of other factors in their structure led to an increase in only certain quality metrics. Their noticeable rise was recorded in the MLR model (6) with a combination of 4 factors: TC $\geq$ 5.9 mmol/l, WHR $\geq$ 0.9 c.u., as well as HDLC and IRI in continuous form. At the same time, the predictive algorithm based on the ensemble of MLR models (7), developed and trained by the Bagging - Bootstrap aggregating method, had the optimal ratio of Sen (0.82) and Spec (0.77) indicators, as well as the maximum AUC value (0,85), corresponding to a high forecast accuracy. This model included a combination of 6 predictive algorithms selected from the list of logistic regressions ranked by the Akaike criterion. The coefficients of the aggregated model were calculated by the weighted averaging method using the formula:

$$\hat{\beta}_{ig} = \frac{\sum_{k=1}^{r} \hat{\beta}_{ik} s_k \Gamma_{ik}}{\sum_{k=1}^{r} s_k \Gamma_{ik}} \tag{1}$$

Where $\hat{\beta}_{ik}$ - coefficient of *i*-th variable in *k*-th model; s_k - weight of the *k*-th model accounting strength of its validity based on the Kullback-Leibler information loss ratio; Γ_{ik} - binary indicator values characterizing the presence of *i* -th predictor in *k*-th model.

The number of ensemble model components was selected according to predictive ability calculations depending on regression models number of included inside ensemble (Fig. 1).

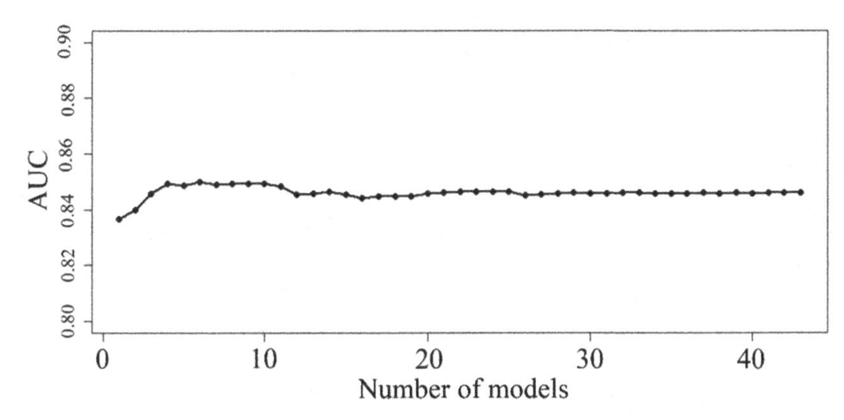

Fig. 1. Accuracy (AUC) dependence by the number of ensemble models

In this ensemble, a combination of 7 factors in categorical form was used as predictors (TC ≥5.9 mmol/l, LDLC > 3.5 mmol/l, WHR ≥0.9 c.u., WHtR ≥ 0.69 c.u., AIP ≥ 3.4 c.u., LAP ≥ 38.5 cm * mmol/l, UA ≥ 356 μmol/l) and 2 - in continuous (HDLC and IRI). Various ensemble model predictors on resulting variable influence degree are shown in the graph (Fig. 2).

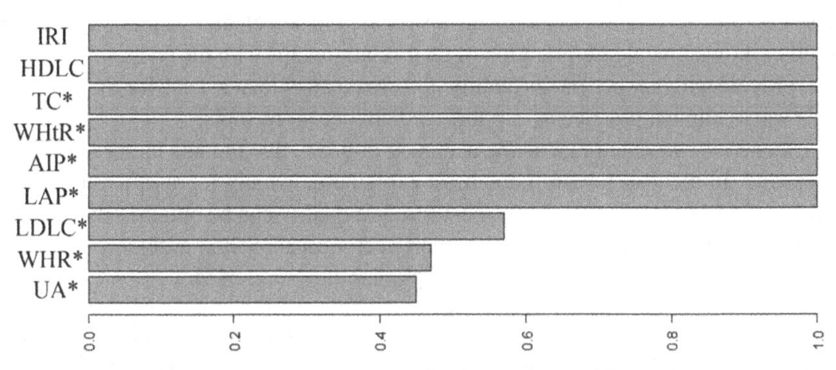

Fig. 2. Relative predictors contribution to the resulting variable

Greatest and equivalent impact on resulting variable (OCAD) were showed by 6 predictors: IRI, HDLC, TC, WHtR, AIP, LAP. Less visible contributions were shown by LDC, WHR и UA. It should be noted that the predictive accuracy of models based on SVM and RF methods was insufficient for any combination of potential predictors.

4 Discussion

Recently, ML methods have been used increasingly as clinical research predictive tools. Their application allows output variables modeling based on input factors, which are characterizing patient clinical and functional status with various diseases, therapy and surgical treatment options. Modern technologies of collection, storage and processing info allowed to create big volumes repositories of biomedical data, including through the use of electronic medical history and patient records including anamnesis of diseases and their outcomes. This data contains certain knowledge about the causal relationships between patient current state, its dynamic changes during disease process - on the one hand, and the likelihood of developing different outcomes - on the other. The indicators for which such relationships were identified are classified as predictors of the corresponding events. If there are indicators threshold values, which are enchanting the predictive potential, they can be attributed to risk factors for predicted events. In contrast to some other areas of knowledge, where the main forecasting goal is the high developed models accuracy, in clinical medicine, in addition to this criterion, evidence of the predictors validity is being used and required along with predictors threshold values specification, degree of influence on the resulting variable assessment and analyzed factors relationships formalization. The presence of such knowledge increases the "explainability" of the ML models and, therefore, increases the confidence in the developed predictive models.

Accuracy is an objective function that determines the models application effectiveness in various fields of knowledge. At the same time, for medical practice not only the accuracy of predicting events is important, but also the ability to explain the causes, conditions and mechanisms of their development. This, in turn, is an important condition for personalizing prevention and therapy programs. Such approach implementation should be based on the algorithms development for predictors search and validation which are allowed to show clinical interpretation of their relationships with the endpoints of observation, provide a higher prognosis quality and create an evidence base for the predictive models use in clinical practice as support medical decisions tools.

It is generally accepted that as the accuracy of predictive models increases, so does their opacity. In medical research, the most explainable widely represented models are logistic models. At the same time, the best forecast quality can be obtained by other ML methods, for example, random forest, support vector machine and ensemble of models, which are the most problematic from the explainability point of view.

In recent years, definitions of ML methods explainability, causality, interpretability, and "confidence" have been given, and several approaches have been proposed to "whiten" the black box of ML models and develop "responsible" artificial intelligence [16]. One of the important explainable artificial intelligence parts is ensuring that in the developed model only predictors with proven effect on the final variable are being used. This task is most easily solved by linear or logistic regression models. In these cases, several approaches are proposed to improve explainability: hypothesis testing for individual predictors, overall assessment of model quality and forecast accuracy [17, 18]. These approaches can be used for models developed using other ML methods: rule-based learning, decision trees, Bayesian classifiers. Despite the fact that these models have the properties of transparency in construction, decomposition and algorithmization, in most cases, it is difficult for clinicians to interpret the relationship between the input data and the endpoint. For example, if continuous predictors in such models directly or inversely affect the resulting variable, then for physician, in addition to this fact, it is necessary to set a threshold, above (or below) which the variable would be describing as the risk factor of a particular event. The absence of such threshold reduces explainability level of even simple models. According to other authors, the complexity of models interpretation is also associated with the consideration lack of the predictors mutual influence on the resulting variable [19, 20].

The high prevalence of NOCAD among persons with suspected CAD intensifies the development of prognostic models, which allows to assess the coronary arteries anatomical status before ICA [3]. It is assumed that these technologies usage would reducing the unnecessary risks of ICA and lowering irrational health care costs. In our study, no hemodynamically significant CA lesions were found in 30.4% of patients during ICA, which prompted the authors to assess the CMR factors predictive potential for OCAD at the stage of pretest diagnosis. The reason for this analysis was the well-known key role concept of these factors in pathogenesis [21]. It was previously shown that combined indices (VAI, LAP), including lipid varieties, differ from isolated indicators of lipid metabolism in a more reliable relationship with CA damage [22]. The data from other paper showed that CAD has a closer association with WHtR and VAI indicators than with LAP [13].

In our work, during a multistage selection procedure, we identified potential predictors of OCAD, including anthropometric and metabolic indices which characterizing patients metabolic status.

Obtained results showed that the predictive value of WHR, WHtR and LAP was higher than VAI, which made it possible to use them in predictive models. Insulin resistance is one of the leading pathogenetic factors of the arterial pool atherosclerotic remodeling. The surrogate markers of this syndrome include IRI [3], which demonstrated significant predictive potential in our study (models 6 and 7). A lot of papers indicate the relationship between CAD and hyperuricemia, which is also one of the informative indicators of CMR [23]. In our study, the serum UA level was linearly and nonlinearly related to OCAD, and its concentration $\geq$356 μmol/L increased the probability of verifying hemodynamically significant CA lesions by 2.2 times (Table 3). Which made it possible to use this indicator as a predictor in the ensemble of MLR models (Table 4). A lipid spectrum imbalance with an increased concentration of LDL cholesterol and a decrease in the level of HDL cholesterol has a proven causal relationship with atherosclerotic CA remodeling [24]. In our research the indicators of atherogenic dyslipidemia at the selection stage demonstrated a high predictive potential and were subsequently used to construct predictive algorithms (Tables 1, 2 and 3). Wherein, the predictive properties of HDL cholesterol were manifested in all developed models, while and LDL cholesterol and AIP - only in the model (7).

A comparative analysis of the algorithms predictive accuracy based on modern ML methods demonstrated the advantages of a 6 models ensemble developed by MLR. The quality metrics of this model had maximum values (AUC – 0,85, ACC – 0,80, Sen – 0,82, Spec – 0,77), which corresponded with high forecast accuracy. In our study, it was shown that the CAD Consortium model provided a forecast accuracy by AUC 0.75. In the DISCHARGE 2020 pilot study, the predictive accuracy of the CAD Consortium scale was AUC 0.73 [25]. The elevation of AUC up to 0.85 was achieved by categorizing individual indicators, new predictors usage and models ensemble application. The results obtained in our study are competitive and comparable to the best predictive indicators in this area.

5 Conclusion

Based on a comprehensive analysis of data characterizing the functional and metabolic patients' status with acute coronary syndrome, the CMR factors were identified and verified as predictors of OCAD and their threshold values were evaluated (TC $\geq$ 5.9 mmol/l, LDLC > 3.5 mmol/l, WHR $\geq$ 0.9 c.u., WHtR $\geq$ 0.69 c.u., AIP $\geq$ 3.4 c.u., LAP $\geq$ 38.5 cm * mmol/l, UA $\geq$ 356 μmol/l).

- The MLR model's ensemble demonstrated the highest prediction accuracy (AUC – 0,85, ACC – 0,80, Sen – 0,82, Spec – 0,77) based on 6 MLR predictive algorithms combination.
- In this study, the models based on SVM and RF had significantly lower predictive accuracy (AUC – 0,74, Acc 0,65, Spec – 0,68, Sen – 0,45 и AUC – 0,77, Acc и Sen – 0,7, Spec – 0,69, respectively).

Prospects for further research in this area are associated with the improvement of predictive models based on expanding the range of predictors and methods of ML, including multilayer artificial neural networks. The limitations of the study associated with an insufficient sample size, limited range of analyzed factors and methods of ML. Conflict of Interest: All authors declare no potential conflict of interest.

References

1. The World Health Organization. The top 10 causes of death (2020). https://www.who.int/ru/news-room/fact-sheets/detail/the-top-10-causes-of-death
2. Sumin, A.N.: The assessment of pretest probability in obstructive coronary lesion diagnostics: unresolved issues. Russ. J. Cardiol. **11**(151), 68–76 (2017). https://doi.org/10.15829/1560-4071-2017-11-68-76
3. Geltser, B.I., Tsivanyuk, M.M., Shakhgeldyan, K.I., et al.: Machine learning for assessing the pretest probability of obstructive and non-obstructive coronary artery disease. Russ. J. Cardiol. **25**(5), 3802 (2020). https://doi.org/10.15829/1560-4071-2020-3802
4. Wang, Z.J., Zhang, L.L., Elmariah, S., et al.: Prevalence and Prognosis of nonobstructive coronary artery disease in patients undergoing coronary angiography or coronary computed tomography angiography: a meta-analysis. Mayo Clin Proc. **92**(3), 329–346 (2017). https://doi.org/10.1016/j.mayocp.2016.11.016
5. Diamond, G.A., Forrester, J.S.: Analysis of probability as an aid in the clinical diagnosis of coronary-artery disease. N. Engl. J. Med. **300**, 1350–1358 (1979). https://doi.org/10.1056/NEJM197906143002402
6. Fihn, S.D., Blankenship, J.C., Alexander, K.P., et al.: 2014 ACC/AHA/AATS/PCNA/SCAI/STS focused update of the guideline for the diagnosis and management of patients with stable ischemic heart disease. J. Am. Coll. Cardiol. **64**(18), 1929–1949 (2014). https://doi.org/10.1016/j.jacc.2014.07.017

7. Genders, T.S., Steyerberg, E.W., Alkadhi, H., et al.: A clinical prediction rule for the diagnosis of coronary artery disease: validation, updating, and extension. Eur. Heart J. **32**, 1316–1330 (2011). https://doi.org/10.1093/eurheartj/ehr014
8. Bittencourt, M.S., Hulten, E., Polonsky, T.S., et al.: European Society of Cardiology-recommended coronary artery disease consortium pretest probability scores more accurately predict obstructive coronary disease and cardiovascular events than the Diamond and Forrester Score: The Partners Registry. Circulation **134**, 201–211 (2016). https://doi.org/10.1161/circulationaha.116.023396
9. Baskaran, L, Danad, I., Gransar, H., et al.: A comparison of the updated Diamond-Forrester, CAD Consortium, and CONFIRM history-based risk scores for predicting obstructive coronary artery disease in patients with stable chest pain. JACC: Cardiovasc. Imaging 12(7 Pt 2), 1392–400 (2019).https://doi.org/10.1016/j.jcmg.2018.02.020
10. Juarez-Orozco, L.E., Saraste, A., Capodanno, D., et al.: Impact of a decreasing pre-test probability on the performance of diagnostic tests for coronary artery disease. Eur. Heart J. Cardiovasc. Imaging **20**, 1198–1207 (2019). https://doi.org/10.1093/ehjci/jez054
11. Knuuti, J., Wijns, W., Saraste, A., et al.: 2019 ESC Guidelines on the diagnosis and management of chronic coronary syndromes: the task force for diagnosis and management of chronic coronary syndromes of the European Society of Cardiology (ESC). Eur. Heart J. **41**, 407–477 (2020). https://doi.org/10.1093/eurheartj/ehz425
12. Montalescot, G., Sechtem, U., Achenbach, S., Members, T.F., et al.: ESC guidelines on the management of stable coronary artery disease: the task force on the management of stable coronary artery disease of the European Society of Cardiology. Eur. Heart J. **34**(38), 2949–3003 (2013). https://doi.org/10.1093/eurheartj/eht296
13. Shalnova, S.A., Deev, A.D., Muromtseva, G.A., et al.: Relation of anthropometric indexes and coronary heart disease. Cardiovasc. Ther. Prevent. **17**(3), 11–16 (2018). https://doi.org/10.15829/1728-8800-2018-3-11-16
14. Geltser, B.I., Orlova-Ilyinskaya, V.V., Vetrova, O.O., et al.: Assessment of cardiometabolic risk factors in various phenotypes of masked hypertension. Cardiovasc. Ther. Prevent. **19**(4), 2422 (2020). https://doi.org/10.15829/1728-8800-2020-2422
15. Chandrashekar, G., Sahin, F.: A survey on feature selection methods. Comput. Electr. Eng. **40**, 16–28 (2014). https://doi.org/10.1016/j.compeleceng.2013.11.024
16. Arrieta, A.B., Díaz-Rodríguez, N., Del Ser, J., Bennetot, A., Tabik, S., Barbado, A., et al.: Explainable Artificial Intelligence (XAI): concepts, taxonomies, opportunities and challenges toward responsible AI. Inf. Fusion **58**, 82–115 (2020). https://doi.org/10.1016/j.inffus.2019.12.012
17. Bursac, Z., Gauss, C.H., Williams, D.K., et al.: Purposeful selection of variables in logistic regression. Source Code Biol. Med. **3**, 17 (2008). https://doi.org/10.1186/1751-0473-3-17
18. Hosmer, D.W., Lemeshow, S., Sturdivant, R.X.: Applied Logistic Regression, p. 398. Wiley, Hoboken (2013)
19. Mood, C.: Logistic regression: why we cannot do what we think we can do, and what we can do about it. Eur. Sociol. Rev. 26(1), 67–82 (2010). www.jstor.org/stable/4060247
20. Lundberg, S.M., Erion, G., Chen, H., et al.: From local explanations to global understanding with explainable AI for trees. Nat. Mach. Intell. **2**, 56–67 (2020). https://doi.org/10.1038/s42256-019-0138-9
21. Guo, F., Moellering, D.R., Garvey, W.T.: The progression of cardiometabolic disease: validation of a new cardiometabolic disease staging system applicable to obesity. Obesity **22**(1), 110–118 (2014)
22. Amato, M.C., Giordano, C., Galia, M., et al.: AlkaMeSy Study Group: Visceral Adiposity Index: a reliable indicator of visceral fat function associated with cardiometabolic risk. Diab. Care **33**, 920–922 (2010). https://doi.org/10.2337/dc09-1825

23. Biscaglia, S., Ceconi, C., Malagu, M., et al.: Uric acid and coronary artery disease: an elusive link deserving further attention. Int. J. Cardiol. **213**, 28–32 (2016). https://doi.org/10.1016/j.ijcard.2015.08.086
24. Mach, F., Baigent, C., Catapano, A.L., et al.: ESC/EAS Guidelines for the management of dyslipidaemias: lipid modification to reduce cardiovascular risk. Eur. Heart J. **41**, 111–188 (2019). https://doi.org/10.1093/eurheartj/ehz455
25. Feger, S., et al.: Clinical pre-test probability for obstructive coronary artery disease: insights from the European DISCHARGE pilot study. Eur. Radiol. **31**, 1–11 (2020). https://doi.org/10.1007/s00330-020-07175-z

Knowledge Engineering

Application of FCA for Domain Model Theory Investigation

Dmitry Palchunov(✉)

Sobolev Institute of Mathematics, Novosibirsk, Russian Federation
palch@math.nsc.ru

Abstract. The article explores the construction of semantic models of subject domains to formalize the existing knowledge about the subject domain and generate new knowledge. Methods of representation and processing of partial knowledge about cases of a given domain are investigated. Formal Concept Analysis has been applied to axiomatize classes of partial models that formally represent knowledge about the domain cases. To solve this problem, the theory of classes of fragments of atomic diagrams of algebraic systems and axiomatizable classes of fragments of atomic diagrams are studied. The apparatus of Boolean-valued and fuzzy models is used to obtain new knowledge about the domain cases.

Keywords: Formal Concept Analysis · Subject domain · Domain theory · Domain case · Fragment of atomic diagram · Axiomatizable class · Theory of a class of models

1 Introduction

The paper explores the application of the Formal Concept Analysis (FCA) to semantic modeling of subject domains. The goal is to develop model-theoretical methods for formalizing the knowledge about the cases of subject domains to further generate new knowledge.

Formal Concept Analysis [1–3] is used to solve problems of axiomatization of classes of partial models. To solve these problems, we pass from partial models to their atomic diagrams, which are fragments of atomic diagrams of algebraic systems.

To generate new knowledge about the subject domain, based on the analysis of the existing knowledge about the cases of this subject domain (domain cases), including fuzzy knowledge and hypotheses, we use the theory of Boolean-valued models and fuzzy models [4–6].

The definitions and information on the Formal Concept Analysis can be found in [7, 8]; the definitions and information on the model theory can be found in [9, 10].

The research was funded by RFBR and Novosibirsk Region, project number 20-47-540005. The study was carried out under the state contract of the Sobolev Institute of Mathematics (project No. 0314-2019-0002).

S. M. Kovalev et al. (Eds.): RCAI 2021, LNAI 12948, pp. 119–134, 2021.
https://doi.org/10.1007/978-3-030-86855-0_9

2 Methods of Formalization of Subject Domains

To develop formal models of subject domains, tools are needed to formalize the knowledge about these subject domains [11–13]. The most general, universal mathematical representation of a domain model is an ***algebraic system***: a basic set and predicates (relations), functions (operations), and constants (distinguished elements that have special names) defined on this set.

Note also that any (n)-ary function (operation) on a set A can be represented by its graph, an $(n + 1)$-ary relation on this set A. Therefore, in this paper, we will use algebraic systems whose signature contains only predicate and constant symbols.

2.1 Problems of Domain Modeling and Related Works

In the early 21st century, the logical technologies of the Semantic Web received a powerful development [14]: Description Logics, the family of knowledge representation languages for authoring ontologies OWL based on them (OWL DL [15]), SWRL (Semantic Web Rule Language) [16] and SQWRL (a query language for OWL), as well as automatic inference systems (logic reasoners) [17, 18], which help search for inconsistencies in descriptions and derive new knowledge from existing ones [19, 20].

However, currently, the use of model theory for the formal description of subject domains has several disadvantages. Here are some of the most significant problems to consider.

The first problem is related to the fact that in model theory, the definition of a predicate is given in terms of its extent. However, in many cases, this approach to defining relationships does not match the tasks being solved. For example, everyone knows what a dog is, anyone can tell a dog from a cat or a squirrel, but few people have an idea about the extent of this predicate: for example, how many dogs live on Earth now. A fairly successful approach to solving this problem is presented by Formal Concept Analysis [21–23], which is used in this paper to solve problems of modeling subject domains.

The second problem stems from the fact that only classes of algebraic systems with the same signature are considered in model theory. In particular, this refers to the concept of an axiomatizable class of algebraic systems: all systems included in an axiomatizable class must have the same signature. The same is true for the classes of algebraic systems axiomatized by sentences of a special form: varieties, quasivarieties, $\forall$- and $\exists$-axiomatizable classes.

However, if we consider formal models of the domain cases, we often deal with a situation where different cases of the same subject domain are described by different sets of concepts. For example, if the domain cases are patient medical records [24, 25, 40, 41], we can see that different patients have data on different sets of tests, they were prescribed different medications, and so on. In this situation, the formal models of these cases should have different signatures. At the same time, in all domain cases, the theory of this subject domain should be true: that is, on algebraic systems, there should be a true set of sentences, the signature of which may not be contained in the signature of these algebraic systems.

The same situation applies to the ontologies: the ontology of the subject domain is correct for all domain cases, while the description of the case normally does not include all the concepts of the ontology of the given subject domain [26, 27, 42].

Another aspect of this problem is that model theory considers homomorphisms, isomorphisms, and elementary equivalence only of algebraic systems with the same signature.

The third significant problem is that an algebraic system represents a static, not a dynamic description of the situation.

To solve these problems, as well as other problems that have not been discussed here, we develop a special field of model theory, the model theory of subject domains, aimed at solving problems of the formal representation of knowledge about subject domains, including ontological knowledge, processing and generation of new knowledge, construction of formal mathematical models of subject domains, classes of domain cases, theories, and ontologies of subject domains (Fig. 1).

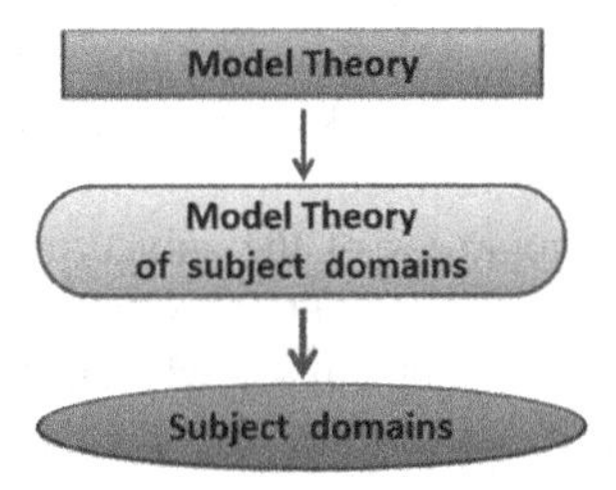

Fig. 1. Model theory of subject domains

2.2 Our Approach to Formalizing Subject Domains

To formalize subject domains, we use our four-level ontological model of knowledge representation [32]. The first level is an ontology, which includes the specification of the meaning of key concepts in the domain. In particular, an ontology can contain a medical nomenclature such as SNOMED CT.

The second level of knowledge representation is general knowledge about a given subject domain. This knowledge is true for all domain cases. For example, this can be knowledge contained in medical articles and monographs, in the regulations of a national healthcare agency, etc.

The third level is the collection of all known domain cases. For example, it could be a set of medical records. The knowledge contained in medical records is fundamentally incomplete. For example, a medical record does not contain the results of all possible tests for a given patient. We formally represent knowledge about the domain cases in the form of finite fragments of atomic diagrams or finite partial models.

Finally, the fourth level of knowledge representation is estimated and probabilistic knowledge, as well as hypotheses. The hypotheses are assumed to be true, but they need further verification. We obtain hypotheses and estimated knowledge based on the analysis of the domain cases using the ontology and general knowledge.

This article focuses on the development of methods for solving the second problem mentioned above: only classes of algebraic systems with the same signature are considered in model theory. Our goal is to define the theory of a class of fragments of atomic diagrams having different signatures, and also to formulate a criterion for such class of fragments of atomic diagrams to be axiomatizable.

3 Axiomatization of Domain Cases

The purpose of this article is to solve the problem of axiomatization of classes of domain cases. At the same time, we consider a situation where knowledge about each case is partial, incomplete. In addition, descriptions of different cases of the same subject domain may contain different sets of key concepts. Examples of such cases are patient medical records [25, 28], precedents of computer attacks [29, 30], and precedents of triggering risks in the risk management. In all of these examples, case descriptions are deliberately incomplete, and each description contains its own set of entities and relationships. If we consider patient histories, these are various patient tests, symptoms, and prescribed medications. In the case of computer attacks, these are various vulnerabilities, types of attacks, consequences, and damage caused.

General knowledge and regularities of the subject domain, including ontological knowledge, are described by sentences containing quantifiers. Within the framework of our consideration, in contrast to general knowledge, knowledge about the domain cases is described by quantifier-free formulas [31]. For example, a patient has given test results; a computer attack has caused given damage.

In real practice, only partial knowledge about domain cases is available to us. This partial knowledge of domain cases can be formally represented using partial models. The definition of a partial model will be provided below. First, let us give the necessary definitions.

We call an algebraic system the tuple

$$\mathfrak{A} = \langle A; P_1, \ldots, P_m, f_1, \ldots, f_k, c_1, \ldots, c_l \rangle,$$

where A is the carrier (or the basic set) of the algebraic system, $P_1, \ldots, P_m$ are predicates, $f_1, \ldots, f_k$ are functions and $c_1, \ldots, c_l$ are constants (distinguished elements) defined on the set A.

The tuple $\sigma = \langle P_1, \ldots, P_m, f_1, \ldots, f_k, c_1, \ldots, c_l \rangle$ is called the signature of the algebraic system $\mathfrak{A}$}. The set of formulas of the signature σ is denoted by $F(\sigma)$, the set of sentences (formulas without free variables) of the signature σ is denoted by $S(\sigma)$.

Each (n)-ary function defined on the system $\mathfrak{A}$ can be represented by its graph, an $(n+1)$-ary predicate; therefore, without loss of generality, we can consider algebraic systems

$$\mathfrak{A} = \langle A; P_1, \ldots, P_m, c_1, \ldots, c_l \rangle$$

of the signature $\sigma = \langle P_1, \ldots, P_m, c_1, \ldots, c_l \rangle$; such algebraic systems are called ***models***.

Definition 1. *The tuple* $\mathfrak{A}^p = \langle A; P_1, \ldots, P_m, c_1, \ldots, c_l \rangle$ *is called a partial model of the signature* $\sigma = \langle P_1, \ldots, P_m, c_1, \ldots, c_l \rangle$ *if the value of any (n)-ary predicate* P_i *on this partial model* $\mathfrak{A}^p$ *is defined as the pair* $P_i^{\mathfrak{A}^p} = \left(P_i^+, P_i^-\right)$, *where* $P_i^+, P_i^- \subseteq |\mathfrak{A}|^n$ *and* $P_i^+ \cap P_i^- = \emptyset$. *Then for the elements* $a_1, \ldots, a_n \in |\mathfrak{A}|$, *if* $(a_1, \ldots, a_n) \in P_i^+$ *then* $\mathfrak{A}^p \models P_i(a_i, \ldots, a_n)$, *if* $(a_1, \ldots, a_n) \in P_i^-$ *then* $\mathfrak{A}^p \models \neg P_i(a_1, \ldots, a_n)$, *and if* $(a_1, \ldots, a_n) \notin \left(P_i^+ \cup P_i^-\right)$ *then the value of the predicate* $P_i(a_1, \ldots, a_n)$ *on the model* $\mathfrak{A}^p$ *is not known (is undefined).*

We use fragments of atomic diagrams of algebraic systems as a tool for formalizing knowledge about the domain cases.

To define an atomic diagram of an algebraic system, it is necessary to enrich the signature σ with new constants, the names of all elements of the system $\mathfrak{A}$. We enrich the signature σ to the signature.

$$\sigma_A = \sigma \cup \{c_a \mid a \in A\},$$

and instead of the system $\mathfrak{A} = \langle A, \sigma \rangle$, we will consider the algebraic system $\mathfrak{A}_A = \langle A, \sigma_A \rangle$, in which $c_a^{\mathfrak{A}_A} = a$.

Let us give the definition of an atomic diagram for algebraic systems of this kind.

Sentence φ is called atomic ($\varphi \in AS(\sigma_A)$) if $\varphi = (c_1 = c_2)$ or $\varphi = P(c_1, \ldots, c_n)$, where $P, c_1, \ldots, c_n \in \sigma_A$. Consider the set

$$\begin{aligned} AD(\mathfrak{A}) = \{\varphi \in S(\sigma_A) \mid \mathfrak{A}_A \models \varphi \text{ and } \varphi \text{ is atomic}, \\ \text{or } \varphi = \neg\psi \textit{ and } \psi \textit{ is atomic}\}. \end{aligned}$$

We call the set of sentences $AD(\mathfrak{A})$ an atomic diagram of the model $\mathfrak{A}$.

Note that here, included in the atomic diagram of the model is not only atomic sentences, but also their negations, precisely because further we will consider not the atomic diagrams themselves, but their subsets, fragments of atomic diagrams. Indeed, if we know the set of all atomic sentences that are true on the model $\mathfrak{A}$, then the fact that the given atomic sentence φ does not belong to this set implies that φ is not true on a model $\mathfrak{A}_A$, and hence $\mathfrak{A}_A \models \neg\varphi$. If we have only partial knowledge about the domain case, represented by a fragment of the atomic diagram Δ, then the fact that $\varphi \notin \Delta$ does not imply that φ is not true on $\mathfrak{A}_A$ and, respectively, that $\mathfrak{A}_A \models \neg\varphi$. Therefore, we include in the atomic diagram and in fragments of atomic diagrams both atomic sentences, which are known to be true in a given case, and negations of atomic sentences, if known to be false.

The definition of the atomic diagram of the partial model $\mathfrak{A}^p$ is similar to the definition of the atomic diagram of the ordinary model:

$$\begin{aligned} AD\left(\mathfrak{A}^p\right) = \{\ \varphi \in S(\sigma_A) \mid \mathfrak{A}_A^p \models \varphi \text{ and } \varphi \text{ is atomic}, \\ \text{or } \varphi = \neg\psi \textit{ and } \psi \text{ is atomic}\}. \end{aligned}$$

Moreover, if neither $P(a_1, \ldots, a_n)$ nor $\neg P(a_1, \ldots, a_n)$ is true on $\mathfrak{A}^p$, then

$$P(a_1, \ldots, a_n), \neg P(a_1, \ldots, a_n) \notin AD\left(\mathfrak{A}^p\right).$$

It is easy to see that the atomic diagram of a partial model is a fragment of the atomic diagram of an algebraic system of the given signature.

Note that the atomic diagram $AD(\mathfrak{A}^p)$ of a partial model $\mathfrak{A}^p$ defines the model $\mathfrak{A}^p$ up to isomorphism. Therefore, the problem of axiomatization of classes of partial models that formalize sets of domain cases is equivalent to the problem of axiomatization of classes of fragments of atomic diagrams of algebraic systems (models).

Therefore, further in the article, to formalize knowledge about the domain cases, we will consider not partial models, but fragments of atomic diagrams of models.

The use of fragments of atomic diagrams to formalize knowledge about the cases of subject domains is quite convenient. First, we can work not with infinite algebraic systems or theories, but with finite sets of sentences (finite fragments of atomic diagrams).

Second, and most importantly, we can seamlessly integrate domain case knowledge from different sources. We can consider combining various fragments, even those with different signatures, and, as a result, get a new fragment of an atomic diagram. This will be done on condition that the fragments being merged not contain conflicting information, which is checked quite simply: fragments of atomic diagrams Δ_1 and Δ_2 contradict each other if and only if there is a sentence φ such that $\varphi \in \Delta_1$ and $\neg\varphi \in \Delta_2$.

There is another important advantage of using fragments of atomic diagrams to describe the knowledge about domain cases. A set of fragments of atomic diagrams represents the knowledge about a set of situations. It is clear that only one of the described situations occurs each time. Therefore, a finite set of fragments of atomic diagrams $\{\Delta_i | i \in I\}$ can be regarded as a disjunction of fragments of Δ_i and each fragment of Δ_i can be considered as a conjunction of atomic sentences and their negations included in it. With this consideration, the following rather useful statement holds:

Remark 1. *For any quantifier-free sentence φ of signature σ_A, there is a finite set of fragments of atomic diagrams $\{\Delta_i | i \in I\}$, which is logically equivalent to the sentence φ.*

Note that the domain cases must satisfy the ontology of this subject domain and the domain theory. On the other hand, by analyzing many known cases, we can generate new knowledge about the subject domain based on those statements that are true for all known cases, thus enriching the part of the theory of this domain known to us. We can formulate such statements as hypotheses and then test them on new cases.

In order to formalize such a process of obtaining new knowledge about the subject domain, it is necessary to give an accurate and sound definition of the truth of the set of sentences (in the general case, containing quantifiers) on a set of fragments of atomic diagrams that represent the known set of domain cases.

4 Axiomatizable Classes of Fragments of Atomic Diagrams

Further, for convenience of presentation, we will identify domain cases with fragments of atomic diagrams describing the knowledge we know about these cases. Consider the signature σ, which contains symbols of all the necessary concepts and some "enclosing" set A (possibly infinite) containing a sufficient number of elements.

For a fragment of atomic diagram Δ and a sentence φ, we define a ***compatibility relation*** between a fragment Δ and a sentence φ and denote it by $\Delta \parallel \varphi$. This relation is an incidence relation in the formal context $(\{\Delta_i | i \in I\}, S(\sigma), \parallel)$ (Fig. 2). If $\Delta \parallel \varphi$ holds, then we say that the sentence φ is compatible with a fragment of the atomic diagram Δ.

Definition 2. *Let $\Delta \subseteq AS(\sigma_A)$ and $\varphi \in S(\sigma)$. Denote*

$$\mathbf{\Delta} \parallel \boldsymbol{\varphi} \text{ if } \Delta \cup \{\varphi\} \nvdash .$$

This definition formally describes the following property: φ is compatible with Δ when we can imagine a situation, partially described by the fragment Δ, for which the statement φ is true. However, φ and Δ can have completely different signatures. This is shown by the following statement.

F	$S(\sigma)$							
	φ_1	φ_2	φ_3	...	φ_k	φ_{k+1}	φ_{k+2}	...
Δ_1	+		+				+	
Δ_2		+		+		+		
...			+					+
Δ_k		+		+			+	
...			+		+			+
Δ_n	+						+	

Fig. 2. Formal context $((\{\Delta_i | i \in I\}, S(\sigma), \parallel), S(\sigma), \parallel)$

Proposition 1. *Let $\Delta \subseteq AS(\sigma_A)$ and $\varphi \in S(\sigma)$. $\Delta \parallel \varphi$ holds if and only if there is a model $\mathfrak{A}$ such that $\mathfrak{A} \models \Delta$ and $\mathfrak{A} \models \varphi$.*

This statement means that the sentence φ is compatible with the fragment of atomic diagram Δ ($\Delta \parallel \varphi$) if and only if there is a completion $\mathfrak{A}$ of the fragment Δ (i.e., $\mathfrak{A} \models \Delta$ and $\mathfrak{A}$ is the complete description of the given situation partially described by the fragment Δ), for which the sentence φ is true: $\mathfrak{A} \models \varphi$. The presence of such a completion $\mathfrak{A}$ indicates that a situation (domain case) is possible where the partial information Δ is true and where the statement φ is true. At the same time, model $\mathfrak{A}$ provides complete information about a possible domain case, about which we know only partial information Δ.

Let $\{\Delta_i | i \in I\}$ be a set of cases of a certain domain (in principle, one can consider an infinite set of indices I). For a fragment of atomic diagram Δ and a set of sentences Γ, we define a ***compatibility relation*** $\Delta \parallel \Gamma$, this relation is an incidence relation in the formal context $(\{\Delta_i | i \in I\}, \wp(S(\sigma))$ (Fig. 3).

Definition 3. *Let $\Delta \subseteq AS(\sigma_A)$ and $\Gamma \subseteq S(\sigma)$. Denote*

$$\mathbf{\Delta} \parallel \mathbf{\Gamma} \text{ if } \Delta \cup \Gamma \nvdash .$$

F	$\wp(S(\sigma))$							
	Γ_1	Γ_2	Γ_3	...	Γ_k	Γ_{k+1}	Γ_{k+2}	...
Δ_1	+		+				+	
Δ_2		+		+		+		
...			+					+
Δ_k		+		+			+	
...			+		+			+
Δ_n	+						+	

Fig. 3. Formal context $(\{\Delta_i | i \in I\}, \wp(S(\sigma)), \|)$

The compatibility of a fragment of the atomic diagram Δ with a set of sentences Γ means that a domain case is possible on which, on the one hand, partial information Δ is true, and on the other hand, all statements from the set of sentences Γ are true.

This definition can be generalized to a compatibility relation between a class (a set) of fragments of atomic diagrams K and a set of sentences Γ. Let us introduce a relation $K \| \Gamma$.

Definition 4. *Let* $K \subseteq \wp(AS(\sigma_A))$ *and* $\Gamma \subseteq S(\sigma)$. *Denote* $\boldsymbol{K \| \Gamma}$ *if for any* $\Delta \in K$ *holds* $\Delta \cup \Gamma \nvdash$.

The compatibility $K \| \Gamma$ means that a set of domain cases is possible, on each of which some known partial information Δ from the set K ($\Delta \in K$) is true, and at the same time all statements from Γ are true on all these possible domain cases.

It is important to note the following point. Consider a class of fragments of atomic diagrams $K \subseteq \wp(AS(\sigma_A))$ and a set of sentences Γ, let a class K be compatible with the set of sentences Γ, that is, $K \| \Gamma$. The fact that a set of domain cases is possible, on each of which some known partial information $\Delta \in K$ is true, and on this set of possible domain cases K, the set of sentences Γ is true, can be interpreted so that the statements from Γ are hypotheses about this domain. Indeed, based on the partial knowledge we have about the domain cases, we can assume the truth of all statements from Γ. These hypotheses should be further tested.

We also note that a situation is quite possible when there are two hypotheses, two statements φ and ψ, compatible with K, i.e., $K \| \varphi$ and $K \| \psi$, and at the same time, statements φ and ψ contradict each other, i.e., $\varphi, \psi, \vDash$; then we cannot accept them at the same time. However, if the class K is compatible with the set of sentences Γ, then all statements from Γ do not contradict each other and, therefore, can all be taken together as hypothetically true statements.

Recall that for the formal context (G, M, I), the operation $()'$ is defined as follows: for $A \subseteq$ G and $B \subseteq$ M we have $(A)' = \{ m \in M \mid g\text{Im} \ \forall g \in G\}$ and $(B)' = \{ g \in G \mid g\text{Im} \ \forall m \in M\}$.

Remark 2. *Let* $K \subseteq \{\Delta_i | i \in I\}$. $K \| \Gamma$ *holds if and only if* $K \subseteq (\Gamma)'$ *holds in the formal context* $(\{\Delta_i | i \in I\}, \wp(S(\sigma)), \|)$.

Our task is to define the concepts of the theory of a class of partial models and an axiomatizable class of partial models. Since, as shown above, the partial model is completely specified by the corresponding fragment of atomic diagram, these tasks are equivalent to the following tasks: to define the concept of the theory of a class of fragments of atomic diagrams and an axiomatizable class of fragments of atomic diagrams.

As shown in [33], axiomatizable classes and theories (of a signature σ) are exactly, respectively, the extents and intents of formal concepts of the formal context $(K(\sigma), S(\sigma), \models)$.

Proposition 2 [33]. *Let $K \subseteq K(\sigma)$ and $T \subseteq S(\sigma)$. The pair (K, T) is a formal concept of the formal context $(K(\sigma), S(\sigma), \models)$ if and only if K is an axiomatizable class and T is the theory of K.*

However, we cannot transfer this property to the case of a formal context $(\{\Delta_i | i \in I\}, S(\sigma), \|)$, that is, we cannot define the theories of classes of fragments of atomic diagrams and axiomatizable classes of fragments of atomic diagrams as extents and intents of formal concepts of this formal context due to the following circumstances.

Remark 3. *a) There is a fragment $\Delta \subseteq AS(\sigma_A)$ and sentences $\varphi, \psi, \in S(\sigma)$ such that $\Delta \| \varphi$ and $\Delta \| \psi$ hold, but $\Delta \| \{\varphi, \psi\}$ does not hold.*

b) Moreover, there is a fragment $\Delta \subseteq AS(\sigma_A)$ and a sentence $\varphi \in S(\sigma) \backslash$ such that $\Delta \| \varphi$ and $\Delta \| \neg\varphi$ hold.

This remark shows that, in the general case, intents of formal concepts of the formal context $(\{\Delta_i | i \in I\}, S(\sigma), \|)$ may be contradictory, and, therefore, we cannot use them to define theories of classes of fragments of atomic diagrams.

Thus, we need to move from considering the relation $\Delta \| \varphi$ of compatibility of fragments of atomic diagrams Δ and sentences φ to considering the relation $\Delta \| \Gamma$ of compatibility of fragments of atomic diagrams Δ and sets of sentences Γ, that is, from the formal context $(\{\Delta_i | i \in I\}, S(\sigma), \|)$ to the formal context $(\{\Delta_i | i \in I\}, \wp(S(\sigma))$ (Fig. 3 and 4).

First, we introduce the concept of a quasi-theory of a fragment of an atomic diagram. Consider a set of fragments of atomic diagrams $F = \{\Delta_i | i \in I\}$, where $\Delta_i \subseteq AS(\sigma_A)$ for $i \in I$ describing domain cases. An arbitrary set of indices I can be considered, although for specific applications, it will be finite.

Definition 5. *Consider the formal context $(\{\Delta_i | i \in I\}, \wp(S(\sigma)), \|)$, let $\Delta \in F$. The set $\boldsymbol{QT(\Delta)} = (\{\Delta\})' = \{ \Gamma \subseteq S(\sigma) \mid \Delta \| \Gamma\}$ is called the* ***quasi-theory****of a fragment of the atomic diagram Δ.*

Obviously, if some set of sentences belongs to the quasi-theory of a fragment of the atomic diagram Δ, then all its subsets also belong to the quasi-theory of Δ. Therefore, it is reasonable to consider only the elements of the quasi-theory $QT(\Delta)$ that are maximal by inclusion.

Proposition 3. *Let $\Delta \subseteq AS(\sigma_A)$ and Γ be a maximal element of the partially ordered set $\langle QT(\Delta), \subseteq \rangle$. Then Γ is a theory.*

Proposition 4. *Let* $\Delta \subseteq AS(\sigma_A)$ *and* $\Gamma \in QT(\Delta)$. *Then there is a theory* $T \supseteq \Gamma$ *such that* T *is a maximal element of the partially ordered set* $\langle QT(\Delta), \subseteq \rangle$.

We denote $\mathbb{T} = \{ \mathrm{T} \subseteq \mathrm{S}(\sigma) \mid \mathrm{T} \text{ is a theory}\}$.

F	$T \subseteq \wp(S(\sigma))$							
	T_1	T_2	T_3	...	T_k	T_{k+1}	T_{k+2}	...
Δ_1	+		+				+	
Δ_2		+		+		+		
...			+					+
Δ_k		+		+			+	
...			⋮		⋮			⋮
Δ_n	+						+	

Fig. 4. Formal context $(\{\Delta_i | i \in I\}, \mathbb{T}, \|)$

Thus, when defining the theory of a fragment of an atomic diagram Δ, only theories of the signature σ compatible with the fragment Δ are of interest (Fig. 4).

Definition 6. *Let* $\Delta \subseteq AS(\sigma_A)$. *The set*

$\boldsymbol{ST}(\Delta) = \{\Gamma \subseteq S(\sigma) \mid \Gamma$ *is maximal with the property* $\Delta \cup \Gamma \nvdash$, *i.e.* $\Delta \| \Gamma\}$ *is called* ***super-theory*** *of a fragment of atomic diagram* Δ.

Corollary 1. *If* $T \in ST(\Delta)$, *then* T *is a theory, that is, a deductively closed set of sentences. Thus,* $(\Delta) \subseteq \mathbb{T}$.

Proposition 5. *Let* $\Delta \subseteq AS(\sigma_A)$ *and* $T \in ST(\Delta)$. *Then* T *is a complete consistent theory:* $T \nvdash$.

Corollary 2. *Let* $\Delta \subseteq AS(\sigma_A)$ *and* T *be a complete theory.* $T \in ST(\Delta)$ *holds if and only if* $\Delta \cup T \nvdash$.

We denote $\mathrm{C}\mathbb{T} = \{ T \subseteq S(\sigma) \mid T$ is a complete theory and $T \nvdash\}$.

Corollary 3. $\mathrm{ST}(\Delta) = (\{\Delta\})'$ *in the formal context* $(\{\Delta | \Delta \subseteq \mathrm{AS}(\sigma)\}, \mathrm{C}\mathbb{T}, \|)$ (Fig. 5).

Let us now consider theories of classes of fragments of atomic diagrams.

Definition 7. *Let* $K_0 = \{\Delta \subseteq AS(\sigma_A) \mid \Delta \nvdash\}$ *u* $K \subseteq K_0$. *The set*

$\boldsymbol{ST}(K) = \{ \Gamma \subseteq S(\sigma) \mid \Gamma$ *is maximal with the property* $K \| \Gamma\}$ *is called* ***super-theory*** *of the class of fragments of atomic diagrams* K.

Proposition 6. *If* $T \in ST(K)$ *then* T *is a theory. Therefore* $(K) \subseteq \mathbb{T}$.

Corollary 4. $ST(K) = (K)'$ *in the formal context* $(K_0, \mathbb{T}, \|)$.

Now we can define the concept of an axiomatizable class of fragments of atomic diagrams.

Definition 8. *Consider the class* $K_0 = \{\Delta \subseteq AS(\sigma_1) \mid \Delta \nvdash\}$. *The class* $K \subseteq K_0$ *is called* ***axiomatizable****if the pair* $(K, ST(K))$ *is a formal concept of the formal context* $(K_0, \mathbb{T}, \|)$(Fig. 6).

F	$CT \subseteq \wp(S(\sigma))$							
	T_1	T_2	T_3	…	T_k	T_{k+1}	T_{k+2}	…
Δ_1	+		+				+	
Δ_2		+		+		+		
…			+					+
Δ_k		+		+			+	
…			+		+			+
Δ_n								

Fig. 5. Formal context $(\{\Delta \mid \Delta \subseteq AS(\sigma)\}, C\mathbb{T}, \|)$

K_0	$\mathbb{T} \subseteq \wp(S(\sigma))$							
	T_1	T_2	T_3	…	T_k	T_{k+1}	T_{k+2}	…
Δ_1	+		+				+	
Δ_2		+		+		+		
…			+					+
Δ_k		+		+			+	
…			+		+			+
Δ_n	+						+	

Fig. 6. Formal context $(K_0,\ \mathbb{T},\ \|)$

5 Boolean-Valued Models Generated by Domain Case Classes

The last section of the article will consider the problem of generating new knowledge based on the analysis of the domain cases known to us. An example of such a task is the generation of new knowledge based on the analysis of patient medical records. The knowledge generated in the analysis of the domain cases are hypotheses that can be further confirmed or refuted (verified or falsified) [34–36]. We cannot obtain guaranteed accurate knowledge since we do not have complete knowledge about all possible cases of a given domain [37]

5.1 Weak Boolean-Valued Models

To generate knowledge based on the analysis of domain cases, we use Boolean-valued and fuzzy models [4, 5]; using such models, imprecise knowledge is formalized [38, 39]. We need to define Boolean-valued models of classes of fragments of atomic diagrams.

Definition 9 [5]. *Let $\mathbb{B}$ be a complete Boolean algebra and let the mapping $\tau : S(\sigma_A) \to \mathbb{B}$ be defined. A triple $\mathfrak{A}_{\mathbb{B}} = A, \sigma_A, \tau$ is called a* ***Boolean-valued model****if the following conditions hold:*

$$\tau(\varphi) = \overline{\tau(\varphi)};\ \ \tau(\varphi \vee \psi) = \tau(\varphi) \cup \tau(\psi);$$

$$\tau(\varphi \,\&\, \psi) = \tau(\varphi) \cap \tau(\psi); \;\; \tau(\varphi \to \psi) = \overline{\tau(\varphi)} \cup \tau(\psi);$$

$$\tau(\forall x \varphi(x)) = \bigcap_{a \in A} \tau(\varphi(c_a)); \;\; \tau(\exists x \varphi(x)) = \bigcup_{a \in A} \tau(\varphi(c_a)).$$

Since fragments of atomic diagrams represent only partial and not complete knowledge about the domain, we need to weaken the conditions of the definition of the Boolean-valued model. Fragments of atomic diagrams are sets of quantifier-free sentences. For this case, we can weaken the requirements for the Boolean-valued model by omitting the conditions necessary for specifying the quantifiers.

Definition 10. *Let* $\mathbb{B}$ *be a Boolean algebra and let the mapping* $\tau : S(\sigma) \to \mathbb{B}$ *be given. A pair* $\mathfrak{A}_\tau = \langle \sigma, \tau \rangle$ *is called a weak Boolean-valued model if the following conditions hold:*

$$\tau(\varphi) = \overline{\tau(\varphi)}; \quad \tau(\varphi \vee \psi) = \tau(\varphi) \cup \tau(\psi);$$

$$\tau(\varphi \,\&\, \psi) = \tau(\varphi) \cap \tau(\psi); \quad \tau(\varphi \to \psi) = \overline{\tau(\varphi)} \cup \tau(\psi);$$

if $\varphi \models \psi$ then $\tau(\varphi) \subseteq \tau(\psi)$.

Theorem 1. *Consider a class* $K \subseteq \{\Delta \subseteq AS(\sigma_A) \mid \Delta \nvdash\}$ *of consistent fragments of atomic diagrams. We define a mapping* $\tau : \mathrm{S}(\sigma) \to \mathbb{B}$ *as follows:*

$$\tau(\varphi) = \{T \mid \textit{there exists } \Delta \in K \textit{ such that } T \in ST(\Delta) \text{ and } \varphi \in T\}$$

for any sentence $\varphi \in \mathrm{S}(\sigma)$.
Then the pair $\mathfrak{A}_\tau = \langle \sigma, \tau \rangle$ *is a weak Boolean-valued model.*

Theorem 2. *Consider a class* $K \subseteq \{\Delta \subseteq AS(\sigma_A) | \Delta \nvdash\}$ *of consistent fragments of atomic diagrams. We define a mapping* $\eta : S(\sigma) \to \mathbb{B}$ *as follows:*

$$\eta(\varphi) = \{(\Delta, T) \mid \Delta \in K, \; T \in ST(\Delta) \; \textit{and} \; \varphi \in T\}$$

for any sentence $\varphi \in S(\sigma)$.
Then the pair $\mathfrak{A}_\eta = \langle \sigma, \eta \rangle$ *is a weak Boolean-valued model.*

5.2 Using the Proposed Model-Theoretical Methods for Generating Knowledge About Subject Domains

The model-theoretical methods developed in this article were implemented in software. A number of program systems have been registered. Some of these systems extract knowledge from natural language texts and represent them in the form of fragments of atomic diagrams, process precedents of computer attacks to solve information security risk management problems for an enterprise, extract knowledge about situations and temporal relationships between them from natural language texts, and extract knowledge from natural language texts for creating smart contracts [31].

Let us provide the examples of knowledge that we can generate by analyzing partial in-formation about domain cases, in particular, medical records.

For instance, consider the following post: "Scientists at Northwestern University in Illinois found that those who drink one or more cups of coffee a day have a 10% lower risk of contracting coronavirus compared to people who do not consume coffee." This statement can be obtained automatically from the Boolean-valued models described in Theorems 1 and 2 if we take the information contained in the medical records, in particular, of coronavirus patients, as the class K. To do this, additional information on patient nutrition must be added to the medical records.

Note that having these Boolean-valued models, it is also possible to automatically extract knowledge that has a more complex formulation. For example, at the age of 40–50 years and with a weight of 70–80 kg, or 100–110 kg in men, the risk of infection decreases by 15%. You can automatically generate much more complex statements, the receipt of which is almost impossible for humans. At the same time, the use of the compatibility relation introduced in the work (on which Theorems 1 and 2 are based) instead of the truth makes it possible to significantly expand the set of precedents (medical records) that we consider for generating and testing hypotheses.

Namely, we can consider medical records that do not include the concepts contained in the verified statement (for example, information about height or weight), but are compatible (or, conversely, incompatible) with this statement. This feature is very useful in many cases.

Currently, based on the use of the methods described in this article, a software system is being developed designed to extract arguments from natural language texts. The extracted knowledge is presented in the form of fragments of atomic diagrams, which allows for a subtle and detailed comparison of the situations on which the argumentation is based.

6 Conclusion

In the article, we have developed model-theoretical methods designed to solve the problems of semantic modeling of domain cases. For a formal representation of knowledge about the domain cases, we used partial models and corresponding fragments of atomic diagrams.

The problem of axiomatization of classes of fragments of atomic diagrams with different signatures is solved. We have examined theories of classes of fragments of atomic diagrams and axiomatizable classes of fragments of atomic diagrams.

To solve the problem of generating knowledge about the subject domain, we have investigated Boolean-valued models generated by classes of fragments of atomic diagrams.

References

1. Kuznetsov, S.O., Poelmans, J.: Knowledge representation and processing with formal concept analysis. Wiley Interdisc. Rev. Data Min. Knowl. Discovery **3**(3), 200–215 (2013)

2. Poelmans, J., Kuznetsov, S.O., Ignatov, D.I., Dedene, G.: Formal concept analysis in knowledge processing: a survey on models and techniques. Source Doc. Exp. Syst. Appl. **40**(16), 6601–6623 (2013)
3. Buzmakov, A., Kuznetsov, S.O., Napoli, A.: Fast generation of best interval patterns for nonmonotonic constraints. In: Appice, A., Rodrigues, P.P., Costa, V.S., Gama, J., Jorge, A., Soares, C. (eds.) ECML PKDD 2015. LNCS (LNAI), vol. 9285, pp. 157–172. Springer, Cham (2015).https://doi.org/10.1007/978-3-319-23525-7_10
4. Pal'chunov, D.E., Yakhyaeva, G.E.: Interval fuzzy algebraic systems. In: Proceedings of the 9th Asian Logic Conference 2005. Mathematical Logic in Asia. World Scientific Publishers, pp. 191–202 (2006)
5. Pal'chunov, D.E., Yakhyaeva, G.E.: Fuzzy logics and fuzzy model theory. Algebra Logic **54**(1), 74–80 (2015)
6. Palchunov, D., Yakhyaeva, G.: Application of Boolean-valued models and FCA for the development of ontological models. In: Proceedings of the 2nd International Workshop on Formal Concept Analysis for Knowledge Discovery (FCA4KD), vol. 1921, pp. 77–87. CEUR Workshop Proceedings (2017)
7. Ganter, B., Wille, R.: Formal Concept Analysis: Mathematical Foundations. Springer, Heidelberg (1999). https://doi.org/10.1007/978-3-642-59830-2
8. Ganter, B., Stumme, G., Wille, R. (eds.): Formal Concept Analysis. LNCS (LNAI), vol. 3626. Springer, Heidelberg (2005). https://doi.org/10.1007/978-3-540-31881-1
9. Chang, C.C., Keisler, H.J.: Model Theory, 3rd edn. North-Holland, Elsevier Science Pub. Co., Amsterdam, New York (1990)
10. Ershov, Y., Palyutin, E.A.: Mathematical Logic. Mir Publishers, Moscow (1986)
11. Gumirov, V.S., Matyukov, P.Y., Palchunov, D.E.: Semantic domain-specific languages. In: 2019 International Multi-conference on Engineering, Computer and Information Sciences (SIBIRCON), pp. 0955–0960. IEEE Press (2019)
12. Bolton, R., et al.: Customer experience challenges: bringing together digital, physical and social realms. J. Serv. Manag. **29**(5), 776–808 (2018)
13. Marmolejo-Saucedo, J.A., Hurtado-Hernandez, M., Suarez-Valdes, R.: Digital twins in supply chain management: a brief literature review. In: Vasant, P., Zelinka, I., Weber, G.-W. (eds.) Intelligent Computing and Optimization: Proceedings of the 2nd International Conference on Intelligent Computing and Optimization 2019 (ICO 2019), pp. 653–661. Springer, Cham (2020). https://doi.org/10.1007/978-3-030-33585-4_63
14. Tomaszuk, D., Wood, D.H.: RDF 1.1: knowledge representation and data integration language for the web. Symmetry **12**(1), 84–88 (2020)
15. Baset, S., Stoffel, K.: OntoJIT: Parsing Native OWL DL into Executable Ontologies in an Object-Oriented Paradigm. Information Management Institute University of Neuchatel, Neuchatel, Switzerland (2016)
16. De'Farias, T.M., Roxin, A., Nicolle, C.: SWRL rule-selection methodology for ontology interoperability. Data Knowl. Eng. **105**, 53–72 (2016)
17. Tsarkov, D., Horrocks, I.: FaCT++ description logic reasoner: system description. In: Furbach, U., Shankar, N. (eds.) Automated Reasoning: Third International Joint Conference, IJCAR 2006, Seattle, WA, USA, August 17-20, 2006. Proceedings, pp. 292–297. Springer, Heidelberg (2006). https://doi.org/10.1007/11814771_26
18. Steigmiller, A., Liebig, T., Glimm, B.: Konclude: system description. J. Web Semant. **27–28**, 78–85 (2014)
19. Palchunov, D.E., Tishkovsky, D.E., Tishkovskaya, S.V., Yakhyaeva, G.E.: Combining logical and statistical rule reasoning and verification for medical applications. In: Proceedings of the International Multi-conference on Engineering, Computer and Information Sciences, (SIBIRCON), pp. 309–313. IEEE Press (2017)

20. Khamparia, A., Pandey, B.: Comprehensive analysis of semantic web reasoners and tools: a survey. Educ. Inf. Technol. **22**(6), 3121–3145 (2017). https://doi.org/10.1007/s10639-017-9574-5
21. Kuznetsov, S.O., Makhalova, T.: On interestingness measures of formal concepts. Inf. Sci. **442**, 202–219 (2018)
22. Makhalova, T., Kuznetsov, S.O., Napoli, A.: MDL for FCA: is there a place for background knowledge? CEUR **2149**, 45–56 (2018)
23. Palchunov, D.E., Yakhyaeva, G.E.: Integration of fuzzy model theory and FCA for big data mining. In: 2019 International Multi-Conference on Engineering, Computer and Information Sciences (SIBIRCON), pp. 0961–0966. IEEE Press (2019)
24. Sharaf-El-Deen, D.A., Moawad, I.F., Khalifa, M.E.: A new hybrid case-based reasoning approach for medical diagnosis systems. J. Med. Syst. **2**(38), 1–11 (2014)
25. Naydanov, C., Palchunov, D.E., Sazonova, P.: Development of automated methods for the critical condition risk prevention, based on the analysis of the knowledge obtained from patient medical records. In: Proceedings of the International Conference on Biomedical Engineering and Computational Technologies (SIBIRCON. SibMedInfo—2015), pp. 33–38. IEEE Press (2015)
26. Staab, S., Studer, R. (eds.): Handbook on Ontologies, 2nd edn. Springer, Heidelberg (2009).https://doi.org/10.1007/978-3-540-92673-3
27. Palchunov, D.E.: Virtual catalog: the ontology-based technology for information retrieval. In: Wolff, K.E., Palchunov, D.E., Zagoruiko, N.G., Andelfinger, U. (eds.) Knowledge Processing and Data Analysis, LNAI 6581, pp. 164–183. Springer, Heidelberg (2011)
28. Palchunov, D.E., Yakhyaeva, G., Yasinskaya, O.: Software system for the diagnosis of the spine diseases using case-based reasoning. Siberian Sci. Med. J. **1**(36), 97–104 (2016)
29. Kim, H.K., Im, K.H., Park, S.C.: DSS for computer security incident response applying CBR and collaborative response. Exp. Syst. Appl. **37**(1), 852–870 (2010)
30. Yakhyaeva, G., Yasinskaya, O.: Application of case-based methodology for early diagnosis of computer attacks. J. Comput. Inf. Technol. **22**(3), 145–150 (2014)
31. Galieva A.G., Palchunov D.E.: Logical methods for smart contract development. In: 2019 International Multi-conference on Engineering, Computer and Information Sciences (SIBIRCON), pp. 0881–0885. IEEE Press (2019)
32. Palchunov, D.E.: Axiomatization of classes of domain cases based on FCA. In: Kuznetsov, S.O., Panov, A.I., Yakovlev, K.S. (eds.) RCAI 2020. LNCS (LNAI), vol. 12412, pp. 3–14. Springer, Cham (2020). https://doi.org/10.1007/978-3-030-59535-7_1
33. Pal'chunov, D.E.: Lattices of relatively axiomatizable classes. In: Kuznetsov, S.O., Schmidt, S. (eds.) ICFCA 2007. LNCS (LNAI), vol. 4390, pp. 221–239. Springer, Heidelberg (2007). https://doi.org/10.1007/978-3-540-70901-5_15
34. Baxter, D., Shepard, D., Siegel, N., Gottesman, B., Schneider, D.: Interactive natural language explanations of Cyc inferences. In: AAAI 2005 International Symposium on Explanation-aware Computing (2005)
35. Shi, W., Barnden, J.A.: Using inductive rules in medical case-based reasoning system. In: Gelbukh, A., de Albornoz, Á., Terashima-Marín, H. (eds.) MICAI 2005. LNCS (LNAI), vol. 3789, pp. 900–909. Springer, Heidelberg (2005). https://doi.org/10.1007/11579427_92
36. Lin, R.H., Chuang, C.L.: A hybrid diagnosis model for determining the types of the liver disease. Comput. Biol. Med. **7**(40), 665–670 (2010)
37. Palchunov, D., Yakhyaeva, G., Dolgusheva, E.: Conceptual methods for identifying needs of mobile network subscribers. In: Proceedings of the 13th International Conference on Concept Lattices and their Applications, vol. 1624, pp. 147–160. CEUR Workshop Proceedings (2016)
38. Yakhyaeva, G.: Logic of fuzzifications. In: Proceedings of the 4th Indian International Conference on Artificial Intelligence, IICAI 2009, pp. 222–239 (2009)

39. Yakhyaeva, G.E.: Application of Boolean valued and fuzzy model theory for knowledge base development. In: Proceedings of the International Multi-conference on Engineering, Computer and Information Sciences, SIBIRCON 2019, pp. 868–871 (2019)
40. Chelsom, J., Dogar, N.: Linking health records with knowledge sources using OWL and RDF. Stud. Health Technol. Inf. **257**, 53–58 (2019)
41. Pogodin, R., Palchunov, D.: The use of model-theoretical methods for automated knowledge extraction from medical texts. In: IEEE 22nd International Conference of Young Professionals in Electron Devices and Materials. IEEE Xplore (2021, to appear)
42. Gribova, V., Shalfeeva, E.: Ontology of anomalous processes diagnosis. Int. J. Intell. Syst. **36**(1), 291–312 (2021)

The Metagraph Model for Complex Networks: Definition, Calculus, and Granulation Issues

Valery Tarassov, Yuriy Kaganov, and Yuriy Gapanyuk(✉)

Bauman Moscow State Technical University, Moscow, Russia
gapyu@bmstu.ru

Abstract. This article attempts to look at complex graph models (specifically, the metagraph model) through the prism of information granulation. The basic provisions and definitions of information granulation are explored. The formal definitions of the metagraph data model and metagraph agent model are given. The examples of data metagraph and metagraph rule agents are discussed. The concept of an active metagraph, aimed for the data metagraph model and metagraph agent model combination, is proposed. It is shown that the metagraph vertex, the metagraph edge, attributes, the metagraph fragment, metagraph agents, and the active metagraph can be represented as a special kind of a metavertex. The metagraph calculus adopted for the information granulation is proposed. The metagraph calculus from the point of view of atomicity definition is described. The granularity of the metagraph model, including the atomicity property, the holonic organization, refinement and coarsening, partial ordering, similarity relationship, partitions and coverings, measures of granularity, the granularity of metagraph agents, are discussed.

Keywords: Information granulation · Granular Computing · Complex graph · Complex network · Metagraph · Metagraph agent · Metavertex

1 Introduction

Currently, the scientific direction of complex networks (complex graphs) is the subject of active research. According to [1], "a complex network is a graph (network) with non-trivial topological features—features that do not occur in simple networks such as lattices or random graphs but often occur in graphs modeling of real systems." The terms "complex network" and "complex graph" are often used synonymously. According to [2] "the term 'complex network,' or simply 'network,' usually refers to real systems while the term 'graph' is generally considered as the mathematical representation of a network." The most significant discrepancies are caused by the term "complex" in relation to graph models. Normally, there are two ways to interpret the term "complex":

We dedicate this article to the blessed memory of our teacher and colleague, Valery Tarassov.
The work is supported by Russian Foundation for Basic Research, project No. 20-07-00770.

S. M. Kovalev et al. (Eds.): RCAI 2021, LNAI 12948, pp. 135–151, 2021.
https://doi.org/10.1007/978-3-030-86855-0_10

1. Flat graphs (networks) of a huge dimension. Such networks may include millions or more vertices. The edges connecting the vertices can be non-directional or directional. Sometimes a multigraph model is used; in this case, two vertices can be connected not by one but by several edges.
2. Complex graphs that use a complex description of vertices, edges, and their location. Often in such models, they refuse the flat arrangement of vertices and edges. It is these models that can be most useful when describing complex data models. One of the most important types of such models is "complex networks (graphs) with emergence." The term "emergence" is used in general system theory. The emergent element means a whole that cannot be separated into its component parts. As far as the authors know, there are currently two "complex networks with emergence" models: hypernetworks and metagraphs. The hypernetwork model [3] is mature, and it helps to understand many aspects of complex networks with an emergence. But the metagraph model is more flexible and convenient than a hypernetwork model for use in artificial intelligence and software engineering [16].

Information granulation is also a significant area of modern research. According to [4], "Information granulation has emerged as one of the fundamental concepts of information processing giving rise to the discipline of Granular Computing. The concept itself permeates through a large variety of information systems. The underlying idea is intuitive and appeals to our commonsense reasoning. We perceive the world by structuring our knowledge, perceptions, and acquired evidence in terms of information granules-entities, which are abstractions of the complex word and phenomena."

The main idea of this article is to look at complex graph models (specifically, the metagraph model) through the prism of information granulation.

The article is organized as follows. Section Two discusses the basic definitions of information granulation. Sections Three and Four focus on the metagraph model and its transformation using metagraph agents. Section Five describes the metavertex as a basic structure of a metagraph model. Section Six proposes the metagraph calculus adopted for the information granulation. Section Seven discusses the granularity of the metagraph model.

2 The Basic Provisions and Definitions of Information Granulation

In this section, we rely heavily on the methodological apparatus given in the article [5]. From the approaches to information granulation presented by the authors of this article, we distinguish those that are suitable for information granulation based on complex graphs:

- According to Merriam–Webster's Dictionary [6], a granule may be defined as "a small particle, especially one of numerous particles forming a larger unit." Thus, the significant property of the granule is ***atomicity***. But the considered definition of atomicity is not specific enough. Let us provide the following definition:
  - **The atomicity definition.** The atomicity of an information element (granule) implies that a given element can be clearly distinguished from the surrounding

elements of the external system, added, removed, or moved to another place in the external system. If, as a result of operations of adding, deleting, or moving an element in the external system, structural violations occur, then the number of such violations must be finite, and the location in the external system for each such violation must be uniquely localized relative to other elements.

- According to [5], granules "could be further decomposed into smaller or finer granules called subgranules. Based on complexity, abstraction level, and size, granules can be measured at different levels. The problem domain, or the universe, exists at the highest and coarsest granule. Granules at the lowest level are composed of elements or basic particles of the particular model that is used." Thus, a significant property of granularity is the ***hierarchical organization*** of the granules.
- The authors of [5] rightly note that "granules are formed based on finer granules due to their distinguishability, similarity, and functionality. We may examine granules from different directions. A group of granules, words, for example, forms a sentence which is also a granule. Similarly, sentence granules can form a paragraph granule, paragraph granules form a section granule, and so on, until we have a book granule." Furthering this idea, we can note that one word can be part of several sentences, sentences can be repeated in different chapters, a chapter can be included in different book editions. Thus, the ***hierarchical organization*** of granules is actually a special case of ***holonic organization***. The holonic organization is often used in the multiagent approach. According to [7], a holon is "the whole, considered at the same time as part of the whole."
- An important consequence of a holonic organization is its ***multivariance***. Being in the middle of the holon hierarchy, one can simultaneously represent the current holon as various combinations of lower-level holons and include the current holon in various upper-level holons, affecting their organization.
- According to L. Zadeh [8], there are two operations to form and separate granules, "***granulation*** involves a decomposition of whole into parts. Conversely, ***organization*** involves an integration of parts into whole." Thus, a significant property of granulation is the ***construction and deconstruction (separation) operations*** for the granules. The authors of [5] also consider the concept of "***higher-order information granules,***" which they determined based on a fuzzy approach. At the same time, according to [9], "the term granulation can be viewed more broadly. Instead of introducing two concepts, i.e., granulation and organization, granulation could be defined as a process of two directions in problem solving: construction and decomposition."
- According to [9], "granular relationships may be classified into two groups: ***inter-relationship and intrarelationship***." Thus, it is essential to separate the internal links in the granules (intrarelationships) and the external links between the granules (interrelationships).

The authors of [5] also consider several operations and relationships between the granules (next, we use the original designations of the authors of the article [5]):

Refinement and Coarsening and Partial Ordering. According to [5], "a granule g_1 is a refinement of another granule g_2, or equivalently, g_2 is a coarsening of g_1, which is denoted by $g_1 \preceq g_2$, or $g_2 \succeq g_1$, if every subgranule or object of g_1 is contained in some subgranules of g_2. The $\preceq$ is a fine relationship and $\succeq$ is a coarse relationship. These relationships are also known as form and enclosure, i.e., g_1 forms g_2 and g_2 encloses g_1."

The authors of article [10] also rightly note that the refinement/coarsening relationships "may not be the case for all granules. Therefore, the fine and coarse relationships are not fully true but partially true. These relationships are called partial fine (p-fine) and partial coarse (p-coarse) relationships. A granule o_1 is p-refinement of another partition o_2, or equivalently, o_2 is a p-coarsening of o_1, which is denoted by $o_1 \sqsubseteq o_2$, or $o_2 \sqsupseteq o_1$, if some subgranules of o_1 are contained in some subgranules of o_2. The $\sqsubseteq$ is a p-fine relationship, and $\sqsupseteq$ is a p-coarse relationship."

Thus, the $\sqsupseteq$ and $\sqsubseteq$ relationships are implementing the holonic organization of granules.

Similarity Relationship. According to [5], "the similarity is a key to form an intrarelationship of a granule. It can also be used to measure closeness among granules. Various distance measures can be used to calculate how similar two granules are." To determine similarity, the authors of [5] propose using the approaches adopted in cluster analysis and distances in metric spaces, e.g., Euclidean or Manhattan distances.

Granulations as Partitions and Coverings. According to [10], "a partition consists of disjoint subsets of the universe, and a covering consists of possibly overlapping subsets. The relationships among these subsets are called partition relationship and covering relationship, respectively. Granular trees can be generated with a partition or covering operations." The formal definitions for partitions and coverings contain the following properties:

3. For all i, $X_i \neq \emptyset$, partitions and coverings are not empty;
4. For all $i \neq j$, $X_i \cap X_j = \emptyset$, partitions are not overlapping, this property holds only for partitions;
5. $\cup X_i = UN$, the union of all partitions or the union of all coverings forms the "universe";
   where X_i – partition or covering; UN – the "universe," a complete set of granules.

Measures of Granularity. The authors of [5] note that "the study of measures of granularity attracted researchers' attention to understand more about the relationship, fineness and coarseness of granules" and propose measures of granularity based on the fuzzy approach.

Based on this section's main provisions and definitions, in the following sections, we will consider the metagraph approach and its correspondence to the granulation approach.

3 The Metagraph Data Model

The metagraph model may be considered as a family of complex graph models. Initially proposed by A. Basu and R. Blanning in 2007 [11], the model later received a number of extensions independently offered by various groups of researchers [15]. For this article, we rely on the "annotated metagraph model." This is a variant of the metagraph model described in the article [12].

The ***metagraph*** model may be described as follows:

$$MG = \langle V, MV, E \rangle, \quad (1)$$

where MG – a metagraph; V – a set of metagraph vertices; MV – a set of metagraph metavertices; E – a set of metagraph edges.

Metagraph vertex is described by a set of attributes:

$$v_i = \{atr_k\}, v_i \in V, \quad (2)$$

where v_i – a metagraph vertex; atr_k – an attribute.

Metagraph edge is described by a set of attributes, the source and destination vertices, and the edge direction flag:

$$e_i = \langle v_S, v_E, eo, \{atr_k\} \rangle, e_i \in E, eo = true|false, \quad (3)$$

where e_i – a metagraph edge; v_S – a source vertex (metavertex) of the edge; v_E – a destination vertex (metavertex) of the edge; eo – an edge direction flag ($eo = true$ – directed edge, $eo = false$ – undirected edge); atr_k – an attribute.

The ***metagraph fragment:***

$$MG_i = \{ev_j\}, ev_j \in (V \cup E \cup MV), \quad (4)$$

where MG_i – a metagraph fragment; ev_j – an element that belongs to the union of vertices, edges, and metavertices.

The ***metagraph metavertex:***

$$mv_i = \langle \{atr_k\}, MG_j \rangle, mv_i \in MV, \quad (5)$$

where mv_i – metagraph metavertex belongs to the set of metagraph metavertices MV; atr_k – attribute, MG_j – metagraph fragment.

Thus, metavertex, in addition to the attributes, includes a fragment of the metagraph. The presence of private attributes and connections for metavertex is a distinguishing feature of the metagraph. It makes the definition of metagraph holonic: metavertex may include a number of lower-level elements and, in turn, may be included in a number of higher-level elements.

The example of the data metagraph (shown in Fig. 1) contains three metavertices: mv_1, mv_2, and mv_3. Metavertex mv_1 contains vertices v_1, v_2, v_3 and connecting them edges e_1, e_2, e_3. Metavertex mv_2 contains vertices v_4, v_5, and connecting them edge e_6. Edges e_4, e_5 are examples of edges connecting vertices v_2-v_4 and v_3-v_5 that are contained in different metavertices mv_1 and mv_2. Edge e_7 is an example of the edge connecting metavertices mv_1 and mv_2. Edge e_8 is an example of the edge connecting vertex v_2 and metavertex mv_2. Metavertex mv_3 contains metavertex mv_2, vertices v_2, v_3, and edge e_2 from metavertex mv_1 and also edges e_4, e_5, e_8, showing the holonic nature of the metagraph structure.

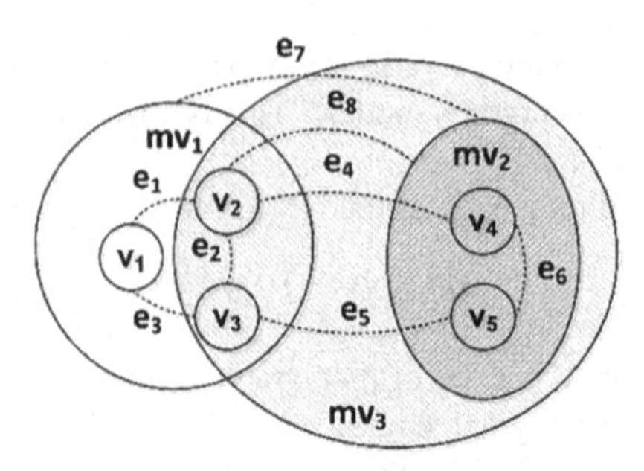

Fig. 1. The example of data metagraph

4 Using Metagraph Agents to Process Metagraph Model

The metagraph data model is intended for complex data descriptions. However, it is not intended for data transformation. The modern approach for data transformation is the multiagent approach [13]. According to [14], the metagraph agent (ag^{MG}) intended for data transformation is proposed. There are two kinds of metagraph agents: the metagraph function agent (ag^{F}) and the metagraph rule agent (ag^{R}). Thus $ag^{MG} = ag^{F} \mid ag^{R}$.

The ***metagraph function agent*** serves as a function with input and output parameters in the form of a metagraph:

$$ag^F = \langle MG_{IN}, MG_{OUT}, AST \rangle, \quad (6)$$

where ag^F – a metagraph function agent; MG_{IN} – an input parameter metagraph; MG_{OUT} – an output parameter metagraph; AST – an abstract syntax tree of a metagraph function agent in the form of a metagraph.

The ***metagraph rule agent*** is rule-based:

$$ag^R = \left\langle MG, R, AG^{ST} \right\rangle, R = \{r_i\}, r_i : MG_j \rightarrow OP^{MG}, \quad (7)$$

where ag^R – metagraph rule agent; MG – a working metagraph, a metagraph based on which the rules of the agent are performed; R – a set of rules r_i; AG^{ST} – a start condition (metagraph fragment for start rule check or start rule); MG_j – a metagraph fragment based on which the rule is performed; OP^{MG} – a set of actions performed on metagraph.

The antecedent of the rule is a condition over the metagraph fragment; the rule's consequent is a set of actions performed on the metagraph. Rules can be classified as open or closed.

The consequent of the open rule is not permitted to change the metagraph fragment occurring in the rule antecedent. In this case, the input and output metagraph fragments may be separated. The open rule is similar to the template that generates the output metagraph based on the input metagraph.

The consequent of the closed rule is permitted to change the metagraph fragment occurring in the rule antecedent. The metagraph fragment changing in rule consequent causes to trigger the antecedents of other rules bound to the same metagraph fragment. But incorrectly designed closed rules systems can cause an infinite loop of metagraph rule agent.

Thus, the metagraph rule agent can generate the output metagraph based on the input metagraph (using open rules) or can modify the single metagraph (using closed rules).

The example of a metagraph agent rule structure is shown in Fig. 2. The metagraph rule agent is represented as a metagraph metavertex. According to the definition, it is bound to the working metagraph MG_1 – a metagraph based on which the rules of the agent are performed. This binding is shown with edge e_4.

The metagraph rule agent description contains inner metavertices that correspond to agent rules (*rule 1 ... rule N*). Each rule metavertex contains antecedent and consequent inner vertices. In the given example, mv_2 is the metavertex bound with the antecedent, which is shown with edge e_2, and mv_3 is the metavertex bound with consequent, which is shown with edge e_3. Antecedent conditions and consequent actions are defined in the form of attributes bound to antecedent and consequent of corresponding vertices.

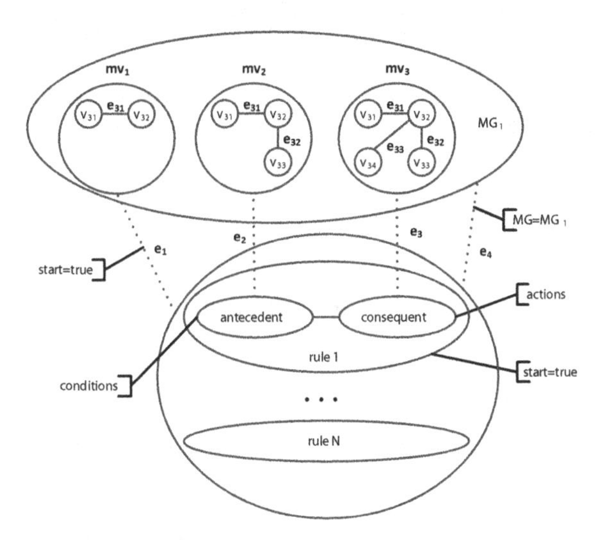

Fig. 2. The example of the metagraph agent rule structure

The start condition is given in the form of the attribute "start = true." If the start condition is defined as a start metagraph fragment, then the edge bound start metagraph fragment to agent metavertex (edge e_1 in the given an example) is annotated with the attribute "start = true." If the start condition is defined as a start rule, then the rule metavertex is annotated with the attribute "start = true" (rule 1 in the given example). Figure 2 shows both cases corresponding to the start metagraph fragment and the start rule.

The distinguishing feature of a metagraph agent is its homoiconicity, which means that it can be a data structure for itself. This is due to the fact that, according to the definition, a metagraph agent may be represented as a set of metagraph fragments, and this set can be combined in a single metagraph. Thus, a metagraph agent can change the structure of other metagraph agents.

In order to combine the data metagraph model and metagraph agent model, the concept of ***active metagraph*** is proposed:

$$MG^{ACTIVE} = \left\langle MG^{D}, AG^{MG} \right\rangle, AG^{MG} = \{ag_i\}, \tag{8}$$

where MG^{ACTIVE} – an active metagraph; MG^{D} – a data metagraph; AG^{MG} – a set of metagraph agents ag_i, attached to the data metagraph.

Thus, an active metagraph allows for the combination of data and processing tools for the metagraph approach. Similar structures are often used in computer science. As an example, we can consider a class of object-oriented programming languages, which contains data and methods of their processing. Another example is a relational DBMS table with an associated set of triggers for processing table entries.

The main difference between an active metagraph and a single metagraph agent is that an active metagraph contains a set of metagraph agents that can use both closed and open rules. For example, one agent may change the structure of an active metagraph using closed rules, while the other may send metagraph data to another active metagraph using open rules. Agents work independently and can be started and stopped without affecting each other.

Both metagraph agents and active metagraph may be constructed using the metagraph calculus described in Section Six.

5 The Metavertex as a Basic Structure of a Metagraph Model

This section shows how the elements of a metagraph model can be reduced to various forms of a metavertex.

5.1 Metagraph Vertex Representation

By definition, a vertex is a special case of a metavertex. The vertex contains nested attributes but does not contain a nested metagraph fragment:

$$(v_i = \{atr_k\}) \equiv \left(mv_i = \left\langle \{atr_k\}, MG_j \right\rangle\right), v_i \in V, mv_i \in MV, MG_j = \emptyset \tag{9}$$

5.2 Metagraph Edge Representation

A metagraph edge can be represented as a special case of a metavertex that contains the source and destination vertices as nested elements. In this case, the direction of the edge can be represented as an attribute of the metavertex. Figure 3 shows an example for representing an undirected edge e_1 as a metavertex MVe_1 (eo = false), and Fig. 4 shows a similar example for a directed edge (eo = true).

In this case, the metagraph edge may also be considered as a restricted form of a hypergraph hyperedge [17]. A hyperedge can contain an arbitrary number of vertices; in this case, the restriction is that there are only two vertices.

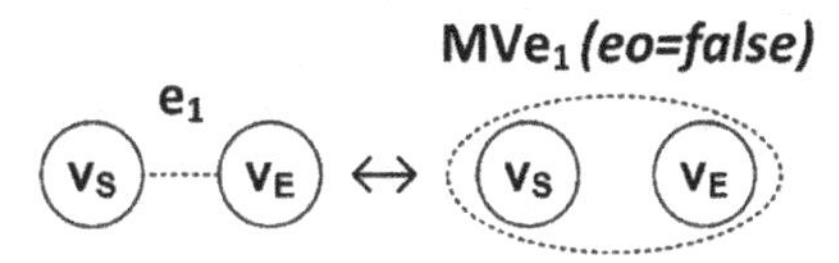

Fig. 3. The representation of an undirected edge as a metavertex

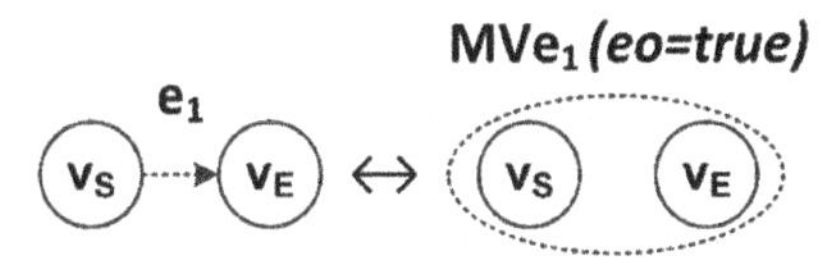

Fig. 4. The representation of a directed edge as a metavertex

5.3 Metagraph Attribute Representation

The attribute may be represented as a special case of a metavertex containing nested vertices for name and value. The edge between name and value vertices may be interpreted as " =" relation.

Figure 5 shows a simple numeric attribute "count = 5" representation. Figure 6 demonstrates an example of the vertex v_1 containing numeric attribute and reference attribute that refers to the metavertex mv_2.

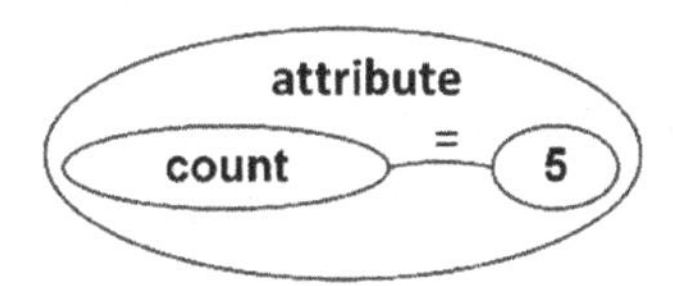

Fig. 5. The representation of an attribute as a metavertex

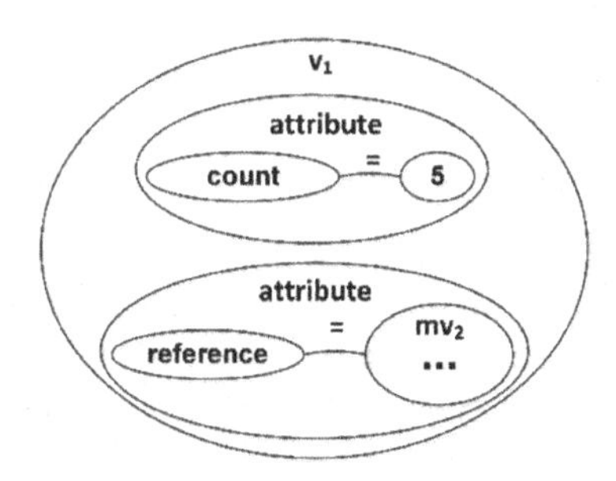

Fig. 6. The representation of a vertex with two attributes as a metavertex

5.4 Metagraph Fragment Representation

A metagraph fragment can contain vertices, metavertices, and edges. Since each of these elements is individually representable as a metavertex, the representations of the elements can be artificially combined into a common metavertex.

The example is shown in Fig. 7. In this case, the metavertex mv_1 with nested vertices v_1, v_2, v_3 and connecting them edges e_1, e_2, e_3 are represented as a set of nested metavertices with the single root mv_1. Edges e_1, e_2, e_3 are represented as edges (Fig. 7, left side) and as metavertices (Fig. 7, right side).

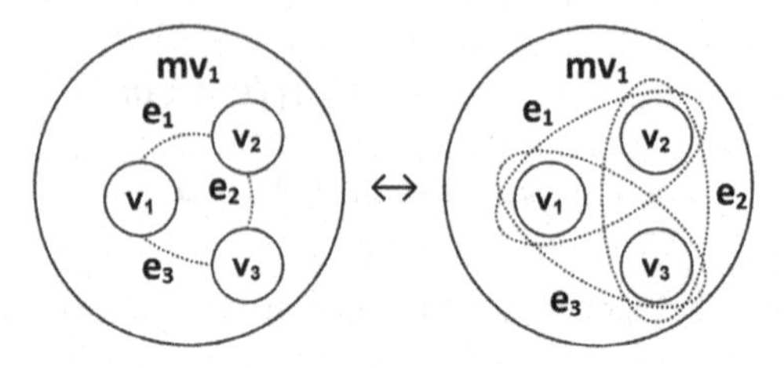

Fig. 7. The example of two equivalent representations for a metagraph fragment

5.5 Metagraph Function Agent Representation

The metagraph function agent contains three metagraphs: an input parameter metagraph, an output parameter metagraph, and an abstract syntax tree in the form of a metagraph. These three metagraphs can be artificially combined into a common metavertex.

5.6 Metagraph Rule Agent Representation

The metagraph rule agent contains a working metagraph, set of processing rules, and start condition for the agent. It is shown in Section Four that processing rules may also be represented in a metagraph form. The start condition may be modeled as an attribute attached to the metavertex or edge. The structure can be artificially combined into a common metavertex.

5.7 Active Metagraph Representation

The active metagraph contains a data metagraph and a set of metagraph agents. It is shown that each agent may be represented in the form of metavertex. This structure can be artificially combined into a common metavertex.

Thus, the elements of a metagraph model can be represented as a metavertex.

6 The Metagraph Calculus

The metagraph calculus is a formal calculus for operating with metagraphs. It is used as the basis for metagraph transformations. This calculus was proposed in [14], and in this article, it is adopted for metagraph granulation.

All calculus constructs are strings divided into left and right parts by the assignment operator, which uses the equal sign "=". To the left of the assignment is the name of the metagraph model element to be constructed, and to the right are metagraph model elements and calculus operators. The "//" syntax is used for comments.

All the operators can use the traditional and prefix forms. The prefix form uses the generally accepted syntax for grouping data using parentheses and commas.

In the following subsections, we consider the basic operators of metagraph calculus.

6.1 Construction Operator

The construction operator is designed to create new metagraph model elements based on existing ones. It is equivalent to the organization operator proposed by L. Zadeh [8].

Constructions of this kind are present in various programming paradigms. In object-oriented programming, these are class constructors; in functional programming, the "cons" operator is designed for recursive list creation.

The syntax symbol for the construction operator is the addition symbol "+" This operator is n-local since a metavertex can include an arbitrary number of vertices and edges.

The formal definition:

$$MG_{RES} = MG_{LHS}\left[+MG_{RHS-i}\right]^{+}, \tag{10}$$

where MG_{RES} – a result metagraph fragment; MG_{LHS} – a left-hand-side metagraph fragment; $MG_{RHS\text{-}i}$ – a repeating right-hand-side metagraph fragment. The repeating part $[]^{+}$ may be considered as a positive iteration (one or more repetitions).

```
// An example of constructing a metavertex mv1
// Traditional form
mv1 = v1+v2+v3+e1+e2+e3
// Prefix form
mv1 = +(v1,v2,v3,e1,e2,e3)
```

Since the metagraph model originally included the concept of an edge, a particular case of the construction operator for creating edges is included in the calculus. In this case, the syntax is "++". The only feature of the "++" syntax is that this variant of the operator is double, that is, it allows for no more than two operands.

The formal definition:

$$e_{RES} = V_{LHS} + +V_{RHS}, \tag{11}$$

where e_{RES} – a result metagraph edge; V_{LHS} – a left-hand-side vertex or metavertex; V_{RHS} – a right-hand-side vertex or metavertex.

```
// Example of constructing the edge e1
// Traditional form
e1 = v1++v2
// Prefix form
e1 = ++(v1,v2)
// Examples of incorrect constructions
// the restriction on operator doubleness is violated
e1 = v1++v2++v3 // Error
e1 = ++(v1,v2,v3) // Error
```

6.2 Deconstruction Operator

The deconstruction operator is designed to deconstruct coarse (higher-level elements) into fine (lower-level) elements. It is equivalent to the granulation operator proposed by L. Zadeh [8]. This operator is very similar to the tuple decomposition operator used in functional programming. In this case, the "left arrow" syntax "<=" is used.

The formal definition:

$$\{MG_{LL-i}\} \Leftarrow MG_{HL}, \tag{12}$$

where MG_{HL} – a higher-level metagraph fragment; $\{MG_{LL\text{-}i}\}$ – a set of lower-level metagraph fragments.

```
// An example of deconstructing a metavertex mv1
v1, v2, v3, e1, e2, e3 <= mv1
```

6.3 Deletion and Transitive Deletion Operators

The delete operator is designed to remove lower-level predicate vertices from upper-level predicate vertices. In this case, the syntax is "-".

The formal definition:

$$\begin{aligned} MG_{RES} &= MG_{HL} - MG_{DEL}, \\ MG_{RES} &= MG_{HL} - *MG_{DEL}, \end{aligned} \tag{13}$$

where MG_{RES} – a result metagraph fragment; MG_{HL} – a higher-level metagraph fragment; MG_{DEL} – a metagraph fragment for deletion.

```
// Example of removing edge e1 from metavertex mv1
// Traditional form
mv1 = mv1-e1
// Prefix form
mv1 = -(mv1,e1)
```

The delete operator in a metagraph model has several limitations. These limitations are associated with ensuring the logical integrity of the elements of the metagraph model:

- **D1_Condition.** Since the edge contains exactly two vertices, none of these two vertices can be removed. In this case, the logical integrity of the edge is violated.
- **D2_Condition.** It is not possible to remove element A from element B if element B contains a nested element C that refers to element A. In this case, the logical integrity of element C is violated. Example of integrity violation:

```
mv1 = v1+v2
mv2 = v1+v2+mv1
mv2 = mv2-v1 // Error - v1 vertex is present in mv1
```

To overcome the second limitation, a transitive deletion operator with the syntax "-*" was introduced into the calculus. In this case, all elements that lose logical integrity as a result of deletion are also transitively deleted. Transitive delete example:

```
mv1 = v1+v2
mv2 = v1+v2+mv1
mv2 = mv2-*v1
// After deletion mv2 = v2
```

Before deletion, element mv2 contains elements v1, v2, mv1. Element v1 is deleted from mv2 upon request. Since the element mv1 nested in mv2 contains a reference to the deleted element v1, mv1 must be transitively deleted from mv2. Therefore, as a result of the transitive deletion operator, mv2 contains only the element v2.

6.4 Metagraph Calculus from the Point of View of the Atomicity Definition

This section will look at the correspondence between the definition of atomicity and metagraph calculus. Consider the individual elements of the definition (selected with bold).

The atomicity of an information element (granule) implies that a given element can be clearly distinguished from the surrounding elements of the external system, added, removed, or moved to another place in the external system.

- All metagraph elements can be clearly distinguished from the surrounding elements.
- The construction operator is used for adding elements.
- The deletion operator is used for removing elements.
- Moving an element can be thought of as removing it from some part of the metagraph and then adding it to another part of the metagraph.

If, as a result of operations of adding, deleting, or moving an element in the external system, structural violations occur, then the number of such violations must be finite, and the location in the external system for each such violation must be uniquely localized relative to other elements.

- In the proposed calculus, the adding operation cannot lead to violations.
- Because moving is a subsequent deletion and addition, then only deletion violations may lead to the moving violations.

- In the proposed calculus, only the deletion operation may lead to violations.
- The number of violations may be infinite if and only if the number of metagraph elements is infinite. But metagraphs with an infinite number of elements are not considered in the proposed approach.
- When an attempt is made to delete elements that violate the conditions D1_Condition or D2_Condition, the metagraph elements that violate these conditions are automatically localized.

Thus, the metagraph calculus fully complies with the definition of atomicity, and the elements of the metagraph model processed using calculus can be considered atomic.

7 The Granularity of the Metagraph Model

This section will examine how the basic provisions and definitions of information granulation from Section Two correspond to the metagraph model.

7.1 Atomicity Property

It is shown in section six that metagraph calculus fully complies with the definition of atomicity, and the elements of the metagraph model processed using calculus can be considered atomic.

7.2 Holonic Organization

It is shown in Section Five that all elements of the metagraph model can be reduced to the metavertex. According to the definition, the metavertices are holonically organized by default. The example is shown in Fig. 1.

The multivariance also holds for metavertices. Being in the middle of the holonically organized metavertices hierarchy, you can simultaneously represent the current metavertex as various combinations of lower-level metavertices and include the current metavertex in various upper-level metavertices.

7.3 Construction and Deconstruction Operations for Granules

The construction and deconstruction operations for granules are implemented using the metagraph calculus for metagraph model elements.

7.4 Higher-Order Information Granules

In the metagraph model, the higher-order information granules are implemented as the organization of the previous organization. Using the construction (organization) operator proposed by L. Zadeh and implemented in metagraph calculus, one can recursively include lower-level metavertices into the higher-level metavertices.

7.5 Interrelationship and Intrarelationship

Both kinds of relationships may be implemented in a metagraph model using edges. If we consider metavertex as a granule, then the edges inside the metavertex are intrarelationships, while the edges between metavertex and outside elements are interrelationships.

If we consider metavertices mv_1 and mv_2 as granules in Fig. 1, then e_1, e_2, e_3, and e_6 are examples of intrarelationships, while e_7 is an example of an interrelationship.

7.6 Refinement and Coarsening and Partial Ordering

If we define the $\sqsubseteq$ relationship for nested metavertices, then we may consider metavertex organization as a partial ordering relationship. Then, for example, in Fig. 1, mv_2 is the p-refinement of mv_3 ($mv_2 \sqsubseteq mv_3$), and mv_3 is the p-coarsening of mv_2 ($mv_3 \sqsupseteq mv_2$).

7.7 Similarity Relationship

The similarity of two metavertices may be defined as a percentage of common nested elements. It is shown in section five that all elements of the metagraph model may be reduced to the metavertex. If mv_1^{SET} is a set of inner metavertices for the metavertex mv_1, and mv_2^{SET} is a set of inner metavertices for the metavertex mv_2, then:

$$Similarity(mv_1, mv_2) = \frac{mv_1^{SET} \cap mv_2^{SET}}{mv_1^{SET} \cup mv_2^{SET}} \tag{14}$$

7.8 Granulations as Partitions and Coverings

We may consider metavertex as the "universe," a complete set of granules. Then partitions and coverings may be considered as inner metavertices, containing lower-level vertices and metavertices.

7.9 Measures of Granularity

It is shown in Section Five that all elements of the metagraph model can be reduced to the metavertex. If mv_1^{SET} is a set of inner metavertices for metavertex mv_1, then measure of granularity for metavertex mv_1 may be defined using the number of inner metavertices:

$$Granularity(mv_1) = \left| mv_1^{SET} \right| \tag{15}$$

For simple vertex $v_1^{SET} = \emptyset$, and $Granularity(v_1) = 0$.

7.10 Granularity of Metagraph Agents

The granularity of a metagraph agent is primarily due to its homoiconicity. The metagraph agent can change both the data metagraph and the structure of other metagraph agents represented as metagraphs.

8 Conclusions

In this article, we look at complex graph models (more precisely, the metagraph model) through the prism of information granulation. All the basic properties of information granulation are holding for the metagraph model.

The metagraph calculus fully complies with the definition of atomicity, and the elements of the metagraph model processed using calculus can be considered atomic.

All elements of the metagraph model may be reduced to the metavertex. Thus, metavertices are holonically organized by default.

The refinement and coarsening, the partial ordering, the similarity, the measure of granularity, partitions and coverings for metagraphs may be described in a natural way using the features of the metagraph model organization.

In the metagraph model, the higher-order information granules are implemented as the organization of the previous organization. Using the construction (organization) operator proposed by L. Zadeh and implemented in metagraph calculus, one can recursively include lower-level metavertices into the higher-level metavertices.

Thus, the metagraph model may be considered as a practical implementation of an abstract information granulation approach.

References

1. Manoj, B.S., Chakraborty, A., Singh, R.: Complex Networks: A Networking and Signal Processing Perspective. Pearson, New York (2018)
2. Chapela, V., Criado, R., Moral, S., Romance, M.: Intentional Risk Management through Complex Networks Analysis. SpringerBriefs in Optimization. Springer, Cham (2015). https://doi.org/10.1007/978-3-319-26423-3
3. Johnson, J.: Hypernetworks in the Science of Complex Systems. Imperial College Press, London (2013)
4. Pedrycz, W., Chen, S.M.: Granular Computing and Intelligent Systems. Springer-Verlag, Berlin Heidelberg (2011)
5. Yao, J.T., Vasilakos, A.V., Pedrycz, W.: Granular computing: perspectives and challenges. IEEE Trans. Cybern. **43**(6), 1977–1989 (2013)
6. Merriam-Webster. http://www.m-w.com/. Accessed on 14 May 2021
7. Tarassov, V.B.: From Multi-Agent Systems to Intelligent Organization. Editorial URSS. Moscow (2002). (in Russian)
8. Zadeh, L.A.: Key roles of information granulation and fuzzy logic in human reasoning, concept formulation and computing with words. In: Proceedings of the Fifth IEEE International Conference on Fuzzy Systems (1996)
9. Yao, J.T.: Information granulation and granular relationships. In: Proceedings of the EEE International Conference on Granular Computing, pp. 326–329. Beijing, China (2005)
10. Yao, J.T., Yao, Y.Y.: Induction of classification rules by granular computing. In: Proceedings of the 3rd International Conference on Rough Sets and Current Trends in Computing, vol. LNAI 2475, pp. 331–338 (2002)
11. Basu, A., Blanning, R.: Metagraphs and Their Applications. Springer, New York (2007). https://doi.org/10.1007/978-0-387-37234-1
12. Tarassov, V.B., Gapanyuk, Y.E.: Complex graphs in the modeling of multi-agent systems: from goal-resource networks to fuzzy metagraphs. In: Kuznetsov, S.O., Panov, A.I., Yakovlev, K.S. (eds.) RCAI 2020. LNCS (LNAI), vol. 12412, pp. 177–198. Springer, Cham (2020). https://doi.org/10.1007/978-3-030-59535-7_13

13. Tarassov, V.B.: Enterprise total agentification as a way to industry 4.0: forming artificial societies via goal-resource networks. In: Intelligent Information Technologies for Industry 2018. AISC, vol. 874, pp. 26–40. Springer, Cham (2018)
14. Gapanyuk, Y.: The metagraph multiagent system based on the semantic complex event processing. Procedia Comput. Sci. **169**, 137–146 (2020)
15. Chernenkiy, V.M., Gapanyuk, Y.E., Nardid, A.N., Gushcha, A.V., Fedorenko, Y.S.: The hybrid multidimensional-ontological data model based on metagraph approach. In: Petrenko, A.K., Voronkov, A. (eds.) PSI 2017. LNCS, vol. 10742, pp. 72–87. Springer, Cham (2018). https://doi.org/10.1007/978-3-319-74313-4_6
16. Gapanyuk, Y.E.: Metagraph approach to the information-analytical systems development. In: CEUR Workshop Proceedings. APSSE 2019 – Proceedings of the 6th International Conference Actual Problems of System and Software Engineering, pp. 428–439, (2019).
17. Voloshin, V.I.: Introduction to Graph and Hypergraph Theory. Nova Science Publishers, New York (2009)

Subjective Expert Evaluations in the Model-Theoretic Representation of Object Domain Knowledge

Gulnara Yakhyaeva(✉) and Vera Skokova

Novosibirsk State University, Novosibirsk, Russia

Abstract. Often, evaluative knowledge about the object area is formulated not only as an objective (statistical) probability but also as a subjective (expert) probability. Expert evaluations may be incomplete or inconsistent with each other. A tool is needed to check the consistency of expertise.

The paper proposes a theoretical-modal formalization of subjective and objective interpretations of probability. This allows us to formulate the criteria for the correctness of the evaluative knowledge received from the experts. The article describes an algorithm for checking the correctness of evaluative knowledge, as well as an algorithm for correcting some incorrectness.

Keywords: Objective probability · Subjective probability · Evaluative knowledge · Precedent model · Fuzzification · Fuzzy model

1 Introduction

The increased interest in artificial intelligence in recent years is associated with the development of new promising technologies, in particular, knowledge discovery in databases, natural language processing, autonomous unmanned intelligent systems, and hybrid human-machine intelligence [1]. A surge in the complexity of knowledge describing various subject areas requires the development of a theory of formalization of the representation of knowledge of object areas.

In [2], a four-level Semantic Model of knowledge representation was proposed. The first level of this model is the object domain ontology. In the language of model theory, an ontology is a signature and an analytical theory of a given object domain. The second level of the Semantic Model is the theory of the object domain This is the general knowledge about the object domain that is true for any precedent of this object domain. The third level is the set of domain precedents that can be considered (known) at the present time. And, finally, the fourth level is a set of probabilistic and evaluative statements, consistent patterns and hypotheses, i.e. sentences that have a fuzzy truth value.

Modeling any object domain inevitably begins with the description of the first level of the Semantic Model, i.e. with a description of the concepts of this object domain [3].

The research was funded by RFBR and Novosibirsk region, project No. 20-47-540005.

S. M. Kovalev et al. (Eds.): RCAI 2021, LNAI 12948, pp. 152–165, 2021.
https://doi.org/10.1007/978-3-030-86855-0_11

However, further description can be continued starting with the formalization of any of the remaining levels. So, for example, when describing mathematical object domains, it is customary to start from the second level of formalization, i.e. descriptions of the set of axioms of the given object domain.

Another, empirical approach is to form a base of precedents of the object domain, with subsequent statistical processing of this base. A striking representative of this approach to knowledge representation is the formal concepts analysis methodology [4]. With this approach, knowledge is formalized in the form of a formal context, and then subjected to various statistical processing (see, for example, [5–8]).

From a model-theoretical point of view, an empirical approach to constructing a Semantic Model is described in the language of Precedent and Boolean-valued models [9]. In Sect. 1 of the article, we present the main definitions and theorems of this approach.

The last approach to the construction of a semantic model of the object domain is based on the initial collection of subjective knowledge of experts with the subsequent "decoding" and interpretation of this knowledge. Section 2 of the article is devoted to the description of the Fuzzy Models, which are the basis for the formalization of the subjective approach to the construction of a Semantic Model of the object domain. The section shows that this approach is a conservative extension of the classical model theory, which does not contradict the Aristotelian logic.

In practice, typically, we have partial expert knowledge about the events of the object domain, so we cannot immediately describe the Fuzzy Model. Moreover, since the experts' evaluations are subjective, they may turn out to be incorrect, i.e. inconsistent with all Fuzzy Models. The theoretical foundations of the checking algorithm the correctness of expert knowledge is described in Sect. 3. The very same checking algorithm the correctness of expert knowledge, as well as the algorithm for correcting some incorrectness, are described in Sect. 4.

2 Precedent Models as Formalization of Frequency Interpretation of Probability

Today, there are three main concepts of the interpretation of probability [10]: the epistemological concept, the frequency (empirical) concept, and the concept of the agent's degree of confidence. The most famous representative of the epistemological approach is the classical interpretation of probability. The main idea of the classical approach is that the world is symmetric, i.e. in a uniform probability distribution between all possible elementary outcomes. Thus, the classical probability of an event is simply a share of the total number of possibilities at which an event occurs.

However, the real (physical) world in most of its manifestations is not symmetrical. Even in the well-known problem of tossing a dice, the elementary outcomes are not equally probable if the dice is weighted down on one side [11]. Thus, the notion of frequency or statistical probability comes to replace the classical interpretation of probability.

One of the basic concepts of the probability theory is the concept of trial, i.e. observation of an event. If different series of trials are carried out under the same conditions, then the relative frequency of the event fluctuates around a certain value, i.e. reveals the property of stability. If a lot of trials have been carried out under the same conditions, then the relative frequency of this event is taken as the statistical (or finite-frequency) probability of an event.

Let us formalize the trial description in the form of an algebraic system $\mathfrak{A} = \langle A, \sigma \rangle$. The signature σ is a set of concepts in the language of which a given object domain is described. Since all trials are carried out under the same conditions, then, obviously, all algebraic systems describing different trials will be defined on the same basic set A and contain the same signature σ. In this work, the focus will be restricted to the case when the signature σ contains only predicate symbols, i.e. the system $\mathfrak{A} = \langle A, \sigma \rangle$ is an algebraic model. Let us introduce the set of constants $C = \{c_a | a \in A\}$ and denote $\sigma_A = \sigma \cup C$. Then any event in the object domain can be formalized in the form of some sentence φ of the signature σ_A. Let denote as $S(\sigma_A)$ the set of all sentences of the signature σ_A, i.e. the set of different events in a given object domain.

If the event $\varphi \in S(\sigma_A)$ has occurred during the trial, then the sentence φ will be true on the algebraic system $\mathfrak{A}$ corresponding to this trial. Thus, on each system, its own meaning of sentences is determined, depending on the trial results. An algebraic system describing a particular trial will be called an object domain precedent [12]. Note that, on the one hand, in the general case, there may be algebraic models of the form $\mathfrak{A} = \langle A, \sigma \rangle$ which are not precedents of the object domain. On the other hand, different trials can be formalized by isomorphic systems.

Let a series of n trials be carried out, which have resulted in a set of precedents

$$\mathbb{E} = \{\mathfrak{A}_1, \ldots, \mathfrak{A}_n\}.$$

Definition 1. *A triple $\mathfrak{A}_{\mathbb{E}} \leftrightharpoons \langle A, \sigma_A, \tau \rangle$ is called a* ***Precedent Model****(generated by the set of trials $\mathbb{E}$) if for any event $\varphi \in S(\sigma_A)$ we have*

$$\tau(\varphi) = \{\mathfrak{A} \in \mathbb{E} | \mathfrak{A} \models \varphi\}.$$

In the Precedent Model, each event is associated with a set of trials on which the event occurred. Note that from a model-theoretic point of view, the model $\mathfrak{A}_{\mathbb{E}}$ is a Boolean-valued model. In this Boolean-valued model, each sentence of the signature σ_A is associated with an element of the Boolean algebra $\rho(\mathbb{E})$ [13].

Definition 2. *A triple $Fuz(\mathfrak{A}_{\mathbb{E}}) \leftrightharpoons \langle A, \sigma_A, \mu \rangle$ is called a* ***Fuzzification*** *of the Precedent Model $\mathfrak{A}_{\mathbb{E}}$ if for any event $\varphi \in S(\sigma_A)$ we have*

$$\mu(\varphi) = \frac{\|\tau(\varphi)\|}{\|E\|}.$$

The truth values of sentences in Fuzzification are numbers from the interval [0, 1], which are interpreted as the objective (frequency) probability of the corresponding events. A more detailed description of the properties of Precedent Models and their Fuzzifications can be found in [14, 15].

Let us define a semantic equivalence relation on the set $S(\sigma_A)$. We say that two sentences $\varphi, \psi \in S(\sigma_A)$ are semantically equivalent (and denote $\varphi \sim \psi$) if on any (classical) model of signature σ_A they take the same truth values. Let us define an order relation on the set $S(\sigma_A)$:

$$\varphi \leq \psi \iff \varphi \sim \varphi \& \psi.$$

Note that the valuation $\mu : S(\sigma_A) \to [0, 1]$ from Definition 2 is a fuzzy measure [16], i.e. has the following properties:

(A) $\mu(\mathbf{1}) = 1$ and $\mu(\mathbf{0}) = 0$;
(B) $\varphi \le \psi \Rightarrow \mu(\varphi) \le \mu(\psi)$, for any $\varphi, \psi \in S(\sigma_A)$.

Following it, we will say that the measure μ is ***additive*** if for any sentences $\varphi, \psi \in S(\sigma_A)$, we have the property:

(C) $\mu(\varphi \vee \psi) = \mu(\varphi) + \mu(\psi) - \mu(\varphi \& \psi)$.

Since we are considering a finite set of trials $\mathbb{E}$, the measure μ will be ***finite***, i.e.

$$\|\mu(S(\sigma_A))\| < \omega,$$

where ω is the smallest infinite cardinal number.

It also follows from Definition 2 that the measure μ is ***rational***, i.e. $\mu(S(\sigma_A)) \subset \mathbb{Q}$. Thus, the following proposition holds.

Proposition 1. The valuation μ of the Fuzzification $Fuz(\mathfrak{A}_{\mathbb{E}})$ of any Precedent Model $\mathfrak{A}_{\mathbb{E}}$ is a fuzzy, additive, finite, rational measure.

The measure μ will be called ***degenerate*** if $\mu(S(\sigma_A)) = \{0, 1\}$. Note that if the valuation μ of the Fuzzification $Fuz(\mathfrak{A}_{\mathbb{E}})$ is a degenerate measure, then the set of precedents $\mathbb{E}$ consists of identical trials formalized by isomorphic models.

Proposition 2. The valuation μ of the Fuzzification $Fuz(\mathfrak{A}_{\mathbb{E}})$ of any Precedent Model $\mathfrak{A}_{\mathbb{E}}$ has the following property:

(D) $\varphi \sim \psi \Rightarrow \mu(\varphi) = \mu(\psi)$, для любы $\varphi, \psi \in S(\sigma_A)$.

Proof of Proposition can be found at paper [15].

Remark 1. *If the mapping $\mu : S(\sigma_A) \to [0, 1]$ has properties (A), (C) and (D) then it also has the property (B).*

Proof. Let $\varphi \le \psi$. Then $\varphi \sim \varphi \& \psi$. Hence,

$$\mu(\varphi) = \mu(\varphi \& \psi) \le \mu(\varphi \& \psi) + \mu(\neg\varphi \& \psi).$$

On the other hand,

$$\mu(\psi) = \mu((\psi \& \varphi) \vee (\psi \& \neg\varphi)) = \mu(\psi \& \varphi) + \mu(\psi \& \neg\varphi) - \mu(\mathbf{0}).$$

Thus, we get that $\mu(\varphi) \le \mu(\psi)$.

Remark 2. *Let the mapping $\mu : S(\sigma_A) \to [0, 1]$ have properties (A) and (D), then property (C) is equivalent to property.*

(E) *For any* $\varphi \in S(\sigma_A)$ *we have*

$$\mu(\varphi) = \mu(\psi_1) + \cdots + \mu(\psi_n),$$

where $\psi_1 \vee \cdots \vee \psi_n$ *is the principal disjunctive normal form (PDNF) of the sentence* φ.

Proof follows from the semantic equivalence properties of formulas.

3 Fuzzy Models as a Formalization of Subjective Probability

The concept of subjective probability was introduced in the 1930s by Frank Ramsey. It implies the degree of confidence of an expert in the occurrence of an event. The concept is used when it is impossible to use the objective probability due to the incompleteness or lack of data on observations in the past, due to the high cost of obtaining the objective probability [17].

B. Kobrinsky noted three main areas of application of the methodology of subjective probability in intelligent systems [18]:

- taking into account in the knowledge base intuitive ideas of a specialist, for example, manifesting in the form of associations;
- display in knowledge base formalisms of an expert's (group of experts') confidence in knowledge;
- reflection at the input of the system of what can be characterized by the term "doubt" in the objective signs and / or subjective information passed through the brain of a specialist in the problem area.

Confidence factors reflecting the dynamics of manifestation of attributes, including figurative ones, and taking into account the severity of linguistic and visual representations, are a condition for increasing the reliability of solutions of fuzzy intelligent systems [19].

According to the methodology of the four-level knowledge representation model, after the construction of the first level, we can proceed to describe the fourth level. Let us formalize the concept of subjective probability using the algebraic system of the signature σ_A.

Definition 3. *A triple* $\mathfrak{A}_\mu = \langle A, \sigma_A, \mu \rangle$ *is called a* ***Fuzzy Model*** *if we have follow properties:*

1. *The mapping* $\mu : S(\sigma_A) \to [0, 1]$ *is the fuzzy measure;*
2. $\varphi \sim \psi \Rightarrow \mu(\varphi) = \mu(\psi)$, *for any* $\varphi, \psi \in S(\sigma_A)$.

The sentence $\varphi \in S(\sigma_A)$ is true on the Fuzzy Model $\mathfrak{A}_\mu$, if $\mu(\varphi) = 1$. It is obvious that any identically true sentence is true on any Fuzzy Model. Thus, the concept of a Fuzzy Model is a conservative extension of the concept of a model in classical predicate logic. Moreover, if the measure μ is degenerate, then the Fuzzy Model $\mathfrak{A}_\mu$ is a model of the classical predicate logic.

Proposition 3. *Let $\mathfrak{A}_\mu = \langle A, \sigma_A, \mu \rangle$ be the Fuzzy Model with non-degenerate measure μ. Let there be functions $f, g : [0, 1]^2 \to [0, 1]$, which for any $\varphi, \psi \in S(\sigma_A)$ satisfy the conditions:*

$$\mu(\varphi \& \psi) = f(\mu(\varphi), \mu(\psi));$$

$$\mu(\varphi \vee \psi) = g(\mu(\varphi), \mu(\psi)).$$

Then

1. $\mu(\varphi) \neq \mu(\neg\varphi)$ *for any* $\varphi \in S(\sigma_A)$*;*
2. *The functions f and g are not monotone.*

Proof. Let us prove the theorem for the function f; the proof for the function g is similar.

1) Let us assume that $\mu(\varphi) = \mu(\neg\varphi) = \alpha$. Then we have

$$\mu(\varphi) = \mu(\varphi \& \varphi) = f(\mu(\varphi), \mu(\varphi)) = f(\alpha, \alpha) = \alpha$$

$$\mu(\mathbf{0}) = \mu(\varphi \& \neg\varphi) = f(\mu(\varphi), \mu(\neg\varphi)) = f(\alpha, \alpha) = 0.$$

   Therefore, f is not a function, i.e. we face a contradiction.
2) Since the measure μ is non-degenerate, there is a sentence $\varphi \in S(\sigma_A)$, such that $0 < \mu(\varphi) < 1$. From item (1) it follows that $\mu(\varphi) \neq \mu(\neg\varphi)$. Let $\mu(\varphi) = \alpha$ and $\mu(\neg\varphi) = \beta$.

   Case 1: $\alpha < \beta$. Then

$$\mu(\varphi) = \mu(\varphi \& \varphi) = f(\alpha, \alpha) = \alpha,$$

$$\mu(\mathbf{0}) = \mu(\varphi \& \neg\varphi) = f(\alpha, \beta) = 0.$$

   Thus, $f(\alpha, \alpha) > f(\alpha, \beta)$.
   Case 2: $\beta < \alpha$. Then

$$\mu(\neg\varphi) = \mu(\neg\varphi \& \neg\varphi) = f(\beta, \beta) = \beta.$$

Thus, $f(\beta, \beta) > f(\alpha, \beta)$.

Hence, the monotonicity property is violated. ■

From item (1) of Proposition 2, it follows that not for every Fuzzy Model $\mathfrak{A}_\mu$, there exist functions f and g with the properties described above. However, if, for example, on the measure μ impose the condition

$$\mu(\varphi) = \mu(\psi) \iff \varphi \sim \psi, \text{for any } \varphi, \psi \in S(\sigma_A),$$

then such functions can be defined. However, according to item (2) in Proposition 2, the functions f and g that implement these dependencies will not be the t-norm and t-conorm, respectively. Therefore, any Fuzzy Model $\mathfrak{A}_\mu$ does not obey the laws of any of the fuzzy logic existing today.

Note that, in general, the valuation μ, introduced in Definition 3 is a homomorphism of partially ordered sets, mapping the Lidinbaum–Tarski algebra $S(\sigma_A)/_\sim$ into the interval $[0, 1]$. In this case, we can interpret the fuzzy value of the truth of the statement as the degree of its reliability. If a probabilistic interpretation is needed, then it is necessary to fulfill the additivity property.

Obviously, each Fuzzification is a Fuzzy Model. However, there are Fuzzy Models that are not Fuzzifications.

4 Expert's Subjective Knowledge

Defining the fuzzy model $\mathfrak{A}_\mu$ we must have knowledge about the subjective probability of all sentences in the set $S(\sigma_A)$. However, an expert (or even a group of experts) may not have such complete knowledge; moreover, the set $S(\sigma_A)$ may be infinite. Nevertheless, there is a finite set of events in the object domain, about the probabilistic values of which an expert can give his expert assessment.

Consider the following example. Let us say we want to predict the spread of coronavirus infection in a Team of n people. We do not have complete knowledge about the possible infection of each of the team members. However, we have the following information (see Table 1):

Table 1. An example of expert knowledge

φ_1	*With a probability of 45%, Petrov is sick with coronavirus*
φ_2	*With a probability of 65%, either Petrov or Ivanov is sick with coronavirus*
φ_3	*With a probability of 80%, the Team has an employee infected with the coronavirus*
φ_4	*With a probability of 30%, if there is at least one infected person in the Team, then all employees are sick with the coronavirus*

Thus, at the input we have a finite set of sentences $S \in S(\sigma_A)$ and the valuation $\eta_S : S \to [0, 1]$. Further, it becomes necessary to solve the following problems:

Problem 1. How to check if the valuation η_S is correct (i.e., realizable)?

Problem 2. If the assessment is incorrect, find the reasons for the incorrectness and invite the expert to reconsider some of his meanings.

Problem 3. If the estimate is correct, then for an arbitrary sentence $\varphi \in S(\sigma_A)\backslash S$, find all possible truth values compatible with the given valuation.

In [20], Problem 3 was partially solved; it was proved that for any sentence $\varphi \in S(\sigma_A)\backslash S$, the set of all possible truth values consistent with this valuation forms an interval. In this work, we will focus on solving the first two problems.

Consider the set of sentences $S \in S(\sigma_A)$. Let σ_S denote the signature of the set of sentences S. Obviously, $\sigma_S \subseteq \sigma_A$. Let $C_S = C \cap \sigma_S$ be the set of constants from S. Define the set $A_S = \{a \in A | c_a \in C_S\}$.

Definition 4. *Consider the set of sentences $S \in S(\sigma_A)$ and the mapping $\eta_S : S \to [0, 1]$. We say that a Fuzzy Model $\mathfrak{B}_\mu = \langle B, \sigma_A, \mu \rangle$* ***agrees*** *with the valuation η_S, if*

1. $A_S \subseteq B$;
2. $\eta_S(\varphi) = \mu(\varphi)$ *for any sentence* $\varphi \in S$.

Definition 5. *The valuation $\eta_S : S \to [0, 1]$ is* ***realizable on the set B*** *if*

1. $A_S \subseteq B$;
2. *Let $\sigma = \sigma_S \backslash C_S$. Then there is a class of precedents $\mathbb{E} = \{\mathfrak{B}_1, \mathfrak{B}_2, \ldots, \mathfrak{B}_n\}$ of the signature σ(i.e. $\mathfrak{B}_i = \langle B, \sigma \rangle$ for any $i = \overline{1, n}$) such that $Fuz(\mathfrak{B}_\mathbb{E})$ agrees with η_S.*

Note that a necessary condition for realizability of the valuation η_S on some set is the condition that the set $\eta_S(S)$ must be a finite subset of rational numbers from the interval [0, 1].

Theorem 1. *Consider the set of sentences $S \in S(\sigma_A)$ and the mapping $\eta_S : S \to [0, 1]$. Let $A_0 = A_S \cup \{a_1, a_2\}$, where $a_1, a_2 \notin A_S$. Then if the signature $\sigma = \sigma_S \backslash C_S$ contains only unary predicates, then for any set* ***B*** *such that $A_S \subset B$ we have*

$$\eta_S \text{ is realizable on the set } A_0 \iff \eta_S \text{is realizable on the set } B.$$

Proof. $\Rightarrow$) Let the valuation η_S be realizable on the set e A_0. Then there is a class of precedents $\mathbb{E} = \{\mathfrak{A}_1, \mathfrak{A}_2, \ldots, \mathfrak{A}_n\}$ such that $Fuz(\mathfrak{B}_\mathbb{E})$ agrees with η_S.

We construct the mapping $h : B \to A_0$ as follows

$$h(b) = \begin{cases} b, & b \in A_S; \\ a_1, & b \in B \backslash A_S. \end{cases}$$

Let us construct the class of precedents $\mathbb{E}' = \{\mathfrak{B}_1, \mathfrak{B}_2, \ldots, \mathfrak{B}_n\}$, where each model $\mathfrak{B}_i = \langle B, \sigma \rangle$ is defined as follows: for any predicate $P \in \sigma$ and for any $b \in B$, we have

$$\mathfrak{B}_i \models P(b) \Leftrightarrow \mathfrak{A}_i \models P(h(b)).$$

Obviously, for any sentence $\varphi \in S$, the following statement holds:

$$\mathfrak{B}_i \models \varphi \Leftrightarrow \mathfrak{A}_i \models \varphi.$$

Let $\mathfrak{A}_\mathbb{E} = \langle A_0, \sigma_{A_0}, \tau_\mathbb{E} \rangle$ и $\mathfrak{B}_{\mathbb{E}'} = \langle B, \sigma_B, \tau_{\mathbb{E}'} \rangle$ be the Precedent Models generated by sets of precedents $\mathbb{E}$ and $\mathbb{E}'$ respectively. Then for any sentence $\varphi \in S$, we have

$$\mathfrak{B}_i \in \tau_{\mathbb{E}'}(\varphi) \iff \mathfrak{A}_i \in \tau_\mathbb{E}(\varphi).$$

Therefore, $Fuz(\mathfrak{B}_{\mathbb{E}'})$ agrees with η_S. Hence η_S is realizable on the set B.

$\Leftarrow$) Let the valuation η_S be realizable on the set B. Then there is a class of precedents $\mathbb{E} = \{\mathfrak{B}_1, \mathfrak{B}_2, \ldots, \mathfrak{B}_n\}$ such that $Fuz(\mathfrak{B}_{\mathbb{E}})$ agrees with η_S.

Let's construct the class of precedents $\mathbb{E}' = \{\mathfrak{A}_1, \mathfrak{A}_2, \ldots, \mathfrak{A}_n\}$, where each model $\mathfrak{A}_i = \langle A_0, \sigma \rangle$ is defined as follows: for any predicate $P \in \sigma$ and for any $a \in A_S$, we have

$$\mathfrak{A}_i \models P(a) \iff \mathfrak{B}_i \models P(a).$$

And also, for the elements $a_1, a_2 \in A_0 \backslash A_S$, we define

$$\mathfrak{A}_i \models P(a_1) \iff \forall b \in B \backslash A_S : \mathfrak{B}_i \models P(b),$$

$$\mathfrak{A}_i \models P(a_2) \iff \exists b \in B \backslash A_S : \mathfrak{B}_i \models P(b).$$

It is not difficult to show that in this case, we will also have the property.

$$\mathfrak{B}_i \models \varphi \Leftrightarrow \mathfrak{A}_i \models \varphi.$$

Therefore, $Fuz(\mathfrak{A}_{\mathbb{E}'})$ agrees with η_S. Hence, η_S is realizable on the set A_0. ■

Consequence 1. *Consider the set of sentences $S \in S(\sigma_A)$and the mapping $\eta_S : S \to [0, 1]$. Let the signature σ_S contain only unary predicates and a finite (or empty) set of constants. Then there are a set of quantifier-free sentences $S' \in S(\sigma_A)$ and the valuation $\eta_{S'} : S' \to [0, 1]$ such that for any set **B**(where $A_S \subset B$), we have*

η_S is realizable on the set B $\iff$ $\eta_{S'}$ is realizable on the set B.

Proof. Let the valuation η_S be realizable on the set B. Then, by Theorem 1, η_S is realizable on the finite set A_0.

Consider a sentence $\varphi \in S$ containing quantifiers. Let us bring it to the prenex normal form. Then, if

$$\varphi \sim Q_1x_1 \ldots Q_{n-1}x_{n-1}\exists x_n \psi(x_1, \ldots, x_n),$$

we replace it with the sentence

$$Q_1x_1 \ldots Q_{n-1}x_{n-1}\left(\bigvee_{a \in A_0} \psi(x_1, \ldots, x_{n-1}, a)\right).$$

And if

$$\varphi \sim Q_1x_1 \ldots Q_{n-1}x_{n-1}\forall x_n \psi(x_1, \ldots, x_n),$$

then we replace it with the sentence

$$Q_1x_1 \ldots Q_{n-1}x_{n-1}\left(\bigwedge_{a \in A_0} \psi(x_1, \ldots, x_{n-1}, a)\right).$$

Repeating this procedure n times (for each quainter), we will replace the sentence φ with a quantifier-free sentence $\varphi^{'}$.

It is not difficult to show that for any finite model $\mathfrak{A} = \langle A_0, \sigma_S \rangle$, we have

$$\mathfrak{A} \models \varphi \iff \mathfrak{A} \models \varphi^{'}.$$

Therefore, for any Fuzzification $Fuz(\mathfrak{A}_{\mathbb{E}}) = \langle A_0, \sigma_A, \mu \rangle$ generated by the class of such models, we have $\mu(\varphi) = \mu\left(\varphi^{'}\right)$.

Replacing in this way all formulas containing quantifiers by the corresponding quantifier-free formulas, we obtain the set $S^{'}$. Obviously, $S^{'}$ will also be realizable on the set A_0. Then, by Theorem 1, $S^{'}$ is realizable on the set B.

■

5 Algorithm for Checking the Correctness of Expert Knowledge

To check expert knowledge for consistency, a software module was developed. It is created in the Java and Kotlin programming languages. The user, employing the dialog box, can define events, describing them in the form of predicate logic formulas, using the operations of conjunction, disjunction, implication and negation, as well as quantifiers of existence and universality. The user writes subjective probabilities of these events in the form of numbers from 0 to 1. The user can enter any number of formulas and their probabilistic values. Figure 1 shows the input of formulas corresponding to the example from Table 1. Next, the resulting formulas are transferred for analysis to the parsing algorithm.

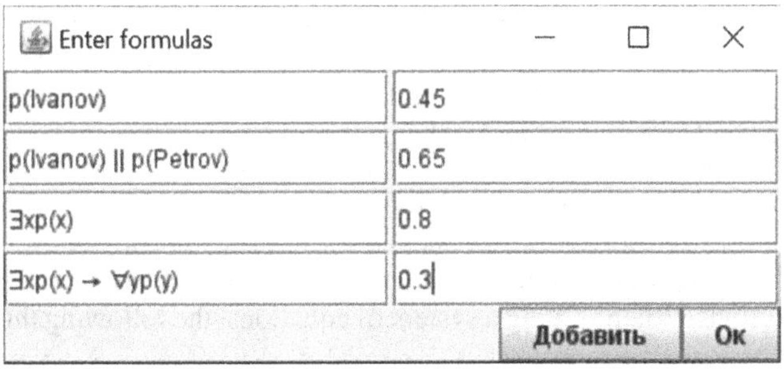

Fig. 1. User input. An example of correct valuation

At the first stage, we construct the signature of the introduced set of formulas: the set of all constants C_σ and the set of all predicates P_σ. After that, according to Theorem 1, we enrich the signature with two new constants a_1 and a_2.

For the example shown in Fig. 1, the following signature is obtained:

$$C_\sigma^{'} = \{Petrov, Ivanov, a_1, a_2\}, P_\sigma = \{p\}.$$

Further, according to Corollary 1, we assume that the formulas are defined on a finite model. Therefore, we open formulas with quantifiers: we replace the universal quantifier with a conjunction, and the existential quantifier with a disjunction. When a quantifier is found in a formula, it is determined which variable and which subformula are under the quantifier. Further, the subformula is replaced by a conjunction or disjunction of subformulas, in which instead of a variable there is one of the constants from the set $C_\sigma^{'}$. These steps are repeated recursively for each sub-formula of the original formula until there are no quantifiers left in the formula.

For our example, the following set of formulas is obtained:

$p(Ivanov)$;

$p(Ivanov) \vee p(Petrov)$;

$p(Ivanov) \vee p(Petrov) \vee p(a_1) \vee p(a_2)$;

$(p(Ivanov) \vee p(Petrov) \vee p(a_1) \vee p(a_2)) \rightarrow (p(Ivanov)\&p(Petrov)\&p(a_1)\&p(a_2))$.

Further, it is necessary to reduce all introduced formulas to the form PDNF of signature $C_\sigma^{'} \cup P_\sigma$. For this, all atomic sentences of signature $C_\sigma^{'} \cup P_\sigma$, are selected and fixed in lexicographic order, and a truth table is created. Next, a system of linear equations is constructed according to the truth table in the following way:

$$\begin{cases} \sum\limits_{j=1}^{m} \alpha_{ij} x_j = \mu_i, i = \overline{1, n}; \\ \qquad \sum\limits_{j=1}^{m} x_j = 1. \end{cases}$$

where n is the number of formulas entered by the user and m is the number of all possible conjuncts containing all atomic sentences of signature $C_\sigma^{'} \cup P_\sigma$. The coefficient α_{ij} is 1 if conjunct j is contained in the complete SDNF representation of sentence i, and 0 otherwise. The coefficient μ_i is the probability value of the i-th sentence. Obviously, $0 \leq \mu_i \leq 1$. The variable x_j is the sought-for probabilistic value of the j-th conjunct. According to Proposition 1 and Remark 2, the set of sentences is realizable if and only if the given system has solutions under the constraints.

$$0 \leq x_j \leq 1 \text{ for any } j = \overline{1, m}$$

An additional program module written in Python using the library z3[1] is responsible for finding solutions. When solving a system of equations, the following three cases may be:.

Case 1. The system has solutions under given constraints.
Case 2. The system has no solutions under the given constraints but has solutions that go beyond the constraints.
Case 3. The system has no solutions.

In the first case, the set of sentences is realizable, and there are no conflicts in it. So, for the example considered in Fig. 1, the following system of linear equations is constructed:

[1] https://github.com/Z3Prover/z3.

$$\begin{cases} x_0 + x_1 + x_2 + x_3 + x_4 + x_5 + x_6 + x_7 = 0.45; \\ x_0 + x_1 + x_2 + x_3 + x_4 + x_5 + x_6 + x_7 + x_8 + x_9 + x_{10} + x_{11} = 0.65; \\ x_0 + x_1 + x_2 + x_3 + x_4 + x_5 + x_6 + x_7 + x_8 + x_9 + x_{10} + x_{11} + x_{12} + x_{13} + x_{14} = 0.8; \\ x_0 + x_{15} = 0,3; \\ x_0 + x_1 + x_2 + x_3 + x_4 + x_5 + x_6 + x_7 + x_8 + x_9 + x_{10} + x_{11} + x_{12} + x_{13} + x_{14} + x_{15} = 1. \end{cases}$$

This system has solutions with given constraints and the software module issues these solutions.

In the second and third cases, the set of sentences with subjective valuations suggested by the user is unrealizable. To resolve the conflict, in both cases, it is necessary to adjust the user valuations.

In the case when the system has solutions outside the constraints, the algorithm of "uniform load distribution" is proposed. For this, at the first step of the algorithm, one arbitrary solution $\langle a_1, \ldots, a_m \rangle$ of the system is selected and its total lower deviation is calculated:

$$\beta = \sum_{j=1}^{m} min\{0, a_j\}.$$

Further, this deviation is evenly distributed over the positive values of the vector:

$$b_j = \begin{cases} 0, & a_j \le 0; \\ a_j + \frac{\beta}{k}, & a_j > 0; \end{cases}$$

where k is the number of positive coordinates in the vector $\langle a_1, \ldots, a_m \rangle$.

Obviously, the vector $\langle b_1, \ldots, b_m \rangle$ satisfies the condition $\sum_{j=1}^{m} b_j = 1$. However, the condition $0 \le b_j \le 1$ for any $j = \overline{1, m}$ may still fail. We repeat this step until all the coordinates of the vector fall into the interval [0, 1].

At the second step of the algorithm, we correct the vector of user estimates $\langle \mu_1, \ldots, \mu_n \rangle$ so that the vector $\langle b_1, \ldots, b_m \rangle$ is a solution to the system of equations.

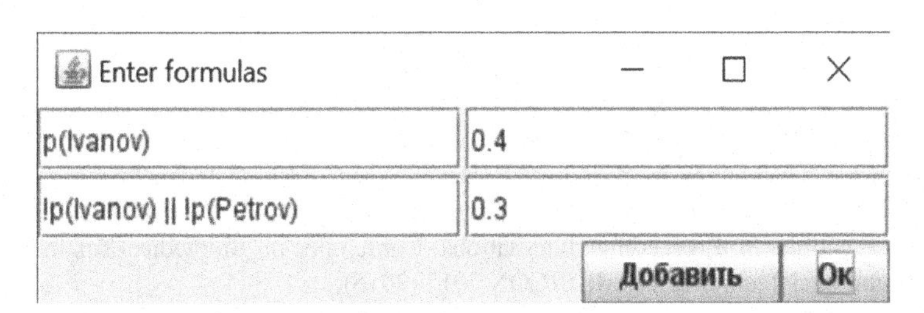

Fig. 2. User input. An example of incorrect valuation

As an example, consider the subjective valuation by the user, shown in Fig. 2. The system recognizes the incorrectness of the valuation and offers a correction option (Fig. 3).

In the case when the constructed system of equations is inconsistent, the algorithm reports that the data entered by the user is incorrect and asks to revise them.

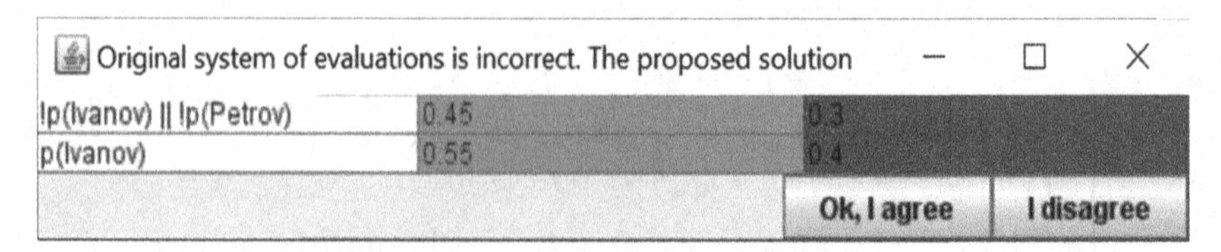

Fig. 3. An example of correcting incorrect expert evaluation

6 Conclusion

The paper describes a model-theoretical formalization of two interpretations of probabilistic knowledge: objective (frequency) probability and subjective (expert) probability. Within the framework of the proposed approach to knowledge are presented in the form of algebraic systems (precedents of the object domain). A Precedent Model of the subject area is built based on precedents. The Fuzzification of the Precedent Model is a model-theoretical formalization of objective probability. Subjective probability is formalized in the form of a Fuzzy Model, which is a conservative extension of the concept of a model in the classical predicate logic.

The consistency check of expert knowledge consists in defining a Fuzzy Model in which this knowledge is invested. If such a model does not exist, then the knowledge gained is considered incorrect (from a logical point of view) and an algorithm for correcting this incorrectness is proposed.

The set of expert valuations is finite and often incomplete. In this regard, it is not always possible to unambiguously describe the Fuzzy Model that formalizes this knowledge. In this case, a class of Fuzzy Models is obtained that are consistent with a given set of expert valuations. In this case, the problem of the ambiguity of generating new evaluative knowledge about the object domain. We have previously proved that such knowledge will be of an interval nature. Further research will be devoted to the development of algorithms for calculating such intervals.

References

1. Sokolov, I.A.: Theory and practice of application of artificial intelligence methods. Her. Russ. Acad. Sci. **89**(2), 115–119 (2019). https://doi.org/10.1134/S1019331619020205
2. Naydanov, C., Palchunov, D., Sazonova, P.: Development of automated methods for the critical condition risk prevention, based on the analysis of the knowledge obtained from patient medical records. In: Proceedings International Conference on Biomedical Engineering and Computational Technologies, SIBIRCON 2015 (2015)
3. Palchunov, D., Yakgyaeva, G.: Representation of Knowledge Using Different Structures of Concepts. CEUR Workshop Proceedings, p. 2729 (2020)
4. Kuznetsov, S.O., Poelmans, J.: Knowledge representation and processing with formal concept analysis. Wiley Interdisc. Rev.: Data Mining Knowl. Discov. **3**(3) (2013). https://doi.org/10.1002/widm.1088
5. Kaytoue, M., Codocedo, V., Buzmakov, A., Baixeries, J., Kuznetsov, S.O., Napoli, A.: Pattern structures and concept lattices for data mining and knowledge processing. In: Bifet, A., et al. (eds.) ECML PKDD 2015. LNCS (LNAI), vol. 9286, pp. 227–231. Springer, Cham (2015). https://doi.org/10.1007/978-3-319-23461-8_19

6. Kuznetsov, S.O., Makhalova, T.: On interestingness measures of formal concepts. Inf. Sci. **442–443**, 202–219 (2018)
7. Palchunov, D., Yakhyaeva, G.: Application of Boolean-valued models and FCA for the development of ontological model. CEUR Workshop Proceedings, pp. 1921 (2017)
8. Palchunov, D.E., Yakhyaeva G.E.: Integration of Fuzzy Model Theory and FCA for Big Data Mining. In: SIBIRCON 2019 - International Multi-Conference on Engineering, Computer and Information Sciences, Proceedings. Novosibirsk, Russia, pp. 0961–0966 (2019)
9. Palchunov, D.E., Tishkovsky, D.E., Tishkovskaya, S.V., Yakhyaeva G.E.: Combining logical and statistical rule reasoning and verification for medical applications. In: Proceedings - 2017 International Multi-Conference on Engineering, Computer and Information Sciences, SIBIRCON 2017, 18–22 September 2017, Novosibirsk, Russia (2017)
10. Rocchi, P.: Interpretations of Probability. In: Janus-Faced Probability, pp. 3–8. Springer, Cham (2014). https://doi.org/10.1007/978-3-319-04861-1_1
11. Carnap, R.: Philosophical Foundations of Physics. Basic Books, New York (1966)
12. Yakhyaeva, G.E.: Application of Boolean Valued and Fuzzy Model Theory for Knowledge Base Development. In: SIBIRCON 2019 - International Multi-Conference on Engineering, Computer and Information Sciences, Proceedings, pp. 0868–0871 (2019)
13. Palchunov, D., Yakhyaeva, G.: Fuzzy logics and fuzzy model theory. Algebra Logic **54**(1), 74–80 (2015)
14. Yakhyaeva, G.: Fuzzy model truth values. In: Proceedings of the 6-th International Conference Aplimat, February 6–9, Bratislava, Slovak Republic, pp. 423–431 (2007)
15. Yakhyaeva, G.: Logic of fuzzifications. In: Proceedings of the 4th Indian International Conference on Artificial Intelligence, IICAI 2009, pp. 222–239 (2009)
16. Beliakov, G., James, S., Wu, J.-Z.: Discrete Fuzzy Measures: Computational Aspects. Springer, Cham (2020). https://doi.org/10.1007/978-3-030-15305-2
17. Dulesov, A.S., Semenova, M.Yu.: Subjective probability in determining the measure of uncertainty of the state of an object. Fundamental research, No.3 (2012). (in Russian)
18. Kobrinsky, B.A.: Approaches to displaying subjectively fuzzy representations of an expert and a user in intelligent systems. Software products and systems. No.4 (1997). (in Russian)
19. Kobrinsky, B.A.: Fuzzy and confidence factors of verbal and visual expert knowledge. Fuzzy systems, soft computing and intelligent technologies. In: Proceedings of the VII All-Russian Scientific and Practical Conference (St. Petersburg, July 3–7, 2017) (2017). (in Russian)
20. Palchunov, D.E., Yakhyaeva, G.E.: Fuzzy algebraic systems. Vestnik NSU. Ser.: Math. Mech. Inf. **10**(3), 75–92 (2010). (in Russian)

Multiagent Systems and Robotics

Q-Mixing Network for Multi-agent Pathfinding in Partially Observable Grid Environments

Vasilii Davydov[2,3], Alexey Skrynnik[1], Konstantin Yakovlev[1,2], and Aleksandr Panov[1,2](✉)

[1] Federal Research Center Computer Science and Control, Russian Academy of Sciences, Artificial Intelligence Research Institute, Moscow, Russia
[2] Moscow Institute of Physics and Technology, Moscow, Russia
panov.ai@mipt.ru
[3] Moscow Aviation Institute, Moscow, Russia

Abstract. In this paper, we consider the problem of multi-agent navigation in partially observable grid environments. This problem is challenging for centralized planning approaches as they typically rely on full knowledge of the environment. To this end, we suggest utilizing the reinforcement learning approach when the agents first learn the policies that map observations to actions and then follow these policies to reach their goals. To tackle the challenge associated with learning cooperative behavior, i.e. in many cases agents need to yield to each other to accomplish a mission, we use a mixing Q-network that complements learning individual policies. In the experimental evaluation, we show that such approach leads to plausible results and scales well to a large number of agents.

Keywords: Multi-agent pathfinding · Reinforcement learning · Mixing Q-network · Grid environment

1 Introduction

Planning the coordinated movement for a group of intelligent agents is usually considered as a separate direction of behavior planning. Two classes of methods for solving this problem can be distinguished: centralized and decentralized. The methods of the first group are based on the assumption of the existence of a control center, which has access to complete information about the states and movements of agents at any time. In most cases, such methods are based either on reducing the multi-agent planning to other well-known problems, e.g. the Boolean satisfiability (SAT-problems) [17], or on heuristic search. Among the latter, algorithms of the conflict-based search (CBS) family are actively developing nowadays. Original CBS algorithm [14] guarantees completeness and optimality. Many enhancements of CBS exist that significantly improve its performance while preserving the theoretical guarantees — ICBS [2], CBSH [5] etc. Other variants of CBS, such as the ones that take the kinematic constraints into account,

S. M. Kovalev et al. (Eds.): RCAI 2021, LNAI 12948, pp. 169–179, 2021.
https://doi.org/10.1007/978-3-030-86855-0_12

target bounded-suboptimal solutions [1] are also known. Another widespread approach to centralized multi-agent navigation is prioritized planning [19]. Prioritized planners are extremely fast in practice, but they are incomplete, in general. However, when certain conditions have been met, the guarantee that any problem will be solved by a prioritized planning method can be provided [3]. In practice, these conditions are often met in the warehouse robotics domains; therefore, prioritized methods are actively used for logistics applications.

Methods of the second class, decentralized, assume that agents are controlled internally and their observations and/or communication capabilities are limited, e.g. they do not have direct access to the information regarding other agent's plans. These approaches are naturally better suited to the settings when only partial knowledge of the environment is available. In this work, we focus on one such setting, i.e. we assume that each agent has a limited field of view and can observe only a limited myopic fragment of the environment.

Among the methods for decentralized navigation, one of the most widely used is the ORCA algorithm [18] and its numerous variants. These algorithms at each time step compute the current speed via the construction of the so-called velocity obstacle space. When certain conditions are met, ORCA guarantees that the collision between the agents is avoided; however, there is no guarantee that each agent will reach its goal. In practice, when navigating in a confined space (e.g. indoor environments with narrow corridors, passages, etc.), agents often find themselves in a dead-lock, when they reduce their speed to zero to avoid collisions and stop moving toward goals. It is also important to note that the algorithms of the ORCA family assume that velocity profiles of the neighboring agents are known. In the presented work, such an assumption is not made, and it is proposed to use learning methods, in particular, reinforcement learning methods, to solve the considered problem.

The use of reinforcement learning algorithms for path planning in partially observable environments is not new [7,15]. In [9], the authors consider the single-agent case of a partially observable environment and apply the deep Q-network [8] (DQN) algorithm to solve it.

In [11], the multi-agent setting is considered. The authors suggest using the neural network approximator that fits parameters using one of the classic deep reinforcement learning algorithms. However, the full-fledged operation of the algorithm is only possible when the agent's experience is replenished with expert data selected based on the optimal path that is built by the classical scheduler. The approach does not use maximization of the general Q function but tries to solve the problem of multi-agent interaction by introducing various heuristics: an additional loss function for blocking other agents; a reward function that takes into account the collision of agents; and other agents' goals encoding in the observation.

We propose solving the problem using reinforcement learning methods. As a methodological base, we suggest using a mixing Q-network, which implements the principle of monotonic improvement of the overall assessment of the value of the current state based on the current assessments of the value of the state of individual agents. Learning the mixing mechanism based on a parameterized approximator allows us to automatically generate rules for resolving conflict patterns when two or more agents pass intersecting path sections. We also propose the implementation of a flexible and efficient experimental environment with trajectory planning for a group of agents with limited observations. The configurability and the possibility of implementing various behavioral scenarios by changing the reward function allow us to compare the proposed method with both classical methods of multi-agent path planning and with reinforcement learning methods designed for training one agent.

2 Problem Statement

The process of interaction between the agent and the environment will be modeled by the partially observable Markov decision process (POMDP). The result of the training will be a policy that maps the agent's observation into the action. This function will generate agent behavior and take into account possible conflict situations.

Markov decision process is described as the set $<S, A, P, r, \gamma>$. $s \in S$ describes a state of the environment. Every step in the environment, an agent executes action $a \in A$ and receives reward with the following reward function $r(s, a) : S \times A \rightarrow \mathbb{R}$. This action initiates a state-transition in the environment $P(s'|s, a) : S \times A \times S \rightarrow [0, 1]$. The agent uses the information received from the environment to automatically generate the policy function $\pi(a|s) : A \times S \rightarrow [0, 1]$. In many cases, it is more efficient to form the value function $Q(a_t, s_t) = r(s_t, a_t) + \mathbb{E}(\sum_{i=1}^{\infty} \gamma^i r(s_{t+i}, a_{t+i}))$, where γ is a discount factor.

The POMDP differs from the standard setting in that a separate set of possible observations of the agent O is introduced, which in the general case, is not the same as the set of states S: $<S, O, A, P, r, \gamma>$. In this case, the agent receives from the environment not its state but some observation o. Accordingly, the strategy and the value function are formed from the observation: $\pi(a|o) : A \times O \rightarrow [0, 1]$, $Q(a_t, o_t) = r(s_t, a_t) + \mathbb{E}(\sum_{i=1}^{\infty} \gamma^i r(s_{t+i}, a_{t+i}))$.

In the problem of pathfinding for a set of agents, the environment is a graph of a regular structure (cellular field), in which a subset of nodes is responsible for obstacles, another subset — positions available to agents, including goals for agents. The task of the agents is to build the optimal (shortest) path to their goal. In this problem, the state $s \in S$ describes the location of obstacles, agents, and goals of agents. Observation $o \in O$ describes information about the location of obstacles, agents, and goals in a radius around a specific agent. Agents can perform actions to move along the X and Y axes along the cell field.

3 Method

In this paper, we propose an original architecture for decision-making and agent training based on a mixing Q-network that uses deep neural network to parameterize the value function by analogy with deep Q-learning (DQN).

In deep Q-learning, the parameters of the neural network are optimized $Q(a, s|\theta)$. Parameters are updated for mini-batches of the agent's experience data, consisting of sets $<s, a, r, s'>$, where s' is the state in which the agent moved after executing action a in the state s.

The loss function for the approximator is:

$$L = \sum_{i=1}^{b}[((r^i + \gamma max_{a^{i+1}} Q(s^{i+1}, a^{i+1}|\theta)) - Q(s^i, a^i|\theta))^2],$$

b is a batch size.

In the transition to multi-agent reinforcement learning, one of the options for implementing the learning process is independent execution. In this approach, agents optimize their own Q-functions for the actions of a single agent. This approach differs from DQN in the process of updating the parameters of the approximator when agents use the information received from other agents. In fact, agents decompose the value function (VDN) [16] and aim to maximize the total Q-function $Q_{tot}(\tau, u)$, which is the sum of the Q-functions of each individual agent $Q^i(a^i, s^i|\theta^i)$.

The Mixing Q-Network (QMIX) [10] algorithm works similarly to VDN. However, in this case, to calculate Q_{tot}, a new parameterized function of all Q-values of agents is used. More precisely, Q_{tot} is calculated to satisfy the condition that Q_{tot} increases monotonically with increasing Q^i:

$$\frac{\delta Q_{tot}}{\delta Q^i} \geq 0 \; \forall i \; 1 \leq i \leq num \, agents,$$

Q_{tot} is parameterized using a so-called mixing neural Q-network. The weights for this network are generated using the hyper networks [4]. Each of the hyper networks consists of a single fully connected layer with an absolute activation function that guarantees non-negative values in the weights of the mixing network. Biases for the mixing network are generated similarly; however, they can be negative. The final bias of the mixing network is generated using a two-layer hyper network with ReLU activation.

The peculiarities of the mixing network operation also include the fact that the agent's state or observation is not fed into the network since Q_{tot} is not obliged to increase monotonically when changing the state parameters s. Individual functions Q^i receive only observation as input, which can only partially reflect the general state of the environment. Since the state can contain useful information for training, it must be used when calculating Q_{tot}, so the state s is fed as the input of the hyper network. Thus, Q_{tot} indirectly depends on the state of the environment and combines all Q-functions of agents. The mixing network architecture is shown in Fig. 1.

The mixing network loss function looks similar to the loss function for DQN:

$$\sum_{i=1}^{b}[(y^i_{tot} - Q_{tot}(\tau^i, u^i, s^i|\theta))^2]$$

$$y_{tot} = r + \gamma max_{t^{i+1}} Q_{tot}(\tau^{i+1}, u^{i+1}, s^{i+1} | \theta^{-}).$$

Here b is the batch size, τ^{i+1} is the action to be performed at the next step after receiving the reward r, u^{i+1} is the observation obtained at the next step, s^{i+1} is the state obtained in the next step. θ^{-} are the parameters of the copy of the mixing Q-network created to stabilize the target variable.

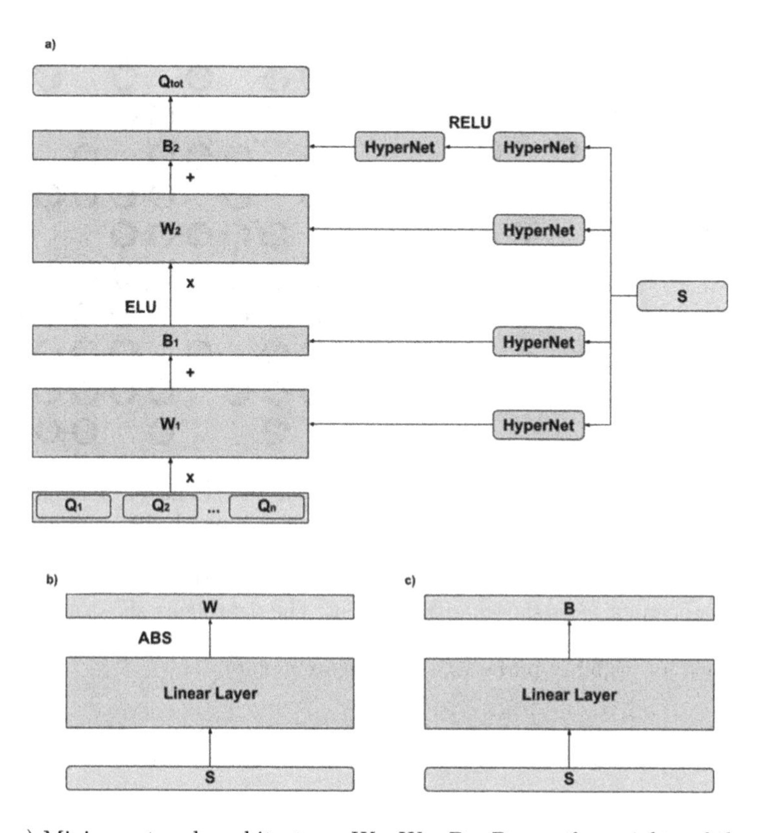

Fig. 1. a) Mixing network architecture. W_1, W_2, B_1, B_2 are the weights of the mixing network; Q_1, Q_2 ... Q_n are the agents' Q values; s is the environment state; Q_{tot} is a common Q Value; b) Hyper network architecture for generating the weights matrix of the mixing Q-network. The hyper network consists of a single fully connected layer and an absolute activation function. c) Hyper network architecture for generating the biases of the mixing Q-network. The hyper network consists of a single fully connected layer.

4 Experimental Environment for Multi-Agent Pathfinding

The environment is a grid field with agents, their goals, and obstacles located on it. Each agent needs to get to his goal, avoiding obstacles and other agents. An example of an environment showing partial observability for a single agent is shown in Fig. 2. This figure also shows an example of a multi-agent environment.

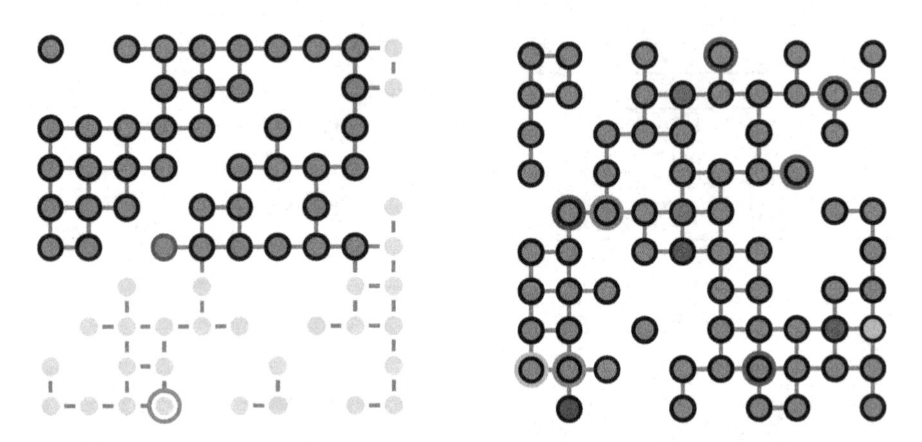

Fig. 2. The left figure shows an example of partial observability for a single agent environment: gray vertices are free cells along the edges of which the agent can move; a filled red circle indicates the position of the agent; the vertex with a red outline is the target of this agent, vertex with red border - projection of the agent's goal. The area that the agent cannot see is shown as transparent. The right figure shows an example of an environment for eight agents, projections of agents' goals and partial observability are not shown for visibility purposes. (Color figure online)

The input parameters for generating the environment are:

- field size $E_{size} \geq 2$,
- obstacle density $E_{density} \in [0, 1)$,
- number of agents in the environment $E_{agents} \geq 1$,
- observation radius: agents get $1 \leq R \leq E_{size}$ cells in each direction,
- the maximum number of steps in the environment before ending $E_{horizon} \geq 1$,
- the distance to the goal for each agent E_{dist} (is an optional parameter, if it is not set, the distance to the goal for each agent is generated randomly).

Obstacle matrix is filled randomly by parameters E_{size} and $E_{density}$. The positions of agents and their goals are also generated randomly, but with a guarantee of reachability.

The observation space O of each agent is a multidimensional matrix: $O : 4 \times (2 \times R + 1) \times (2 \times R + 1)$, which includes the following 4 matrices. *Obstacle matrix*: 1 encodes an obstacle, and 0 encodes its absence. If any cell of the agent's field of view is outside the environment, then it is encoded 1. *Agents' positions matrix*: 1 encodes other agent in the cell, and 0 encodes his absence. The value in the center is inversely proportional to the distance to the agent's goal. *Other agents' goals matrix*: 1 if there is a goal of any agent in the cell, 0 — otherwise. *Self agent's goal matrix* if the goal is inside the observation field, then there is 1 in the cell, where it is located, and 0 in other cells. If the target does not fall into the field of view, then it is projected onto the nearest cell of the observation field. As a cell for projection, a cell is selected on the border of the visibility area, which either has the same coordinate along with one of the axes as the target cell or if there are no such cells, then the nearest corner cell of the visibility area is selected. An example of an agent observation space is shown in Fig. 3.

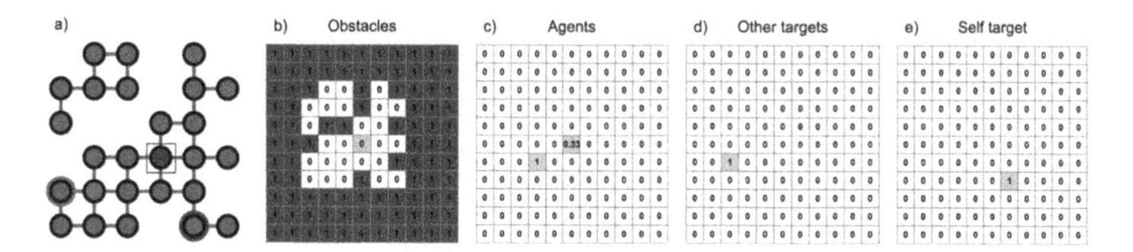

Fig. 3. An example of an observation matrix for a purple agent. In all observation cells, 1 means that there is an object (obstacle, agent, or goal) in this cell and 0 otherwise. a) Environment state. The agent for which the observation is shown is highlighted; b) Obstacle map. The central cell corresponds to the position of the agent, in this map the objects are obstacles; c) Agents map. In this map, the objects are agents; d) Other agents' goals map. In this map, the objects are the goals of other agents; e) Goal map. In this map, the object is the self-goal of the agent.

Each agent has five actions available: stay in place and move vertically (up or down) or horizontally (right or left). An agent can move to any free cell that is not occupied by an obstacle or other agent. If an agent moves to a cell with its own goal, then it is removed from the map and the episode is over for it.

Agents receive a reward of 0.5 if they follow one of the optimal routes to their goal, −1 if the agent has increased its distance to the target, and −0.5 if the agent stays in place.

5 Experiments

This section compares QMIX with the Proximal Policy Optimization (PPO), single-agent reinforcement learning algorithm [13]. We chose PPO because it showed better results in a multi-agent setting compared to other modern reinforcement learning algorithms. Also, this algorithm significantly outperformed other algorithms, including QMIX, in the single-agent case.

The algorithms were trained on environments with the following parameters: $E_{size} = 15 \times 15$, $E_{density} = 0.3$, $E_{agents} = 2$, $R = 5$, $E_{horizon} = 30$, $E_{dist} = 8$. As the main network architecture of each of the algorithms, we used architecture with two hidden layers of 64 neurons, with ReLU activation function for QMIX and Tanh for PPO. We trained each of the algorithms using 1.5M steps in the environment.

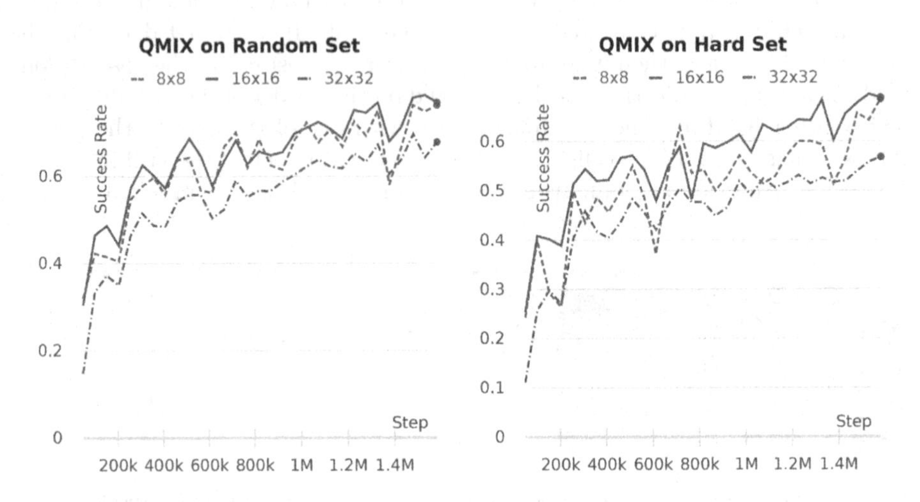

Fig. 4. The graphs show separate curves for different environment sizes. For environment sizes 8×8; 16×16; 32×32, we used 2, 6, 16 agents, respectively. The left graph shows the success rate for the QMIX algorithm in random environments. The right graph shows the success rate for the QMIX algorithm in complex environments.

The results of training of the QMIX algorithm are shown in Fig. 4. We evaluated the algorithm for every 10^5 step on a set of unseen environments. The evaluation set was fixed throughout the training. This figure also shows evaluation curves for complex environments. We generated a set of complex environments so that agents needed to choose actions cooperatively, avoiding deadlocks. An example of complex environments for an environment size of 8×8 is shown in Fig. 5. This series of experiments aimed to test the ability of QMIX agents to act sub-optimally for a greedy policy, but optimal for a cooperative policy.

The results of the evaluation are shown in Table 1 for random environments and in Table 2 for complex environments. As a result of training, the QMIX significantly outperforms the PPO algorithm on both series of experiments, which shows the importance of using the mixing network for training.

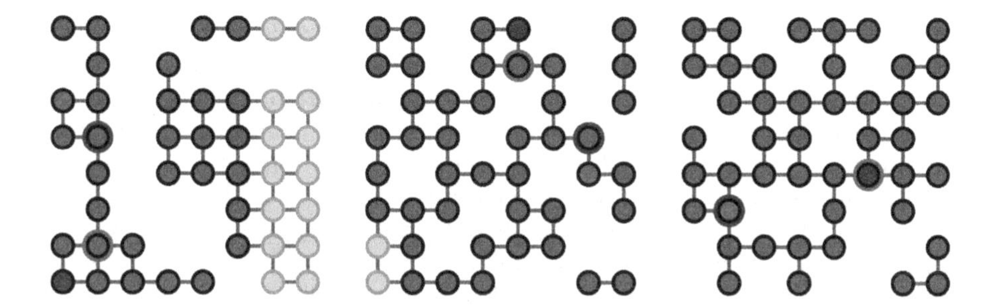

Fig. 5. Examples of complex 8×8 environments where agents need to use a cooperative policy to reach their goals. In all examples, the optimal paths of agents to their goals intersect, and one of them must give way to the other. Vertices that are not visible to agents are shown as transparent.

Table 1. Comparison of the algorithms on a set of 200 environments (for each parameter set) with randomly generated obstacles. The last two columns show the success rate for PPO and QMIX, respectively. The results are averaged over three runs of each algorithm in each environment. QMIX outperforms PPO due to the use of the mixing Q-function Q_{tot}.

E_{size}	E_{agents}	R	$E_{horizon}$	E_{dist}	$E_{density}$	PPO	QMIX
8 × 8	2	5	16	5	0.3	0.539	**0.738**
16 × 16	6	5	32	6	0.3	0.614	**0.762**
32 × 32	16	5	64	8	0.5	0.562	**0.659**

Table 2. Comparison on a set of 70 environments (for each parameter set) with complex obstacles. The last two columns show the success rate for PPO and QMIX, respectively. The results are averaged over ten runs of each algorithm in each environment. QMIX, as in the previous experiment, outperforms PPO.

E_{size}	E_{agents}	R	$E_{horizon}$	E_{dist}	$E_{density}$	PPO	QMIX
8 × 8	2	5	16	5	0.3	0.454	**0.614**
16 × 16	6	5	32	6	0.3	0.541	**0.66**
32 × 32	16	5	64	8	0.5	0.459	**0.529**

6 Conclusion

In this work, we considered the problem of multi-agent pathfinding in the partially observable environment. This formulation with incomplete information makes it impossible to apply the classical methods of multi-agent pathfinding, but it allows for the use of reinforcement learning algorithms. It was proposed to apply a mixing Q-network with a neural network approximation to solve this problem, which selects the parameters of a unifying Q-function that combines the Q-functions of individual agents. An experimental environment was developed for launching experiments with learning algorithms. In this environment, the efficiency of the proposed method was demonstrated and its effectiveness outperforms the on-policy reinforcement learning algorithm design only for the single-agent case. It should be noted that the comparison was carried out under conditions of limiting the number of episodes of interaction between the agent and the environment. If such sample efficiency constraint is removed, the on-policy method can outperform the proposed off-policy Q-mixing network algorithm. In future work, we plan to combine the advantages of better-targeted behavior generated by the on-policy method and the ability to take into account the actions of another agent when resolving local conflicts using QMIX. The model-based reinforcement learning approach seems promising, in which it is possible to plan and predict the behavior of other agents and objects in the environment [6,12]. We also assume that using adaptive task composition for agent training (curriculum learning) will also give a significant performance boost for tasks with a large number of agents.

References

1. Barer, M., Sharon, G., Stern, R., Felner, A.: Suboptimal variants of the conflict-based search algorithm for the multi-agent pathfinding problem. In: Proceedings of The 7th Annual Symposium on Combinatorial Search (SoCS 2014), pp. 19–27 (July 2014)
2. Boyarski, E., et al.: ICBS: Improved conflict-based search algorithm for multi-agent pathfinding. In: Proceedings of The 24th International Joint Conference on Artificial Intelligence (IJCAI 2015), pp. 740–746 (2015)
3. Čáp, M., Novák, P., Kleiner, A., Selecký, M.: Prioritized planning algorithms for trajectory coordination of multiple mobile robots. IEEE Trans. Autom. Sci. Eng. **12**(3), 835–849 (2015)
4. Ha, D., Dai, A., Le, Q.V.: Hypernetworks. In: Proceedings of the International Conference on Learning Representations (2016)
5. Felner, A., Li, J., Boyarski, E., Ma, H., Cohen, L., Kumar, T. S., Koenig, S.: Adding heuristics to conflict-based search for multi-agent path finding. In: Proceedings of the 28th International Conference on Automated Planning and Scheduling (ICAPS 2018), pp. 83–87 (2018)
6. Gorodetskiy, A., Shlychkova, A., Panov, A.I.: Delta schema network in model-based reinforcement learning. In: Goertzel, B., Panov, A.I., Potapov, A., Yampolskiy, R. (eds.) AGI 2020. LNCS (LNAI), vol. 12177, pp. 172–182. Springer, Cham (2020). https://doi.org/10.1007/978-3-030-52152-3_18
7. Martinson, M., Skrynnik, A., Panov, A.I.: Navigating autonomous vehicle at the road intersection simulator with reinforcement learning. In: Kuznetsov, S.O., Panov, A.I., Yakovlev, K.S. (eds.) RCAI 2020. LNCS (LNAI), vol. 12412, pp. 71–84. Springer, Cham (2020). https://doi.org/10.1007/978-3-030-59535-7_6
8. Mnih, V., et al.: Human-level control through deep reinforcement learning. Nature **518**(7540), 529–533 (2015)
9. Panov, A.I., Yakovlev, K.S., Suvorov, R.: Grid path planning with deep reinforcement learning: preliminary results. Procedia Comput. Sci. **123**, 347–353 (2018)

10. Rashid, T., Samvelyan, M., Schroeder, C., Farquhar, G., Foerster, J., Whiteson, S.: Qmix: monotonic value function factorisation for deep multi-agent reinforcement learning. In: International Conference on Machine Learning, PMLR, pp. 4295–4304 (2018)
11. Sartoretti, G., et al.: Primal: pathfinding via reinforcement and imitation multi-agent learning. IEEE Robot. Autom. Lett. **4**(3), 2378–2385 (2019)
12. Schrittwieser, J., Hubert, T., Mandhane, A., Barekatain, M., Antonoglou, I., Silver, D.: Online and Offline Reinforcement Learning by Planning with a Learned Model (2021)
13. Schulman, J., Wolski, F., Dhariwal, P., Radford, A., Klimov, O.: Proximal policy optimization algorithms. arXiv preprint arXiv:1707.06347 (2017)
14. Sharon, G., Stern, R., Felner, A., Sturtevant., N.R.: Conflict-based search for optimal multiagent path finding. Artif. Intell. J. **218**, 40–66 (2015)
15. Shikunov, M., Panov, A.I.: Hierarchical reinforcement learning approach for the road intersection task. In: Samsonovich, A.V. (ed.) BICA 2019. AISC, vol. 948, pp. 495–506. Springer, Cham (2020). https://doi.org/10.1007/978-3-030-25719-4_64
16. Sunehag, P., et al.: Value-decomposition networks for cooperative multi-agent learning based on team reward. In: Proceedings of the 17th International Conference on Autonomous Agents and Multiagent Systems (2017)
17. Surynek, P., Felner, A., Stern, R., Boyarski, E.: Efficient sat approach to multi-agent path finding under the sum of costs objective. In: Proceedings of the 22nd European Conference on Artificial Intelligence (ECAI 2016), pp. 810–818. IOS Press (2016)
18. van den Berg, J., Guy, S.J., Lin, M., Manocha, D.: Reciprocal n-body collision avoidance. In: Pradalier, C., Siegwart, R., Hirzinger, G. (eds.) Robotics Research. Springer Tracts in Advanced Robotics, vol. 70, pp. 3–19. Springer, Berlin (2011). https://doi.org/10.1007/978-3-642-19457-3_1
19. Yakovlev, K., Andreychuk, A., Vorobyev, V.: Prioritized multi-agent path finding for differential drive robots. In: Proceedings of the 2019 European Conference on Mobile Robots (ECMR 2019), IEEE, pp. 1–6 (2019)

Subdefinite Computations for Reducing the Search Space in Mobile Robot Localization Task

Anton Moscowsky(✉)

National Research Center "Kurchatov Institute", Moscow, Russia
Moskovsky_AD@nrcki.ru

Abstract. The paper describes the application of the technology of subdefinite computations for the problem of localizing a mobile robot by landmarks. The application of subdefinite computations together with probabilistic approaches is considered using the example of a histogram filter. It is shown that the use of this technology can significantly increase the computational efficiency by reducing the space in which the search for the position of the robot takes place. The experimental results are obtained by simulation.

Keywords: Localization · Mobile robot · Probabilistic approaches · Histogram filter · Subdefinite computations

1 Introduction and Problem Statement

The task of localization—determining the position in space—is a cornerstone in mobile robotics since it is necessary for the navigation task, which allows the robot to plan movement in space and build on this higher-level behavior. This paper considers the classical problem of localization by a set of beacons with known coordinates. Despite the development of sensors and methods of automatic mapping from their data, the task of localization by landmarks is still relevant. The importance stems from the fact that localization by beacons usually requires less expensive equipment, both sensor and computing. In the simplest case, a simple camera and an on-board computer such as the Raspberry Pi are enough. Methods that work with static maps are usually more fault-tolerant, which is important for a number of tasks and is acceptable in cases where the robot moves in the same, sometimes specially prepared, environment. Thus, localization by static beacons, for example, is actively used in underwater robotics (acoustic methods LBL (Long Baseline) [1]). In general, the robot knows the map with the positions of the landmarks, and its sensors can measure the distance to the landmark and/or the angle to the landmark. One way to solve such problems is a direct geometric approach known as the triangulation method [2], however, due to the sensor errors, there are a number of modifications for this method [3–5]. Another geometric approach to localization [6] allows robot position tracking and able to work in conditions of unsynchronized data.

S. M. Kovalev et al. (Eds.): RCAI 2021, LNAI 12948, pp. 180–196, 2021.
https://doi.org/10.1007/978-3-030-86855-0_13

Probabilistic approaches are most common as of today; they are described in detail in the book by S. Thrun [7]. The histogram filter and the particle filter are particularly relevant to this problem among the probabilistic approaches. They implement direct and random search for a position of a robot in space. As the area of space in which the robot operates increases, so does the number of calculations for both algorithms, or the accuracy of the methods decreases. On the other hand, if it was possible to apply an algorithm that, according to the input data, could narrow the search area, then this would have a positive effect on both the speed and accuracy of the approaches under consideration. In this paper, an approach is explored that could reduce the search space. It is based on subdefinite computations (SD computations) developed by A.S. Narin'yani [8, 9], which are traditionally related to artificial intelligence technologies. This work is a development of the ideas of applying SD computations to the localization problem, presented by V.E. Karpov [10].

2 Probabilistic Approaches to the Localization Problem

As mentioned above, today the predominant direction in the localization of mobile robots is probabilistic approaches. Among them, the most common varieties of the Kalman filter in practice, such as EKF [11] and UKF [12], and particle filter varieties, such as AMCL (Adaptive Monte Carlo Localization). Less common are discrete filters: Histogram and Binary Bayesian. This whole class of approaches is predicated on calculating the probability of a robot's position based on its mathematical models of observation and movement. A number of recent works are aimed at training such models using machine learning [13, 14].

The particle filter is a random directional search method. The space, in which the robot is, is filled randomly with "particles," each of which represents a hypothesis about the position of the robot. A limitation of the particle filter is that the accuracy and rate of convergence is directly related to the number of particles. So, the larger the space, the more particles are required, and, consequently, the computational cost increases, too.

In contrast to the particle filter, the histogram filter is a method of full search of areas of space. The search space is divided with some step into a finite number of components, and for each component, its own weight is calculated. The component with the highest weight is determined as the position of the robot. Unlike a particle filter, this approach "goes over" the entire space, eliminating situations where the random search method misses the area of the real position of the robot. Unfortunately, this is achieved at the cost of a significant increase in computational load. Also, in most cases, such an enumeration is redundant since the movement of the robot for adjacent intervals of the algorithm is usually small, but the entire area has to be calculated.

So, the effectiveness of the application of some probabilistic methods is largely determined by the initial sizes of the search spaces. Further, the paper considers one of the promising mechanisms for narrowing the search areas based on the use of the procedure of subdefinite computations.

3 Proposed Approach

3.1 Subdefinite Computations

Subdefinite computations (SD computations or subdefinite models) were proposed by A.S. Narin'yani and represent a universal computational model built on iterative refinement of variables. The main element is a subdefinite variable (SD variable), which describes a set of possible values, among which there is a real value. The SD variable can be either a discrete set of values or intervals [15]. Its extension is a multi-interval, which contains a set of interval SD variables. For SD variables, subdefinite operations are defined that allow manipulation with them. Refinement of SD variables occurs due to the so-called assignment functions, which express some variables in terms of others. Also, in the computational model, there are validation functions that evaluate the result of the assignment functions before updating the value of the SD variable. In the model, based on the specifics of the problem, constraints can be specified that SD variables must satisfy. Thus, the computational model is a four:

$$M = (V, R, W, C), \tag{1}$$

where V are parameters from a given area in the form of a set of SD variables, R is a set of constraints, W is a set of assignment functions, and C is a set of validation functions. When the model is defined, the computation process can be described by the algorithm **subdefinite_proc**.

An algorithm of the SD computation process. The input are model M parameters (1), the output are updated values of SD variables set V.

```
1:    Algorithm subdefinite_proc(V, R, W, C)
2:        S = W
3:        while S ≠ Ø
4:           f = S[0]
5:           remove f from S
6:           vo = output var of f from V
7:           vi = input vars of f from V
8:           vn = f(vi)
9:           va = vi ← vn
10:          if va ≠ vi
11:             rl = func. from R for which vo is input
12:             for r in rl
13:                voi = other vars input of rl
14:                if not r(va, voi)
15:                   continue while
16:                end if
17:             end for
18:             vn = va
19:          end if
20:          fl = functions from W for which vn is input
21:          for f in fl
22:             if f ∉ S
23:                add f to S
24:             end if
25:          end for
26:       end while
27:    return V
```

The algorithm is a sequential application of the assignment functions until the narrowing of the values of the SD variables occurs. In line 9 of the algorithm **subdefinite_proc**, the operation marked with symbol '⟵' is the operation of assigning a new value to the SD variable. The update takes place in such a way that the new value of the SD variable cannot go beyond the old value, i.e. at each step, the uncertainty range of the variable should not increase.

3.2 Application to the Problem of Localization

Since the position of the robot is unknown in the localization problem, it will be expressed in terms of SD variables. For example, if a mobile robot moves in two-dimensional space its position is determined by three SD variables: the position along the X-axis, along the Y-axis, and rotation θ:

$$V = \{^*X, {}^*Y, {}^*\theta\}, \tag{2}$$

the * mark to the left of a variable name indicates that it is a subdefinite one. SD variables are intervals (or multi-intervals) and are initialized according to the initial knowledge of the position of the robot. The area in which the robot operates forms the constraints R (1), in such a way:

$$A_{min} \leq {}^*A \leq A_{max}, \; A = \{X, Y, \theta\}.$$

For the orientation, the domain is usually equal to $(-\pi, \pi]$, and, therefore, always after changing the angular variable, subsequent normalization to this interval is required.

The core idea of using the SD calculations mechanism of the localization problem is illustrated in Fig. 1. An example of a robot moving along a wall with doors widely is used to illustrate localization techniques in [7]. The robot is able to determine if it is in front of the door and estimate its movement. Because the task is one-dimensional, then the position is described only by one SD variable *X.

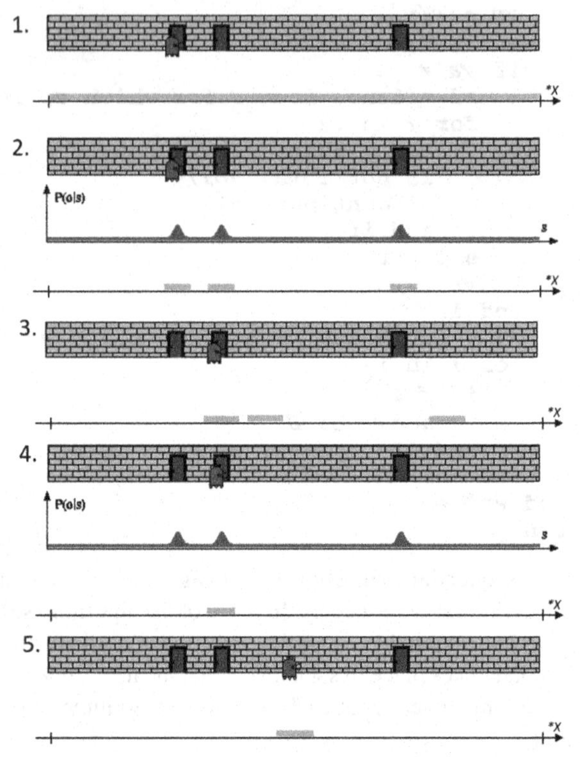

Fig. 1. An illustration of the application of the SD computation method to the problem of mobile robot localization. In diagram 1, *X is initialized with the whole area. In diagram 2, the robot detects the door, and *X narrows down to a multi-interval of three intervals. In diagram 3, the robot is moved, and the multi-interval is also moved and expanded, taking into account the error in determining the displacement. In diagram 4, the robot again detects the door, thereby narrowing the *X value to an interval. In diagram 5, the robot moves again, causing the *X value to change.

Considering the 2D localization task, there are N landmarks in the space with known positions. The robot's sensors are able to determine the distance r_i and the angle (bearing) α_i. These measurements are made with some error, usually characterized by the standard deviation σ_r and σ_α. To use the error in the computational process, the standard deviation can be converted into an SD variable, following the three-sigma rule:

$$^*\Delta b = [-3\sigma b, 3\sigma b], \ b = \{r, \alpha\}. \tag{3}$$

Further, the relationship between the coordinates of the landmarks and measured distance and bearing with the location of the robot is considered. The i-th landmark with coordinates in (X_{oi}, Y_{oi}) sets the following distance dependence, following the equation of the circle:

$$({}^*X - X_{oi})^2 + ({}^*Y - Y_{oi})^2 = (r_i + {}^*\Delta r)^2, \tag{4}$$

and bearing dependence:

$${}^*\theta = \arctan\left(\frac{Y_{oi} - {}^*Y}{X_{oi} - {}^*X}\right) - (\alpha_i + {}^*\Delta\alpha). \tag{5}$$

Then, in order to write down the assignment functions (1), it is required to express each of the main SD-variables (2) from Eqs. (4) and (5):

$${}^*X = \pm\sqrt{(r_i + {}^*\Delta r)^2 - ({}^*Y - Y_{oi})^2} + X_{oi}, \tag{6}$$

$${}^*Y = \pm\sqrt{(r_i + {}^*\Delta r)^2 - ({}^*X - X_{oi})^2} + Y_{oi}, \tag{7}$$

$${}^*X = \frac{({}^*Y - Y_{oi})}{\tan({}^*\theta + {}^*\Delta\alpha + \alpha_i)} + X_{oi}, \tag{8}$$

$${}^*Y = ({}^*X - X_{oi})\tan({}^*\theta + \alpha + {}^*\Delta\alpha) + Y_{oi}. \tag{9}$$

Each visible landmark adds five Eqs. (5–9) to the set W (1). The $\pm$ sign in (6) and (7) indicates that the output in these functions is a multi-interval expansion of SD variable. This means that all other calculations also require the use of multi-intervals.

The validation functions C (1) helps determine the inconsistency of the data from the sensors, preventing the assignment functions to make conflicting refinements. So, for example, in functions (6) and (7) there is a square root; therefore, the sub-root expression should not be less than zero. This requirement generates two validation functions.

When every component of the computational model M (1) is determined, then, using algorithm **subdefinite_proc**, it is possible to determine the area of the robot's position. However, the process of localizing a mobile robot must be carried out constantly since the robot is usually in motion. In this case, the area calculated at the previous step might be used for the initial approximation at the new step. If the robot is moving, then the area should also expand in the direction of movement of the robot. Usually, mobile robots have the ability to estimate their speed through odometry, inertial sensors, or directly from control commands. Let the robot move during the time dt with a linear velocity v and an angular velocity w, which are determined with an error σ_v and σ_w. Based on this, the initial area at the new step is calculated as follows:

$$\begin{aligned} {}^*\theta_{t+dt} &= {}^*\theta t + (w + {}^*\Delta w)dt \\ {}^*X_{t+dt} &= {}^*X_t + (v + {}^*\Delta v)\cos({}^*\theta t + dt)dt \\ {}^*Y_{t+dt} &= {}^*Y_t + (v + {}^*\Delta v)\sin({}^*\theta t + dt)dt \end{aligned} \tag{10}$$

SD variables of errors $(\Delta v, \Delta w)$ are calculated similarly to (3). In this case, the resulting region must be tested for the R (1) constraints. Such "tracking," on the one hand, reduces the number of calculations and increases the accuracy of the method, while, on the other hand, creating situations where the algorithm can "get stuck" in an incorrectly refined region. Most often, an incorrect specification of an area can occur, as in other localization algorithms, due to a discrepancy between the real errors and errors used in calculations. There is also the problem of the robot kidnapping, usually describing a situation when the robot was moved without its participation (external influence). Such situations can be determined by applying the validation functions *C* (1) to the region obtained at the previous step. If this area has not passed this check, then, at the current step, it is worth using as an initial approximation of SD variables the maximum possible intervals that satisfy the constraints *R* (1).

An algorithm of subdefinite localization process. The input are a set of SD variables *V*, constraints *R*, maximum possible area *Vmax*, landmarks data *O*, robot speed *v* and *w*, and time interval *dt*. The output are updated values of *V*. Function **updates_with_motion** implements formulas (10), function **update_from_landmarks** implements formulas (5–9).

```
1:   Algorithm SD_localization(V, R, Vmax, O, v, w, dt)
2:      V = update_with_motion(V, v, w, dt, R)
3:      W, C = update_from_landmarks(O)
4:      for c in C
5:         if not c(V)
6:            V = Vmax
7:         end if
8:      end for
9:      V = subdefinite_proc(V, R, W, C)
10:  return V
```

The algorithm **SD_localization** forms regions in which, according to the input data and concepts of errors, the robot is located. How much the area will be narrowed depends on the amount of input data, their nature (for example, two landmarks that are very apart from each other narrow the area more than those located next to each other) and the magnitude of the errors. Further, this area can be fed to the input of an algorithm that searches for a specific position.

3.3 Features of the Application

Narin'yani's calculation process is based on substitution of some SD variables in the assignment function from *W* and subsequent update. SD variable substitution usually consists of lower and upper limit substitution:

$$^{*}A = [A_{min}, A_{max}],\ \mathrm{f}(^{*}A) = [\min(\mathrm{f}(A_{min}), \mathrm{f}(A_{max})), \max(\mathrm{f}(A_{min}), \mathrm{f}(A_{max}))] \quad (11)$$

However, this is true only for functions that are monotone on the interval $[A_{min}, A_{max}]$. Functions (2.5–2.9) are not, therefore, a change in the approach to their calculation is required. In fact, (11) is the definition of the range of values of a function on a segment, but for a non-monotonic function, this turns into the definition of an infimum and supremum on a segment:

$$\mathrm{f}(^{*}A) = \left[\inf_{[Amin,\, Amax]}(\mathrm{f}),\ \sup_{[Amin,\, Amax]}(\mathrm{f})\right] \quad (12)$$

Moreover, in the cases under consideration, functions (5–9) depend on several variables. Accordingly, the infimum and supremum for them should be found over the entire domain of definition. However, using formulas (6) and (7), multi-intervals are calculated, and a simple application of formula (12) will combine them into one interval, which will lead to a decrease in the accuracy of the method. Therefore, instead of (12), it is required to search for the range of values also in the form of a multi-interval. This search is implemented by the Monte Carlo method (algorithm **ROV_Monte_Carlo**).

The algorithm **ROV_MonteCarlo. The** input are an assignment function f, a set of input SD variables *V*, and parameter *Nrolls*, determining how many times the process will run. The output is a multi-interval of a range of values of f on domain *V*. Function **get_random_sub_domain** returns a random subdomain of input SD variables.

```
1:    ROV_MonteCarlo(f, V, Nrolls)
2:       S = Ø
3:       s = f(V)
4:       add s to S
5:       for Nrolls
6:          v = get_random_sub_domain(V)
7:          s = f(v)
8:          add s to S
9:       end for
10:      for s in S
11:        for s1 in S from s
12:           if s    s1 ≠ Ø
13:              s = s U s1
14:              remove s1 from S
15:           end if
16:      end for
17:   return s
```

During the algorithm, random intervals belonging to the input SD variable are generated. A set of ranges of values for all intervals is calculated for the assignment function. Further, the intervals will be combined according to the sign of intersection, thus forming a set of non-intersecting intervals at the output. The accuracy of algorithm **ROV_MonteCarlo**, like any algorithms based on the Monte Carlo principle, depends on the number of attempts. In fact, the presented algorithm replaces line 8 in the algorithm **subdefinite_proc**.

3.4 Localization Only by Bearing

In the previous sections, the problem of localization by the distance and the bearing to the landmark was considered. However, there are situations where only the bearing to the landmark is known. This can be either localization by a camera, which is not equipped with rangefinders and works with objects, the distance to which cannot be measured geometrically, or the task of determining a position by radio bearing. Equation (4) in this case is absent, and only by using (5, 8, 9), it is not possible to refine it to a sufficient level without having a good initial approximation for the robot orientation, for example, according to the compass readings.

To solve this problem, is required to define an additional set of dependencies. They can be obtained if two landmarks are observed simultaneously, and the theorem of sines (13) is applied to a triangle with vertices in the position of the robot and these landmarks (Fig. 2):

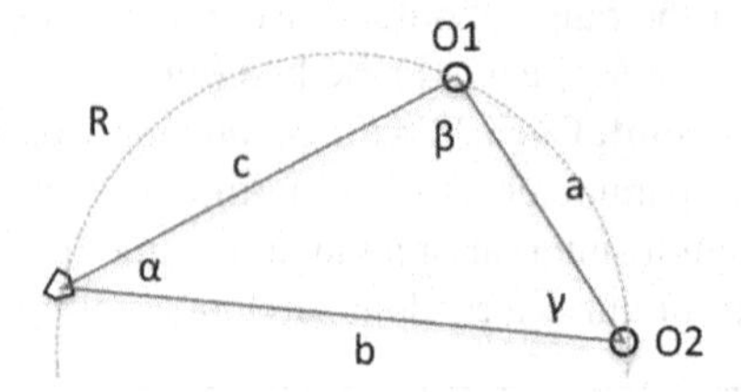

Fig. 2. A triangle formed by a robot and two landmarks

$$\frac{a}{\sin\alpha} = \frac{b}{\sin\beta} = \frac{c}{\sin\gamma} = 2R. \tag{13}$$

In Eq. (13), only the angle α (measurements of the robot), the distance a (the distance between the landmarks) is known. It helps calculate the radius of the circumscribed circle R, which is also an SD variable since angle α is also determined with some error (3):

$$^{*}R = \frac{\alpha + {}^{*}\Delta\alpha}{2a}.$$

Distances b and c are expressed in terms of the position of the robot, defined in terms of SD variables:

$$^{*}b = \sqrt{(X_{O1} - {}^{*}X)^2 + (Y_{O1} - {}^{*}Y)^2},$$

$$^{*}c = \sqrt{(X_{O2} - {}^{*}X)^2 + (Y_{O2} - {}^{*}Y)^2}.$$

It is also known that the sum of α, β and γ is equal to π. Then, if β and γ will be taken as SD variables, then following assignment functions can be written:

$$^{*}X = \sqrt{(2{}^{*}R\sin({}^{*}\beta))^2 - (Y_{O1} - {}^{*}Y)^2} + X_{O1}, \tag{14}$$

$$^{*}Y = \sqrt{(2{}^{*}R\sin({}^{*}\beta))^2 - (X_{O1} - {}^{*}X)^2} + Y_{O1}, \tag{15}$$

$$^{*}X = \sqrt{(2{}^{*}R\sin({}^{*}\gamma))^2 - (Y_{O2} - {}^{*}Y)^2} + X_{O2}, \tag{16}$$

$$^{*}Y = \sqrt{(2{}^{*}R\sin({}^{*}\gamma))^2 - (X_{O2} - {}^{*}X)^2} + Y_{O2}. \tag{17}$$

$$^{*}\beta = \pi - {}^{*}\gamma - (\alpha + {}^{*}\Delta\alpha),\ {}^{*}\gamma = \pi - {}^{*}\beta - (\alpha + {}^{*}\Delta\alpha), \tag{18}$$

$$^*\beta = \arcsin\left(\frac{^*b}{2^*R}\right), {}^*\gamma = \arcsin\left(\frac{^*c}{2^*R}\right). \quad (19)$$

Because functions (19) contain an arcsine, they generate the additional correctness checking functions, which requires under-sine expressions lay in interval $[-1, 1]$. This set of functions is applicable to each pair of landmarks; however, to reduce computations with a large number of landmarks, a limited number of pairs could be taken, choosing pairs based on some additional considerations, for example, pairs with the maximum value of α, pairs of landmarks that are maximally or minimally distant from the robot, or apart, etc.)

3.5 Combination with Histogram Filter

In general, the histogram filter splits the search area with a certain step and calculates the weight for each sub-area. The implementation of the histogram filter used in the work is presented by the algorithm **histogram_filter.**

The algorithm **histogram_filter** for localization by landmarks. The input are previous step grid G, landmarks data O, robot angle a, robot speed v and w, time interval dt, and mixture coefficient k. The output is a robot pose. The function **shift_grid** shifts the grid values by the movement of the robot, **blur_grid** performs a Gaussian blur of the grid, **empty_grid** initializes an empty grid of the specified size, **update_from_landmark** calculates the weights of the cells based on the landmark data using the formula (20), **norm_grid** normalizes the grid, **get_max_cell** returns the coordinates of the cell with the maximum weight.

```
1:     Algorithm histogram_filter(G, O, a, v, w, dt, k)
2:        Go = shift_grid(G, a, v, w, dt)
3:        Go = blur_grid(Go)
4:        Gn = empty_grid(sizeof(G))
5:        for o in O
6:           Gn = update_from_landmark(Gn, o)
7:        end for
8:        Gn = norm_grid(G)
9:        G = (1-k)Go + kGn
10:       G = norm_grid(G)
11:       x, y, j = get_max_cell(G)
12:    return x, y, j
```

It is important that in the problem under consideration, at each step, there are space constraints obtained using **SD localization** algorithm, and it is possible not to carry out calculations over the entire region with histogram filter. Then it is proposed to initialize a new filter at each step, which covers only the range of values of the obtained constraints. And in order to obtain greater smoothness of localization and to avoid jumps between values of similar weights, it is worth transferring to the filter the position of the robot obtained at the previous step and shifted by its movement.

The algorithm **SD_histogram_filter**, variation of histogram filters which works with output of **SD_localization** algorithm. The input are a set of SD variable V, landmarks data O, robot speed v and w, time interval dt, and previous robot pose xp, yp, θp. The output is a new robot pose. Functions **empty_grid**, **update_from_landmark**, **get_max_cell** are described in the algorithm **histogram_filter**, **motion_update** - displaces the position of the robot, taking into account its movement, **update_from_pose** - updates the grid weights according to the formula (20), **get_max_prob** - returns the maximum grid weight.

```
1:     Algorithm SD_histogram_filter(V, O, v, w, dt, xp,
yp, jp)
2:       xn, yn, jn = motion_update(xp, yp, jp, v, w,
dt)
3:       P = Ø
4:       for v in V
5:          G = empty_grid(sizeof(v))
6:          G = update_from_pose(xn, yn, jn)
7:          for O in o:
8:            G = update_from_landmark(o)
9:        end for
10:         x, y, j = get_max_cell(G)
11:         p = get_max_prob(G)
12:         P[p] = x, y, j
13:       end for
14:       x, y, j = max(P)
15:       return x, y, j
```

To calculate the cell weights in Algorithms 4 and 5, the normal distribution is used:

$$p(dx) = \frac{1}{\sqrt{2\pi}\sigma} e^{-\left(\frac{dx}{\sigma}\right)^2}, \tag{20}$$

applied to landmark distance and landmark angle errors:

$$dr_{ij} = r - \sqrt{(X_o - x_{ij})^2 + (Y_o - y_{ij})^2},$$

$$d\theta_{ij} = \theta - arctan\left(\frac{Y_o - y_{ij}}{X_o - x_{ij}}\right).$$

4 Experiments

To carry out numerical experiments, the algorithms presented in the work were implemented in python3. The histogram filter was implemented to find solutions in three-dimensional space (x, y, Θ) within a given constraints. Using the vectorization of the NumPy library has greatly reduced the computation time of the filter. In the tasks set, a histogram filter with a division of 0.2 m along the coordinate axes and 0.15 rad along the angular axes was used.

4.1 Simple Simulation

The primary performance was checked in a simple model written in python3 with visualization using the Matplotlib library. The robot moves at constant speeds (v = 0.1 m/s, w = 0.012 rad/s) in a space of 20 × 20 m. Three classical problems of determining the position by landmarks were simulated: 1) localization by camera, 2) localization of the format LBL (underwater acoustic localization variant), and 3) radio bearing localization. When localizing by camera, the robot determines the distance to landmarks and the angle to them in a certain sector. With LBL, the robot determines only the distances to landmarks, with radio bearing—only the angle to them. The robot received data only within the specified boundaries and with the addition of Gaussian noise (Table 1). Each experiment had its own set of assignment functions W.

Table 1. Simulation parameter summary

	$N_{landmark}$	r_{max}, m	α_{max}, rad	σ_r, m	σ_α, rad	W
Camera	100	5	$\pi/3$	0.1	0.01	(5–9)
LBL	15	15	π	0.1	–	(6, 7)
Radio Bearing	20	15	π	–	0.01	(5, 8, 9, 14–19)

Landmarks in the space of one experiment were placed randomly, one experiment consisted of 1,000 steps, where each step represented a half-second interval. The data obtained were simultaneously given to the histogram filter (the algorithm **histogram_filter**) applied to the entire area and to the proposed SD localization method (the algorithm **SD_localization**), followed by refinement with the histogram filter (the algorithm **SD_histogram_filter**). Each experiment for each typical task was repeated 10 times on a computer with an Intel Core i5–4670 3.4 Ghz processor.

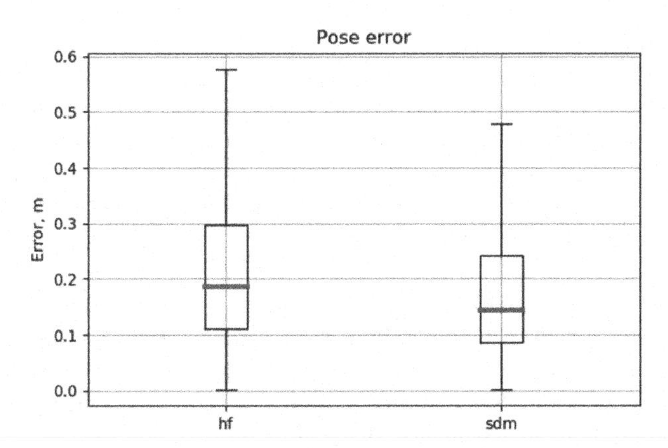

Fig. 3. A comparison of the error distribution in robot position determination in the localization by camera task

In the problem of localization by camera data, the proposed method of SD localization showed a slight increase in the accuracy in determining the position and angle; in Fig. 3, the distribution of the error is shown using boxplots. Hereinafter, the classic version of this diagram is used, where the dimensions of the rectangle show the first and third quartiles, the line inside the rectangle is the median, and the lines outside the rectangle are the interquartile range with 1.5 coefficient.

In terms of time, usage of SD localization also yielded a benefit. According to the diagram in Fig. 4, the unit step time for the SD localization (the whole step time divided by the number of visible landmarks) varies more than for the histogram filter. This is due to the fact that the computation process itself is iterative and ends when the condition of stopping is met.

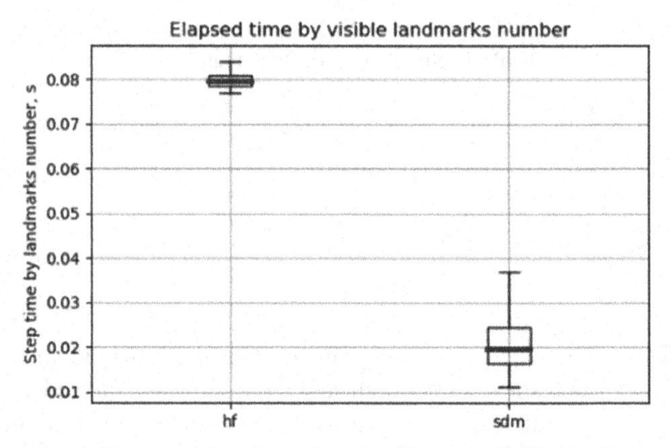

Fig. 4. A comparison of the execution time of an algorithm step divided by the number of visible landmarks in the localization by camera task

Figure 5 shows how the area of constraints decreases in relation to the number of visible landmarks. The area of constraints is obtained by multiplying the total lengths of the variables $^*X$ and $^*Y$ (2).

For the other two considered tasks, the summary of simulation is given in Table. 2. In the task that simulates the LBL underwater acoustic localization approach, an improvement in accuracy is also achieved over the histogram filter. For the LBL problem, the angle comparison was not carried out since it is impossible to determine it from distance data alone. At the same time, for this task, the histogram filter shows higher performance since, unlike in the other two tasks, it searches among two variables instead of three.

In the most difficult localization problem, based on bearing to landmarks, the proposed method also showed better mean of position determination, but was worse at angle determination. This can be explained by the fact that in the algorithm **histogram_filter**, in contrast to the algorithm **SD_histogram_filter**, the values from the previous step are taken into account with an asymmetric shape of their distributions.

Average temporal characteristics are lower for SD localization, however; one step is even more "blurred" in space than in other tasks because it depends not only on the

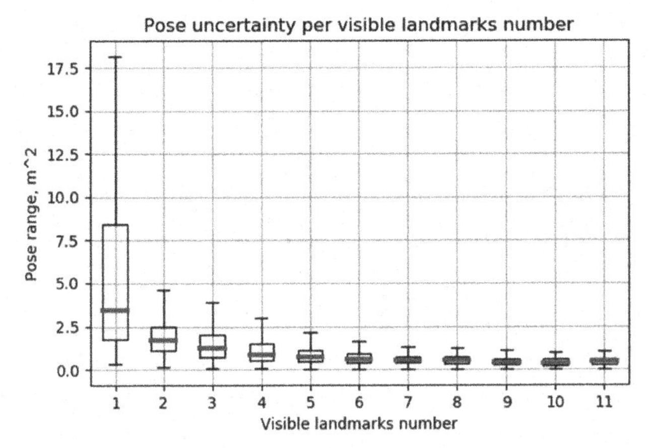

Fig. 5. A dependence of the distribution of the uncertainty region for the position in the localization by camera task

number of landmarks, but also on their relative position since landmarks with close angles to each other are ignored in terms of Eqs. (14–19).

Also, for localization by radio bearing, it is important to have at least three observable landmarks (Fig. 6) since two landmarks according to Fig. 2 form a circle of solutions.

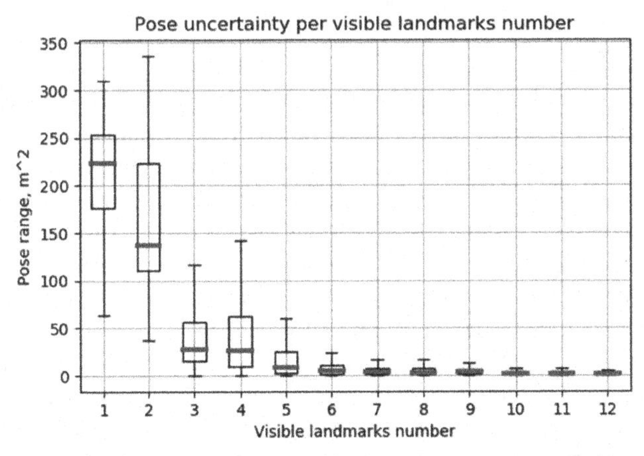

Fig. 6. A dependence of the distribution of the area of uncertainty for robot position from the number of visual landmarks in the localization by radio bearing task

The summary of the simulation of all tasks and some additional indicators for the SD localization method are presented in Table. 2. The best performance figures for each task are marked with bold type.

Table 2. Simulation results summary

Task	Camera		LBL		Radio Bearing	
Method	HF	SDL	HF	SDL	HF	SDL
Mean error of position determination, m	0.36	**0.2**	0.16	**0.11**	1.11	**0.6**
Standard error of position determination, m	0.8	**0.24**	0.32	**0.07**	2.25	**1.38**
Mean error of angle determination, rad	0.01	**0.006**	–	–	**0.001**	0.01
Standard error of angle determination, rad	0.33	**0.13**	–	–	0.3	**0.08**
Mean method step time, s	0.5	**0.12**	0.01	**0.06**	0.61	**0.55**
Standard error of method step time, s	0.21	**0.07**	**0.002**	0.02	**0.18**	0.25
The share of the actual position falling into the uncertainty area, %	–	100	–	99.99	–	96.99
Average size of the area of uncertainty of position, m^2	–	1.24	–	0.77	–	19.1
Average size of the area of uncertainty of angle, rad	–	0.32	–	–	–	0.34
Average ratio of the area of uncertainty to the entire area, %	–	0.04	–	0.19	–	2.24

4.2 Gazebo Simulation

To test the overall performance of the method under conditions closer to reality, experiments were carried out in the Gazebo (v. 11.) simulation environment. This environment represented a real robotic polygon. The implemented approach was designed as a node of the ROS Noetic framework. A model of the robot YARP-5 was used that had been initially created for research in the field of group and social [16] robotics. The robot was equipped with a camera and encoders and operated in an area with ArUco tags placed along the perimeter (Fig. 7 on the left). The problem of localization by camera was solved, similar to that described in the previous section.

The robot moved around the polygon using navigation mechanisms (Fig. 7 on the right), performing the task of finding objects that imitate food. The position localization error had the following values: median –0.18 m, first and third quartiles –0.14 and 0.26 m, angle error –0.005, –0.04, 0.06 rad, respectively. The average size of the uncertainty area was 0.28 m^2 and 0.15 rad, and on average, related to the entire area as 0.18%. The ratio of the number of visible landmarks to their total number is shown in Fig. 8, where it can be seen that the robot determined its position very steadily, starting from three landmarks. The area of the region of uncertainty averaged 0.008 m, which was lower than the desired step of the histogram filter, making it possible not to use it in such cases, but take the center of the region as the position of the robot.

Fig. 7. A gazebo model of the testing ground for the YARP-5 robot with ArUco tags (left) and the robot's route (right): in the filled dots, the robot made a full turn in place

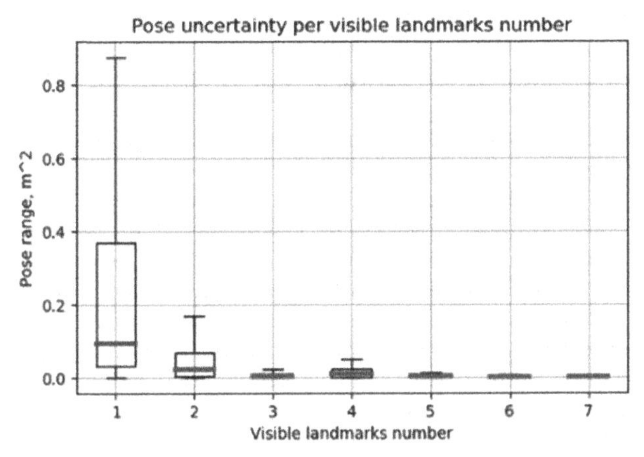

Fig. 8. A dependence of the distribution of the area of uncertainty for the position in the localization by camera task in the Gazebo environment

5 Conclusion

It was shown that the use of SD calculations in the localization by visual landmarks problem greatly reduces the area (Table 2), in which the search is carried out by probabilistic methods. Reducing the search area leads to a reduction in the total computation time of the algorithm. There was also an increase in localization accuracy compared to the classic histogram filter. Further research in this field will focus on the implementation of a particle filter that operates within the constraints obtained during SD-localization and testing the approaches on real YARP-5 robots. Another important issue requiring research and experimentation is the transition to a full-fledged three-dimensional localization of the robot with six degrees of freedom.

References

1. Su, X., et al.: A review of underwater localization techniques, algorithms, and challenges. J. Sensors **2020**, 1–24 (2020)
2. Betke, M., Gurvits, L.: Mobile robot localization using landmarks. Robot. Autom. IEEE Trans. **13**, 251–263 (1997)
3. Ebied, H., Witkowski, U., Abdel-wahab, M.: Robot Localization based on Visual Landmarks, vol. 2. Pp. 49–53 (2008)
4. Font, J.M., Batlle, J.A.: Mobile robot localization. revisiting the triangulation methods. IFAC Proc. **39**(15), 340–345 (2006)
5. Pierlot, V., Van Droogenbroeck, M.: A new three object triangulation algorithm for mobile robot positioning. IEEE Trans. Robot. **30**(3), 566–577 (2014)
6. Detweiler, C., et al.: Passive mobile robot localization within a fixed beacon field. Springer Tracts Adv. Robot. **47**. 425–440 (2008)
7. Thrun, S., Wolfram, B., Fox, D.: Probabilistic Robotics (Intelligent Robotics and Autonomous Agents). The MIT Press (2005)
8. Narin'yani, A.S., Subdefinite models: a big jump in knowledge processing technology. In: Proceedeings East-West Conference on AI: from theory to practice, EWAIC, vol. 93. pp. 7–9 (1993)
9. Нариньяни А.С. Введение в недоопределенность. Информационные технологии. 2007. № 4. P. 1–32.
10. Карпов В.Э. О некоторых особенностях применения недоопределенных моделей в робототехнике // Международная научно- практическая конференция «Интегрированные модели и мягкие вычисления в искусственном интеллекте» (28–30 мая 2009) Сб. научных трудов.Т.1. М.: Физматлит, pp. 520–532 (2009)
11. Ahmad, H., Namerikawa, T.: Extended Kalman filter-based mobile robot localization with intermittent measurements. Syst. Sci. Control Eng. Taylor & Francis **1**(1), 113–126 (2013)
12. Martinelli, F.: Robot localization: Comparable performance of EKF and UKF in some interesting indoor settings, In: 2008 Mediterranean Conference on Control and Automation - Conference Proceedings, MED'08, pp. 499–504 (2008)
13. Jonschkowski, R., Rastogi, D., Brock, O.: Differentiable Particle Filters: End-to-End Learning with Algorithmic Priors. Science and Systems (2018)
14. Jonschkowski, R., Brock, O.: End-to-End Learnable Histogram Filters. Computer Science (2017)
15. Telerman, V., Ushakov, D.: Data types in subdefinite models. In: Calmet, J., Campbell, J.A., Pfalzgraf, J. (eds.) Artificial Intelligence and Symbolic Mathematical Computation, pp. 305–319. Springer Berlin Heidelberg, Berlin, Heidelberg (1996). https://doi.org/10.1007/3-540-61732-9_65
16. Karpova, I., Karpov, V.: Some mechanisms for managing aggressive behavior in group robotics. In: 29th DAAAM International Symposium on Intelligent Manufacturing and Automation, Zadar, Croatia, EU, 24h-27th October 2018 (2018)

Enhancing Exploration Algorithms for Navigation with Visual SLAM

Kirill Muravyev[1,2](✉), Andrey Bokovoy[1], and Konstantin Yakovlev[1,2]

[1] Artificial Intelligence Research Institute, Federal Research Center for Computer Science and Control of Russian Academy of Sciences, Moscow, Russia
{bokovoy,yakovlev}@isa.ru

[2] Moscow Institute of Physics and Technology, Dolgoprudny, Russia

Abstract. Exploration is an important step in autonomous navigation of robotic systems. In this paper we introduce a series of enhancements for exploration algorithms in order to use them with vision-based simultaneous localization and mapping (vSLAM) methods. We evaluate developed approaches in photo-realistic simulator in two modes: with ground-truth depths and neural network reconstructed depth maps as vSLAM input. We evaluate standard metrics in order to estimate exploration coverage.

Keywords: Exploration · Vision-based simultaneous localization and mapping · Simulation · Robotics

1 Introduction

Making robotic systems fully autonomous is an important problem for modern researchers [6,12,20,25]. In order to operate autonomously, the system needs to know it's position on the map (environment). If the environment is unknown, the map is need to be built first. This step can be done by manually controlling the robotic system, however that's not always possible due to operating conditions, e.g. poor signal for remote control. So, one way of solving this problem is using Simultaneous Localization and Mapping (SLAM) with exploration algorithms.

SLAM algorithms are used to build the map of an unknown environment and retrieve robot's current position by utilizing different sensors. There are a lot of different sensors for SLAM to operate with, such as: GPS [5], lidar [9,14], inertia measurement unit (IMU) [19,27] and cameras [1,17]. The choice of the sensors is done considering the operating environment, robot's size or weight restrictions and etc.

In GPS-denied environment, popular sensor of choice is monocular camera. Modern monocular vSLAM algorithms use convolutional neural networks to reconstruct depth maps [3,26]. Those depth maps are suitable as an input for

---

This research was supported by the Ministry of Science and Higher Education of the Russian Federation, project No. 075-15-2020-799.

S. M. Kovalev et al. (Eds.): RCAI 2021, LNAI 12948, pp. 197–212, 2021.
https://doi.org/10.1007/978-3-030-86855-0_14

RGB-D vSLAM algorithms. However, these algorithms still suffer from problems that are common for all vSLAM algorithms: incorrect scale, localization errors during rotations without translation and poorly detailed environment.

The second important part of autonomous navigation is **exploration** [4,23]. At each step of localization and mapping the algorithms decide where robot needs to go in order to explore more unknown space and map it. Modern algorithms are versatile and usually work with 2D maps and poses (SLAM output). However, to increase the robustness of autonomous navigation with vision-based SLAM, we need to consider vSLAM problems in exploration algorithms. In this work we introduce such enhancements and evaluate them in photo-realistic simulated environment.

This paper is organized as follows: Sect. 2 describes current state of research in visual SLAM and autonomous exploration. Section 3 states the exploration problem formally. Section 4 describes proposed exploration pipeline detailly. Section 5 presents the experimental setup and the results of the experiments in both RGB-D and monocular modes. Section 6 concludes.

2 Related Work

Exploration is crucial for autonomous navigation in unknown environment, so there exists a vast variety of methods and algorithms aimed at solving this task. We focus on methods that work in conjunction with visual SLAM or work with visual sensors. This section gives brief overview.

In early works authors used known information about operating environment. For example, in [21] knowledge about geometric forms of floor, walls, ceiling and etc. is used in order to extract frontiers directly from the images. The goal point is chosen at the most informative place on the map based on the extracted information. In order to find the shortest path, Dijkstra's pathplanning algorithms is used. The algorithm is tested on real robot in indoor environment, so the developed visual servo control is applied in order to reach the destination. Regardless being able to solve small and medium-scale exploration tasks, this approach is applicable to indoor exploration only and not robust to environment changes and large scale exploration.

In [7] authors use exploration with graph-based stereo SLAM. However, in order to perform shortest pathplanning, local semi-continuous metric space is used in opposite to following the nodes of the graph. Authors also implemented visual odometry failure recovery in order to improve the final quality of the localization and exploration. The algorithm is able to navigate autonomously for 30 min (limited by robot's battery) in real indoor environment.

Another approach that utilizes monocular vSLAM is presented in [24]. Semi-dense LSD-SLAM [10] algorithm is used for mapping and localization of micro aerial vehicle (MAV). As an exploration algorithm authors introduce star discovery. This approach is used in order to overcome the visual odometry drift and errors during rotation without motion (common problem for monocular vSLAM). The exploration algorithm is pretty straightforward: MAV performs star discovery on spot, then the farthest point on the frontier in line of sight is chosen as a new star discovery point, then the robot proceeds to this point. This approach require a lot of free space in order to perform a star rotation. That limits the application area of this algorithm drastically.

More recent approach [11] introduces an enhancement to frontier search by making use of heading information and coarse graph representation of the map in order to improve map coverage and reduce time of exploration. The algorithm is tested on wheeled robot platform. Authors report that the robot were able to explore large office ($250\,\mathrm{m}^2$) with different obstacles in 7 min. Regardless this algorithm originally works with laser scanner only, the introduced approach can be adopted for vSLAM autonomous exploration.

3 Problem Statement

The exploration problem that we consider is described as follows. A robot equipped with only visual sensors (monocular, stereo or RGB-D camera) is located in unknown environment of restricted area (usually indoor space). Its task is to construct a 2D map of whole environment while moving through it.

At each step t, a robot is given by observation I_t - an image from its camera. Using this observation, exploration algorithm tracks its location, maps information from the observation and decides where to move to explore and map new space. The output of the algorithm A at step t is M_t - a map of explored part of environment, and an action a_t - an intention to move somewhere:

$$A(I_t, M_{t-1}) = (M_t, a_t)$$

A map is represented as 2D matrix and consists of free, occupied and unexplored cells. Each cell of this matrix represents a small square of fixed size (e.g. 5×5 cm). The matrix is also provided with position of its top-left corner in global coordinate system. At initial step, the map is an empty matrix.

$$M_t = (P_t \in \{0, 1, -1\}^{H \times W}; (x_t, y_t) \in \mathbb{R}^2); \quad M_0 = (\emptyset; (0, 0))$$

An action is represented as a robot pose shift:

$$a_t = (dx, dy, \delta)$$

It is the command for robot "move on distance (dx, dy) (relatively to its current position) and rotate by angle δ". To simplify our model, we consider only four possible actions: move forward ($a_t = (dx, 0, 0)$), turn left ($a_t = (0, 0, \delta)$), turn right ($a_t = (0, 0, -\delta)$), and remain on the spot ($a_t = (0, 0, 0)$).

To measure exploration efficiency, absolute and relative coverage metric are commonly used. The value of the absolute metric is the area of explored map at certain time steps t. The value of the relative metric is the percentage of environment space that has been explored at certain time steps t:

$$C_{abs} = \{|(i,j) : M_t^{i,j} \geq 0|\}, t \in T \tag{1}$$

$$C_{rel} = \{\frac{|(i,j) : M_t^{i,j} \geq 0|}{|(i,j) : M^{i,j} \geq 0|}\}, t \in T \tag{2}$$

where M is ground-truth map of the whole environment.

4 Method Overview

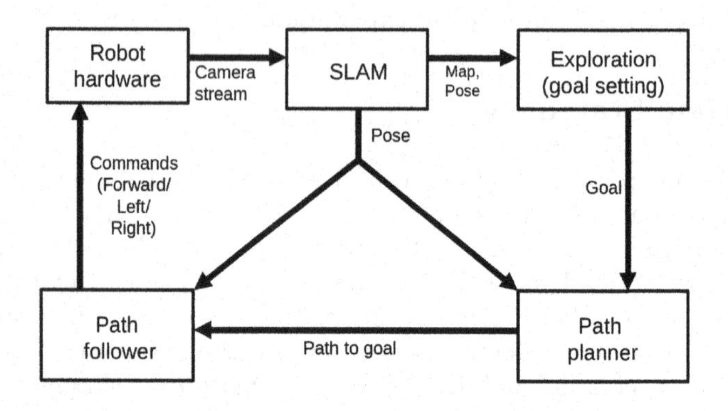

Fig. 1. A scheme of proposed exploration pipeline

We propose fully autonomous exploration pipeline for robots equipped with visual sensors. Our pipeline consists of four parts:

- **SLAM** module takes data from robot's camera and estimates its trajectory and 2D map of environment simultaneously in real time
- **Exploration** module takes current estimated robot position and SLAM-builded map, and chooses goal where the robot should go
- **Path planning** module builds path from robot to goal position in SLAM-produced map
- **Path following** module takes current robot position and path to goal and sets low-level commands to robot's controller: where to move now - forward, left, or right

To simplify implementation on real robots and interaction between modules, we integrate our pipeline with Robot Operation System (ROS)[1]. Full scheme of the pipeline is shown at Fig. 1.

[1] http://www.ros.org.

4.1 SLAM

We chose RTAB-MAP algorithm [16] to perform real-time simultaneous localization and mapping. Our choice is motivated by RTAB-MAP has open-source ROS implementation[2] and has wide range of adjustable parameters. It takes stereo or RGB-D images as input and outputs robot's trajectory and map of environment in both 2D and 3D. Trajectory is stored as a set of 6 DoF poses, 2D map is stored as occupancy grid (a matrix of free, occupied and unknown cells), and 3D map is stored as point cloud.

Off-the-shelf RTAB-MAP algorithm works only with stereo or RGB-D input. To run it in monocular mode, we use fully-convolutional neural network (FCNN) like [3] to predict depth of images from camera. Experiments conducted in work [2] show that RTAB-MAP with CNN-predicted depths is able to successfully build a map of indoor scene in most of cases. Average absolute mapping error was about 0.7 m, and most of it was the scale error. After scale correction, average error reduced to 0.3 m.

4.2 Exploration: Base Version

Fig. 2. An example of frontier-based exploration work. The black area are occupied map cells, white area are free map cells, blue lines are frontiers, red arrow is robot's pose, and large yellow arrow is the goal chosen by exploration. Green rounds represent cost of frontiers – the bigger round, the more profitable the frontier (Color figure online)

[2] http://wiki.ros.org/rtabmap_ros.

For goal setting, we use frontier-based exploration algorithm [15] based on `explore_lite` ROS package[3]. The algorithm from this package looks for frontiers between free and unknown space on 2D SLAM-builded map. To find these frontiers, breadth first search (BFS) in map cell neighborhood graph is used. A centroid of the most "profitable" frontier is marked as goal for robot. An example of frontiers and goal is shown at Fig. 2.

Lets describe goal search formally. Let $p \in \mathbb{R}^2$ be current robot position and $F_1, \ldots, F_N$ be frontiers found by BFS. Each frontier is represented as set of points on 2D map:

$$F_i = \{f_{i,1}, \ldots, f_{i,n_i}\};\ f_{i,j} \in \mathbb{R}^2,\ j = 1, \ldots, n_i$$

A frontier looks like a chain of cells on occupancy map, i.e. points $f_{i,j}$ and $f_{i,j+1}$ are located in neighbor map cells. Centroid of a frontier is geometrical mean of all its points:

$$centr_i = \frac{1}{n_i} \sum_{j=1}^{n_i} f_{i,j}$$

Frontier cost is a combination of its breadth (i.e. its size in cells) and distance from robot position to it:

$$cost_i = \alpha ||centr_i - p||_2 - \beta n_i \tag{3}$$

Breadth is added to cost function with sign "-" because broader frontiers are usually more useful for exploration: the broader frontier is, the more new space we may explore beyond it.

The resultant goal is the centroid of frontier with lowest cost:

$$goal = centr_{\arg\min_i cost_i} \tag{4}$$

The described cost function has significant drawbacks. First, the distance between robot and frontier is measured without obstacle map in mind. So, the path to lowest-cost frontier may be very long that may lead to large exploration time. Second, this cost function does not consider robot's orientation. In context of visual SLAM, large on-the-spot turns may cause localization fails, so the angle that robot should turn is also critically important. To eliminate these drawbacks, we modify the cost function and introduced some other enhancements into exploration algorithm. The proposed enhancements are described below.

4.3 Exploration: Our Enhancements

To increase stability and speed of exploration and adapt it to vision-based SLAM methods, we made some enhancements into `explore_lite` algorithm.

[3] http://wiki.ros.org/explore_lite.

First, we changed cost function of frontiers. Instead of euclidean distance between robot and frontier, we used length of robot-frontier path in 2D occupancy map. Also we added orientation - the angle between robot's direction and direction from robot to frontier (i.e. how much should robot turn before it starts moving to the frontier). Our cost estimation formula may be written as follows:

Let $q \in \mathbb{R}^2$ be robot orientation vector, and $\pi = (p_0, p_1, \ldots, p_k)$ be path from robot to centroid of i-th frontier of size n_i. In path π, p_0 is the robot position, and p_k is the centroid of $i - th$ frontier. Our cost function is

$$cost_i = \alpha \sum_{j=0}^{k} ||p_{j+1} - p_j||_2 - \beta n_i + \gamma |\angle(q, p_1 - p_0)| \tag{5}$$

where α is coefficient for path length, β is coefficient for frontier size, and γ is coefficient for turn angle between robot orientation and direction to frontier.

Second, we added some post-processing of SLAM-builded map. We noticed that map constructed by visual SLAM method may contain small fake gaps in obstacles caused by occlusions or low camera resolution. In this case, path planner may find invalid path to goal. So we reduced map resolution from default 0.05 m to 0.1 m. We performed it by max pooling method with cell type order "unknown < free < occupied". Additionally, we expanded all the obstacles by 1 cell (marked all cells near obstacles as occupied cells).

Also we added a kind of "bump detector" into our exploration algorithm. When path follower sends command "move forward" to robot, and SLAM tracks no forward motion for certain time (e.g. 1 s), we mark map cell ahead robot position as occupied. This trick lets robot not to stuck before invisible obstacle (e.g. small box on the floor in case of tall robot).

Described map post-processing let us significantly decrease amount of fake gaps and non-traversable paths suggested by planner. That makes exploration faster and more stable.

4.4 Path Planner

For path planning from robot to goal, we use Theta* algorithm [18]. This algorithm has high computational efficiency and supports any-angle paths. So, Theta* paths on occupancy grid are shorter and much smoother than paths of traditional algorithms like Dijkstra [8] or A* [13] (see Fig. 3). The path smoothness is critically important for visual SLAM systems because sharp movements may make vSLAM unstable.

The path planner takes post-processed occupancy map, robot and goal positions, and outputs sequence of points that represents robot-goal path. Each point of this sequence is located in free map cell, and each segment between two neighbor points passes through free cells. To track map and pose updates, re-planning is launched with fixed frequency, 5 Hz.

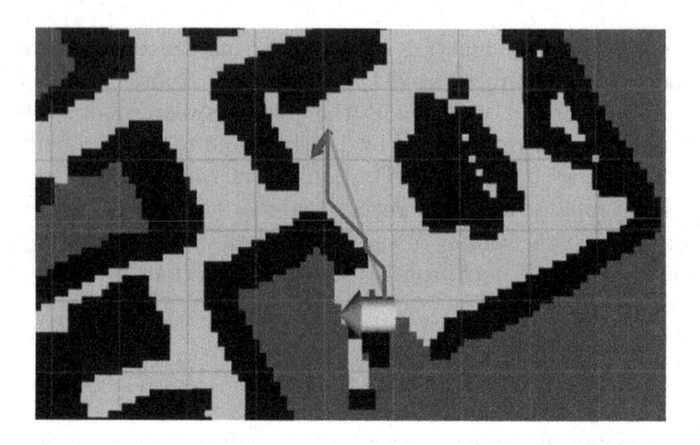

Fig. 3. An example of A* path (red) and Theta* path (green) (Color figure online)

4.5 Path Follower

To move robot along proposed path, we use simple and straightforward algorithm. We compare robot orientation and direction from robot pose to the next point of the path. If the angle between robot orientation and direction to path point is under some threshold (e.g. less than 5° in absolute value), we move robot forward. If it is above the threshold and is negative, we turn robot left. If it is above the threshold and is positive, we turn robot right.

To increase speed and stability of exploration, we also use some heuristics in path follower. First, at start of exploration, the follower sends only "turn left" command until robot rotates 360°. The "look around" makes exploration faster and sometimes more stable.

Second, in case of vSLAM tracking loss, we launch the following program: rotate 180° left, move a bit forward, and rotate 180° left again. This trick helps robot to return into place stored in SLAM's memory and restore SLAM tracking.

5 Experiments

5.1 Experimental Setup

We evaluated our pipeline in both RGB-D and monocular modes. In RGB-D mode, images and precise depths from simulator were sent as input for the SLAM module. In monocular mode, a fully-convolutional neural network (FCNN) was used to estimate depth maps from images. Images with these FCNN-predicted depths were sent as input for SLAM.

We evaluated our exploration pipeline in photo-realistic indoor environment of Habitat simulator [22]. For our experiments we used scenes of Gibson dataset [28]. This dataset was collected in real indoor environments with high-

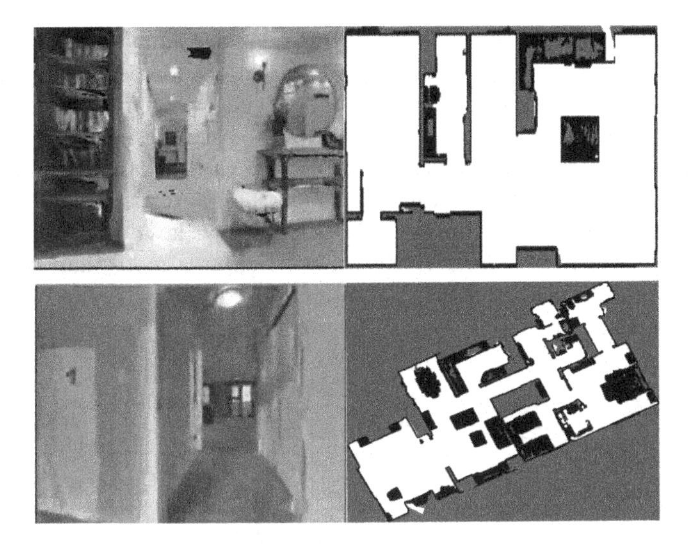

Fig. 4. Images and maps of some scenes of Gibson dataset

precision Matterport camera[4] and accurate algorithmic post-processing. That let us receive realistic image and precise depth map from each point of scene.

Gibson dataset contains about 500 scenes. Most of them are apartments or living houses. Many scenes have defects like gaps in textures that may cause exploration fails and incorrect quality estimation. Also, many scenes have several floors, so 2D SLAM does not work on them. Therefore we selected only 31 scenes for our experiments – the scenes without stairs and texture defects. Area of selected scenes varied from 28 to 251 m^2. An example of images and maps of these scenes is shown in Fig. 4.

To measure exploration efficiency, we used coverage metric - the area of map space explored at certain time. We measured both absolute and relative area. The area values were measured for different time from start – from 15 s to 240 s.

Another efficiency metric that we computed was the number of scenes where exploration was finished in 240 s, and average finish time on these scenes. We considered exploration as finished when explored area was more than 95% of total scene area.

Also we counted number of SLAM tracking losses over all the scenes to measure exploration stability.

5.2 Results with RGB-D Input

For broad evaluation of the whole exploration pipeline and our enhancements in RGB-D mode, we carried out a set of experiments on selected scenes with precise depths at SLAM module input. First, we tested our pipeline with unchanged

[4] https://matterport.com/.

`explore_lite` algorithm as exploration module. Second, we added a "bump detector" and tested our pipeline again. Next, we added obstacle expanding into map post-processing to test its effect. And finally, we included the last our enhancement - added orientation coefficient into cost function. To make metric values more stable, we launched exploration with each enhancement 5 times on all scenes, and averaged metric values through these 5 tests.

To examine behaviour of our exploration in both large and small environments, we selected 13 relatively large scenes (with area more than 60 m^2), and 18 scenes with area under 60 m^2. We estimated coverage metrics on large and small scenes separately.

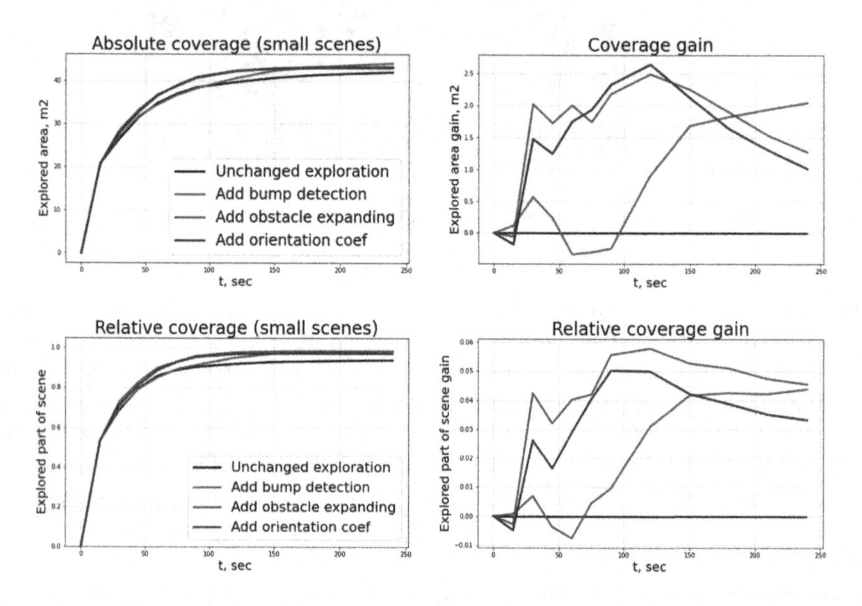

Fig. 5. Coverage of exploration on small scenes: top left – absolute coverage values, top right - absolute coverage gain (compared to unchanged `explore_lite` algorithm, bottom left – coverage relative to total scene area, bottom right – gain of relative coverage (compared to unchanged `explore_lite` algorithm)

The coverage results on small scenes are shown at Fig. 5. At full experiment time (240 s), unchanged `explore_lite` algorithm covered about 94% of scene area at average. With adding bump detection, 240-s covered area increased to about 97%. Obstacle expanding and orientation coefficient had no significant effect to total covered area, but had significant positive effect to exploration speed - the area covered in 90 s increased from 91% to 96%.

The coverage values for exploration on large scenes are shown at Fig. 6. Differences at large scenes were more noticeable than on small ones (see for example Fig. 7). With unchanged exploration, total covered area was at average 78% in relative value and 85 m^2 in absolute value. With adding an imitation of "bump detector", the covered area increased to 80% and 86 m^2 respectfully. With adding

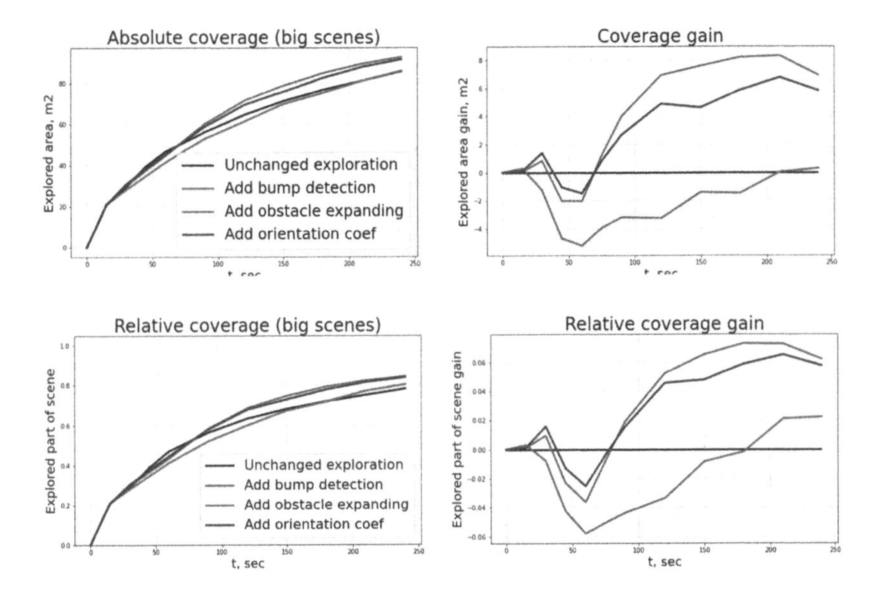

Fig. 6. Coverage of exploration on large scenes: top left – absolute coverage values, top right – absolute coverage gain (compared to unchanged `explore_lite` algorithm, bottom left - coverage relative to total scene area, bottom right – gain of relative coverage (compared to unchanged `explore_lite` algorithm

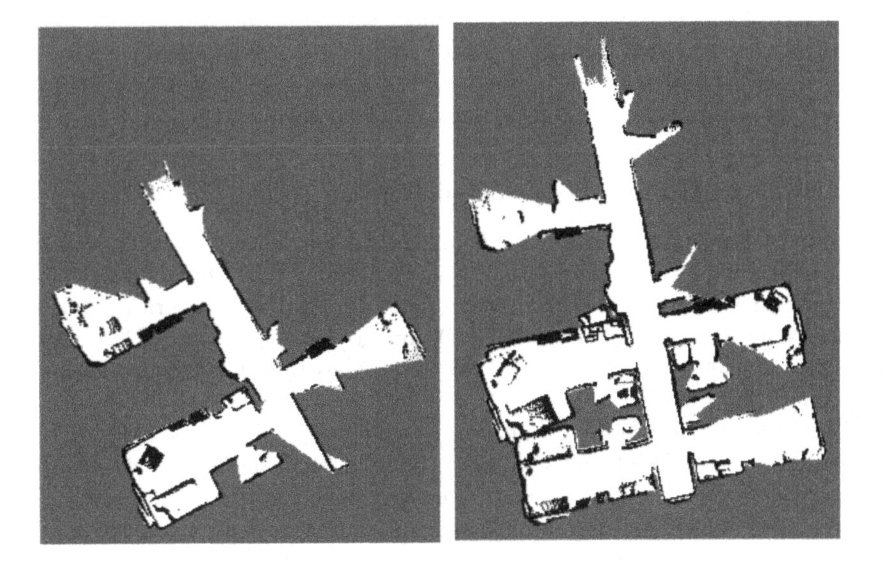

Fig. 7. Maps builded by SLAM during 240 s of exploration on a large scene. Left – with unchanged exploration, right – with all our enhancements

obstacle expanding, the coverage increased to 84% and 92.5 m^2. But adding orientation coefficient made no progress in coverage - explored area remained at level of 84%.

Table 1. Stability and efficiency metric values for exploration with different enhancements

Enhancement	N of SLAM losses	N of finished scenes	Avg. finish time, s
No	14.2	21.6	213
Bump detection	13.8	21.75	205
Obstacle expanding	10.0	23.4	165
Orientation coef	10.4	23.2	157

The results of SLAM stability and exploration efficiency evaluation are shown in Table 1. Bump detection and obstacle expanding had great positive effect to all of the metrics. Adding orientation coefficient to cost function did not influence SLAM stability, but reduced a bit average finish time - from 165 s to 157 s. Such weak effect of orientation coefficient may be probably caused by large amount of "dead ends" in scenes selected for evaluation. So, robot had to turn around many times in these dead ends regardless of frontier cost function. This hypothesis may be checked by experiments on large scenes with spacious rooms.

Overall, proposed enhancements of exploration algorithm improved quality for all of estimated metrics. With introduction of a kind of "bump detector", obstacle expanding, and orientation coefficient of cost-function, average part of explored area increased by 3% on small scenes and 6% on large scenes. Also these enhancements reduced number of SLAM losses by almost 1.5 times and reduced average exploration finish time from 213 s to 157 s.

5.3 Results with FCNN-predicted Depths

To examine our pipeline in monocular mode, we carried out some experiments on selected scenes. We used pre-trained network from [3] for depth prediction. To adapt this network to simulated environment and Habitat camera parameters, we fine-tuned it on approximately 38000 image-depth pairs from 25 scenes of our selected collection. The other 6 selected scenes were used for evaluation of the exploration pipeline.

The experiments showed that our exploration pipeline is able to work autonomously and build plausible map (see Fig. 8) in monocular mode. However, errors in neural depth estimation caused some errors in constructed map. For example, a narrow doorways sometimes were mapped as continuous wall (see Fig. 9). Due to such inaccurate mapping, the planner could not find paths to far goals, and exploration algorithm explored only part of scene area. Coverage metric values are shown in Fig. 10. Average explored part of area reached 44% (compared to 77% with exploration in RGB-D mode).

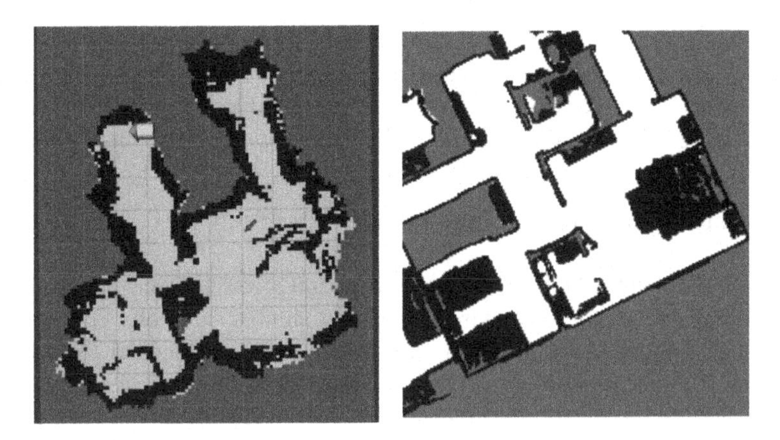

Fig. 8. An example of map constructed during exploration with FCNN depths (left) compared to ground-truth map (right)

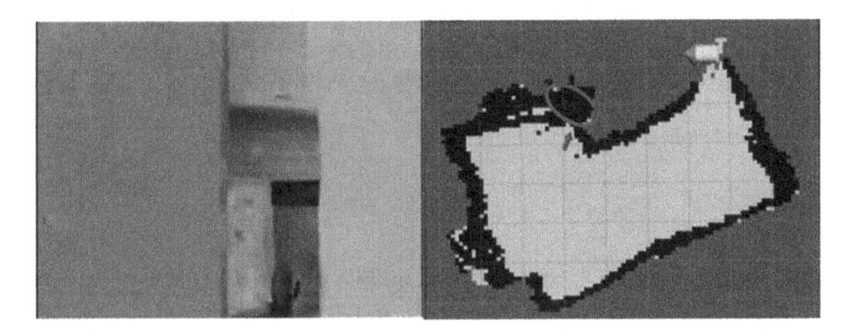

Fig. 9. Example of inaccurate mapping with FCNN-predicted depths. On the camera view (left part of picture), small doorway is observed. But on the map (right part of the picture), the doorway is marked as a wall (see red ellipsis) (Color figure online)

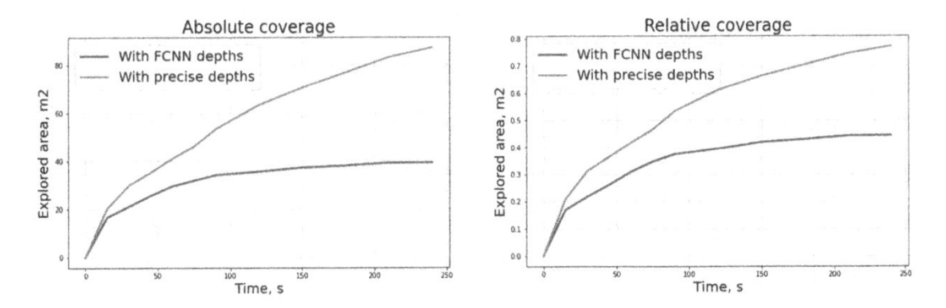

Fig. 10. Comparison of exploration with FCNN-predicted depths and exploration with precise depths: absolute coverage (left), and relative scene coverage (right)

Overall, our tests showed that proposed exploration pipeline is able to work in monocular mode with neural depth estimation, but inaccurate depth prediction may lead to mapping errors and incomplete area coverage. These errors may be eliminated with more thorough neural network fine-tuning and fine adjustment of SLAM parameters. A video with demonstration of exploration with our enhancements and FCNN-predicted depths is available at https://drive.google.com/file/d/1QJWmjR9Y2VWbycZVwz3Y6Dl9Rzkp-zjB/view?usp=sharing.

6 Conclusion and Future Work

We introduced novel enhancements to exploration algorithm and evaluated them in photo-realistic simulated environment. We showed that our enhancements increase the area of the explored space, reduce the time needed for full scene exploration and reduce number of tracking losses with vSLAM operating ground-truth depth map. We also tested our approach in monocular mode, with FCNN-predicted depth maps. The results show that the exploration algorithm with our enhancements is able to explore about a half of environment in monocular mode.

In future we plan to carry out more research into monocular vSLAM to increase its accuracy and exploration coverage. Possible ways of increasing vSLAM quality are usage of novel time-consistent FCNN architectures, global depth correction with geometric methods, and thorough vSLAM map post-processing.

References

1. Asadi, K., et al.: Vision-based integrated mobile robotic system for real-time applications in construction. Autom. Constr. **96**, 470–482 (2018)
2. Bokovoy, A., Muraviev, K., Yakovlev, K.: Map-merging algorithms for visual SLAM: feasibility study and empirical evaluation. In: Kuznetsov, S.O., Panov, A.I., Yakovlev, K.S. (eds.) RCAI 2020. LNCS (LNAI), vol. 12412, pp. 46–60. Springer, Cham (2020). https://doi.org/10.1007/978-3-030-59535-7_4
3. Bokovoy, A., Muravyev, K., Yakovlev, K.: Real-time vision-based depth reconstruction with nvidia jetson. In: 2019 European Conference on Mobile Robots (ECMR), pp. 1–6. IEEE (2019)
4. Burgard, W., Moors, M., Fox, D., Simmons, R., Thrun, S.: Collaborative multi-robot exploration. In: Proceedings 2000 ICRA. Millennium Conference. IEEE International Conference on Robotics and Automation. Symposia Proceedings (Cat. No. 00CH37065), vol. 1, pp. 476–481. IEEE (2000)
5. Burschka, D., Hager, G.D.: V-GPS (slam): vision-based inertial system for mobile robots. In: IEEE International Conference on Robotics and Automation, 2004. Proceedings, ICRA 2004, 2004, vol. 1, pp. 409–415. IEEE (2004)
6. Choi, J., Park, J., Jung, J., Lee, Y., Choi, H.T.: Development of an autonomous surface vehicle and performance evaluation of autonomous navigation technologies. Int. J. Control Autom. Syst. **18**(3), 535–545 (2020)
7. Dayoub, F., Morris, T., Upcroft, B., Corke, P.: Vision-only autonomous navigation using topometric maps. In: 2013 IEEE/RSJ International Conference on Intelligent Robots and Systems, pp. 1923–1929. IEEE (2013)
8. Dijkstra, E.W., et al.: A note on two problems in connexion with graphs. Numerische mathematik **1**(1), 269–271 (1959)

9. Droeschel, D., Behnke, S.: Efficient continuous-time slam for 3D lidar-based online mapping. In: 2018 IEEE International Conference on Robotics and Automation (ICRA), pp. 5000–5007. IEEE (2018)
10. Engel, J., Schöps, T., Cremers, D.: LSD-SLAM: large-scale direct monocular SLAM. In: Fleet, D., Pajdla, T., Schiele, B., Tuytelaars, T. (eds.) ECCV 2014. LNCS, vol. 8690, pp. 834–849. Springer, Cham (2014). https://doi.org/10.1007/978-3-319-10605-2_54
11. Gao, W., Booker, M., Adiwahono, A., Yuan, M., Wang, J., Yun, Y.W.: An improved frontier-based approach for autonomous exploration. In: 2018 15th International Conference on Control, Automation, Robotics and Vision (ICARCV), pp. 292–297. IEEE (2018)
12. Gonzalez, A.G., Alves, M.V., Viana, G.S., Carvalho, L.K., Basilio, J.C.: Supervisory control-based navigation architecture: a new framework for autonomous robots in industry 4.0 environments. IEEE Trans. Ind. Inf. **14**(4), 1732–1743 (2017)
13. Hart, P.E., Nilsson, N.J., Raphael, B.: A formal basis for the heuristic determination of minimum cost paths. IEEE Trans. Syst. Sci. Cybern. **4**(2), 100–107 (1968)
14. Hening, S., Ippolito, C.A., Krishnakumar, K.S., Stepanyan, V., Teodorescu, M.: 3D LiDAR SLAM integration with GPS/INS for UAVS in urban GPS-degraded environments. In: AIAA Information Systems-AIAA Infotech@ Aerospace, p. 0448 (2017)
15. Hörner, J.: Map-merging for multi-robot system (2016). https://is.cuni.cz/webapps/zzp/detail/174125/
16. Labbé, M., Michaud, F.: RTAB-Map as an open-source lidar and visual simultaneous localization and mapping library for large-scale and long-term online operation. J. Field Robot. **36**(2), 416–446 (2019)
17. Lemaire, T., Berger, C., Jung, I.K., Lacroix, S.: Vision-based slam: stereo and monocular approaches. Int. J. Comput. Vis. **74**(3), 343–364 (2007)
18. Nash, A., Daniel, K., Koenig, S., Felner, A.: Theta ∧*: any-angle path planning on grids. AAAI. **7**, 1177–1183 (2007)
19. Nützi, G., Weiss, S., Scaramuzza, D., Siegwart, R.: Fusion of IMU and vision for absolute scale estimation in monocular slam. J. Intell. Robot. Syst. **61**(1), 287–299 (2011)
20. Papachristos, C., Khattak, S., Mascarich, F., Alexis, K.: Autonomous navigation and mapping in underground mines using aerial robots. In: 2019 IEEE Aerospace Conference, pp. 1–8. IEEE (2019)
21. Santosh, D., Achar, S., Jawahar, C.: Autonomous image-based exploration for mobile robot navigation. In: 2008 IEEE International Conference on Robotics and Automation, pp. 2717–2722. IEEE (2008)
22. Savva, M., et al.: Habitat: a platform for embodied AI research. In: Proceedings of the IEEE/CVF International Conference on Computer Vision, pp. 9339–9347 (2019)
23. Sim, R., Roy, N.: Global a-optimal robot exploration in slam. In: Proceedings of the 2005 IEEE International Conference on Robotics and Automation, pp. 661–666. IEEE (2005)
24. von Stumberg, L., Usenko, V., Engel, J., Stückler, J., Cremers, D.: Autonomous exploration with a low-cost quadrocopter using semi-dense monocular slam. arXiv preprint arXiv:1609.07835 (2016)
25. Tang, L., Wang, Y., Ding, X., Yin, H., Xiong, R., Huang, S.: Topological local-metric framework for mobile robots navigation: a long term perspective. Auton. Robots **43**(1), 197–211 (2019)

26. Tateno, K., Tombari, F., Laina, I., Navab, N.: CNN-SLAM: real-time dense monocular slam with learned depth prediction. In: Proceedings of the IEEE Conference on Computer Vision and Pattern Recognition, pp. 6243–6252 (2017)
27. Vidal, A.R., Rebecq, H., Horstschaefer, T., Scaramuzza, D.: Ultimate slam? Combining events, images, and IMU for robust visual slam in HDR and high-speed scenarios. IEEE Robot. Autom. Lett. **3**(2), 994–1001 (2018)
28. Xia, F., Zamir, A.R., He, Z., Sax, A., Malik, J., Savarese, S.: Gibson env: real-world perception for embodied agents. In: Proceedings of the IEEE Conference on Computer Vision and Pattern Recognition, pp. 9068–9079 (2018)

Natural Language Processing

Relying on Discourse Trees to Extract Medical Ontologies from Text

Boris Galitsky[1], Dmitry Ilvovsky[2], and Elizaveta Goncharova[2](✉)

[1] Oracle Inc., Redwood Shores, Redwood City, CA, USA
boris.galitsky@oracle.com
[2] National Research University Higher School of Economics, Moscow, Russia
{dilvovsky,egoncharova}@hse.ru

Abstract. We explore the role of discourse analysis in ontology construction. While extracting candidate phrases to form ontology entries from text, it is important to pay attention to which discourse units these phrases occur in. It turns out that not all discourse units are equal in terms of their contribution to forming ontology entries. We survey text mining and ontology information extraction techniques in medical domain and select the ones where advanced linguistic analysis including the discourse level is leveraged the most to produce a robust and efficient ontology. We evaluate the consistency of the resultant ontology and its role in assuring high search relevance using several real-life medical datasets and prove the importance of introducing discourse information into the ontology construction.

Keywords: Medical ontology · Discourse analysis · Text mining · Question answering

1 Introduction

Building and adapting medical ontologies is a complex task that requires substantial human effort and close collaboration between domain experts (e.g. health professionals) and knowledge engineers. Even if automatic ontology construction techniques are mature enough to support this task [22], they provide only partial solutions, and manual interventions from healthcare professionals will always be necessary if high quality is expected. The use of ontologies in medicine is mainly focused on the representation of medical terminologies. Healthcare professionals use them to represent knowledge about symptoms and treatments of diseases. Pharmaceutical enterprises use ontologies to represent information about drugs, dosages, and allergies.

Ontologies are a foundation for numerous Decision Support Systems (DSS) used to support medical activities; therefore, the quality of the underlying ontologies affects the performance of DSSs that rely on them. In consequence, automatically-built medical ontologies (including schema knowledge and individuals descriptions) must be validated by domain experts. However, healthcare professionals are usually not fluent in ontology management and must be

S. M. Kovalev et al. (Eds.): RCAI 2021, LNAI 12948, pp. 215–231, 2021.
https://doi.org/10.1007/978-3-030-86855-0_15

assisted by knowledge engineers during the validation process, which can potentially extend errors and inconsistencies.

Extracting medical or clinical information from health records, which contain important items such as eligibility criteria, a summary of diagnosing results, and prescribed drugs, is an important task, especially with the adoption of electronic health records (EHR). These records are normally stored as free-form text documents and contain valuable unstructured information that is essential for better decision-making for a patient's treatment. Gaining insight from a tremendous amount of unstructured clinical data has been a critical and challenging issue for medical organizations. Having an automated system that is able to read patients' medical reports, extract medical entities, and analyze the extracted data is not only desirable but also a necessary component of medical organizations' routine. The challenging part of this task is how to extract and encode the unstructured data to improve an overall healthcare system.

Information extraction (IE) and text mining (TM) is a potentially suitable technique here. There are three major elements that should be extracted from these clinical records: entities, attributes, and relations between them [20]. Automatic recognition of medical entities in the unstructured text is a key component of biomedical information retrieval systems. Its applications include analysis of unstructured medical text, such as the one presented in EHR [2] or obtained from the medical social networks, and knowledge discovery from biomedical literature [15]. The extracted medical terminologies are often structured as ontologies, with the relations connecting the entities and a list of synonyms for each term.

Ontologies are a critical component for these tasks, and the quality and consistency of an ontology automatically extracted from text determine the overall DSS accuracy. The bottleneck of building concise, robust, and complete ontologies is the lack of a mechanism to extract ontology entries from reliable, authoritative parts of documents. Building ontologies, one needs to use reliable text fragments expressing the central point of a text and avoid constructing entries from additional comments, clarifications, examples, instances, and other less significant parts of the text. To overcome this challenge, we rely on discourse analysis (that has been proven useful for a number of natural language processing tasks, such as argumentation mining [13], text classification [12], and summarization [33]) to select discourse units that yield relevant ontology entries. In this paper, we present the ontology construction system that consists of several text mining blocks significant for providing efficient and complete medical ontology.

The paper is organized as follows. The first section is devoted to reviewing existing techniques for ontology construction and their limitation. Then the discourse structure, which is introduced to overcome these limitations, is defined and explained. Section 3 shows the overall system architecture for the ontology construction, which is followed by a more detailed description of the main system's components (Sects. 4–7). In Sect. 8, we provide the experiment scenarios and analyze the obtained results. We conclude in Sect. 9.

2 Related Work

2.1 Ontology Extraction in Medical Domain

Usually, an ontology presents the information as the sets of entities bound by a relation [4]. Information presented in this format is useful for many applications (mining biomedical text, ontology learning, and question answering). Ontologies structure knowledge as a set of terms with edges between them labeled by the type of relation to evoke meaningful information.

Retrieving relevant phrases that can be considered as an ontology entry is a critical component in medical ontologies construction. Initially, rule-based methods that apply lexical or syntactical templates to form the ontology entities have been used for this task. Further, they have been replaced with machine learning approaches, and lately, deep learning (DL) models have become the most popular in this domain.

The rule-based approaches provide a high level of control on the entities added into the ontology, as the syntactic or lexical templates are usually proposed by the domain expert. In [31], the authors utilize syntactical patterns to retrieve medical key phrases. These phrases are, first, grouped w.r.t. their informativeness with different weights assigned to them, and then the most relevant ones form the ontology entries. The weight of each key phrase is calculated via pair-wise mutual information. In [29], the authors propose a novel method to retrieve significant key phrases based on a naive Bayesian learning algorithm. The specificity of the approach is that it requires many statistical features and several domain-specific features to extract medical key phrases. More recent [1] introduces a method to retrieve key phrases based on heuristics that collaborate natural language processing (NLP) techniques, statistical knowledge, and the internal structural pattern of terms. In addition, DBpedia is utilized to align the terms that may be relevant to the candidate key phrases extracted from the original document. The candidate key phrases are ranked in accordance with several metrics, including the term frequency, then the candidates with the highest rank are treated as the ontology entry. The fact that expert knowledge is required to create relevant templates or generate informative features is the main disadvantage of these techniques.

In [27], the authors compare the performance of statistical and semantic approaches to medical concept extraction, and key phrases identification, specifically. They have implemented conditional random fields (CRF) for clinical named entities extraction and used MetaMap [3], an automotive system that utilizes external medical knowledge to get crucial features from texts. The authors have noticed that the use of only CRF classifier performs much better than rule-based MetaMap relying on external knowledge. However, they also have mentioned that the machine-learning method is highly dependent on the annotated training corpora, therefore, better results are obtained for well-represented classes that the model has seen during the training procedure. Finally, the authors have shown that the best performance in entity extraction is obtained from the combination of a CRF classifier with some lexical features and semantic features obtained from the domain knowledge-based method using MetaMap.

Recently, state-of-the-art results for a number of NLP tasks have been achieved by DL models. As ontology construction requires processing textual data, DL models have been adjusted to this domain. Named entity recognition (NER) models are widely applied to medical documents to retrieve candidates for ontology entries. For example, in [16], the authors combine BiLSTM and CRF models (BiLSTM-CRF) to retrieve named entities on Chinese electronic medical records. They notice that medical entities retrieval is still a big challenge for the medical domain as, first, there is no uniform standard to name medical entities; second, there may be several names for one entity, and, third, new entities are constantly being created, which is hard to follow with the predefined set of rules. The combination of BiLSTM model joining with a CRF layer introduced in the work improves the performance of NER for medical texts. In [24], the authors propose a modification of the well-known transformer-based BERT architecture to better combine general and clinical knowledge learned in the pre-training phase, and show that this model provides good performance on various medical datasets. We should mention that all these approaches are data-driven and require huge labeled medical datasets for models training that are not always available. Besides, the authors have noticed that DL models trained on some highly specialized datasets are failed to be generalized for other domains. In [2] the authors developed the novel hybrid DL-based approach, called Neural Concept Recognizer (NCR) which includes an additional neural dictionary manager that learns to generalize to novel synonyms for concepts to overcome this challenge.

The system introduced in this work includes several modules for constructing and validating medical ontologies. We apply discourse analysis to the entry recognition component of the ontology construction system. Analysis of the text discourse structure allows the system to pay more attention to relevant text fragments that yield ontology entries.

2.2 Discourse Organization of the Text

To construct the ontology from a large amount of unstructured data, which is the common way to represent information, one should be able to retrieve relevant entities from the text and identify the type of relations connecting them. We believe that this goal could be achieved by processing the discourse structure of the text.

The discourse organization of the text shows how discourse units (text spans) are related to each other. Discourse analysis reveals this structure and describes the relations that hold between text units in the document. One of the most popular theories that describe the discourse structure is Rhetorical Structure Theory (RST) [23]. RST divides a text into minimal atomic units, called Elementary Discourse Units (EDUs), and retrieves the rhetorical relation, such as *Elaboration*, *Explanation*, *Causes*, etc., that holds between these atomic text spans. RST forms a tree representation of discourse called a Discourse Tree (DT). In DT, the EDUs are the leaves, and rhetorical relations are edges. EDUs linked by a rhetorical relation are also distinguished based on their relative importance in conveying the author's idea: the nucleus is the central part, whereas the satellite is a supportive part.

Discourse analysis leverages language features, which allow speakers to specify that they are:

- talking about something they have talked about before in the same discourse;
- indicating a relation that holds between the states, events, beliefs, etc. presented in the discourse;
- changing to a new topic or resuming one from earlier in the discourse.

Discourse can be structured by its topics, each comprising a set of entities and a limited range of things being said about them. The topic structure is common in the expository text found in schoolbooks, encyclopedias, and reference materials. A topic can be characterized by the question it addresses. Each topic involves a set of entities, which may (but do not have to) change from topic to topic. This aspect of structure has been modeled as entity chains [5]: each a sequence of expressions that refer to the same entity. A place, where a sequence of entity chains terminates and another set begins can be used as an indicator that the discourse has moved from one topically oriented segment to another. This is important for tuple extraction logic in the process of ontology formation from the text. Thus, it seems reasonable to leverage such information in the ontology construction.

Modern discourse parsers that construct DT are DL-based. Due to the availability of the large annotated discourse corpora for many languages, especially English, discourse parsers [17,19,21] provide reliable and correct DT for the text. Manually annotated Ru-RSTreebank corpus [26] has been recently introduced which resulted in the creation of discourse parser for Russian [9]. The availability of state-of-the-art discourse parsers for different languages makes the discourse-based models universal, so they could be applied to different texts without modifications.

3 System Architecture

In this section, we present the overall description of discourse-enhanced ontology extractor from texts. The architecture of the system is shown in Fig. 1. For a corpus of texts, we apply Candidate Ontology Entry Extractor (COEE), which is the first block of the introduced system. It first performs discourse parsing and yields DT. This DT is then subject to a rule-based extractor of EDUs appropriate for tuple formation.

It happens in multiple steps, first, the EDU with the central entity is extracted and other associated EDUs are labeled as appropriate for tuple formation. Then, all nucleus EDUs are considered and if they constitute a too short phrase, they are merged with the respective nucleus to form a single DT node. Finally, all nucleus EDUs outside of EDUs associated with the central entity is included in the list of EDUs appropriate for tuple formation. As a result, we obtain the list of phrases from which the tuples will be formed as candidates

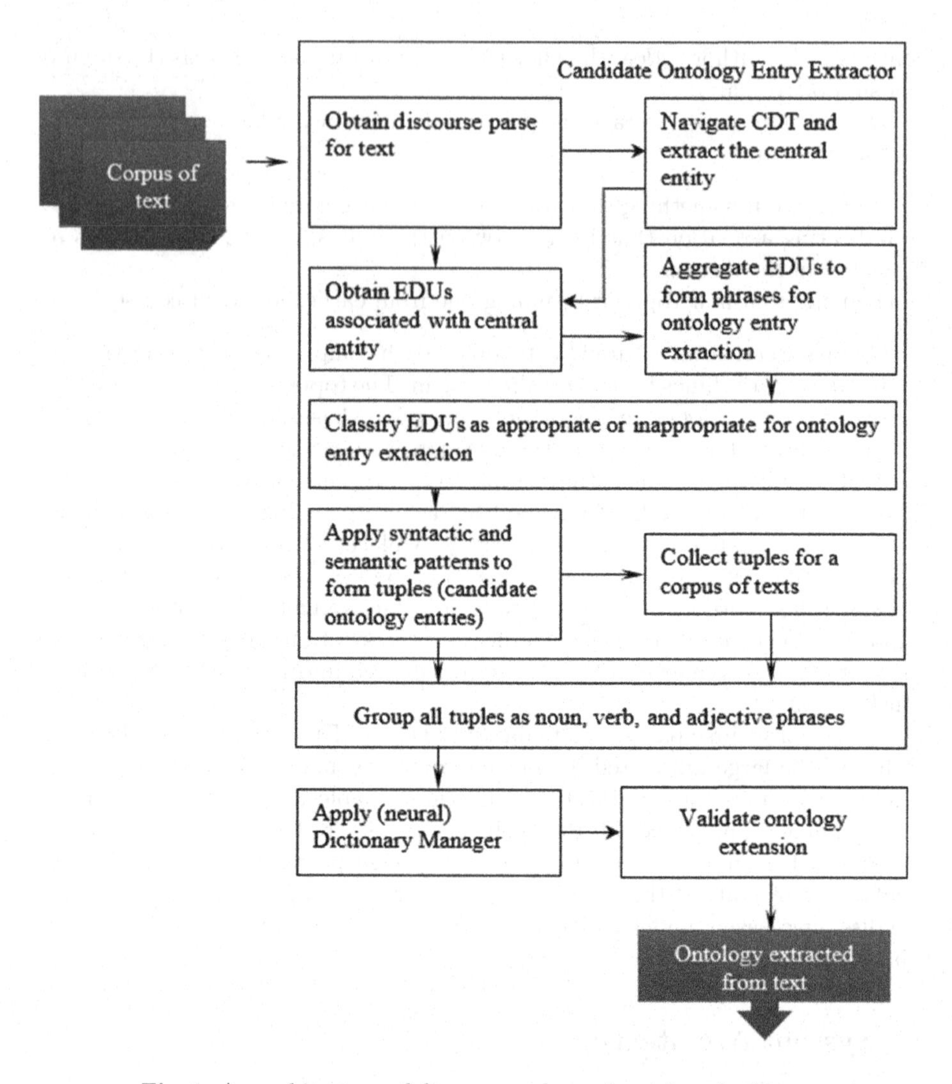

Fig. 1. An architecture of discourse-enhanced ontology builder.

for inclusion into the ontology. Hence, the COEE pipeline includes the following transformations:

Text $\longrightarrow$ DT $\longrightarrow$ list-of-EDUs $\longrightarrow$ list-of-phrases $\longrightarrow$ list-of-tuples.

We apply syntactic templates to extract a tuple such as ⟨*predicate, subject, object*⟩ from a phrase. As a result, the output of the COEE is a list of tuples for a given text. Before grouping, these tuples need to be accumulated for all texts in a corpus.

The grouping component combines tuples of the same sort so that tuples can be matched to each other to produce reliable, informative ontology entries, minimizing inconsistencies. Noun phrases are grouped with the noun ones, verb with the verb, and propositional with the prepositional phrases.

The aggregation component that follows next performs tuples generalization to avoid too specific, noisy entries that cannot be reliably applied with sufficient confidence. Dictionary manager that includes identification of synonyms helps in generalizing tuples that have the same meaning but different words expressing it. Also, specific ontology types have certain generalization rules for values like space or proper names which are generalized in a different way than entities expressed in words (see Sect. 5). Finally, we validate the ontology to keep the ontology up to date. Let us consider all of these stages in more detail.

4 Candidate Ontology Entry Extractor

4.1 Discourse-Level Support for Ontology Construction

The main novel component of the introduced system is the discourse-aware entry extractor. We take a text and its discourse tree and explore which phrases can potentially form an ontology entry. Let us consider a piece of text where discourse relations are crucial for ontology construction. We take a paragraph from the

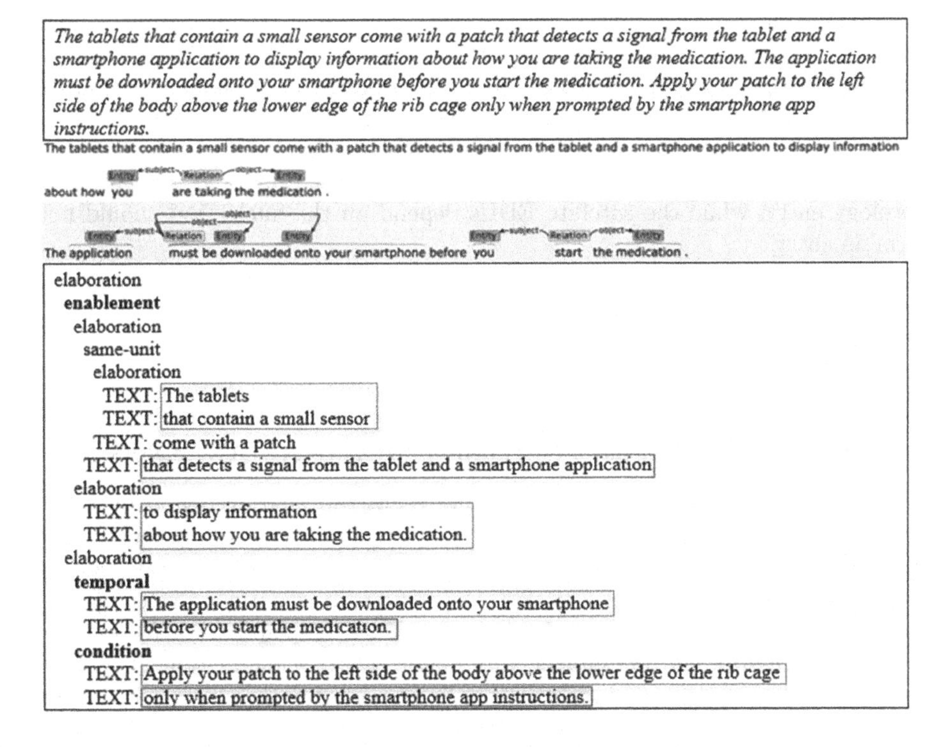

Fig. 2. Text paragraph, its DT, and entity graph showing that not all phrases are equally good to extract tuples to form ontology entries. (Color figure online)

MedlinePlus website[1] and show that not all phrases are good to extract tuples to form ontology entries (see Fig. 2).

A typical syntactic and semantic approach to the entity/tuple extraction considers all highlighted phrases equally. However, some of these phrases are central to this text and, therefore, should serve as a source for relation extraction. At the same time, the rest of the phrases are meaningful in the context of central phrases and should not be used for relation extraction in a stand-alone mode to avoid extracting relations that should not be generalized [11,14].

In Fig. 2, green bolded rectangles show central phrases where extracted relations are informative and express the central topic of this text. Red rectangles show the rest of the phrases which should not yield entity tuples as they are informative only being attached to the central phrases.

In the constructed discourse tree, we see that the central phrase *"tablet-contain-sensor"* corresponds to the nucleus EDU of the top-level rhetorical relation of *Enablement.* This phrase talks about the *"tablet"* which is a central topic of this text, and its predicate *"contain a small sensor"*. Another important phrase associated with the main entity node *"The tablets"* is *"to display information about how you are taking the medication"*.

The satellite EDUs contain phrases that cannot be properly interpreted in a stand-alone mode. For example, *"Come with a patch that detects a signal"* must be interpreted in the context of the *"tablet"*. Otherwise, a hypothetical ontology entry *detect (patch, signal)* is too general and does not necessarily hold on its own. A consistent ontology should not generalize from this expression.

As we proceed from the central entity, navigating the discourse tree, we observe that nucleus EDUs are interpretable on their own and can form an ontology entry, while the satellite EDUs depend on the nuclei and should not form an entry.

Thus, having analyzed the discourse structure of the observed text paragraph, we are able to extract the following entries:

contain (tablet, sensor (small));
display (information (take (people, medications)).

4.2 Rhetorical Relations Determining Informative Text Spans

Let us now look closer at how each type of rhetorical relation defines whether or not the part of the input text contains a candidate ontology entry. For nucleus-satellite *Elaboration* relation, we index the nucleus part as informative and assume that the satellite part is too specific to be mentioned in the ontology. For *Enablement* relation, we have the following template *"To achieve some state [NUCLEUS]—do this and that [SATELLITE]"*. A query that should be asked with the constructed ontology may be of the form *"how to achieve some state?"* but less likely be of the form *"what can I achieve doing this and that?"*. Therefore, we treat the nucleus of *Enablement* relation as a relevant part.

[1] https://medlineplus.gov/druginfo/meds/a603012.html.

We expect the relations such as *Contrast* or *Condition* to be processed as follows: the EDU which expresses facts that actually hold (and not the satellite part facts which are unusual, unexpected, unanticipated) are considered as relevant. *Attribution* acts in a similar way: the nucleus fact is important and may occur in a factoid question, and the satellite part (on whom this is attributed to) is usually a detail.

The *Same-Unit* and *Joint* relations are symmetric and should not affect our selection of relevant text portions.

For *Contrast*, a satellite is good because it is an expression with elevated importance. For *Evidence*, just nucleus is good because the statement is important but its backup is unlikely to be queried.

If the second discourse unit in the *Elaboration* relation describes the same state of affairs as the first one (in different words), or, at a certain level of abstraction, says the same thing, then both nucleus and satellite would form meaningful answers. In the original formulation of RST, usually, an additional requirement for *Elaboration* is imposed that the satellite is more detailed and longer. The broadest definition *Elaboration* also includes in special cases such relation as *Reformulation* or *Restatement*, *Summary*, *Specification* and *Generalization*.

Explanation gives the cause or reason why the state of affairs presented in the context sentence takes place, or why the speaker believes the content of that sentence holds, or why the speaker chose to share information with us; these cases correspond to the three types of causal relations identified. For the cases of content level causality, epistemic causality, and speech act causality satellite should not form an entry [14].

Rhetorical relations *Evidence*, *Justify*, *Motivation*, *Enablement*, *Evaluation*, *Background* all overlap in their function with *Explanation*, but vary in goals and means of giving reasons. For example, *Evidence* is given in order to increase the hearer's belief in a claim.

There are the most popular rhetoric relations that could be identified by state-of-the-art discourse parsers. Following the introduced rules we analyze DT obtained from the discourse parser proposed by Joty et al. [19], and retrieve the candidate text fragments from the nucleus or satellite EDUs based on the type of rhetoric relation they are connected by.

4.3 Relation Extractor Based on Syntactic Parsing

Having revealed the candidate text spans to form the ontology entries, we then aim to process them to extract relevant tuples. This task could be achieved by applying dependency parser. Dependency parser reveals syntactical structure of the input text and presents it in the tree format. This parser analyzes the grammatical structure of the text and provides the relations that hold between "root" words and their dependents. The relations are standard grammatical relations existing in the observed language, such as *subject*, *object*, etc.

In the work, we use open information extraction library ClausIE [10] to derive knowledge tuples for ontology engineering. This library relies primarily on Stanford dependency parser [8] and analyzes grammatical sentence structure to evoke knowledge triples. Not only can explicit knowledge triples be derived from this method, but also implied, embedded knowledge can also be evoked. ClausIE is domain-independent and, compared to other well-known domain-independent open IE approaches, performs significantly better.

ClausIE is applied to the candidate text fragments, which are the combination of relevant EDUs retrieved from the previous COEE block. The knowledge tuples are derived in RDF-like format, i.e. *predicate(subject, object)* triplets. For example, a sentence *"The human papillomavirus virus (HPV) leads to cervical cancer"* would produce an explicit triple *"leads to" ("The human papillomavirus virus", "cervical cancer")* and an implicit triple *"is" ("human papillomavirus virus", "HPV")*.

5 Phrase Aggregator

To accumulate the obtained tuples for all the texts in a corpus and form meaningful ontology entries, we imply a phrase aggregator. This component takes a list of tuples, where the subject and object are represented by the words or phrases, and merges synonymous and related phrases to form concise ontology entries. The aggregator outputs a hierarchical structure of phrase entities obtained by means of generalization of phrase instances. We use the following phrase filtering rules:

1 Only extract noun, verb, and prepositional phrases.
2 Exclude phrases with sentiments because they can occur in opinionated context.
3 Exclude name entities since they cannot be generalized across properties. However, we include a specific type of such proper nouns in connection with relation specific to health domain such as *affect/cure/drug-for/followed-by* and others.
4 Numbers and prepositions are excluded.
5 There is a limit on phrase length.
6 Too frequent phrases and too rare phrases are removed.
7 Phrases that start with an article if they are short are avoided.
8 Strings which are not words are cleaned/normalized (e.g., *is* $\longrightarrow$ *to be*).

For sentiment analysis, we use Stanford CoreNLP pipeline to perform the rules introduced above. Stanford CoreNLP sentiment component [30] is utilized to assess the sentimental power of each word in the phrase.

Once the phrases are extracted, they are clustered and aggregated to obtain reliable, repetitive instances. Phrases which only occur once are unreliable and considered to be the *noise*. For example, let us consider the following phrases: *"insulin-dependent diabetes mellitus"*, *"adult-onset dependent diabetes mellitus"*, *"diabetes with almost complete insulin deficiency"*, and *"diabetes with almost complete insulin deficiency and strong hereditary component"*, the hierarchy obtained for them is shown in Fig. 3.

Head noun extraction occurs as follows. If two phrases have the same head noun, we combine them into a category. If two phrases within a category have other nouns or adjectives in common besides the head noun, we form a subcategory from these common nouns. In this regard, we follow the cognitive procedure of induction, finding a commonality between data samples retaining the head noun, such as *diabetes*. Hence we have the following class, subclasses and sub-subclasses: *diabetes* $\longrightarrow$ *mellitus* $\longrightarrow$ *insulin-dependent*.

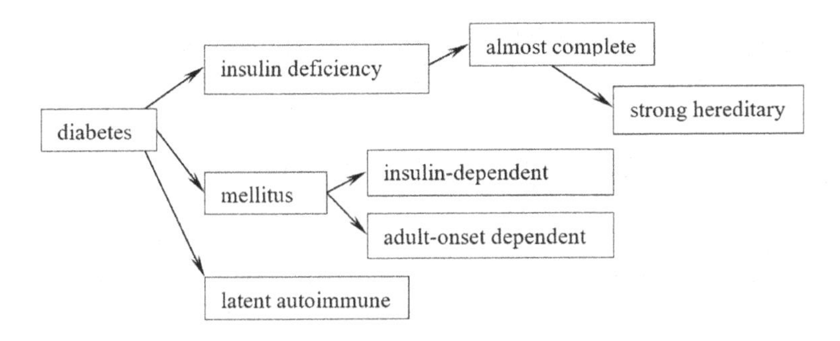

Fig. 3. Phrase hierarchy formed by the aggregator.

6 Neural Dictionary Manager

Neural dictionary manager (NDM) is launched on the final step of ontology construction. NDM is applied to the entity recognition in large unstructured text, which optimizes the use of ontological structures and can identify previously unobserved synonyms for concepts in the ontology. The input of the neural dictionary manager is a word or a phrase. The manager computes the probability of an entity in the ontology matching it. The manager includes a text encoder, which is a neural network that maps the query phrase into a vector representation, and an embedding matrix with rows corresponding to the ontology concepts.

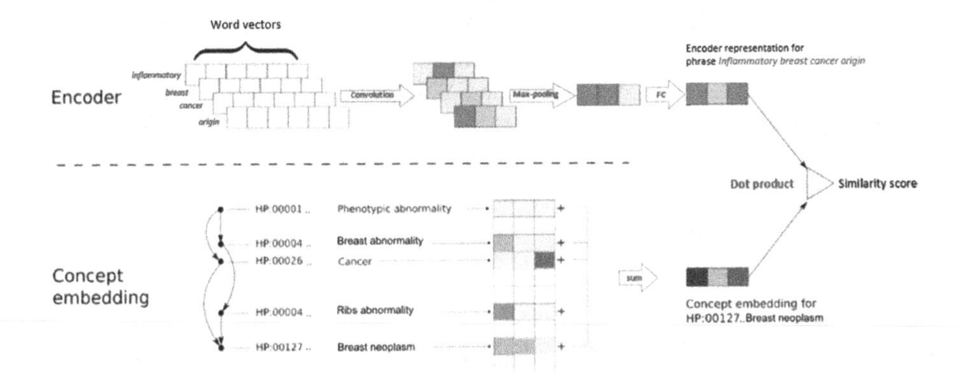

Fig. 4. Architecture of the neural dictionary model.

The architecture of the neural dictionary model that we imply in the system is shown in Fig. 4 [2]. The Encoder flow is at the top, and the flow for computing the embedding for a concept is shown at the bottom. A phrase is first represented in the Encoder by its word vectors, which are then processed by a convolution layer into a new space. A max-over-time pooling layer is employed to merge the set of vectors into a single one. After that, a fully connected layer maps this vector into the final representation of the phrase. To use the NDM for entity recognition in a sentence or larger text, all n-grams of one to seven words are extracted from the text. The neural dictionary manager is used to match each n-gram to an entity. Irrelevant n-grams are removed from the list of candidates when their matching score (the softmax probability provided by the neural dictionary model) is lower than a threshold.

7 Validating Ontology

As a final block of the introduced system, we observe the validation procedure. This procedure is relevant for validating ontologies constructed automatically from medical texts (e.g., clinical guidelines) or re-validating ontologies (constructed manually or automatically) since medical knowledge evolves quickly over time. The following relations can be validated:

- a class A is a subclass of B;
- property P is a sub-property of Q;
- D is the domain class for property P;
- R is the range class for property P;
- I is an individual of class A;
- the property P links the individuals I and J.

To validate the ontology, we utilize question answering (Q/A) schema relying on the domain expert knowledge. The first step of the introduced schema consists of auto-generation of NL questions list from the ontology to be validated. These questions are submitted to domain experts who provide an agreement decision (*Yes/No*) and textual feedback. The next step consists of interpreting expert's feedback to validate or modify the ontology.

Following the idea introduced in [6], we construct manually question templates associated with each type of ontological element. A question template consists of a regular textual expression with the appropriate variables over ontology nodes. For instance, the pattern "Do the SYMPTOMS that PATIENT has correspond to DISEASE?" is a textual pattern with three variables: {SYMPTOMS, PATIENT, and DISEASE}. This question template aims to validate a specific illness with the patient's symptoms.

8 Evaluation

8.1 Dataset

Evaluation of the ontology construction procedure is quite a challenging task as criteria vary from the domain and application areas. There are several complex domains-specific medical Q/A datasets such as MCTest [28], biological process modeling [7], BioASQ [32], etc. which are available for the analysis, but limited in scale (500-10K). To track the contribution of each ontology construction step, we combine five datasets of varying complexity of questions, texts, and their associations. The utilized Q/A datasets are described in Table 1.

Table 1. The Q/A datasets used for evaluation of the ontology construction

Name	Description	Number of Q/A pairs
Medical-Question-Answer-Datasets	Several sources for medical question and answer datasets from HealthTap.com	1600000
MedQuAD	Medical Q/A pairs created from 12 NIH websites. The collection covers 37 question types associated with diseases, drugs, and other medical entities such as tests	50000
Medical Q/A data	Medical Q/A datasets gathered from eHealth Forum and HealthTap websites	–
PubMedQA [18]	Biomedical question answering dataset collected from PubMed abstracts produced by re-purposing existing annotations on clinical notes	275000
emrQA [25]	Generated domain-specific large-scale electronic medical records datasets produced by re-purposing existing annotations on clinical notes	1 million questions-logical form and 400,000+ Q/A evidence pair

8.2 Assessment of Ontology Consistency

When ontology entries are extracted arbitrarily from noisy data, some entries contradict each other. The frequency of contradiction indirectly indicates the error rate of tuple extraction and overall ontology formation. An example of contradicting entries are ⟨*bird, penguin, fly*⟩ vs ⟨*bird, penguin, not fly*⟩ and ⟨*frog, crawl, water*⟩ vs ⟨*frog, swim, water*⟩ (the third argument should be distinct).

We extract ontology entries from the answers. Then, in the resultant ontology, given each entry, we attempt to find other entries which contradict the given one. If at least one entry is found, we consider the given entry *inconsistent*. The portion of inconsistent entries for the whole ontology is counted and shown as a percentage of all ontology entries. As a baseline, we evaluate an ontology whose entries are extracted from all text parts and left without any refinement. Then we apply various enhancement steps presented in the paper and track if they affect the ontology consistency.

Table 2 presents the percentage of the inconsistent entries in the ontology, thus, we assess how each ontology improvement step affects its resultant consistency. The inconsistency values are normalized for the total number of ontology entries as each refinement step reduces the number of entries, pruning ones determined to be unreliable.

Table 2. Assessment of ontology consistency.

Dataset	Baseline: individual entries extraction	Syntactic parser	w. dictionary manager	w. discourse	w. ontology validation
Medical-Question-Answer-Datasets	7.6	2.8	2.4	1.7	0.8
MedQuAD	6.2	2.3	1.9	1.4	1.1
Medical Q/A data	7.0	2.4	1.7	1.7	1.0
PubMedQA	6.9	3.8	2.9	1.6	0.8
emrQA	11.1	4.9	3.2	2.2	1.3

We observe that adding rules for extracting ontology entries make the resultant ontology cleaner, more robust, and consistent. Employing all means to reduce inconsistencies achieves the contradiction rate of less than 1% of inconsistent ontology entries in most domains. The hardest domains to achieve inconsistency are MedQuAD and emrQA. The worst performance occurs for electronic medical records (the bottom row).

8.3 Assessment of Search Improvement Due to Ontology

We also evaluate the accuracy of search (in percent) on several health-related datasets when this search is supported by an ontology. We vary the complexity of ontological support, steps employed to improve/validate it, and ontological sources (see Table 3). As we have the single best answer for each evaluation dataset, search relevance is measured with the F1 metric. Our baseline search is a default tf-idf method without ontology involvement. We add the ontology at the various construction steps according to the ontology construction system architecture (Fig. 1).

One can observe that there is a small improvement in search relevance (F1) with each enhancement in ontology construction. Such an improvement in the range of 2% may be hard to differentiate from a random deviation. However, the overall improvement due to ontologies is significant and accounts for above 10%. Our ablation experiments show that each step in discourse processing, aggregation, matching, and validation is important and should not be skipped.

Table 3. Assessment of ontology quality via search relevance.

Dataset	Baseline: individual entries extraction	Syntactic parser	w. dictionary manager	w. discourse	w. ontology validation
Medical-Question-Answer-Datasets	78.3	82.3	84.1	85.3	86.1
MedQuAD	75.1	80.4	81.6	83.0	85.0
Medical Q/A data	80.2	83.1	85.8	86.7	86.3
PubMedQA	77.5	82.0	84.2	86.0	87.2
emrQA	76.0	81.2	82.9	83.9	86.4
Improvement		**5.7**	**8.1**	**9.8**	**11.3**

9 Conclusion

Advanced systems for supporting clinical decision is especially enticing in the emergency department. These systems require highly accurate solutions due to the situation is crucial. The use of text mining has played an important role in the development of medical ontologies that support decision-making in emergency services, and its application is already an incipient reality. Despite the rapid development of TM techniques that support the extraction of relevant data from electronic medical records and ontology construction procedures, the latter still suffers from the redundancy and inconsistency of the data retrieved.

In this paper, we introduced the system for automated ontology construction. We reviewed major text mining techniques leveraged for this task and observed an ontology construction bottleneck as selecting portions of documents good for ontology construction. We explored how discourse analysis helps in retrieving the relevant text spans that could be comprised into the ontology as the entry.

Our evaluation showed that relying on discourse analysis indeed improves the quality of an ontology with respect to a lower number of inconsistencies and higher relevance of the resultant search. We conclude that once we extract ontology entries from important and informative parts of text instead of extracting them from all text, the reliability of the resultant ontology for search and decision-making grows.

References

1. Amer, E., Fouad, K.M.: Keyphrase extraction methodology from short abstracts of medical documents. In: 2016 8th Cairo International Biomedical Engineering Conference, CIBEC 2016 (2016)

2. Arbabi, A., Adams, D.R., Fidler, S., Brudno, M.: Identifying clinical terms in medical text using ontology-guided machine learning. JMIR Med. Inform. **7**, e12596 (2019)
3. Aronson, A.R.: Effective mapping of biomedical text to the UMLS Metathesaurus: the MetaMap program. In: Proceedings of AMIA Symposium (2001)
4. Banko, M., Cafarella, M., Soderland, S., Broadhead, M., Etzioni, O.: Open information extraction from the web. In: IJCAI International Joint Conference on Artificial Intelligence, pp. 2670–2676 (2007)
5. Barzilay, R., Lapata, M.: Modeling local coherence: an entity-based approach. Comput. Linguis. **34**, 1–34 (2008)
6. Ben Abacha, A., Da Silveira, M., Pruski, C.: Medical ontology validation through question answering. In: Peek, N., Marín Morales, R., Peleg, M. (eds.) AIME 2013. LNCS (LNAI), vol. 7885, pp. 196–205. Springer, Heidelberg (2013). https://doi.org/10.1007/978-3-642-38326-7_30
7. Berant, J., et al.: Modeling biological processes for reading comprehension. In: Proceedings of the 2014 Conference on Empirical Methods in Natural Language Processing (EMNLP), pp. 1499–1510. Association for Computational Linguistics, Doha, Qatar (2014)
8. Chen, D., Manning, C.: A fast and accurate dependency parser using neural networks. In: Proceedings of the 2014 Conference on Empirical Methods in Natural Language Processing (EMNLP), pp. 740–750. Association for Computational Linguistics, Doha, Qatar (2014)
9. Chistova, E., et al.: RST discourse parser for Russian: an experimental study of deep learning models. In: van der Aalst, W.M.P., et al. (eds.) AIST 2020. LNCS, vol. 12602, pp. 105–119. Springer, Cham (2021). https://doi.org/10.1007/978-3-030-72610-2_8
10. Corro, L., Gemulla, R.: ClausIE: clause-based open information extraction. In: WWW 2013 - Proceedings of the 22nd International Conference on World Wide Web, pp. 355–366 (2013)
11. Galitsky, B.: Improving relevance in a content pipeline via syntactic generalization. Eng. Appl. Artif. Intell. **58**, 1–26 (2017)
12. Galitsky, B., Ilvovsky, D., Kuznetsov, S.O.: Text classification into abstract classes based on discourse structure. In: Proceedings of the International Conference Recent Advances in Natural Language Processing, pp. 200–207. Incoma Ltd., Shoumen, Bulgaria, Hissar, Bulgaria (2015)
13. Galitsky, B., Ilvovsky, D., Kuznetsov, S.O.: Detecting logical argumentation in text via communicative discourse tree. J. Exp. Theor. Artif. Intell. **30**, 637–663 (2018)
14. Galitsky, B.A., Dobrocsi, G., de la Rosa, J.L., Kuznetsov, S.O.: Using generalization of syntactic parse trees for taxonomy capture on the web. In: Andrews, S., Polovina, S., Hill, R., Akhgar, B. (eds.) ICCS 2011. LNCS (LNAI), vol. 6828, pp. 104–117. Springer, Heidelberg (2011). https://doi.org/10.1007/978-3-642-22688-5_8
15. Gonzalez, G., Tahsin, T., Goodale, B., Greene, A., Greene, C.: Recent advances and emerging applications in text and data mining for biomedical discovery. Briefings Bioinform. **17**, 33–42 (2015)
16. Ji, B., et al.: A hybrid approach for named entity recognition in Chinese electronic medical record. BMC Med. Inform. Decis. Making **19**, 149–158 (2019)
17. Ji, Y., Eisenstein, J.: Representation learning for text-level discourse parsing. In: Proceedings of the 52nd Annual Meeting of the Association for Computational Linguistics (Volume 1: Long Papers), pp. 13–24. Association for Computational Linguistics, Baltimore, Maryland (2014)

18. Jin, Q., Dhingra, B., Liu, Z., Cohen, W.W., Lu, X.: PubMedQA: a dataset for biomedical research question answering. CoRR abs/1909.06146 (2019). http://arxiv.org/abs/1909.06146
19. Joty, S., Carenini, G., Ng, R., Mehdad, Y.: Combining intra- and multi-sentential rhetorical parsing for document-level discourse analysis. In: ACL 2013–51st Annual Meeting of the Association for Computational Linguistics, Proceedings of the Conference, vol. 1 (2013)
20. Jusoh, S., Awajan, A., Obeid, N.: The use of ontology in clinical information extraction. J. Phys. Conf. Series **1529**, 052083 (2020)
21. Li, J., Li, R., Hovy, E.: Recursive deep models for discourse parsing. In: Proceedings of the 2014 Conference on Empirical Methods in Natural Language Processing (EMNLP), pp. 2061–2069. Association for Computational Linguistics, Doha, Qatar, October 2014
22. Liu, J., Kuipers, B., Savarese, S.: Recognizing human actions by attributes. CVPR **2011**, 3337–3344 (2011)
23. Mann, W., Thompson, S.: Rethorical structure theory: toward a functional theory of text organization. Text Talk **8**, 243–281 (1988)
24. Nejadgholi, I., Fraser, K.C., De Bruijn, B., Li, M., LaPlante, A., El Abidine, K.Z.: Recognizing UMLS semantic types with deep learning. In: Proceedings of the Tenth International Workshop on Health Text Mining and Information Analysis (LOUHI 2019), pp. 157–167. Association for Computational Linguistics, Hong Kong (2019)
25. Pampari, A., Raghavan, P., Liang, J., Peng, J.: emrQA: a large corpus for question answering on electronic medical records. In: Proceedings of the 2018 Conference on Empirical Methods in Natural Language Processing, pp. 2357–2368. Association for Computational Linguistics, Brussels, Belgium (2018)
26. Pisarevskaya, D., et al.: Towards building a discourse-annotated corpus of Russian. In: Kompjuternaja Lingvistika i Intellektualnye Tehnologii, vol. 1 (2017)
27. Khin, N.P.P., Lynn, K.T.: Medical concept extraction: a comparison of statistical and semantic methods. In: 2017 18th IEEE/ACIS International Conference on Software Engineering, Artificial Intelligence, Networking and Parallel/Distributed Computing (SNPD), pp. 35–38 (2017)
28. Richardson, M., Burges, C., Renshaw, E.: MCTest: a challenge dataset for the open-domain machine comprehension of text. In: EMNLP 2013–2013 Conference on Empirical Methods in Natural Language Processing, Proceedings of the Conference, pp. 193–203 (01 2013)
29. Sarkar, K.: A hybrid approach to extract keyphrases from medical documents. Int. J. Comput. Appl. **63** (2013)
30. Socher, R., et al.: Recursive deep models for semantic compositionality over a sentiment treebank. In: EMNLP 2013–2013 Conference on Empirical Methods in Natural Language Processing, Proceedings of the Conference (2013)
31. Song, M., Tanapaisankit, P.: Biokeyspotter: An unsupervised keyphrase extraction technique in the biomedical full-text collection. Intell. Syst. Ref. Libr. **25** (2012). https://doi.org/10.1007/978-3-642-23151-3_3
32. Tsatsaronis, G., et al.: An overview of the BIOASQ large-scale biomedical semantic indexing and question answering competition. BMC Bioinform. **16**, 138 (2015)
33. Wang, X., Yoshida, Y., Hirao, T., Sudoh, K., Nagata, M.: Summarization based on task-oriented discourse parsing. IEEE/ACM Trans. Audio Speech Lang. Process. **23**, 1358–1367 (2015)

TITANIS: A Tool for Intelligent Text Analysis in Social Media

Ivan Smirnov[1], Maksim Stankevich[1](✉), Yulia Kuznetsova[1], Margarita Suvorova[1], Daniil Larionov[1,2], Elena Nikitina[1], Mikhail Savelov[3], and Oleg Grigoriev[1]

[1] Federal Research Center "Computer Science and Control" Russian Academy of Sciences, Moscow, Russia
{ivs,stankevich,suvorova,dslarionov}@isa.ru
[2] National Research University Higher School of Economics, Moscow, Russia
[3] Moscow Institute of Physics and Technology, Moscow, Russia
savelov.me@phystech.edu

Abstract. This paper introduces TITANIS, a new social media text analysis tool specifically designed to assess the reaction of social media users to global events from a psycho-emotional point of view. The tool offers an expanded set of text parameters and natural language processing methods suitable for working with texts from social media. In addition to the widely used NLP approaches, such as tf-idf and sentiment analysis, TITANIS includes psycholinguistic, semantic, discursive, and other types of analysis that allow detecting more peculiarities in the texts of users with different psycho-emotional states. The paper describes the structure of the tool and provides insight into the methodological background of its functionality. To demonstrate some capabilities of TITANIS, we applied it to the Pikabu data to analyze the user reaction to the period of self-isolation and the COVID-19 informational background on social media.

Keywords: Social media analysis · Natural language processing · Machine learning · COVID-19

1 Introduction

The current stage in the development of the social and human sciences is characterized by the formation of a scientific field of "computational science" in which human behavior is investigated using new methods of collecting, processing, and analyzing data [17]. Knowledge progress and improvement of practice in sociology, political science, economics, psychology, linguistics, pedagogy, medicine, history, cultural studies, ethnography, etc. is expected through the use of Big Data and software improvements including the AI tools [10,33,34]. Unlike traditional methods of obtaining social and humanitarian information, Big Data

The reported study was funded by RFBR and EISR, project number 21-011-31638.

S. M. Kovalev et al. (Eds.): RCAI 2021, LNAI 12948, pp. 232–247, 2021.
https://doi.org/10.1007/978-3-030-86855-0_16

results from the use of various high-tech means and preprocessing of the generated content.

Social media provides essential data for computational social science. The importance of network discourse research is determined by the fact that at present, network communication can strongly influence public opinion and behavioral patterns, consolidation and division, moods and values of society and social groups. Numerous studies show that social media and networking services are powerful tools for disseminating information and play a key role in social and political mobilization around the world [46].

On social media, people can express their opinions on the most pressing issues of our time, and receive criticism or support. Almost instantaneous cross-posting and unlimited volumes of accumulated information create an information base for intensifying the formation of public opinion. The effect of "collectivization" of actions [49] arises, opinions are generalized, "crystallized" [47], and spread. Another reason for the growing role of social media is emotional contagion when one person's emotions and behaviors directly trigger similar emotions or behaviors in others. Widespread emotionally charged content shapes emotions as the thoughts and actions of a wide range of people. In this way, real human behavior can be inspired by online communication.

We are introducing TITANIS (Tool for Intelligent Text Analysis in Social media), a new mining tool for texts from social media. TITANIS is designed to solve not only academic tasks but also many practical ones: monitoring the psycho-emotional states of society and social groups, the dynamics of social, political, and economic activity of the population, reliable assessment of opinions, moods, and intentions, etc. The development of such tasks is an urgent task that unites social sciences and informatics, and one of the leading areas of joint research is the analysis of social media. We also present an experimental application of TITANIS to Pikabu data related to the COVID-19 pandemic, namely, in response to self-isolation (lockdown).

2 Related Work

Researchers have been analyzing social media for over a decade. For example, there are even various communities and organizations, such as the International Network for Social Network Analysis (INSNA, insna.org/about-us), that host events and post news, scientific/technical articles, and book reviews on social media analysis.

From social networks, you can get data related to the user (age, gender, geolocation, hobbies, etc.), as well as information about the structural properties of the network itself. For example, you can measure the impact of different people and the relationships between members, find communities on a specific topic, and more [16]. While some data can be obtained directly from user profiles, some socio-demographic parameters of users can be determined by analyzing the content they consume [23].

Social media data provides data collection capabilities that can be used to solve a variety of research problems. This can be a global task that requires collecting a huge amount of data, for example, downloading all social media records for a certain period of time. In practice, this data can be used to prevent terrorist attacks and identify covert criminal organizations [8], predict accidents and natural disasters [38], and track the spread of diseases [18,28]. In addition to the complexity of processing such volumes of data, researchers may face other difficulties in accessing such data, which are associated with the policies of large social networks.

The problem of assessing mental health of social network users has attracted more and more attention in the last decade [5,39,48]. In general, research related to this topic usually deals with a machine learning problem, where a model predicts whether users experience a certain mental state by analyzing social media posts. Most often, these models parse text features from user messages and profile-level information.

Some of the social media-based tasks might require much less data. For example, analysis of the interests of a particular user, their social circle, and personal characteristics. In the commercial field, it can be used in HR analytics, where companies assess the psychological characteristics of potential job candidates, and their behavior in professional networks [3,21]. Another popular challenge in recent years is link prediction, where recommendation systems predict whether a user will like a given post [27].

There are also a number of tasks that do not require an analysis of the structure of a social network. For example, the problem of brand analytics, when companies want to know what users write about them [13]. To do this, sometimes it is enough to consider individual posts from the network without analyzing the graph structure of the network itself. To provide some examples of existing tools, we can mention: Brand analytics, Brand24, Mention, SemanticForce, etc.

Some of the existing tools for social media analysis provide functionality for examining the structures of social media graphs and are intended primarily for commercial purposes. For example, NodeXL has functions for visualizing the network, evaluating network metrics, and opinion mining from text [40]. A similar tool NetMiner [14] can extract words from unstructured text data and filter them by speech tags and tf-idf metrics. Another open-source software package, Pajec [31], allows you to analyze large networks and find applications in social media analytics. A list of social media mining tools with short descriptions can be found at [2].

There are many different tools for social media analysis and there are many studies that use social media data to to solve various research problems. However, we found that tools that help analyze social networks are not enough to study the psycho-emotional side of activity on social networks and, for example, to study the specifics of the population's reaction to global events. Moreover, most of the existing tools are not designed to work with Russian-speaking social media and the Russian language. To fill these gaps, we directed our research toward the implementation of TITANIS.

3 TITANIS Design and Components

TITANIS is a Python library that provides feature extraction modules and communicates with multiple Docker containers hosting parsers and trained models. The components are integrated through a flexible language analysis pipeline and sequential invocation of feature extractors and final models.

At the core, TITANIS supports five language analysis modules, easily combinable and configurable for a given set of tasks and parameters. The tool is based on the IsaNLP library[1] allowing to combine both custom and third-party core NLP analyzers into flexible end-to-end pipelines. We attempt to minimize the number of various NLP analyzers called when multiple tasks are requested. Thus, we attempt to optimize the runtime of the tool.

Tokenization. Input text is split into tokens using the UDPipe [44] tokenizer. A single tokenization method is used across all tasks to optimize text preprocessing time.

Morphology and Lemmatization. Different morphology-sensitive methods in our tool are originally trained using different morphological analyzers. Therefore, they call several analyzers for normalization and morphological feature prediction in the final system. TITANIS supports Mystem [36] and UDPipe morphological analyzers and lemmatizers.

Syntax. By default, for syntax parsing, TITANIS uses the UDPipe 2.5 model for the Russian language. It is chosen as our tool because (1) it is the most time-efficient syntax parser for Russian with decent performance at the moment, and (2) it performs tokenization, morphological analysis, and syntax parsing jointly.

SRL. For basic semantic role labeling in frustration analysis, we employ the IsaNLP SRL Framebank parser proposed in [26]. We also propose an original method of emotion-aware semantic role labeling, discussed in Sect. 4.2.

RST Discourse Parsing. In TITANIS, we use the RST parser for Russian proposed in [6].

TITANIS provides an easy way to install the language parsers and psycho-emotional analyzers on any modern operating system that supports Docker service. All model-based components are packaged as Docker containers, enabling easy installation and deploying different analyzers on remote machines equipped with more RAM and processing power to improve performance further. The open access version of TITANIS with limited functionality available at github[2]. The full version can be requested by contacting *ivs@isa.ru.*

4 TITANIS Functionality

The analysis of psycho-emotional states in the texts of social media requires advanced NLP approaches including in-depth linguistic parsing and psycholinguistic processing. In this section we describe key functions of TITANIS.

[1] https://github.com/IINemo/isanlp.
[2] https://github.com/tchewik/titanis-open/.

4.1 Psycholinguistic Analysis

The proposed tool allows you to calculate a wide range of different text markers. Some of the markers can be identified as psycholinguistic indicators of the text, which can reflect the specificity of the emotional or mental state of the author [25]. For example, these markers include:

- the ratio of the number of verbs to the number of adjectives (Trager Coefficient);
- the ratio of the number of infinitives to the total number of verbs;
- frequency of use of the first-person plural pronouns;
- frequency of the first-person verbs in the past tense.

We can also highlight a number of vocabulary-based indicators that reflect the frequency of words from different vocabularies: thematic (e.g. healthcare terms, environmental terms, political terms), sentiment/mood-based (e.g. motivation vocabulary, anxiety vocabulary, hostile vocabulary).

Both psycholinguistic and vocabulary indicators have previously been used as features for a variety of tasks, such as predicting depression by analyzing essays and social media posts [41,42].

4.2 Analysis of Emotional Structure

To better understand the emotions in the text, including determining the cause and who is experiencing the emotion, we use methods of semantic role labeling. Semantic role labeling in our case is based on Professor G. Zolotova's syntactic theory [32,50].

To determine the cause and who is experiencing emotions, we described emotional transitive and reflexive verbs and their substantive and adverbial correlates (derivates), such as "*удивлять - удивить - удивляться - удивиться - удивление - удивительно*" (different forms of *to surprise*), with a total number of 487 lexemes. Emotional lexemes in the linguistic storage are identified by their stems and composed as nets (about 90 micro-groups). Predicate lexemes of an emotional class express the emotional state of a person and semantically imply two semantic participants (roles): an obligatory experiencer and a cause (causator) as a mandatory argument (in the case of transitive, or causative, verbs) or a close syntactic neighbor of an emotional construction (in most cases). This allows us to find out who (the experiencer) goes through special emotional states during certain socially significant events, critical periods, and situations and why this happens(the cause). In addition, the types of emotions involved can be easily classified and psychologically interpreted as different linguistic designations (part of speech, verb aspect, transitive/reflexive verb) of the same emotional state and are stored together as mentioned above.

The method for semantic role labeling [37] is based on a set of predefined rules, a vocabulary of predicative words, and on morphological and syntactic analysis. The algorithm itself can be broken down into five steps:

1. Filtering – we filter texts that do not contain predicates from the provided vocabulary
2. Sentence splitting and clause extraction
3. Extracting predicate-argument structures from clauses
4. Enrichment of texts with morphological information. Labeling semantic roles by applying the provided rule set
5. Application of linguistic constraints to eliminate ambiguity.

Each rule in the set is designed to retrieve one semantic role. It is defined by a set of features that must be present in predicate and argument words if they have this semantic role. The features of the predicate are as follows: reflexivity; if the predicate is a deverbal noun; if the predicate is a status category. The rule can be designed in such a way that it matches a certain normal form of the predicate word. Features of argument words include: animacy; case; existence of specific preposition. In addition, any rule has a set of predicates to which it can be applied. This set can be wide (any predicate from the dictionary) or narrow, up to any non-empty set of predicate normal forms.

4.3 Analysis of Discourse Structure

Discourse structure analysis can help us reveal the additional information about the argumentation structure of the social media texts, specific to emotional states. It is generally accepted that text is not just a chain of sentences; it is connected [19]. One of the theories modeling discourse as a hierarchical structure is the Rhetorical Structure Theory [29]. According to the RST, text is organized into a hierarchical non-projective tree in which smaller discourse units (text spans) are embedded in larger ones. "Canonical" elementary discourse units (EDU) describe events or states, and, therefore, syntactically, typical EDUs are simple clauses [22]. DUs are combined into higher-level spans if there is a rhetorical relation between them. Relations can be multinuclear (symmetrical, e.g. Contrast, Sequence) or mononuclear (asymmetrical, e.g. Cause-Effect, Solutionhood).

We use various discourse features, extracted from the RST parser output: the number of discourse units (DU), the number of discourse trees, the number of elementary discourse units (EDU) included in the first tree, the number of EDUs included in the last tree, the number of EDUs not included in the trees, the average length of a DU in words, the average length of an EDU in words, the average length of a parse tree, the proportion of multinuclear rhetorical relations, the proportion of unique first EDU words, the average ratio of the right constituent length to the left constituent length, the proportion of simple sentences among the EDUs, the frequency of occurrences of certain rhetorical relations (e.g., elaboration, interpretation-evaluation), the frequency of occurrences of consecutive rhetorical relations pairs (e.g., elaboration -> Interpretation-evaluation).

4.4 Frustration Detection

To measure the manifestation of frustration in social media posts, we implemented a machine learning model that was trained on two types of social media posts tagged by experts: frustrated posts and calm posts. The initial dataset consisted of 6,235 (3,027 frustrated and 3,208 calm) text messages posted by 101 users of social media (Pikabu). Prediction models were created by fine-tuning BERT neural networks [9]: RuBERT pretrained on Russian Wikipedia and news and Conversational RuBERT by DeepPavlov pretrained on subtitles and social networks [4]. The best model was able to achieve 77% of accuracy in the problem of predicting posts written in frustrated condition.

5 Empirical Research

5.1 The Task

The social media influence increases especially when the society's vitality depends on a population moods and emotions, and the behavior of large groups is controlled by a huge amount of conflicting information. For example, it has been shown that the emotions spreading during the current COVID-19 pandemic crisis are predominantly negative, which damages the emotional climate and can lead to a deterioration in the state of society as a whole [43]. The coronavirus crisis is prompting research on collective mental health and "collective therapy" to provide some necessary practical guidance to overcome the crisis [20]. During an "Infodemic," social media can be used to understand public opinion in real time and to refine the public policy based on users' interest and emotions [30]. The need to research the economic, political, social, and humanitarian impact of COVID-19 is driving improvements in social media data processing and text analysis tools.

Our current research is aimed at identifying the differences between social media posts written during the pandemic and during quiet times. The challenge was to use our tools to find the text markers that distinguish between "COVID" and "pre-COVID" messages, assess the significance of the differences, and interpret them.

5.2 Pikabu.ru Dataset

The texts for our analysis were selected from the entertainment website Pikabu.ru. Entertainment websites are considered a "mirror" of public sentiment, and a kind of gauge of social sentiment [49]. The architecture of Pikabu.ru is similar to Reddit.com, one of the most popular objects of sociological, political, and psychological research [1,7,15].

A preliminary review of the discussions on Pikabu.ru showed that since March 1, 2020, the pandemic has been relatively actively discussed in the communities related to the following topics: News, Medicine, Science, and Education. The set of posts from selected communities published on Pikabu.ru from March

1, 2020, to July 5, 2020, contains 3,665 posts and 280,788 comments to those posts. Messages from these communities were flagged as pandemic-related if the words "coronavirus," "pandemic," "epidemic," "quarantine," or "self-isolation" were included in its tags. A set of posts from the same period in 2019 was collected with the aim of forming a control corpus to study the specifics of the "covid" discourse. The control corpus includes 2,020 posts and 143,329 comments. Some descriptions of the collected texts are presented in Table 1.

Table 1. Posts collected in 2019 and 2020.

Year	2019	2020
# posts	2,002	3,665
# posts with covid tags	–	1,108
Avg. words per post	370	284
Avg. sentence per post	28	22

5.3 Psycholinguistic Aspect

Noteworthy changes in psycho-linguistic markers between 2019 and 2020 were received for posts, not for comments. We performed Student's T-test to compare posts from 2019 with those from 2020. In the posts analyzed, the most significant difference ($p < 0.0001$) is obtained for the thematic word groups (TGW) most closely related to COVID-19, namely "Public Health Service" (virus, hospital, respirator, ambulance, etc.). In 2020, people are much more likely to use relevant vocabulary in their posts. Accordingly, the relative number of unique words increased, which can also be explained by the use of special health-related vocabulary in messages. Posts have become shorter: the number of unique words and the number of words in general, clauses, and sentences decreased significantly ($p < 0.0001$) compared with 2019. As shown in [11], a decrease in the number of words can be interpreted as a manifestation of depression. The rest of the markers can be divided into **social**, **cognitive**, and **affective sets**.

Social Set: The frequency of lexemes from TGW "Negative Sociality" (semantics of inequality, social barriers, insincerity, marginality, crime and persecution) increases ($p<0.0001$), and from TGW "Positive Sociality" (semantics of support and social resources, including family) falls accordingly ($p \approx 0.0015$). These shifts in consensus indicate a relative degradation of social cohesion in the face of pandemic and quarantine stress.

Cognitive Set: The vocabulary frequency of the two TGWs "Cognitive Activity and Communication" ($p < 0.0001$) and "Positive Rational Assessment" ($p \approx 0.029$) decreases, reflecting a relative decrease in the ability to process information rationally.

Affective Set consists of lexical (TGW "Negative emotions and bodily states" or "Lexicon of suffering"), syntactic, and traditional psycho-linguistic markers. In addition to the already discussed decrease in the absolute number of words, an increase in the relative "Number of unique words/number of words," as well as an increase in the Trager Coefficient (both $p < 0.0001$), and a decrease in the relative proportion of third-person verbs ($p \approx 0.025$) in texts may indicate the depression of authors [11]. The Trager Coefficient's own increase means, according to the explanation accepted in psycho-linguistics, increased agitation and affectation. An increase in the Coefficient of Readiness to Action ($p \approx 0.001$) is interpreted similarly [35]. In [24] a simultaneous increase in the Trager Coefficient and the Coefficient of Readiness to Action, accompanied by an increase in Negative Sociality, is interpreted as a sign of a narcissistic tendencies. Taken together, the listed affective shifts between 2019 and 2020 can be characterized as an anxiety excitement complex emergence. Mean values and confidence interval for some text markers are presented in Fig. 1.

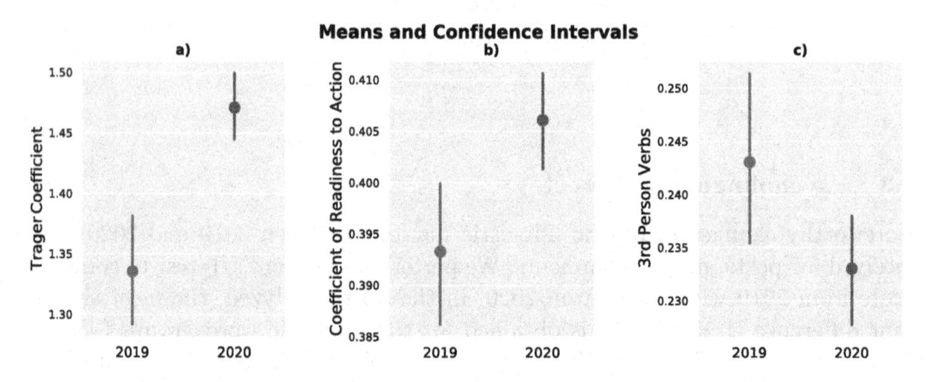

Fig. 1. Mean and confidence interval for **a)** Trager Coefficient, **b)** Coefficient of Readiness to Action and **c)** third-person pronouns ratio in user posts between 2019 and 2020.

From the point of view of the markers under consideration, in general, the obtained shifts represent a pattern characteristic of the shock stage of experiencing a catastrophe, the signs of which are a drop in the constructiveness of thinking and an increase in the level of depression and anxious phobic symptoms [12]. At this stage, sociability is rather suppressed, and the focus is on the object that destroyed the usual way of life—in our case, the COVID-19 pandemic with its individual consequences.

5.4 Semantic Aspect

The emotive predicate groups were studied for changes in the frequency of their words for the period 2019–2020. For each year, predicate groups were selected, the frequency of which to the number of all predicates in the analyzed texts was at least 0.02 in rounding.

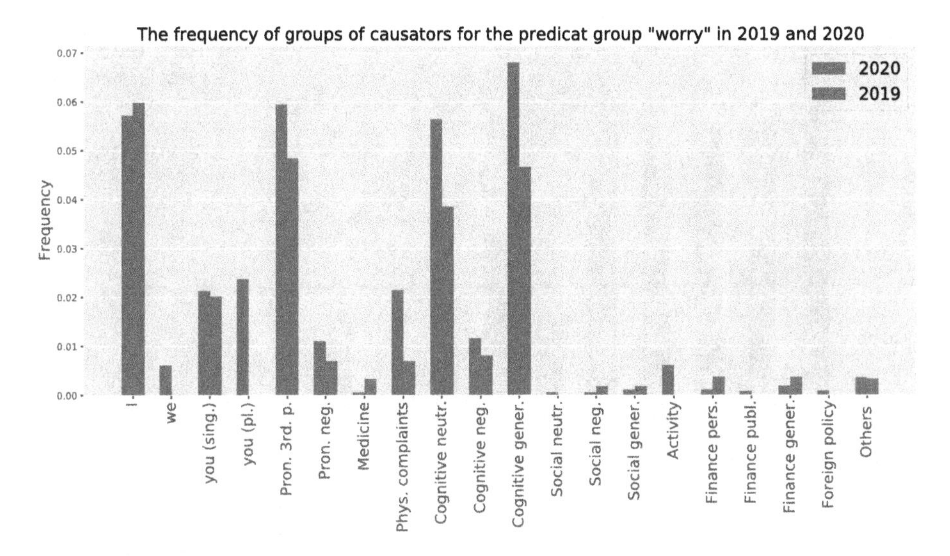

Fig. 2. The frequency of groups of causators for the predicate group *worry* in 2019 and 2020.

We demonstrate some of the capabilities of the predicate analysis method using the example of the predicate group "worry" as the most dynamic of the analyzed, and one of the syntactic roles—the causator (the reason that causes the state named by the predicate). Since the use of lexical means of negation in conjunction with predicates is currently not taken into account, an object in the causator role of "worry" can mean, as the author says in the text, that this object has caused anxiety in someone or that it has stopped to be, or never was, a cause for worry.

The words appearing in the analyzed texts as worry causators (i.e., arguments for the worry predicates) were divided by the expert into the following semantic groups: medicine (*medicine, prevention, surgeon*); complaints about physical condition (*pain, dizziness, varicoses*); cognitive sphere: neutral (*question, presence, situation*); cognitive sphere: negative (*loss, problem, absence*); social sphere: neutral (*madam, philistine, bio-positivist*); social sphere: negative (*bastard, surveillance, bungler*); activity (*diploma, work, job*); personal finance (*income, wage, pension*); public finance (*welfare, public debt, deficit*); foreign policy (*Iceland, colonization, Ukraine*). Groups of personal pronouns (plural/singular) as well as negative pronouns (*nobody, nothing*) were analyzed separately. Words that do not belong to any of the categories were combined into the "others" group (a total of six arguments in 2019, and of 14 arguments in 2020). The total frequencies for the predicate groups are shown in Fig. 2.

According to the data obtained, in general, the worry causators have become more diverse (47 arguments in 2019 versus 111 arguments in 2020), as well as the groups of causators (there were no groups in the social sphere: neutral, activity, public finance, and foreign policy in 2019).

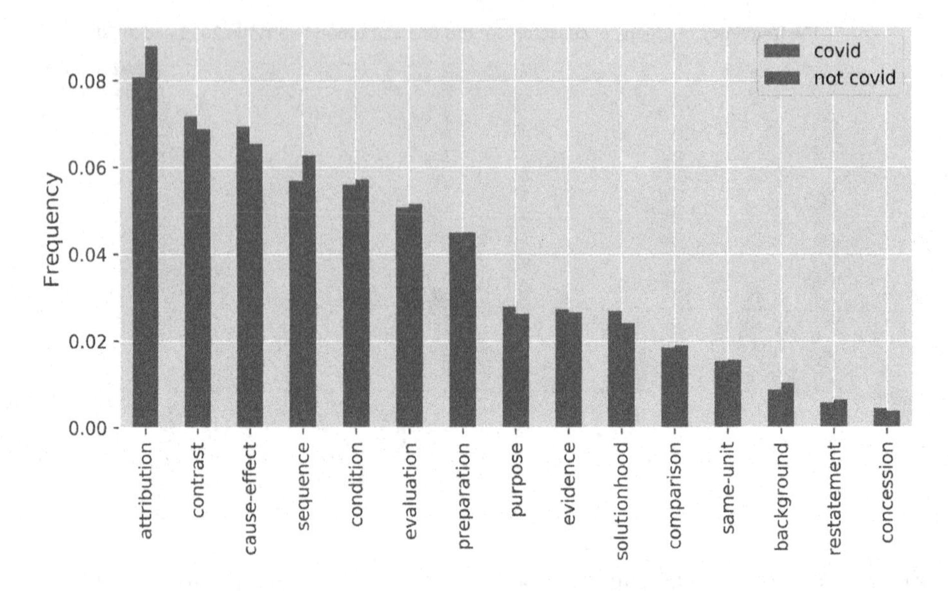

Fig. 3. Frequency of rhetorical relations for different classes in relation to all occurrences of relations in texts of a given class. Elaboration (27% of instances) and Joint (16% of instances) relations are excluded as the most frequent and least informative.

The most specific changes directly related to the pandemic situation include an increase in the frequency of arguments from the "complaints about physical condition" group, and the emergence of an "activity" group that was not identified for worry predicates in 2019. The range of health complaints has increased markedly from 13 arguments in 2019 to 37 arguments in 2020. Particularly interesting is the inclusion of arguments that are most likely directly related to COVID-19: pandemic, anosmia, cough, fever, etc. Life difficulties caused by a pandemic and quarantine are reflected in concerns about some usual activities and primarily work.

Thus, the use of predicate analysis made it possible to identify in the texts written during the COVID-19 pandemic a noticeable shift in the focus of attention to somatic reality, its current state, and potential threats.

5.5 Discourse Aspect

The subcorpus of long texts for discourse features investigation consists of 6,710 (40% covid-related) posts and 489,460 (30% covid-related) comments.

In "COVID" texts the Attribution (reference to the source of information) relation is less frequent (see Fig. 3). As shown in [45], the Attribution is significantly more frequent in the news genre than, for example, in blogs. There are fewer "COVID" texts in the news genre in the current dataset than non covid texts This may explain the lower quantity of the Attribution relation. In addition, in "COVID" texts, the difference between news and blogs genres is not so significant, i.e. the opposite opinion is more common on covid blogs.

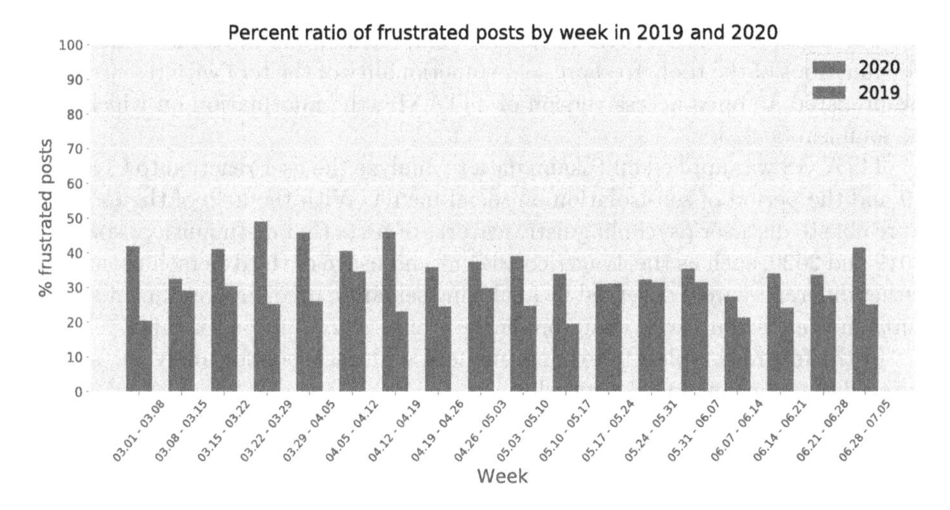

Fig. 4. Percent ratio of frustrated posts by weeks in 2019 and 2020.

Some discourse relations have a higher frequency in "COVID" texts, for example, Solutionhood. In this relation, a problem is presented in the satellite, and its solution is proposed in the nucleus. The problem often can be formulated as a question. Since emotional texts often contain appeals to the audience and questions, including rhetorical ones, the Solutionhood relation becomes more frequent.

The discourse parser regards all interrogative discourse units as Solutionhood. However, this is not always the case. For example, a rhetorical question can be an evaluation of a previous statement and is the Interpretation-Evaluation relation.

5.6 Frustration Level

The frustration detection model was applied on the Pikabu.ru posts collected from March 1 to July 5 in both 2019 and 2020. In total, after removing short texts from observations, we labeled 1,786 posts for 2019 and 3,313 posts for 2020. The share of posts labeled as frustrated in 2019 is 26% and 38% in 2020. It is worth mentioning that the proportion of frustrated posts within posts which has "covid" tags is almost equal to 50%. The percentage proportion of frustrated posts by weeks in 2019 and 2020 is presented in Fig. 4.

6 Conclusion

This paper introduces TITANIS, a new social media text analysis tool specifically designed to assess the reaction of social media users to events from a psycho-emotional point of view. The tool offers functionality to perform psycholinguistic, semantic, discursive, and other types of analysis that allow detecting peculiarities in the texts of users with different psycho-emotional states.

The paper describe TITANIS design, components, and methods behind the key functions of the tool. To share some functionality of the tool with researchers, we prepared an open-access version of TITANIS, the information on which can be found in Sect. 3.

TITANIS was applied on Pikabu data to analyze the user reaction to COVID-19 and the period of self-isolation on social media. With the help of the tool, we were able to discover psycholinguistic features of texts that distinguish posts from 2019 and 2020, such as the Trager coefficient and usage of third-person pronouns. Other differences were observed by analyzing semantic predicate-argument structures in the Pikabu texts, using predicate group "worry" as an example.

In the future, we plan to expand our tool with methods for analyzing structured discussions on social networks.

References

1. Aggarwal, A., Gola, B., Sankla, T.: Data mining and analysis of reddit user data. In: Gunjan, V.K., Suganthan, P.N., Haase, J., Kumar, A. (eds.) Cybernetics, Cognition and Machine Learning Applications. AIS, pp. 211–219. Springer, Singapore (2021). https://doi.org/10.1007/978-981-33-6691-6_24
2. Ahmed, W.: Using social media data for research: an overview of tools. J. Commun. Technol. **1**(1), 77–94 (2018)
3. Bai, S., Zhu, T., Cheng, L.: Big-five personality prediction based on user behaviors at social network sites. arXiv preprint arXiv:1204.4809 (2012)
4. Burtsev, M., et al.: DeepPavlov: open-source library for dialogue systems. In: Proceedings of ACL 2018, System Demonstrations, pp. 122–127 (2018)
5. Chancellor, S., De Choudhury, M.: Methods in predictive techniques for mental health status on social media: a critical review. NPJ Digital Med. **3**(1), 1–11 (2020)
6. Chistova, E., et al.: RST discourse parser for Russian: an experimental study of deep learning models. In: AIST (2020)
7. Choi, D., Han, J., Chung, T., Ahn, Y.Y., Chun, B.G., Kwon, T.T.: Characterizing conversation patterns in reddit: from the perspectives of content properties and user participation behaviors. In: Proceedings of the 2015 ACM on Conference on Online Social Networks, pp. 233–243 (2015)
8. Choudhary, P., Singh, U.: A survey on social network analysis for counter-terrorism. Int. J. Comput. Appl. **112**(9), 24–29 (2015)
9. Devlin, J., Chang, M.W., Lee, K., Toutanova, K.: BERT: pre-training of deep bidirectional transformers for language understanding. arXiv preprint arXiv:1810.04805 (2018)
10. DiMaggio, P.: Adapting computational text analysis to social science (and vice versa). Big Data Soc. **2**(2), 2053951715602908 (2015)
11. Enikolopov, S., Medvedeva, T., Vorontsova, O.: Linguistic characteristics of texts of people with different mental status. Bulletin of the Moscow State Regional University 3 (2019)
12. Enikolopov, S., Boyko, O., Medvedeva, T., Vorontsova, O., Kazmina, O.Y.: Dynamics of psychological reactions at the start of the pandemic of COVID-19. Psychol.-Educ. Stud. **12**(2), 108–126 (2020)

13. Fan, W., Gordon, M.D.: The power of social media analytics. Commun. ACM **57**(6), 74–81 (2014)
14. Furht, B.: Handbook of Social Network Technologies and Applications. Springer Science and Business Media (2010). https://doi.org/10.1007/978-1-4419-7142-5
15. Garg, R., Kim, J.: Impact of reddit discussions on use or abandonment of wearables. In: Taylor, N.G., Christian-Lamb, C., Martin, M.H., Nardi, B. (eds.) iConference 2019. LNCS, vol. 11420, pp. 444–455. Springer, Cham (2019). https://doi.org/10.1007/978-3-030-15742-5_43
16. Ghani, N.A., Hamid, S., Hashem, I.A.T., Ahmed, E.: Social media big data analytics: a survey. Comput. Hum. Behavior **101**, 417–428 (2019)
17. Guba, K.: Big data in sociology: new data, new sociology? Sociologiceskoe Obozrenie **17**(1), 213–236 (2018)
18. Gupta, A., Katarya, R.: Social media based surveillance systems for healthcare using machine learning: a systematic review. J. Biomed. Inform. 103500 (2020)
19. Hobbs, J.: On the coherence and structure of discourse. Technical report 37 (1985)
20. Iglesias-Sánchez, P.P., Vaccaro Witt, G.F., Cabrera, F.E., Jambrino-Maldonado, C.: The contagion of sentiments during the COVID-19 pandemic crisis: the case of isolation in Spain. Int. J. Environ. Res. Public Health **17**(16), 5918 (2020)
21. Jin, L., Chen, Y., Wang, T., Hui, P., Vasilakos, A.V.: Understanding user behavior in online social networks: a survey. IEEE Commun. Mag. **51**(9), 144–150 (2013)
22. Kibrik, A.A., Podlesskaya, V.: Night dream stories: a corpus study of spoken Russian discourse. Languages of Slavonic Culture, Moscow (2009)
23. Kosinski, M., Stillwell, D., Graepel, T.: Private traits and attributes are predictable from digital records of human behavior. Proceed. National Acad. Sci. **110**(15), 5802–5805 (2013)
24. Kovalev, A.K., Kuznetsova, Y.M., Penkina, M.Y., Stankevich, M.A., Chudova, N.V.: Possibilities of automatic text analysis in the task of determining the psychological characteristics of the author. Exp. Psych. (Russia) **13**(1), 149–158 (2020)
25. Kuznetsova, Y., Smirnov, I., Stankevich, M., Chudova, N.: Creating a text analysis tool for socio-humanitarian research. Part 2. The RSA machine and the experience in using it. Sci. Tech. Inf. Process. **47**(6), 374–382 (2020)
26. Larionov, D., Shelmanov, A., Chistova, E., Smirnov, I.: Semantic role labeling with pretrained language models for known and unknown predicates. In: Proceedings of the International Conference on Recent Advances in Natural Language Processing (RANLP 2019), pp. 619–628 (2019)
27. Liben-Nowell, D., Kleinberg, J.: The link-prediction problem for social networks. J. Am. Soc. Inform. Sci. Technol. **58**(7), 1019–1031 (2007)
28. Loscalzo, S., Yu, L.: Social network analysis: Tasks and tools. In: Social Computing, Behavioral Modeling, and Prediction, pp. 151–159. Springer (2008). https://doi.org/10.1007/978-0-387-77672-9_17
29. Mann, W.C., Thompson, S.A.: Rhetorical structure theory: toward a functional theory of text organization. Text-interdis. J. Study Discourse **8**(3), 243–281 (1988)
30. Medford, R.J., Saleh, S.N., Sumarsono, A., Perl, T.M., Lehmann, C.U.: An "infodemic": leveraging high-volume twitter data to understand early public sentiment for the coronavirus disease 2019 outbreak. In: Open Forum Infectious Diseases. Oxford University Press (2020)
31. Mrvar, A., Batagelj, V.: Analysis and visualization of large networks with program package Pajek. Complex Adapt. Syst. Model. **4**(1), 1–8 (2016)
32. Osipov, G., Smirnov, I., Tikhomirov, I.: Relational-situational method for text search and analysis and its applications. Sci. Tech. Inf. Process. **37**(6), 432–437 (2010)

33. Platonova, S.: Chetvertaya paradigma nauchnykh issledovaniy i sotsiogumanitarnyye nauki [the fourth paradigm of scientific research and social sciences and humanities]. Zhurnal sotsiologii i sotsialnoy antropologii, pp. 7–24 (2020)
34. Resnyansky, L.: Conceptual frameworks for social and cultural big data analytics: answering the epistemological challenge. Big Data Soc. **6**(1), 2053951718823815 (2019)
35. Sboev, A., Gudovskikh, D., Rybka, R., Moloshnikov, I.: A quantitative method of text emotiveness evaluation on base of the psycholinguistic markers founded on morphological features. Procedia Comput. Sci. **66**, 307–316 (2015)
36. Segalovich, I.: A fast morphological algorithm with unknown word guessing induced by a dictionary for a web search engine. MLMTA, pp. 273–280 (2003)
37. Shelmanov, A., Smirnov, I.: Methods for semantic role labeling of Russian texts. In: Computational Linguistics and Intellectual Technologies. Proceedings of International Conference Dialog, pp. 607–620 (2014)
38. Singh, J.P., Dwivedi, Y.K., Rana, N.P., Kumar, A., Kapoor, K.K.: Event classification and location prediction from tweets during disasters. Ann. Oper. Res. **283**(1), 737–757 (2019)
39. Skaik, R., Inkpen, D.: Using social media for mental health surveillance: a review. ACM Comput. Surveys (CSUR) **53**(6), 1–31 (2020)
40. Smith, M.A., et al.: Analyzing (social media) networks with NodeXl. In: Proceedings of the Fourth International Conference on Communities and Technologies, pp. 255–264 (2009)
41. Stankevich, M., Kuznetsova, Y., Smirnov, I., Kiselnikova, N., Enikolopov, S.: Predicting depression from essays in Russian. In: Komp'juternaja Lingvistika i Intellektual'nye Tehnologii, pp. 647–657 (2019)
42. Stankevich, M., Smirnov, I., Kiselnikova, N., Ushakova, A.: Depression detection from social media profiles. In: Elizarov, A., Novikov, B., Stupnikov, S. (eds.) DAMDID/RCDL 2019. CCIS, vol. 1223, pp. 181–194. Springer, Cham (2020). https://doi.org/10.1007/978-3-030-51913-1_12
43. Steinert, S.: Corona and value change. The role of social media and emotional contagion. Ethics Inf. Technol. 1–10 (2020). https://doi.org/10.1007/s10676-020-09545-z
44. Straka, M., Straková, J.: Tokenizing, POS tagging, lemmatizing and parsing ud 2.0 with udpipe. In: Proceedings of the CoNLL 2017 Shared Task: Multilingual Parsing from Raw Text to Universal Dependencies, pp. 88–99 (2017)
45. Toldova, S., Davydova, T., Kobozeva, M., Pisarevskaya, D.: Discourse features of blogs in subcorpus of russian ru-rstreebank. Computational Linguistics and Intellectual Technologies. In: Proceedings of the International Conference Dialogue 2020, pp. 747–761 (2020)
46. Varol, O., Ferrara, E., Ogan, C.L., Menczer, F., Flammini, A.: Evolution of online user behavior during a social upheaval. In: Proceedings of the 2014 ACM Conference on Web Science, pp. 81–90 (2014)
47. Volosnikov, R.: The influence of social media on the formation and functioning of public opinion. Sociol. Almanac **10**, 82–90 (2019)
48. Wongkoblap, A., Vadillo, M.A., Curcin, V.: Researching mental health disorders in the era of social media: systematic review. J. Med. Internet Res. **19**(6), e228 (2017)

49. Zagidullina, M.: Entertaining web-site as indicator of public sphere: hash tag politics on pikabu.ru. Political Linguis. J. **65**(5), 189–193 (2017)
50. Zolotova, G.A., Karaulov, Y.N.: Sintaksicheskii slovar': Repertuar elementarnykh edinits russkogo sintaksisa [Syntactic Dictionary: Repertoire of Elementary Units of Russian Syntax]. Nauka (2001)

Approach to the Automated Development of Scientific Subject Domain Ontologies Based on Heterogeneous Ontology Design Patterns

Yury Zagorulko(✉), Elena Sidorova, Irina Akhmadeeva, Alexey Sery, and Galina Zagorulko

A.P. Ershov Institute of Informatics Systems of Siberian Branch of the Russian Academy of Sciences, Novosibirsk, Russia
zagor@iis.nsk.su

Abstract. Our practice has shown that for the development of ontologies of scientific subject domains (SSD), the use of ontology design patterns (ODPs) is especially effective. This is due to the fact that the ontology of any SSD contains, as a rule, a large number of typical fragments that are well described by the ODPs. In addition, since these patterns greatly facilitate the development of an SSD ontology, it is possible to involve experts in the modeled SSD not possessing the skills of ontological modeling, which, in turn, speeds up the development of an SSD ontology. In order to obtain an ontology that describes a given SSD fully enough, it is necessary to process a huge number of publications related to this SSD. We can facilitate and accelerate the process of populating an ontology with information from these sources using lexico-syntactic patterns. The paper presents an approach to automating the development of the SSD ontologies based on a set of heterogeneous ontology design patterns. This set includes two kinds of patterns: (a) patterns intended for ontology developers and (b) lexico-syntactic patterns automatically built on the basis of (a), capable of automatically populating the ontology with the information extracted from natural language texts.

Keywords: Ontology design patterns · Content patterns · Automatic generation of lexico-syntactic patterns · Ontology population

1 Introduction

At present, ontologies are recognized as the most effective means of formalizing and systematizing knowledge and data in scientific subject domains (SSD), by which we mean subject areas covering a certain scientific discipline or area of scientific knowledge in all of its aspects, including the objects and subjects of research characteristic of it, methods used in it, scientific activity performed in it and results obtained.

The development of a domain ontology is a rather complex and time-consuming process. To simplify and facilitate it, various methods and approaches have been proposed and applied [1–3]. Recently, an approach using Ontology Design Patterns (ODPs) [4] – documented descriptions of practical solutions to typical problems of ontological

S. M. Kovalev et al. (Eds.): RCAI 2021, LNAI 12948, pp. 248–263, 2021.
https://doi.org/10.1007/978-3-030-86855-0_17

modeling – has been intensively developed. Our practice has shown that the ODPs are especially effective for the development of the SSD ontologies [5–9]. This is due to the fact that an SSD ontology contains, as a rule, a large number of typical fragments, which are well described by the ODPs. In addition, as using these patterns greatly facilitates the development of an SSD ontology, it is possible to involve experts in the modeled SSD not possessing the skills of ontological modeling, which, in turn, speeds up the development of an SSD ontology.

If we need to obtain an ontology giving a full description of an SSD, ontology development is further complicated by the necessity to process an immense number of relevant publications. To facilitate and accelerate this process, methods are being developed for the automatic population of an ontology based on natural language texts [10, 11], including those using lexico-syntactic patterns of ontological design [12, 13].

The paper describes an approach proposed by the authors to automate the construction and population of SSD ontologies, based on heterogeneous ODPs. A feature of this approach is that the development and initial filling of the SSD ontology is carried out by knowledge engineers and experts in the SSD, who use such ODPs as content patterns and structural patterns. Further population of the SSD ontology, i.e. adding new instances of concepts/relations into it [10], is performed automatically using lexico-syntactic patterns (LSPs) built on the basis of the above-mentioned types of the ODPs and the current version of the SSD ontology.

The rest of the paper is organized as follows. The second section presents the ODPs ontology, which is the conceptual basis of a system for automated construction of SSD ontologies using heterogeneous ODPs. The third section is devoted to the description of this system. The fourth section describes the process of constructing lexico-syntactic patterns based on the content patterns and structural patterns included in the system, the dictionary of general scientific lexicon and the current version of the ontology. The fifth section is devoted to the issues of ontology population using the LSPs constructed. In the conclusion, we summarize the results of the implementation and use of this approach and outline the prospects for its development.

2 The ODPs Ontology

As it was said above, the ODPs ontology is the conceptual basis of the system for automated construction of SSD ontologies using heterogeneous ODPs. It is built using the basic ontologies of scientific activity, scientific knowledge, and information resources, earlier developed by the authors (see Sect. 3 and [6]), and includes (see Fig. 1) a systematization of the ODPs and description of (a) their properties and constituent elements, (b) methods of their application, and (c) publications and information resources related to the topic "Ontology design patterns".

The ODPs can be systemized (classified) on the following grounds: by the types of ontological modeling problems to be solved, by the purpose (by the types of applied problems to be solved), and by application areas, i.e. subject areas for which ODPs are created.

As a basic systematization of the ODPs in this ontology, the authors have taken the systematization by the types of ontological modeling problems to be solved. Systematization on other grounds is reflected in the properties of the patterns, in one way or another. When developing a systematization of patterns according to the problems being solved, the authors relied on the classification proposed in the NeOn research project [14]. According to it, ODP patterns are divided into six main types: Structural ODPs, Correspondence ODPs, Content ODPs, Reasoning ODPs, Presentation ODPs, and Lexico-Syntactic ODPs. In turn, Structural ODPs are subdivided into Architectural ODPs and Logical ODPs; Correspondence ODPs, into Alignment ODPs and Reengineering ODPs; and Presentation ODPs, into Naming ODPs and Annotation ODPs.

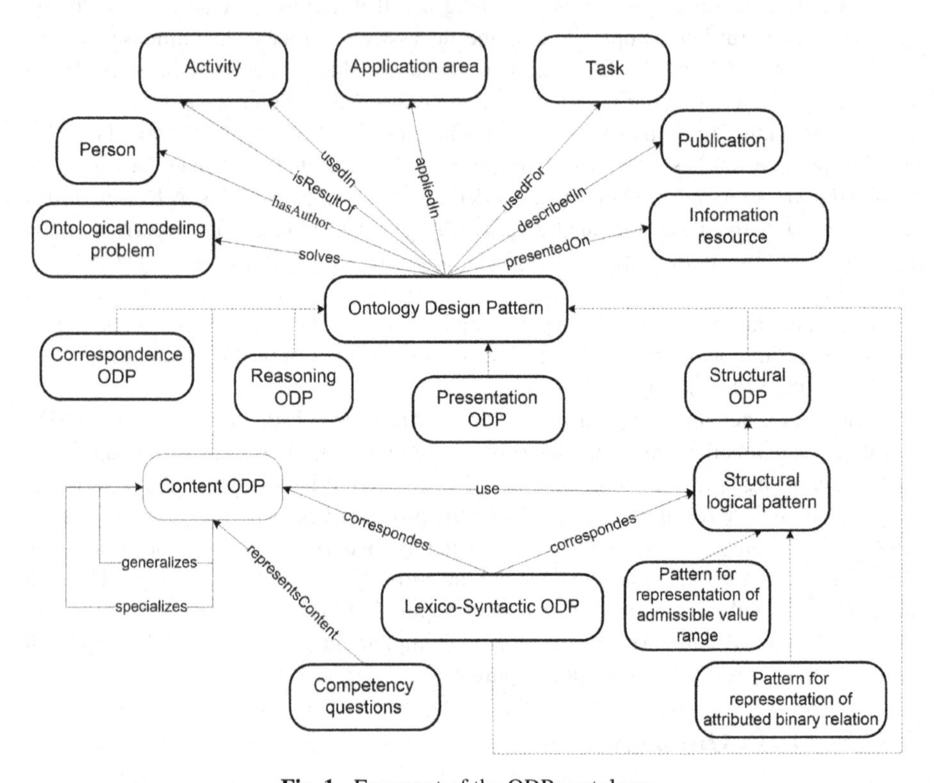

Fig. 1. Fragment of the ODPs ontology.

The core of the ODPs ontology is constituted by the *Ontological Design Pattern* class, which specifies the ODPs' basic properties, and its subclasses representing the above types of patterns. These classes are *Structural Pattern, Content Pattern, Presentation Pattern,* etc.

ODPs properties are described on the basis of the format proposed on the portal of the ODPA Association [15]. In accordance with it, the description of a pattern includes information about its author and application area (scope), its textual description, graphical representation, links to other patterns, a set of scenarios and examples of use. The content pattern is additionally supplied with a set of Competency questions [16] reflecting its content.

We have supplemented the pattern description format with some information elements serving to describe the context for the development and use of ODPs. For these purposes, we included the following classes in the ODPs ontology: *Scope (Subject domain), Activity, Task, Publication, Person, Organization, Information resource,* etc. To associate patterns with the instances of these classes, we have included in the ODPs ontology corresponding relations allowing associating patterns with subject areas, persons, organizations and projects in which they are used, as well as with the publications and information resources where they are described.

The content patterns may be connected by the "generalizes" and "specializes" relations. These relations correspond to the operations that can be used to customize a particular pattern to the modeled SSD [4].

The patterns most completely presented in the ODPs ontology are these implemented in the proposed system for the automated construction of SSD ontologies [5]: Structural logical patterns, Content patterns, Presentation patterns and Lexico-syntactic patterns.

The need to use structural logical patterns arose due to the lack of expressive means in the OWL language for representing complex entities and structures relevant for the construction of the SSD ontologies, in particular, n-ary and attributed binary relations (binary relations with attributes), as well as the ranges of admissible values determined by an ontology developer.

The pattern of the representation of the range of admissible values is intended for setting the possible values of the properties of a class (as a rule, strings), when the entire set of such values is known in advance and, therefore, can be fixed at the development stage.

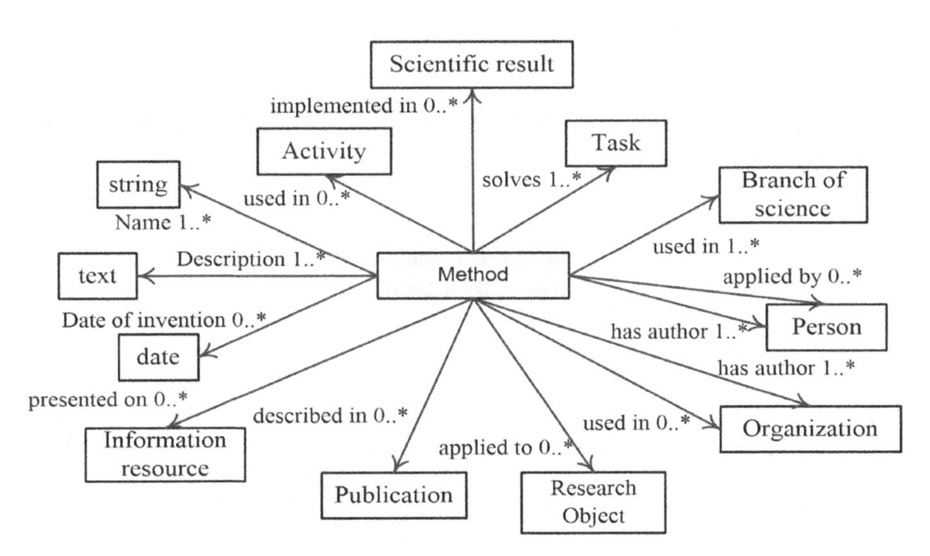

Fig. 2. Pattern for representing the concept "Method".

Content patterns are intended to support a uniform and consistent presentation of concepts and their properties used in the modeled SSD. We have developed these patterns for the concepts common to most scientific subject domains: *Research object, Research subject, Method, Task, Division of Science, Scientific Result, Activity (Scientific Activity), Project, Person, Organization, Publication, Information resource,* etc. For each of these patterns, we have defined a set of Competency questions. These questions have helped to identify the composition of the mandatory and optional ontological elements of the pattern and to describe the requirements for them presented in the form of axioms and constraints.

In addition, we have defined, for each pattern representing the SSD concept, a set of key attributes to identify uniquely a specific instance of the concept.

As an example, consider a pattern for representing the concept "Method" (see Fig. 2). Representing the elements of the description of this pattern are such mandatory ontology classes as *Task, Branch of science, Person and Organization*, such optional classes as *Activity, Scientific result,* etc., as well as the relations "used_in", "implemented_in", "solves", etc. Note also that the Method pattern has one key attribute *Name*.

The following set of Competency questions represents the content of the Method pattern:

What is the name of the method?
When was the method proposed?
In what activity is the method used?
In what scientific results is the method implemented?
What tasks are solved using the method?
In which divisions of science is the method used?
Who is the author of the method?
Who (what persons) applies the method?
In which organizations is the method applied?
To what objects of research is the method applied?

3 The Architecture of the System for the Automated Development of SSD Ontologies

The system for the automated development of SSD ontologies based on heterogeneous ontology design patterns (SADO) includes the following components (Fig. 3): the ODPs ontology, ODPs repository, repository of basic ontologies, general scientific dictionary, ontology editor, data editor, information-analytical Internet resource, and a system for automatic ontology population based on lexico-syntactic patterns (LSP).

The ODPs repository is built on the basis of the ODPs ontology and includes the ODPs implementations. Content patterns, presentation patterns and structural logical patterns are implemented in the OWL language, while the lexico-syntactic patterns are represented in a specialized template description language [17].

The SADO system supports the method of constructing SSD ontology based on basic ontologies containing the most general concepts characteristic of most scientific subject domains. In this regard, the system includes a repository of basic ontologies including the ontology of scientific knowledge, ontology of scientific activity, basic ontology of tasks and methods, and basic ontology of information resources. All basic ontologies have OWL specifications. For the most important concepts of basic ontologies, we have developed content patterns to facilitate and simplify the construction of an ontology of a specific SSD.

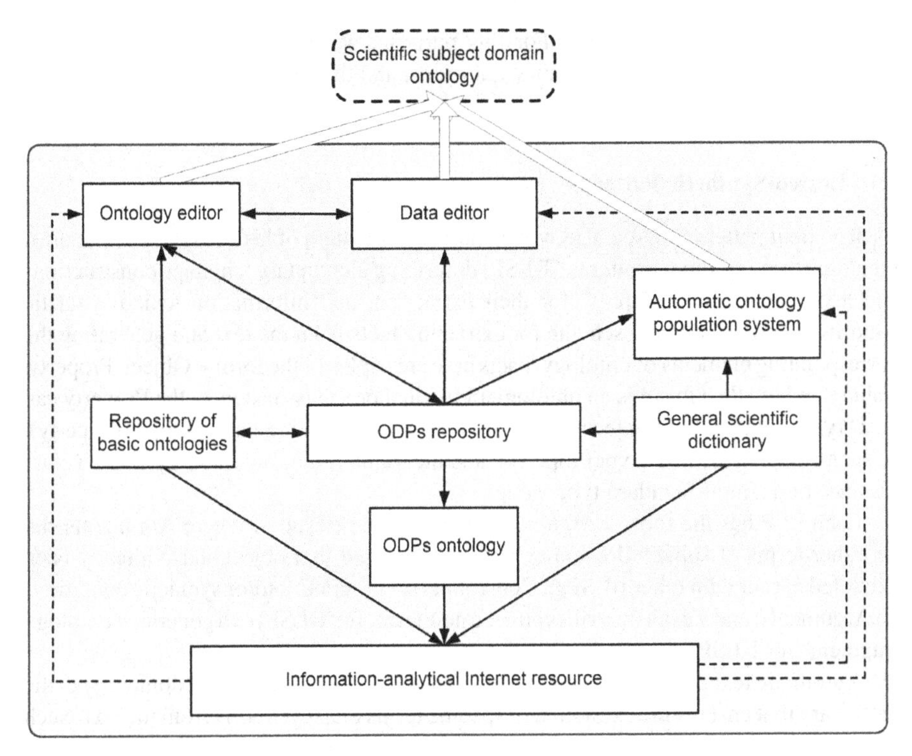

Fig. 3. The architecture of the SADO system.

As the ontology editor, the SADO system currently uses the popular Protégé editor. To support a more convenient use of the ODPs, the system also includes a data editor that allows you to populate the SSD ontology by concretizing (instantiating) the content patterns included in the pattern repository.

The general scientific dictionary contains the lexicon typical of most scientific subject domains. It is used to build lexico-syntactic patterns based on content patterns included in the repository.

The information-analytical Internet resource (IAIR) is designed to systematize all information about the ODPs and provide content-based access to it. Systematization of this information and content-based access to it is organized on the basis of the ODPs ontology. In addition, the IAIR, in fact, is the user interface of the SADO system, providing users with access to all editors supporting the development of the SSD ontology, as well as to the automatic ontology population system based on the LSP.

4 Automatic Generation of Lexico-Syntactic Patterns

Implementation of automatic ontology population requires a set of lexico-syntactic patterns (LSP) describing various ways of presenting information corresponding to each

Content ODP in scientific texts. For this purpose, we use a Content ODP description in OWL, appropriate competency questions, and the corresponding SSD ontology fragment.

4.1 Lexico-Syntactic Patterns

Each content pattern is associated with a multi-level system of lexico-syntactic patterns, including terminological patterns (T-LSP) describing elementary language constructions and lexico-syntactic "samples" for their extraction, and information lexico-syntactic patterns (I-LSP) defining a scheme for extracting facts from the text and generating the corresponding elements of ontology. Facts here are triples of the form <Object, Property, Value>, where the Object is an ontology individual or a class instance, the Property can be a "type" relation linking the individual to the class, a relation name (ObjectProperty), or an attribute name (DatatypeProperty), and the Value can be an ontology class, a class instance or a simple standard type value.

Each LSP has the form <Arguments, Constraints, Result>, where Arguments can be either terms of subject domain or objects (provided that objects have already been extracted earlier with other I-LSPs), Constraints set semantic and/or syntactic conditions on Arguments, and Result describes either a new term (for T-LSP) or a generated ontology fragment (for I-LSP).

Automatic text processing using lexico-syntactic patterns requires a domain-specific dictionary that ensures the extraction of specific terms of a given SSD from the text. Such a dictionary expands the general scientific dictionary included in the SADO system.

Thus, the general scientific terms will include such words as *method, task, object of study, define, calculate, apply*. Examples of the SSD terms are *temperature, hydrocarbon gas, self-ignition*.

Each term of the domain-specific dictionary found in the text is provided with grammatical and semantic information, which is further used when the LSP is applied. Semantic information in the vocabulary is represented by a system of lexico-semantic classes or features, which correspond to the labels of ontological entities (class, attribute, relation). Examples of such semantic features formed on the basis of the Content ODP describing the concept "Method" are: METHOD, TASK, METHOD.*Name*, METHOD.*Description*, METHOD.*solves*, METHOD.*Name*, etc.

4.2 Principles of LSP Generation

Let us consider what kind of data the LSP generation algorithm relies on.

The SSD ontology provides information about classes, their properties (attributes and relations), and about individuals and their properties. The labels of all these ontology entities can be used to populate the dictionary and form a system of lexico-semantic features for the markup of terms.

The ODPs ontology includes descriptions of Content ODPs, in which the labels of all attributes and relations linking the class with standard data types and other classes of the ontology, competency questions, and a list of key attributes of the class are presented. The labels of class attributes and relations are represented by language expressions, which are markers introducing properties in the text. Competency questions expressed in natural language allow us to set initial syntactic constraints on facts to be extracted, which can later be refined using a corpus of texts. The information about the key attributes of the class is needed to generate new objects based on the values of these attributes extracted from the text.

The set of all class properties (attributes and relations) defines the structure of the corresponding SSD objects, and each property can be analyzed independently of the other properties and described by a separate set of LSPs.

Structural Logical ODPs can be part of the Content ODP and express more complex relationships between entities in the ontology. At the moment, the ODPs ontology contains two Structural Logical ODPs that serve to represent the ranges of admissible values and attributed binary relations. We consider such relations as a group of related binary relations and describe them by a set of I-LSP.

The corpus of scientific texts serves as a source of domain vocabulary used by specialists of the SSD considered. Not only typical entity labels are extracted from the corpus, but also specific indicators for further entity extraction.

Thus, the use of ontological knowledge and data makes it possible to identify the knowledge of the language of the subject domain and the ways of the linguistic description of ontological entities in texts necessary for information extraction and ontology population. Formalization of this knowledge in the form of the system of LSPs will allow us to apply existing technologies of automatic text processing for the solution of the task.

Let us take a closer look at the ways of representing and generating the elements of the system of LSPs.

The vocabulary of the SSD terms is formed from string literals presented in the domain ontology, which include the labels of classes, attributes, relations, values of attributes, as well as the values specified using the ODP for representing the ranges of admissible values.

Terminological patterns (T-LSPs), which are lexico-syntactic patterns formed from terms, markers, semantic and syntactic constraints, are used to extract the domain terms not presented in the vocabulary. Three types (groups) of such templates are considered to solve the tasks.

The first group provides extraction of individual labels based on a central word or term using syntactic rules for noun phrases identification. Thus, in the example (1), the T-LSP allows the extraction of noun phrases, the head of which is a word orüre METHOD, for example: *method for the calculation of the limits of unstable detonation of natural gas.*

$$[<\text{Adj}>*,\ <\text{METHOD}>,\ [<\text{Adj}>*,\ <\text{N, GEN}>]*] \Rightarrow \text{METHOD.Name} \qquad (1)$$

This T-LSP includes three arguments: 1) a group of adjectives, 2) a term of the lexico-semantic class (feature) METHOD, and 3) a noun phrase collected by a nested T-LSP of the form [<Adj>*,<N, GEN>]*; constraints are a) the semantic class of the 2nd argument, b) the genitive case for the nested T-LSP used as the 3rd argument; the result of this T-LSP defines the lexico-semantic feature METHOD.Name for all terms extracted with this T-LSP.

The second group of T-LSPs is formed using relation indicators, which are usually predicates from the general scientific vocabulary, mapped to attribute labels and relation labels of Content ODP, or predicates extracted from the competency questions. For example,

$$[< \text{METHOD.Name} >' \textit{defined as}' \ \$x \ < \text{NP}^* >] \Rightarrow \text{METHOD.Description} \quad (2)$$

This pattern is a template with a variable ($x) that provides the extraction of N-grams, which are a sequence of noun phrases used to populate the Description attribute for the Method class.

Another type of pattern is used to find new predicate terms that serve to extract relations (terms that allow the same relation to be extracted are considered conditional synonyms):

$$\begin{aligned}&[< \text{METHOD.Name} >, \$x < \text{VP} >, < \text{RESEARCH\_OBJECT.Name} >] \\ &\Rightarrow \text{METHOD.Application}\end{aligned} \quad (3)$$

This pattern allows us to extract conditional synonyms for the predicates *'examine'*, *'is applied to'*, *'extract'* that serve to find the relation between the method and the object of study in the text.

I-LSPs are used to extract facts and create new objects. Three types of I-LSPs are suggested.

I-LSPs of the first type (initializing) create objects based on terms that have a lexico-semantic feature matching either the label of a class or the label of a key attribute of that class:

$$\begin{aligned}&[< \text{METHOD} >] \Rightarrow \text{create Method()} \\ &[< \text{METHOD.Name} >] \Rightarrow \text{create Method(Name : arg1)}\end{aligned} \quad (4)$$

The group of patterns (4) provides the creation of objects of the *Method* class. The first pattern creates an "empty" object, which is typical in situations where the text contains a reference to the previously mentioned object. The second pattern fills in the key attribute *Name* for an object of the *Method* class, using a term with the corresponding lexico-semantic feature METHOD.Name. This is possible when the name is extracted with one of the T-LSPs (as in example (1)).

For each relation (ObjectProperty) represented in the Content ODP, an I-LSP is formed that links objects by means of predicates. This type of pattern is described by three arguments - two objects of corresponding classes and a predicate term (group of terms). The predicates considered are a) relational names, b) verbs extracted from competency questions, and c) predicates extracted from the corpus using T-LSP, e.g. (3). All predicates have a corresponding lexico-semantic feature in the domain vocabulary. Consider the following example:

[Method(),<METHOD.Application>,Research object() ⇒
arg1::Method(applies_to:arg3) (5)

This pattern allows us to extract relations of the form *Method<applies to > Research object* if there is a term of lexico-semantic class METHOD.Application in the text between the mentions of these two objects. The result of applying this pattern is the creation of a new relation between an object of the *Method* class (arg1) and an object of the *Research object* class (arg3).

In practice, however, we need to specify additional syntactic constraints between the predicate and the term group, which may differ for specific predicate words. In this case the patterns look different:

[Method() <NOM>, *'is applied to'*, Research object () <DAT>] ⇒
arg1::Method(applied_to: arg3)

[Method() <NOM>, *'examine'*, Research object () <ACC>] ⇒
arg1::Method(applied_to: arg3) (6)

[Research object() <NOM>, *'examined'*, Method() <DAT>] ⇒
arg1::Method(applied_to: arg3)

In the same way the I-LSPs for attribute extraction (DatatypeProperty) are formed. The only difference is that the 3rd argument is a term belonging to the lexico-semantic class associated with this attribute:

[Method(), *'defined as'*, <METHOD.Description>] ⇒
arg1::Method(Description:arg3.Norm) (7)

This pattern populates the Description attribute for objects of the *Method* class using the N-grams collected by T-LSP from example (2).

4.3 LSP Generation Algorithm

The LSP generation process for each content pattern consists of 3 stages: a dictionary building, T-LSPs generation and I-LSPs construction (see Fig. 4).

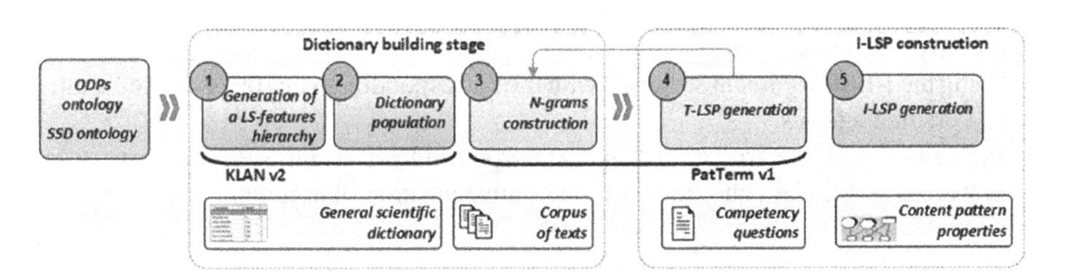

Fig. 4. The LSP generation scheme.

The dictionary building stage (steps 1–3) includes:

- analyzing hierarchical and structural relationships between the classes of the SSD ontology and generating a set of lexical and semantic features of the dictionary on their basis;

- extracting names of classes, attributes and relations from the content pattern, and extracting the names of extra classes and values of the attributes of individuals from the SSD ontology;
- getting normal forms of all names (using morphological and surface-syntactic analysis) and adding them to the subject vocabulary with appropriate lexical and semantic features;
- forming the N-grams from the normal forms of terms for which we cannot assemble noun phrases.

The LSPs generation stage consists of constructing T-LSPs and I-LSPs substages. At the T-LSPs construction substage (step 4), the following tasks are addressed:

- generating T-LSPs for assembling noun phrases, the vertices of which are class names (or their synonyms/quasi-synonyms); each pattern is formed on the basis of a template (see example (1)) with the replacement of the vertex with the corresponding term or indicating a certain lexico-semantic class as the vertex of the term;
- analyzing the issues of assessing competence and names of attributes/class relations, extracting predicate terms and their agreement with the terms of the general scientific dictionary (thereby expanding the list of synonyms or quasi-synonyms for a given predicate);
- generating T-LSPs based on predicate terms and relationship structure (see examples (2) and (3));
- analyzing T-LSPs occurrences in the corpus of texts expressing attributes/relations, and clarification of syntactic conditions for the agreement of predicate terms with actants.

The I-LSPs construction substage (step 5) addresses the following tasks:

- analyzing the structure of the content pattern, extracting the set of all binary connections between the components of the pattern and preparing the I-LSP template for each type of connection;
- filling the I-LSP argument structure with the corresponding types of associated entities and predicate terms,
- analyzing I-LSP occurrences in the text corpus and generating syntactic restrictions, as well as positional conditions for the relative position of arguments.

5 LSP-Based Ontology Population

To validate the proposed approach experimentally, we are developing an ontology populating system, which implements an ontology populating process as a pipeline starting from a raw text and ending with the LSP-based assembling of facts. When developing the system, we use various tools and technologies that we have developed to address NLP problems. They are KLAN, a vocabulary extraction tool [17, 18], PatTerm (Pattern-based Term extractor), a pattern-based text analysis tool [18], and FATON, a fact assembler [19].

The KLAN system allows for morphological and surface-syntactic text analysis, creating, on its basis, domain-specific dictionaries, and further extracting vocabulary terms from other texts. Also, the general scientific dictionary has been developed using the KLAN system. The PatTerm system is utilized for the LSP-based extraction of terms, and for the building T-LSPs given the list of literals. The FATON system is aimed to assemble facts, given the I-LSPs and a set of terms extracted by the KLAN and PatTerm systems.

Therefore, the LSP-generating and ontology populating system combines various technologies, and incorporates them into the single process of LSP-based ontology population (Fig. 5). It consists of an ontology integration module and two subsystems, which are an LSP generation subsystem and an LSP-based information retrieval subsystem.

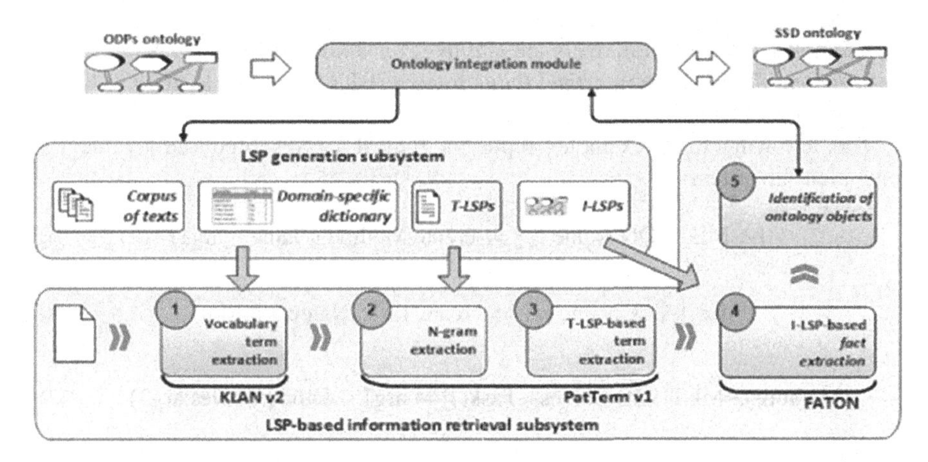

Fig. 5. The architecture of the LSP-based ontology populating system.

As stated in the previous chapter, the LSP generation subsystem facilitates constructing both terminological and informational lexico-syntactic patterns, as well as constructing a domain-specific dictionary necessary for using these patterns.

The LSP-based information retrieval subsystem is developed as a pipeline of data processors running sequentially. It implements a 5-staged ontology populating algorithm.

At stage 1, KLAN extracts vocabulary terms from text, enriching them with grammatical and semantic characteristics. At stages 2 and 3, the PatTerm system extracts N-grams created by the LSP generation subsystem and then extracts some new terms using T-LSPs with variables. The FATON system utilizes a multi-agent algorithm (stage 4) to pass through the set of terms searching for the arguments matching the I-LSPs provided. If arguments match an I-LSP, the algorithm checks whether they satisfy the constraints, and if they do, a new fact or object is assembled.

At the last stage (stage 5), all the objects constructed are identified, i.e. compared with the individuals in ontology. If an ontology individual matches some object, it is updated using object information. All new objects are added to the ontology as individuals.

The subsystems interact with the scientific subject domain ontology via the ontology integration module, which supports ontology-oriented programming from the owlready2

[20] library. In order to cover the ontologies designed using structural logical patterns, such as "Attributed binary relation" or "Admissible value range", we have extended the module with new features that allow working with complex properties just as well as with standard ones from the OWL language.

We have validated the approach proposed on a corpus of Russian texts with a length of 1 to 5 sentences. These texts are brief descriptions of various methods used in Decision Support Systems. Based on the content pattern "Method" and the ontology of Scientific Domain "Decision Support in weakly formalized areas," [21] we have created a domain-specific dictionary consisting of 214 terms marked with 21 lexical-semantic features, and 82 I-LSPs for extracting instances of the *Method* class and their properties. We have used the labels (rdfs:label) of the properties of the *Method* class, along with the values of the properties of the instances of this class and classes related to it, to generate a hierarchy of lexical-semantic features.

Examples of term-feature pairs are *additive convolution* (METHOD.Name), *knapsack problem* (TASK.Name), *artificial intelligence* (BRANCH_OF_SCIENCE.Name), *solves problem* (METHOD.solves), etc.

The following three examples represent typical I-LSPs produced by the LSP generation subsystem:

$$[< \text{METHOD.Name} >] \Rightarrow \text{create Method (Name : arg1)} \tag{8}$$

$$[< \text{TASK.Name} >] \Rightarrow \text{create Task (Name : arg1)} \tag{9}$$

$$\textbf{[Method(),<METHOD.Solves>,Task()]} \Rightarrow \textbf{arg1::Method(Solves:arg3)} \tag{10}$$

Figure 6 shows how the following text from out corpus was processed (in Russian): "*Support Vector Machines solves classification and regression analysis tasks by constructing a nonlinear plane that separates solutions.*"

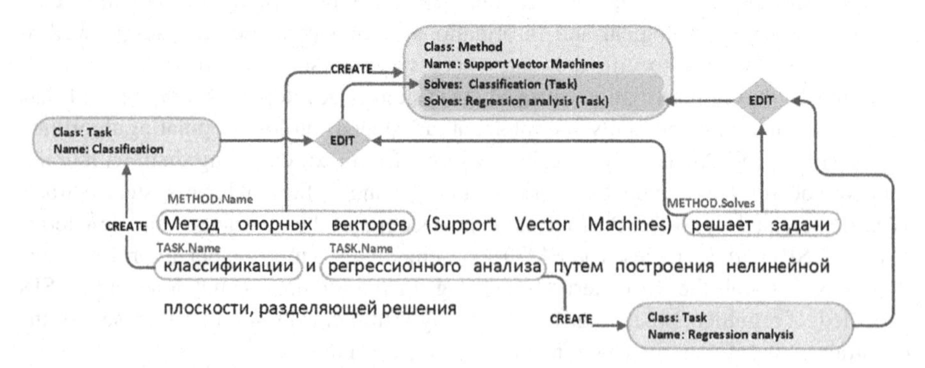

Fig. 6. LSP-based text processing (in Russian).

The algorithm found four terms having lexical-semantic features METHOD.Name, TASK.Name and METHOD.solves. Corresponding to the initializing I-LSPs (8) and

(9), three instances were created: one instance of the *Method* class and two instances of the *Task* class. Then, according to the I-LSP (10), the *"Support Vector Machine"* instance was linked with the instances of *Tasks* it solves, which are *"Classification"* and *"Regression Analysis"*.

6 Conclusion

The paper describes an approach proposed by the authors to automate the construction and population of scientific subject domains ontologies, based on heterogeneous ontology design patterns, including lexico-syntactic patterns.

A feature of this approach is that the development and initial filling of the SSD ontology is carried out by knowledge engineers and experts in the SSD using such ODPs as content patterns and structural patterns. Further population of the SSD ontology can be performed automatically with lexico-syntactic patterns built on the basis of content patterns included in the system repository and the current version of the SSD ontology. That is, the main difference between our approach and other approaches [12, 13, 22] using LSPs is that in our approach LSPs are generated automatically.

It should also be noted that you cannot develop an ontology once and for all. You need to keep it continuously up to date. To solve this problem, LSPs can be used, which automatically populate the ontology with appropriate information from new publications and information resources.

This approach has shown its practical utility in the development of ontologies for various scientific subject areas ("Support for solving computationally complex problems on supercomputers" [18], "Decision Support in weakly formalized areas" [9, 21], etc.).

In the near future, it is planned to develop a specialized pattern editor to support the presentation and construction of the ODPs in the form of graphs.

Acknowledgment. The research has been supported by Russian Foundation for Basic Research (project no. 19–07-00762).

References

1. Sure, Y., Staab, S., Studer, R.: Ontology engineering methodology. In: Staab, S., Studer, R. (eds.) Handbook on Ontologies. IHIS, pp. 135–152. Springer, Heidelberg (2009). https://doi.org/10.1007/978-3-540-92673-3_6
2. De Nicola, A., Missikoff, M.: A lightweight methodology for rapid ontology engineering. Commun. ACM **59**, 79–86 (2016)
3. Sattar, A., Salwana, E., Surin, M., Ahmad, M.N., Ahmad, M., Mahmood, A.K.: Comparative analysis of methodologies for domain ontology development: a systematic review. Int. J. Adv. Comput. Sci. Appl. **11**(5), 99–108 (2020)
4. Blomqvist, E., Hammar, K., Presutti, V.: Engineering ontologies with patterns: the extreme design methodology. In: Hitzler, P., Gangemi, A., Janowicz, K., Krisnadhi, A., Presutti, V. (eds.) Ontology Engineering with Ontology Design Patterns. Studies on the Semantic Web, vol. 25, pp. 23–50. IOS Press, Amsterdam (2016)

5. Zagorulko, Y., Borovikova, O., Zagorulko, G.: Development of ontologies of scientific subject domains using ontology design patterns. In: Kalinichenko, L., Manolopoulos, Y., Malkov, O., Skvortsov, N., Stupnikov, S., Sukhomlin, V. (eds.) DAMDID/RCDL 2017. CCIS, vol. 822, pp. 141–156. Springer, Cham (2018). https://doi.org/10.1007/978-3-319-96553-6_11
6. Zagorulko, Y., Borovikova, O., Zagorulko, G.: Pattern-based methodology for building the ontologies of scientific subject domains. In: Fujita, H., Herrera-Viedma, E., (eds.) New Trends in Intelligent Software Methodologies, Tools and Techniques. Proceedings of the 17th International Conference SoMeT_18. Series: Frontiers in Artificial Intelligence and Applications, vol. 303. Amsterdam, IOS Press (2018)
7. Glinskiy, B., et al.: Building ontologies for solving compute-intensive problem. J. Phys.: Conf. Ser. **1715**, 012071 (2021)
8. Snytnikov, A.V., Glinskiy, B.M., Zagorulko, G.B., Zagorulko, Y.A.: Ontological approach to formalization of knowledge in computational plasma physics. J. Phys.: Conf. Ser. **1640**, 012013 (2020)
9. Zagorulko, Y., Zagorulko, G.: Features of development of internet resource for supporting developers of intelligent decision support systems. Open Semant. Technol. Intell. Syst. **8**, 63–67 (2018)
10. Petasis, G., Karkaletsis, V., Paliouras, G., Krithara, A., Zavitsanos, E.: Ontology population and enrichment: state of the art. In: Paliouras, G., Spyropoulos, C.D., Tsatsaronis, G. (eds.) Knowledge-Driven Multimedia Information Extraction and Ontology Evolution. LNCS (LNAI), vol. 6050, pp. 134–166. Springer, Heidelberg (2011). https://doi.org/10.1007/978-3-642-20795-2_6
11. Ganino, G., Lembo, D., Mecella, M., Scafoglieri, F.: Ontology population for open-source intelligence: a GATE-based solution. Softw.: Pract. Exp. **48**(12), 2302–2330 (2018)
12. Maynard, D., Funk, A., Peters, W.: Using lexico-syntactic ontology design patterns for ontology creation and population. In: Proceedings of the Workshop on Ontology Patterns (WOP 2009), collocated with the 8th International Semantic Web Conference (ISWC-2009). vol. 516, pp. 39–52. CEUR Workshop Proceedings (CEUR-WS.org) (2009)
13. Ijntema, W., Sangers, J., Hogenboom, F., Frasincar, F.: A lexico-semantic pattern language for learning ontology instances from text. Journal of Web Semantics **15**, 37–50 (2012)
14. Gangemi, A., Presutti, V.: Ontology design patterns. In: Staab, S., Studer, R. (eds.) Handbook on Ontologies. IHIS, pp. 221–243. Springer, Heidelberg (2009). https://doi.org/10.1007/978-3-540-92673-3_10
15. Association for Ontology Design & Patterns. http://ontologydesignpatterns.org, Accessed on 20 July 2021
16. Karima, N., Hammar, K., Hitzler, P.: How to document ontology design patterns. In: Advances in Ontology Design and Patterns. Studies on the Semantic Web, vol. 32, pp. 15–27. IOS Press, Kobe, Japan (2017)
17. Sidorova, E.: Ontology-based approach to modeling the process of extracting information from text [In Russian]. Ontol. Design. **8**(1), 134–151 (2018)
18. Sidorova, E., Akhmadeeva, I.: The software environment for multi-aspect study of lexical characteristics of text. In: Selected Papers of the XX International Conference on Data Analytics and Management in Data Intensive Domains (DAMDID/RCDL 2019). CEUR Workshop Proceedings, vol. 2523, pp. 306–315 (2019)
19. Garanina, N., Sidorova, E., Bodin, E.: A multi-agent text analysis based on ontology of subject domain. In: Voronkov, A., Virbitskaite, I. (eds.) PSI 2014. LNCS, vol. 8974, pp. 102–110. Springer, Heidelberg (2015). https://doi.org/10.1007/978-3-662-46823-4_9
20. Lamy, J.-B.: Owlready: Ontology-oriented programming in Python with automatic classification and high level constructs for biomedical ontologies. Artif. Intell. Med. **80**, 11–28 (2017)

21. Zagorulko, G.: Development of ontology for intelligent scientific internet resource decision-making support in weakly formalized domains [In Russian]. Ontol. Design. **6**(4), 485–500 (2016)
22. de Cea, G.A., Gomez-Perez, A., Montiel-Ponsoda, E., Suarez-Figueroa, M.C. Using linguistic patterns to enhance ontology development. In: Proceedings of the International Conference on Knowledge Engineering and Ontology Development (KEOD 2009), pp. 206–213. Funchal - Madeira, Portugal, October 6–8, 2009. INSTICC Press (2009)

Fuzzy Models and Soft Computing

The PC-Algorithm of the Algebraic Bayesian Network Secondary Structure Training

Nikita Kharitonov[1(✉)], Maxim Abramov[2], and Alexander Tulupyev[1,2]

[1] St. Petersburg State University, St. Petersburg, Russia
nak@dscs.pro

[2] St. Petersburg Federal Research Center of the Russian Academy of Sciences, St. Petersburg, Russia

Abstract. Algebraic Bayesian networks and Bayesian belief networks are one of the probabilistic graphical models. One of the main tasks which need to be solved during the networks' handling is the model structure training. This paper is dedicated to the automation of this process for algebraic Bayesian networks.

This work relates to the PC-algorithm for algebraic Bayesian network secondary structure training. The algorithm is based on the PC-algorithm for Belief Bayesian networks training. The algorithm pseudo-code and usage example are described. The provided algorithm helps investigate the full-automated machine learning of algebraic Bayesian networks. Earlier, the structure was provided by experts.

Keywords: Algebraic bayesian networks · Bayesian belief networks · Probabilistic graphical models · Structure training · PC-algorithm

1 Introduction

Algebraic Bayesian networks and Bayesian belief networks relate to the class of probabilistic graphical models. The latter are used in different research fields for system modeling and prediction of its behavior [4,10,11]. The difference of algebraic Bayesian from other models is that they allow using interval probability estimates.

One of the main tasks solved during the machine learning is model training. For algebraic Bayesian networks, this task has two subtasks: the model structure training and probability estimates training. The second task has several solutions, for example, [3]. But the automated solution of the first task has not been presented yet. This work is dedicated to the automation of the algebraic Bayesian network structure training.

This research was supported by the St. Petersburg Federal Research Center of the Russian Academy of Sciences, the government task No. 0073-2019-0003 and by St. Petersburg State University, project No. 73555239.

S. M. Kovalev et al. (Eds.): RCAI 2021, LNAI 12948, pp. 267–273, 2021.
https://doi.org/10.1007/978-3-030-86855-0_18

The fact that both the algebraic Bayesian network and Bayesian belief network have similar probabilistic semantics allows us to generate an algebraic Bayesian network from a Bayesian belief network. In this research, this fact is used for creating an algorithm for generating the secondary structure of the algebraic Bayesian network based on a PC-algorithm. The algorithm's pseudo-code and example of usage are also described.

2 Related Works

As has been mentioned above, algebraic Bayesian networks [12,13] are related to the class of probabilistic graphical networks. The latter are used in a lot of applied research, for example, in medicine and social science [4,10,11].

The main idea of algebraic Bayesian networks is the decomposition of information in a network into smaller strongly-related parts called knowledge patterns. The mathematical model of a knowledge pattern can be the ideal of conjuncts, disjuncts, or quanta set (the set of all possible conjunctions under the given variables). The whole network can be presented as a set of knowledge patterns. This representation is called the secondary structure of algebraic Bayesian networks.

All the knowledge patterns in a given network have one of the possible representations. In [12,13], it is shown that for all representations, it is possible to convert one representation to another, and transformation matrices are provided.

Each of the knowledge pattern's elements has probability estimation. Nilsson's approach [5–7] for the introduction of probabilities is used; a sample space for probability space is the set of quanta. Therefore, the information in the knowledge pattern is represented as a probabilities distribution (Figs. 1, 2, 3).

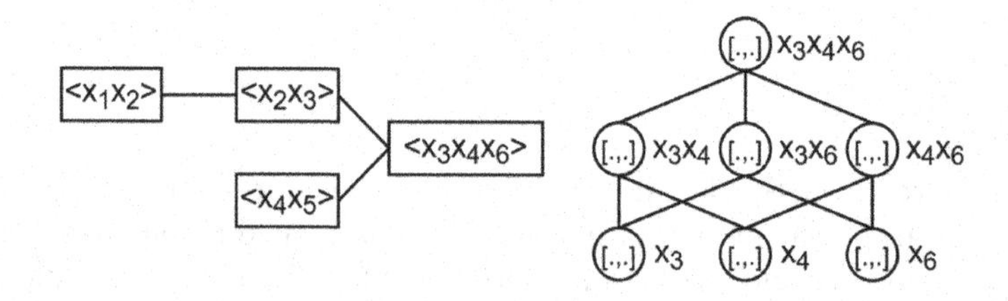

Fig. 1. The example of an algebraic Bayesian network and knowledge pattern presented as the ideal of conjuncts. [.,.] is some interval estimate of conjunct probability.

One of the main tools of algebraic Bayesian networks is the possibility to process interval probability estimates of elements. In that case, the information in the networks is represented as a set of probabilities distributions.

The main operations in algebraic Bayesian networks are a priori and a posteriori inference [14,15]. The former allows one to receive the probability of some event, which is described by a probabilistic formula. The latter helps update the estimates in networks with a new incoming information.

First, it is required to build a network. The work [3] presents approaches for receiving probabilities estimates in network based on some data set. This paper focuses on the training of network structure on information, which is represented as a set of statistically received statements about the conditional independence of variables.

3 PC-Algorithm

Bayesian belief networks [8] are also related to the class of probabilistic graphical models. Conditional independence and d-separation are the probabilistic basis for them.

Bayesian belief network graph presentation is a directed graph without cycles. Each of the nodes contains variable x and a set of conditional probabilities on x given variables, which are in parent nodes.

The d-separation is one of the main definitions in Bayesian networks theory.

Let's consider graph G and graph path p. p is d-separated by the set of nodes A only when:

- p contains chain $i \rightarrow m \rightarrow j$ or fork $i \leftarrow m \rightarrow j$, such as $m \in A$;
- p contains collider $i \rightarrow m \leftarrow j$, such as $m \notin A$ and $children(m) \notin A$.

The main feature of d-separation is: each two d-separated nodes are conditionally independent; each two conditionally independent nodes are d-separated.

One of the main ways for Bayesian belief network generation is a PC-algorithm [9].

The main steps are as follows [12]:

1. Build the undirected graph $G = (V, E)$ with all possible nodes.
2. $k := 0; \forall x, y \in V DSep(x, y) := \emptyset$.
3. while $\exists x, y$ that number of neighbors more than k:
   (a) Foreach pair of neighbors x, y
      i. if $\forall S \in V : |S| = k; x, y \notin S; p(XY|S) = 0$,
         then delete edge between x and y; $DSep(x, y) = DSep(x, y) \cup S$.
   (b) k := k + 1
4. foreach undirected chain $x - y - z$
   (a) if $y \notin DSep(x, z)$,
      then replace chain on collider $x \rightarrow y \leftarrow z$.
5. Repeat
   (a) forall undirected edges $y - z$:
      i. if $x - y$ becomes a part of undirected chain $x - y - z$, step 3 hasn't give a result and then $x - y$ become $x \rightarrow y$,
         then $y \leftarrow z$;
      ii. if $y \leftarrow z$ creates a cycle,
         then $y \rightarrow z$.
6. Return result

There is an example of PC-algorithm usage. Suppose that before the algorithm call, the next data was received using statistical methods (pic.1a):

- U is independent of V;
- U, V are conditionally independent of W given X;
- W is independent of X;
- W, X are conditionally independent of Y given Z.

At the first step, the undirected graph with all possible nodes is built (Pic. 1b).

At the second step, edges are removed in pair U, V and pair W, X (pic. 1c).

At the third step, for each two connected nodes A, B, all the edges are removed to vertices C, such as A conditionally independent B given C (pic. 1d).

At the fourth step, for all three A-B-C, the collider is built (pic. 1e).

At the fifth step, the left edges are built (pic. 1f).

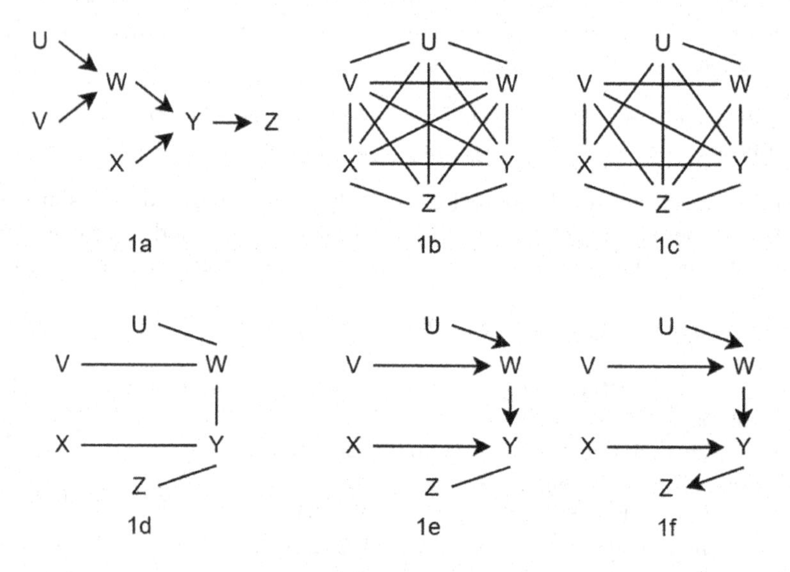

Fig. 2. The PC-algorithm for belief bayesian network generation

4 Generation of an Algebraic Bayesian Network Based on the Bayesian Belief Network

The probabilistic semantics of algebraic Bayesian networks coincides locally with the semantics of Bayesian belief networks [12]. This fact allows us to build an algebraic Bayesian network based on the available Bayesian belief network.

A priori inference allows us to receive the probability estimates of elements, which cannot be calculated from the data in the Bayesian belief network directly.

Knowledge patterns are built on the nodes of the Bayesian belief network: the collider $x \to y \leftarrow z$ will be converted into a knowledge pattern $[x, y, z]$, and chains $x \to y \to z$ and forks $x \leftarrow y \to z$ will be converted into two knowledge patterns $[x, y], [y, z]$.

5 PC-Algorithm for Algebraic Bayesian Networks

The process mentioned above allows us to modify the existing PC-algorithm for the Bayesian belief network to obtain an algebraic Bayesian network.

We will consider the algebraic Bayesian network as a set of knowledge patterns during the network building process. This representation allows us to easily find the connection between them.

The first three steps of the PC-algorithm will be the same.

At the fourth step, instead of creating a collider, the knowledge pattern with three atoms is built.

The fifth step of the algorithm will have the only one point because the algebraic Bayesian network has no directed edges: both nodes x, y, which have an edge between them and are not in a knowledge pattern yet, are added to a new knowledge pattern $[x, y]$.

Here is the pseudo-code of a PC-algorithm for an algebraic Bayesian network generation:

1. Build the undirected graph $G = (V, E)$ with all possible nodes.
2. $k := 0; \forall x, y \in V DSep(x, y) := \emptyset; ABN := \emptyset$.
3. while $\exists x, y$ that number of neighbors more than k:
   (a) Foreach pair of neighbors x, y
      i. if $\forall S \in V : |S| = k; x, y \notin S; p(XY|S) = 0$,
         then delete edge between x and y; $DSep(x, y) = DSep(x, y) \cup S$.
   (b) k := k + 1
4. foreach undirected chain $x - y - z$
   (a) if $y \notin DSep(x, z)$,
      then $ABN = ABN \cup [x, y, z]$. Remove edges $x - y$ and $y - z$.
5. Repeat
   (a) forall undirected edges $x - z$:
      $ABN = ABN \cup [x, y]$. Remove edge $x - y$.
6. Return result

The removal of the edges is required to avoid an infinitive cycle.

Let us show the example of the algorithm usage. The input data are the same as in Section Two of the paper. The steps 1–3 are also the same, as in the PC-algorithm for Bayesian belief networks (pic. 2a-2c.).

At the fourth step, two knowledge patterns with three atoms are built.

At the fifth step, the final knowledge pattern is built.

The PC-algorithm for the algebraic Bayesian network structure generation has smaller complexity than the PC-algorithm for the Bayesian belief network structure generation because it is not necessary to store the edges' direction,

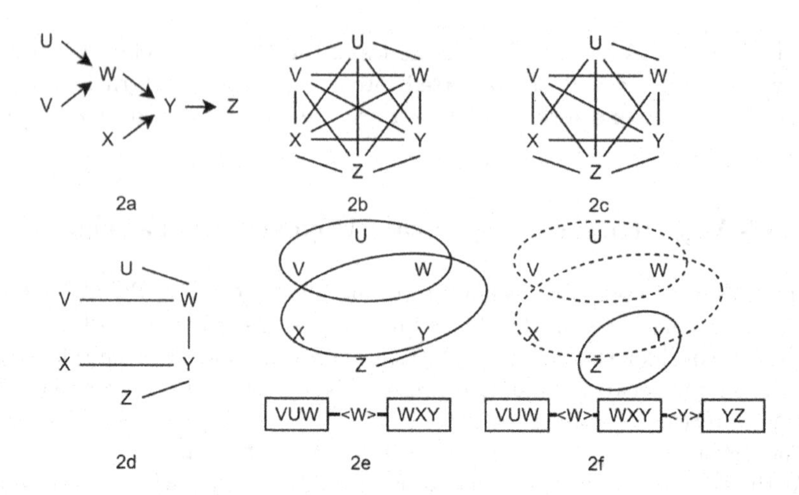

Fig. 3. The PC-algorithm for algebraic bayesian network structure generation

and a less complex fifth step. Also, there is a good opportunity for the algorithm optimisation by using parallel computing.

The complexity of the PC-algorithm for the generation of an algebraic Bayesian network structure depends on data coherence. If the coherence is weak, more edges will be deleted at the third step, and fewer operations will be done at the following steps.

The algebraic Bayesian network generated by the algorithm has only two- and three-atomic knowledge patterns. This also has an optimisation effect because the complexity of operations in a knowledge pattern grows exponentially with the number of atoms in it.

6 Conclusion

The paper describes the PC-algorithm for the generation of an algebraic Bayesian network structure. This is the first algorithm for algebraic Bayesian network structure training based on the input data. The provided algorithm allows one to investigate the full-automated machine learning of algebraic Bayesian networks. Earlier, the structure was provided by experts.

The next steps of the research are the optimisation of the algorithm with parallel computing and its practical use in the area of social engineering attacks [1,2].

References

1. Khlobystova, A., Abramov, M.: The models separation of access rights of users to critical documents of information system as factor of reduce impact of successful social engineering attacks. CEUR Workshop Proc. **2782**, 264–268 (2020)
2. Bushmelev, F., Abramov, M., Tulupyeva, T.: Adaptive method of color selection in application to social media images. CEUR Workshop Proc. **2782**, 252–257 (2020)

3. Kharitonov, N.A., Maximov, A.G., Tulupyev, A.L.: Algebraic bayesian networks: naïve frequentist approach to local machine learning based on imperfect information from social media and expert estimates. In: Kuznetsov, S.O., Panov, A.I. (eds.) RCAI 2019. CCIS, vol. 1093, pp. 234–244. Springer, Cham (2019). https://doi.org/10.1007/978-3-030-30763-9_20
4. Liang, R., Liu, F., Liu, J.: A belief network reasoning framework for fault localization in communication networks. Sensors **20**(3), 1–21 (2020). art. 6950
5. Nilsson, N.J.: Probabilistic logic. Artif. Intell. **28**, 71–87 (1986)
6. Nilsson, N.J.: Logic and artificial intelligence. Artif. Intell. **47**, 31–56 (1991)
7. Nilsson, N.J.: Probabilistic Logic Revisited. Artif. Intell. **59**, 39–42 (1993)
8. Pearl, J.: Causality: Models, Reasoning, and Inference. Cambridge University Press, Cambridge (2000)
9. Spirtes, P., Glymour, C., Scheines, R.: Causation, Prediction, and Search, 2nd edn. MIT Press, Cambridge (2001)
10. Steijn W.M.P., Van Kampen J.N., Van der Beek D., Groeneweg J., Van Gelder P.H.A.J.M.: An integration of human factors into quantitative risk analysis using bayesian belief networks towards developing a QRA+. Saf. Sci. **122**, 104514 (2020)
11. Toropova, A., Tulupyeva, T.: Comparison of behavior rate models based on bayesian belief network. In: Dolinina, O., et al. (eds.) ICIT 2020. SSDC, vol. 337, pp. 510–521. Springer, Cham (2021). https://doi.org/10.1007/978-3-030-65283-8_42
12. Tulupyev, A.L., Nikolenko, S.I., Sirotkin, A.V.: Bayesian Belief Networks: Probabilisticlogic Approach. Nauka, Saint-Petersburg SPb. (2006). (in Russian)
13. Tulupyev, A.L., Sirotkin, A.V., Nikolenko, S.I.: Bayesian Belief Networks. SPbSU Press, Saint-Petersburg (2009). (in Russian)
14. Zolotin A.A., Malchevskaya E.A., Kharitonov N.A., Tulupyev A.L.: Local and global logical-probabilistic inference in the Algebraic Bayesian networks: matrix-vector description and the sensitivity questions. Fuzzy systems and soft calculations, Tver: TvGTU, pp. 133–150 (2017) (in Russian)
15. Zolotin, A.A., Tulupyev, A.L.: Sensitivity statistical estimates for local a posteriori inference matrix-vector equations in algebraic bayesian networks over quantum propositions. Vestnik St. Petersburg Univ. Math. **51**(1), 42–48 (2018). https://doi.org/10.3103/S1063454118010168

Logistic-Based Design of Fuzzy Interpretable Classifiers

Alexander Dolgiy[1(✉)], Sergey Kovalev[1,2], Anna Kolodenkova[3], and Andrey Sukhanov[1,2]

[1] JSC NIIAS, Moscow, Russia
a.suhanov@rfniias.ru
[2] Rostov State Transport University, Rostov-on-Don, Russia
[3] Samara State Technical University, Samara, Russia

Abstract. The paper develops an idea of fuzzy evidential classifiers based on modification of logistic regression model and Dempster–Shafer methodology. The proposed approach is integrating the additional linguistic variable into the classifier. This variable considers different shades of truth for class membership hypotheses and enriches available information for decision-making. It leads to identification of pre-failure states and detecting anomalies, inconsistency, and incorrectness in the initial data. As a result of the research, linguistic log-regression model is shown, and its components are justified. The inference procedure based on the model is illustrated. In the end, a simple example of implementation is also shown.

Keywords: Logistic regression · Linguistic scale · Dempster–Shafer scheme · Fuzzy evidential classifier

1 Introduction

Nowadays, classifiers are widely used in the implementations of image recognition and machine learning. Classifiers are the special mathematical models that are used to group observed objects into classes reflecting their affinity scale. The most popular classifiers are decision trees [1], fuzzy neural nets [2], Bayes classifier [3], and k-nearest neighbor model [4]. As well, in practice (particularly, in diagnostics), the logistic regression-based classifiers are implemented [5]. However, the overall shortcoming of the above-mentioned models is that it is impossible to interpret the operations of decision justification, assessment of the impact of different uncertain factors, justification of conflict decisions, and anomalous observations. Besides, traditional mathematical models do not provide manual operations during the training phase to correct a classifier, which is sometimes required for human-machine systems with an increased level of reliability and security. To exclude these shortcomings, in recent years, the design techniques

The work was supported by RFBR grants Nos. 19-07-00263, 19-07-00195, 19-08-00152, 20-07-00100, and 20-37-51002.

S. M. Kovalev et al. (Eds.): RCAI 2021, LNAI 12948, pp. 274–285, 2021.
https://doi.org/10.1007/978-3-030-86855-0_19

for interpretable mathematical models have been developed [6, 7]. Interpretable classifiers take the particular interest. These classifiers can find the practical implementations for knowledge retrieval, anomaly detection, heterogeneous data fusion, and interactive decision-making systems. An interpretable classifier is a classification model, algorithm and result of which are represented via a convenient form for a user.

To increase the classifiers' interpretability, one of the ways is to develop hybrid evidential classifiers that are based on a combination of several techniques. In particular, the combination of belief function theory of Dempster–Shafer (DS) [8, 9] together with mathematical models based on logistic regression [10] can be used. The evidential classifier splits the evidence of input data vector into probabilistic mass functions with their further combination based on the Dempster rule. Then, the resulting function is used for decision-making. Due to the generality and expressiveness of the formalism of evidence functions, evidence classifiers provide receiving more informative results than conventional ones. This expressiveness can be used for quantitative estimation of uncertainty and for increased interpretability of classification models.

In recent years, a set of evidential classifiers has been developed for the wide range of implementations [11, 12, 21]. In [13], the classifiers, which are based on the models using class-conditional distributions and general Bayes theory, are considered. In [3, 15], authors show the extensions of Bayes' theorem, where mass functions m_j are constructed based on distances to train samples or prototypes. In [14], the evidential classifier, which is based on k-nearest neighbor, is proposed and, in [15–20], its variations are presented. In [22], the evidential neural classifier is proposed, where mass functions are constructed based on the distances to prototypes.

The current work develops the idea of fuzzy evidential classifiers based on the modification of logistic regression model and DS techniques. The proposed approach is the extension of the classifier in the form of an additional linguistic variable whose values characterize different truth values of class membership hypotheses and enrich the available information for decision-making.

2 Elements of DS Theory

Let $Q = \{q_1,..., q_k\}$ be the universal set of hypotheses about considered facts (true or false hypotheses). Let 2^Q be the exponential set characterizing a plurality of subsets from set Q. Probability function of mass distribution (m-function) is the mapping m: $2^Q \to [0, 1]$ such that:

$$\sum\nolimits_{A \subseteq Q} m(A) = 1 \text{ and } m(\emptyset) = 0 \tag{1}$$

Practically, Q is considered as a hypothesis set and mass function m is considered as some evidence regarding the truth of these hypotheses. Each $m(A)$ means the rate of unit probability mass for hypothesis A. Each subset $A \subseteq Q$ ($m(A) > 0$) is called the focal set regarding m.

Two functions, belief and plausibility, are connected with mass function m. These functions present the interval of possibility for the groups from Q, and they are computed as follows:

$$
\begin{aligned}
Bel(A) &:= \sum_{B \subseteq A} m(B), \\
Pl(A) &:= \sum_{B \cap A \neq \emptyset} m(B) = 1 - Bel(\overline{A}).
\end{aligned}
\tag{2}
$$

Bel(*A*) is interpreted as the support rate of *A*, and *Pl*(*A*) is interpreted as the "non-support" rate of *A*.

The key element of the DS technique is the combination rule of *m*-functions representing pieces of independent evidence regarding the truth of hypotheses. Using the DS rule, two *m*-functions (m_1 and m_2) are combined into the unified *m*-function, which is also called the orthogonal sum [8, 9]:

$$
(m_1 \oplus m_2)(A) := \frac{1}{1-k} \sum_{B \cap C = A} m_1(B) m_2(C) \tag{3}
$$

Where $A \subseteq Q$, $A \neq 0$ and $(m_1 \oplus m_2)(\emptyset) = 0$. The value of *k* has a sense of the conflict rate of the *m*-function and is defined as follows:

$$
k = \sum_{B \cap C = \emptyset} m_1(B) m_2(C)
$$

Although, the DS rule is commutative and associative, it has exponential complexity. Computations via the DS rule are essentially simplified for special *m*-functions called *m*-singletons.

Mass function *m* is called a singleton if it has the following form:

$$
m(A) = s, m(Q) = 1 - s, \tag{4}
$$

where $A \subset Q$, $A \neq 0$, $s \in [0, 1]$ is the support rate of *A*.

For the *m*-singleton, the weight function is defined as [9]:

$$
w(A) := -\ln(1 - m(A)). \tag{5}
$$

The value of *w* is the weight of evidence, which is connected with *m*. For *m*-singletons, the following property of the orthogonal sum takes place.

Property. For *m*-singletons m_1 and m_2 with the identical focal set *A*, their orthogonal sum is also *m*-singleton and weights obtained via DS-rule are summed. Let the *m*-singleton with focal set *A* and weight *w* be designated as A^w. Then, this property can be presented as follows [23]:

$$
A^{w_1} \oplus A^{w_2} = A^{w_1 + w_2}. \tag{6}
$$

The mass function is called separable if it can be decomposed into the orthogonal sum of simple *m*-functions. Therefore, the separable *m*-function can be written as:

$$
m = \bigoplus_{\emptyset \neq A \subset \Theta} A^{w(A)}, \tag{7}
$$

where $w(\cdot)$ is the mapping of form $2^Q\{\emptyset, Q\} \rightarrow [0, +\infty)$.

In such a way, the evidence weights are summed when the DS rule is applied.

3 Classification Model Based on Logistic Regression

This model is developed for solving the problem of classification of d-scaled feature vectors $\mathbf{x} = (x_1, \ldots, x_d)$ into K classes $Q = \{q_1, \ldots, q_k\}$ based on the analysis of linear regression (log-regression equations). Linear regression establishes the dependency between logistic probabilities of the occurring class q_i in the form of an affine function:

$$\ln P_k(\mathbf{x}) = \boldsymbol{\beta}_k^T \mathbf{x} + \beta_{k_0} k = 1, \ldots, K, \tag{8}$$

where $p_k(\mathbf{x}) = P(q_k|\mathbf{x})$ is the posterior probability of q_k; $\beta_k \in \mathbb{R}^d$ and $\beta_{k0} \in \mathbb{R}$ are the parameters depending on q_k. The posterior probability of q_k can be expressed from (8) as:

$$P(q_k|\mathbf{x}) = \frac{\exp(\boldsymbol{\beta}_k^T \mathbf{x} + \beta_{k_0})}{\sum_{l=1}^{K} \exp(\boldsymbol{\beta}_l^T \mathbf{x} + \beta_{l_0})}. \tag{9}$$

The transformation of linear combinations of features $\beta_k^T x + \beta_{k0} \in R\boldsymbol{\beta}_k^T \mathbf{x} + \beta_{k_0} \in \mathbb{R}$ into probabilities belonging to [0; 1] based on (9) is called softmax-transform.

For the known training set of samples $\{(\mathbf{x}_i y_i)\}^n{}_{i=1}$, parameters β and β_0 are generally estimated as a maximization of conditional logarithmic plausibility:

$$\sum_{i=1}^{n} \sum_{j=1}^{k} [\delta^j_{Q(\mathbf{x}_i)} \ln p_j(\mathbf{x}_i) + (1 - \delta^j_{Q(\mathbf{x}_i)}) \ln(1 - p_j(\mathbf{x}_i)]. \tag{10}$$

Classifiers of logistic regression define solution areas separated by hyperplanes.

4 Evidential Classifier

The work of the evidential classifier is based on the idea of the representation of each feature x_j from input vector $\mathbf{x}$ as the independent evidence referred to one or the other class with the further conjunction based on the DS rule (3).

In the evidential classifier, the log-regression function computed for each class q_k and feature x_j is considered as the independent evidence referring q_k. This function is sometimes called the weight function, which is computed as:

$$w_{jk} = \beta_{jk} x_j + \beta_{0k}. \tag{11}$$

The weight function acts as evidence referring q_k or as one referring adjunct $\neg q_k$ depending on the sign of (11).

Based on (11), the weights of evidence are computed for q_k and $\neg q_k$. They are titled w_{jk}^+ and w_{jk}^- and equal to positive and negative parts of (4.1). As a result, two singlet m-functions $m_{jk}^+ := \{\theta_k\}^{w_{jk}^+}$ and $m_{jk}^- := \{\bar{\theta}_k\}^{w_{jk}^-}$ for each value of x_j and q_k are formed. When the features are combined via the DS rule, their weights are summed on the basis of (6) separately for the positive parts and negative ones of the weight function (11). As a result, the following combined weight functions are obtained for q_k:

$$m_k^+ := \bigoplus_{j=1}^{J} m_{jk}^+ = \{\theta_k\}^{w_k^+},\ m_k^- := \bigoplus_{j=1}^{J} m_{jk}^- = \{\bar{\theta}_k\}^{w_k^-},\ w_k^+ := \sum_{j=1}^{J} w_{jk}^+,\ w_k^- := \sum_{j=1}^{J} w_{jk}^-. \tag{12}$$

The resulting class probabilities $P_m(q_k)$ inducted by m-functions are computed based on softmax-transform:

$$p_m(q_k) = \frac{\exp\left(\sum_{j=1}^{J} \beta_{jk}\mathbf{x} + \beta_{0_k}\right)}{\sum_{l=1}^{K} \exp\left(\sum_{j=1}^{J} \beta_{jl}\mathbf{x} + \beta_{0_l}\right)}. \tag{13}$$

5 Linguistic Scale for Hypotheses of Class Membership

For the classification of vectors $\mathbf{x} \in \mathbf{X}$ belonging K classes $Q = \{q_1,\ldots, q_K\}$, let $g{:} =$ "$\mathbf{x} \in q_k$" be the hypothesis that $\mathbf{x}$ belongs to $q_k \in Q$ and $Thr = Thr_k$ be the linguistic variable (LV) "TRUTH" characterizing truth value of this hypothesis. Thr has a set of linguistic values (LVals) $\eta_1,\ldots,\eta_n$ reflecting the different truth degree of g. The LVals form linguistic scale L, where they are in descending order referring the truth property of g. Simultaneously, the property of uncertainty is increased when the truth property is decreased. Uncertainty characterizes the ambiguity that $\mathbf{x}$ belongs to q_k. In other words, it shows the possibility that $\mathbf{x}$ belongs not only to q_k but also to other classes from Q, which can formally be expressed as:

$$\text{"}\exists V \subseteq Q \ \ \mathbf{x} \in \{q_k \cup V\}\text{"}. \tag{14}$$

It is obvious that an increase of uncertainty of g leads to the extension of subset V surrounding q_k. In the limit case corresponding to complete uncertainty of g, V equals Q. It actually means the equal possibility of $\mathbf{x}$ belonging to any class from Q. In this case, the truth measure of g becomes minimal and uncertainty one becomes maximal. Full uncertainty of hypothesis that $\mathbf{x}$ belongs to q_k is represented by another limit fuzzy term η_n on linguistic scale L.

In this way, LVals $\eta_1,\ldots,\eta_n$ form a bipolar scale, where the limit left LVal η_1 reflects the absolute truth of membership hypothesis of $\mathbf{x}$ to q_k and the limit right one reflects full uncertainty or a lack of knowledge about $\mathbf{x}$ belonging to any class. LVal lying between η_1 and η_n on scale L represent intermediate estimates of truth for hypothesis $x \in q_k$. As an example, four-valued scale $L_4{:} =$ [True, Almost True, Possibly True, Unknown] can be considered.

It should be noted that as opposed to the traditional bipolar truth scale, where limit values reflect opposite properties, which are True or False, the above-mentioned scale is unipolar with absent intermediate point interpreted as "Neither true, nor false." Here, the distance from the first point of scale means the grade of truth, and the distance from the last point means the grade of uncertainty.

Let the approach to formalization of linguistic scale L be considered on the basis of a combination of class membership hypotheses.

Let LVal η_1 characterizing absolute truth of $\mathbf{x} \in q_k$ be designated as $g_1 := \mathbf{x} \in q_k$. Further, let it be presented in form $V_1 = \{q_k\}$. Following value η_2 brings some uncertainty into hypothesis g_1 and characterizes the possibility of $\mathbf{x}$ belonging not only to q_k (or V_1), but also to some subset $V_2 \subset Q$ that can be presented as hypothesis $g_2 := \mathbf{x} \in V_2$.

Therefore, LVal η_2 extending uncertainty of η_1 can be represented by hypothesis $g_1 \vee g_2$, or, in terms of the DS theory, by a complex hypothesis $\{g_1, g_2\}$. In turn, by analogy, η_3 extends the uncertainty of previous LVal η_2 on scale L and characterizes the fact of $\mathbf{x}$ belonging to some class subset V_3 "surrounding" the set $\{V_1 \cup V_2\}$, which is presented by hypothesis $g_3 := \mathbf{x} \in V_3$. Therefore, η_3 extending the uncertainty of the previous η_2 is represented as a complex hypothesis $\{g_1, g_2, g_3\}$. As a result, ordered hypothesis set $\{g_1\}$, $\{g_1, g_2\}$,...,$\{g_1,..., g_n\}$ corresponding to set $\eta_1,...,\eta_n$ is obtained during the extension of the area of considered hypotheses.

In terms of the DS theory, set $\{g_1\}$, $\{g_1, g_2\}$,...,$\{g_1,..., g_n\}$ forms the focal set of strictly nested truth hypotheses: $\{g_1\} \subset \{g_1, g_2\} \subset,..., \subset \{g_1,..., g_n\}$.

As shown below, this property of a linguistic scale allows one to essentially simplify calculations for the hypotheses' combination.

6 Combination of Simple *m*-Functions

Let $\Re = \{g_1, \ ..., \ g_n\}$ be the hypothesis set and $2^{\Re}$ be the exponential one.

For evidence a, which is given on $2^{\Re}$, let mass function m_a: $2^{\Re} \to [0, 1]$ be called the simplest if the focal set (subset with non-zero mass) forms the set of strictly nested hypotheses such as:

$$m(g_{i1}) + m(g_{i1}g_{i2}) + \ldots + m(g_{i1}g_{i2}\ldots g_{in}) = 1 \tag{15}$$

It is obvious that set $\{g_1\}$, $\{g_1, g_2\}$,...,$\{g_1,..., g_n\}$ formed in the previous section is the evidence with the simplest mass function.

Let $\overline{g}_i = \{g_1, \ ..., \ g_i\}$ be the designation for complex hypothesis $\{g_1,..., g_i\} \in 2^{\Re}$.

For the pieces of evidence having the simplest mass functions, the important property can be given.

Property. For evidence a on hypothesis set $2^{\Re}$ with the simplest function m_a, belief probability of hypothesis equals the sum of mass for all, including strictly nested hypotheses:

$$Bel(\overline{g}_i) = \sum_{j=1}^{i} m(\overline{g}_j) \ . \tag{16}$$

Statement 1. For two pieces of evidence, a and b having the simplest m-functions m_a and m_b, mass function of the combined evidence is also simplest and can be computed via difference of products for belief probabilities:

$$m_{ab}(\overline{g}_i) = Bel_a(\overline{g}_i)Bel_b(\overline{g}_i) - Bel_a(\overline{g}_{i+1})Bel_b(\overline{g}_{i+1}),\ i = 1, ..., n.$$

Let the following expression be called the belief weight (identically to (5)):

$$w(Bel) = -\ln(1-Bel). \tag{17}$$

Statement 2. For two pieces of evidence, a and b having the simplest m-functions m_a and m_b, the belief weight of combined evidence is computed via the sum of including ones:

$$w(Bel_{a\oplus b}) = w(Bel_a) + w(Bel_b). \tag{18}$$

Due to the conventional sum function, the possibility of an evidence combination represented in the form of simplest mass functions essentially simplifies calculations and provides the linear complexity of corresponding algorithms.

7 Calibration of the Linguistic Scale

The machine learning theory considers calibration as the procedure matching the values of numerical features to class membership. In the model of the DS classifier considered above, the calibration of x_j is the calculation of weight w_{jk} (11) and the assignment of the sign to q_k or $\overline{q}_k$. Then, the probability of class membership $P(q_k|x_j)$ is calculated based on (13).

In the developed linguistic-logistic model, calibration is considered as matching numerical values $x_j \in \mathbf{x}$ and linguistic values η_i of hypotheses $\overline{g}_i$ to probabilities.

$P(\overline{g}_i|x_j)$.

Let $\mathbf{x} = (x_1, \ldots, x_j)$ be the input vector. $q_k \in \{q_1,\ldots, q_k\}$, each x_j represents evidence referred to $\mathbf{x}$ belonging to q_k. The weight of this evidence is defined by log-regression (11):

The probabilities of hypotheses are connected with (11) by the following logistic dependency:

$$P(q_k|x_j) = \frac{1}{1 + \exp(-w_{jk})}. \tag{19}$$

For log-regression function w, let $w_{\min} = -6$ and $w_{\max} = 6$ be the threshold values characterizing minimal probability of class membership $P \cong 0$ and maximal one $P \cong 1$. For these threshold values, operating range $[x_{\min}; x_{\max}]$ showing change of feature x is defined on the basis of (19). It is obvious, for the given log-regression function w (because it is monotonous for each x outside $[x_{\min}; x_{\max}]$), probabilities $P(q_k|x)$ take extreme values such as $\forall x > x_{\max}\ P(q_k|x) = 1$ and $\forall x < x_{\min}\ P(q_k|x) = 0$. Therefore, the following probabilities take place outside operating range:

$$P(g_1|x) = 1 \text{ for } x > x_{j\max}, P(\overline{g}_n|x) \text{ for } x < x_{\min} \tag{20}$$

Inside the operating range, the calibration of the linguistic scale of truth hypotheses $\overline{g}_i$ is performed by separating operating range $[x_{\min}; x_{\max}]$ into n identical intervals $[x^i_{\min}; x^i_{\max}]$, which correspond to n hypotheses $\overline{g}_i$ and setting local logistic regression w_i for each subinterval. Local log-regressions w_i are linear weight functions of type (4.1) passing through threshold points $(x^i_{\min}, w_{\min})$ and $(x^i_{\max}, w_{\max})$ of corresponding subintervals $[x^i_{\min}; x^i_{\max}]$. The probabilities of x belonging to hypotheses of truth are defined on the basis of local log-regression equations for the corresponding subintervals:

$$P(q_k, \overline{g}_i|x) = \frac{1}{1 + \exp(-w_i)}, \tag{21}$$

$$P(q_k, \overline{g}_{i+1}|x) = 1 - P(q_k, \overline{g}_i|x). \tag{22}$$

Therefore, for each subinterval $[x^i_{\min}; x^i_{\max}]$, two neighbor hypotheses $\overline{g}_i$ and $\overline{g}_{i+1}$ are defined. Here, the calibration of $\overline{g}_i$ is performed via (21) and the calibration of $\overline{g}_{i+1}$ is made via (22). Inside each subinterval $[x^i_{\min}; x^i_{\max}]$, a decrease of x leads to a monotone decrease of $P(q_k, \overline{g}_i|x)$ and a simultaneous increase of $P(q_k, \overline{g}_{i+1}|x)$ that provides a "smooth transition" of probability from one more defined hypothesis to the following less defined one. Such interchange is quite natural because each following hypothesis $\overline{g}_{i+1}$ has more uncertainty in respect to $\overline{g}_i$ on the linguistic scale and the decrease of x leads to increased uncertainty. As x is changed inside $[x_{\min}; x_{\max}]$ from $x_{\max}$ to $x_{\min}$, the change of membership intervals is obtained from $[x^1_{\min}; x_{\max}]$ to $[x_{\min}; x^n_{\max}]$. Figure 1 illustrates the process of the calibration of feature scale X for three linguistic hypotheses of truth $\eta_1 = \{g_1\}$, $\eta_2 = \{g_1, g_2\}$, $\eta_3 = \{g_1, g_2, g_3\}$.

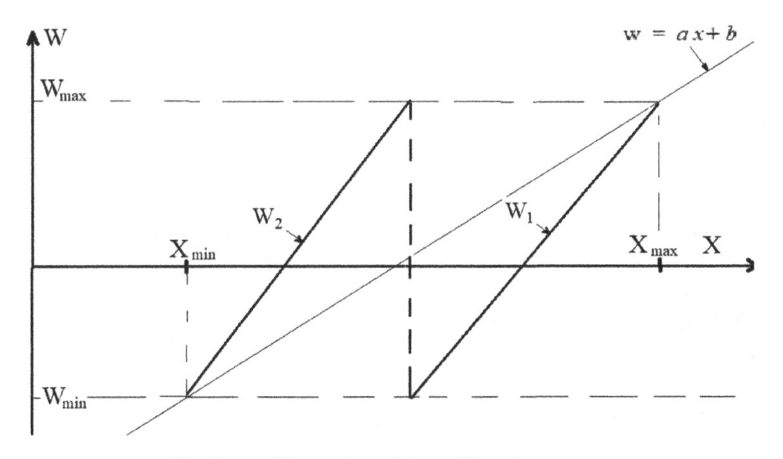

Fig. 1. An illustration of the calibration process

8 Linguistic Log-Regression Model

Formally, linguistic log-regression DS-model (LLRds) is represented by the tuple:

$$LLRds := \langle Q, \mathbf{X}, \{w_{jk}\}, \{\eta_i\} \rangle,$$

where Q is the class set, $\mathbf{X}$ is the feature space, $\{w_{jk}\}$ is the set of log-regression weight functions, and $\{\eta_i\}$ is the set of truth LVal for class membership hypotheses.

If vector $\mathbf{x}$ is obtained at the input of LLRds, each included feature x_j is considered as evidence referred class $q_k \in Q$. For each q_k and x_j, weight $w'^{i}_{jk}(\overline{g}_i)_j$ is computed and transformed into $P(\overline{g}_i, q_k|x_j)$ on the basis of (20–23). As a result, the simple m-function m_{jk} is computed for each q_k and x_j. Then, the obtained m-functions are transformed into belief weights $w(Bel(\overline{g}_i))$, which are combined for each q_k and x_j using simple sum on the basis of statement 2 mentioned above. The resulting beliefs are transformed into the distribution of unit probability mass $m(\overline{g}_i, q_k) = P(\overline{g}_i, q_k|\mathbf{x})$ based on the opposite to (6.3). Probability distributions $P(\overline{g}_i, q_k)$ are then used in the inference mechanism for making final decisions regarding $\mathbf{x}$ belonging to one or the other class.

9 LLRds-Based Inference

The resulting decision-making about an input vector belonging to one or the other class is made based on the analysis of linguistic hypotheses probabilities of class membership $P(\overline{g}_i, q_k)$.

Particularly, the modification of the pignistic Bet-transform [10] can be used for choosing the membership class of $\mathbf{x}$ using redistribution of general probability mass of complex hypothesis $\mathrm{m}(\overline{g}_i) = m\{g_1,\ldots, g_i\}$ uniformly between all components. In this case, pignistic probability $Bet(q_k)\mathrm{Bet}(\mathrm{q_k})$ obtained for each class q_k and reflecting $\mathbf{x}$ belonging to q_k is computed as the sum of $m(\overline{g}_i)$ divided by their size:

$$Bet(q_k) = m(g_1) + m\{g_1, g_2\} : 2 + \ldots + m\{g_1, g_n\} : n. \tag{23}$$

Based on (9.1), decision-making is performed as a choice of the class with maximal *Bet*.

In LLRds, due to new variables, decision-making becomes more flexible and considers different shades of truth and uncertainty of hypotheses, which are represented in an interpretable linguistic form. To implement such mechanism, let the scheme of a fuzzy inference based on production rules "IF-THEN" be used, where the rules represent the connection between linguistic truth values and corresponding decisions regarding the class membership of an input vector.

Let $P(\overline{g}_i, q_k)$ be obtained for all n hypotheses for all K classes. For this case, model of decision-making is presented in the form of fuzzy rules, where antecedents are combinations of linguistic truth values η_i of classes q_k and consequents are the corresponding numbers of the membership classes:

$$R_i : \mathrm{IF}(q_1 = \mathrm{h}_{i1}) \text{ AND}, \ldots, \text{ AND} (q_K = \mathrm{h}_{iK}) \text{ THEN } q_{iK+1}. \tag{24}$$

Therefore, each rule R_i establishes the correspondence between one of possible combinations of truth LVal for competitive classes and the class considered the best for the current rule. Inference is performed for each rule on the basis of conjunction of probabilities $P(\eta_{ij})$ included into the antecedent and the assignment of the obtained fuzzy estimation to the class considered in the consequent. In this case, the probabilities of hypotheses are interpreted as fuzzy estimations of truth hypotheses. Concluding the procedure, the obtained fuzzy estimations are combined for each class, and the class with the highest estimation is chosen.

Let the diagnostic model including two state class of a device (Broken, Unbroken) be considered as the implementation example. Let Truth (T), Almost Truth (AT), Unknown (U) be the linguistic values used as the hypotheses. For these conditions, the maximal number of fuzzy rules in the model of decision-making is $3 * 3 = 9$. The most obvious are the following rules:

$$\text{IF (Unbroken} = \text{T) AND (Broken} = \text{U) THEN Unbroken}$$
$$\text{IF (Unbroken} = \text{U) AND (Broken} = \text{T) THEN Broken}$$

It should be noted that LLRds is able to consider more complex informational situations of choice, which are presented, for example, by the following fuzzy inference rules:

$$\text{IF (Unbroken} = \text{AT) AND (Broken} = \text{T) THEN Pre} - \text{failure}$$
$$\text{IF (Unbroken} = \text{U) AND (Broken} = \text{U) THEN Uncertainty}$$
$$\text{IF (Unbroken} = \text{T) AND (Broken} = \text{T) THEN Anomaly}$$

In conclusion, let it be noted that LLRds is the generalization of the conventional log-regression model, which can be considered a particular case of LLRds with linguistic scale L_1 containing the single hypothesis of absolute truth g_i. However, the introduction of a multi-valued linguistic scale increases the expressiveness of the model and extends its abilities thanks to the emergence of a new class with informative features, which can be useful for decision-making. As a result, the obtained decisions may become more interpretable and justified. For LLRds, decision-making is formed by experts as fuzzy systems considering a specific subject area and particular properties of informational situations.

10 Conclusion

The paper proposes a new approach to the design of interpretable fuzzy classifiers based on the truth granulation of class hypotheses. A method for calibrating linguistic estimates of the truth of hypotheses is proposed, based on which a mechanism for hypotheses combination according to the Dempster–Shafer scheme is implemented. Taking into account the specifics of the simplest mass functions for class hypotheses, computationally efficient linear algorithms for hypotheses combination according to the Dempster–Shafer scheme are achieved.

The inclusion in the classification model of a linguistic truth scale for class hypotheses increases the expressiveness of the model and expands its capabilities thanks to the emergence of a new class of informative features involved in decision-making. In particular, the proposed example of fault diagnosis allows to make decisions about undefined or transient states of the device, identify pre-failure states and detect the failures arising together with anomalies, inconsistencies, and incorrectness in sensor data.

The introduction of a linguistic scale into the logistic model makes it possible to identify the significance of individual features for decision-making based on the analysis of the truth of hypotheses presented in an interpretable linguistic form.

References

1. Levitin, A.V.: Restrictions on the Power of Algorithms: Decision Trees. Algorithms. Introduction to Development And Analysis, pp. 409–417. Williams (2006)
2. Wang, Z., Wang, R., Gao, J., Gao, Z., Liang, Y.: Fault recognition using an ensemble classifier based on Dempster–Shafer Theory. Pattern Recogn. **99**, 107079 (2020)
3. Smets, P.: Belief functions: the disjunctive rule of combination and the generalized Bayesian theorem. Int. J. Approx. Reason. **9**, 1–35 (1993)
4. Gong, C., Zhi-gang, S., Wang, P.-H., Wang, Q.: Cumulative belief peaks evidential K-nearest neighbor clustering. Knowl.-Based Syst. **200**, 105982 (2020). https://doi.org/10.1016/j.knosys.2020.105982
5. Denoeux, T., Destercke, S., Cuzzolin, F., Martin, A.: Logistic regression revisited: belief function analysis. Belief Func.: Theory Appl. **11069**, 57–64 (2018)
6. Magdalena, L.: Fuzzy systems interpretability: What, Why and How. In: Lesot, M.-J., Marsala, C. (eds.) Fuzzy Approaches for Soft Computing and Approximate Reasoning: Theories and Applications: Dedicated to Bernadette Bouchon-Meunier, pp. 111–122. Springer International Publishing, Cham (2021). https://doi.org/10.1007/978-3-030-54341-9_10
7. Kovalev, S.M., Dolgiy, A.I.: Interpretability of fuzzy temporal models. Adv. Intell. Syst. Comput. **874**, 223–234 (2019)
8. Dempster, A.P.: Upper and lower probabilities induced by a multivalued mapping. Ann. Math. Stat. **38**, 325–339 (1967)
9. Shafer, G.: A Mathematical Theory of Evidence. Princeton University Press, Princeton, N.J. (1976)
10. Denoeux, T.: Analysis of evidence-theoretic decision rules for pattern classification. Pattern Recogn. **30**, 1095–1107 (1997)
11. Su, Z.-G., Wang, P.-H.: Improved adaptive evidential k-NN rule and its application for monitoring level of coal powder filling in ball mill. J. Process Control **19**, 1751–1762 (2009)
12. Guettari, N., Capelle-Laiz´e, A.S., Carr´e, P.: Blind image steganalysis based on evidential k-nearest neighbors. 2016 IEEE International Conference on Image Processing, pp. 2742–2746 (2016)
13. Chen, X.-L., Wang, P.-H., Hao, Y.-S., Zhao, M.: Evidential KNNbased condition monitoring and early warning method with applications in power plant. Neurocomput. **315**, 18–32 (2018)
14. Denoeux, T., Smets, P.: Classification using belief functions: the relationship between the case-based and model-based approaches. IEEE Trans. Syst. Man Cybern B **36**, 1395–1406 (2006)
15. Appriou, A.: Probabilit´es et incertitude en fusion de donn´ees multisenseurs. Revue Scientifique et Technique de la D´efense **11**, 27–40 (1991)
16. Denoeux, T.: A k-nearest neighbor classification rule based on Dempster-Shafer theory. IEEE Trans. Syst. Man Cybern. **25**, 804–813 (1995)
17. Jiao, L., Pan, Q., Feng, X., Yang, F.: An evidential k-nearest neighbor classification method with weighted attributes. In: Proceedings of the 16th International Conference on Information Fusion, pp. 145–150 (2013)
18. Liu, Z.-G., Pan, Q., Dezert, J.: A new belief-based K-nearest neighbor classification method. Pattern Recogn. **46**, 834–844 (2013)
19. Lian, C., Ruan, S., Denoeux, T.: An evidential classifier based on feature selection and two-step classification strategy. Pattern Recogn. **48**, 2318–2327 (2015)
20. Lian, C., Ruan, S., Denoeux, T.: Dissimilarity metric learning in the belief function framework. IEEE Trans. Fuzzy Syst. **24**, 1555–1564 (2016)
21. Su, Z.-G., Denoeux, T., Hao, Y.-S., Zhao, M.: Evidential K-NN classification with enhanced performance via optimizing a class of parametric conjunctive t-rules. Knowl.-Based Syst. **142**, 7–16 (2018)

22. Denoeux, T.: A neural network classifier based on Dempster-Shafer theory. IEEE Trans. Syst. Man Cybern. A **30**, 131–150 (2000)
23. Smets, P.: The canonical decomposition of a weighted belief. In: International Joint Conference on Artificial Intelligence, pp. 1896–1901 (1995)

Intelligent Systems

Knowledge-Based Diagnostic System With a Precedent Library

Nikolay Blagosklonov[1](✉), Valeriya Gribova[2], Boris Kobrinskii[1], and Elena Shalfeeva[2]

[1] Federal Research Center "Computer Science and Control" of the Russian Academy of Sciences, Moscow, Russian Federation
nblagosklonov@frccsc.ru, bak@isa.ru

[2] Institute of Automation and Control Processes of the Far Eastern Branch of the Russian Academy of Sciences, Vladivostok, Russian Federation
{gribova,shalf}@iacp.dvo.ru

Abstract. The hypothesis of the presumptive diagnosis before laboratory confirmation is especially important in orphan (rare) hereditary diseases. It is possible to solve this problem using computer-based decision support systems based on knowledge. However, in medical practice, there are cases of an atypical clinical picture in patients with fuzzy manifestations of features. In such cases, it is possible to increase the diagnostic accuracy using a precedent approach. The concept of "synthetic precedent" is introduced, which is the result of the transformation of an atypical case into a synthesized description. The paper presents methods for constructing synthetic precedents of two types. The precedents of the first type are created as a result of extension with the fuzzy boundaries for ordinal variables. The precedents of the second type are received by softening the requirement for the number of necessary signs of a patient to match an atypical case from the precedent library. An approach to the creation of a hybrid system, including a traditional knowledge base and a precedent library, is proposed and demonstrated. The use of the hybrid system increases the accuracy of early diagnosis of orphan diseases in childhood.

Keywords: Hybrid decision support system · Expert knowledge · Precedent approach · Fuzzy · Knowledge base · Precedent library · Orphan diseases

1 Introduction

The preliminary diagnosis (before laboratory confirmation) is especially important in the practice of a physician in general and in orphan (rare) diseases of hereditary genesis particularly. The process of identifying these diseases is associated with several specific nuances. Many diseases manifest (appear clinically for the first time) at an early age, sometimes even at birth. Although, of course, there are also late forms, but much less often. Therefore, pediatricians are the first medical professionals to see such patients, and the main role in timely and accurate diagnosis is assigned to geneticists.

S. M. Kovalev et al. (Eds.): RCAI 2021, LNAI 12948, pp. 289–302, 2021.
https://doi.org/10.1007/978-3-030-86855-0_20

Molecular genetic testing should be performed to definitively confirm the diagnosis. This type of laboratory research is quite expensive, so the physician needs to form a narrow range of differential diagnostic hypotheses for further testing. There are no clear criteria for the number of preliminary diagnoses, but, of course, the physician should follow the principle of expediency, so that the correct diagnosis is present among the list of tested hypotheses, and at the same time, redundancy of assumptions should be avoided.

Due to the low incidence of hereditary diseases in the population, a physician can personally observe a very small number of patients with each nosological form (more than 6,000 genetic diseases are known in total). Therefore, a physician for many years of active practice will not encounter most hereditary diseases. Lack of personal experience makes it difficult to advance a preliminary diagnosis when meeting such patients.

The diversity of clinical manifestations of rare diseases poses another challenge for physicians. There are many phenotypic features of these diseases. The severity of signs is influenced by factors such as the patient's age, genetic polymorphism (diversity) of signs, and ethnicity. Variations in the age of signs' manifestation add to the difficulties. Differential diagnosis is also complicated by the fact that many signs may be similar in different diseases. However, at the same time, they have varying degrees of severity and characteristic combinations with a specific age of manifestation.

In creating decision support systems that assist a physician at the stage of advancing a preliminary diagnosis, developers need to take into account these peculiarities of orphan pathology.

Based on the analysis of previously created systems for the diagnosis of hereditary diseases [1–5] in [6], an approach is proposed to create a decision support system using an ontological representation to form a knowledge base for the diagnosis of these rare diseases of hereditary genesis. The knowledge base formation process is described in detail in [7]. The preliminary extraction of knowledge was carried out based on the analysis of literature with subsequent clarifying by experts of the subject area, structuring and formalization with the participation of a cognitologist. In [7, 8] a fuzzy knowledge model was proposed, which included expert estimates for modality coefficients and confidence factors for two characteristics of signs—manifestation and severity—as well as comparative analysis algorithms for confirming and ranking differential diagnostic hypotheses. The cloud implementation of the proposed solutions is performed on the IACPaaS platform [9]. At present, the system for the diagnosis of orphan hereditary lysosomal diseases is under trial operation; knowledge models and algorithms for searching for hypotheses are being specified and improved.

In this regard, a team of authors is actively discussing further ways of developing the system. As one of these areas, the possibility of a hybrid approach to diagnostics based on knowledge and precedents is being investigated. The aim of this paper is to describe a hybrid approach to diagnostics of orphan diseases.

2 Overview of Diagnostic Systems for Hereditary Diseases

Earlier, computer systems have already been created to assist physicians diagnose patients with rare hereditary diseases. They can be conditionally divided into two classes:

information-reference systems and knowledge-based systems. The former includes such reference resources as Online Mendelian Inheritance in Man (OMIM), The Genetic and Rare Diseases Information Center (GARD), The Human Phenotype Ontology (HPO), OrphaNet. These resources are online databases that list diseases and their symptoms. They contain information about the specific defective genes that determine the onset of the disease, and list laboratory and molecular genetic tests which are necessary to confirm the disease. Except for information and reference support, these services cannot help in the daily practice of a geneticist at the stage of pre-laboratory examination of a patient.

Although semantic similarity metrics for measuring phenotypic resemblance between queries and inherited diseases, annotated with HPO, can be used to rank disease candidates in differential diagnosis, suggesting the clinical features that best differentiate diagnoses [1]. Also, worth mentioning is the Australian POSSUM system with a database of metabolic diseases, multiple malformations, teratogenic and chromosomal syndromes, and their images, focused on learning and diagnostic tasks [2].

Among previously created knowledge-based systems, DIAGEN and GenDiag can be distinguished. The GENDIAG expert system developed in France included over 2,000 hereditary diseases and syndromes [3]. The database contained information about 3,000 different features. For such feature, the system used weighting factors characterizing the frequency of occurrence and importance for diagnosis. The knowledge base was organized in a tree structure. The system used the methods of the theory of fuzzy sets. The Russian system DIAGEN [4] was created in the late 1980s. The knowledge base of the DIAGEN system included 1,200 hereditary diseases manifested clinically in childhood. The thesaurus for their description included more than 1,500 features. Knowledge was organized as associations. Above the attribute space of symptoms, relations were introduced that characterized their main properties: frequency, causal, phenotypic, and others. A structural graph (morphophysiological relationships), a cause-and-effect graph (pathogenetic mechanisms), and a phenotypic similarity graph (close or synonymous concepts) were built based on the feature proximity function. A single "resulting" graph was based on fuzzy logic concepts. The weight of the newly produced arc was calculated using the modified Shortliffe scheme. Based on the diagnostic results, the physician received a list of hypotheses-diagnoses, had the opportunity to peruse the list of signs characterizing these diseases, the specific defects, and view photos of patients with similar diagnoses. The diagnostic results were saved to the system archive and could be used in the future to identify new cases.

The Face2Gen system is currently operational, and the Ada DX is being developed. Face2Gene [5] is a diagnostic system that includes the search for diseases by features and also uses the recognition of disease-specific masks (dysmorphological manifestations) from photographs of the patients. To work with images, neural network technologies are used. For each disease, specific classifiers are created—gestalt syndromes. The photograph of each patient is converted into an impersonal face descriptor, which is then compared to the gestalts of the syndromes to quantify the similarity (scoring). The search for diseases by signs and the possibility of detailed acquaintance with diseases in this system are implemented through integration with the London Dysmorphology Database and

London Neurogenetics Database, which were previously independent software products [10].

Ada DX system [11] is currently in the prototype stage. This German system is based on a probabilistic reasoning engine, which is used to infer the probability of disease based on the scores provided in the knowledge base. The knowledge base was created by physicians as part of a specially developed approach to integrating knowledge from medical literature. Models of diseases and associated symptoms are added to the knowledge base and modeled according to data from the peer-reviewed medical literature. The knowledge base consists of models of diseases common in the population and several hundred rare diseases. The system generates two ranked lists of differential diagnoses based on the entered symptoms and patient characteristics. The first list is ranked according to estimates of the probability of diseases. The second list is ranked according to the assumed correspondence of the totality of symptoms to diseases, regardless of their probabilities. Disease probabilities and conformity assessments are displayed to the physician in two columns of the system interface. The physician is also provided with links to similar cases in the Ada DX database.

The Spanish computer-aided system for the primary diagnosis of rare diseases uses two approaches: (a) Monte Carlo modeling of symptom descriptions made by clinicians in the ORPHANET system and (b) the use of web prototypes [12]. In this system, symptoms that are not in the database or are not causally related to the presumed disease are not considered for diagnosis.

Almost all known systems for diagnosing hereditary diseases rely on expert knowledge. The impossibility of forming large enough data sets for orphan diseases due to the rarity of this pathology prevents one from raising the task of using machine learning methods in their diagnosis based on the features observed by physicians.

For especially complex cases of diseases with an incomplete picture of the manifestation of relevant signs, which can be conventionally considered as precedents, special systems are usually used. However, there is no information in the available literature sources about such case-based systems for the diagnosis of a rare pathology. At the same time, it seems possible to investigate this problem.

In the general case, to implement precedent-based systems, the nearest neighbor method and its different variations are used, for example, a method for finding a solution based on precedents using the domain ontology [13], an expert inputting threshold values for the degree of similarity of precedents, a method for extracting precedents based on decision trees, etc. [13–15]. To refine precedents, an approach based on semantic indexing of cases is often used. It allows one to consider the knowledge of experts in a specific subject area, i.e., the coefficients of the importance of the parameters, the identified dependencies, etc. However, the process of indexing becomes more complicated as the number of cases in the precedent library grows and the need to perform indexing dynamically remains [15]. One of the important problems in the implementation of intelligent systems based on precedents is the specification of the term "suitable" case [16].

In many cases, to represent precedents, its representation is used as a set of parameters with specific values and a decision-diagnosis: CASE = (x1,…, xn, R), where x1,…, xn are the parameters of the situation describing this precedent; X1,…, Xn are the areas of admissible values of the corresponding parameters, R is the diagnosis [15]. However, for such a subject area as medicine, this is a simplification since often a key factor in diagnosing diseases is considering the development of the process over time. Hereditary metabolic diseases are characterized by a change in the clinical picture at different age periods.

A promising approach for diagnostic systems for difficult-to-differentiate diseases is the integration of technologies using knowledge bases with the search for decisions based on precedents. The experience of such integration has been tested in various subject areas, in particular, with the ontological approach [14, 17, 18]. It cannot be ruled out that this technology may, in certain cases, contribute to an increase in the efficiency of diagnostics of fuzzy clinical descriptions in poorly structured areas, which include orphan diseases.

3 Materials and Methods

By "precedent" we mean an atypical/unique case that does not fit the classical description or known variants of the clinical picture of the disease. The main challenge faced by case-based systems designers is how to provide real-time diagnostics on a large (and ever-increasing) amount of data—the precedent library. However, a fundamental feature of the use of precedents in the diagnosis of orphan diseases is their small number. At the same time, due to the specificity of this class of pathology, each reliable case of such a disease should be used either to confirm the quality of the knowledge base or to correct it, or for use in diagnostics by analogy if the knowledge base cannot provide the required level of identification (due to, for example, the absence of all the necessary signs of the disease). Due to the particularly pronounced rarity of unique cases of orphan diseases, the source of information will be indicated in the precedent library for each case.

At the same time, in contrast to the use of prototypes in [12], the description of an atypical case can be transformed by experts or automatically using a special algorithm into a so-called synthetic precedent to increase the chance of proposing an appropriate hypothesis at the earliest possible stage of the disease. Under the term "synthetic precedent" we mean a certain generalized concept by analogy with a synthetic dataset, which has begun to be actively used in medical applications. Such a "synthetic precedent" is the result of the transformation of an atypical case into a synthesized description, which makes it possible to exclude the appeal to the nearest neighbor method.

3.1 Precedents Representation Methods

The analysis of the degree of correspondence of several dozen reliable cases of patients with mucopolysaccharidosis from scientific publications with descriptions of a typical clinical picture by experts gave basis to put forward a hypothesis about the practical utility of using synthetic precedents.

This is a new approach to using precedents, provided they are few in number and combined with the classical approach to building knowledge-based decision support systems.

The construction of a synthetic precedent assumes the "expansion" of an atypical case with "fuzzy boundaries", which allows replacing the "mathematical" assessment of proximity when searching for similar cases with a meaningful expansion of the ranges of feature values at the time of saving the description in the precedent library. In this regard, in terms of its form, a synthetic precedent can be considered as a symptom complex for a certain disease.

Each precedent is classified according to two criteria: consideration of dynamics and construction methodology. Considering the dynamics, atypical cases are divided into simple and temporal, that is, without taking into account the dynamics and taking into account age-related changes. Due to the absence of the dynamics of observation of real patients at present, only simple precedents were used in the work. According to the construction methodology, precedents are of the first and second types, which will be discussed in detail below.

3.2 Synthetic Precedents Constructing

Synthetic precedents can be constructed using two different methods. The first method allows one to expand the boundaries of ordinal scales (for example, age), while the second helps to vary the number of features that should be in a new patient similar to a precedent.

Method for Constructing Synthetic Precedents of the First Type. For each case (from the precedent library), build a corresponding synthesized precedent of the "first type" (with the modality of each feature "main"). Using simple precedents (such as CASE = (x1,..., xn, R)), build a generalization as follows. If the i-th feature has an ordinal scale of values (not binary), expand the value encountered in the precedent. To the "description" of the synthesized precedent (intended for argumentation of the decision) indicate—"some similarity to the case <*reference to the precedent-original*>").

One of the criteria in medicine is the dependence of individual manifestations of diseases on the patient's age. In orphan diseases, this also applies to the manifestation and level of severity of symptoms. A synthetic precedent should be associated with a criterion—an age close to that atypical case based on which it is built. An example of a generic use case of this type is shown in Fig. 1.

Method for Constructing Synthetic Precedents of the Second Type. For each precedent for which several deviating features are indicated (presumably more than four features; as indicated in paper the problem is reduced to "modeling common sense," i.e. the formation of a synthetic precedent of the "second type" (with grouping) as a symptom complex with many features that were in a particular atypical case, pro-vided that there is an incomplete coincidence (on one feature). For example, to select a characteristic majority, the values "4 out of 5 signs should be in the patient" can be set. To the description for the reasoning of the decision, indicate: "pay attention to the case <*reference to the precedent-original*>". An example of a synthesized precedent of the second type is shown in Fig. 2.

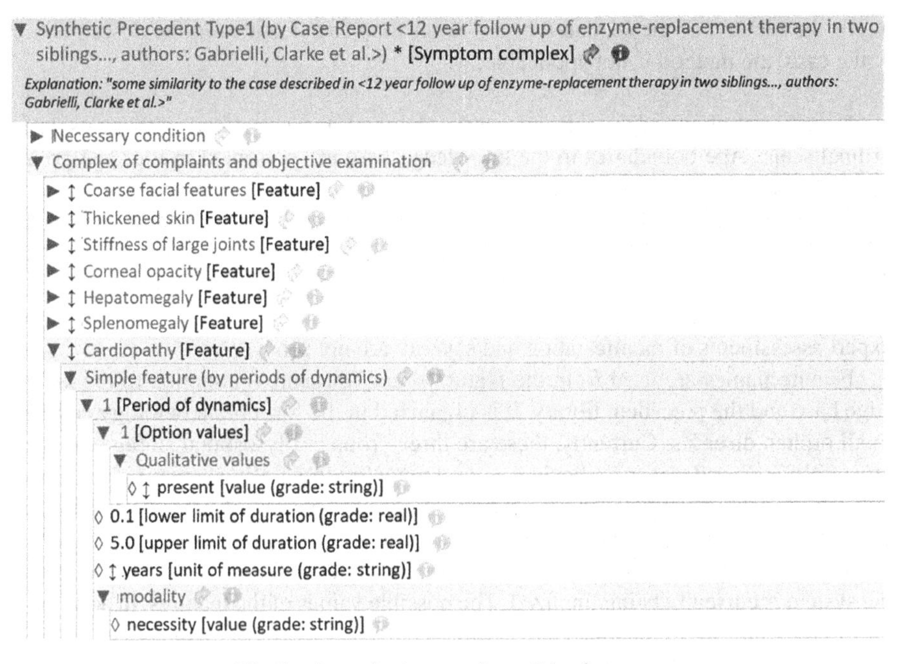

Fig. 1. A synthetic precedent of the first type

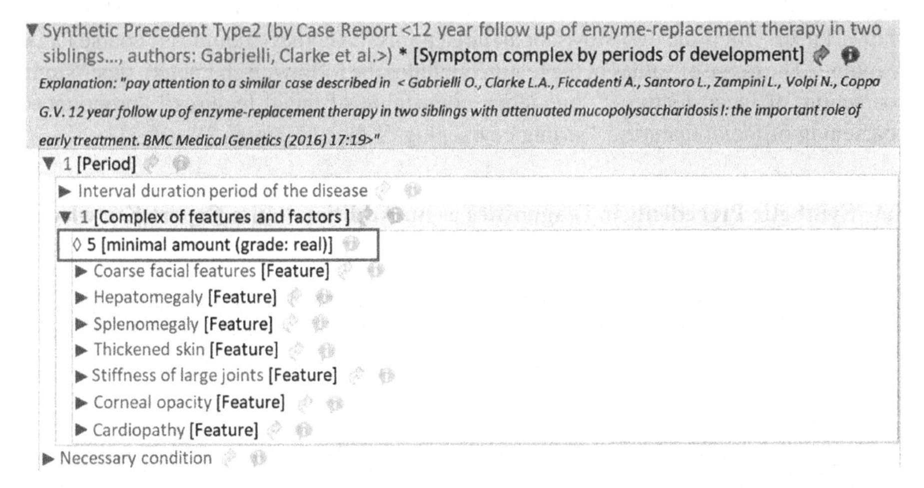

Fig. 2. A synthetic precedent of the second type.

The limitations on the use of these methods for constructing synthetic precedents are the following conditions:

- For the method of the first type — the absence of features with a numerical or ordinal scale, the method is not applicable.

- For the method of the second type — fewer than four features in the description of the case, the method is not applicable.

Knowledge about orphan diseases was obtained and structured without using an ordinal scale. Age boundaries in the knowledge base are presented in four age groups (that is, on a categorical scale). The precedents use the patient's age on an ordinal scale of years-months. To indicate the presence of a feature in the clinical picture of the disease within the age group, in the current version, a binary scale "present"/"absent" was used. Thus, when constructing a synthetic precedent of the first type, it is necessary to use features that are encountered in an atypical case with the modality of "main," while expert assessments of manifestation and severity are not set.

Feature names are used from the feature space (thesaurus) common to the knowledge base and the precedent library. It is organized in the form of an ontology common to all orphan diseases. Currently, these are three groups of lysosomal storage diseases: mucopolysaccharidoses, gangliosidoses, and mucolipidoses. When creating a new synthetic precedent, after specifying a verified diagnosis, the list of possible features for selection is filtered depending on the disease group.

To implement the possibility of expanding the values of features, the terminology of the system is currently being finalized. The possible values of the features, in addition to the binary scale, are supplemented by various characteristics of the symptoms, for which an ordinal scale will be used. For example, for the feature "stiffness of large joints," the physician will be asked to additionally indicate the upper or lower extremities and the number of affected large joints. Expanded values in this example are "elbow," "shoulder," "hip," "knee," "multiple dysostosis, or all large joints." Another example is "coarse facial features." The range of values of the feature includes the following characteristics: "slight coarsening of facial features," "moderate coarsening of facial features," "pronounced coarsening of facial features," "strong coarsening of facial features."

3.3 Synthetic Precedents in Diagnostics as an Addition to the Expert Knowledge Base

The decision support system puts forward hypotheses predicated on knowledge base rules, forming an explanation for each of them using the comparative analysis algorithm [7]. After completing the work of the knowledge base, the search for a match is carried out for a new case in the precedent library (excluding the coincidence by secondary signs). When forming the explanation, it is indicated as "found a similar case" for an extended (fuzzy) age interval. In the future, the expansion of the values of features by their attributes (characteristics) will be carried out. Proximity can be established either by proximity on a numerical scale or by falling into one category, for example, "period up to 1 year"). The probability of an exact match in age is extremely small, but this option cannot be ignored.

Then a search for a match is carried out in the library of synthetic precedents with the formation of an explanation based on the description. Thus, it becomes possible to expand the chances of the presence of hypotheses in general or to increase the number of hypotheses with arguments that will not mislead the physician.

To implement a precedent approach in diagnostics using the obtained precedents libraries, an appropriate software component is required. The architecture of the developed hybrid decision support system includes:

- the knowledge base for diagnostics by clinical forms, formed by a cognitologist based on expert knowledge,
- the precedent library for identified atypical cases within clinical forms,
- the decision support component (inference) based on the knowledge base,
- the case-based decision support component,
- and the synthetic precedents-based decision support component.

The description of the ontology (as a semantic network of medical terms and relationships), together with the thesaurus of features, was formulated with the participation of experts in such a way that further, on its basis, specialists can regularly transfer new or refined knowledge within the framework of this domain. The proposed ontological approach provides seamless integration of the two diagnostic approaches.

Cases that do not fully comply with the rules in the knowledge base are sent to the precedent library under the obligatory condition that information about the finally established (verified) diagnosis should come from the attending physicians. Only after that, it becomes possible to create on this basis a synthetic precedent for a given nosological form.

4 Result: The Hybrid Service

The implementation of the two methods is carried out in the ontological (specialized) framework of the IACPaaS platform, which gives cloud access to the tools of transferring knowledge for storage and systematization (on a unified ontological basis), development tools for complexes of scientific and applied intellectual services and the means of their use.

The hybrid approach to solving differential diagnostics problems predicated on a knowledge base and on an analysis of precedents makes it possible to provide the user with more hypotheses (among which the correct one is more likely) or to refine the solution obtained by one method using the solution obtained by another method.

The use of a specialized environment of the IACPaaS platform allows an expert to form knowledge using context-sensitive knowledge editors (where information is represented in the view of a network of terms), and software component developers can use a set of technologies for assembling intelligent services (which significantly increases the speed of developing a complex of artificial intelligence systems). The use of hybrid systems will improve the quality of decision support for physicians.

4.1 Examples of Using the Hybrid Approach

The first case [19] is a 4.5-year-old female child. This is an atypical case of Hurler syndrome. The patient has the following symptoms described in the publication:

- coarse facial features,
- thickened skin,
- stiffness of large joints,
- corneal opacity,
- hepatomegaly,
- splenomegaly,
- and cardiopathy.

According to expert knowledge, at this age, the main features include not only coarse facial features, stiffness of large joints, hepatomegaly, splenomegaly, and cardiopathy, but also:

- short neck,
- mental retardation,
- and hernias.

Features that are considered necessary, in addition to corneal opacity, are: growth retardation, macroglossia, and hearing loss. Thickened skin is one of the minor features.

For Hurler's syndrome, it is necessary to note the absence of several important features.

The expert knowledge approach indicates the need for these features to confirm the correct diagnosis (Fig. 3).

Fig. 3. The case of Hurler syndrome

If, based on this atypical case, synthetic precedents of both types are constructed (Fig. 4), then when a patient with a similar set of features meets in medical practice, the system will fundamentally increase the chance to put forward the desired hypothesis.

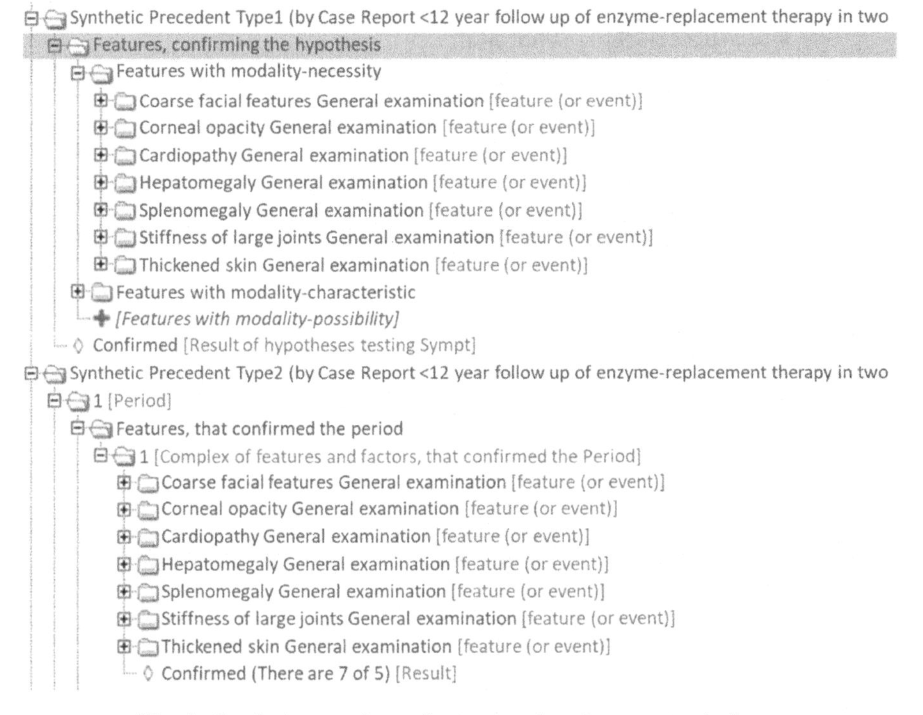

Fig. 4. Synthetic precedents of two types, based on one atypical case

The second case [20] is a one-month-old male infant. This is an atypical case of Sly syndrome. Observed signs included:

- coarse facial features,
- growth retardation,
- hepatomegaly,
- and splenomegaly.

According to the expert knowledge in the system, at this age, the main symptoms include coarse facial features and hernias.

The knowledge-based approach clearly indicates the lack of one of the diagnostic criteria for the advancement of a confirmed hypothesis. Also, one sign is missing for differentiation from another clinical form, which can be seen in Fig. 5.

If, based on of this atypical case, synthetic precedents of both types are constructed (Fig. 6), then when a patient with a similar set of features re-meets in a hybrid system, the probability of putting forward a corresponding hypothesis about a similar diagnosis increases.

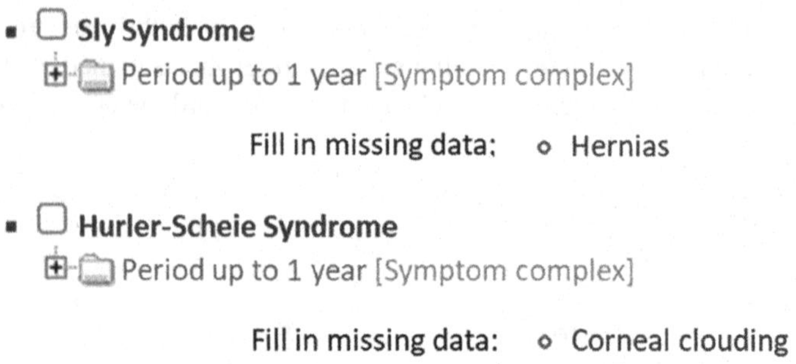

- **Sly Syndrome**
  Period up to 1 year [Symptom complex]

  Fill in missing data: ○ Hernias

- **Hurler-Scheie Syndrome**
  Period up to 1 year [Symptom complex]

  Fill in missing data: ○ Corneal clouding

Fig. 5. An intelligent system request for a missing differentiating feature

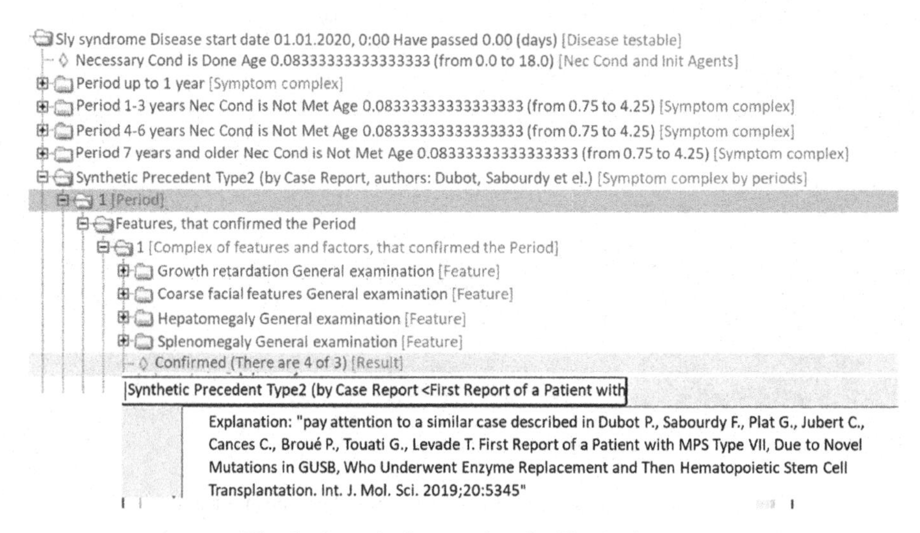

Fig. 6. A synthetic precedent for Sly syndrome

5 Conclusion

The hybrid intelligent medical system that includes the knowledge base and the precedent library can provide diagnostic hypotheses more efficient. Based on the experience of working with different classes of diseases on the IACPaaS platform, the inclusion of synthetic precedents, along with the original descriptions of atypical cases (original-use case), provides improved recognition. For rare diseases with unclear symptoms, precedents play a prominent role. Expanding the boundaries of the manifestation of signs in the age range and in terms of their severity in the synthesized precedent should be of particular importance. The implementation of synthetic precedents can be carried out in different ways, including considering the modality of features or a certain incompleteness of the description. Thus, in a hybrid system, the formation of hypotheses can take place in three stages: based on the rules of the knowledge base, according to original precedents, and according to synthesized precedents.

Acknowledgements. This work was carried out with partial financial support from the Russian Foundation for Basic Research RFBR (project No. 19–29-01077, 18–29-03131).

References

1. Köhler, S., et al.: Clinical diagnostics in human genetics with semantic similarity searches in ontologies. Am. J. Hum. Genet. **4**(85), 457–464 (2009). https://doi.org/10.1016/j.ajhg.2009.09.003
2. Fryer, A.: POSSUM (Pictures of Standard Syndromes and Undiagnosed Malformations). J. Med. Genet. **1**(28), 66–67 (1991)
3. Ayme, S., Caraboenf, M., Gouvernet, J.: GENDIAG: A computer assisted syndrome identification system. Clin. Genet. **5**(28), 410–411 (1985)
4. Kobrinsky, B., Kazantseva, L., Feldman, A., Veltishchev, J.: Computer diagnosis of hereditary childhood diseases. Med. Audit. News **4**(1), 52–53 (1991)
5. Allanson, J.E., Cunniff, C., Hoyme, H.E., McGaughran, J., Muenke, M., Neri, G.: Elements of morphology: Human malformation terminology for the head and face. Am. J. Med. Genet. A **149A**, 6–28 (2009). https://doi.org/10.1002/ajmg.a.32612
6. Kobrinskii, B.A., Blagosklonov, N.A., Demikova, N.S., Gribova, V.V., Shalfeeva, E.A., Petryaeva, M.N.: The possibility of applying the ontological approach to the diagnosis of orphan diseases. In: Yarushkina, N.G., Moshkin V.S. (eds.) Seventeen National conference on artificial intelligence with international participation CAI-2019, vol.2, pp. 47–55. UlSTU, Ulyanovsk, Russia (2019). (in Russian)
7. Blagosklonov, N.A., Kobrinskii, B.A.: Model of integral evaluation of expert knowledge for the diagnosis of lysosomal storage diseases. In: Kuznetsov, O.P., Kuznetsov, S.O., Panov, A.I., Yakovlev, K.S. (eds.) Proceedings of the Russian Advances in Artificial Intelligence 2020, vol.2648, pp.250–264. CEUR Workshop Proceedings, Moscow, Russia (2020)
8. Kobrinskii, B.A.: Certainty factor triunity in medical diagnostics tasks. Sci. Tech. Inf. Process. **46**, 321–327 (2019)
9. Gribova, V.V., Kleschev, A.S., Moskalenko, F.M., Timchenko, V.A., Fedorischev, L.A., Shalfeeva, E.A.: IACPaaS cloud platform for the development of intelligent service shells: current state and future evolution. Softw. Syst. **3**(31), 527–536 (2018). https://doi.org/10.15827/0236-235X.123.527-536. (in Russian)
10. Winter, R.M., Baraitser, M.: The London Medical Database. Oxford University Press, Oxford (2006)
11. Ronicke, S., Hirsch, M.C., Türk, E., Larionov, K., Tientcheu, D., Wagner, A.D.: Can a decision support system accelerate rare disease diagnosis? Evaluating the potential impact of Ada DX in a retrospective study. Orphanet J. Rare Dis. **14**, 69 (2019). https://doi.org/10.1186/s13023-019-1040-6
12. Alves, R., et al.: Computer-assisted initial diagnosis of rare diseases. Peer J. **4**, e2211 (2016). https://doi.org/10.7717/peerj.2211
13. Varshavskiy, P.R., Alekhin, R.V.: Ar Kar Myo, Zo Lin Khaing: implementation of a case-based module for intelligent systems. Softw. Syst. **2**(110), 26–31 (2015). https://doi.org/10.15827/0236-235X.109.026-031. (in Russian)
14. Denisova, E.A., Gubanova, G.F., Lezhenina, S.V., Chernyshov, V.V.: Model of case-based reasoning system for female infertility diagnosis. Int. J. Appl. Fundam. Res. **7**, 123–128 (2018). (in Russian)
15. Varshavskii, P.R., Eremeev, A.P.: Modeling of case-based reasoning in intelligent decision support systems. Sci. Tech. Inf. Process. **5**(37), 336–345 (2010). https://doi.org/10.3103/S0147688210050096

16. Nazarenko, G.I., Osipov, G.S., Nazarenko, A.G., Molodchenkov, A.I.: Intelligent systems in clinical medicine. Case-based clinical guidelines synthesis. Inf. Technol. Comput. Syst. **1**, 24–35 (2010). (in Russian)
17. Prentzas, J., Hatzilygeroudis, I.: Combinations of case-based reasoning with other intelligent methods. Int. J. Hybrid Intell. Syst. CIMA **6**(4), 189–209 (2009)
18. Avdeenko, T.V., Makarova, E.S.: The decision support system in it-subdivisions based on integration of cbr approach and ontology. Vestnik of Astrakhan State Technical University. Ser.: Manage. Comput. Sci. Inf. **3**, 85–99 (2017). https://doi.org/10.24143/2072-9502-2017-3-85-99
19. Gabrielli, O., Clarke, L.A., Ficcadenti, A., Santoro, L., Zampini, L., Volpi, N., Coppa, G.V.: 12 year follow up of enzyme-replacement therapy in two siblings with attenuated mucopolysaccharidosis I: the important role of early treatment. BMC Med. Genetic. **17** (2016). https://doi.org/10.1186/s12881-016-0284-4
20. Dubot, P., et al.: First report of a patient with MPS Type VII, due to novel mutations in gusb, who underwent enzyme replacement and then hematopoietic stem cell transplantation. Int. J. Mol. Sci. **20**, 5345 (2019)

Semiotic Models in Monitoring and Decision Support Systems

Alexander Kulinich(✉)

V. A. Trapeznikov Institute of Control Sciences, RAS, Moscow, Russian Federation
alexkul@rambler.ru

Abstract. The paper considers an approach to the construction of decision support systems based on the use of the subject area semiotic models and methods of natural language processing. The peculiarity of the proposed approach lies in the fact that the unstructured linguistic information of the Internet is used as the knowledge base of the semiotic model. The structuring of this information is carried out based on a subjective qualitative semiotic model of the situation, built by an expert, and the use of natural language processing methods for texts relevant to the subject area, which are obtained from the Internet. The functional structures of decision support systems in the tasks of monitoring the situation state, making decisions, and supporting the modeling results interpretation in conditions of uncertainty are given. Qualitative assessments of the possibility of implementing decision support systems based on a subjective semiotic model and natural language processing methods are given. Conclusions based on the results of experiments with a software model of the system for the decision support problem are presented, confirming the effectiveness of this approach.

Keywords: Decision-making · Semiotic system · Subjective model · Natural language processing · System architecture

1 Introduction

Currently, methods of supporting decision-making in complex socio-economic and political systems under uncertain conditions can be divided into several classes. The first class of methods (Data Mining) is based on obtaining domain objective laws by extracting knowledge from data presented in numerical scales.

In social and political situations, the initial information can be presented in the form of opinions, points of view, argumentation, and other linguistic information. Parameterization of such information for its further analysis is not an easy task. In this case, Text Mining technology is used, which allows one to structure large amounts of text information into classes that include semantically similar information. After highlighting semantically close texts, the task of the analyst and the expert is to understand these texts, to give their expert assessment, based on which a decision will be made.

Another class of methods is based on the direct extraction of expert knowledge, which is presented in models for choosing the best solution or in models for predicting

S. M. Kovalev et al. (Eds.): RCAI 2021, LNAI 12948, pp. 303–316, 2021.
https://doi.org/10.1007/978-3-030-86855-0_21

the situation's development. These methods use the subjective experts' preferences, their assessments, knowledge of the subject area laws, etc. However, at the same time, difficulties arise in constructing a mathematical model of a situation and measuring its parameters. In conditions of uncertainty, such a model is a conceptual simulation model built by an expert and qualitatively reflecting the basic laws of the situation. In such conditions, the situation model is difficult to verify, and, therefore, the modeling results, which are difficult to interpret in terms of the subject area, turn out to be unreliable.

In this work, we are trying to combine the technology of qualitative subjective modeling and the technology of obtaining relevant information from the Internet, using various methods of processing unstructured linguistic information. At the same time, a qualitative subjective model is used as a template for obtaining relevant information from the Internet.

The following tasks are considered: monitoring the situation state and obtaining forecasts of its development; decision support for situation control with the decision's interpretation and searching for their precedents on the Internet. The semiotic model of the subject area proposed in [1] is used as a qualitative subjective model of the situation.

2 Semiotic Model of the Situation

The semiotic model of the situation [1] is a model representing the expert's knowledge about dynamical systems, whose element is the sign model by G. Frege [2]. The sign model connects the real world (denotation) with mental representations of the world (knowledge) in the form of the sign name (symbol) and the sense that determines its main features (properties).

The semiotic model describes the situation in three aspects: syntactic, semantic, and pragmatic. The syntax is responsible for representing the relationship between signs that describe reality. Semantics studies the relationship between signs and what they mean in the real world, while pragmatics is responsible for the relationship between signs and those who use them.

Syntactic model. The syntactic model defines a set of domain parameter names $F = \{f_i\}$. For each parameter, a set of values is known, $Z = \{Z_i\}$ in the form of an ordered set of linguistic values, i.e. $Z_i = \{z_{i1},...z_{iq}\}$, $z_{iq+1} \succ z_{iq}$, $q = 0...n-1$. The vector of values of all parameters of a situation at time t, $Z(t) = (z_{1e},...,z_{nq},)$ is called its state.

In the syntactic model, the cause-and-effect relation W is defined, given on the sets of parameter values. For all parameters of the situation, we write this relation as logical-linguistic equations [3] in the form of a mapping:

$$W : Z(t) \rightarrow Z(t + 1),$$

where $Z(t) \in Z_i \times Z_i$.

That is, the syntactic model is defined by the following tuple:

$$\langle F,\ Z,\ W,\ Z(t)\rangle, \tag{1}$$

where F is a parameter set, Z is a set of sets of parameter values, W is a cause-and-effect relationship on a set of parameter values, and $Z(t)$ is a state — a vector of values of all parameters.

Semantic model. In the semantic model of the subject area, possible states of the syntactic model (1) are presented in the form of a partially ordered set of named classes of states.

That representation is based on the interpretation of the space of possible states of the dynamic system $SS = \underset{i}{\times} Z_i$ as semantic space (Semantic Space).

In the feature semantic space, the situation states are presented as concepts. Real situations are determined by the names and vectors of the values of the attributes that determine their content (sense). In semantic spaces, situations with close values of parameters form classes of states and relations (class-subclass) are defined between the classes, i.e. the conceptual structure is determined.

In [4], a method was proposed for structuring the state space SS of a dynamic system (1) into nested subspaces of possible states $SS(d^H) \subset SS$, which have artificial names d^H, $SS(d^H) \Leftrightarrow d^H$, which define the system states class (1).

It was shown that the names d^H, which define the subspaces of states $SS(d^H)$, form a partially ordered set of names $\{d^H\}$ of state classes $CF = (\{d^H\}, \leq)$, which is called a qualitative conceptual framework and which defines a qualitative ontology of the subject area for which the syntactic model was built (1).

Thus, the semantics of the syntactic model (1) is determined by a qualitative conceptual framework:

$$CF^* = \left(\left\{d^{H*}\right\}, \leqslant\right), \tag{2}$$

where $d^{H*} \Leftrightarrow SS(d^{H*})$, the symbol $\Leftrightarrow$ means that the name uniquely identifies the area of the semantic space $SS(d^{H*}) \subset SS$, $V(d^{H*}) = \{Z^*(t)\}$ - the volume of the sign d^{H*}, including the states $Z^*(t)$ belonging to its area $SS(d^{H*})$, i.e. $Z^*(t) \in SS(d^{H*})$.

The pragmatic model. In semiotics, the pragmatic is responsible for the relationship between signs and those who use them. The pragmatic model examines the usefulness assessment of the system state for the decision-maker. The assessment is based on determining the coefficients of the expert's preferences α_{ij} relative to the values of the parameters in the state vector ($Z(t)$).

The state estimate $O(Z(t))$ is represented by a linear convolution:

$$\mathrm{O}(\mathrm{Z}(t)) = \sum_j \alpha_{ij} x_j(t), j = 1, \ldots, \mathrm{n}. \tag{3}$$

where $x_j(t) \in [0,1]$ is the mapping φ of the features' linguistic values $z_j(t)$ onto the numerical axis segment [0,1], that is, $\varphi{:}z_j(t) \rightarrow x_j(t) \in [0,1]$, $z_j(t) \in Z(t)$, $O(Z(t)) \in [0,1]$.

All three models are related to each other by common parameters, and, therefore, changes in the state of any of them will lead to a change in the states of other models.

The peculiarity of semiotic models is that in conditions of uncertainty and incompleteness of knowledge, they allow one to represent a set of alternative syntactic models of a situation in the form of a partially ordered set of names of states classes of a semantic model — a conceptual framework of the subject area.

The advantage of subjective qualitative semiotic models is the low labor intensity of their construction, while the disadvantage is the complexity of their verification and the multiplicity of subjective interpretations of the modeling results. It is proposed to "mitigate" this shortcoming of semiotic models by using natural language processing methods in the tasks of predicting the development of the situation state and interpreting possible solutions.

3 Methods and Approaches for Natural Language Processing

There is a lot of research and development aimed at solving the problems of natural language processing (NLP):

Information Retrieval is information search, whose purpose is to identify information relevant to the user's request. The result of Information Retrieval is a set of texts received from the information retrieval system. However, the formation of a query for an information retrieval system requires an expert to have knowledge of the subject area and experience in the keywords selection in the preparation of queries, which should reflect his knowledge of this area.

Knowledge Acquisition is a technology for acquiring knowledge, whose tasks are automatic abstracting and annotation, identification of keywords, and construction of ontologies. Knowledge Acquisition suggests a complete analysis of the text and the presentation of the sentence meaning in the text corpus. However, a complete analysis of each sentence is algorithmically complex and applicable to subject areas with a small corpus of text [5].

Information Extraction involves extracting information of a certain type from a text and presenting it in a certain format. This technology, a monitoring technology, is used to replenish the database. The Information Extraction technology is more complex than Information Retrieval, but it is considered effective because it saves the expert's time and allows one to present the result in a certain format, convenient for further processing [6]. It is believed that [7] Information Retrieval as a search for relevant documents and Information Extraction as a search for information within a document complement each other.

Thus, the result of the Information Retrieval technology is a set of documents relevant to the request, Knowledge Acquisition is knowledge about the subject area, and the Information Extraction technology is a set of facts that are represented as entities (personalities, organizations, etc.) and complex events, including several entities and the relationship between them.

Text Mining is a kind of Data Mining aimed at processing text data to reveal hidden laws in the text corpus. Text Mining relies mainly on statistical methods and machine learning [8]. Text Mining can be used in conjunction with Information Extraction to analyze information obtained from text [9].

Distributive text analysis can be considered a subclass of Text Mining. This is a language research method based on the study of the environment (distribution) of text units and does not use information about the lexical or grammatical meaning of these units. In distributive analysis, each word in a text is represented as a vector of words used in conjunction with this word in a given context. Words in this vector are characterized by a number that determines the frequency of their joint occurrence. The analysis of the text is based on the distributive hypothesis that words in similar contexts have similar meanings of vectors of the words' joint use [10].

It is believed that Natural Language Processing methods can complement each other in the analysis of natural language texts and various combinations of their use allow one to solve various applied problems requiring linguistic analysis [11, 12], etc.

Further, we will consider these methods of linguistic analysis for the tasks of monitoring the situation state and making decisions based on qualitative subjective semiotic models of the situation.

4 The Architecture of a Semiotic Decision Support System

The architecture of control systems based on applied semiotics [13–15], was formed in the framework of studies of situational control systems for complex objects and includes the following subsystems:

- an interpreter of the input language, which translates the unstructured information of the environment into the system internal language;
- an analyzer, which carries out a preliminary classification of the current situation into situations that require and do not require control;
- a classifier, which generalizes and reduces the current situation to one or more classes of typical situations included in the knowledge base and allowing one-step control actions;
- a correlator, which organizes the process of forming control actions on the con-trolled object, adequate to the current situation and the current world model in the system knowledge base.

This architecture involves the development of a structured knowledge base that includes many classes of typical situations. The sequential transmission of the operation results from the interpreter, analyzer, and classifier, and then the correlator forms a control cycle for the operation of the semiotic architecture of the system.

The differences in the architecture considered in this work are that the unstructured information of the Internet is used as a knowledge base for the semiotic system operation. This requires an analysis of possible options for constructing a semiotic architecture and a preliminary analysis of its quality. Within the framework of the proposed architecture, the task solution is considered: monitoring the situation state and supporting decision-making.

4.1 Situation Monitoring

Monitoring is understood as the process of observing and registering the state of an object or situation. When the state of a technical object is observed, the parameters of which can be measured and represented in numerical scales, the implementation of the monitoring process normally does not cause difficulties. When monitoring social and political situations, many parameters of which are presented in linguistic scales reflecting the opinions, points of view, behavior of social groups or individual politicians, the program implementation of monitoring the situation state becomes much more complicated.

The use of complete linguistic analysis (Knowledge Acquisition) to determine the situation state, which involves morphological, syntactic, and semantic analysis of the text, resulting in a semantic network of concepts in the subject area, turns out to be inappropriate due to the complexities of natural language processing.

The generalized architecture of the system for solving the problem of monitoring the situation state using natural language processing technologies and based on a subjective semiotic model is shown in Fig. 1.

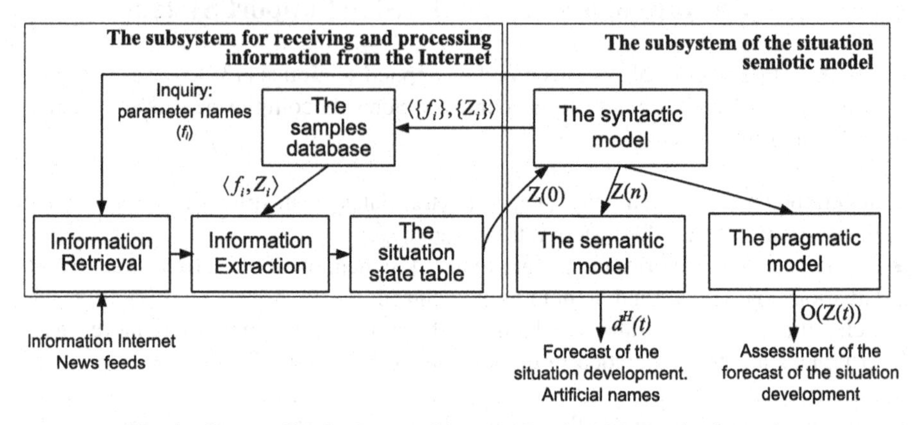

Fig. 1. A generalized system architecture for situation monitoring tasks

There are two main subsystems here:

- the subsystem for receiving and processing information from the Internet;
- and the subsystem of the situation semiotic model.

It is believed that the expert has built a subjective semiotic model of the situation. The parameters of this semiotic model are used as parameters of the subsystem for receiving and processing unstructured information on the Internet.

The names $f_i \in F$ of the situation parameters of the semiotic model are used when forming a request for the Information Retrieval subsystem. This allows one to get text information about the current state of the situation. The names of the situation parameters of the semiotic model $f_i \in F$ and their possible linguistic values Z_i are used to build a database of samples necessary for the operation of the Information Extraction subsystem.

The result of the Information Extraction subsystem is the vector of the situation parameters obtained as a result of extracting linguistic values, $Z^* = (z^*_{1h},\ldots, z^*_{nq})$, $z^*_{ij} \in Z_i$. This vector is normalized, φ: $Z^* \rightarrow X^*$, $X^* = (x^*_{1h},\ldots, x^*_{nq})$, $x^*_{ij} \in [0, 1]$, and transferred to the situation state table.

If the newly obtained state Z^* differs from the current $Z(0)$, then in the semiotic model, the following is calculated: the forecast of the situation development in the syntactic model is a vector of values Z(n); in the semantic model, the state class name ($d^H \in CF^*$); in a pragmatic is the assessment of the new state $O(Z^*)$.

Information Retrieval and Information Extraction technologies are being researched by many scientists who offer various methods and algorithms for their implementation. Analyzing the assessments of the quality of these technologies, it is possible to understand the quality of the proposed monitoring approach based on the semiotic model.

The Information Retrieval technology is presented in the form of a set of internet search services that allow one to retrieve relevant information from the Internet based on queries formulated using a semiotic model.

The quality of this technology, the completeness, and the relevance of information obtained upon request are ensured by the developers of these services, and the ability to use the results is supported by libraries for different programming languages. This allows them to be used in the software development of end-users solving specific problems.

The Information Extraction technology is more complex to implement. This technology extracts information from the text, the template of which is presented in the samples database. The samples database is built based on the semiotic model parameters. For simple structured texts in which the sample can be recognized, the performance of this subsystem is considered satisfactory.

However, with an unstructured text in a natural language for the operation of this system, it is necessary to solve some specific linguistic problems: the named entities' definition, the coreference resolution, the construction of patterns, relationships, scenarios. All these tasks are complex; for example, even an approximate solution of the coreference problem is possible only in some subject areas, provided that the knowledge base of this area is used [16]. Thus, according to the results of the prestigious Message Understanding Conference (MUC-6), the best results in solving the coreference problem reached 59% completeness with 72% accuracy. At the same time, the results of human performance were estimated at 80% [5].

These indicators are considered a certain limit of the quality of this technology when analyzing unstructured text, reflecting the properties of a natural language. Further improvement of the quality of this subsystem is associated with high costs [17].

Currently, there are a large number of commercial systems that implement the Information Extraction technology, most of which involve preliminary preparation, structuring of the text corpus, and extraction of numerical information about the values of some parameters.

Of interest are open-source systems for natural language processing, for example, the Gate (General Architecture for Text Engineering) modular system developed at the Faculty of Informatics of the University of Sheffield (UK) [18]. For the Information Extraction task based on the Gate architecture, the ANNIE (A Nearly-New IE system) application was developed [19].

Methods of extracting generic relations from the text to enrich taxonomies, thesauri, and ontologies of the subject area are of interest, too. Numerous international conferences (competitions) of algorithms for extracting hyperonyms from text [20] were organized for automatic or automated replenishment of existing taxonomies for English and other Western European languages [21, 22].

At the Dialogue-2020 conference, the task of extracting hyperonyms for the automated replenishment of the Russian taxonomy (thesaurus) RuWordNet was set [23].

The task was to find hyperonyms for some targeting word (noun or verb) based on the analysis of the text corpus [24].

Most of the methods proposed by the developers are combined methods based on calculating the vectors of the joint occurrence of the target word and the word set of the text corpus [24]. The selection of a set of candidate hyperonyms from the co-occurrence vector is carried out using various techniques (weighting words based on heuristics, finding the proximity of word vectors of the text corpus, and vectors of known taxonomies and thesauri marked up manually).

To highlight hyperonyms, additional sources of information are also used in the form of dictionaries (for example, Wiktionary), lexical templates, pre-trained multilingual neural networks (R-BERT) [25], and others [24].

At present, the use of the Information Extraction technology in the tasks of monitoring the state of a situation together with a subjective semiotic model is advisable in cases of preliminary structuring of the text corpus. In this case, a significant part of the analyst's routine work is removed.

4.2 Decision-Making Based on a Semiotic Model of the Situation

The result of the monitoring subsystem is the assessment of the situation development forecast $O(Z(n))$. If, in the situation development forecast, the estimate $O(Z(t))$ is worse than the current one $O(Z(0))–O(Z(n)) > 0$, then, in this case, the decision-making problem arises with the aim of the pragmatic model $O(Z(t))$.

In [26], the decision-making problem was reduced to solving an inverse problem in a semiotic model. The essence of the solution lies in the sequential transfer of solutions to the inverse problem from the pragmatic model to the syntactic model, and then to the semantic model. The target situation in the pragmatic model is defined as the difference between the forecast and current estimates, $O(Z(t))$. In this case, the solution of the inverse problem in a semiotic system is presented in the form of a conceptual framework of solutions — a partially ordered set of artificial names of solution classes.

The task of the decision-making subsystem based on the semiotic model is to search the Internet for interpretations of artificial names of decision classes and their explanation.

The generalized architecture of the system for solving the problem of decision-making using text processing technologies and based on the subjective semiotic model is shown in Fig. 2.

The decision-making system includes the main subsystems:

- the subsystem of the semiotic model;
- the subsystem for processing unstructured information on the Internet;
- and the subsystem for the development of alternatives to solutions and their explanations.

Subsystem for Processing Unstructured Information on the Internet

Text Corpus. The tasks of the retrieval of information on the Internet (Information Retrieval) in this case differ from its tasks in monitoring.

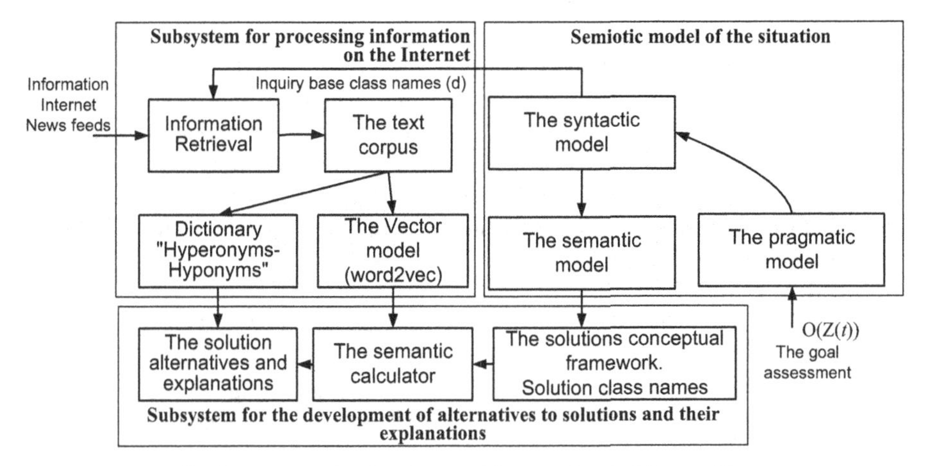

Fig. 2. A generalized system architecture for decision-making

Whereas only "fresh" news is highlighted during monitoring, when making decisions, the task is to obtain as much information relevant to the query as possible.

A request to search for information on the Internet is formed using a semiotic model and includes the names of the basic concepts of the semiotic model. The result of the subsystem is a text corpus that is relevant to the name of the basic concept of the semiotic model.

Dictionary "Hyperonyms-Hyponyms." The subsystem for extracting generic relations from the text corpus is built based on lexical-syntactic templates. A lexical-syntactic template is a structural sample of a linguistic structure, reflecting its lexical and surface-syntactic properties.

In the general case, the template determines the sequence of elements of which the described linguistic structure should consist and sets the conditions for the grammatical agreement of these elements [27].

The lexical-syntactic templates are used to create a dictionary of generic relations in the text corpus. In this dictionary of hyperonyms-hyponyms, sentences have been added to explain each generic relationship. The dictionary has the following structure:

$$\langle \text{HYPER, HYPO, Context} \rangle. \tag{4}$$

where HYPER, HYPO are the sets of hyponyms and hyperonyms of the domain, Context is the set of sentences in which these generic relations were defined.

Vector model. The vector model of the text corpus is obtained using the word2vec distributive text analysis technology [28] by training the neural network with sentences of the text corpus.

The vector model is the word vectors of the text corpus with the characteristics of their joint use in this context. That is, the vector $R_i = (w_i/r_{i1},\ldots, w_n/r_{in})$ is defined, which characterizes the joint occurrence r_{ij} of the word w_i with other words $(w_i,\ldots, w_n)$.

In the word2vec distributive analysis technology, the *positive*(•) and *negative*(•) operations with word vectors are defined, which makes it possible to determine new vectors corresponding to the sense of the joint use of words from the dictionary.

The operation *positive*(w_t,..., w_s) defines a words' vector that characterizes the new meaning of the joint use of words in the argument of this operation, and the operation *negative*(w_q,..., w_n) defines a words' vector that characterizes the new meaning, in which there are no words included in the argument of this operation. In other words, the following function is defined:

$$\text{w2v}(positive(w_t, \ldots, w_s);\ negative(w_q, \ldots, w_n)) = \text{R}^*_w, \tag{5}$$

where $R^*_w = (w_i/r_{i1},\ldots, w_n/r_{in})$ is a vector of words characterizing the new meaning of the joint use of words $(w_t,\ldots, w_s)$, $(w_q,\ldots, w_n) \in W$, and W is a domain dictionary.

Subsystem for the Development of Solution Alternatives and Their Explanations

Conceptual framework of solutions. The formal solution of the inverse problem gives a set of classes of solutions, structured in the form of a qualitative ontology, a conceptual framework of solutions. However, these solutions are signs that have a name and content, and are expressed in the form of mathematical signs that have no interpretation in the subject area.

The solution of the inverse problem is represented as a solution vector $A = (a_1,\ldots,a_n)$, $a_i \in \{1,0,-1\}$, where a_i characterizes the estimate of the value of the *i-th* parameter (f_i) in the solution of the inverse problem: (+1) parameter is present (large value), (-1) parameter is absent (small value).

To solve the problem of interpretation, the method of composite artificial names was proposed [26]. A composite artificial name of a generalized solution class is a name that includes the name of the base concept (d^0) and the evaluation of the values (a_i) of the distinguishing features of the generalized solution class. Those, the composite artificial name is the concatenation: $d^0 \& a_i \& f_i$.

Semantic calculator. The semantic calculator is designed to determine the vector of the joint use of words included in the solution of the inverse problem, obtained using a semiotic model. The work of the semantic calculator is based on a trained distribution model of the domain and is represented as a function whose arguments are artificial names of decision classes.

Thus, the solution of the inverse problem is transferred to the semantic calculator in the form of a solution vector $A = (a_1,\ldots, a_n)$. Substituting the solution vector of the inverse problem into expression (5), we have:

$$\text{w2v}\left(positive(w_t|a_t = 1, \ldots, w_s|a_s = 1);\ negative(w_q|a_q = -1, \ldots, w_n|a_n = -1)\right) = \text{R}^*_w, \tag{6}$$

where the vector of words $R^*_w = (w_i/r_{i1},\ldots, w_n/r_{in})$ reflects the sense of the joint use of words included in the function arguments (6), which determine the inverse problem solution.

Solution alternatives and explanations. Decisions in a semiotic system are the possible names of decision classes. To reduce the "linguistic noise" of the word vectors obtained in the semantic calculator, in this vector we leave words that can potentially be names of decision classes. To do this, we find the intersection of hyperonyms from the dictionary (4) and words in the solution vector R^*_w.

Then we represent the possible names of the class of solutions in the form of a tuple:

$$\langle (\mathrm{W} \cap \mathrm{HYPER});\ \mathrm{Context} \rangle,$$

where the intersection of the set $W = \{w_i\} \in R^*_w$ and the set HYPER from the dictionary (4) gives a set of solution classes names, and Context (the text of the sentence) will help to choose the right word.

5 Experiments

Experimental verification of the proposed architecture was carried out for the decision support subsystem.

A semiotic model of the socio-political situation was developed. The syntactic model defines: basic concepts: Power (d_1^0), Population (d_2^0), Economy (d_3^0), Oligarchs (d_4^0); parameters of these concepts, $f_i \in F$; possible values of the parameters $Z_i \in Z$ and the causal network W.

For a given goal, when solving the inverse problem for the basic concept "Oligarchs" with the parameters "Level of dissatisfaction" and "Level of patriotism," the value of the parameter "Level of dissatisfaction" increased. That is, we got a new concept d_4^1 with a high value of the "Level of dissatisfaction" parameter. In the semantic model, this solution is formally represented by the vector - $A_4 = (1, 0)$, which is denoted by the artificial name d_4^1 = "Dissatisfied oligarchs".

The problem is to find an interpretation of this solution in the subject area. For this, a software layout was developed in Python3, which includes the following subroutines:

- extracting relevant information from the Internet for building a text corpus (information was read from 150 URLs, in addition, the text of a book dedicated to the Russian oligarchs [29] was included in the text corpus;
- the dictionary "Hyperonyms-Hyponyms" is formed from the text corpus using lexical-syntactic templates (when constructing templates, the program of morpho-logical analysis of the Russian language Pymorphy2 [30] was used). The diction-ary is stored in an SQLite-3 database;
- the vector model of the text corpus (word2vec program was used, the results of which are saved in the SQLite-3 database);
- development of solution alternatives and their explanations (SQL queries to the SQLite-3 database are used to obtain names of solution classes with comments).

To find the interpretation of the inverse problem solution d_4^1 = "Dissatisfied oligarchs," we normalize and substitute it into the semantic calculator (6):

$$\mathrm{w2v}(\mathit{positive}(\ll \mathit{Oligarchs} \gg,\ \ll \mathit{Dissatisfaction} \gg)) = \mathrm{R}^*_w.$$

As a result, we get a vector of words that reflects the sense of this solution:

R^*_w = (*Harm\0.904; Fact\0.885; Respondent\0.873; Expert\0.872; Annexation\0.866; Regret\0.863; Position\0.852; Factor\0.844; Trend\0.833; Claim\0.830; Distrust\0.817; Efficiency\0.813; Advantage\0.808; Request \ 0.805; Reason \ 0.805;…;*).

Next, we get the possible names of the decision classes by intersecting the vector of words R^*_w with the subject area hyperonyms:

($W \cap$ HYPER) = (*Harm \ 0.904; Fact \ 0.885; Regret \ 0.863; Position \ 0.852; Claim \ 0.830; Distrust \ 0.817; Character \ 0.806;…;*).

The example shows that to the inverse problem solution with the name "Dissatisfied oligarchs," the word "Harm" is the closest, the joint occurrence is 0.904. Therefore, the possible name for the solutions class is "Harmful oligarchs."

Decision classes can be obtained expertly by analyzing the context of the hyperonym. For example, the word "Distrust" with a joint occurrence of 0.817 has the following context: "There was a steady mutual distrust between this category of business and the conditional "collective Putin": the former always feared the seizure of property, and the "collective Putin"— disloyalty." Analyzing this context, the expert identified a new decisions class — "Distrustful oligarchs."

Thus, the proposed semiotic architecture of the decision support system allows one to obtain alternatives to the names of decision classes and choose a solution by analyzing the text that substantiates this choice.

Note that the corpus of the example text included about 30,000 sentences characterizing various aspects of the subject area. Using this approach allowed us to determine the possible names of the solutions classes by analyzing a significantly smaller number of sentences. This determines the effectiveness of the method, which consists of reducing routine analytical work and increasing the intellectual productivity of an expert.

6 Conclusion

The paper proposes an architecture of a semiotic decision support system under conditions of uncertainty. In the proposed architecture, the unstructured linguistic information of the Internet is used as a knowledge base. Subsystems for monitoring the situation state and supporting decision-making, which include a semiotic model of the situation, and subsystems for extracting unstructured information from the Internet and processing it using well-known methods of natural language processing are considered. Experimental verification of the decision-making subsystem has shown that the effectiveness of the proposed approach lies in the reduction of routine analytical work, which increases the intellectual productivity of an expert.

Further studies will be aimed at improving the quality of the proposed approach using methods for increasing the volume of the text body, available dictionaries of hyperonyms-hyponyms and additional semantic analysis of sentences that include words of the decision vector.

References

1. Kulinich, A.A.: Semiotic approach in modeling and decision-making in Ill-defined complex situations. In: Proceedings of the 11-th International Conference "Management of Large-Scale System Development", pp. 1–5. IEEE, Moscow (2018)
2. Frege, G.: On sense and nominatum. In: Readings in Philosophical Analysis (1949)
3. Pospelov, D.A.: Logiko-lingvisticheskiye modeli v sistemakh upravleniya [Logical-linguistic models in control systems] (in Russian), Energiya (1981)
4. Kulinich, A.A.: Conceptual frameworks of ontologies for Ill-structured problem domains. Sci. Tech. Inf. Process. **42**(6), 411–419 (2015). https://doi.org/10.3103/S0147688215060027
5. Appelt, D.E.: Introduction to information extraction. AI Commun. **12**(3), 161–172 (1999)
6. Cunningham, H.: Information Extraction, Automatic. Encyclopedia of Language and Linguistics, 2nd edn. Elsevier, New York (2006)
7. Gaizauskas, R., Wilks, Y.: Information extraction: beyond document retrieval. J. Doc. **54**(1), 70–105 (1998)
8. Hearst, M.: What is text mining? http://www.ischool.berkeley.edu/~hearst/text-mining.html. Accessed 23 Jul 2021
9. Nahm, U.Y., Mooney, R.: A mutually beneficial integration of data mining and information extraction. In: Proceedings of the Seventeenth National Conference on Artificial Intelligence AAAI-2000, pp. 627–632, Austin, Texas (2000)
10. Sahlgren, M.: The distributional hypothesis. From context to meaning. distributional models of the lexicon in linguistics and cognitive science (Special issue of the Italian Journal of Linguistics), Rivista di Linguistica **20**(1), 33–53 (2008)
11. Brewster, C., Ciravegna, F., Wilks, Y.: Knowledge acquisition for knowledge management. In: Proceedings IJCAI 2001 Workshop on Ontology Learning, Seattle (2001)
12. Cullota, A., McCallum, A., Betz, J.: Integrating probabilistic extraction models and data mining to discover relations and patterns in text. In: Proceedings of the main conference on Human Language Technology Conference of the North American Chapter of the Association of Computational Linguistics, pp. 296–303, New York (2006)
13. Pospelov, D.A., Osipov, G.S.: Prikladnaya semiotika [Applied Semiotics]. Novosti iskusstvennogo intellekta [News of Artificial Intelligence]. (in Russian), p. 1 (1999)
14. Pospelov, D.A.: Situatsionnoye upravleniye: teoriya i praktika [Situational control: theory and practice] (in Russian), Nauka (1986)
15. Ehrlich, A.I.: Approach to development of systems for modeling, simulating and decision making support in system engineering. In: Architectures for Semiotic Modeling and Situation Analysis in Large Complex Systems: Proceedings of the ISIC Workshop - the 10th IEEE International Symposium on Intelligent Control, pp. 375–381, Monterey (Cal), USA (1995)
16. Rubashkin, V.S.: Predstavleniye i analiz smysla v intellektual'nykh informatsionnykh sistemakh – [Representation and analysis of sense in intelligent information systems] (in Russian), Nauka (1989)
17. Grishman, R.: Information extraction: Techniques and challenges. In: Pazienza, M.T. (ed.) SCIE 1997. LNCS, vol. 1299, pp. 10–27. Springer, Heidelberg (1997). https://doi.org/10.1007/3-540-63438-X_2
18. Cunningham, H. et al.: GATE: a framework and graphical development environment for robust NLP tools and applications. In: Proceedings of the 40th Anniversary Meeting of the Association for Computational Linguistics (ACL 2002), Philadelphia (2002)
19. Gate's ANNIE system. http://gate.ac.uk/ie/annie.html. Accessed 23 Jul 2021
20. Camacho-Collados, J. et al.: SemEval-2018 task 9: hypernym discovery. In: Proceedings of the 12th International Workshop on Semantic Evaluation, pp. 712–724. ACL (Association for Computational Linguistics), New Orleans (la), Stroudsburg (pa) (2018)

21. Jurgens, D., Pilehvar, M.T.: SemEval-2016 task 14: semantic taxonomy enrichment. In: Proceedings of the 10th International Workshop on Semantic Evaluation, pp. 1092–1102 (2016)
22. Bernier-Colborne, G., Barriere, C.: CRIM at SemEval-2018 task 9: a hybrid approach to hypernym discovery. In: Proceedings of the 12th International Workshop on Semantic Evaluation, pp. 725–731. Association for Computational Linguistics, New Orleans, Louisiana (2018)
23. Loukachevitch, N.V., Dobrov, B.V.: RuThes linguistic ontology vs. Russian wordnets. In: Proceedings of the Seventh Global Wordnet Conference, pp. 154–162 (2014)
24. Nikishina I., et al.: RUSSE'2020: Findings of the first taxonomy enrichment task for the Russian language. In: Proceedings of International Conference on Computational Linguistics and Intellectual Technologies Dialog-2020, pp. 579–595 (2020)
25. Tikhomirov, M. et al.: Combined approach to hypernym detection for thesaurus enrichment. In: Computational Linguistics and Intellectual Technologies: Papers from the Annual Conference "Dialogue", pp. 736–746 (2020). https://doi.org/10.28995/2075-7182-2020-19-736-746
26. Kulinich, A.: An inverse problem solution in semiotic systems under uncertainty. In: Proceedings of 1st International Conference on Control Systems, Mathematical Modelling, Automation and Energy Efficiency (SUMMA), pp. 235–240. IEEE, Lipetsk, Russia (2019)
27. Bolshakova, E., Efremova, N., Noskov, A.: LSPL-patterns as a tool for information extraction from natural language texts. In: Markov, K., et al. (eds.) New Trends in Classification and Data Mining, pp. 110–118, Sofia, ITHEA (2010)
28. Mikolov, K., et al.: Distributed representations of words and phrases and their compositionality. In: Advances in Neural Information Processing Systems: Proceedings of 27th Annual Conference on Neural Information Processing Systems, pp. 3111–3119, Nevada, USA (2013)
29. Hoffman, D.: Oligarchs. Wealth and Power in the New Russia. Corpus (2010)
30. Korobov, M.: Morphological Analyzer and Generator for Russian and Ukrainian Languages. In: Khachay, M.Y., Konstantinova, N., Panchenko, A., Ignatov, D.I., Labunets, V.G. (eds.) AIST 2015. CCIS, vol. 542, pp. 320–332. Springer, Cham (2015). https://doi.org/10.1007/978-3-319-26123-2_31

Cognitive Patterns for Semantic Presentation of Natural-Language Descriptions of Well-Formalizable Problems

Sergey Kurbatov[1], Igor Fominykh[2], and Aleksandr Vorobyev[2](✉)

[1] Research Centre of Electronic Computing, Moscow, Russia
[2] National Research University MPEI, Moscow, Russia
abvorobyev@bk.ru

Abstract. The paper suggests and develops a method for creating cognitive patterns for well-formalizable problems described in a natural language. The method takes into account the full set of human cognitive abilities: the understanding of a natural language in the light of a well-formalizable problem, its formalization for an automatic solution, a graphical display of the solution, and its psychological aspects. The method is focused on a holistic approach to applied artificial intelligence systems considered in terms of interdisciplinarity. We have conducted an experimental study of the method capabilities on a set of geometric problems. Our experiment has included the modification of the source text at the level of morphology, syntax, and significant objects of a geometric problem followed by the preparation of a drawing. We have suggested an extension of the experiment to the problems with physical content.

Keywords: Cognitive patterns · Well-formalizable problems · Natural language · Geometric problems · Automated solution

1 Introduction

The problem of a cognitive approach based on consideration of the cognitive aspects of the processes of perception, thinking, cognition, explanation, and understanding is a fundamental challenge. Due to this fact, its study has been in progress from the mid-20th century to the present and covers various areas and using various methods. A cognitive approach has been used in epistemology (theory of knowledge), psychology, linguistics, and neurophysiology, aiming to overcome interdisciplinary barriers.

The advent of computer technology and cybernetics led, in the 1950s–1960s, to a cognitive revolution—a change in the scientific paradigm according to [1]. This cognitive revolution was associated with a rapid development of the theory and practice of artificial intelligence (AI), which made it possible to simulate on a computer the processes studied using the cognitive approach. It was assumed that the systems of computer presentation

This study was supported by the Russian Foundation for Basic Research (project No. 18-07-00098 A, No. 20-07-00439 A, No. 18-29-03088 A).

S. M. Kovalev et al. (Eds.): RCAI 2021, LNAI 12948, pp. 317–330, 2021.
https://doi.org/10.1007/978-3-030-86855-0_22

of knowledge developed in artificial intelligence (at the present stage—well-developed ontologies) will provide high adequacy of cognitive process simulations. It was also assumed that it was enough to simulate a cognitive process on a computer and not to study its functioning in humans.

However, the reality proved more complicated, and numerous obstacles arose. Let us list the typical ones:

1. Difficulties in categorizing ontology concepts and underestimating the role of metaphors, which was noted, in particular, by Lakoff [2].
2. Tough binding of developed AI application systems to specific subject areas.
3. Poor explanatory capabilities for decisions made by the system.
4. A virtual lack of common sense with a computer, which allows most humans to make the right decisions and right assumptions without using strict logic and calculations.

The above difficulties can lead to significant practical constraints, such as deficiencies in explanations that do not satisfy bankers and investors — they need a more convincing substantiation for their loan or investment decisions.

Therefore, integrating cognitive methods and AI systems in an interdisciplinary aspect is now an urgent task. The purpose of this paper is to develop and research a method for creating cognitive patterns for the semantic presentation of well-formalizable problems described in a natural language (NL).

In this formulation, the method takes into account the full set of human cognitive abilities: understanding a natural language in terms of a well-formalizable problem, creating a semantic presentation for an automated solution, the graphical support for the solution, and its psychological aspects. The cognitive patterns developed by us differ from widely used cognitive maps by their orientation toward linguistic processing, by using the original language of semantic presentation, and advanced graphic support (interactive visualization [3]). The features of this method are discussed in more detail below in the "Related Studies" section.
Research and development related to both NL processing and automated problem solving have made significant progress to date. However, an integrated, interdisciplinary approach that combines an in-depth linguistic study, well-developed explanatory capabilities, and cognitive aspects of user interaction with a computer is still in its infancy. It is toward this approach that we are developing the suggested method to resolve the contradiction between the freedom of NL descriptions and a strict formalization.

2 General Description

The suggested method is based on our experimental study of an automatic problem-solving system with an NL interface [4]. The system includes a linguistic processor, an ontology-oriented solver, and interactive visualization tools. The cognitive patterns developed as part of this method should substantially support all stages of the system functioning (NL processing, automatic solution, visualization). The general structure of the cognitive pattern is shown in Fig. 1.

The central component includes a generalized semantic description of the cognitive pattern, links to the reference NL description, formulas, and data for interactive visualization.

The general logic of working with cognitive patterns is as follows:

1. A natural-language description of the problem is processed by a linguistic processor which generates index information (syntactic structure and keywords) based on which a relevant cognitive pattern is found.
2. The pattern's variables are assigned specific values extracted from the text (or by default).
3. Data from the pattern is transmitted to the solver (for visualization and search for a solution).

It is advisable to interpret the suggested patterns as frames focused on resolving contradictions between hard-to-formalize aspects of a natural language and the strict requirements of well-formalizable problems. Interactive visualization is used for more transparency and persuasiveness of solutions.

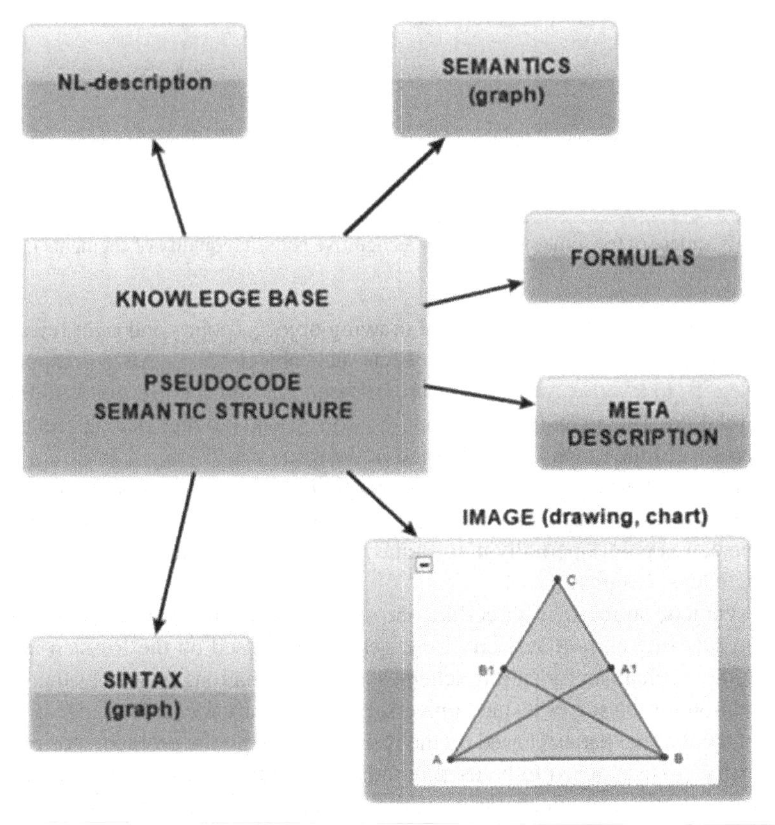

Fig. 1. General structure of the cognitive pattern

A fragment of pseudocode corresponding to the cognitive structure describing a triangle with medians can be as follows:

```
point A  start  AB segment
point B  end  AB segment
point A1   to BC segment, etc.
```

A fragment of the semantic graph for this pseudocode is shown in Fig. 2.

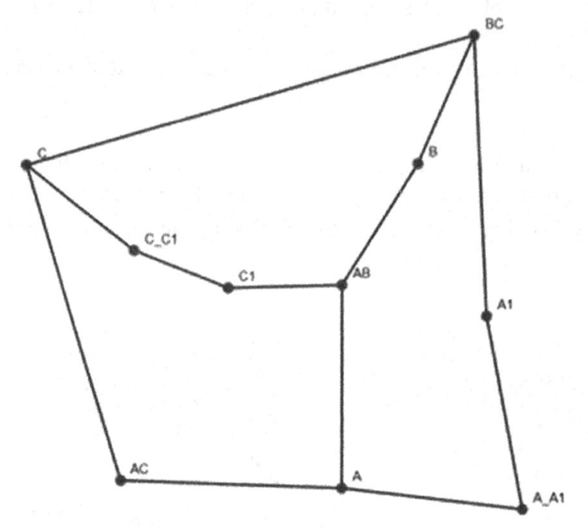

Fig. 2. A fragment of the semantic graph for a cognitive pattern (equality of segments is omitted)

The graph vertices correspond to the drawing objects (points and right lines), while the arcs correspond to the relations between such objects. E.g., AB corresponds to a triangle leg, B, to a vertex, whereas the arc between AB and B corresponds to the "end-of-line" relation. The arc between AB and C1 corresponds to the "belong" relation. All other elements of the graph are interpreted in the same way.

Knowledge about medians is presented partially in the semantic structure (equality of the corresponding segments on the legs, the ratio of 2:1 of the median segments at their intersection point), partially in formulas (equation of the median length in terms of the triangle legs' lengths).

The syntactic structure is a tree-like one and generated in advance while playing an important role (the current version of the system is focused on the Russian language; however, the mechanism for calling schemes, their designations, as well as the semantic representation for the solver is quite universal.). It is mainly focused on speeding up the choice of a cognitive pattern based on the results of parsing the problem's original text. Additionally, it is supposed to be used in a dialogue with the user. A semantic pattern makes the solver's work much easier, while an interactive visualization allows one to work with both structures.

Note that the solver can work with a semantic presentation only, not with syntax structures or graphical scripts. A description of the solver functioning is beyond the scope of the presented research. In short, the solver chooses some action (a construction operation or a theorem) based on the current semantic structure. The choice is made heuristically and depends on the subject area. Next, the action is executed and a new semantic structure is generated. The process ends when the required result is found, there are no more possible actions, or the search resources are exhausted. Heuristics are organized according to G. Polya's methodology [5].

In his concept, not only the actual solution of problems is important but also the related aspects:

- How a formal statement of the problem is extracted from an NL wording
- What means are involved for its solution and for what reasons
- What plausible reasoning is used
- What inductive and empirical considerations we are guided by when searching for a solution
- How to generalize the solution, etc.

Therefore, Polya focused specifically on the cognitive aspects of the solution.

As a matter of principle, RDF models, languages like OWL (Web Ontology Language), and various graph visualization systems (CytoScape, yEd, Gephi, Visual Graph) can be used to describe semantics. Depending on the intended solver, formulas reflecting the subject area patterns can be represented using predicate calculation means. Surely, in a specific implementation, one should assess thoroughly the complexity of solutions. In particular, plugins that allow integrating heterogeneous systems are usually very difficult to implement.

3 Materials and Methods

To test and study the capabilities of the cognitive pattern method, we have performed a computer implementation of a cognitive pattern for the subject area of geometry. The semantic component pseudocode contains strings such as "type-1 obj-1 rel type-2 obj-2," where type describes the object type (a reference to ontology), obj-nn is the object's unique name, and rel is a relation between objects, e.g., "point A on segment BC."

The semantic presentation serves as the basis for an extension that describes larger constructs, such as "ABC triangle." Using such extensions, a generalized semantic description of a cognitive pattern is created, containing template variables (#A#B#C). In the problem text, e.g., "In XYZ triangle…," these variables are assigned specific values (#A = X, #B = Y, #C = Z). Then, the cognitive pattern interpreter generates a text file that provides visualization (a sketch of the problem drawing). Visualization tools are JavaScript, JSXGraph, and MathJax libraries [6, 7]. The latter library provides displaying of a mathematical notation and is comparable to LaTeX in terms of its expressive capacity.

Syntax and semantics graphs are provided with similar display capacities. It is important that the stages of working with a cognitive pattern are supported by interactive visualization. By clicking on an object (a point, a segment, a circle, a concept, a syntactic or semantic relationship, etc.), the user can get information regarding such an object. This style allows us to follow the system solutions at the content and conceptual level.

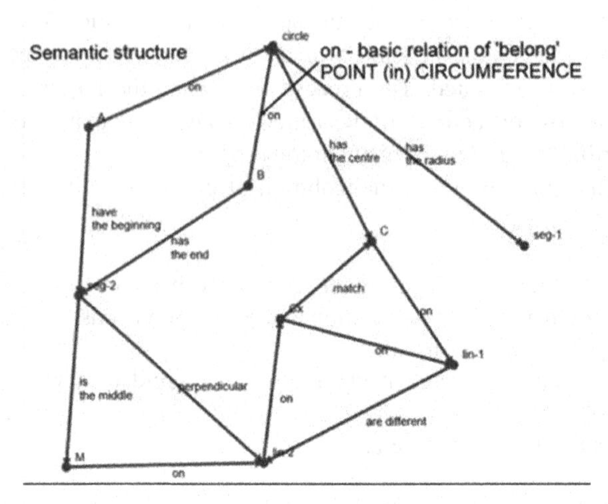

Fig. 3. Semantic structure synthesized by the solver (interactive visualization of the "on" relation)

The semantic graph for solving this problem is shown in Fig. 3. By mouse click, the user gets information regarding the "on" relation (this is the basic "belong" relation between a point and a circle).

4 Results and Discussion

The empirical basis for testing the above implementation has included more than 500 problems from the collection [10]. For each problem, we have manually prepared descriptions for visualization—creating a problem drawing. Following the analysis of descriptions, we have designed several dozen cognitive patterns, which collectively cover almost the entire corpus of problems. Let us explain the features of working with cognitive patterns using two examples.

One of the designed cognitive patterns for problems with medians has the following NL description: "The triangle medians are drawn down to the legs with given lengths." Here is a description with template variables: "#A#B#C triangle with #A#C base and #A#D and #C#E medians. #A#B = #a. #B#C = #b." Keywords for the pattern are triangle, medians, two triangle legs are equal, respectively, drawn, omitted, leg midpoints, angle between medians, are equal, =.

The problem text: "Two triangle legs are 6 cm and 8 cm, respectively. The medians drawn to these legs are perpendicular. Find the triangle area." Based on this text, 10 strings are generated for extended structures. As a result of visually rendering this text, a drawing sketch is displayed on the screen, Fig. 4, the left triangle.

The sketch does not fully reflect the problem conditions: the perpendicularity of medians is not reflected. To adjust the drawing, we use the "fine-tuning" script which, through iterations, provides perpendicularity, Fig. 4, the right triangle. The comments on the triangle legs reflect the semantics of medians (points E and S are the segment midpoints; the medians at the intersection point are divided as 2:1). Note again that the use of a pattern greatly simplifies both the transition from the problem text to the semantic presentation and building up a drawing.

There are no vertex names in the above text—for the drawing, they are taken by default. However, the description may be as follows: "… XYZ triangle … XA and ZB… medians"; instead of specific values (6 and 8); symbolic values are allowed, etc. This pattern has been tested for texts where such descriptions are allowed, and the vocabulary has also been changed. Examples of paraphrasing this problem are given in [8], and some examples of the empirical base, in [9].

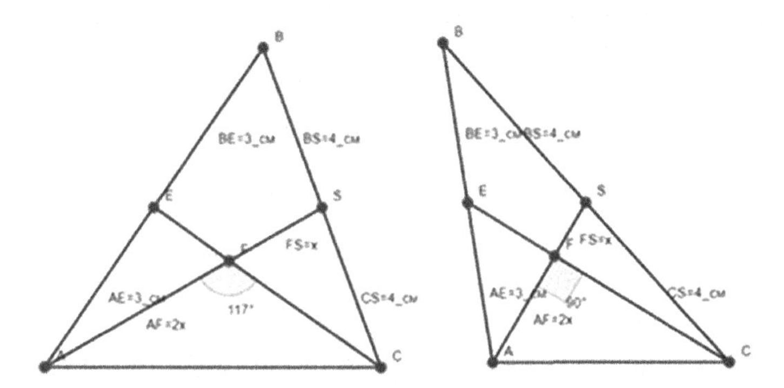

Fig. 4. The drawing before and after "fine-tuning" (the problem of medians)

The second problem text: "In ABCD trapezoid, the lower base AD is two-fold larger than the upper one, that is equal to *a*; angle *A* at the base is 45°, and the circles drawn on the legs as diameters touch each other. Find the trapezoid area." Figs. 5 and 6 show the drawings before and after "fine-tuning," and below is the "fine-tuning" script with comments.

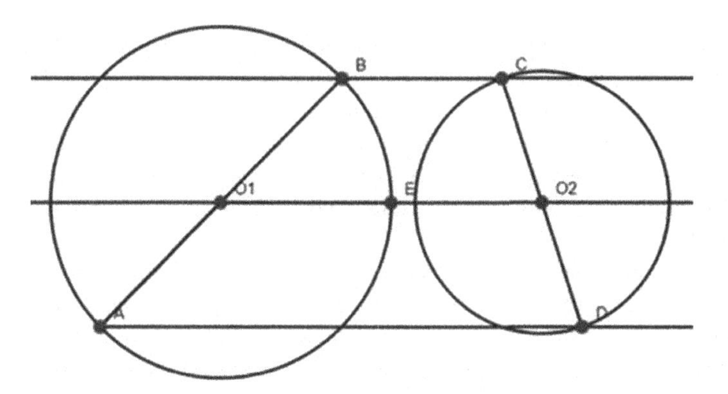

Fig. 5. The drawing before "fine-tuning" (the problem of trapezoid and circles)

The “fine-tuning” implemented in an NL: move point O2 along right line O1_E until the intersection of a circle with radius O2_E with the right lines along which the trapezoid bases are situated.

Comments to the script text:

The initial radius O2_E is taken to be equal to the first circle radius (O1_E). AX and q are the right lines along which the trapezoid bases are situated. O2 is the second circle radius; in the process of iterations, it moves along the middle line of the trapezoid. The iteration step is d_x; the termination condition is equality of segments E_O2 = C_O2 = D_02 (at a given accuracy of 0.02).

The fine-tuning for the problem of external and internal tangents to two circles is described in [3]. In the process of fine-tuning, the angle between the tangents and the diameters of the circles was changed.

Here is the problem text: “Two circles with radii r and R (r < R) are situated so that one of their common internal tangents is perpendicular to one of their external tangents. Find the area of the triangle formed by these tangents and one more internal tangent.”

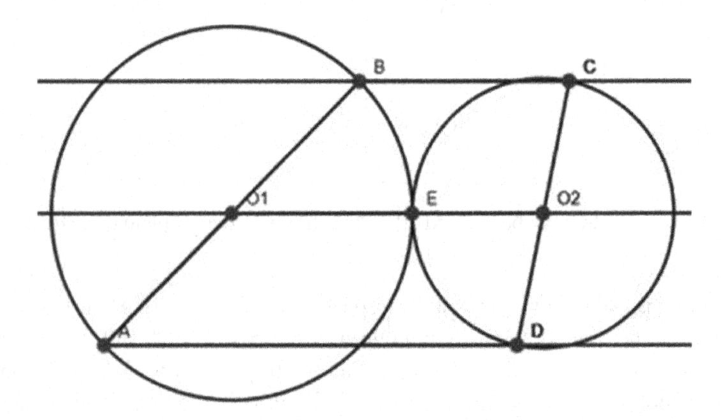

Fig. 6. The drawing after “fine-tuning” (the problem of trapezoid and circles)

The NL description of a cognitive pattern for similar problems is as follows: “Two circles with radii *r* and *R* (r < R) have external and internal tangents.” The semantic pseudocode contains 11 strings describing the above pattern (four right lines and two circles). After fine-tuning (perpendicularity requirement), the drawing is modified. Next, the following string is added to the pseudocode: “right line pr-1 is perpendicular to right line pr-3,” and the following string is added to the NL description: “Internal tangent is perpendicular to the external one.”

In the current version of the system for the selected cognitive pattern, we have developed various options for fine-tuning the drawing, depending on the parameters set in the problem text. Note that a cognitive pattern does not guarantee a solution, but a correct drawing allows us to make assumptions based on empirical data (plausible reasoning in G. Polya’s style [5]).

A cognitive pattern can include various cases (in semantic presentation, they correspond to the OR operation). An example of such a pattern is given below; the text and the drawing of a real problem for the pattern are given in [10], problem 1.1.8.

The NL description of the pattern is as follows: "An arbitrary point is taken on the triangle base or on its extension. Two circles are drawn through this point, the triangle vertex, and the base vertices." The graphics extension is given below:

```
BEG-ALL
3 drawing operators
L-BR1: BR1-1 BR1-2 BR1-3 (on the base, to the left of
B, to the right of C)
//
BR1-1 BEG: a point on the base BC
3 drawing operators
BR1-1 END:
//
BR1-2 BEG: a point on the extension BC from point B
4 drawing operators
BR1-2 END:
//
BR1-3 BEG: a point on the extension BC from point C
4 drawing operators
BR1-3
L-BR1 END
END-ALL
```

Real drawing operators are omitted; only their numbers are indicated instead of them. The BEG-ALL and END-ALL brackets delimit all pattern operators. Operators after BEG-ALL are common in all cases. The list after L-BR1 is based on three possible cases for the drawing (BR1–1 BR1–2 BR1–3). The general presentation of the bracket is BRi-j, where i is the solution number, and j is the solution case. Numbering is important for the solver that can generate multiple solutions with different cases.

Each case corresponds to an individual drawing that the browser renders independently. Figure 7 shows the first two cases of the drawing; the third is rendered similarly.

The results obtained have confirmed our assumption that using cognitive patterns dramatically reduces the load on the linguistic processor and the solver. In this case, the system functioning is more transparent, and the software debugging is greatly facilitated.

Psychological aspects in the current implementation take into account the naturalness of the drawing, the balance between brevity and the number of solution steps, an appeal to geometric intuition (it looks like these right lines are perpendicular/parallel — try to prove it).

The subject area of geometry allows us to test the mechanism of working with cognitive patterns, but the pattern designing method is not tied to a specific area. Thus, to demonstrate visualization capabilities, we added the following string to the system: type-1 obj-1 rel_ type-2 obj-2, describing some formula. Here, exp_mm is the unique expression name; ar_nn is arity; the term is the terminal element. The cognitive pattern describing this formula should be interpreted as the "Integral" frame with four template

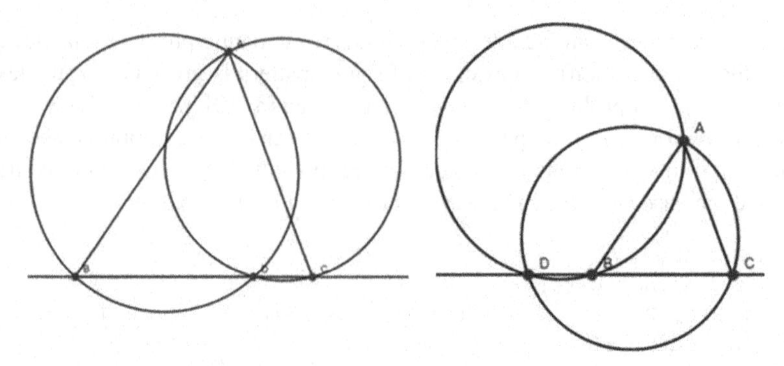

Fig. 7. The first two cases of drawing for a cognitive pattern

variables. In terms of contents, the variables correspond to the upper limit, the lower limit, the integrand function, and the differential.

Based on this semantic presentation, the system generated the following text:

```
integral (minus-inf,plus-inf,(e EXP minus((x EXP
2))),dx).
```

After appropriate recoding, the system generated the following text:

```
examle_07 = "\\[   \\int\\limits_{- \\infty} ^
{\\infty} e^{-x^{2}} dx  \\]" ;
```

The variable examle_07 is displayed in a text object with MathJax support (MathJax notation is similar to that used in LaTex). The visualization result is shown in Fig. 8.

$$\int\limits_{-\infty}^{\infty} e^{-x^{2}} dx$$

Fig. 8. Formula visualization from semantic presentation

Surely, a full-fledged semantic description will require a corresponding extension of the ontology.

Note that we are talking about dynamic visualization of a formula from a declarative semantic presentation. In a cognitive pattern, this presentation (with an accuracy of up to the object names) is prepared in advance; but it can be formed during the solver operation. For instance, when solving some problem (drawing a right-angled triangle based on a hypotenuse and a bisector), the solver synthesized a semantic presentation. Similarly, to the situation with an integral, the recoding of this presentation generates a text (in a LaTeX style):

```
s_rez = " X = \\frac {- L + \\sqrt{L^{2} +
(2*\\sqrt{2}*R)^{2} } } {2} " ;
```

The s_rez variable is then sent to a JSXGraph text object using the useMathJax:true specifier. The visualization result is shown in Fig. 9.

$$X = \frac{-L + \sqrt{L^2 + (2 * \sqrt{2} * R)^2}}{2}$$

Fig. 9. Visualization of the semantic representation synthesized by the solver

In addition to geometry, which provided a significant empirical corpus, we considered some problems with physical content. In particular, we considered a problem related to the photoelectric effect. Here is the problem text: "In an experiment to study the photoelectric effect, light with a frequency of $\nu = 6.1 \cdot 1{,}014$ Hz falls on the cathode surface, as a result, a saturation current of 2 mA arises in the circuit. What is the incident light power P, if on average, one of 20 photons incident on the cathode knocks out one electron?" The text basically matches the description of a demo problem in physics — the Unified State Exam (profile level, No. 9331).

The reference graphic for the cognitive pattern (similar to the triangle with medians in Fig. 1) is a typical photocurrent graph.

After choosing this scheme, the formulas' variables included in the pattern are assigned specific values. The basic formulas describe the charge and mass of an electron, $mv^2/2 < eU_r$ (retarding voltage and kinetic energy of photoelectrons), etc. The formulas are related to the pattern keywords: electron, amount of charge, quantum, photon, quantum energy, radiation frequency, Planck's constant, etc.

The designed pattern includes seven main and four auxiliary formulas and 15 keywords. Keywords from the problem text should both facilitate the choice of a pattern and the choice of promising formulas (for the subsequent launch of an automated solution). The formulas are displayed in a graphical notation similar to the above example with an integral.

We have also considered problems with electrical circuits, capacitor circuits, and mechanical problems (for example, elastic and inelastic collision). For these problems, we have analyzed the feasibility of developing cognitive patterns supported by graphics and formulas corresponding to the problem semantics. Surely, a full-fledged implementation of such patterns will require the ontology to be significantly improved with including basic physical concepts thereto, such as space, time, mass, force, etc.).

5 Related Studies

Research and development related to both NL processing and automated problem solving have made significant progress to date. However, an integrated, interdisciplinary approach, that combines an in-depth linguistic study, well-developed explanatory capabilities, and cognitive aspects of user interaction with a computer, is still in its infancy. It is towards this approach that we are developing the suggested method to resolve the contradiction between the freedom of NL descriptions and a strict formalization.

Historically, the elements of this approach were outlined in classic papers by Schenck [11] and Vinograd [12]. However, the difficulties in creating appropriate software (limited, "fragile," underdeveloped means of adaptation, etc.) have reduced interest in similar studies. Further research on NL processing was conducted in different areas: translation systems; access to NL databases, automated referencing. Huge volumes of textual information on the Internet have driven the research on its structuring, in particular, for their subsequent use in data mining systems. Among modern large-scale NL processing systems, widely known is Watson.

In-game situations requiring an understanding of an NL at a non-trivial level, this system could outperform humans in answering difficult questions. It was declared that Watson would be able to solve sophisticated practical problems related to linguistic processing. However, an attempt to use Watson for medical purposes (oncology) uncovered serious complications. Definitely, this only reveals the system's limitations, but in no way diminishes the scientific and practical significance of Watson. Another large-scale system—Wolfram—features an interpreter operator providing an understanding of NL queries. However, its capabilities are limited (the authors worked with version 11.3, which has not yet implemented the data input in Russian).

The use of interactive geometric environments in the educational process with elements of cognitive methods is discussed in [13]. The authors rightly point out the need to involve the figurative component of thinking in the process of providing geometric proofs. However, the examples given in the monograph are controversial in terms of complexity and clarity, i.e., cognitive characteristics as such. In the field of education, an important advantage of the suggested method, as compared to the approach described in the monograph, is an open software code. This advantage also applies to all studies focused on dynamic geometric environments but based on closed systems, such as the well-known GEOGEBRA.

When choosing the implementation tools, we have considered the CytoScape, yEd, and Gephi systems in terms of the possibility of entering graphs from EXCEL or using XML files. Ultimately, we chose JSXGraph, taking into account its cross-platform nature, an open-source code, a large number of examples, and the availability of the MathJac library, which provides a mathematical notation for visualization.

The related studies of recent years have introduced texts in an NL and solved geometric and algebraic problems [15–18]. However, their linguistic tools, transparent and convincing explanations, the capabilities of interactive visualization are more limited than those developed in the suggested method.

In recent years, ELMo and BERT models have also been developed, the project [19]. ELMo is based on a recurrent neural network, BERT is based on the so-called attention mechanism. BERT is the closest in terms of subject matter, but both models are focused on a different concept of understanding the text. They successfully answer questions, predict the next word of the text, etc., but they do not form a semantic representation on which the solver can work.

6 Conclusion

The main contribution of this paper to solving the fundamental issue of a cognitive approach to the holistic process of understanding a problem described in a natural language, its solution, and the visual perception is as follows:

1. We have suggested and developed a method for designing cognitive patterns for well-formalizable problems described in a natural language.
2. The method takes into account the full set of human cognitive abilities: understanding of a natural language in the light of a well-formalizable problem, its formalization for an automated solution, a graphical visualization of the solu-tion, and its psychological aspects.
3. We have tested the method on a set of geometric problems and suggested an extension of the experiment to physical problems.
4. The method is focused on the concept of G. Polya, the famous researcher and teacher.
5. The use of cognitive structures greatly simplifies linguistic processing and sup-ports the solver's functioning.

In the applied area, our research is focused on creating brand-new educational systems based on AI methods, developing intellectual assistants for students, teachers, authors of textbooks and teaching materials, tutors. Some experiments with the system for educational purposes are described in [14].

References

1. Kuhn, T.: The Structure of Scientific Revolutions. Chicago, 1962; 2edn. Chicago, 1970. HOL interactive theorem prover (2018)
2. Lakoff, G.: Metaphors We Live By. University of Chicago Press. 2003 edition contains an 'Afterword', 2003 (1980)
3. Naidenova, X., Kurbatov, S., Ganapolsky, V.: Cognitive models in planimetric task text processing. Int. J. Cogn. Res. Sci. Eng. Educ. (ISSN: 2334–847X)
4. Kurbatov, S.S., Fominykh, I.B., Vorobyev, A.B.: ontology-controlled geometric solver. In: Kuznetsov, S.O., Panov, A.I., Yakovlev, K.S. (eds.) Artificial Intelligence. RCAI 2020. LNCS, vol. 12412. Springer, Cham (2020). https://doi.org/10.1007/978-3-030-59535-7_19
5. Polya, G.: Mathematical Discovery: On Understanding, Learning and Teaching Problem Solving, p. 432. Wiley, Hoboken (1981)
6. Dynamic mathematics with JavaScript, JSXGraph is a cross-browser JavaScript library for interactive geometry, function plotting, charting, and data visualization in the web browser. – http://jsxgraph.uni-bayreuth.de/wp/index.html
7. MathJax is a cross-browser JavaScript library that displays mathematical notation in web browsers, using MathML, LaTeX and ASCIIMathML markup. – https://github.com/mathjax/MathJax/releases/tag/3.1.2
8. Screenshot-1. http://www.eia--dostup.ru/APP-1.pdf
9. Screenshot-2. http://www.eia--dostup.ru/APP-2.pdf
10. Kulanin, E.D.: 3000 konkursnyh zadach po matematike. Geometriya, Ileksa (2018)
11. Schenk, R.C., Goldman, N.M., Rieger, C.J., Riesbeck, C.K.: Conceptual information processing. Norh-Holland Publishing Company, Amsterdam (1975)

12. Winograd, T.: Understanding Natural Language. Academic Press, New York (1972)
13. Sergeeva, T.F., Shabanova, M.V., Grozdev, S.I.: Fundamentals of Dynamic Geometry, p. 152. Publishing house ASOU, Russia (2016).(in Russian)
14. Sergey, S., Kurbatov, I.B., Fominykh, A.B.: Vorobyev applied aspects of the integrated problem solving system with natural language interface. In: Conference: 2020 V International Conference on Information Technologies in Engineering Education (Inforino), IEEE Computer Society (2020)
15. Gan, W., Yu, X.: Automatic understanding and formalization of natural language geometry problems using syntax-semantics models. Int. J. Innov. Comput. Inf. Control ICIC **14**(1), 83–98 (2018)
16. Seo, M., Hajishirzi, H., Farhadi, A., Etzioni, O., Malcolm, C.: Solving geometry problems: combining text and diagram interpretation. http://geometry.allenai.org/assets/emnlp2015.pdf
17. Shi, S., Wang, Y., Lin, C.-Y., Liu, X., Yong Rui, Y:. Automatically solving number word problems by semantic parsing and reasoning. In: Proceedings of the 2015 Conference on Empirical Methods in Natural Language Processing. Lisbon, Portugal, 17–21 September, pp. 1132–1142 (2015)
18. Wang, K., Su, Z.: Automated geometry theorem proving for human-readable proofs. In: Proceedings of the Twenty-Fourth International Joint Conference on Artificial Intelligence. Buenos Aires, Argentina, 25–31 July (2015)
19. AllenNLP 2.5.0. https://pypi.org/project/allennlp/

Detecting Anomalous Behavior of Users of Data Centers Based on the Application of Artificial Neural Networks

Igor Saenko[1(✉)], Igor Kotenko[1], Fadey Skorik[2], and Mazen Al-Barri[2]

[1] Saint-Petersburg Federal Research Center of the Russian Academy of Sciences (SPC RAS), Saint-Petersburg, Russia
{ibsaen,ivkote}@comsec.spb.ru

[2] Saint-Petersburg Signal Academy, Saint-Petersburg, Russia
work_bk@bk.ru

Abstract. The paper discusses an approach to detecting anomalies in the behavior of users of data centers, using a specialized analytical unit based on artificial neural networks. It is proposed to use transaction log records of the databases that are part of the data center as data sets for analysis. An experimental evaluation of the proposed approach is made for several types of analytical units, which include several artificial neural networks. Experiments have demonstrated the high efficiency of the proposed approach.

Keywords: Applied intelligent systems · Anomaly detection · Artificial neural network · Data center · Analytical unit

1 Introduction

The issues of detecting anomalous user behavior in automated control systems have been relevant over the past decades. Up until today, they do not have unambiguous answers, as new technologies for information processing appear.

One of these technologies, which is becoming widespread in many areas, is cloud technology associated with the use of collective data processing centers, which are otherwise called data centers (DCs). DCs play an important role in control systems for various purposes. They constitute the information and technical basis of the cloud infrastructure since they support a repository of heterogeneous information that is utilized by users in their own interests [1]. For this reason, DCs are the objects that security violators primarily target to obtain information or disrupt the operation of the centers. However, these violators can be both internal and external [2].

The problem of detecting anomalies in the behavior of DC users is not least associated with the constant increase in their distribution and the complexity of the topology, as well as the updating of hardware and software. This, in turn, causes certain problems in administration and significantly increases the requirements for the qualifications of personnel.

S. M. Kovalev et al. (Eds.): RCAI 2021, LNAI 12948, pp. 331–342, 2021.
https://doi.org/10.1007/978-3-030-86855-0_23

Currently, firewalls, anti-virus tools, intrusion detection systems, monitoring systems [3], and access control systems [4, 5] are used to ensure DC information security. At the same time, when building information security systems, various methods of searching for anomalies can be used, which have varying degrees of efficiency. However, these anomalies are usually found in network traffic. But network traffic anomalies do not reflect the incorrect, abnormal user behavior when working with databases. These actions can only be detected by analyzing the database logs. Such an analysis, aimed at identifying anomalous behavior of DC users, is currently either not being carried out or not being carried out in full. This is largely due to the peculiarities of the datasets that form the database log records, and the complexity of using the most known classifiers and machine learning methods for their analysis (SVM, Bayesian networks, k-means, random forest, logistic regression, etc.) [6]. Also, the issues of using artificial neural networks in the context of analyzing user actions and preventing various attacks or abuses provoked by them have not yet been properly considered.

The approach proposed in this paper is focused on detecting anomalies in the database logs and is based on the use of analytical units containing artificial neural networks. Based on the analysis of known works devoted to the search for anomalies in DCs, it can be argued that this approach is being implemented for the first time. This determines the *main contribution* and the *scientific novelty* of this work.

The further structure of the paper is as follows. Section 1 analyzes the state of research in the field of analysis and search for anomalies. Section 2 discusses the issues of obtaining datasets for training and testing neural networks. Section 3 describes the structure of the proposed analytical unit containing the neural network module and the procedure for its functioning. The experimental results on the detection of anomalies are presented and discussed in Sect. 4. The Conclusion contains general conclusions and directions for further research.

2 Existing Methods of Analysis and Search for Anomalies

Popular methods for detecting anomalies in the actions of data center users can be summarized in several large groups:

1. Tests based on the data model. The result of the tests is the identification of points that have a significant deviation from the constructed model. These points are anomalies [7–9].
2. Calculation of metrics. As an example, we can consider the calculation of the distance to the k-th neighbor, thereby determining the deviation from the norm [10, 11].
3. Determination of anomalies using statistical tests [12, 13]. Typically, these methods are used to identify individual anomalies.
4. Methods for finding anomalies based on the induction and clustering of the problem into smaller fragments [14, 15].
5. Machine learning techniques such as ellipsoidal data fit [16] or support vector machines [17].
6. Anomaly detection by calculating an average score based on the results of several detection algorithms [18, 19].

Methods based on patterns of network attacks [20], context search [21], and analysis of the state of signatures [22] are also distinguished.

From the analysis of known methods for detecting anomalies, it can be concluded that anomalies in the behavior of DC users can be classified as follows:

- allocation of a separate data instance, anomalous in relation to other data instances
- allocation of a separate data instance, anomalous in a certain context
- identifying a dataset that is anomalous with respect to other data, and each individual instance of that dataset is not anomalous.

These properties of anomalies will be used further in the construction of artificial neural networks.

3 Obtaining Initial Data for an Artificial Neural Network

As the initial data for training and subsequent operation of artificial neural networks, it is advisable to use the results of the analysis of the transaction logs of the databases used in the DC, converted into numerical form.

Typically, the transaction log is stored as one or more continuously updated files. The log contains information about database events and user queries in text form. By default, the following information is included:

- Date of the request
- Request time
- Request source
- Information about the event (request).

In the paper, the transaction logs of the database of the educational portal of the educational institution, which includes about 4,000 tables, whose sizes varied from ten to several hundred records, were used as a source for forming the dataset of the initial data. Up to several hundred users could access the database at the same time, and their access rights varied depending on the category of the account.

The initial data for the operation of the neural network is formed as follows.

First, there is an accumulation of information about the frequency of user calls to the database and to specific tables, types of queries, and their frequency.

Highlighted is a typical range of time of day in which this user works with the database.

The address information about the source of the request (the recipient of the data sample) is saved.

Upon completion of the accumulation of a certain amount of data, their statistical processing is performed. The processing results are used to generate a training (control) sample of numbers used to train (operate) an artificial neural network.

For correct training of an artificial neural network and minimization of the output layer error, before starting training, it is advisable to accumulate at least 15,000 records in the training dataset.

An example of an entry in the database transaction log is shown in Fig. 1. Before the keyword 'statement', the record contains information about the date and time of the request. This word contains the text of the SQL query with which the user accessed the database.

```
2021-03-05 15:13:27.677 MSK [836454] LOG:  statement: /
*pga4dash*/
     SELECT 'session_stats' AS chart_name, row_to_json(t) AS
chart_data
     FROM (SELECT
        (SELECT count(*) FROM pg_stat_activity WHERE datname =
(SELECT datname FROM pg_database WHERE oid = 13426)) AS "Total",
        (SELECT count(*) FROM pg_stat_activity WHERE state =
'active' AND datname = (SELECT datname FROM pg_database WHERE oid
= 13426))  AS "Active",
        (SELECT count(*) FROM pg_stat_activity WHERE state =
'idle' AND datname = (SELECT datname FROM pg_database WHERE oid =
13426))  AS "Idle")
```

Fig. 1. A sample database transaction log entry

Converting transaction log records to numeric form is as follows.

First, when analyzing a specific query, the record is decomposed into separate components.

A sample of the form [0, 0, 0, ..., 0] is formed. The dimension of the sample determines the size of the input layer of the neural network. The selection is initialized to zeros.

Then an initial analysis of the request time is performed. If the user's hit falls into the previously saved range of hits, the value 1 is assigned to a certain value in the sample. Otherwise, the degree of deviation in the range of values [0, 1] is calculated.

Next, the source of the request is determined and the degree of correspondence of the source address to the subnet from which the user's requests previously came is calculated. The value of the correspondence of the address information saved earlier in the range [0, 1] is set. The result obtained also falls into the sample of the original data (into the dataset).

Then the content of the database query is analyzed. Based on the accumulated statistical data, the probability of a user accessing the table indicated in the query is calculated, which is set in the range [0, 1].

Similarly, the probabilities of using queries of a certain type (SELECT, UPDATE, INSERT INTO, etc.) are set, as well as the probabilities of accessing certain fields in the table in a query. The obtained data is also included in the sample of the initial data for the neural network.

Accordingly, for each sample of initial data, a sample of output values of neural data is formed, which determines the type of user behavior.

To simulate anomalous user behavior, certain changes were made to the transaction logs, which were later used to form training and control datasets, in total, making up no more than 2% of the total number of records.

The essence of the changes was as follows:

- For users who do not have the permission to write and modify data, UPDATE, INSERT INTO, CREATE TABLE, DROP TABLE records have been added.
- There were added user calls to certain records in the service tables of the database, and tables that they had never previously accessed.
- There were added the requests typical for individual users, but at unusual times for work, for example, after working hours, or from network addresses from which they had not previously accessed the database.

In addition to the above, no more changes were made to the transaction logs and to the datasets obtained on their basis.

4 The Structure of the Analytical Unit for Detecting Anomalies

To detect anomalies in the actions of DC users, it is advisable to use the implemented software analytical units. The analytical unit includes (Fig. 2):

- the module for transforming the initial data
- the module of artificial neural networks
- the module for interpreting the obtained results.

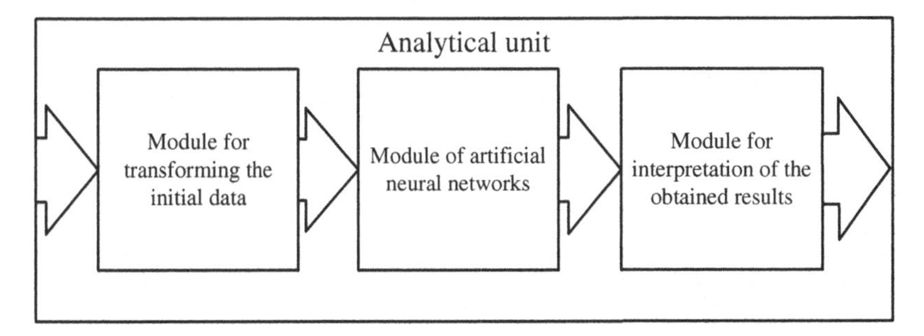

Fig. 2. Generalized structure of the analytical unit

The module for transforming the initial data performs the function of reading the necessary records from the database transaction log and converts their contents into numerical form, followed by the formation of samples that act as initial data for the operation of the neural network.

If necessary, the initial data is normalized within the limits [0, 1]. For this purpose, for example, a sigmoidal logistic function is used, which has the following form:

$$\tilde{x}_{ik} = \frac{1}{e^{-a(x_{ik}-x_{ci})} + 1}, \tag{1}$$

where x_{ik} and $\tilde{x}_{ik}$ are the initial and normalized values of the k-th data element of the i-th interval, respectively; x_{ci} is the center of the normalized i-th interval; a is the function slope parameter.

When forming a training dataset, it is necessary to process the obtained samples by a human expert to form pairs of input/output datasets necessary for training the neural network.

The module of artificial neural networks includes one or more neural networks that perform, after appropriate training, the functions of transforming the numerical samples obtained in the module for transforming the initial data. The transformation is carried out to a form close to one of the output datasets on which these neural networks were previously trained.

The generalized structure of an artificial neural network is shown in Fig. 3. It includes three modules.

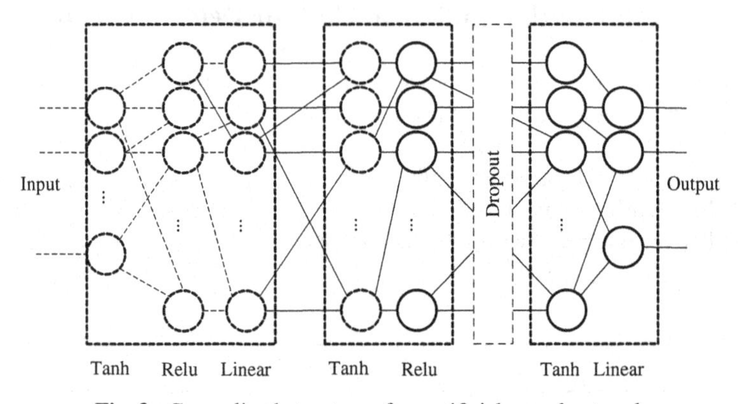

Fig. 3. Generalized structure of an artificial neural network

Each of the modules includes:

- a number of layers of neurons with linear (stepwise) or nonlinear (hyperbolic tangent) activation functions
- layers with a filtering (Relu) function
- a separate module (Dropout) that removes redundant connections between layers of neurons.

For neural networks with the proposed structure, it is advisable to use the adaptive learning step method (Adadelta) as a learning method [23]. This method allows you to get quality results in a reasonable period of time.

Adadelta method uses an exponential moving average to estimate the second moment of the gradient g_t. The parameters are updated as follows:

$$g_{t+1} = \gamma g_t + (1 - \gamma)\nabla f_i(\Theta_t)^2, \tag{2}$$

$$v_{t+1} = -\frac{\sqrt{x_t + \varepsilon}\,\nabla f_i(\Theta_t)}{\sqrt{g_{t+1} + \varepsilon}}, \tag{3}$$

$$x_{t+1} = \gamma x_t + (1 - \gamma)v_{t+1}^2, \quad (4)$$

$$\Theta_{t+1} = \Theta_t + v_{t+1}, \quad (5)$$

where f_i is the function calculated on the i-th part of the data, t is the iteration step, x_t is the moving average, and γ is the hyperparameter.

The module for interpreting the obtained results acts as a filter that determines the proximity of the result obtained at the output of the artificial neural network to the reference values previously set by the human expert for the training dataset.

5 Detection of Anomalies in the Actions of DC Users

To implement an approach to detecting anomalies in the actions of DC users, it is advisable to place an analytical unit on a DC computer network node with the ability to obtain data from the database transaction log in a time mode close to real. The place of the analytical unit in the structure of the DC is shown in Fig. 4.

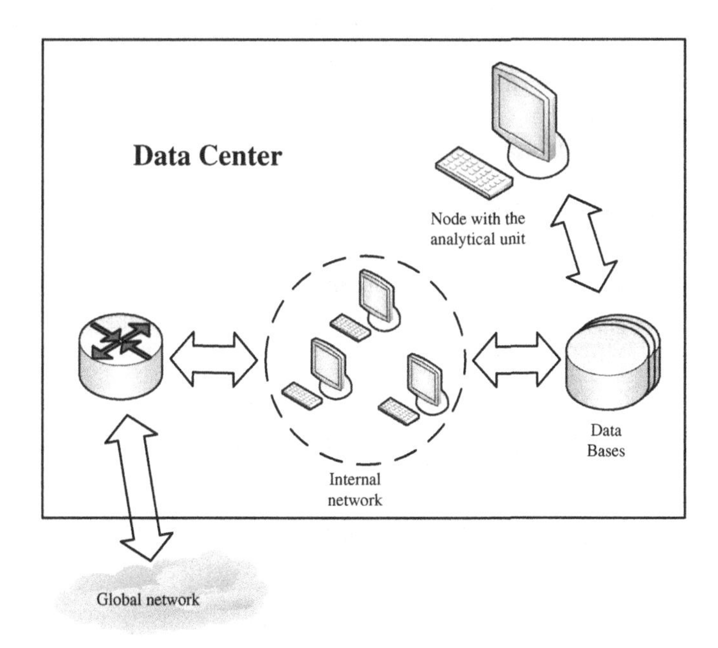

Fig. 4. The place of the analytical unit in the structure of the DC

Three types of analytical units were used for testing, including one, two, and three artificial neural networks, respectively. Each neural network was trained using different datasets. The size of the data sets varied from 15,000 to 30,000 records. The experiments were carried out on a typical computer with the parameters Intel CPU 1.86 GHz, RAM 4.0 Gb. The application that implements the analytic unit was written in Python (Django framework). The test dataset was generated by adding abnormal records to the normal dataset. Anomalous records were generated randomly by duplicating existing records and changing the names of data tables in SQL queries.

Python was used as a programming language for the implementation of the analytical block. To implement artificial neural networks, the PyTorch library was used. The experiments were carried out on a computer with the following characteristics: Intel Core i5 processor, DDR4 16 GB RAM, GeForce RTX 3060 video card, and 128 GB SSD.

The basic structure of the artificial neural network at the initial stage of experiments includes seven layers of fixed dimension. The first (input) layer has 12 neurons with a nonlinear activation function (hyperbolic tangent). The second and third layers similarly include 12 neurons each with nonlinear (Relu) and linear (step) activation functions. The fourth, fifth, and sixth layers consist of 18 neurons each. For these layers, nonlinear activation functions are used: for the fourth and sixth layers - hyperbolic tangent, and for the fifth layer - Relu. To the connections between the neurons of the fifth and sixth layers, the dropout function is applied. The seventh layer is an output and consists of one neuron with a linear activation function.

The test dataset was generated by randomly adding abnormal entries to the transaction logs. Then, based on the augmented transaction log, the corresponding dataset was formed.

Tests were performed on datasets of different sizes which contained 15,000, 25,000, or 30,000 records.

Table 1 shows the results of testing the analytical unit which includes one, two or three artificial neural networks, which were trained on datasets of different sizes, containing 15,000, 25,000, or 30,000 records.

Table 1. Analytical units testing results.

Number of neural networks	Dataset volume, 10^3	False interpretation of the result, %
1	15	41
	25	25
	30	19
2	15	37
	25	19
	30	14
3	15	20
	25	12
	30	9

The "False interpretation of the result" is defined as the sum of the *False Positive Rate* (*FPR*) and *False Negative Rate* (*FNR*). *FPR* and *FNR* are defined as follows:

$$FPR = FP/N, \quad (6)$$

$$FNR = FN/N, \tag{7}$$

where N is the size of the testing sample, $N = TP + TN + FP + FN$, TP is the number of correct positive decisions, TN is the number of correct negative decisions, FP is the number of erroneous positive decisions, and FN is the number of erroneous negative decisions.

The dependence of the false interpretation of the result (learning errors) on the iteration number of the training sample is shown in Fig. 5.

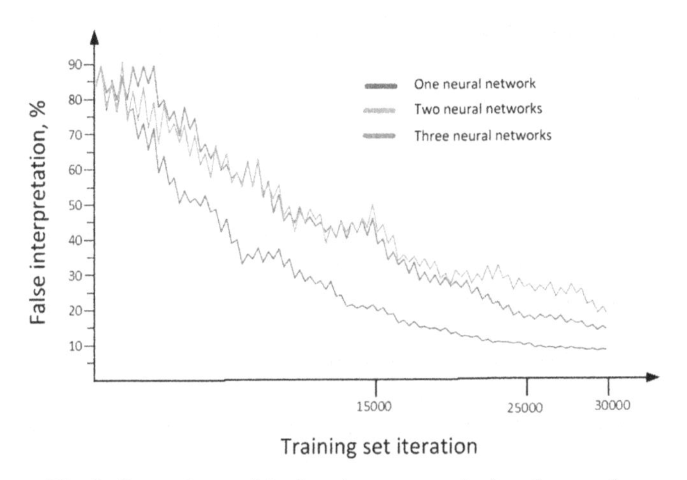

Fig. 5. Dependence of the learning error on the iteration number

Table 2 shows the time spent on training neural networks, depending on their number and the size of the training sample. The table shows the values of the average training time, calculated from the results of three tests. The software implementation of each analytical unit made it possible to train artificial neural networks simultaneously, in parallel streams.

Table 2. Training times for various datasets.

Number of neural networks	Dataset volume, 10^3	Training time, sec.
1	15	552
	25	920
	30	1104
2	15	994
	25	1656
	30	1987
3	15	1988
	25	3312
	30	3975

Analysis of the obtained experimental results allows us to draw the following conclusions. The best result in terms of the accuracy of detecting anomalies in the behavior of DC users was shown by the analytical unit, which includes three artificial neural networks that were trained on a dataset of 30,000 records. The learning error decreases as the number of iterations increases. The training accuracy can be doubled if not one, but three artificial neural networks are used in the analytical unit.

Analyzing the data on the training time, we can draw the following conclusion. The training time of the analytical unit increases with an increase in the size of the dataset according to a linear law. This pattern is easy to see if we compare the training times with each other for dataset sizes equal to 15,000 and 30,000, and a different number of neural networks. So, with one neural network, these times are equal, respectively, 552 and 1,104 s, with two neural networks — 994 and 1,987 s, with three neural networks — 1,988 and 3,975 s. It turns out that a twofold increase in the size of the dataset also doubles the training time.

At the same time, the dependence of the training time on the number of neural networks in the analytical unit is non-linear. More precisely, it obeys the power dependence. So, if we consider the experimental data obtained for a dataset with a volume of 15,000 records, then you can easily see that the transition from one neural network in the analytical unit to two neural networks increases the training time by about two times. At the same time, the transition from two to three neural networks also doubles the training time. It turns out that the transition from one to three neural networks leads to an increase in the training time already four times. This dependence can be seen for the other two datasets, with volumes of 25,000 and 30,000 records.

Thus, cross-checking the output data of different neural networks and their further generalized interpretation can significantly improve the final result of the analytical unit. In this case, the complexity of the structure of the artificial neural network is not required and, accordingly, there will be no increase in labor costs for training artificial neural networks.

6 Conclusion

The paper considered an approach to detecting anomalous behavior of DC users based on the application of artificial neural networks, included in a specialized software-implemented analytical unit located on one of the nodes of the DC local area network.

Based on the results of the analysis of the results obtained, it is possible to use the analytical unit in its current form as an auxiliary tool for detecting various kinds of anomalies, including anomalies in the transaction logs of the DC databases.

Directions for further research are associated both with a change in the structure of an artificial neural network (in order to reduce the labor costs that need to be spent on training and further functioning of a neural network without losing the quality of the results of its work), and with the complication or change in the structure of the modules for transforming the initial data and interpreting the results obtained, which can lead to an increase in the accuracy of determining anomalies.

Acknowledgement. This research is being supported by the grant of RSF No. 21-71-20078 in SPC RAS.

References

1. Kotenko, I., Polubelova, O., Saenko, I.: Data repository for security information and event management in service infrastructures. In: Proceedings of the International Conference on Security and Cryptography - SECRYPT (ICETE 2012), pp. 308–313 (2012). https://doi.org/10.5220/0004075303080313
2. Kant, K., Meixing, L., Jajodia, S.: Security considerations in data center configuration management. In: 2011 4th Symposium on Configuration Analytics and Automation (SAFECONFIG), pp. 1–9 (2011). https://doi.org/10.1109/SafeConfig.2011.6111676
3. Zhang, X., Zhang, Z.: Data center integrated monitoring based on performance monitoring of server and application system. In: 2010 International Conference on Computer and Communication Technologies in Agriculture Engineering, pp. 491–493 (2010). https://doi.org/10.1109/CCTAE.2010.5544335
4. Ferraiolo, D., Gavrila, S.., Jansen, W.: On the unification of access control and data services. In: Proceedings of the 2014 IEEE 15th International Conference on Information Reuse and Integration (IEEE IRI 2014), pp. 450–457 (2014). https://doi.org/10.1109/IRI.2014.7051924
5. Wiboonrat, M.: Distribution control systems for data center. In: 2015 IEEE/SICE International Symposium on System Integration (SII), pp. 789–794 (2015). https://doi.org/10.1109/SII.2015.7405080
6. Branitskiy, A., Kotenko, I., Saenko, I.B.: Applying machine learning and parallel data processing for attack detection in IoT. In: in IEEE Transactions on Emerging Topics in Computing. https://doi.org/10.1109/TETC.2020.3006351
7. Kurt, M.N., Yılmaz, Y., Wang, X.: Sequential model-free anomaly detection for big data streams. In: 2019 57th Annual Allerton Conference on Communication, Control, and Computing (Allerton), pp. 421–425 (2019). https://doi.org/10.1109/ALLERTON.2019.8919759

8. Ramapatruni, S., Narayanan, S.N., Mittal, S., Joshi, A., Joshi, K.: Anomaly detection models for smart home security. In: 2019 IEEE 5th Intl Conference on Big Data Security on Cloud (BigDataSecurity), IEEE Intl Conference on High Performance and Smart Computing, (HPSC) and IEEE Intl Conference on Intelligent Data and Security (IDS), pp. 19–24 (2019). https://doi.org/10.1109/BigDataSecurity-HPSC-IDS.2019.00015
9. Wang, E., Song, Y., Xu, S., Guo, J., Qu, P., Pang, T.: A detection model for anomaly on ADS-B data. In: 2020 15th IEEE Conference on Industrial Electronics and Applications (ICIEA), pp. 990–994 (2020). https://doi.org/10.1109/ICIEA48937.2020.9248249
10. Djenouri, Y., Belhadi, A., Lin, J.C., Cano, A.: Adapted K-nearest neighbors for detecting anomalies on spatio-temporal traffic flow. IEEE Access **7**, 10015–10027 (2019). https://doi.org/10.1109/ACCESS.2019.2891933
11. Guo, Z.-X., Shui, P.-L.: Anomaly based sea-surface small target detection using K-nearest neighbor classification. IEEE Trans. Aerosp. Electron. Syst. **56**(6), 4947–4964 (2020). https://doi.org/10.1109/TAES.2020.3011868
12. Turner, R., Ghahramani, Z., Bottone, S.: Fast online anomaly detection using scan statistics. In: 2010 IEEE International Workshop on Machine Learning for Signal Processing, pp. 385–390 (2010). https://doi.org/10.1109/MLSP.2010.5589151
13. Zhang, J., Paschalidis, I.C.: Statistical anomaly detection via composite hypothesis testing for Markov models. IEEE Trans. Signal Process.**66**(3), 589–602 (2018). https://doi.org/10.1109/TSP.2017.2771722
14. Papalexakis, E.E., Beutel, A., Steenkiste, P.: Network anomaly detection using co-clustering. In: 2012 IEEE/ACM International Conference on Advances in Social Networks Analysis and Mining, pp. 403–410 (2012). https://doi.org/10.1109/ASONAM.2012.72
15. Dromard, J., Owezarski, P.: Integrating short history for improving clustering based network traffic anomaly detection. In: 2017 IEEE 2nd International Workshops on Foundations and Applications of Self* Systems (FAS*W), pp. 227–234 (2017). https://doi.org/10.1109/FAS-W.2017.152
16. Moshtaghi, M., Rajasegarar, S., Leckie, C., Karunasekera, S.: Anomaly detection by clustering ellipsoids in wireless sensor networks. In: 2009 International Conference on Intelligent Sensors, Sensor Networks and Information Processing (ISSNIP), pp. 331–336 (2009). https://doi.org/10.1109/ISSNIP.2009.5416818
17. Zhang, X., Gu, C., Lin, J.: Support vector machines for anomaly detection. In: 2006 6th World Congress on Intelligent Control and Automation, pp. 2594–2598 (2006). https://doi.org/10.1109/WCICA.2006.1712831
18. Yin, A., Zhang, C.: BOFE: anomaly detection in linear time based on feature estimation. In: 2018 IEEE International Conference on Data Mining Workshops (ICDMW), pp. 1128–1133 (2018). https://doi.org/10.1109/ICDMW.2018.00162
19. Pratap, U., Canudas-de-Wit, C., Garin, F.: Average state estimation in presence of outliers. In: 2020 59th IEEE Conference on Decision and Control (CDC), pp. 6058–6063 (2020). https://doi.org/10.1109/CDC42340.2020.9303809
20. Han, M., Kim, I.: Anomaly detection method using network pattern analysis of process. In: 2015 World Congress on Internet Security (WorldCIS), pp. 159–163 (2015). https://doi.org/10.1109/WorldCIS.2015.7359435
21. Farshchi, M., et al.: Contextual anomaly detection for a critical industrial system based on logs and metrics. In: 2018 14th European Dependable Computing Conference (EDCC), pp. 140–143 (2018). https://doi.org/10.1109/EDCC.2018.00033
22. Atefi, K., Yahya, S., Rezaei, A.,Hashim, S.H.B.M.: Anomaly detection based on profile signature in network using machine learning technique. In: 2016 IEEE Region 10 Symposium (TENSYMP), pp. 71–76 (2016). https://doi.org/10.1109/TENCONSpring.2016.7519380
23. Li, D., Qiao, Z., Song, T., Jin, Q.: Adaptive natural policy gradient in reinforcement learning. In: 2018 IEEE 7th Data Driven Control and Learning Systems Conference (DDCLS), pp. 605–610 (2018). https://doi.org/10.1109/DDCLS.2018.8515994

Tools for Designing Intelligent Systems

A Study of the Feasibility of Creating of a Real-Time Neural Network Infrared Ground Objects Recognition System

Andrey Maltsev(✉), Anatoly Nekleenov(✉), Dmitriy Otkupman(✉), and Victoria Ostashenkova(✉)

JSC Research and Production Enterprise "Impulse", Moscow, Russian Federation
{maltsev_ai,nekleenov_an,otkupman_dg,ostashenkova_vk}@impuls.ru

Abstract. The problem of implementation of a real-time neural network thermal imaging recognition system, built on widely available components, and allowing placement on a small-sized carrier, is considered. The main criteria for choosing hardware and software parts were the data processing speed and high accuracy of the classification of the detected ground objects.

Keywords: Thermal imaging system · Single-board computer · Convolutional neural network

1 Introduction

Object recognition systems based on thermal imaging are increasingly used in a wide range of industries, including security and defense. This trend is due to advances in the high-performance computing systems production and the emergence of small size and relatively large-format uncooled microbolometer detectors. Thermal imaging systems, unlike optical electronic imaging systems operating in the visible range, provide round-the-clock observations and are less dependent on weather conditions, including interference from dust and smoke.

Considerable progress is also occurring in the development of object recognition algorithms. Until recently, the only really working autonomous recognition systems were based on correlation-extreme algorithms, which required a high-quality reference image of the target object and were strictly limited by the angle of view of this reference sample. In the majority of modern weapon guidance systems, object recognition is performed by the operator. The task of creating a fully autonomous system capable of recognizing and selecting an object only on the basis of information about its visual characteristics is still under research.

Apparently, the breakthrough in creating autonomous recognition systems for military applications will be associated with intelligent systems based on Artificial Neural Networks (ANN). Particularly, the most popular among modern ANN models are the convolutional neural networks (CNN), which can successfully detect objects on the image and demonstrate high performance. If sufficient computing power is available, it

S. M. Kovalev et al. (Eds.): RCAI 2021, LNAI 12948, pp. 345–353, 2021.
https://doi.org/10.1007/978-3-030-86855-0_24

is not so difficult to create a recognition system based on modern neural network technologies. Difficulties arise in practical cases, when it is necessary both to fit the thermal module with computing system into a limited size space, and to provide real-time operation speed. The most common types of such cases are the autonomous target seekers, which can detect, recognize, and track objects within tight computational time limits. In [1], the results of a pilot study of a prototype of an autonomous infrared object recognition system based on domestic components — a lens and a thermal module — are described. In this research, the video signal, received from a thermal imaging camera, placed on the moving and vibrating drone, was processed by the ground-based conventional computing system with a recognition algorithm based on the neural network of the YOLOv3 architecture. This solution leaves open the question of the possibility of creating an autonomous recognition system, operating in real time, which is required for practical applications.

2 Research Procedure

In the study of the possibility of autonomous real-time recognition of ground objects, data from field studies of the prototype of the above-mentioned infrared detection system were used. The research methodology consisted in the adjustment of the parameters of the neural network algorithm and in choosing and setting up a computing module capable of providing the required computation speed.

Figure 1 shows the functional relationship between the field and laboratory parts of the investigations. The optical system with a microbolometer thermal imaging module, a single-board computer, and a wireless transmitter were placed on an unmanned aerial vehicle (UAV). The transmitter by wireless line sent primary processed video footage to the ground-based part of the system, where the video stream was recorded on the storage device. In a new study, these videos were used to emulate the infrared camera video signal in the laboratory.

The hardware and software parts of laboratory studies of the detection system performance consist of a single-board computer as a prototype of an on-board computer and a program that implements a neural network recognition algorithm. In laboratory research, it was important to simulate the original signal of the matrix receiver so that the computational load on the on-board computer was close to real conditions.

The signal simulation of the microbolometer thermal imaging module was based on video clips recorded from a drone during field trials. These recordings were played using a video player, to whose output a special video capture device (frame grabber) was connected, which transmitted a video stream to the computer in the digital video camera format via a USB port. This solution provided the repeatability of operating conditions for various configurations of the hardware and software parts of the recognizer and also excluded the influence of the video decoding process on the performance of the on-board computer.

The main parameters for choosing the on-board computer were small size, high-performance, and relatively low-cost. The dimensions of the used computing module with the carrier board were L $\times$ H $\times$ W $=$ 87 $\times$ 48 $\times$ 50 mm, while the weight was 195 g.

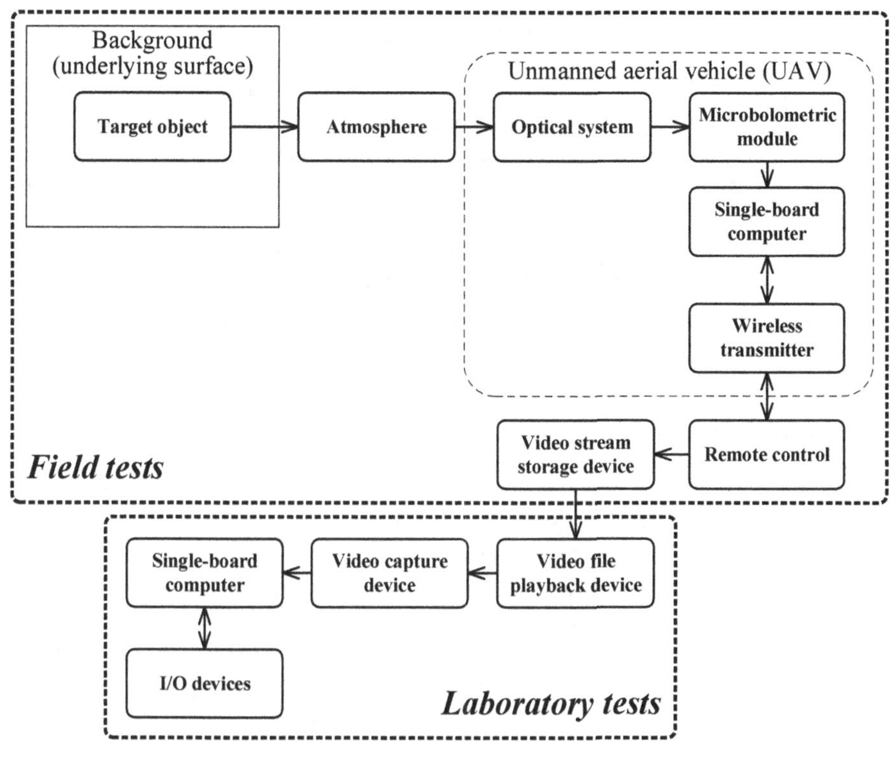

Fig. 1. A functional design of field and laboratory studies

The main parameters and characteristics of the autonomous thermal recognition system are given in Table 1.

Table 1. Parameters and characteristics of the recognition system

Optical system		Thermal imaging module		Single-board computer	
Focal length	100 mm	Technology	VO_x	Performance	1 TFLOP/s
F-Number	1.4	Format	640 × 480	GPU	256-core NVIDIA Maxwell™
Spectral range	8–14 μm	Pixel size	17 μm	CPU	Quad-Core ARM® Cortex®-A57 MPCore
Angular field of view	6.2° × 4.7°	Noise equivalent temperature difference	<60 mK	Memory	4 GB 64-bit LPDDR4

As opposed to [1], where real-time object recognition was not a priority, recognition speed is important in this work, so a lightweight (faster but less accurate) popular YOLO-tiny [2] version 4 [3] network architecture was chosen, pre-trained on visible range images from the classical COCO dataset [4] with weights and configuration files available from the repository [5]. The main parameters of the network used were as follows: the dimensions of input images — 416 × 416, the precision of floating-point calculations — 16-bit (FP16); object recognition was performed for each frame separately (batch size = 1). Retraining the network on a FLIR [6] publicly available dataset of infrared images of vehicles did not improve the accuracy and confidence of recognition. For this reason, a special training set of infrared images is currently being developed. It includes both real infrared images from thermal imaging cameras and synthesized images.

3 Research Results

Two poor-quality daytime video clips were selected for the study. The first clip (video recording 1) was recorded from relatively steady positioned unmanned aerial vehicle. It contains an underlying surface "heterogeneous meadow — dirt road" as background and van as the target object, maneuvering from the "front-view" to the "side-view" position. The second clip (video recording 2) with the "one-two-storey houses — fences — paved roads — standing cars»" background was recorded from the rapidly maneuvering UAV. This video has significant motion blur and image jitter. Examples of video frames are shown in Figs. 2.

a) video recording 1 (starting, intermediate, and end position of the van)

b) video recording 2 (selected frames that significantly differ in image quality; all three fragments contain cars marked with ellipses).

Figs. 2. Frames of analyzed video recordings

The recognition algorithm analyzes every video frame, selects objects similar to the target (the vehicle, in our case), and determines the confidence (the correct recognition probability) — Fig. 3.

The frame rate of the video clips is 25 frames per second. Thus, within one frame (40 ms), the processes of frame analysis, selection of target-like objects, determination of confidence, and selection of the object that best matches the specified target class must be started and fully completed.

Fig. 3. Visualization of the recognition process. The detected object is framed by rectangles; object class and the recognition confidence value are shown on the top of them (car 0.38; truck 0.63).

It should be noted that even with a relatively smooth motion of the unmanned carrier, there is significant instability of the image from frame to frame. To illustrate the degree of instability, the relative coordinates X, Y of the position of the center of the detected object in the frame were calculated. $X = 0$, $Y = 0$ is the upper left frame corner, and $X = 1$, $Y = 1$ is the lower right corner. Figure 4 shows the results of calculations for frames of video recording 1.

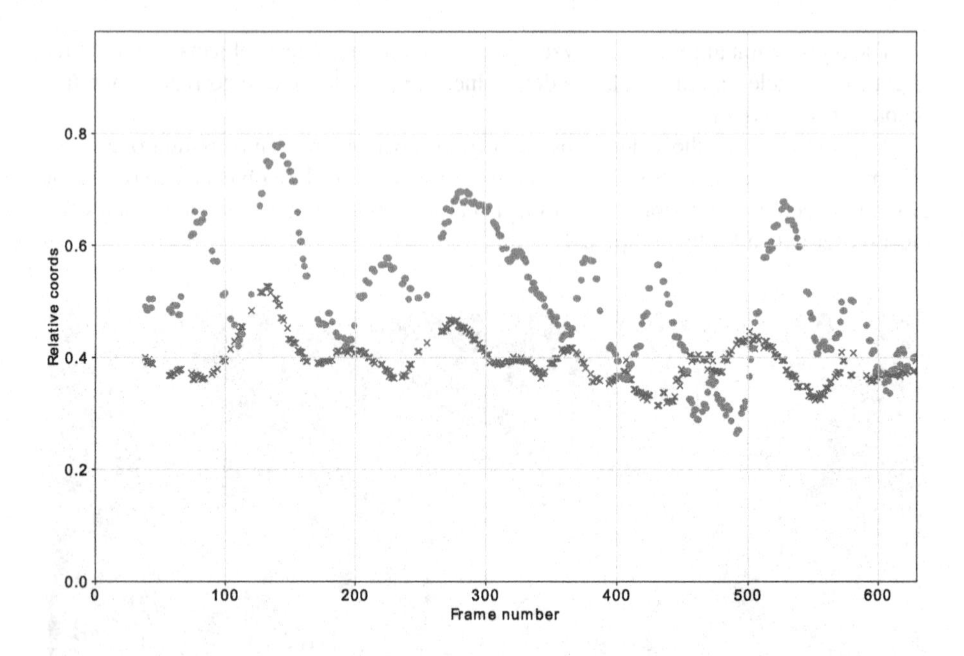

Fig. 4. Changing the position of the center of the target object in the frame due to the instability of the camera for video recording 1

Figures 5 show the results of neural network analysis of video recordings. Frame numbers lie on the abscissa axis, and the confidence value of target recognition and the frame analysis time are shown on the ordinate axis. Dashed lines indicate the recognition threshold (5%) and the real-time frame analysis limit (40 ms). Gaps in the histogram correspond to situations where the maximum recognition confidence of the object is below the 5% threshold.

The time-processing graphs show an initial transient process, during which the frame analyzing time is above the average. The lack of target recognition at this time in Fig. 5a appears to be due to the more difficult recognition of the "front-view" position of the target object. This confirms the increase in recognition confidence as the object is turned to the "side view."

Lower values of the object recognition confidence in Fig. 4b was expected due to the poor quality of video recording 2. However, this example demonstrates the ability of a neural network algorithm to recognize a target even in difficult conditions.

The analysis time per frame for both videos did not exceed 40 ms, even for video recording 2, where up to two objects were simultaneously recognized in the frame. In general, from the point of view of the task of this study, the possibility of implementing the "lens — thermal imaging matrix — computing module — neural network algorithm" system for real-time object recognition has been confirmed.

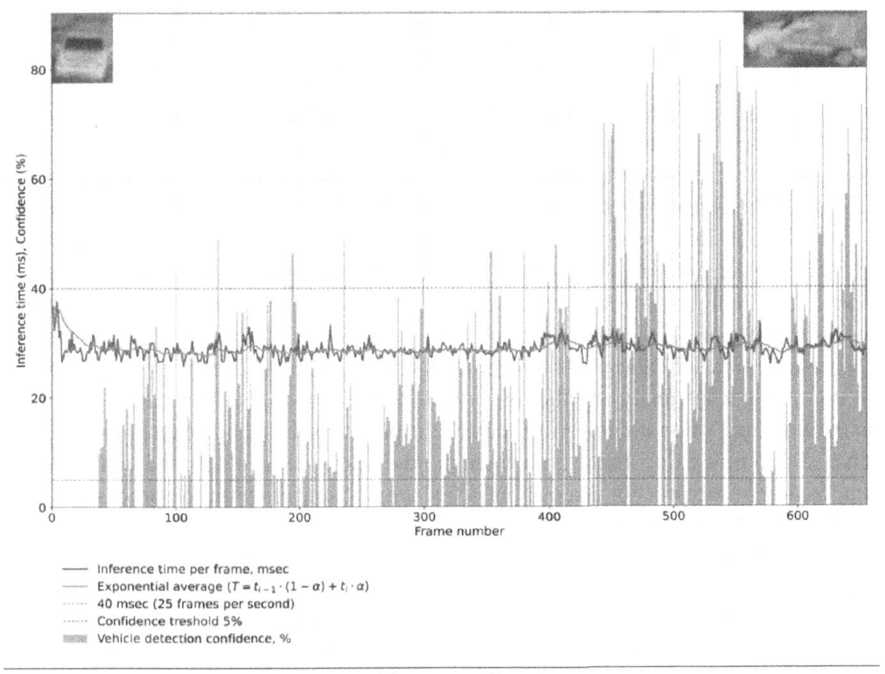

a) video recording 1

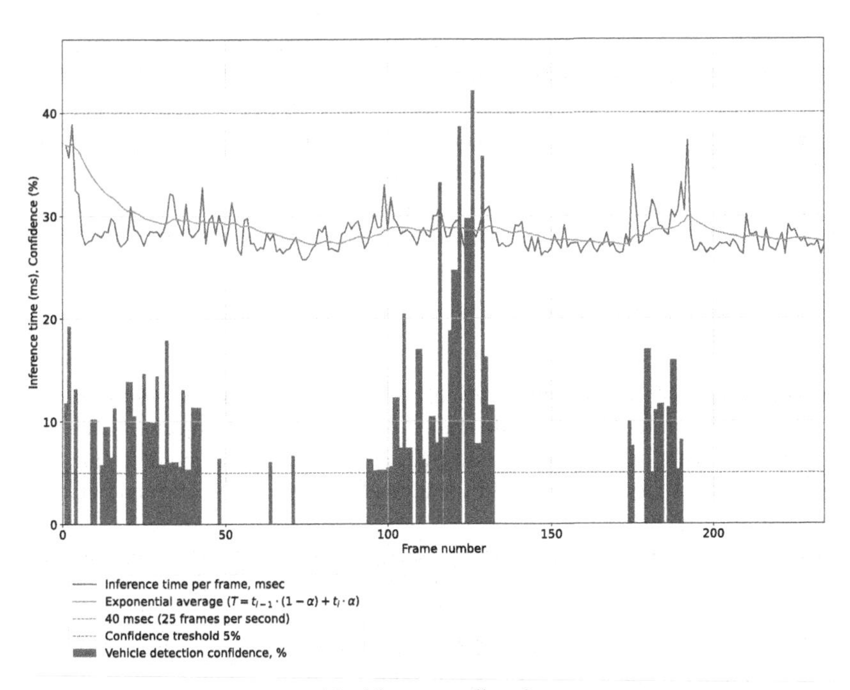

b) video recording 2

Fig. 5. Results of processing video recordings by a neural network algorithm

Experiments show that the processing speed of a single frame depends on its content, including the presence or absence of detectable objects in it. The processing time of the frames of the field study recordings is in the range of about 25.7–38.3 ms, which corresponds to the processing speed range of 38.9–26.2 frames per second.

A characteristic feature of the recognition system is also a slightly increased processing time for the first frames of the video signal, which is clearly seen in the graphs in Figs. 5. When the network detects a target object in the field of view, the algorithm for its identification is launched, somewhat slowing down the speed of image processing. This is clearly seen in the graph in Fig. 5b: in the areas corresponding to the presence of an object in the field of view (the presence of a histogram column), the average frame processing time increases by several milliseconds. On the hardware used, this increase in processing time still allows for real-time object recognition. The system performance was compared when analyzing the finished video file recorded earlier during field tests and the emulated video stream. After starting the program, the recognition process occurs with a certain time delay. In the case when the signal source is an encoded video file, the initialization of the process takes about 4.5 s, while the average frame processing time is 31.25 ms, which corresponds to a processing speed of about 32 frames per second. In the case when the signal source is an emulated video stream received by the computer via a USB port, the initialization time of calculations in the process of establishing communication with the signal source increases, and the average time for obtaining the first processing result is about 5.5 s from the start of the calculations. However, at the same time, the frame processing time is less, it is 29.4–28.6 ms, which corresponds to a speed of 34–35 frames per second. This acceleration is due to the absence of additional load on the computer caused by the processes of reading and decoding video frames.

To control the operation of the algorithm on the on-board computer, the recognition process was accompanied by displaying the result with drawing rectangular frames and additional detection indicators around the identified objects. Disabling this results visualization mechanism, which is not required during operation in the autonomous mode, provides an additional performance boost. In this mode, the average processing time of a single frame is about 25–26 ms, which corresponds to a speed of 40–38 frames per second.

4 Conclusion

1. A laboratory modeling technique was used to study the possibility of implementing a neural network system for real-time recognizing ground objects. Video recordings made during field experiments were used to simulate in laboratory the thermal imaging camera video stream fed in real conditions to the input of an autonomous recognition system.
2. The applied technique ensures the repeatability of operation conditions, excludes the influence of the processes of reading and decoding video frames on the system performance, and allows for the use of various video banks to evaluate the performance of the detection system built on different hardware and software parts.
3. The laboratory recognition system was built based on a high-performance single board computer with a graphics accelerator and recognition algorithm based on neural network YOLOv4-tiny (416 × 416, FP16, batch size = 1).

4. Studies have shown that the widely available small-sized components can be used to implement an autonomous system for real-time recognizing of ground objects with a frame rate of at least 25 frames per second.

References

1. Maltsev, A.I., Otkupman, D.G., Ostashenkova, V.K., Ostanin, M.V.: Experimental study of a prototype for an autonomous infrared system for ground object recognition. J. Almaz – Antey Air Space Defence Corp. **1**, 93–102 (2021). https://doi.org/10.38013/2542-0542-2021-1-93-102
2. Redmon, J., Divvala, S., Girshick, R., Farhadi, A.: You only look once: unified, real-time object detection. CVPR: OpenCV People Choice Award, 1–10 (2016). arXiv:1506.02640 [cs.CV]
3. Bochkovskiy, A., Wang, C.-Y., Liao, H.-Y.M.: YOLOv4: optimal speed and accuracy of object detection. computer vision and pattern recognition (cs.CV). Image and Video Processing (eess.IV), 1–17 (2020). arXiv:2004.10934v1 [cs.CV]
4. Lin, T.-Y., et al.: Microsoft COCO: common objects in context. In: Fleet, D., Pajdla, T., Schiele, B., Tuytelaars, T. (eds.) ECCV 2014. LNCS, vol. 8693, pp. 740–755. Springer, Cham (2014). https://doi.org/10.1007/978-3-319-10602-1_48
5. Github. AlexeyAB: Yolo v4, v3 and v2 for Windows and Linux. https://github.com/AlexeyAB/darknet
6. FREE FLIR Thermal dataset for algorithm training. https://www.flir.com/oem/adas/adas-dataset-form

The Implementation of the Ontological Approach to Control of the Processes of Designing Integrated Expert Systems Based on the Problem-Oriented Methodology

Galina Rybina(✉) and Aleksandr Slinkov

National Research Nuclear University MEPhI, Moscow, Russia

Abstract. This work focuses on the experimental studies of a new technology for the development of integrated expert systems (IES) based on the further development of the problem-oriented methodology and intelligent software environment of the AT-TECHNOLOGY workbench through the integration of an ontological approach to software design for applied IES and methods of intelligent planning and management of IES development processes with different architectural typology.

The description of prototyping methods for applied IES is based on the use of the basic components of the model of an intelligent software environment with an emphasis on expanding one of the components, the technological knowledge base, through the development of an ontology of typical IES architectures and the implementation of interaction with the intelligent planner.

Keywords: Integrated expert systems · Problem-oriented methodology · AT-TECHNOLOGY workbench · Intelligent software environment · Intelligent planner · Technological knowledge base · Ontology model · Applied ontology · Standard design procedure · Reusable components

1 Introduction

Methods of intelligent planning and their integration with knowledge engineering methods, proposed and described in detail in [1, 2], underlie the development and research of intelligent technology for constructing one of the most widespread and practically significant classes of applied intelligent systems — integrated expert systems (IES) — the demand for which, in modern conditions where unprecedented attention is paid to the use of methods and technologies of artificial intelligence (AI), has increased significantly, especially taking into account the priority areas of development and use of technologies defined by the Decree of the President of the Russian Federation (No. 490 of October 10, 2019).

To construct an IES, a problem-oriented methodology has been created, dynamically developed, and actively used [3], whose fundamental feature is the conceptual and

This work was supported by RFBR (project No. 18-01-00457).

S. M. Kovalev et al. (Eds.): RCAI 2021, LNAI 12948, pp. 354–364, 2021.
https://doi.org/10.1007/978-3-030-86855-0_25

software modeling of the architecture of the developed applied IES (static, dynamic, training) at all levels of concretization of integration processes in IES with an orientation on the most common types of non-formalized tasks (NF-tasks), technology-relevant knowledge-based systems (KBS (ES)).

Accordingly, the toolkit of the Workbench type (AT-TECHNOLOGY workbench) is constantly being improved and experimentally investigated in practice, on the basic functional platform of which several generations of tools have already been created that provide automated and intellectual support for the development of applied IESs with expandable functionality and scalable architecture, practically at all stages of the life cycle (LC) of building and maintaining an IES (a detailed description of the methodology and intellectual software environment of the AT-TECHNOLOGY workbench is given in [1] and various publications of recent years).

The modern experience in the application of the problem-oriented methodology and the prototyping technology of applied IES that has developed over the years already has several dozen IES of various architectural typologies, developed for the tasks of diagnostics, design, planning, management, and training; however, the stages of analysis of system requirements and design still remain the most difficult and time-consuming stages of the life cycle, both due to the constant complication of the complexity, volume, and logic of the tasks being solved and due to the significant influence of the human factor and the risks of errors.

Therefore, in recent studies, great attention has been paid to the creation of methods and means of intellectual support for the life cycle stages performed by knowledge engineers (knowledge analysts) by using the methods of intellectual planning [2, 4, 5], which generally reflected the beginning of the transition from automation to intellectualization of the basic processes for designing IES software. As a conceptual basis of intelligent technology, the concept of an intelligent software environment model introduced in [3] was used, whose main components are a technological knowledge base (KB) and an intelligent planner, and their implementation is carried out as part of the AT-TECHNOLOGY workbench (formal aspects are described in [1]).

It should be noted here that an important final result of the period of accumulation of large expert and technological experience in constructing models of various IES architectures for specific problem domains (PD) and the selected types of problems to be solved within the framework of a single unified methodology and constantly developing component functionality of the AT-TECHNOLOGY workbench was the opportunity to naturally form the basis for creating a technological knowledge base, including a set of standard procedures and ready-made solutions at various stages of prototyping IES, including for their reuse [6] in the form of separate software and information components of the AT-TECHNOLOGY workbench, which implement the basic functionality of the IES various architectural typologies (static, dynamic, educational, etc.)

Another, no less important factor is associated with the increasingly important role of integration processes arising from the joint use of semantically heterogeneous objects, components, tools, etc. For example, the degree of complication of software development management processes for applied IES at certain stages of the life cycle using an intelligent planner and a technological knowledge base depends on the sources of knowledge used and the integration of various technologies for the automated acquisition (identification) of knowledge from experts, natural language texts (Text Mining technologies), DB (technologies Data Mining, Deep Data Mining, etc.).

Since, normally, these technologies arose and developed independently of each other, today such autonomy makes it much more difficult to jointly use them in the development, maintenance, and monitoring of such voluminous resources as a knowledge base, a database, and other software tools. Therefore, the problems of integrating the methods and technologies of Text Mining, Data Mining, etc., as well as research in the field of creating tools and technologies for distributed knowledge acquisition [7] are among the most urgent today, as evidenced by a number of works, for example, [8–10], etc.

A similar problem of integrating models, methods, and software tools arises when designing software for dynamic IES [11], in particular, when using specific methods of simulation modeling and a subsystem for modeling the external world (environment), which determine the logic of decision-making based on the implementation of joint functioning processes with basic IES components in real time, as well as in training IES and web IES [12], for the construction of which a significant number of separate software and information components of the AT-TECHNOLOGY workbench with spaced functionality, fragments of various knowledge bases, databases, and hypertext textbooks are used etc.

Therefore, in the context of solving the integration problem, one of the possible approaches to the further development of the means of the intelligent software environment of the AT-TECHNOLOGY workbench is to expand the technological knowledge base by developing and including in its composition an ontology of typical architectures of applied IES, which will support the semantic level of organizing the interaction of the intelligent planner with a set of information and software resources of the technological knowledge base in the form of standard design procedures, reusable components, etc.

Based on these goals, the main emphasis is further placed on the discussion of issues related to the experimental software research of control processes for prototyping of applied IES based on the application of a new ontological approach together with the developed methods and means of intellectual planning.

In general, the appeal of using the ontological approach in software engineering today has increased significantly, and in domestic practice, there is also a significant surge in interest both in the general issues of creating ontological models of software design processes, for example, [6, 13], and in the development of methods and tools for ontological modeling of specific design processes, as well as specifications of the systems being developed [14, 15], etc.

Within the framework of the new direction, positioned as Ontology-Based-Software-Engineering (OBSE) or Ontology-Driven-Software-Engineering (ODSE), various semantic models for the design of software systems are created, including ontological modeling of software development control processes, for example, [16–20], etc.

As a rule, all semantic models of the processes of creating software systems and/or their components are based on a specific classification of the used ontology models, and specific methods for implementing ontological models of design processes are proposed, for example [16, 20, 21]. Work is actively underway to create tools for ontological engineering, in particular [22] and others. Nevertheless, such important aspects as reducing the intellectual burden on knowledge engineers and developers of intelligent systems at various stages of the life cycle are considered much less. At best, the issues of creating a certain universal ontology of knowledge are discussed, for example, about diagnostic processes in various PDs [23].

The focus of this work is a new stage of research on the intellectualization of prototyping processes for applied IES, associated with the expansion of the functional and semantic capabilities of the basic components of the model of an intelligent software environment through the development and use of the applied ontology of standard IES architectures as part of the technological knowledge base, as well as the means that ensure its construction, storing and efficient interaction with an intelligent planner.

2 Some Features of Intellectualization of IES Prototyping Processes

To determine the place and role of the ontology of typical IES architectures, we will briefly consider at the conceptual level some of the features of methods and approaches developed for intellectual support of prototyping processes for applied IES (a formal description of all models and algorithms is given in [1, 2]).

The basic declarative component of the model of an intelligent software environment is a technological knowledge base, which contains knowledge about the accumulated experience of designing IES in the form of a set of standard design procedures (SDP) and reusable components (RUC). An important operational component of the model of the intelligent program of the environment is the means of intelligent planning of the actions of knowledge engineers, which ensure the generation and execution of plans for constructing prototypes of IES, i.e. smart planner developed by integrating smart planning models and methods with knowledge engineering methods applied in the field of IES.

The initial data for generating IES prototype development plans are the IES prototype architecture model, described using the hierarchy of extended data flow diagrams (EDFD) [3], and the technological knowledge base containing many SDP and RUC. Accordingly, the model of IES prototyping processes [2] includes the function of planning the actions of engineers based on knowledge to obtain the current IES prototype for a specific PD. Thus, the statement of the problem of intelligent planning of IES prototyping processes is considered in the context of this model, and to implement an effective method for planning the actions of knowledge engineers, a well-known approach related to planning in the state space [4] was used.

The main task of the intelligent planner is to automatically generate plans (global and detailed [2]) based on the IES architecture model and a set of SDPs from the technological knowledge base, which significantly reduces the risks of erroneous actions of knowledge engineers. The implementation of the tasks of the plan is carried out using a set of operational RUC (each planned task is associated with a specific function of a particular RUC). Operating the SDP as the main algorithmic element, the intelligent planner at each moment of time makes a detailed construction of the IES development plan, depending on the current state of the project (the type of NF task reflected on the architecture model), the features of the PD, the presence of data storage devices on the architecture model, etc.

The general architecture of the AT-TECHNOLOGY workbench is built in such a way that all functionality is distributed, i.e. It is "distributed" into components registered in the environment of the workbench and operating under the control of an intelligent environment, which makes it possible to use a large group of RUCs (about 70 components that implement the capabilities of both operational and information RUC) within the intellectual technology of IES construction.

In its most general form, any SDP describes the sequence and methods of using certain means when creating applied IES of various architectural typologies, as well as the conditions and sequence for performing individual stages, depending on which the following are distinguished: SDP that do not depend on the type of task (for example, related to the processes of acquiring knowledge from various sources - experts, NL-texts, databases); SDP, depending on the type of problem (for example, building the components of training IES); SDP associated with RUC, i.e. procedures containing information about the life cycle of the RUC from the beginning of its adjustment to the inclusion in the prototype of the IES, as well as information about the tasks solved by this RUC, the necessary settings and, possibly, their values.

The main essence of the developed method for generating a knowledge engineer's action plan is to perform a sequence of transformations of the architecture model of the current IES prototype, performed in 4 stages [2]: obtaining a generalized EDFD in the form of a graph; generation of exact coverage (i.e., a set of SDP instances with mutually disjoint fragments containing all the vertices of the graph) using heuristic search; generation of a knowledge engineer action plan based on the received detailed coverage; generating a plan view.

All of the above steps are performed by an intelligent planner that fully implements the functionality associated with planning IES prototyping processes. With the help of the preprocessor of the EDFD hierarchy, preprocessing of the EDFD hierarchy is performed by transforming it into one generalized diagram of maximum detail. The task of covering the detailed EDFD with the available SDP is implemented using the global plan generator, which, based on the technological knowledge base and the constructed generalized EDFD, ensures the fulfillment of the task, as a result of which an accurate coverage is built, which is subsequently converted into a global development plan.

The detailed plan generator provides detailing of each element of the coverage, i.e. on the basis of the obtained EDFD coverage and technological knowledge base, each element of the coating is detailed, thereby forming a preliminary detailed plan. Then, based on the analysis of available RUC and their versions (data on which are requested from the development process control component), using the plan interpretation component, a detailed plan is formed, in which each task is addressed to a specific call of a specific RUC and can be performed by a knowledge engineer. With the help of the component for constructing the final plan, the necessary representation of the plan is formed for its use by other components of the intelligent software environment (component of the plan visualization, etc.).

The conducted studies have shown that the creation of a technology for using an intelligent software environment for building prototypes of applied IES and the efficiency of its use in order to reduce the intellectual load on knowledge engineers largely depends not only on the level of complexity of the architecture models designed by the IES, but is also significantly determined by the degree of accessibility. SDP and RUC when searching and initializing them. Therefore, the appearance in the technological knowledge base of a large number of semantically heterogeneous RUCs with implicitly expressed functionality and specifications led to an increase in the complexity of the search and increased the negative effect of non-optimal choice of solutions. Therefore, the composition of the technological knowledge base was expanded by building an applied ontology of typical IES architectures. Figure 1 shows a general diagram of the prototyping process for applied IESs using an intelligent planner and technological knowledge base.

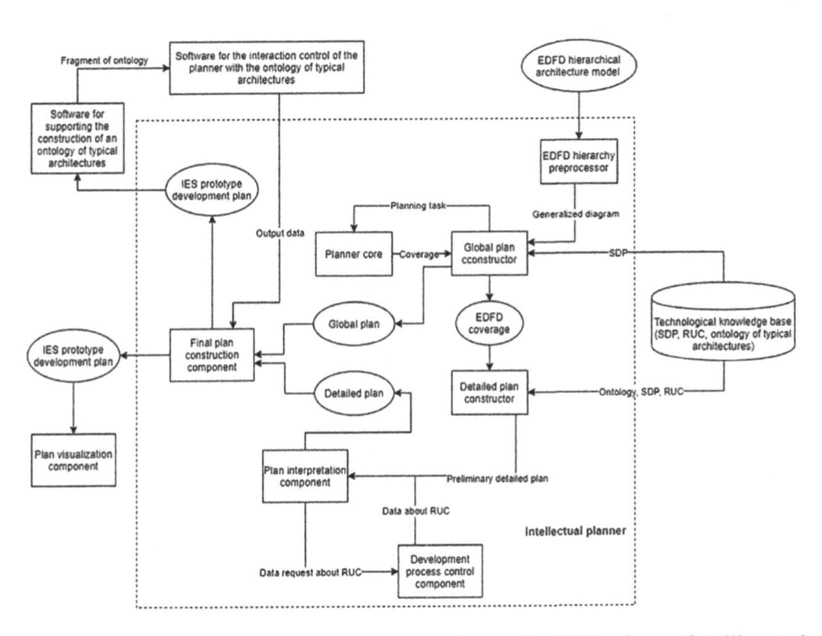

Fig. 1. General diagram of the prototyping process for applied IES using an intelligent planner and technological knowledge base

Now let us consider in more detail the most important aspects related to the construction of an ontology of typical IES architectures, which, based on the extended classification based on the subject of conceptualization [21], can be classified as applied ontologies.

3 Description of the Basic and Modified Ontology Models

As a basic ontology model for constructing an applied ontology of typical IES architectures, we took a model in the form of a semantic network, developed within the framework of a problem-oriented methodology for constructing IES [1], and which was effectively used and developed to create ontologies of various courses/disciplines in within the framework of the Chamber of Commerce and Industry "Construction of training IES". For example, modern versions of ontologies for individual courses/disciplines are actively used to organize web testing of students and conduct practical and laboratory exercises, including through the implementation of basic components and software in the form of procedural and information RUCs tied to elements of the ontology (detailed description presented in [12]).

In this case, it is important that in a simplified form the semantic network is described as: $M = \langle V, U, C \rangle$, where V is a set of ontology elements that admit any typology and specifications within the framework of the task at hand; $U = \{uj\} = \{\langle V_{kj}, V_{lj}, R_j \rangle\}$, j = 1,..., m is the set of links between ontology elements, where V_{kj} is the parent vertex, V_{lj} is the child vertex, R_j is the link type, and $R = \{ R_z\}$, where z = 1,..., Z, R_1 is a connection of the "part-whole" type (aggregation), which means that the child vertex is part of the parent vertex; R_2 is a link of the "association" type, which means that in order to master the concept of a parent node, it is necessary to own the concept of a child node; R_3 - "weak" connection, means that to own the concept of a parent node, possession of the concept of a child node is desirable, but not necessary; $C = \{C_i\}$, i = 1,..., a - the set of hierarchical links between the elements of the ontology, while $C_i = \langle V_k, V_l \rangle$, where V_k is the parent element, V_l is the child element in the hierarchical structure of the ontology.

Based on the development of formal specifications (concretizations) of the basic RUC model [3] for all currently used RUC and their versions, as well as an analysis of various models of IES architectures and main CCIs, the above-described basic model was modified, in accordance with which the current the version of the applied ontology is represented in the form $Oarch = \langle M_{om}, F_{arch} \rangle$, where M_{om} is a modified model of typical IES architectures; F_{arch} is a set of basic and modified operations (procedures) for constructing ontology elements, implemented in the form of software components, each of which, in accordance with the requirements of the intelligent software environment of the AT-TECHNOLOGY workbench, is designed as an operational RUC.

The modified model is a semantic network described in the form: $M_{om} = \langle V_{om}, U_{om}, P_{Dom} \rangle$, where V_{om} is a set of elements of an architecture model (M_{ies}), built on the basis of the ideas of deep integration of components (at all levels of integration), and each element includes name of the ontology vertex, weight (in the range 0... 100) and information about the RUCs used U_{om} is a set of links of several types between elements of the M_{ies} model (parent and child nodes of the ontology), and the semantics of the types of these links can vary widely (aggregation, association, hierarchy, strong, medium and weak links, etc.) and be interpreted depending on the SDP used; P_{Dom} (optional) a lot of special data, i.e. information of a different nature, specifying the features and/or non-standard approaches to the development of individual components of the IES prototype (parameters, texts, codifiers, information about external subsystems, components, applications, etc.).

Accordingly, to support the construction of an applied ontology of typical IES architectures, based on this model, special tools were developed to implement the necessary functionality, as well as software tools were created to control the interaction of an intelligent planner with the ontology of typical architectures (Fig. 1). Let us briefly consider some aspects related to the construction of this ontology.

4 Features of the Construction of an Applied Ontology of Typical IES Architectures

As noted above, the main goal of this stage of research in the context of integrating the implemented methods and means of intelligent planning with the ontological approach was the construction of an applied ontology of a new type based on taking into account the features of architecture models designed by IES and the features of component-wise functionality in the form of a set of RUCs. The architecture model of the IES prototype, represented in the form of the EDFD hierarchy, is one of the most important components of the project, since its structure largely determines the composition of the IES prototype and its functional and integration capabilities to support the solution of a specific class of problems.

The elements of the EDFD hierarchy are characterized by such data types as: NF-operation (*NF*); Formalized Operation (*Fo*); Essence (*E*); Storage (*S*), etc. It is essential that the multilevel integration processes reflected in the EDFD hierarchy result in the appearance of architectural elements at different nesting levels, which leads to different architectural solutions in the process of building detailed plans, including the use of RUC. Accordingly, the same elements of the architecture can have different logical and informational capabilities; therefore, RUCs that implement this functionality for identical elements also work in different ways.

Proceeding from this, the structure of the applied ontology of typical IES architectures, as well as the algorithms and procedures for its creation and storage, should be developed so as to provide the possibility of attracting and flexible adjustment of the corresponding RUCs for performing planned tasks depending on the features of the architecture model designed by the IES, and some the knowledge engineer can perform independently or in conjunction with an expert.

Therefore, it is the semantic network as a model of the ontology of typical IES architectures, and not the general vocabulary of concepts, which is most often used in most information processing systems of the ontological type, that makes it possible to significantly strengthen the semantics of the network vertices and display relations not only of the taxonomic type, but also more complex connections between models of SDP, RUC and IES architectures, as well as use powerful functionality when interpreting relations and vertices (ontology elements).

In the general case, the structure of the applied ontology of typical IES architectures is represented as follows: at the top level of the ontology there are various IES architectures (the level of typical architectures); then the architecture elements are located (this level, as follows from the ontology model, contains an unlimited number of sublevels, depending on the nesting of the components that make up the architecture elements); then the operations that are performed by the components of the architecture elements are presented; at the lower level of the ontology there are RUCs that implement the operations of the components of the architecture elements.

In the current version of the applied ontology of typical IES architectures, three types of links between ontology elements are programmatically supported: a "part-whole" link (aggregation) for linking ontology elements located at different but adjacent levels; a link of the "association" type for linking ontology elements that are at the same level; "Weak" link, for linking elements that are both at adjacent levels and at the same level. In addition to these types of links, there are also implemented interlevel links between ontology elements located at different levels.

In Fig. 2. for the Chamber of Commerce and Industry "Construction of training IES" [12], as an example, an element of applied ontology is shown - a component of the formation of educational and training tasks (ETT) and its various connections with other elements, in particular: connections of the *RT* type for specific methods/operations (*TR*) implemented as a set of operational RUCs; relationships of the *RK* type to identify the degree of achievement of specific target competencies (*K*) as a result of the use of ETT and hierarchical relationships of the *CK* type between competencies; connections of the *RC* type for a possible, but optional connection of the ETT with a hypertext textbook (or its separate chapters), which, similarly to the ETT, is a separate component of more general means of forming educational influences.

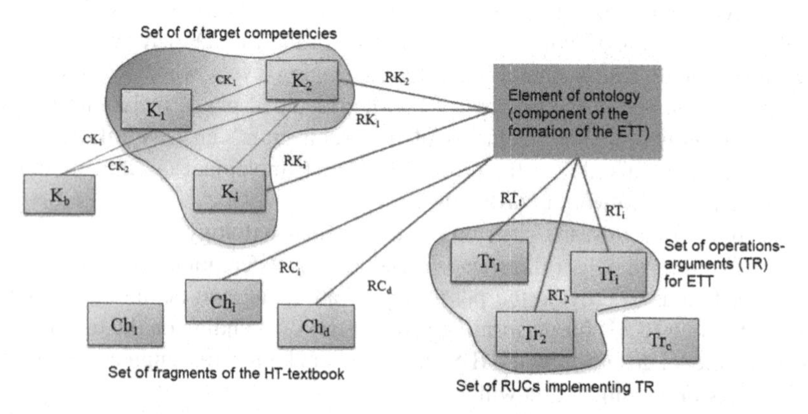

Fig. 2. An example of various links of the element "Component of the formation of ETT" with other elements of the ontology of typical IES architectures.

Now let's briefly review some of the implementation features. Since the ontology of typical architectures is part of the technological knowledge base, it has access to data on the SDP and RUC. The technological knowledge base is stored in the form of an XML document, in which the methods of describing all elements using tags are determined. First, a description of 4 types of SDP elements is presented: operation - function, unformalized operation - *nffunction*, entity - *entity*, storage - *store*. This is followed by a description of the connections between the elements - flow, after which a description of the SDP fragments - fragment is given, and then the chronology of the execution of the SDP fragments is described in the case of their coverage of the maximum granularity of the EDFD elements as a result of the work of the intelligent planner -

network. Thus, the RUCs must implement the functionality of the SDP fragments in the order in which these fragments cover the elements of the EDFD of maximum detail.

Since the applied ontology of typical architectures includes various models of IES architectures and their elements (subsystems/tools/components), the following operations can be performed on elements of architecture models as on elements of an ontology: initialization of adding a new architecture to the ontology; adding architecture elements to the ontology; removal of architectural elements from the ontology; sampling of ontology elements; unification of ontologies.

In addition, it is possible to replenish the technological knowledge base by adding new SDP or changing the format available using a special language based on XML, as well as replenishing the set of operational RUC.

5 Conclusion

In general, it can be stated that the experimental base in the form of accumulated information and software for applied IES, developed on the basis of the problem-oriented methodology and the AT-TECHNOLOGY workbench that supports it, turned out to be a successful "testing ground" for the further development of research in the development of intelligent planning technology. and management of the processes of building intelligent systems, including on the basis of the ontological approach.

The technological transition from "automation" to "intellectualization" of labor-intensive design processes and maintenance of information and software for applied IES was accomplished by creating conditions for the effective use of an intelligent planner, in particular, the development of a technological knowledge base (SDP, RUC, ontology of typical IES architectures) and then carrying out full-scale research on the creation of intelligent technology for constructing applied IES.

References

1. Rybina, G.V.: Intellektual'nye sistemy: ot A do YA. Seriya monografij v 3 knigah. Kniga 1. Sistemy, osnovannye na znaniyah. Integrirovannye ekspertnye sistemy. - M.: Nauchtekhlitizdat, p. 224 (2014)
2. Rybina, G.V., Blohin, Y.U.M.: Metody i programmnye sredstva intellektual'nogo planirovaniya dlya postroeniya integrirovannyh ekspertnyh system. Iskusstvennyj intellekt i prinyatie reshenij. **1**, 2–28 (2018)
3. Rybina, G.V.: Teoriya i tekhnologiya postroeniya integrirovannyh ekspertnyh sistem. Monografiya, M.: Nauchtekhlitizdat, p. 482 (2008)
4. Nau, D.S.: Current trends in automated planning. AI Magazine **28**(4), 43–58 (2007)
5. Osipov, G.S.: Metody iskusstvennogo intellekta. M: Fizmatlit (2011)
6. Lavrishcheva, E.M.: Programmnaya inzheneriya. Paradigmy, tekhnologii i CASE-sredstva. M.: Izdatel'stvo YUrajt, p. 280 (2016)
7. Rybina, G.V., Slinkov, A.A., Buyanov, D.R.: The combined method of automated acquiring of knowledge from various sources: the features of development and experimental research of the temporal version. In: The Proceedings of the 18th Russian Conference in «Artificial Intelligence», RCAI 2020, Moscow, Russia, pp. 15–25. Oct 10–16 2020

8. Aggarwal, C.C., Zhai, C.: Mining Text Data, p. 535. Springer, New York (2012). https://doi.org/10.1007/978-1-4614-3223-4
9. Aljawarneh, S., Anguera, A., Atwood, J.W., Lara, J.A., Lizcano, D.: Particularities of data mining in medicine: lessons learned from patient medical time series data analysis. Eurasip J. Wirel. Commun. Netw. (1), Article 260 (2019)
10. Efimenko, I.V., Khoroshevsky, V.F.: Identification of promising high-tech solutions in big text data with semantic technologies: energy, pharma, and many others (chapter 16. advanced methods). In: Daim, T. (ed.) Innovation Discovery. Network Analysis of Research and Invention Activity for Technology Management, Alan Pilkington (2018)
11. Rybina, G.V.: Dinamicheskie integrirovannye ekspertnye sistemy: tekhnologiya avtomatizirovannogo polucheniya, predstavleniya i obrabotki temporal'nyh znanij. Informacionnye izmeritel'nye i upravlyayushchie sistemy. T.16. **7**, 20–31 (2018)
12. Rybina, G.V.: Intellektual'naya tekhnologiya postroeniya obuchayushchih integrirovannyh ekspertnyh sistem: novye vozmozhnosti. Otkrytoe obrazovanie. Tom 21. **4**, 43–57 (2017)
13. Horoshevskij, V.F.: Proektirovanie sistem programmnogo obespecheniya pod upravleniem ontologij: modeli, metody, realizacii. Ontologiya proektirovaniya, Tom 9. **4**(34), 429–448 (2019)
14. Shalfeeva, E.A.: Vozmozhnosti ispol'zovaniya ontologij pri razrabotke i soprovozhdenii programmnyh sistem. In: Shalfeeva, E.A. (ed.) Vladivostok: IAPU DVO RAN, p. 1 (2011)
15. Pustovalova, N.V.: Postroenie soglasovannoj modeli trebovanij dlya processa programmnoj inzhenerii. In: Pustovalova, N.V., Avdeenko, T.V. (eds.) Trudy SPIIRAN. Vypusk 44, pp. 31–49 (2016)
16. Happel, H.: Applications of ontologies in software engineering. In: Happel, H., Seedorf, S. (eds.) Proceedings of the 2nd International Workshop on Semantic Web Enabled Software Engineering, ESE 2006, pp. 1–14 (2006)
17. Happel, H.J.: KOntoR: An ontology-enabled approach to software reuse. In: Happel, H.J., Korthaus, A., Seedorf, S., Tomczyk, P. (eds.) Proceedings of SEKE 2006: the 18th International Conference on Software Engineering & Knowledge Engineering, California, pp. 349–354, July 5–7 2006
18. Bossche, M.V.: Ontology driven software engineering for real life applications. In: Bossche, M.V., Ross, P., MacLarty, I., van Nuffelen, B., Pelov, N.: In: Proceedings of 3rd International Workshop on Semantic Web Enabled Software Engineering, SWESE 2007, Innsbruck, Austria (2007)
19. Liao, L.: Software process ontology and its application. In: Liao, L., Qu, Y., Leung, H.K.N. (eds.) Studies on the Semantic Web, vol. 17: Semantic Web Enabled Software Engineering, pp. 207–217, IOS Press (2014)
20. Jabar, M.A.: General domain ontology in enterprise software development process. In: Jabar, M.A., Khalefa, M.S. (eds.) Int. J. Eng. Adv. Technol. **8**(3S), 398–402 (2019)
21. Calero, C., Ruiz, F., Piattini, M. (eds.): Ontologies for Software Engineering and Software Technology, 1st edn, p. 340. Springer, Heidelberg (2006). https://doi.org/10.1007/3-540-34518-3
22. Olszewska, J.I.: ODYSSEY: software development life cycle ontology. In: Olszewska, J.I., Allison, I.K. (eds.) Proceedings of International Joint Conference on Knowledge Discovery, Knowledge Engineering and Knowledge Management, Seville, Spain, pp. 303–311, 18–20 Sept 2018
23. Gribova, V.V., SHalfeeva, E.A.: Ontologiya diagnostiki processov. Ontologiya proektirovaniya **4**(34), 449–461 (2019)

A Module for Industrial Safety Inspection Planning Based on Self-organization

Alexander Berman(✉), Olga Nikolaychuk, Alexander Pavlov, and Alexander Yurin

Matrosov Institute for System Dynamics and Control Theory, Siberian Branch of the Russian Academy of Sciences, Irkutsk, Russia

Abstract. The paper considers the application of the principles of self-organization for the automation of the business process of industrial safety inspection (ISI). Self-organization refers to the process of ordering elements (components) in an information system due to internal factors, without specific external influence. Self-organization is parametric and structural in nature. The architecture of the system as a whole and the main aspects of the main module, namely, scheduler, which provides self-organization of an open multicomponent information system of the ISI, are described. An ontological model of the object of expertise, the task, the method, and the operation that implements it, as the basis of self-organization, is proposed. The model and algorithms for implementing the scheduler are detailed. In particular, the algorithms of the main operations are described: the formation of the task description, the methodology for solving the problem, and the "intelligent" task execution. It also lists the principles of formation and describes the main local rules of the knowledge base of the scheduler, which are responsible for describing the methodology, the decision process, the coordination of expert opinions, and self-learning. A conceptual description of the implementation of the scheduler based on the components of the software platform is given. Some results of application of the considered approach for the problem of technical diagnostics of ISI are given: fragments of the generated software, forms of the user interface demonstrating the description of the object of expertise, local rules, methods and results of self-organization.

Keywords: Ontology · Self-organization of information systems · Industrial safety inspection

1 Introduction

The creation of information systems that provide automation of business processes remains one of the most relevant areas of information technology development. The paper considers the application of the principles of self-organization to automate the business process of industrial safety inspection.

The purpose of the industrial safety inspection (ISI) is to confirm compliance with the industrial safety requirements of hazardous production facilities, buildings and structures, and technical devices used in hazardous enterprises. As part of the ISI, a 100%

S. M. Kovalev et al. (Eds.): RCAI 2021, LNAI 12948, pp. 365–379, 2021.
https://doi.org/10.1007/978-3-030-86855-0_26

inspection of the equipment is required to identify potentially hazardous areas and make appropriate decisions to avoid failures. The quality of the ISI affects the number of losses in emergencies, the cost of diagnostics, as well as periodic and restorative repairs. The ISI includes some tasks from the stage of work planning and documentation analysis to the stage of making technical decisions on repairs and forming a conclusion of the inspection.

The ISI task does not have a mass character; rather it is unique. It is caused by the properties of the object of inspection and its state at the current time; these factors define the composition of the works (operations) and methods of their implementation. Another feature of the ISI task is the interaction of experts who are specialists in various domains, which leads to the interdisciplinary nature of the task and the need to coordinate the opinions of expert groups. These factors indicate the complexity and, to some extent, the uncertainty of the process of solving the problem.

Multicomponent open intelligent information systems [1] are the best way to solve this class of tasks. These systems contain a set of components that can be extended depending on the occurrence of new requirements and limitations of the business process; this fact can be considered as a dynamic change of the external environment. These extensions allow one to solve tasks of various disciplines with an unlimited set of methods, processing heterogeneous information in terms of the degree of formalization, dynamically forming the architecture of components for solving the task under consideration.

In this paper, we describe the structure and functions of the module of a multicomponent information system that provides dynamic planning of the ISI based on the principle of self-organization. Self-organization is understood as the process of ordering elements (components) in an information system due to internal factors, without specific external influence. It is proposed to implement this module predicated on a rule-based expert system; its knowledge base describes the possible behavior of an information system based on information about the state of its functioning. The state of the process is described in terms of the concepts of the top-level ontology of the domain under consideration. The key concepts are the scientific discipline, the object of investigation, the physical processes of the object, the properties of the object, the task, the method, etc.

The application of the principles of self-organization for the automation of the ISI will allow us to endow the information system with the properties of adaptability and autonomy. In turn, the system with these properties will increase the efficiency of the ISI, at least by reducing labor costs and improving the quality of results.

Currently, some systems automate the ISI business process [2], some of them using artificial intelligence methods [3]. In general, the management of this business process is carried out by the top managers of the organization that performs the ISI. The disadvantage of such implementation is the influence of the human factor at the organizational level when coordinating and making decisions at each stage of the examination; it is also necessary to note the lack of opportunities for accumulating, reusing, and processing the knowledge of the team, where decision-making largely depends on the level of professionalism of this team. As a result, there are violations in the performance of work, non-compliance with the work plan, errors, and shortcomings in the results of the ISI.

The application of the principles of self-organization (including technical) is one of the ways to create software that has the properties of self-adaptivity, self-structuring, self-diagnosis, and self-configuration [1, 4–7] is the task of structural and parametric software synthesis. The algorithms for controlling the synthesis procedure use the apparatus of differential equations [9], descriptions of ontology and non-deterministic automata [7], logical rules [10], and set-theoretic apparatus [11], etc.

There are examples of applying the principles of self-organization when creating research prototypes of software in various fields, in particular, automation of technological processes, a smart factory for industry 4.0 [8], a configuration of document management systems [12], transport process management, calculation of operating modes for heat and mass transfer equipment [9], assessment of the state of electrical equipment [13], flood prediction [1], etc.

2 The Architecture of the Multicomponent Information System

The multicomponent tool for solving interdisciplinary problems has the following architecture [14]:

$IS = (E, Dt, Knl, Ont, Object, Task, Slv, R_{IS}, Pln, UI)$,

where *IS* is a tool, *E* are experts, *Dt* are databases, *Knl* are knowledge bases, *Ont* is an ontology of the subject and domain areas, $Ont \rightarrow \{Object, Task, Dt, Knl, R\_Is\}$, *Task* are the tasks, *Object* is the object of investigation, *Slv* are "solvers" (components), R_{IS} are the relationships between *IS* components, in particular, between experts and tasks, between tasks, between tasks and "solvers", *Pln* is an intelligent scheduler that provides the operation of a *SAlg* self-organizing algorithm for solving a multidisciplinary task based on *LRule* local rules, and *UI* is a user interface.

Among the "solvers" are the basic ones and the ones created by a user $Slv = \{Slv_{Base}, Slv_{User}\}$. We list the basic "solvers" necessary for implementing the main operations of data and knowledge processing: data management (Slv^{Dt}), ontological modeling (Slv^{Ont}), rule-based reasoning (Slv^{Knl}), organization of two-way data exchange (Slv^{Com}), a dialog interaction with a user (Slv^{UI}), operation specifications based on visual workflow notation (Slv^{Op}).

User "solvers" have been created for conducting ISI, for example, Slv^{DP} is an expert system that determines the types of degradation processes and the causes of their occurrence, Slv^{Pln_IST} is an expert system for forming an ISI plan, etc.

3 Ontology

It is proposed to use the following hierarchy of ontologies to implement the process of self-organization: the top-level ontology for describing system concepts independent of domains, the subject and task ontologies for describing domain concepts, and task-specific concepts.

The top-level ontology in the domain-specific aspect defines the concept of the object of investigation (or analysis, or design, or activity, hereinafter referred to as investigation), and it describes the properties of this object, also indicates the relationships with the concepts of scientific disciplines, aspects of the investigation and physical processes inherent in the object.

In general, the process of ontological modeling of concepts for which it is necessary to provide the possibility of long-term storage of information consists of the design and implementation stages. A description of the structure and relationships of the necessary set of concepts is created on the design stage. Data structures for the obtained model and the selected DBMS are created in the implementation stage. The ontological modeling component (Slv^{Ont}) automates this process in the context of the selected DBMS (PostgreSQL currently), in addition, to testing (rapid prototyping) of the resulting models at the design stage, the concept instance mechanism is used. This mechanism provides working with the conceptual model as a relational database through its implementation of the *IDBControlInterface* interface (declared in Slv^{Dt}). In this case, the concept instance uses the concept as a meta description, and is a container for the concept property and its value pairs:

$$\begin{aligned} Instance &= \{Concept,\ ID,\ \{\ ValueOfProperty\}\} \\ ID &= Literal \\ ValueOfProperty &= \{PropertyOfConcept,\ Value\} \\ Value &= Literal \mid Instance. \end{aligned}$$

Maintaining the relevance of information about the concepts of the ontology after the implementation stage is carried out by obtaining a description of the structure of the concepts included in the object under investigation using the data management component (Slv^{Dt}).

Thus, the proposed method of formalization of the object under investigation allows us, on the one hand, to quickly test the developed models and, on the other hand, to avoid losing the relevance of the ontology due to the accumulation of changes in the database structure.

The ISI task is characterized by the uncertainty of the object of investigation (this uncertainty is resolved only by the time the work begins), a small (literally single) number of similar objects, and a different set of investigated elements. At the same time, the specificity of the ISI determines a large number of general characteristics, namely: technical requirements, technical condition, mechanical, physical, and chemical properties of the object and its elements, the hierarchy of the object structure. These facts lead to the need for a specialized model of the object of investigation, which allows one, on the one hand, to take into account the presence of common properties, and on the other to provide the necessary degree of variability.

The model of the object under investigation has the following form:

$$\begin{aligned} &Object = \{Name, \left[ParentObject\right], Classifier, \{PropertyWithValue\}\} \\ &Classifier = \{Name, \left[Classifier\right], \{ClassifierRelatedProperty\}\} \\ &ClassifierRelatedProperty = \{ID, DescriptionOfProperty\} \\ &PropertyWithValue = \{DescriptionOfProperty,\ Value\}, \end{aligned}$$

where *Name* is the name of the object, *ParentObject* is a reference to a higher element of the hierarchy, *Classifier* is a classifier, $\{PropertyWithValue\}$ is a set of object properties and their values considered in this ISI; in this set, a list of property descriptions is defined using the classifier. The classifier has a hierarchical structure and allows one to define a set of properties of the investigated object for each level of the hierarchy.

The proposed model allows one to store data uniformly for all types and kinds of equipment.

The top-level ontology in the task-specific aspect defines the concept of the task including a description of the task properties and the relationships with the concepts and laws of scientific disciplines, as well as methods and means of solving tasks.

The task model has the following form:

$$Task = \{Name, \{Discipline\}, \{Concept\}, \{Parameter\}, \{DomainLaw\}, \{Method\}, \{Solver\}, \{Task\}, State\},$$

where *Name* is the name of the task, *Discipline* is the list of disciplines, *Concept* is the list of concepts of the task, *Parameter* is the input and output parameters of the task, *DomainLow* is the name of the regularities (lows) of the discipline used to solve the task, *Method* is the methods of solving the task, *Solver* is the software modules that implement the methods, and *State* is the description of the state of the process of solving the task at the current time, in particular: forming, reformulating, queued, executing, completed, insufficient data, and incomplete information.

The formalization of the method for solving the task is carried out based on the model of operations. This model allows one to describe the implementation of the method in the form of a composite operation:

$$Method \to OpC$$
$$OpC = Name,\ Alg,\ \left\{Parameter^{OpC}\right\}.$$

The elements of the algorithm are described by the structure:

$$Alg = \{DataElement,\ OpB,\ OpC,\ Operator\}.$$

DataElement is the data processed by the algorithm, *OpB, OpC* is the basic and composite (based on basic) operations, *Operator* is the operators of the interaction of operations.

$$DataElement = \{Constant|Parameter\}$$
$$Operator = O_{DT}|\ O_{CT}|\ O_{If}|\ O_{L}|\ O_{B}.$$

O_{DT}, O_{CT}, O_{If}, O_{L}, O_{B} are the data transfer, control transfer, IF, Loop, Group operators.

$$Constant = \{Literal|Concept|Instance\}$$
$$Parameter = Name, Input|Output$$
$$Parameter = Parameter^{OpC}|Parameter^{OpB}$$
$$Name = Literal.Input = Value\ \{Value\}$$
$$Value = Constant\ |\ Output.$$

$$Output = Literal\{Literal\} | \; Concept\{Concept\} | \; Instance\{Instance\}$$

$$OpB = Location, \; Name, \; \left\{Parameter^{OpB}\right\}$$

$$Location = Literal.$$

Then the algorithm is described by possible combinations of operations:

$$Alg = \left\{\{DataElement\}O_{DT}\left(OpC|OpB \mid O_{If} \mid O_{L} | \; O_{B}\right)\right\},$$
$$\left\{\left(OpC|OpB \mid O_{If} \mid O_{L} | \; O_{B}\right)O_{CT}\left(OpC|OpB \mid O_{If} \mid O_{L} | \; O_{B}\right)\right)\right\}.$$

Let's detail the task model taking into account the operation model:

$$Solver = OpB$$
$$State = \{ValueOfParameter\}$$
$$ValueOfParameter = Parameter, \; Value.$$

Thus, we suggest a domain specialist at the stage of designing a task-specific system to describe the hierarchy of existing tasks of the domain. For each of them, at least one solving method can be implemented in the form of a composite operation. In turn, the operation descriptions will be used either to run with the interpreter or to generate the source code of the target software.

The domain ontology on the top-level conceptual structures allows one to describe any objects of investigation. The task ontology allows one to describe any tasks.

Let's consider an example of the ISI ontology for the following object (*Object*):

- *Name*: vertical welded propane column
- *Classifier:* column
- *DescriptionOfProperty: Value:*80 m^2,
- *DescriptionOfProperty:* technical characteristics during operation, Value:

  - *DescriptionOfProperty:* design pressure, Value: 1,7 MPa,
  - *DescriptionOfProperty:* design temperature, Value: 150 C,
  - *DescriptionOfProperty:* agent used, Value:

  - *DescriptionOfProperty:* name, Value: propane,
  - *DescriptionOfProperty:* properties, Value: corrosive, toxic, explosive.
  - etc.

The task ontology of ISI includes a description of the methodology of the business process, which consists in solving tasks (stages): work planning, analysis of technical documentation, formation of a map of initial data, development of the ISI program, technical diagnostics, and analysis of results, testing, calculation of strength and residual life, making technical decisions on repairs, and forming a conclusion.

The ISI uses models of the basic types of tasks that describe the works (activities):

- carrying out fieldworks (for example, diagnostics), entering data on the results of work, and forming a document based on the results of work;

- formation of the final document based on the results of several works;
- the input of initial data, solving computational tasks by an adequate method (for example, strength calculation), and formation of a document based on the results of the work;
- coordination of the opinions of the expert group, which consists of collecting information about alternatives, expert opinions about these alternatives, and devel-oping a decision based on group decision-making methods.

Let us present an example of a description of the *Task* diagnostics task:

- *Name:* performing work on diagnosing a technical device,
- *Disciplines:* technical diagnostics,
- *Concepts:* a work, a work scheme, a technical device, an expert, etc.
- *Parameters:*
  - *Input:* a technical device
  - *Output:* diagnostic results, report (document)
- *DomainLaws:* diagnostic schemes for technical devices
- *Methods:* a composite operation "diagnostics of a technical device"
- *Solvers:* data management component (SlvDt),
- *Tasks:*
  - selection of tools,
  - selection of regulatory and technical documentation (NTD),
  - definition of the diagnostic scheme,
  - input of the diagnostic results,
  - formation of the document.
- Inherited tasks:
  - *Name task* – visual and measurement control
  - *Name task* – thickness measurement
  - *Name task* – flaw detection
  - *Name task* – study of metal properties
  - *Name task* – hydraulic tests, etc.

4 Scheduler

The proposed formal model of composite operations allows us to represent the functionality of the target software system as a set of such operations. In this case, its software implementation can be acquired automatically using a specialized interpreter or generator. At the same time, the process of software implementation of the interpreter and/or generator depends only from the proposed model of operations and does not include any specifics of the tasks being implemented. During execution, the interpreter converts the selected composite operation along with its nested ones of such kind into a sequence of basic operations, that provides the implementation of the desired behavior on run (The generator works similarly, but instead of directly executing it generates code in the selected programming language. The article further uses the concept of an interpreter.)

$I(OpC) \rightarrow (OpB_1, \ldots, OpB_N)$,

where I is the interpreter.

One of the ways for granting the software system with the self-organization capabilities is the implementation of the ability to dynamically change the algorithms of the tasks to be solved. The implementation of this ability is proposed to be accomplished by extending the functionality of the interpreter with the planning function. Thus, the self-organization algorithm has the following structure:

$SAlg = (Task^*, ActionList, Exe, OpC_{Sys}, OpC_{Serv}, KB_{Sys})$,

where $Task^*$ is the ID of the task to be solved,

$ActionList\,(Task^*) \rightarrow OpC_1, \ldots, OpC_M$,

where *ActionList* is the execution plan that consists of operations of a given level (in our case, these are the basic operations or composite operations) and that represents the subject or system tasks considered as non-decomposable tasks,

$Exe\,(OpC) = (ActionList\,(OpC), I(OpC))$,

where *Exe* is the execution block for performing operations;

KB_{Sys} (*LRule*) is a system knowledge base for managing the process of solving a task (supports process of the formalization and "intelligent" solution of the task); the knowledge base allows one to formalize the types of possible actions of the algorithm in the form of a set of special templates, and specific actions in the form of facts of these templates, which provides control of the solution process at the branching points, for example, to choose a method for solving a task from a set of alternatives, a method for obtaining source data, evaluating the results of solving the task, etc.;

OpC_{Sys} are system operations for forming a task description, forming a methodology for solving a task, task execution, resolving the incompleteness of a task, and training the system;

OpC_{Serv} are service operations for managing the plan (adding, deleting, changing the priority of the operation), requesting information from the user.

Thus, the input data for the *SAlg* is the task ID, which is used to search for the related composite operation. Based on the description of found composite operation, the planning unit prepares the primary solution plan, in form of the operations sequence with priority in accordance with the original execution order, taking into account the nesting of composite operations.

Here is a more detailed description of the algorithms of the main operations.

Operation for forming the task description:

1. Enter the name of the task. The operation uses the functions of the user interac-tion component (getting a literal value).
2. The choice of disciplines related to the task. The operation uses the functions of the user interaction component (getting a set of identifiers from a given database object).

3. The choice of concepts related to the task. The operation uses the functions of the user interaction component (getting a set of identifiers from a given database object; a more complicated version uses the result of the previous operation to limit the search space).
4. Enter a description of the task parameters. The operation cycles through the func-tion of the user interaction component (data entry of the specified database ob-ject).
5. Description of the sub-tasks. The operation circulates and recursively refers to it-self.
6. Selection of the solvers used. The operation uses the functions of the user interac-tion component (getting a set of identifiers from a given database object).
7. Create task-related knowledge bases. The operation uses the functions of the user interaction component (entering data of a given database object, getting a set of identifiers from a given database object, creating rules).
8. Description of the methodology for solving the task.

Operation "Formation of the methodology for solving the task":

1. Enter the name of the methodology element. Creating the corresponding compo-site operation.
2. Formalization of the input and output parameters of the methodology stage.
3. Description of the algorithm of the methodology element. The operation cycles through the functions of the user interaction component (creating composite operations).
4. Coordination of the received description of the stage between the group of experts.
5. Assessment of the completeness of the methodology description. If there are steps that are not described, go to step 1.
6. Formalize the criteria for evaluating the results obtained.

Operation "Intelligent task execution":

1. Create an action plan based on the structure of the task, the plan contains sub-tasks and operations of the first level of nesting. Actions (plan elements) can be tasks and operations.
2. Check the status of the plan. If the plan is empty, then go to step 5.
3. Performing a priority action. The choice of a priority action (In the simplest case, just another action, with the complication, it is possible to use a special operation or an expert system). If the selected action is an operation, then it just executes. If an action is a task and it has several methods of solving it, then the method is se-lected, for example, based on an expert system, and the composite operation cor-responding to the selected method is started.
4. Evaluation of the result obtained, with an inadequate solution, it is possible to ad-just the plan, interact with the user, etc.

The implementation of the functional blocks of the scheduler is proposed to be implemented in the form of composite operations using the functionality of the Slv^{Op} component. Its implementation is based on the *OpC* composite operation model. The Slv^{Op} component provides the ability to use both an imperative and declarative way for determining the behavior of a composite operation. The first option is provided by visual construction of the necessary algorithm from an available set of basic and composite operations. The second is implemented by the opportunity to apply rule-based reasoning method to solve domain-specific task at the specified points of algorithm. In this case, the knowledge base related to situation and the facts describing it would be transferred as parameters.

5 Local Rules

The main component of the planning module is the knowledge base, which describes the local rules of self-organization.

The structure and content of local rules are determined by various aspects:

- the basics of system analysis (for example, the stages of system analysis-the definition of the object of analysis, the description of its structure, the definition of the problem/task, the choice of the method of solving the task, the assessment of the effectiveness of the solution);
- strategies for implementing the information system (for example, generating source data based on information from the domain ontology, loading the infor-mation processing component based on information from the domain ontology);
- information from the ontology of the domain area, which describes the tasks and stages/algorithms for solving it;
- group decision theory;
- representations and methods of information processing (data and knowledge);
- properties of the information system (for example, the property of self-learning);
- model-oriented approach (for example, MDD steps-model description, description of transformation rules, code generation).

Based on these aspects, the following rule blocks responsible for the processes are identified:

- description of the methodology for solving the task,
- formation of the process of solving the task,
- coordination of opinions by the expert group,
- self-learning of the system.

The methodology in this paper will be called a general sequence of actions, the elements of which represent the main stages of solving a certain problem (interdisciplinary).

Each stage is formalized as an instance of the task model, the sub-tasks of which ensure the achievement of one of the particular goals of the methodology. The process of describing the methodology is proposed to be implemented using the service composite operation "formation of the methodology for solving the task." The regularities of the process of describing the elements of the methodology within this operation are contained in a specialized knowledge base:

IF State (TaskName = Methodology definition; Status < > completed) THAN Addition to the plan (Task (Name = Defining the methodology element))

IF State (Task Name = Defining the methodology element; Status = incomplete information) THEN Resolving the incomplete task (Task (Name = Defining the methodology element)).

The introduction of the stage of information coordination by a group of experts in the task solving process is due to the need to automate this process, to ensure its support by methods of group decision-making, and to accumulate information about the decision-making process: alternatives, reasons for their formulation, opinions of group members, etc. The approval process is necessary when the elements of the methodology are found to be incomplete, i.e. the its description is insufficient to solve the task. Their incompleteness can be associated with the incompleteness of data and knowledge, methods and tools for solving tasks. This aspect implements the rule:

IF State (Status = completed, resultStatus = unsatisfactory) THEN the Resolution of the incomplete task (State (Task Name)).

Self-learning is an important property of an information system, especially if the process of solving a task uses heterogeneous information and depends on the human factor. One of the main problems in organizing self-learning is the lack of high-quality data, which creates the need to implement such a system function to accumulate structured information about the process of solving the task. This is what the rule is for:

IF State (Task Name = Definition of the methodology element; Status = change of wording) OR State (Status = completed; resultStatus = satisfactory) THEN System Training (State (TaskName))

6 Implementation Example

There is problem of automating the process of planning ISI, in the conditions of the existence of uncertainties due to the properties of the object under study and its technological inheritance. Its solution can be carried out by providing the possibility of gradual refinement or modification of the action plan, depending on the incoming information and analysis of the results of the work already performed, based on the proposed approach.

The object of the ISI study includes a number of the following standard properties: technical requirements, technical characteristics, and a technical condition, the contents of which are determined on the basis of the selected classifiers. In addition, individual levels in the hierarchy of the elements of the object of study may additionally contain properties related to the mechanical, chemical, and physical features of the latter.

The ISI methodology is described by a sequence of stages (see Fig. 1). The algorithm (sequence) of the technical diagnostics stage largely depends on the properties of the object of research and the results of previous examinations. It is at this stage that we will demonstrate the results of the proposed approach, when a technical diagnostic program is formed on the basis of a knowledge base describing the causal relationships between work and manufacturing technology, identified degradation processes as a result of previous diagnoses, etc. The model and the opcode snippet are shown below (see Fig. 2). For example, the ISI objects propane column and tank are selected, and on the basis of the proposed approach, the work sequences with the corresponding sequence of tasks are formed (see Fig. 3). Here is an example of the rule for decision-making on the content of the work: IF the object of inspection (the type of object is a column) And the degradation process (name - low-cycle fatigue OR corrosion cracking OR multi-cycle fatigue OR hydrogen cracking) THAN the work (type of work - technical diagnostics, name - flaw detection).

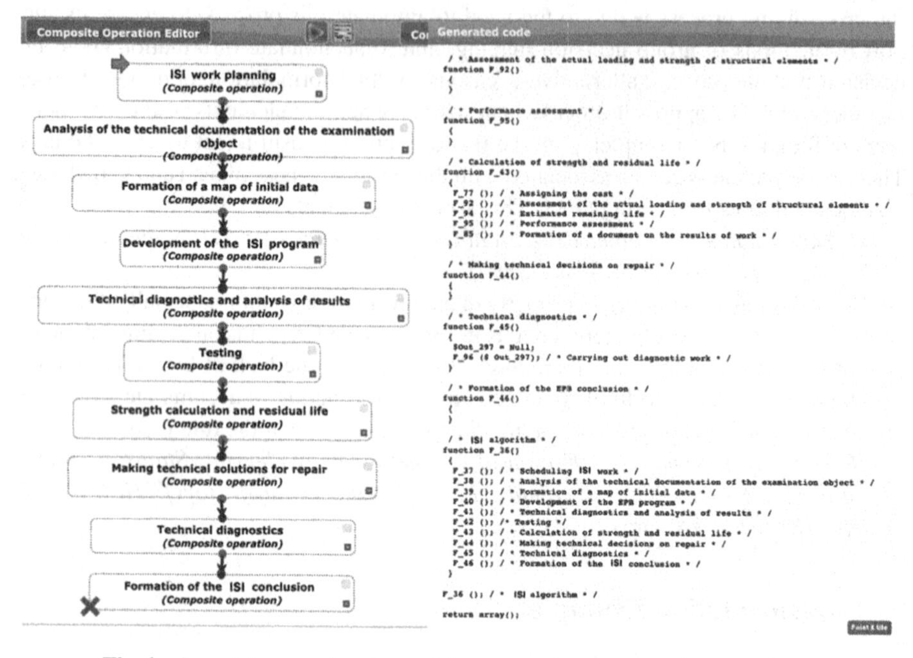

Fig. 1. A model and code snippet of the composite operation "ISI algorithm"

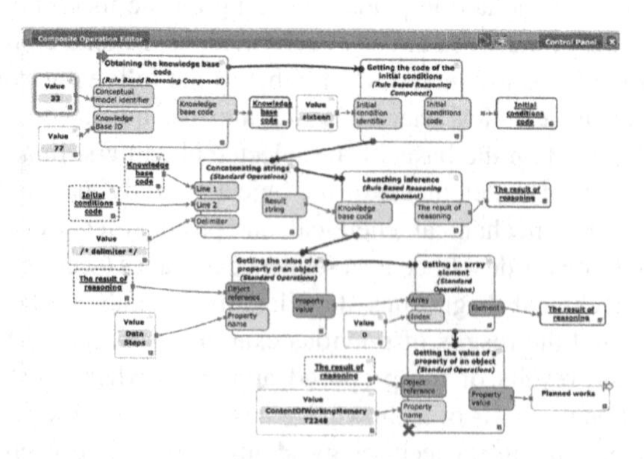

Fig. 2. A model of the composite operation "Performing diagnostic work"

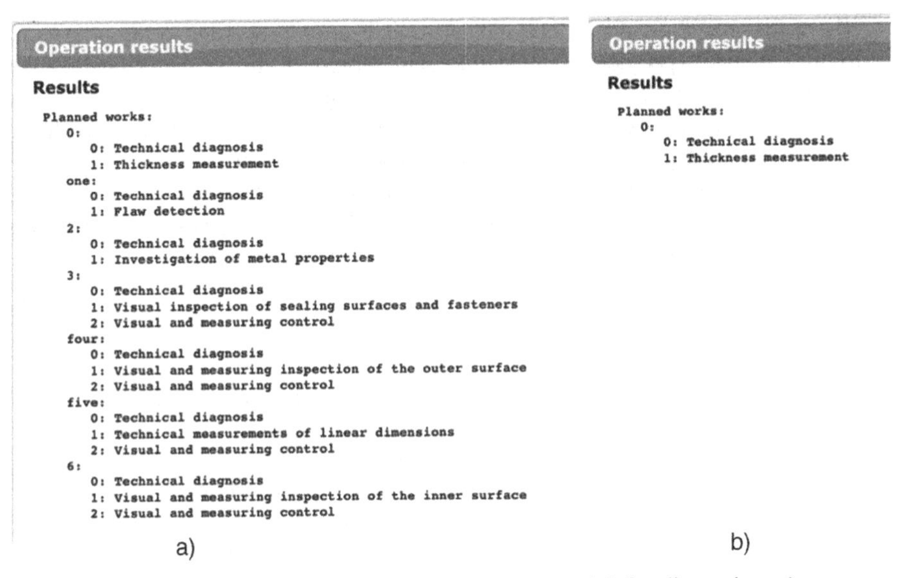

Fig. 3. Automatically generated sequences of operations (tasks) for diagnosing: a) a propane column; b) a tank

7 Conclusion

Thus, the implementation of the properties of self-organization when performing domain-specific functions of the scheduler is based on the following features:

- Using a single model for the actions (operations) performed. The presence and explicit use of the model of operations (actions) performed by the software system allows one to use them as data for processing, and to dynamically form sequences of operations to shape the desired behavior of the software system.
- Computing infrastructure based on a "command queue." This feature allows one to solve the same task in different ways on the same software system infrastruc-ture, for example, changing the order of actions or implementing actions under the influence of the properties of the objects being processed and/or the state of the software system itself.
- Use of rule-based reasoning capabilities in the context of performing actions (operations). It is proposed to use an imperative-declarative way of describing behav-ior, when some blocks of the algorithm of a domain-specific function are appeals to expert systems that solve the tasks of evaluating the results obtained or choos-ing the direction of further actions. This method allows one to effectively use the strengths of both methods, so, for example, it is more convenient to set a general sequence of actions when solving a certain task in the form of an imperative se-quence of calling operations, and it is more convenient to evaluate the results ob-tained from a subject point of view with the help of expert knowledge in the form of an appropriate knowledge base.

These features allow one to provide self-organization properties to the process of performing domain-specific scheduler functions. Moreover, the degree of intellectualization can be dynamically changed, first creating a simpler imperative framework of the algorithm, and then expanding and supplementing it with subject-based knowledge bases based on the experience of using domain-specific functions.

The application of the principles of self-organization in solving ISI tasks will improve the quality of the results of this process by automating the processes of solving tasks and coordinating the knowledge of experts from various subject areas.

References

1. Gorodetsky, V.: Self-organization and multi-agent systems. II. Applications and development technology. Izvestiya RAS. Theory Control Syst. **3**, 55–75 (2012)
2. Gimranova, P., Valekzhanin, D.: Optimization of the process of issuing industrial safety expert opinions with the use of modern technologies software and analytical complexes. Enigma **3**(21), 82–95 (2020)
3. Berman, A., Nikolaichuk, O., Yurin, A., Kuznetsov, P.: Support of decision-making based on a production approach in the performance of an industrial safety review. Chemical and. Petroleum Petrol. Engineering Eng. **1–2**(50), 730–738 (2015)
4. Bellman, K., Botev, J., Tomforde, S.: Self-improving system integration: Mastering continuous change. Future Generation Gen. Computer Comput. Systems **4**(117), 29–46 (2021)
5. Krupitzer, C., Roth, F., VanSyckel, S., Schiele, G., Becker, C.: A survey on engineering approaches for self-adaptive systems. Perv. Mob. Comput. **17**(PB), 184–206 (2015)
6. Wagner, M.: Self-Adaptive Systems: A Systematic Literature Review Across Categories and Domains. University of Adelaide, Preprint (2020)
7. Zhevnerchuk, D.: Generalized method of synthesis of multicomponent interoperable structures based on ontology and nondeterministic finite automaton. Information Inf. Technologies Tech. **2**(25), 67–74 (2019)
8. Wang, S., Wan, J., Zhang, D., Li, D., Zhang, C.: Towards smart factory for industry 4.0: a self-organized multi-agent system with big data based feedback and coordination. Comput. Netw. **101**, 158–168 (2016)
9. Malygin, E., Krasnyansky, M., Tugolukov, E., Alekseev, S.: Structural and parametric synthesis of a decision support system in the design and operation of heat and mass transfer equipment. Vestnik TSTU **3**(25), 350–359 (2019)
10. Yurin, A., Berman, A., Nikolaychuk, O.: Knowledge structurization and implementation of the self-organization principle in the case of substantiation of conceptual properties for complex technical systems. In: CEUR Workshop Proceedings: Proceedings of 2nd Scientific-Practical Workshop Information Technologies: Algorithms, Models, Systems (ITAMS 2019), vol. 2463, pp. 93–101 (2019)
11. Masloboev, A.: Cognitive technology of dynamic formation and configuration of problem-oriented multi-agent virtual spaces. Vestnik MSTU **4**(16), 748–760 (2013)
12. Obukhov, A.: Approaches to automating the process of structural-parametric synthesis of information systems. In: Lvov, A., Svetlov, M. (eds.) VI International Scientific Conference Problems of control, processing and transmission of information (CPTI-2018), pp. 637–640. Publishing house, Saratov State Technical University named after Yuri Gagarin, Saratov (2019)

13. Eltyshev, D.: On the development of an intelligent expert diagnostic system for assessing the condition of electrical equipment. Systems Syst. Methods and Technologies. **3**(35), 57–63 (2017)
14. Nikolaychuk, O., Pavlov, A., Stolbov, A.: The software platform architecture for the component-oriented development of knowledge-based systems. In: Proceedings of 41st Intern. Convention on Information and Communication Technology, Electronics and Microelectronics (MIPRO 2018), pp. 1064–1069 (2018)

Author Index

Printed in the United States
by Baker & Taylor Publisher Services